Her Way

Mary-Ellen Kulkin

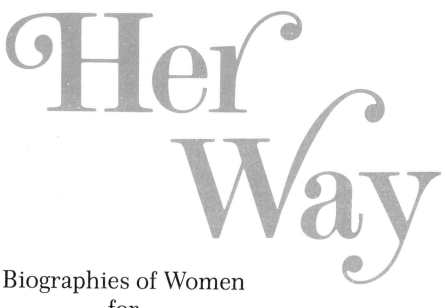

Her Way

Biographies of Women
for
Young People

American Library Association

Chicago 1976

Illustrations by
TIM BASALDUA

Printed in the United States of America

Library of Congress Cataloging in Publication Data

Kulkin, Mary-Ellen, 1932-
  Her way.

  SUMMARY: A collection of 260 short profiles and bibliographies of notable women throughout history and an additional bibliography of over 300 collective biographies of
women.
  1. Women—Biography—Juvenile literature.
2. Women—Juvenile Literature—Bio-Bibliography.
[1. Women—Biography.   2. Women—Bio-Bibliography]
I. Title.

HQ1123.K75   920.72 [920] 76-25861
ISBN 0-8389-0221-9

To my mother,

MIRIAM BAUM GREENBERGER,

for many reasons,
but mostly
because
I love her.

Contents

ACKNOWLEDGMENTS

Many people, in the course of my work on this book, have encouraged me and offered suggestions.

I am particularly grateful to Betsy Baldwin, who, as my editorial and research consultant, not only judiciously used her blue pencil, but also was an enormous help in much of the conceptualization that went into the book.

Several people at the City University of New York were extremely helpful. Particular thanks go to Professor Kathy Chamberlain in whose Women's Studies class I first considered writing this guide, and to professors Sophie Cambria, Sheila Kaplan, Abby Kleinbaum, Ruby Leavitt, and Leigh Marlowe whose interest in the book and in me meant so much.

Others who shared their wisdom and expertise and made valuable suggestions were Bill Adler, Daniel Baldwin, Annette Bodzen, Herb Bloom, Jeffrey Colen, Jeanne Goodstein, Professor James Haskins, Stephanie B. Koplin, Professor Gerda Lerner, Dorothy Markinko, and Bonnie Oberman. A special thanks to Barbara Seamon for her initial encouragement and introduction to the feminist movement.

My appreciation to my children—Betsy, Peter, and Vicki —for their uncomplaining tolerance, suggestions, and encouragement, and to Eddie for putting up with it all.

My everlasting gratitude goes to all those who, when I had doubts, never wavered in their beliefs that I would finish school, meet editorial deadlines, and get the laundry done. They, like the women in this book, taught me that life is more than just "muddling through" and that even the smallest achievements can be major triumphs.

Introduction

Some of my happiest childhood days were spent reading —exciting mysteries about Nancy Drew and novels about girls who tried to be different. Our generation cheered the girls who disguised themselves as boys to get on football teams, and we were inspired by the tales of wives of famous men. It never occurred to us to be angry when our football heroines found out it was more fun to get a new Easter hat than a new helmet. We believed that things were supposed to be that way.

It also seemed natural that the biographies we read told of intelligent and educated women who put aside their own personal ambitions and desires to further the careers of their husbands or who were faced with a choice: career or family. These last appeared to be mutually exclusive, although for many of us, reality proved differently. There were women who had successfully combined both, but few novels or biographies we read seemed to confirm this.

Time went on, World War II was past, and I proudly read the alumnae register of my small all-girls' high school.

Our graduates have become lawyers, doctors, teachers, writers, editors, actresses, researchers, secretaries, photographers, laboratory technicians. Many of them have been active in various kinds of paid and volunteer social and war work. They have taught Red Cross classes and driven trucks.

However, the real goals became clear as the book continued:

> Most important of all, they have married and raised
> families, for marriage is the career which gives an
> educated woman the greatest opportunity to make
> a lasting contribution to American society.

This school was administered by two remarkable unmarried women, only recently retired, who still speak proudly of their early days as feminists. So pervasive was the stereotype of women in our culture, that thirty years ago these otherwise intrepid educators permitted those comments about women to be included in the school's fiftieth anniversary publication.

Women have had the vote for over fifty years and they now constitute an ever-expanding part of the labor force. Ninety percent of all women work sometime during their lives and nearly half of the women between the ages of eighteen and sixty-five are in the labor force. Girls, as well as boys, need to learn from early childhood that they will at some time in their lives make decisions about life-styles, jobs, and careers. Few will simply remain at home as did some of their mothers and most of their grandmothers. Girls need many experiences that will provide them with the kind of exposure to adult careers that has long been available to boys. This kind of exposure and experience occurs in many ways. For some children it is simply through contact with family members and friends, interaction with other adults whose occupations are visible, and, of course, through the media. Other children are exposed, through books and other educational channels, to historical and biographical materials about political and sports figures, inventors, and artists.

Exposure to adults of worth and achievement may have

an effect upon a child's ultimate decision as to what to do with his life, but this is certainly not the only reason we want children to have such experiences. If a child has opportunities to actually get to know adults through real-life or literary exposure, and can acquire some feelings of confidence about his or her abilities, or can have personal horizons widened which allow a fuller appreciation of life, then the efforts expended in providing such opportunities are well spent.

Biographies are one important instrument for creating models and inspirations for young people. The lack of suitable models can have a distinct effect upon the child who *does* read and finds few people with whom to identify and emulate.

I grew up in the 1940s thinking that the only woman athlete was Babe Didrikson, the only woman scientist Marie Curie, and that other than Clara Barton, Florence Nightingale, and some queens and first ladies, the only other women of note were movie actresses. That last bit of information was gleaned from fan magazines, but the weekly newsreels in the local movie houses hinted that Eleanor Roosevelt was more than a White House hostess. My older sister could recall the newspaper and radio reports of Amelia Earhart's disappearance, but otherwise my knowledge of prominent women was confined to the wives, mothers, and daughters of the famous men learned about in school. Until quite recently I suspected that the highlight of Abigail Adams's life was when she hung the laundry in the East Room of the White House, and the only thing I knew about Harriet Beecher Stowe was that she wrote *Uncle Tom's Cabin* and was supposed to have been "the little lady who started that big war." I mistakingly believed that the suffragists were man-hating spinsters. And I was a vociferous reader!

Ignorance about successful women seemed to be the hallmark of the time, for in the early 1950s a group of New York City high school students was asked to name the best-known American black woman. When the results were tabulated it was found that this was neither Harriet Tubman, Phillis Wheatley, Mary McLeod Bethune, nor Marian Anderson, but Aunt Jemima! Yet, I have recently discovered, there were many privately printed biographies of outstanding black men and women which were sold door-to-door in the South, and which found their way into branch libraries in all-black neighborhoods in the North as well. The relative scarcity of biographies of women in my childhood was a reflection of that era's emphasis on motherhood and homemaking rather than on careers for women, and it meant that girls, unlike their brothers, could not find true-life models who would inspire them.

In the last few decades a great many individual and collective biographies of women for youngsters have been published. Some, though, were woefully inadequate. They were poorly written, cursorily researched, and often depicted the subjects primarily in relation to men—as wives, daughters, or mothers. Such books offer little in the way of positive role-models for young girls. Fortunately, many of these books were poorly received at publication and have now gone out of print. Some still remain because they fill some sort of need: either they are part of a series successful with purchasers who do not want to bother to read each book before recommending it, or they deal with someone about whom no other juvenile biography has been written. It would be better, though, for a child to read nothing about a particular person, than to read a biography that is distorted or misleading. Each biography should stand by itself, not by comparison to others of the same subject, and should not be considered worthwhile because it is the only biography of the subject.

What makes a good biography?

A good biography should be readable and accurate and give a sense of the person and the society in which he or she lived. It should show a person's strengths and weaknesses. A biography that is so laudatory or so burdened with moral lessons can have a discouraging effect upon a child who aspires to be like the subject and therefore creates for himself or herself an unrealistic and impossible task.

A biography should employ a style that is appropriate to the subject. A fast-moving journalistic style is suitable in a biography of Billie Jean King or Nellie Bly, but would be tasteless in a biography of Beatrix Potter or Phillis Wheatley.

While a biography for a child may not include the bibliography used by the author in research (instead offering a selection of recommended and related titles to the reader), evidence of research can be seen by the discerning critic. The adult considering a juvenile biography should ideally read some documented source material on the subject and should search for pieces of evidence that the author has not relied solely on secondary or tertiary sources. Occasionally, a juvenile biographer simply "rewrites" in simpler terms the subject's autobiography which may long be out of print or only available privately. Wherever possible, the biographies evaluated in this guide have been checked for accuracy.

A good biography should be accurate and free of distortions, but it may at times be necessary to omit some of the truth about a person because it seems to be inappropriate, incomprehensible, or irrelevant to the reader for whom the biography is intended. Recently there has been a trend to tell children the truth about all matters, in terms they can understand. This seems to be a healthy and realistic approach, and writers who use it should be applauded. Children today, because of their exposure to television and films as well as popular journalism, are not as easily shocked as children of earlier generations. Certainly, it is far better for them to read about a subject tastefully in a biography than it is to learn later that they have been deceived. Children, as well as adults, tend to believe what they read in a book they find in a bookstore or library. The book's permanency and bold print gives it an air of authenticity and authoritativeness which may be lacking in other media. The truth, and the whole truth if possible, is an important part of biographies for young people.

A good biography can be a literary work, rather than just a collection of chronological facts put into a readable sequence. By judicious selection and organization, and by actually capturing the spirit and essence of the subject, many biographies for young readers can hold their own next to a fine work of fiction. Whether or not the subject was a real person almost seems unimportant in such a book. That it combines biography and history is simply an extra dividend. However, anyone helping a child to choose a biography should remember that some children prefer books that may appear to the adult to be little more than a curriculum aid. To such children, reading is simply a way of gathering information on a topic that interests them. Other children shy away from this straightforward textbook approach, willing to read this kind of book only if it is required. They want a good story, and for this youngster, the fictionalized or anecdotal biography is a better choice. The introduction of conversations and private musings can give a biography the aura of fiction, but as long as this is not done too heavily and does not cause distortions or intrusions, it is a widely accepted style. For the reader whose interest seems to be captured only by dialogue and "stories," biographies of this sort can be most enjoyable and profitable.

The adult considering a biography for a young reader should keep the particular child's preference in mind. One should be wary of the elitist idea that a library's primary task is to help form taste, and remember that reading should not only be fun, but should fill needs for all children. Since biographies are a favorite topic for children and teachers, it is important that many kinds be available.

Those that constitute real literature pose no problem, but we should not be too fast to reject those biographies that are easy to read, are for reluctant readers, or have as their subject people who are currently in the media. Such "superstars" are often of enormous, even if transitory, interest to children and may be worthwhile. These books, too, must be written in appropriate style, be accurate and objective. One would be just as guilty of elitist and snobbish ideas by saying that these books need not meet the same standards as the more traditional books.

No discussion of biographies as a literary genre would be complete without mention of some existing series. Fortunately, children do not usually sit down and read every title in a series such as the Bobbs-Merrill Childhood books. The third- or fourth-grader who set upon such a task would not only have no time for the multiplication table or bike-riding and tree-climbing, but would undoubtedly get bored very soon. However, a considerable diet of such books is a distinct possibility; for children do often gravitate to the familiar and, having read one or two such biographies, will easily find others on the shelf, for the books even look alike! The child who reads several of these may soon fear that he or she or one's friends are doomed to mediocrity, for the children in the series, while sometimes dull and conventional, well-behaved and emotionally stable, *also* show an amazing proclivity for their eventual accomplishments; future doctors seem to be able to cure ailing pets and friends even before they reach kindergarten. More likely than not the readers will see little of themselves in the books. Wise librarians, teachers, and parents should try to steer children towards other biographies if these series are being read exclusively· As is pointed out in the individual evaluations in this guide, there are some exceptionally good titles, while others are really unacceptable as biographies even if they provide adequate historical background·

It should also be realized that some subjects lend themselves better to the childhood treatment format than others. The childhood of Babe Didrikson or Helen Keller can easily provide absorbing and inspirational reading, for these were interesting children. On the other hand, many other women led rather uneventful childhoods, and some did little of interest or great consequence until mid-life.

Children may find in a well done biography a direct reinforcement of their own ambitions and goals or they can sufficiently identify with the subject in such a way as to make their own goals seem possible. Elizabeth Blackwell, a nineteenth-century woman who overcame almost insurmountable societal obstacles to become a physician, may prove as inspirational to the girl who dreams of becoming a train conductor as it does to the scientifically oriented girl who wants to go to medical school. A youngster may find it easiest to identify with a person of like background but a child *can* draw analogies: the stutterer who aspires to become a television newscaster may find inspiration in learning that Olympic field and track athlete Wilma Rudolph was crippled as a small child.

A good biography is nonsexist. Any biography that emphasizes and praises a traditional stereotyped role for men or women, thus covertly or overtly attempting to perpetuate these values, is sexist. A book that focusses on a woman's household and domestic achievements, physical attractiveness, charm, and gentle subservience to the exclusion of her contributions to society, her initiative, courage, and intelligence is sexist. Biographies that denigrate a man because he does not display independence, courage, and dominance, or does not assume the financial support of women, are also sexist.

Sexism in a book can be subtle and yet pervasive. An example of this is the author who criticizes or even apologizes because the males and females do not perform their traditional roles and duties. A biography whose subject retires from a career to go back to stove and nursery because "that's what she was always meant to do" promotes the most insidious sexism of all.

A good biography for young readers should never take a patronizing, stereotyped, or negative view of any group or class of people. Sexism, racism, and classism are prejudicial notions which seriously detract from the worth of any book, but are particularly deplorable when found in children's literature.

A biography should not only give a reader a sense of person, time, and place, it must be careful to discuss such matters in terms of the subject's society. Achievements or lack of them should not be judged by today's values and life-styles, but in the context of the subject's own life. However, the author can, and should, remind young readers directly or subtly that times have changed (or have not changed, if such is the case), and that Ms. X's actions—while commonplace today—were extremely courageous or unusual then, or that Ms. Y was not really defaulting on her ambitions when she did not pursue a goal that she might have if she were living today. Incidents of racism need to be explained in a similar fashion—many older books that dealt with blacks and Indians reflected the way the dominant society saw them. We do not advocate changing or distorting what *really* happened; an explanation, not an apology, is needed for today's reader. The young reader may have scant or no understanding of any time longer ago than last year, and he often needs to be reminded of values and mores of the larger world in which a subject lived.

Although a biography of anyone can be written interestingly and well, the author certainly is working under a disadvantage when the subject is simply an appendage to someone else. Some subjects are almost foolproof, for even a simply written, matter-of-fact account of the life of Harriet Tubman or Amelia Earhart is likely to be more than adequate. Similarly, biographies of first ladies and movie actresses if written honestly and objectively may not really be inspirational or serve as role-models for young readers. In evaluating the biographies in this guide, I have tried to avoid evaluating the subject rather than the biography, but it is sometimes a difficult task. One cannot completely separate the two, unless the criteria are limited simply to seeking out good prose. But, as is clear, many more things must be considered in evaluating biography.

This guide has tried to be comprehensive; that is, inclusive of all biographies of women published for children which are currently (through October 1975) in print. Some biographies are so highly fictionalized as to really be more fiction than biography. Occasionally such books have been excluded here, unless the publisher and libraries consistently classify them as biographies. Some memoirs written by women who have chosen one period of their life to write about have also been omitted, for although biographical, they do not seem to be true biographies in the real sense of the word. However, many such memoirs—Anne Frank's *Diary of a Young Girl*, for example—have been selected for inclusion, either because of their style, or because the subject seems of particular interest and relevance to readers today. Many of these memoirs were not written for children or originally published for them, but they have so often found their way to the children's room of libraries that they seem extremely worthy of consideration.

Although this book serves chiefly as a guide to biographies published for children, I have also included a number of books that publishers or librarians consider "young adult" titles. It must be remembered, however, that these books constitute a "grey area." They are often adult titles with special appeal to young people, either because of their subject matter and/or because they are not very demanding as to difficulty or length. Young people will read a full-length, even scholarly adult biography of someone who is of special interest to them, whether or not it is on their school reading list, but may shy away from a popular type of adult biography if the subject is someone whose life has no relevance to theirs. Thus, these books labelled "young adult" are titles that have been so designated for various reasons, not necessarily because they were written for such an audience. For this reason, I have been selective in these titles, choosing those that are especially worthwhile.

The following pages include short profiles of 260 women. Each profile is followed by a complete list of individual biographies which are intended for preschool through high school youngsters. The profiles are useful for both the youngster and the adult seeking to choose a biography. Children's librarians find that children like best the biographies of individuals with whom they are already familiar through television, textbooks, or their teachers. Children do not spontaneously choose books about individuals unknown to them. Thus, these brief profiles can help one to become acquainted with the numerous women of whom one or more full-length biographies have been written.

Collective biographies fall into many categories. Usually the subjects are linked together by some common thread, either of occupation, ethnicity, or simply gender. These are suitable for children wanting simply encyclopedia-like portraits or those readers with a desire for less than full-length portraits, either because of time or attention limits, because they want to learn about many similar people, or because they are searching for a subject about whom they wish to learn more.

Approximately three hundred collective biographies which include a profile of one or more women are also included, and here, as in the individual biographies, all books intended for preschool through high school readers are listed, as well as a selected number of adult titles.

The index lists the approximately eight hundred women included in individual and collective biographies with their identification. Two appendixes precede the index and are entitled "Women Classified by Nationalities" and "Classified List of Selected Biographical Subjects." The latter is a list by occupation or other descriptive category.

Each book has been considered and evaluated on the basis of good literary merit, historical and personal accuracy, freedom from racism and sexism, and whether it is interesting and appropriate for the age and grade level for which it is intended. Each is then assigned a rating. These ratings and a brief critical review of each book are supplemented with other bibliographical information. The ratings are as follows:

*** Highly Recommended

** Recommended

* Acceptable

†† Unacceptable

A book rated *highly recommended* is well written; competently researched; objective, accurate, and interesting; and suitable to the age, grade, or interests of the reader for whom it is intended. It is free of sexism and racism.

A book rated *recommended* may be somewhat flawed in literary quality and/or be slightly sexist, or may simply lack in degree some of the qualifications found in highly recommended titles.

Acceptable books are usually more seriously flawed but worthy of consideration. Usually nonsexist, they still do not expand the emotional or intellectual growth of the reader. Superficiality, overfictionalization, dullness, and insufficient information or clarity of the subject's contributions or achievements may be one or more of the characteristics that contribute to this rating.

Unacceptable books usually have no redeeming qualities. They are either very poorly written, inaccurate, extremely sexist or racist, or quite frequently a combination of these.

These evaluations point out the merits and shortcomings in every biography of a woman intended for children, and will guide the interested adult or youngster in choosing those that show women in an independent, full-dimensional light.

Books, particularly biographies, mirror society. They can also contribute to creating or changing individual values, or they can reinforce existing ones. We can help children choose as models some of the remarkable women described on the following pages so that they may see themselves and others as nonstereotyped, multifaceted human beings. The authors who have competently and inspirationally presented these women within the pages of good biography are helping shape the world of tomorrow. They have begun an important job. Now it is up to us to see that their message is received by young readers.

Individual Biographies

ABIGAIL SMITH ADAMS
1744–1818
Feminist, First Lady, and mother of a president

One of America's earliest spokeswomen for women's rights, Abigail Adams wrote letters to her husband at the Continental Congress in Philadelphia, reminding him that the founding fathers should consider women in the new laws. She criticized proclamations of peace and good will to men, because they still insisted that men retain absolute power over their wives. She was ignored, even when she suggested that women might rebel if they were not represented in the new government and given an opportunity for equal education.

During the ten years John Adams was away serving the new nation, Abigail Adams took complete charge of their farm as well as their growing family. So outstanding an administrator was she, that later the farm supported the family with a regular income. Her husband, John Adams, was the second—and her son John Quincy Adams the sixth —president of the United States.

** *Kelly, Regina Z.* ABIGAIL ADAMS Illus. Houghton Mifflin, 1962. (grades 4-6)
  Somewhat bland biography conveys Abigail Adams's intelligence and intellect, but omits her interest in women's rights.

** *Peterson, Helen* ABIGAIL ADAMS: DEAR PARTNER Illus. Garrard, 1967. (grades 2-5)

Brief and simply written biography depicting Abigail Adams's quick mind and amazing independence does not also convey her concern for women's rights.

†† *Wagoner, Jean* ABIGAIL ADAMS: GIRL OF COLONIAL DAYS Illus. Bobbs–Merrill, 1949. (grades 3-7)

Sexist biography limits itself exclusively to Abigail Adams's childhood. Narrow definitions of sex roles as they existed in the eighteenth century are depicted without comments, thus reinforcing them for young readers. The brief section of the book devoted to Abigail as an adult fails to show her independence—her ideas and contributions are dismissed as follows: "Through John, Abigail felt as if she were a part of the exciting events of the time." The entire biography is so highly fictionalized that it is difficult to distinguish accurate facts.

LOUISA JOHNSON ADAMS
1775–1852

Musician, linguist, and First Lady

Louisa Adams could speak several languages, play the harp and spinet, and read Plato in the original Greek. Before her husband, John Quincy Adams, became the sixth president of the United States, he represented the government in many European countries. One time, Louisa Adams spent forty days travelling across war-ravaged Europe alone with her young son.

In Washington, Louisa Adams's skills as a hostess were apparent, and when she later became First Lady, she performed her expected duties with great finesse.

4

†† *Kerr, Laura* LOUISA: THE LIFE OF MRS. JOHN QUINCY ADAMS
Funk & Wagnalls, 1964. (grades 7-11)
A rather trivial, slightly sexist biography which offers few
insights into the talents, strengths, or independent qualities
of Louisa Adams. The historical background is adequately
introduced, but the biographical portrayal is weak. Her husband's remark, "You are still a little girl and I love you for it,"
hardly seems in keeping with her true characteristics.

JANE ADDAMS
1860–1935

*Settlement house founder, social reformer, and
winner of Nobel Peace Prize*

Born to wealth and privilege, Jane Addams spent her life
seeking solutions to problems that beset society. Hull
House, the settlement house she founded in Chicago in
1889, still stands. Her innovations to help improve the
living conditions of slum-dwellers influenced the entire
social work and welfare field.

By paving the way herself, she encouraged other women
college graduates to enter professions relating to social
problems. Her unusual administrative ability and magnetic
personality attracted and inspired others, and together they
worked to implement meaningful labor and social reforms.

She was a strong supporter of women's rights and suffrage and a founder of the American Civil Liberties Union.
Ms. Addams's ceaseless efforts in behalf of peace were recognized when in 1931 she became the first American
woman to win the Nobel Peace Prize.

5

*** *Grant, Matthew G.* JANE ADDAMS Illus. Creative Education/ Children's Pr., 1973. (grades 2-4)

Very simple but comprehensive account of the life of Jane Addams is illustrated with colorful, vivid, eye-catching pictures. Despite its brevity, and the demands of a limited vocabulary and short sentences, the spirit of the woman and her accomplishments emerge.

*** *Judson, Clara* CITY NEIGHBORS: THE STORY OF JANE ADDAMS Illus. Scribner, 1951. (grades 4-9)

Convincingly fictionalized biography is limited mostly to Jane Addams's childhood and early days at Hull House. Based on extensive research as well as personal acquaintance, it is informative and inspiring without being eulogistic in tone.

*** *Keller, Gail* JANE ADDAMS Illus. Crowell, 1971. (grades 1-4)

Brief and easy enough for early readers to read alone, this really outstanding biography is also good for reading aloud to young children. Even in this short book, the warmth and contributions of Jane Addams are made magnificently clear.

*** *Meigs, Cornelia* JANE ADDAMS: PIONEER FOR SOCIAL JUSTICE Illus. Little, 1970. (grade 7 and up)

Authoritative, carefully researched, and extremely well-written. Insightful and informative, it deals with many issues such as fair labor practices, child labor abuses, and Jane Addams's relationships with other pioneers in labor and social work. Valuable for older readers as well as mature junior high readers.

*** *Peterson, Helen* JANE ADDAMS: PIONEER OF HULL HOUSE Illus. Garrard, 1965. (grades 2-5)

Stirring, easy-to-read narrative, though brief, gives a full and interesting portrait of Jane Addams.

*** *Wise, Winifred E.* JANE ADDAMS OF HULL HOUSE Illus. Harcourt, 1935. (grade 7 and up)

Excellent, colorful, and well-researched biography makes clear Jane Addams's good fortune in growing up in a household where a woman's mind was treated as worthy of cultivation. Her many accomplishments are warmly detailed.

†† *Wagoner, Jean B.* JANE ADDAMS: LITTLE LAME GIRL Illus. Bobbs–Merrill, 1944. (grades 3-7)

Rather sexist book deals almost exclusively with Jane Addams's childhood. Overfictionalized, it reinforces the stereotypic sex roles of children and adults. Scant attention is paid to later accomplishments, and even these details are needlessly sugarcoated.

SAINT AGNES
291–304

According to legend, Christian-born Agnes was only thirteen when, preferring martyrdom, she refused to marry a Roman noble. Condemned to death for her action, she was tied to a stake, but when the wood refused to burn, her head was cut off with a sword.

Saint Agnes's Eve, when country girls are supposed to discover their future husbands, is named for her. A church was later built over her burial place near Rome.

* *Berardi, M. R.* SAINT AGNES Illus. Daughters of St. Paul, 1964. (grades 4-6)

Highly fictionalized book is based on the legend of Saint Agnes, showing her to be strong-willed and independent in thought, but at the same time desirous of martyrdom.

LOUISA MAY ALCOTT
1832–1888
Author

Before the publication of *Little Women* made her famous and wealthy, Louisa May Alcott worked as a Civil War army nurse, seamstress, domestic servant, teacher, and governess. Her father, a prominent educator and philosopher, introduced her to many of the greatest thinkers of the day, and although he provided his family with much intellectual nourishment, he did not provide them with much of an income.

Ms. Alcott's childhood was happy in spite of poverty. Determined to lessen her mother's enormous burdens, she went to work early, and later, drawing upon her many experiences, wrote and sold short stories.

When *Little Women* was first published it became an immediate success, not only with the young people for whom it was intended, but with adults too. Semiautobiographical, it gave a vivid picture of the values and ideals of the nineteenth-century American middle-class family, and pioneered the portrayal of adolescence in fiction.

Though never drawn into an active role in the suffrage movement, Louisa May Alcott was eager for women to have opportunities to enter all the professions and when Massachusetts allowed women to vote for certain local issues she was the first to register.

*** *Colver, Anne* LOUISA MAY ALCOTT: AUTHOR OF LITTLE WOMEN Illus. Garrard, 1969. (grades 4-7)

In this excellent biography, Louisa May Alcott and her family emerge as warm, compassionate people and Ms. Alcott's spirit and achievements are dramatically described.

*** *Fisher, Aileen, and Rabe, Oliver* WE ALCOTTS Illus. Atheneum, 1968. (grades 6-10)

This carefully researched and well-written book is not only a biography of Louisa May Alcott, it is also a family story being told by Mrs. Alcott. It offers valuable insights into the personalities of Louisa's parents. While this device limits somewhat the scope of the book, it adds warmth and personality.

*** *Meigs, Cornelia* INVINCIBLE LOUISA Illus. Little, 1933. (grade 6 and up)

Fast-moving, exceptionally well-written with sensitivity and sympathy, this book gives an accurate portrait of Louisa May Alcott's early life and literary successes. The author gives background information on the social, intellectual, and historical period and carefully introduces Louisa May Alcott's family and their illustrious friends and associates.

*** *Papashvily, Helen* LOUISA MAY ALCOTT Illus. Houghton Mifflin, 1965. (grades 4-7)

Louisa is portrayed as an independent child and her parents as rare human beings with warmth, compassion, and a genuine interest in their children's ideas and activities. Movingly told, the book cites Louisa's accomplishments and shows how she took over many of the financial problems that beset her family.

†† *Wagoner, Jean* LOUISA MAY ALCOTT: GIRL OF OLD BOSTON Illus. Bobbs–Merrill, 1943. (grades 3-7)

Sexist, overfictionalized biography focusses on the childhood of Louisa May Alcott. Stereotyping of sex, class, and race pervades the text, and Alcott's later accomplishments are insufficiently reported.

9

MARIAN ANDERSON
1902–

American concert singer

Marian Anderson began singing during childhood, performing first in churches in Philadelphia, and later in schools, colleges, and eventually in concert halls all over the world. In 1939 she became a symbol of discrimination against black people when the Daughters of the American Revolution, owners of Constitutional Hall in Washington, D.C., refused her its use for a concert. This action so enraged First Lady Eleanor Roosevelt (page 243) that she resigned from the organization.

Marian Anderson gave a concert in Washington anyway. On Easter Sunday, 1939, the Lincoln Memorial became an outdoor integrated theater as seventy-five thousand blacks and whites stood together watching and listening to her, while millions more listened on their radios at home.

In 1955 Marian Anderson became the first black performer to appear with the Metropolitan Opera Company. She has taken an active role in promoting social understanding in the world by acting as a goodwill ambassador for the State Department and serving as a delegate to the United Nations.

*** *Tobias, Tobi* MARIAN ANDERSON Illus. Crowell, 1972. (grades 1-5)

Superb biography in which Ms. Anderson emerges as a fine singer and human being who has faced many obstacles because she is black. Symeon Shimin's illustrations are especially effective in conveying the character and personality of Marian Anderson and those around her.

** *Anderson, Marian* MY LORD, WHAT A MORNING Illus. Viking, 1956; Avon, 1964. (grade 7 and up)
Fine adult autobiography written simply enough for young readers. Warm and moving, it does not completely convey the extent of Ms. Anderson's accomplishments, for she is a modest reporter.

** *Newman, Shirlee* MARIAN ANDERSON: LADY FROM PHILADEL-PHIA Illus. Westminster, 1966. (grades 5-11)
This biography does not place sufficient emphasis on the extent of racism that Marian Anderson has faced nor on her independence and amazing courage. However, it is warm, extremely readable, and faithful to the events of her life.

MAYA ANGELOU
1929–
Author, actress, dancer, director

After a childhood spent in both California and the South, Maya Angelou became a producer, director, dancer, actress, and author. She toured Europe and Africa for the State Department and, at the request of the late Dr. Martin Luther King, was the northern coordinator for the Southern Christian Leadership Conference.

She is active now in film and theater production: her direction of the movie version of her autobiography makes her the first black woman to direct a Hollywood film.

11

*** *Angelou, Maya* I KNOW WHY THE CAGED BIRD SINGS Random, 1970. (grade 9 and up)

Stirring autobiography comes alive on each page with its vivid portrayal of the growing independence of a young black child and teenager. A shocking scene of sexual violence, an integral part of Maya Angelou's life, may make this book unsuitable for some readers. This is a remarkable book not only for its content, but for its fine literary prose. An adult title that can easily be read by emotionally mature junior high and high school students.

━━━━━━━━━━━━━━━━━━━━━━━━━━━━━━━━━━━

MARIE THERESE CHARLOTTE ANGOULEME
1778–1851

*Daughter of French King Louis XVI
and Queen Marie Antoinette*

Marie Therese was only one year old when the revolution broke out in France. She spent the second year of her life imprisoned with her family in the Tuileries Palace and after the execution of both her parents in 1793 became known as the "orphan of the temple," living in exile in various countries.

After the defeat of Napoleon and the restoration of the French monarchy in 1815, Marie Therese returned to her native country and served as a kind of "first lady"—first to her uncle, King Louis XVIII, and then to his successor, King Charles X.

Marie Therese's husband Louis, the son of Charles X, never became king, for once again revolution spread throughout France and in 1830 Charles abdicated in favor of the liberal Duke Louis-Phillipe.

Prominent throughout her life, Marie Therese Charlotte Angouleme was both admired and despised for her connection to the Bourbon monarchs of France.

** *Desmond, Alice Curtis* MARIE ANTOINETTE'S DAUGHTER Illus. with photographs, maps, and diagrams. Dodd, 1967. (grade 9 and up)
Very well researched and documented, mostly nonsexist, convincingly fictionalized biography affords readers a thoughtful examination of Marie Therese's life and the society in which she lived. Well-written and interesting, it is a sympathetic though well-balanced portrait of the life of Marie Antoinette's daughter.

ANNE, QUEEN OF ENGLAND
1665–1714
Ruler of England, 1702–14

A deeply religious Protestant, Anne, daughter of James II and Anne Hyde, ruled England for twelve years. During that period the war between England and France, known as "Queen Anne's War," resulted in England acquiring new territory; the Act of Union unified Scotland and England under the name Great Britain; and Queen Anne's Bounty was created to provide a yearly income for the Church of England.

Anne's marriage to George, Prince of Denmark, was marked by maternal tragedies. At least fourteen pregnancies ended in miscarriage or infant mortality, and the one son who survived infancy died at the age of eleven.

Queen Anne's kindness and consideration for others, her conscientious fulfillment of public duties, and her great devotion to the church are admired and praised, but some critics claim she lacked any great ability or intelligence.

** *Hodges, Margaret* LADY QUEEN ANNE: A BIOGRAPHY OF QUEEN ANNE OF ENGLAND Illus. Farrar, 1969. (grade 7 and up)
    Carefully researched biography only moderately conveys the full life and personality of Queen Anne. Skillfully written and interesting, it is basically faithful to her life.

MARY ANNING
1799–1847

Fossil collector

Mary Anning started her career as a fossil collector when as a youngster she helped her father collect petrified shells and mollusks near their home in the seashore town of Lyme Regis in England. Together they would climb the cliffs and hammer and chisel to remove the fossils they would then sell to tourists.

When Mary's father died she continued to collect and sell these natural curiosities to help support her family. She was only twelve when she discovered the huge creature that scientists named *Ichthyosaurus*, meaning fish-lizard. Later she found the first specimen of *Plesiosaurus*, meaning nearly-like-a-lizard, and the flying reptile, *Pterodactyl*, which means wing-finger.

14

Although she was not formally schooled in geology she devoted herself full-time to the study of fossils and her contributions to the field of geology were acknowledged by the most prominent people in the profession.

Museums all over the world have exhibited Mary Anning's fossil findings; many can be seen at the British Museum of Natural History in London.

*** *Blair, Ruth Van Ness* MARY'S MONSTER Illus. Coward, 1975. (grades 3-7)

Fascinating, historically sound, though highly fictionalized account of Mary Anning's search for "curiosities" surrounding her seaside home which led to her discovery of important fossils. The persistence and seriousness of her pursuit are made clear, despite the correct indications that Mary Anning was not a geologist or a scientist in the true sense of the word. Life in the early nineteenth century is vividly depicted, and the black-and-white illustrations further enhance the text.

SUSAN BROWNELL ANTHONY
1820–1906

American suffragist

Susan B. Anthony's Quaker upbringing taught her that women and men are equal under God, and she devoted most of her long life trying to realize this equality for American women. First as an abolitionist and a temperance leader, later as a participant in the movement to grant women rights over their children and property, she eventually put all of her extraordinary energies and abilities into the suffrage movement. With Elizabeth Cady Stanton (page 266) Ms. Anthony organized the movement, published a newspaper, and worked tirelessly to change women's restrictive role in society.

Susan Anthony was arrested for voting in the 1872 presidential election. She refused to pay the fine levied on her, hoping for imprisonment and the opportunity to take the case to the Supreme Court. However, her hopes were dashed when the charges against her were ignored.

Not until 1920, fourteen years after her death, were women able to vote in all elections in the United States. The Nineteenth Amendment to the Constitution, which granted this long overdue right, is sometimes called the "Susan B. Anthony Amendment," in honor of the woman whose long, tireless efforts helped women's suffrage become a reality.

*** *Noble, Iris* SUSAN B. ANTHONY Messner, 1975. (grades 6-9)

Outstanding biography of Susan Anthony has a thoroughly feminist focus. Although there is a great deal of information packed into it about the entire women's movement, as well as much about Elizabeth Stanton, with whom Ms. Anthony was closely linked, it is truly Anthony's story. Much of the history of the movement often omitted from biography is included here. The book ends by saying that perhaps the ghost of Anthony is now hovering over modern women, telling them the fight has not yet been won.

*** *Peterson, Helen S.* SUSAN B. ANTHONY: PIONEER IN WOMEN'S RIGHTS Illus. Garrard, 1971. (grades 3-6)

Nonfictionalized, straightforward, and accurate account of the life of Susan Anthony has a strong feminist focus, but is occasionally stilted. Ms. Anthony emerges as a strong, courageous leader in this absorbing biography.

*** *Salsini, Barbara* SUSAN B. ANTHONY: A CRUSADER FOR WOMEN'S RIGHTS SamHar Pr., 1972. (grade 7 and up)

Excellent informative account of the life of Susan Anthony is brief (30 pages), but covers all the important events of her life and of the times. Ms. Anthony is revealed as a warm human being as well as an outstanding crusader.

** *Grant, Matthew G.* SUSAN B. ANTHONY Illus. Creative Education/Children's Pr., 1974. (grades 2-5)

Colorfully illustrated biography is strongly feminist, but superficial because it attempts to cover too many details in a brief narrative. Easy-to-read, and generally good, it may serve older reluctant readers better than younger elementary school children.

* *Monsell, Helen* SUSAN B. ANTHONY: GIRL WHO DARED Illus. Bobbs–Merrill, 1954. (grades 3-7)

Nonsexist, but overly fictionalized account of the childhood of Susan Anthony. Her adult accomplishments are depicted fairly accurately but they lack something in depth and spirit.

MARGARET SHIPPEN ARNOLD
1760–1804

Loyalist during Revolutionary War, wife of traitor

Margaret "Peggy" Shippen Arnold, the wife of the notorious American Revolutionary traitor Benedict Arnold, was an intelligent, articulate, attractive woman from a Philadelphia social family. During her lifetime it was believed that she was innocent of any participation or even knowledge of her husband's treason, but recent research indicates she was fully aware of his activities, and probably encouraged and even suggested such a course of action.

17

She was an ardent Loyalist who was ambitious, determined, and sympathetic to all things English. Generally well-liked, after the discovery of her husband's treason she was scorned by many who had known her, although they never doubted her innocence. She and Benedict moved to England at the close of the Revolutionary War where she brought up her five children. Although he had been financially well rewarded by the British government, Arnold's poor business investments and extravagances left her an almost penniless widow. With frugality and fortitude she managed to pay off his debts and to maintain herself with dignity until her own death.

* *Lomask, Milton* BEAUTY AND THE TRAITOR: THE STORY OF MRS. BENEDICT ARNOLD Macrae, 1967. (grade 9 and up)
    Well-written, thoroughly researched, fictionalized account of the life of Peggy Shippen Arnold focusses on her marriage to the traitor Benedict Arnold and on his activities. Though she emerges as an intelligent and self-determined woman, this well-balanced account is, nonetheless, more his story than hers.

JACQUELINE AURIOL
1917–

French aviator

Flying was a hobby for Jacqueline Auriol until the day she crashed. Her entire face was crushed and she was almost killed, but her determination to become a professional pilot and her characteristic spirit and courage sustained

18

her through her long ordeal. After more than fifteen operations, her face was restored and, despite sexual discrimination, she enrolled in a school for test pilots.

Jacqueline Auriol became the world's only officially qualified woman test pilot, and is a five-time winner of the women's world flying speed record.

*** *Auriol, Jacqueline* I LIVE TO FLY Illus. with photographs. Dutton, 1970. (grade 9 and up)

Fast-moving autobiography chronicles Auriol's flying career since her near fatal accident. Informally written and greatly enhanced by photographs, this book reveals her determination and courage. Dramatic and inspiring for adults as well as young readers, the book describes what it is like to be a test pilot and to be a woman in the usually male field of aviation. Some aspects of her personal life are discussed, and the reader is introduced to her husband and her father-in-law, Vincent Auriol, one-time president of France.

JANE AUSTEN
1775–1817

British novelist

Jane Austen's sheltered, quiet, and rather uneventful life in an English parsonage did not restrict her from becoming a great novelist. The youngest daughter of a clergyman, she spent her entire life in small, quiet English country towns, and her novels reflect these communities and the middle-class people who resided in them.

19

Although she is best known for her novel *Pride and Prej-udice*, her other novels—*Sense and Sensibility, Mansfield Park*, and *Emma*—have also achieved lasting literary fame and popularity. Jane Austen's genius lay in her remarkable ability to observe and then imaginatively represent the lives of small provincial families, without relying on great passion, religious themes, or crimes.

†† *Brown, Ivor* JANE AUSTEN AND HER WORLD Illus. with photographs. Walck, 1966. (grade 8 and up)
    Title of this rather sexist book implies that this is a biography, but most of it deals with the period and only a small part with her life. It is implied that Austen "failed" for never marrying.

▶━0━●━0━0━0━0━0━0━0━0━0━●━●━0━0━0━0━0━●━0━0━0━0━●━0━●━●━0━0━0━0━0━0━0━●━●━◀

PEARL BAILEY
1918–

Singer and actress

Pearl Bailey danced and sang in her minister father's revivalist church before she was even three years old. During World War II she toured the country as an entertainer with the USO. In 1946 she made her Broadway debut in *St. Louis Woman*, an all-black musical, and won an award as the season's best newcomer. Since then she has performed in other Broadway shows, movies, and nightclubs, and made recordings. The high point of her career came in 1967 when she headed an all-black cast in a new Broadway pro-

20

duction of the musical comedy *Hello, Dolly!*, for which she received many awards.

*** *Bailey, Pearl* THE RAW PEARL Harcourt, 1968. (grade 9 and up)
   Adult autobiography is distinguished for its down-to-earth, highly readable style which appeals to reluctant as well as more enthusiastic readers. This book is not ghostwritten as are so many personal narratives by celebrities; Ms. Bailey's own distinctive style and manner are captured on each page.

LUCILLE BALL
1911–

Award-winning television and film actress and president of Desilu Productions

Lucille Ball, one of the most talented and funniest women in show business today, is also a successful business-woman.

She started her career in vaudeville and on the stage, and then went to Hollywood where she moved from small parts into leading ones. Already familiar to movie and radio fans, she became very famous when she and her husband, Desi Arnaz, starred in their television series, "I Love Lucy." From its start in 1950 they owned the series' production company, Desilu.

When in 1953 the real-life Lucille Ball was expecting a baby, the television Lucy also rushed to the hospital to give birth. That episode was seen by the largest audience of a commercial show up to that time.

Lucille Ball has since appeared in other series, television specials, and movies. She has won numerous awards, including two Emmy awards.

In 1962 she bought out her former husband's share of Desilu and turned the then-losing outfit into a profitable one, proving that she is definitely not the scatterbrained character she frequently portrays.

* *Cohen, Joel H.* LAUGH WITH LUCY: THE STORY OF LUCILLE BALL Illus. with photographs. Scholastic, 1974. (grades 4-7)
Enjoyable, fast-moving biography of the performer is somewhat superficial and written in fan-magazine style. The focus is on her career as comedienne and mother, with no discussion of her business enterprises. Much of the book also tells the plots and stories of her television shows.

EMILY DUNNING BARRINGER, M.D.
1876–1961

First American woman ambulance surgeon

Emily Dunning Barringer graduated second in her class at medical school and won first place in competitions for positions at two leading New York hospitals, but was denied both appointments because of her sex. A year later she became the first woman intern in a city hospital. The men on the staff conspired to make her quit, but she refused to be intimidated. She raced to emergencies in a horse-drawn ambulance, attracting much attention and comment as the first and only woman ambulance surgeon.

During her long medical career she served as president of the American Medical Women's Association, and during World War II worked to see that women doctors got equal status with men doctors in the armed services.

*** *Noble, Iris* FIRST WOMAN AMBULANCE SURGEON Messner, 1962. (grades 6-10)

Exciting and inspiring biography discusses Dr. Barringer's childhood and years of study culminating in her exciting but difficult year of internship at New York's Bellevue Hospital. It also discusses her later years of accomplishment. The stereotypes of sex roles are also explored.

** *Dunnahoo, Terry* EMILY DUNNING: A PORTRAIT Reilly & Lee, 1970. (grades 4-7)

An interesting, good biography, it is somewhat lacking in the drama and excitement that Dr. Barringer displayed in her own life. However, it is a fairly accurate account that is easy to read.

▬•▬0▬•▬0▬•▬0▬•▬0▬•▬0▬•▬0▬•▬0▬•▬0▬•▬0▬•▬0▬•▬0▬•▬0▬•▬0▬•▬0▬•▬0▬•▬0▬•▬0▬•▬0▬•▬0▬•▬0▬•▬0▬•▬0▬•◀

ETHEL BARRYMORE
1879–1959

American actress

Ethel Barrymore and her two brothers John and Lionel were known as "the American royal family of the theater." She was a star for over fifty years, appearing on the stage and in motion pictures. Acknowledged as the head of the family, she was, her brother Lionel said, "always on hand when the chips were down."

She was a pioneer in the organization of the actors' union, Actors Equity Association, and organized benefits and performances to raise funds during its first long strike.

Ms. Barrymore received many honors, including an Academy Award in 1944, and continued to perform until she was almost eighty years old.

** *Fox, Virginia* ETHEL BARRYMORE: A PORTRAIT Reilly & Lee, 1970. (grades 4-6)
   Basically faithful to her life, this biography focusses on Barrymore's role as head of the family as well as on her professional career. However, the author fails to excite the reader in this slightly bland biography.

* *Newman, Shirlee* ETHEL BARRYMORE: GIRL ACTRESS Illus. Bobbs–Merrill, 1966. (grades 3-7)
   Emphasis on childhood prevents Ethel Barrymore from emerging as the strong, independent woman she later became. Implication is that she had little to do with making the decision to become an actress, but that she was "predestined" to it. Though it has no real sexism or sex-stereotyping, this biography lacks any real significance.

CLARA BARTON
1821–1912

Founder of the American Red Cross

Clara Barton, the founder of the American Red Cross, was a shy and lonely child who early showed an interest and talent for nursing. She began teaching school at eighteen, and founded one of New Jersey's first public schools where she quickly noticed the salary and promotion inequities between men and women. Later she maintained a close association with leaders of the women's rights movement and made clear her strong support for suffrage and equal pay for equal work.

During the Civil War, Clara Barton distributed first aid supplies. She often went right into the lines of fire to aid the injured, earning herself the title "angel of the battlefields." She initiated the practice of preparing and distributing lists of those dead or missing in action.

After the war Ms. Barton was acclaimed as a great patriot, humanitarian, and war heroine. Later, in Europe, she became involved in war relief and the newly formed Red Cross. She worked indefatigably urging the United States to form an American Red Cross, and when this was finally accomplished, Clara Barton was chosen as the first president, a post she held for twenty-three years.

Her lifetime devotion to the service of humanity made her the best-known and most honored woman of her time.

*** *Boylston, Helen* CLARA BARTON: FOUNDER OF THE AMERICAN RED CROSS Illus. Random, 1955. (grades 4-6)

Excellent biography clearly states Ms. Barton's contributions to humanity. Focusses on her early work in nursing but also details her founding of the American Red Cross.

*** *Grant, Matthew G.* CLARA BARTON Illus. Creative Education/Children's Pr., 1974. (grades 3-6)

Generously illustrated, this biography gives a fine portrayal of Clara Barton's life and also describes the services of the Red Cross in peace as well as war. Easy-to-read, and quite brief, it has appeal to reluctant readers as well as young, enthusiastic ones.

*** *Mann, Peggy* CLARA BARTON: BATTLEFIELD NURSE Illus. Coward, 1969. (grades 3-5)

Well-rounded biography treats the fact that women were not given equal treatment with men during this period. Though easy-to-read, this biography has a high interest level which makes it suitable for older readers, too. Clara Barton's nursing contributions are made clear, and the book also chronicles her efforts to establish the Red Cross in America and to extend its work to peacetime.

*** *Nolan, Jeannette* STORY OF CLARA BARTON OF THE RED CROSS Messner, 1941. (grade 6 and up)

Excellent biography gives an absorbing portrayal of Clara Barton and discusses the prejudices against women with which she had to contend throughout her life. Her contributions are made clear in this warm and moving biography.

*** *Rose, Mary C.* CLARA BARTON: SOLDIER OF MERCY Illus. Garrard, 1961. (grades 2-5)

In this nonfictionalized biography Clara Barton's achievements are movingly told with great sincerity. Her early shyness and the emotional support she gained from her family are stressed.

* *Stevenson, Augusta* CLARA BARTON: GIRL NURSE Illus. Bobbs–Merrill, 1946. (grades 3-6)

Highly fictionalized but sugar-coated account of Clara Barton's childhood is based on true events and situations which Clara Barton revealed in her own writings. Her later achievements are presented well, but too briefly.

DAISY BATES
1920–

Civil rights worker

Daisy Bates, perhaps more than anyone else, is responsible for the successful integration of Little Rock High School in 1957. Ms. Bates had been the state president of the National Association for the Advancement of Colored People (NAACP) when the United States Supreme Court ruled in 1954 that segregation in public schools was unconstitutional.

The governor of Arkansas refused to comply with the decision, but Daisy Bates with other leaders of the black community decided to fight back. Her life was in constant danger and the newspaper she and her husband owned was forced out of business. Daisy Bates stood firm, giving courage to the students and parents involved in the struggle, and today blacks and whites go to school together in Little Rock.

*** *Bates, Daisy* LONG SHADOW OF LITTLE ROCK McKay, 1962.
(grade 8 and up)
   Although Daisy Bates relates the story of the struggle for school integration in Little Rock, this is essentially a personal memoir, providing a dignified but moving account of Bates's own life.

27

KATHERINE LEE BATES
1859–1929

American poet and professor

Katherine Lee Bates wrote the poem "America the Beautiful" on a trip across the country, inspired by the view from the top of Pikes Peak in Colorado.

She was the youngest in her family and for financial reasons the only one to attend college. After her graduation from Wellesley College she studied literature at Oxford University in England. Ms. Bates taught new approaches to the study of English literature, served as chairman of Wellesley's English department, and wrote critical reviews, articles, and poetry.

** *Myers, Elisabeth P.* KATHERINE LEE BATES: GIRL POET Illus. Bobbs–Merrill, 1961. (grades 3-7)
   Good biography focusses on the childhood of Katherine Lee Bates, giving a vivid picture of the times and of life in a family that valued education and independence. Bates's later achievements are stated briefly and accurately.

LAURA BAUGH
1955–

Professional golfer

Professional golfer Laura Baugh began hitting golf balls when she was four years old. At age seven she won her first of four consecutive National Peewee Championships.

Golf remained the main interest for young Laura, and she twice won the Los Angeles Women's Championship when she was fourteen and fifteen. At sixteen she became the youngest person ever to win the United States Women's Amateur Championship. However, she could not join her high school's golf team because it was for boys only.

She was an excellent student with a particular interest in the sciences, but decided to turn professional rather than continue her studies in college. During her first year of touring she was named "rookie of the year" by *Golf Digest*.

Laura Baugh's popularity with golf fans is due not only to her ability but also to her great attractiveness. Her air of self-assurance and confidence is unusual for someone so young, and her beauty alone could easily have launched her on a successful modelling career. She has taken advantage of this natural endowment by lending her name to the endorsements of many products, and as a result, is one of the few women golfers to have earned $100,000 in a single year.

** *Jacobs, Linda* LAURA BAUGH: GOLF'S GOLDEN GIRL Illus. with photographs. EMC, 1975. (reading level, grades 4-6; interest level through high school)

Mostly nonsexist, the author has some trouble avoiding focus on the subject's beauty and charm. There is something slightly old-fashioned and eulogistic in the writing, but the book still gives a good overall picture of the subject and offers warm and personal glimpses of her private life. The large number of illustrations greatly enhances the book.

GERTRUDE BELL
1868–1926

Administrator, author, and expert on Arabian affairs

Oxford University graduate Gertrude Bell was the author of the first recorded journey through the Arabian desert and wrote several other books about her experiences and archaeological explorations there.

During World War I, Gertrude Bell served as a major interpreter and political intelligence operator for Central Arabia, and is credited with being almost single-handedly responsible for the selection of Faisal as king. In her later years she was appointed Honorary Director of Antiquities of a museum she helped to create in Baghdad, Iraq.

** *Kamm, Josephine* GERTRUDE BELL: DAUGHTER OF THE DESERT Vanguard, 1956. (grade 7 and up)
This well-documented, straightforward, nonfictionalized narrative is an in-depth account of the life of Englishwoman Gertrude Bell. At times too detailed for the general reader, it also lacks some vitality.

SAINT BERNADETTE OF LOURDES
1844–1879

When young Bernadette was only fourteen she saw eighteen visions of the Virgin Mary in a grotto near her home in Lourdes, in southern France. Although no one else saw the vision, those who observed her seeing it were convinced of the extraordinary event. A miraculous spring that appeared at the time of her vision has been considered responsible for many spiritual and physical healings.

Bernadette became a nun at Nevers, France, where her spiritual generosity and courage made her loved by all. From early childhood she was sickly, and at thirty-five she finally succumbed to tuberculosis.

In 1933 she was named a saint by the Roman Catholic church.

* *Daughters of St. Paul* LIGHT IN THE GROTTO: THE LIFE OF ST. BERNADETTE Illus. Daughters of St. Paul, 1967. (grades 3-7)
Very readable, well-paced biography of Saint Bernadette is marred because it places emphasis not only on her religious devotion, but also on her excessive passivity and willingness to denigrate herself.

* *Daughters of St. Paul* ST. BERNADETTE Illus. Daughters of St. Paul, 1958. (grades 3-6)
Colorfully illustrated, brief, readable story of Bernadette closely follows her life as it has been documented. Her goodness, innocence, but also her passivity are clearly shown.

SARAH BERNHARDT
1844–1923

French actress

"Divine Sarah," as she was known, was one of the world's most famous actresses, equally adept at classic tragedies and modern melodramas. Sarah Bernhardt toured England, the United States, and European countries where audiences clamored to see her, even when they could not understand her native French.

Even though a leg amputation prevented her from walking or standing unaided, Ms. Bernhardt continued to perform, and during World War I she entertained the soldiers in the trenches.

The Legion of Honor was conferred upon her in 1914.

*** *Skinner, Cornelia Otis* MADAME SARAH Illus. Houghton Mifflin, 1967. (grade 9 and up)

Full-length, adult biography gives an objective, elucidating account of the life of one of the world's most fascinating women. The author, an actress as well as writer, brings unusual insight into her examination of the life of Bernhardt.

MARTHA BERRY
1866–1942

Educator, philanthropist, and founder
of Appalachian schools

Beginning with a Sunday school for a few neighboring mountain children in Georgia, Martha Berry eventually built an educational complex that today includes over one hundred buildings scattered over thousands of acres in Mount Berry, Georgia.

Her ideas of education were unusual for her time, for she believed that young people would benefit from practical and vocational learning as well as academic studies. Thus, Berry students not only learned and practiced the newest methods in agriculture and homemaking, but also made the school almost self-supporting by their labor. Martha Berry also had a unique gift for raising funds, a quality which allowed Berry College to become established within twenty years.

*** *Blackburn, Joyce* MARTHA BERRY: A BIOGRAPHY Illus. Lippincott, 1968. (grades 7-9)
   Outstanding, fast-moving, and faithful biography vividly recreates the life of this warm, compassionate woman who did so much for the people of Appalachia and for students from all over the world.

*** *Kane, Harnett, and Henry, Inez* MIRACLE IN THE MOUNTAINS: PORTRAIT OF MARTHA BERRY Doubleday, 1956. (grade 9 and up)
   One of the authors, Ms. Henry, was a long-time associate of Martha Berry, and has given her readers an excellent,

first-hand, well-balanced account of the life of the educator and philanthropist. Though an adult book, it is readable, fast-moving, and suitable for young readers.

*** *Myers, Elisabeth P.* ANGEL OF APPALACHIA: MARTHA BERRY Messner, 1968. (grades 6-10)
Fine portrayal of Martha Berry is highly fictionalized but accurate, providing a good, honest account of the life of the educator.

*** *Phelan, Mary* MARTHA BERRY Illus. Crowell, 1972. (grades 1-4)
Excellent, brief, introductory biography conveys a good sense of Martha Berry's accomplishments, humanity, and personality.

MARY McLEOD BETHUNE
1875–1955

Educator and advisor to presidents

Her parents and fourteen older brothers and sisters were born in slavery, but Mary McLeod Bethune, the first free-born member of the family, was encouraged by her parents to go to school. Intending to use her education to help other blacks, particularly young people, she founded a small school which through her persistent efforts eventually became Bethune-Cookman College.

Ms. Bethune won many honorary degrees, was a founder of the National Council of Negro Women, and was a leader in many political, religious, civic, and business organizations. She served Presidents Coolidge, Harding, Roosevelt, and Truman in advisory positions on many matters relating to blacks, youth, and women.

34

*** *Carruth, Ella Kaiser* SHE WANTED TO READ: THE STORY OF MARY MCLEOD BETHUNE Illus. Abingdon, 1966. (grades 3-7)
Dramatic and inspiring biography provides a good picture of a woman who achieved greatness despite numerous obstacles.

*** *Radford, Ruby L.* MARY MCLEOD BETHUNE Illus. Putnam, 1973. (grades 2-4)
Extremely good biography throws interesting light on Bethune's work in civil rights as well as in education. Easy-to-read, it is a stirring, dramatic portrait.

*** *Sterne, Emma Gelders* MARY MCLEOD BETHUNE Illus. Knopf, 1957. (grades 7-11)
Fast-moving, interesting biography incorporates background of Ms. Bethune's African roots into the compelling narrative of a distinguished lifetime helping her people.

** *Peare, Catherine Owens* MARY MCLEOD BETHUNE Vanguard, 1951. (grades 7-10)
Good biography is a moving and inspirational account of Bethune's achievements, but an implication that she was different and thus superior to other blacks detracts from its value.

* *Burt, Olive* MARY MCLEOD BETHUNE: GIRL DEVOTED TO HER PEOPLE Illus. Bobbs–Merrill, 1970. (grades 3-6)
Good, moving, and worthwhile biography focusses on the subject's youth, but is marred by comparisons between young Mary and other less gifted or ambitious black children. Insufficient information is given regarding her adult achievements.

MARY ANN BICKERDYKE
1817–1901

Civil War hospital worker

While organizing the distribution of a relief fund to servicemen in the early stages of the Civil War, Mary Ann Bickerdyke was shocked to discover the terrible conditions at combat hospitals. She spontaneously began caring for the wounded, while also cooking, distributing supplies, and doing laundry.

"Mother" Bickerdyke, as she became known, was proficient at raising funds and demonstrated tremendous competence and energy in all her endeavors. Although she gained much love and respect from the soldiers, her impatience with military inefficiency and bureaucracy made many dislike and fear her.

After the war, she worked in a home for poor women and children, helped unemployed veterans settle on farms, raised funds for victims of a locust plague, worked for the Salvation Army, assisted veterans in obtaining their pensions, and helped in the organization of the Women's Relief Corps. In 1886, Mary Ann Bickerdyke's efforts were belatedly recognized by Congress when she was awarded a $25-a-month pension.

*** *DeLeeuw, Adele* CIVIL WAR NURSE: MARY ANN BICKERDYKE
Messner, 1973. (grades 6-9)
The subject's fighting spirit is clearly evident in this excellent biography. The history of the time is incorporated into the text, and the reader is made privy to the bureaucracy and

redtape that existed in the army even at that time. The author describes Ms. Bickerdyke's individualist style with humor, but never becomes patronizing.

―――――――――――――――――――――――――――――――――

ELIZABETH BLACKWELL, M.D.
1821–1910

First woman in America to receive a medical degree

Elizabeth Blackwell, determined and well-qualified to become a doctor, was turned down at many medical schools. She was finally accepted at the Geneva Medical School of New York where her admission had been left to the students by an indecisive administration. The male students thought it was a hoax, but no longer considered it such when, as the first woman to receive a medical degree, she graduated at the head of her class. She opened a private dispensary in New York which later became the New York Infirmary and College for Women.

Elizabeth Blackwell inspired and helped many other young women to become doctors, both in the United States and in England. During the Civil War she and her younger sister, Dr. Emily Blackwell, helped select and train nurses. As a pioneer in stressing preventive medicine, sanitation, and public health, Dr. Elizabeth Blackwell has left a legacy not only to all the women doctors who followed her, but to her entire profession.

*** *Baker, Rachel* FIRST WOMAN DOCTOR: STORY OF ELIZABETH BLACKWELL, M.D. Messner, 1944. (grade 6 and up)

Superb biography has become almost a classic. Bound to spark the imagination and inspire would-be doctors, it is a dramatic, well-written biography which pays tribute to the courage and persistence of Elizabeth Blackwell.

*** *Latham, Jean Lee* ELIZABETH BLACKWELL: PIONEER WOMAN DOCTOR Illus. Garrard, 1975. (grades 3-5)

Lively, dramatic portrayal of Elizabeth Blackwell clearly conveys her determination to become a doctor and to open roads for other women. Her early nonsexist education and her later interest in preventive medicine are included in the easy-to-read text, and there is a welcome discussion that she did not always want to become a doctor. Many portrayals of Dr. Blackwell indicate that it was an early ambition, which it was not.

*** *Wilson, Dorothy Clarke* LONE WOMAN: THE STORY OF ELIZABETH BLACKWELL Illus. Little, 1970. (grade 9 and up)

An adult, full-length biography gives a detailed portrait of Elizabeth Blackwell, recreating in depth her long and productive life. Written with authenticity it is, for young readers, a definitive biography of the first woman to receive a medical degree in the United States.

** *Clapp, Patricia* DR. ELIZABETH: A BIOGRAPHY OF THE FIRST WOMAN DOCTOR Lothrop, 1974. (grades 6-9)

A good biography. However, the author has chosen to write Dr. Blackwell's story as a diary and in doing so has introduced a sense of artificiality into the text. Although generally nonsexist for the emphasis is on Dr. Blackwell as an independent, goal-oriented individual, the few "romantic" aspects of her life are somewhat stereotyped.

** *Grant, Matthew G.* ELIZABETH BLACKWELL: PIONEER DOCTOR Illus. Creative Education/Children's Pr., 1974. (grades 2-4)

Attractively and abundantly illustrated, the extremely easy-to-read, brief text attempts to cover all the salient aspects of Elizabeth Blackwell's life. This it does accurately and objectively. However, it lacks emotion and therefore she does not emerge in a warm, humanistic, and inspirational manner.

** *Heyn, Leah* CHALLENGE TO BECOME A DOCTOR: THE STORY OF ELIZABETH BLACKWELL Illus. Feminist Pr., 1971. (grades 4-8)

Written from a feminist perspective, this biography carefully points out sexual inequities and discrimination. The writing is at times somewhat uneven and stilted, detracting from an otherwise fine biography.

* *Henry, Joanne* ELIZABETH BLACKWELL: GIRL DOCTOR Illus. Bobbs–Merrill, 1961. (grades 3-7)

Nonsexist, highly fictionalized biography focusses on the childhood of Elizabeth Blackwell. Although of dubious accuracy, the book gives a good picture of her close-knit family.

NELLIE BLY
(Elizabeth Cochrane Seaman)
1867–1922

Journalist and reformer

Elizabeth Cochrane Seaman, or "Nellie Bly" as she called herself, began her colorful newspaper career when she wrote an indignant letter to a newspaper editor who opposed the idea of suffrage and careers for women. The editor was so impressed with her ability that he hired her as a reporter, thus beginning Nellie Bly's sensational reporting of the need for reforms in factories, slums, and prisons.

Nellie Bly completed one of her best-known series of articles after feigning insanity and being committed to a psychiatric ward in a New York hospital so that she could expose the brutal and neglectful treatment accorded the inmates. Her social reforms were somewhat overshadowed by her spectacular record-breaking trip around the world: daily reports of this trip were avidly followed by her readers. Nellie Bly, one of the best-known and most adventurous figures in the history of American journalism, was a pioneer in opening doors for women to enter the profession.

*** *Baker, Nina* NELLIE BLY, REPORTER Scholastic, 1972. (grades 4-6)
    Colorful biography moves quickly and reveals Nellie Bly's resourcefulness, independence, and journalistic ability.

*** *Graves, Charles* NELLIE BLY: REPORTER FOR THE WORLD Illus. Garrard, 1971. (grades 3-5)
    Very readable, this biography clearly indicates Nellie Bly's pioneer spirit as well as her skills as a reporter. Lively and exciting, it is a dramatic inspiring story.

*** *Hahn, Emily* AROUND THE WORLD WITH NELLIE BLY Illus. Houghton Mifflin, 1959. (grades 6-9)
    Remarkably good feminist biography reveals Nellie Bly's anger at discovering how many obstacles to achievement were placed before women. Her efforts to overcome much of this prejudice and to become a successful reporter are clearly demonstrated.

ELIZABETH PATTERSON BONAPARTE
1785–1879

Society belle, businesswoman, sister-in-law of Napoleon

Elizabeth Patterson was an attractive, well-to-do, eighteen-year-old American girl from Baltimore when she fell in love with and married Jerome Bonaparte, the younger brother of Napoleon Bonaparte. Napoleon, desiring his brothers to marry royalty, refused to recognize or accept this marriage and in defiance of the Pope, annulled it. Young Madame Bonaparte returned to her family home in Baltimore with her small son and spent the rest of her long life attempting to get her son, and later her grandson, recognized as heirs to the French throne. Although she never accomplished this, her determination, her shrewd business investments, and her devotion to her cause attracted much comment and attention.

* *Desmond, Alice Curtis* BEWITCHING BETSY BONAPARTE Illus. with photographs. Dodd, 1958. (grade 9 and up)

Highly fictionalized, well-written, and interesting, but occasionally sexist biography gives a good social history. Elizabeth Bonaparte emerges, only in her last years, as an independent self-actualizing individual.

JOSEPHINE BONAPARTE
1763–1814
Empress of France, wife of Napoleon I

Josephine, the wife of Napoleon I of France, was born on the island of Martinique in the Caribbean Sea. She met Napoleon Bonaparte when he was a rising young army officer after the French Revolution. They were married, and when he declared himself emperor of France in 1814, she was crowned empress.

They did not have any children (although she had two from a previous marriage) and Napoleon, eager to have an heir and to link himself with a Royal House, divorced her and married Marie Louise, daughter of the emperor of Austria.

* *Mossiker, Frances* MORE THAN A QUEEN: THE STORY OF JOSEPHINE BONAPARTE Illus. Knopf, 1971. (grades 7-9)
  Flattering, often one-sided biography draws some interesting explanations and comparisons between eighteenth- and twentieth-century attitudes towards women's education.

ROSA BONHEUR
1822–1899

French painter, first woman to win Grand Cross
of the Legion of Honor

Rosa Bonheur's artist father encouraged her talent and even before she was out of her teens she had a painting exhibited at the Paris Salon, the most important yearly exhibition of the works of living French artists.

Most of her subjects were animals, and she visited slaughterhouses and owned many animals so that she could study their muscular movements.

Bonheur's paintings were remarkable for their accuracy, drama, and power. Her most famous work, the huge life-like *The Horse Fair*, has had special appeal to youngsters, and has been widely reproduced. It hangs now in the Metropolitan Museum of Art in New York City.

** *Price, Olive* ROSA BONHEUR: PAINTER OF ANIMALS Illus. Garrard, 1972. (grades 4-6)

    Good biography is somewhat stilted and lacks the excitement and vitality displayed by the subject. However, it does offer a good accurate study of the artist, and the accompanying illustrations and reproductions, though rather ordinary, add to the book's interest.

CHER BONO
1947–

Singer and actress

Cher Bono, part Cherokee, Armenian, Turkish, and French, grew up in Los Angeles. Her dream of show business success was realized when she married Sonny Bono and as a team they started on the road to stardom. In 1965 they had five records on the best-seller charts, an achievement only equalled by Elvis Presley. Their popularity with teenage fans was due to their young image as well as their talent.

Cher designed and then marketed many of the innovative clothes they wore. Despite the prevalence of the drug culture among other performers and fans, she and Sonny campaigned against drugs and made an antimarijuana film for the federal government which was distributed to schools. From the summer of 1971 to mid-1974 they starred in their own television show. Now divorced from Sonny, Cher continues her career and feels she needs the opportunity to achieve success on her own.

** *Jacobs, Linda* CHER: SIMPLY CHER Illus. with photographs. EMC, 1975. (reading level, grades 4-6; interest level through high school)

A good biography which describes the performer's life from childhood through her teenage marriage and huge success. The book describes her need to achieve personal and professional autonomy in a life without Sonny Bono. Many photographs of her on and off television contribute greatly to the book.

REBECCA BOONE
1739–1813

Frontierswoman, wife of Daniel Boone

Pioneer and frontier life was difficult for all women, but because Rebecca Boone was married to the famed frontiersman and Indian fighter named Daniel Boone, her life was harder than most. She learned to manage without basic necessities, to handle firearms, and, though she could neither read nor write, to work with her husband to pay off their enormous debts. Rebecca Boone raised a family of nine children and cared for a second motherless family of six.

** *De Gering, Etta* WILDERNESS WIFE: THE STORY OF REBECCA BRYAN BOONE Illus. McKay, 1966. (grades 6-9)

Good biography of a courageous pioneer woman is written in colorful frontier colloquialism. Told from the perspective of pioneer family life, it is not so much a personal biography as it is a good picture of the period. Daniel Boone's own activities are not dwelled upon, though they are briefly discussed, and a bibliography, maps, and complete documentation add to the value of the book.

EVANGELINE BOOTH
1865–1950

General of the Salvation Army

"Little Eva," as General Evangeline Booth was called, grew up in England in a family whose whole life centered around their evangelistic organization, the Salvation Army. While other children played house or played school, Evangeline and her brothers and sisters played at preaching and talked of saving the souls of sinners.

While still in her teens, Evangeline became an effective administrator and leader, earning the title "angel of the slums." She was a dramatic lecturer and later organized the Salvation Army's first all-women band. Her various posts took her to Canada and later the United States where she worked to create hospitals, clinics, community centers, nurseries, and lodgings for the homeless. Later, as General of the International Organization, Evangeline Booth travelled to eighty countries and colonies.

*** *Lavine, Sigmund* EVANGELINE BOOTH: DAUGHTER OF SALVATION Illus. Dodd, 1970. (grade 7 and up)

Outstanding portrait of Evangeline Booth combines biography with the story of the developing Salvation Army. General Booth is seen in a full-dimensional light, as a competent, compassionate, and successful woman.

MARGARET BOURKE-WHITE
1905–1971

Photojournalist, first woman to become an
accredited war correspondent

Photographer Margaret Bourke-White's first assignments were to photograph steel mills and other industries in the United States. Her interest in people and places took her all over the world where she photographed poor farmers, unemployed urban dwellers, the famous and the unknown. With her camera she reported wars, social upheavals, and political revolutions for *Life* magazine and her photographs filled several books.

During World War II, as the first woman to become an accredited war correspondent, she earned the rank of lieutenant colonel. During her lifetime, Bourke-White received many awards and honors for her depictions of the depression in the United States, the emerging industrialization of Russia, the growing munitions industry in Germany, poverty in India, racial discrimination in South Africa, World War II, and the horrors of the concentration camps.

A twenty-year heroic struggle with the crippling effects of Parkinson's disease ended with her death in 1971.

*** *Bourke-White, Margaret* PORTRAIT OF MYSELF Illus. with
photographs. Simon & Schuster, 1963. (grade 9 and up)
    Excellent autobiography intended for adults is also interesting and comprehensible to much younger readers. Written after illness forced her to stop photographing, the book reflects the independence and courage of this remarkable woman.

*** *Callahan, Sean, ed.* THE PHOTOGRAPHS OF MARGARET BOURKE-WHITE Illus. with photographs. New York Graphic Society, Ltd., 1972. (all ages) Introduction by Theodore M. Brown.

Large, handsome adult volume of Bourke-White's photographs includes a skillfully and interestingly written biographical introduction. Though clear and to the point it may prove difficult reading for some younger teens, but the photographs that constitute the major part of this book will be of interest to readers of any age. The volume would be a fine accompaniment to any full-length or shorter profile intended for young readers.

*** *Noble, Iris* CAMERAS AND COURAGE: MARGARET BOURKE-WHITE Messner, 1973. (grade 8 and up)

In an unusually fine biography Bourke-White emerges as the courageous, talented, and fiercely independent woman she was. The author combines information about photography, the depression, Gandhi's nonviolent movement in India, World War II, Parkinson's disease, and the process of rehabilitation with a good personal and professional portrayal of an indomitable woman.

BELLE BOYD
1844–1900

Confederate spy, actress, and lecturer

At the start of the Civil War, Virginia-born Belle Boyd worked to raise funds for the South. Later she used her fine equestrian skills and knowledge of the surrounding area as well as her intelligence to become a valuable spy for the Confederacy.

She was frequently caught, but after gaining release resumed her activities. Her exploits were reported in the newspapers and soon Belle Boyd became as notorious in the North as she was famous in the South.

After the war, Ms. Boyd wrote a book about her experiences, became an actress, and later a popular lecturer in both the North and South.

** *Nolan, Jeannette* BELLE BOYD: SECRET AGENT Messner, 1967. (grade 6 and up)

Biography provides a picture of Belle Boyd that shows her to be heroic, assertive, and intelligent. Lacking in some of the vitality and excitement displayed by Ms. Boyd herself, the book is, nevertheless, a good, satisfactory account of her life.

ANNE DUDLEY BRADSTREET
1612–1672

Early American poet

English-born Anne Bradstreet came to the New World with her husband and family when she was eighteen years old. Despite the hardships of colonial life and eventual care of her eight children, she managed to find time for extensive reading and the writing of poetry.

Nature, history, or family were the usual themes of her poetry, and in one poem she comments on those "who say my hands a needle better fits," and continues, "If while I do prove well, it won't advance/They'll say it's stol'n, or else it was by chance."

She wrote primarily for her own satisfaction and the

pleasure of her family, but a collection of her poetry which was published in England marked her as a first poet of the American colonies.

** *Dunham, Montrew* ANNE BRADSTREET: YOUNG PURITAN POET
Illus. Bobbs–Merrill, 1969. (grades 3-7)
    Good biography highlights the childhood and youth of Anne Bradstreet, and despite fictionalization is a reasonably faithful account of her life. Young Anne emerges as highly intelligent, and her father is portrayed as willing and eager to encourage her education when he hires tutors for her in England.

MARY BRECKINRIDGE
1877–1965

Founder of the Frontier Nursing Service in Kentucky

After completing nurses' training, wealthy and socially prominent Mary Breckinridge took further degrees at Columbia University in New York and studied midwifery in the British Isles. After her return to the United States she used her skills and funds to establish the Frontier Nursing Service in Kentucky, where she spent the remainder of her life giving medical attention to the poor of that rural area.

Mary Breckinridge and her nurses rode horseback to bring their care to all who needed it, delivering babies and nursing infants, children, and adults in the primitive conditions of isolated areas.

*** *Wilkie, Katherine, and Moseley, Elizabeth* FRONTIER NURSE: MARY BRECKINRIDGE Messner, 1969. (grade 7 and up)
Smooth narrative dramatically and inspirationally traces the life of this capable, compassionate nurse who gave unselfishly of herself and inspired others to do the same.

LAURA BRIDGMAN
1829–1889

First educated blind deaf-mute

A serious illness completely destroyed Laura Bridgman's senses of hearing and sight, and to a great extent, taste and smell, when she was two years old. Her plight came to the attention of Dr. Samuel Gridley Howe of the famed Perkins Institution, a school for the blind in Boston. She enrolled there as a student, and he began the revolutionary experiment of educating a blind deaf-mute. Detailed reports of this success were later carefully studied by Anne Sullivan before she began to teach deaf and blind Helen Keller (page 157).

Laura Bridgman remained at Perkins all her life, performing simple duties, selling her handiwork, occasionally teaching sewing, maintaining an extensive correspondence, and communicating with the young students at Perkins, all of whom learned the manual alphabet.

** *Hunter, Edith Fisher* CHILD OF THE SILENT NIGHT Illus. Houghton Mifflin, 1963. (grades 3-6)
Warm, sensitive biography reveals Laura Bridgman to be

a persevering and intelligent young woman. Convincingly, but not overly fictionalized, the book closely follows her young life and relates the tireless efforts of those who helped her.

THE BRONTËS

Charlotte Brontë (pen name Currer Bell) 1816–1855
Emily Brontë (pen name Ellis Bell) 1818–1848
Anne Brontë (pen name Acton Bell) 1820–1849

Nineteenth-century British novelists

Life on the isolated bleak Yorkshire moor with their eccentric clergyman father was restrictive and lonely for the Brontë sisters. With their brother Bramwell they wrote imaginative stories which furnished their lives with excitement and drama.

The young Brontë girls attended an oppressive, harsh boarding school which only increased their loneliness and misery, and this and their later experiences as governesses and teachers are reflected in their romantic novels.

Charlotte Brontë's *Jane Eyre* and Emily Brontë's *Wuthering Heights* are today's most widely read Brontë novels. Like the other Brontë works, these not only provided rare insights into the role of women in nineteenth-century England but also served as models for many other romantic and Gothic novels.

*** *Vipont, Elfrida* WEAVER OF DREAMS: THE GIRLHOOD OF CHARLOTTE BRONTË Illus. Walck, 1966. (grades 7-9)

In this splendid biography, Charlotte Brontë expresses resentment at the stereotyped notions of a girl's role. This book is beautifully written, focussing on the youth of the Brontës and detailing the imaginary world in which they lived.

** *Kyle, Elisabeth* GIRL WITH A PEN: CHARLOTTE BRONTË Holt, 1964. (grades 5-9)
  Extremely well-written but highly fictionalized biography portrays the early life of Charlotte Brontë from her late teen years to the publication of *Jane Eyre*. Much information is provided about the close bond that existed between the young Brontës and their lively imaginations are conveyed.

ELIZABETH BARRETT BROWNING
1809–1861

British poet

Elizabeth Barrett Browning could read Homer in the original Greek when she was only eight years old, and at age fourteen she had written an epic poem. An accident left her a semi-invalid, and she was completely dominated by her unreasonable, wealthy father. She was already a popular poet when she met Robert Browning. They fell in love and she escaped from her home to marry him. Her unforgiving father refused to see or hear from her again.

Elizabeth continued to write and publish poetry and corresponded with many other women writers. She never became active in the women's rights movement, but her long poem, *Aurora Leigh*, deals sympathetically with women's rights and unwed mothers. Her long work, *The Cry of the Children*, helped awaken England to the terrible conditions of child labor. However, it is for her *Sonnets from the Portuguese* that Elizabeth Browning is best known today.

53

*** *Burnett, Constance* SILVER ANSWER: A ROMANTIC BIOGRA-
PHY OF ELIZABETH BARRETT BROWNING Illus. Knopf, 1955.
(grades 7-11)
Fine biography emphasizes the oppression to which young
Elizabeth Barrett was subjected, as well as drawing a thought-
ful portrait of her later life, her work, and her marriage.

*** *Lupton, Mary Jane* ELIZABETH BARRETT BROWNING Feminist Pr., 1972. (grade 9 and up)
Written from a feminist perspective, this adult book is a
critical treatment of Browning's work, as well as a personal
biography. Substantially documented, it contains much information not found in most other popular sources. A discussion
of *Aurora Leigh* is interesting and useful, and despite the
scholarly treatment the biography is fairly brief and quite
suitable for high school students.

** *Waite, Helen* HOW DO I LOVE THEE? Macrae, 1953. (grades
7-11)
Though stylistically uneven, this is a moving biography.
The portrait of the poet lacks sufficient depth, but her work
is discussed well and there are many quotations from her
sonnets and letters.

PEARL BUCK
1892–1973

Author

American-born Pearl Buck grew up in China where her
missionary parents provided her with an education that
combined the cultures of China and America. Throughout
her long and active lifetime she worked to promote understanding between the East and West.

She began writing as a youngster and during her career

published more than eighty major works. She wrote for children and for adults, often using the Orient as a setting. A frequent theme of her novels is women and their place in the world. Her nonfiction was on many subjects, and she published innumerable magazine articles.

Pearl Buck's most famous novel, *The Good Earth*, won her the Pulitzer Prize in 1931. In 1938 she won a Nobel Prize for literature and commented, "In my country it is important that this award has been given to a woman."

Ms. Buck, herself a mother of a retarded child, worked, through both her writing and organizations, to help retarded children. She also founded the Pearl S. Buck Foundation to help children of mixed heritage.

*** *Block, Irvin* THE LIVES OF PEARL BUCK: A TALE OF CHINA AND AMERICA Illus. with photographs. Crowell, 1973. (grades 7-10)

Beautifully written, warm, personal biography focusses on Pearl Buck as an independent, brilliant compassionate woman. Interwoven into the biography are the plots of some of her best-known works, and her literary style is carefully commented upon. Ms. Buck emerges as the multidimensional woman she was, and her mother too is depicted as a remarkably courageous and independent woman.

*** *Buck, Pearl S.* MY SEVERAL WORLDS: A PERSONAL RECORD (abridged for young readers) Day, 1954. (grades 6-9)

Very fine book relates some of Buck's experiences in China and America. She acknowledges how grateful she is that her schooling was equal to that offered boys: "we were not corrupted by home economics or cookery or any such soft substitute for hard thinking . . . the theory was . . . that any educated woman can read a cookbook or follow a dress pattern."

*** *Schoen, Celin V.* PEARL BUCK: FAMED AMERICAN AUTHOR OF ORIENTAL STORIES SamHar Pr., 1972. (grade 7 and up)

Extremely brief (thirty pages) but excellent nonfictional-ized biography deals with Pearl Buck's personal and professional life. Emphasis is on her experiences rather than on her works, and the book provides a thoughtful examination of one of America's most prolific writers.

* *Myers, Elisabeth P.* PEARL BUCK: LITERARY GIRL Bobbs–Merrill, 1974. (grades 3-7)

Mediocre biography of the author is thin in characterization and rather uninspiring. Reasonably accurate as far as the basic facts are concerned, it attempts to give a picture of Chinese life in the early twentieth century, but never really succeeds in bringing the culture to life.

ABBIE BURGESS
1839–1892

Lighthouse keeper

The Burgess family lived on a small island where young Abbie's father was the lighthouse keeper. The mother was ill so teenager Abbie took care of her sisters and ran the household. When her brother left the island she helped her father with his duties and, during a two-year period when violent storms kept her father on the mainland, she alone tended the whale oil lamps on the lighthouse towers. Her commitment to that difficult and often hazardous task helped save many passing ships.

After her own family left the island, she assisted the family who took over the job. She later married the new lighthouse keeper's son and the two left to take over another lighthouse.

** *Jones, Dorothy and Sargent, Ruth S.* ABBIE BURGESS: LIGHT-
HOUSE HEROINE Funk & Wagnalls, 1969. (grades 7-10)

The major events in this good biography are true, but much of the story is fictionalized. Abbie Burgess emerges as a young woman with unusual courage and a sense of responsibility to her family and to the duties of managing a lighthouse. The early chapters are particularly inspirational; the later ones are somewhat more romantic when young Ms. Burgess meets and marries the young son of the new lighthouse keeper.

FRANCES HODGSON BURNETT
1849–1924
Author

Living in poverty in the Tennessee mountains was a radical change for Frances Hodgson Burnett's once wealthy British family, but teenager Frances ambitiously tried to help by raising chickens, starting a school, and giving music lessons. However it was the short stories which she sold to magazines that started her on the road to literary and financial success.

Among her short stories and novels for children and adults was the enormously popular, now little-read *Little Lord Fauntleroy*. The novels *Sarah Crewe* and *The Secret Garden* continue to be read and loved by each new generation of readers.

** *Burnett, Constance B.* HAPPILY EVER AFTER: A PORTRAIT OF FRANCES HODGSON BURNETT Vanguard, 1965. (grade 7 and up)

A good biography written by the subject's daughter-in-law is a thoughtful, documented, and honest examination of the personal life of the popular author. Lacking in the drama and excitement found in Burnett's own novels, the biography may have more appeal to adults interested in children's literature than to children themselves.

●-O-●-O-●-O-●-O-●-O-●-O-●-O-●-O-●-O-●-O-●-O-●-O-●-O-●-O-●-O-●-O-●-O-●-O-●-O-●-O-●-O-●-O-●-O-●-O-●-O-●

RACHEL CARSON
1907–1964

Marine biologist, conservationist, and author

Rachel Carson's rare gift for writing and her knowledge of marine biology led her to become the first woman scientist to write for the United States Bureau of Fisheries. Her books *Under the Sea Wind, The Sea Around Us,* and *Edge of Sea* were well received, but when *Silent Spring* was published in 1962, her plea for biological control (instead of chemical control) of insects and pests enraged and threatened the huge chemical industry. The manufacturers of DDT and similar products tried to denounce her as an emotional, nonscientific crank, but she succeeded in alerting the public and the President's Science Advisory Committee to the poisonous nature of pesticides.

Ms. Carson received many honors and awards for her work. Unfortunately she died in 1964, before the present American environmental drive, which, to a large extent, is due to the principles and discoveries which were her life's work.

*** *Brooks, Paul* RACHEL CARSON AT WORK Illus. with photographs. Houghton Mifflin, 1972. (grade 9 and up)

Excellent, full-length, adult biography of Rachel Carson offers an account of her personal life, but focusses on her scientific work. A distinguished, competent treatment of great interest to those readers with knowledge of the sciences. Extensive quotations from her works add considerably to the value of this thoroughly researched, well-documented work.

*** *Latham, Jean Lee* RACHEL CARSON: WHO LOVED THE SEA Illus. Garrard, 1973. (grades 2-5)

Very fine biography reveals Rachel Carson's rare combination of writing and scientific background and shows her to be a crusader and pioneer in ecology awareness. The criticism of her work by the pesticide industry is not indicated here, but Carson's consciousness of herself as a pioneer woman in her particular scientific field is clearly shown. She emerges as a warm person, devoted to her family, energetic, and resourceful.

*** *Sterling, Philip* SEA AND EARTH: THE LIFE OF RACHEL CARSON Illus. Crowell, 1970. (grades 5-8)

Outstanding, thoroughly researched and documented biography offers a well-rounded portrait of the woman who combined her literary and scientific talents with a courageous desire to enlighten the public and who became one of the most influential people of our times. The author writes with clarity, revealing Carson's contributions but also depicting her as a warm human being.

ROSEMARY CASALS
1948–

*Tennis champion, advocate of equal rights
for women in tennis*

Professional tennis champion Rosemary Casals learned to play tennis on San Francisco's public courts. Her father began teaching her when she was eight, and by the time she was fifteen she had won almost every junior title in California. While she was a high school student she was invited to coach the girls' tennis team, and after graduation won almost every important title in women's tennis.

At five feet, two inches, Rosemary Casals is short for a tennis player, but she compensates for this with her fast running and scrambling. With her frequent doubles partner, Billie Jean King, Ms. Casals organized the professional women's boycott of major tournaments to demand equal rights, prize money, and center court time. In 1973 she won the Family Circle Cup Crystal Trophy and $30,000, then the biggest prize in the history of women's tennis.

** *Jacobs, Linda* ROSEMARY CASALS: THE REBEL ROSEBUD Illus. with photographs. EMC, 1974. (reading level, grades 4-6; interest level through high school)

The somewhat pedestrian approach and occasional apologies for the subject's caustic wit detract from an otherwise excellent biography. The author has traced Ms. Casal's life from the beginning of her interest in tennis, and goes into careful detail about the politics of women's tennis.

MARY CASSATT
1845–1926

American painter

When American-born Mary Cassatt decided to become a serious artist, she defied the social convention that a woman just use her talents for decorative purposes. She studied first in Philadelphia, then in Paris, and became one of the greatest painters of children and women. The mothers in her paintings are frequently depicted as active individuals, not idle as usually painted by other artists.

Although not an Impressionist herself, Ms. Cassatt worked closely with them, and due to her efforts, many French Impressionist paintings were acquired by collectors in the United States.

Mary Cassatt received many awards for her work and was a highly successful artist in her lifetime. Today her works hang in museums throughout the world.

*** *McKown, Robin* THE WORLD OF MARY CASSATT Illus. Crowell, 1972. (grades 5-8)

Outstanding nonfictionalized biography of interest to the student of art as well as to the general reader. The book combines the development of the French Impressionists with the life story of the woman who worked with them and introduced their work to the United States.

*** *Myers, Elizabeth* MARY CASSATT: A PORTRAIT Illus. Reilly & Lee, 1971. (grades 4-7)

Absorbing biography gives a personal and professional

account of the life of the artist. Written for a wide audience, the book will appeal to casual readers who have no special interest or knowledge of art, as well as to those with a background in that area.

** *Wilson, Ellen* AMERICAN PAINTER IN PARIS: A LIFE OF MARY CASSATT Illus. Farrar, 1971. (grade 5 and up)
   Good biography gives straightforward account of the life of the American artist, but does not fully capture the spirit of her life or times. The author indicates that Ms. Cassatt, in her later years, regretted not marrying and having children.

WILLA CATHER
1873–1947

American writer

The author of *O Pioneers!*, *My Antonia*, and other prairie novels grew up in Nebraska where she learned to love the outdoors, and became interested in science and literature. At college, Willa Cather's talent for writing became apparent, and after graduation she worked for newspapers and magazines. After her first novel was published, Ms. Cather decided to forego her magazine job and to write fiction only. Her novels deal mainly with American experiences, and specifically with the American drive to achieve and express individuality.

Ms. Cather received many honorary degrees and awards, and though she directed that none of her novels be made into films or anthologized in textbooks, her works remain popular with young people as well as adults. Their appeal lies in her style, subject matter, and ability to recapture the not-so-distant past.

*** *Bonahm, Barbara* WILLA CATHER Illus. Chilton, 1970. (grade 7 and up)

Outstanding biography thoughtfully discusses Willa Cather's life as well as the famous and talented people with whom she associated. Her works are briefly described, a device which succeeds in encouraging youngsters to read her novels or to reconsider them with new insights.

*** *Franchere, Ruth* WILLA: THE STORY OF WILLA CATHER'S GROWING UP Illus. Crowell, 1958. (grade 5 and up)

Sympathetic, well-paced biography of Willa Cather is for youngsters not yet ready to read her works. The emphasis is on her childhood and youth, but the author perceptively describes the young girl who will later become a fine writer. A moving and exciting book, it offers a good picture of the last years of frontier life and of a family who encouraged their daughter to express herself.

** *Brown, Marion and Crone, Ruth* WILLA CATHER: THE WOMAN AND HER WORKS Illus. Scribner, 1970. (grade 7 and up)

A good, mature biography gives a detailed, substantial account of the life of Willa Cather. Despite occasional slow-moving sections of the book, a good portrait of the writer emerges.

CATHERINE OF ARAGON
1485–1536

Queen of England

Catherine of Aragon, daughter of Ferdinand and Isabella of Spain, was widowed at sixteen by the eldest son of England's King Henry VII. Several years later she married the king's younger son who by then had assumed the throne to become Henry VIII. Despite her opposition,

Henry VIII later broke with the Roman Catholic church and annulled their union. She subsequently passed the rest of her life in seclusion and in religious devotions.

Catherine of Aragon was a well-educated, cultured woman who showed extraordinary courage under great misfortunes and difficulties.

** *Roll, Winifred* THE POMEGRANATE AND THE ROSE: THE STORY OF KATHERINE OF ARAGON Prentice-Hall, 1970. (grade 7 and up)

Good nonfictionalized book combines biography with history. Fine historical treatment, giving a perceptive picture of a woman living in a very difficult situation.

CATHERINE THE GREAT
1729–1796

Empress of Russia, 1762–96

Catherine the Great was an obscure German princess who went to Russia to marry the Grand Duke Peter. When he became emperor of Russia, she led a revolt to remove him from the throne, and became empress of Russia. She ruled with absolute power for thirty-five years, during which time she extended the Russian borders, took away power from the church, and introduced some local government throughout the empire.

Catherine fostered the love of the French language and culture and was herself a good sculptor and painter. She wrote a history of Russia, memoirs, comedies, and stories in French and Russian. After her death her son succeeded her as emperor of Russia.

*** *Noble, Iris* EMPRESS OF ALL RUSSIA: CATHERINE THE GREAT
    Messner, 1966. (grade 7 and up)
       Extremely well-balanced, interesting account of the life of Catherine the Great. Convincingly fictionalized, the biography provides a thoughtful examination of the historical period as well as the personality of Catherine.

EDITH CAVELL
1865–1915

Nurse and World War I spy

English-born Edith Cavell trained as a nurse in London and later went to Belgium to head that country's first nursing school and national nursing program. When World War I broke out, the Germans occupied Belgium. Edith Cavell's hospital treated German and Allied soldiers, but as a member of the underground resistance movement, she aided the escape of hundreds of Allied soldiers. Her activities eventually became known by the Germans, who apprehended her and sentenced her to death by a firing squad. Edith Cavell was regarded as a martyr in England. After the war, services were held for her in Westminster Abbey and today a statue of her stands near Trafalgar Square in London.

*** *Grey, Elizabeth* FRIEND WITHIN THE GATES: THE STORY OF
EDITH CAVELL Illus. Houghton Mifflin, 1961. (grades 5-9)
Excellent biography places emphasis on Cavell's earlier
years as a nurse, but also vividly depicts her efforts on behalf
of the Allies during World War I.

*** *Elkon, Juliette* EDITH CAVELL: HEROIC NURSE Messner,
1956. (grade 6 and up)
Dramatic, stirring account of the life of this heroic nurse
skillfully conveys her dedication to human life and values.

** *DeLeeuw, Adele Louise* EDITH CAVELL: NURSE, SPY, HEROINE
Illus. Putnam, 1968. (grades 5-7)
Good biography focusses on Ms. Cavell's activities during
World War I, and though fairly sensitive and lively, lacks
some substance.

LYDIA MARIA CHILD
1802–1880

Author and abolitionist

Lydia Maria Child sacrificed a career as a popular and
financially successful author to devote herself to abolitionist writings. When her strong denunciation of slavery and
racial inequalities entitled *An Appeal in Favor of that Class
of Americans Called Africans* was published in 1833 and
angered book dealers, they stopped carrying her other
books. Ms. Child wrote pamphlets and other books against
slavery and became the only American woman newspaper
editor when she took over the publication of the *National
Anti-Slavery Standard*.

Lydia Maria Child was a prolific writer and a woman of

boundless energy. Besides fictional works, she wrote on such varied subjects as homemaking, child care, society, and history. She was also the editor of the first American periodical for children.

*** *Meltzer, Milton* TONGUE OF FLAME: THE LIFE OF LYDIA MARIA CHILD Crowell, 1965. (grade 7 and up)
    Thoroughly and competently researched biography gives a vivid portrait of the era as well as a thought-provoking portrait of the woman who risked her career to attack slavery. An appendix lists not only works about Ms. Child, but also those by her, adding to the value of an already fine book.

SHIRLEY CHISHOLM
1924–

American congresswoman

Shirley Chisholm is the first black woman to serve in Congress. She is the representative of a New York City district and from the start of her first term has been the outspoken advocate of bills that criticize military spending, encourage day care, revise social security laws, and encourage equality between races, ethnic groups, and men and women.

A brilliant student in Jamaica where she spent some of her early childhood and in Brooklyn where she grew up, Chisholm has earned graduate degrees in education and served as a supervisor of day care centers in New York. As a member of the New York State Assembly she figured importantly in legislation which supported education.

As a congresswoman, Ms. Chisholm became well known throughout the nation and was a serious candidate in the 1972 presidential primary. Although she did not win a place on the November ballot, a large number of supporters had joined her on the "Chisholm Trail" and she earned the respect and admiration of the nation.

*** *Brownmiller, Susan* SHIRLEY CHISHOLM Illus. with photographs. Archway, 1970. (grades 4-8)

Outstanding feminist biography of the dynamic congresswoman has appeal for older reluctant readers as well as younger ones. Ms. Chisholm's childhood, youth, and adult accomplishments are well presented against the background of New York and the Caribbean where she spent her earliest years.

*** *Chisholm, Shirley* UNBOUGHT AND UNBOSSES Houghton Mifflin, 1970. (grade 7 and up)

Excellent autobiography was not written for youngsters but is clear, thought-provoking, and inspiring for them. The prose is not difficult to understand, and young competent readers will be engrossed in this intimate portrayal of the career of the first black congresswoman.

*** *Haskins, James* FIGHTING SHIRLEY CHISHOLM Illus. with photographs. Dial, 1975. (grade 6 and up)

Outstanding book—the epitome of a good biography. Dialogue is used effectively and there is clear evidence of the author's thorough research into the subject's life. The essential spirit of Shirley Chisholm emerges as the author traces her life from early childhood to her political career. The author is fully aware of his subject as a black and as a woman and uses these facts to underline her minority status clearly and often, but never self-consciously. An appendix to the book lists her legislative accomplishments, further enhancing the biography.

*** *Hicks, Nancy* THE HONORABLE SHIRLEY CHISHOLM: CON-
GRESSWOMAN FROM BROOKLYN Lion, 1971. (grades 5-9)
Excellent portrait of Ms. Chisholm is a straightforward
narrative, employing good journalistic style. Young readers
will find it easy to follow; older ones will also find it interesting.

EUGENIE CLARK
1922–
Ichthyologist and oceanographer

Even as a child in New York City, Eugenie Clark was interested in fish. She visited the aquarium regularly and soon
knew her life's work would be in science, with fish as a
specialty. She majored in zoology at college, earned a master's and a doctorate degree, and won many fellowships
and scholarships including a Fulbright.

As an ichthyologist and oceanographer, Dr. Clark undertook underwater research expeditions throughout the
world and has developed a major marine laboratory in
Florida.

*** *Clarke, Eugenie* LADY AND THE SHARKS Illus. with photographs. Harper, 1969. (grade 9 and up)
Adult, personal narrative is more oriented towards the
scientific reader, but its fast-moving, readable style is not
weighted down with complicated terminology or concepts.
Provides a good biography for the general reader of a woman
who has carved out an exciting life for herself in marine
biology.

69

*** *Clark, Eugenie* LADY WITH A SPEAR Illus. with photographs. Harper, 1953; Ballantine, 1974. (grade 8 and up)

Interesting adult biography will have special appeal to those interested in various fields of marine biology. The author discusses her childhood and youth, and general readers will find this to be a fast-moving, immensely readable story of a woman's exciting life.

CLEOPATRA

69 B.C.–30 B.C.

Queen of Egypt, 51 B.C.–30 B.C.

When seventeen-year-old Cleopatra ascended to the Egyptian throne she was expected to rule jointly with a younger brother. However, aided by Rome's Julius Caesar, she gained absolute authority over Egypt. Her reign ended after her forces, combined with those of Mark Antony, were defeated by Octavian. Rather than be faced with going to Rome as a prisoner, Cleopatra took her life by placing an asp to her bosom.

Today she is remembered for her legendary love affairs with Julius Caesar and Mark Antony, and for her courage and beauty. She was the last regent of the dynasty of Ptolemies, after which Egypt became a province of Rome.

* *Leighton, Margaret* CLEOPATRA, SISTER OF THE MOON Farrar, 1969. (grades 7-9)

Well-written, fictionalized biography of Cleopatra shows her maintaining her power through seductive means, and portrays her as passive and dependent on men.

†† *Crayder, Teresa* CLEOPATRA Coward, 1969. (reading level, grade 4; interest level, grades 6-12)

Poorly written, sexist biography is intended for reluctant readers. Youngsters whose reading background is composed of fan magazines and true romances may be comfortable but will not have their horizons widened by this biography. Focus is on Cleopatra's need for Caesar's approval and her romantic interests rather than on any of her political accomplishments.

JACQUELINE COCHRAN

1910(?)–

Aviator and businesswoman

After a childhood marked by physical and emotional hunger, almost no schooling, and work in the cotton mills, Jacqueline Cochran became a beauty shop operator.

In 1932 she decided to learn to fly, and within a few years was winning air races and setting records for speed, distance, and altitude. During World War II she served as director of the Women Auxiliary Service Pilots (WASP).

Although flying has been one of her chief interests, she also founded and heads a highly successful cosmetic business, has taken an active part in politics, has worked as a correspondent for a leading national magazine, and has served as an officer in several aeronautic associations.

As a pilot her achievements have seldom been surpassed. In 1953 she became the first woman to break the sound barrier, and since then has set many jet speed records for both men and women. Among her numerous awards for aviation are the Air Force Association Award, the Distinguished Flying Cross, and the French Legion of Merit. In 1971 she became the only living woman to be included in the Aviation Hall of Fame. Her outstanding accomplishments in business have been widely acknowledged, and she twice has been named "Woman of the Year in Business."

*** Fisher, Marquita O. JACQUELINE COCHRAN: FIRST LADY OF FLIGHT Illus. Garrard, 1973. (grades 3-5)
Fast-moving, anecdotal, and brisk narrative traces Ms. Cochran's life from her early impoverished childhood to her success as an aviator and businesswoman. Easy-to-read, this book is warm and dramatic, and includes most of the major accomplishments of Cochran's life.

KATHARINE CORNELL
1898–

Actress and theater manager

Since 1925 Katharine Cornell has been a theatrical star and the recipient of many awards and honorary doctorate degrees. Ms. Cornell has played a wide variety of roles in her long career and has won wide critical acclaim for her performances in *Romeo and Juliet*, *Antony and Cleopatra*, and as Elizabeth Barrett Browning in *The Barretts of Wimpole Street*. She has managed most of her own productions and often has been directed by her producer-husband, Guthrie McClintic.

During World War II she toured army bases bringing live performances to servicemen who had never before seen professional theater. Katharine Cornell is among the few successful actresses who has spent much of her time performing on the road. For this dedication to her career and to her audiences, and for her extraordinary talent, Ms. Cornell has received the respect and devotion of theater lovers across the United States.

*** *Malvern, Gladys* Curtain Going Up: the story of katharine cornell Messner, 1943. (grade 7 and up)
Outstanding biography of the great actress and manager Katharine Cornell clearly shows that the theater is not all glamour, but entails hard work, intellect, loyalty, and perseverance. Exciting to read as a novel, the biography is faithful to the life of Ms. Cornell, and has appeal for all readers, not only those interested in the theater.

LOTTA CRABTREE
1847–1924

Actress, child star of the gold rush days

When she was quite young, Lotta Crabtree's parents moved to California searching for gold. Her mother ran a boardinghouse at which Lotta met an actress who taught her to sing and dance. By the time she was eight years old, Lotta was appearing professionally at saloon theaters, variety halls, and amusement parks throughout the West. The gold miners adored the child star and her earnings supported her family.

Her fame and popularity spread to the midwestern and eastern states, and Lotta Crabtree became the highest paid actress in America. She invested her earnings soundly, and, at her death, left a huge estate to various philanthropic causes.

** *Place, Marian T.* LOTTA CRABTREE: GOLD RUSH GIRL Illus. Bobbs–Merrill, 1958. (grades 3-7)
   Extremely readable, but overly fictionalized biography of Lotta Crabtree clearly depicts her as a child of unusual talent, intelligence, and resourcefulness. Only a brief portion of the book deals with her adult life, but the youngster's accomplishments do provide enough material for a good biography.

ELLEN CRAFT
c.1826–c.1897

Fugitive slave, abolitionist

Light-skinned Ellen Craft and her husband escaped from slavery by travelling north in disguise. Ms. Craft dressed as a man and assumed the role of a deaf and ill white master, while her husband posed as a slave. They escaped detection and found refuge with Quaker abolitionists in Philadelphia. They settled first in Boston, where they became leading figures in the antislavery movement. They then moved to Great Britain to raise a family.

After the Civil War they returned to the United States and bought a large plantation in Georgia on which they established an industrial school for blacks. Ellen Craft and her husband played major roles in abolitionist and freed-men societies and were greatly admired by their contemporaries.

*** *Freedman, Florence* Two Tickets to Freedom Illus. Simon & Schuster, 1971. (grades 4-7)
    Unusually fine narrative is thoroughly researched, well-documented, and gives a vivid, realistic picture of the era. The escape of the Crafts from slavery reads almost like a suspense novel, but it is based on contemporary sources and is faithful to the truth. Illustrations by Ezra Keats add immeasurably to the book's value.

PRUDENCE CRANDALL
1803–1889

Educator, abolitionist, and feminist

When Prudence Crandall accepted a black student in her Connecticut school, white parents and financiers withdrew their children and support. Like most Quakers, she opposed slavery and this incident strengthened her abolitionist convictions. Ms. Crandall consequently re-opened her school to train middle-class and well-to-do northern black women to be teachers. The local citizens strenuously objected and, when she refused to close the school, they harassed her and arrested her on a trumped-up charge. When these measures failed, the townspeople broke windows, polluted the well, and attempted to set the school on fire. Mob action finally forced Prudence Crandall to close her school and to move west with her husband. There she taught and worked in the women's rights movement.

*** *Yates, Elizabeth* Prudence Crandall: woman of courage Illus. Dutton, 1955. (grade 7 and up)
Touchingly written account of the life of an unusually heroic woman and of the episodes that precipitated her finally closing her school and leaving Connecticut. The issues of the day are clearly depicted, as is the faith Ms. Crandall's father had in her. Their truly unusual relationship is well described.

** *Fuller, Edmund* Prudence Crandall: an incident of racism in nineteenth-century connecticut Illus. with photographs. Wesleyan Univ. Pr., 1971. (grade 8 and up)
Short scholarly book is a detailed, thoroughly researched and documented chronicle of the violent opposition in Connecticut to Prudence Crandall's school for black girls. Though it is her story, it is not as much a biography as it is a historical document.

MARIE CURIE
1867–1934

Discoverer of radium, first woman to win Nobel Prize in sciences, first person to win Nobel Prize twice

Despite a strong academic background in the sciences, Marie Curie was denied admission to the University of Warsaw because of her sex. After experiencing years of political and financial hardships in Czarist-ruled Poland, she went to Paris to study at the Sorbonne and graduated there with honors in physics and mathematics.

After her marriage to scientist Pierre Curie, Marie successfully integrated her scientific career with marriage and motherhood. The Curies won the 1903 Nobel Prize in physics for their work on radioactivity, and after her husband's tragic death, Marie Curie succeeded him as a professor at the University of Paris, becoming the first woman to hold such a position. In 1911, Marie Curie again won the Nobel Prize, the first person to win the award twice.

Marie Curie was honored throughout the world for her discovery of radium and its contribution to medicine. Ironically, it was long exposure to its penetrating rays that caused her death in 1934.

*** *Bigland, Eileen* MADAME CURIE Illus. S. G. Phillips, 1957. (grades 5-9)

Very fine inspiring narrative of Marie Curie's life clearly describes her contributions to science and does a competent job of explaining radium and scientific techniques to readers unfamiliar with such terms and principles.

*** *Curie, Eve* MADAME CURIE Illus. Doubleday, 1949. (grade 8 and up)

Outstanding biography written by Marie Curie's daughter is a thorough, analytical account, in which the subject emerges as a multidimensional woman—scientist, teacher, wife, and mother.

*** *DeLeeuw, Adele* MARIE CURIE: WOMAN OF GENIUS Illus. Garrard, 1970. (grades 4-7)

Outstanding narrative biography gives a good, clear portrait of the woman whose contributions to science have been recognized throughout the world.

*** *Henriod, Lorraine* MADAME CURIE Illus. Putnam, 1970. (grades 2-4)

Unusually fine biography gives a simple but inspiring account of Marie Curie's life. The limitations imposed on women are discussed, and her contributions to science are clearly described.

*** *McKowan, Robin* MARIE CURIE Illus. Putnam, 1971. (grades 4-8)
    Excellent account of Marie Curie's life is warm and inspiring, succinctly depicting her many accomplishments.

** *Henry, Joanne* MARIE CURIE: DISCOVERER OF RADIUM Illus. Macmillan, 1966. (grades 4-6)
    Nonfictionalized narrative gives account of Marie Curie's life, carefully explaining many scientific principles and focussing on her professional work. She emerges as thoroughly competent, although her accomplishments seem to have developed in partnership with her husband, rather than independently.

―――――――――――――――――――――――――――――――――――――

ELIZABETH CUSTER
1842–1933

Author, lecturer, wife of a general

When well-educated, young Elizabeth Bacon married General George Armstrong Custer, the youngest general in the Union Army, she undertook a life that would often test her courage. Frequently the only officer's wife to follow the regiment, she contended with freezing weather in North Dakota and summer heat and mosquitoes in Fort Lincoln.

After her husband was killed at the famous Battle of the Little Big Horn, known also as "Custer's Last Stand," Elizabeth Custer wrote *Boots and Saddles*, the story of their life. So successful was this book, that she wrote others and became a popular lecturer.

She survived the general by fifty-seven years, during which time she prevented the publication of anything that would have tarnished his reputation or memory.

Elizabeth Custer was a member of a circle of prominent literary figures which included Mark Twain, and was active in the movement to preserve old frontier forts.

* *Randall, Ruth Painter* I, ELIZABETH: A BIOGRAPHY OF THE GIRL WHO MARRIED GENERAL GEORGE ARMSTRONG CUSTER Illus. with photographs. Little, 1966. (grade 7 and up)

Extremely well-written, thoroughly researched, and rather romantic biography depicts Ms. Custer as a woman with more than average fortitude and perseverance. She is described strictly as a wife, which was her main role until she became a widow. However, only a very small section of the book is devoted to the last half-century of her life. Thus her many accomplishments are given short shrift in an otherwise good book.

VIRGINIA DARE
1587–?

First child born to British parents in the New World

Virginia Dare's parents had sailed from Plymouth, England, and though intending to settle on Chesapeake Bay, landed at Roanoke Island in Virginia where the baby girl was born.

There is little known about the later lives of Virginia Dare and that small group of colonists, but Virginia has been immortalized in American literature and art.

* *Bothwell, Jean* LADY OF ROANOKE Holt, 1965. (grades 7-9)

Classified as biography, this is actually a historical novel based on the few known facts of Virginia Dare's life. The remainder of the book is fiction and, as such, is quite adequate, reasonably nonsexist, and gives a good picture of the times.

†† *Stevenson, Augusta* VIRGINIA DARE: MYSTERY GIRL Bobbs–Merrill, 1957. (grades 3-7)

So highly fictionalized, it should not be considered biography. Except for some interesting background information on Indians, the book lacks any accuracy. Virginia Dare is taken by the Indians and remains with them always. Somewhat sexist in its approach, the biography serves only as a picture of the times and an exercise in reading.

ANGELA DAVIS
1944–

Philosophy instructor, radical activist

Considered a brilliant student at Brandeis University and the University of California, Angela Davis was later fired from her job as a philosophy instructor at the University of California for her activities in radical movements and membership in the Communist party.

In 1970 Angela Davis was cited by the Federal Bureau of Investigation as one of the ten most wanted criminals for murder, kidnapping, and criminal conspiracy. After she was apprehended, a movement to free her was organized by people who believed that her trial was not so much for any specific crime as it was for her political views. After a long costly trial, the all-white jury returned a verdict of not guilty.

*** *Finke, Blythe F.* ANGELA DAVIS: TRAITOR OR MARTYR OF THE FREEDOM OF EXPRESSION? SamHar, 1972. (grades 7-10)
Very fine, extremely brief, well-balanced biography of Angela Davis succinctly describes her childhood, youth, and political activities. An excellent bibliography of periodicals and magazines is included, enhancing the value of the twenty-five-page book.

FRANCIS REED ELLIOT DAVIS
1882–1964

First black nurse in the American Red Cross

Francis Elliot Davis's father was the son of a former slave and an Indian, and her white unmarried mother the daughter of a minister. Her mother died when Francis was five and she went to live with various black foster families, some of whom were indifferent to her. Later, a white family, for whom she did domestic work, befriended her and helped her to gain an education and to become a nurse.

Highly skilled, intelligent, and dedicated, Francis Davis became the first black nurse to be officially enrolled in the American Red Cross. She worked in the Henry Street Settlement House, served tirelessly through the 1918 flu epidemic, and constantly fought prejudice in schools, hospitals, and the United States Army nurse corps.

*** *Pitrone, Jean* TRAILBLAZER: NEGRO NURSE IN THE AMERICAN RED CROSS Harcourt, 1969. (grade 6 and up)
Stirring, informal biography competently and completely

details Davis's life. She emerges as a figure of rare determination and fortitude. The author also presents, in this extremely readable book, a good picture of prejudices against blacks.

MARGUERITE deANGELI
1889–

Children's book author and illustrator

After studying for a career as a concert singer, Marguerite deAngeli turned to her earlier interest in drawing. While her children were young she began writing and illustrating books for youngsters, often using her own children, and later her grandchildren, as models for her characters. Her books have won almost every award in the book industry, including the coveted Newberry Medal. *Bright April, The Door in the Wall, Up the Hill,* and *The Book of Nursery and Mother Goose Rhymes* are among her works which have remained popular throughout generations of new readers.

** *DeAngeli, Marguerite* BUTTER AT THE OLD PRICE Illus. with photographs and reproductions of her work in color. Doubleday, 1971. (grade 6 and up)

    Well-written, but sometimes dry autobiography may be of greater interest to adults than to the youngsters for whom it seems to be intended. Although not as exciting as her work for children, it has much warmth and honesty.

MARY DECKER
1958–

Track star

Since her teenage days, Mary Decker has not only been winning track events by wide margins, but has also been running faster than many of the boys in top track competition.

At age fifteen, the five-foot-tall, ninety-five-pound teenager was competing in adult races and setting many world records. She was invited to participate in all important indoor track meets (including the Millrose Games at Madison Square Garden), not as a high school competitor, but as a regular participant.

Mary Decker has set indoor records for the 1000- and 880-yard runs. She excels both outdoors on dirt and cinder tracks and indoors on hardwood boards. Frequently her only real competition proves to be the clock.

She is enthusiastically devoted to her sport and runs several miles each day in practice. The young star draws capacity crowds at all events in which she appears.

* *Jacobs, Linda* MARY DECKER: SPEED RECORDS AND SPAGHETTI
Illus. with photographs. EMC, 1975. (reading level, grades 4-6; interest level through high school)
Insufficient emphasis on her sports training and achievements and too journalistic an approach to her life detract from what might have been a very good portrait of the young

track and field star. The author seems to be saying that despite an extraordinary talent she is just an ordinary teenager. The discussion of her career is reasonably thorough but is somewhat subordinated to other facets of her life. Numerous photographs of Ms. Decker greatly enhance the text.

GRAZIA DELEDDA
1875–1936

Italian author, winner of Nobel Prize for literature

By the time Nobel Prize winner Grazia Deledda was ten years old her formal education had ended. Even though her father was the mayor of Nuoro, Sardinia, she received no more education than other girls of her town. Recognizing her intelligence, her father encouraged her to continue to read and learn on her own.

Her first story was published while she was a teenager and because it told of love and violence the townspeople greeted it and her with hostility. This did not deter Ms. Deledda, and by the time she was twenty she had a novel and many shorter works published. Her writing then and later was inspired by Sardinian peasants, traditions, and life-styles. Despite numerous family tragedies, Grazia Deledda continued to write and publish as well as to correspond with leading authors, editors, critics, and journalists of the day.

After her marriage she moved to Rome, where in 1908 she opened the Congress of Italian Women and supported the suffragist movement. A very popular and highly acclaimed author, she wrote until the end of her life. She published 33 novels and 250 short stories. Grazia Deledda was nominated several times for a Nobel Prize, and in 1926 became the only Italian woman, and second of only six women, to win it for literature.

*** *Balducci, Carolyn* A SELF-MADE WOMAN: BIOGRAPHY OF NOBEL PRIZE WINNER GRAZIA DELEDDA Houghton Mifflin, 1975. (grade 9 and up)
   Beautifully written prose captures the spirit of the gifted writer Grazia Deledda. Although the focus is on her own life, it is seen within the context of her large family and childhood in Sardinia, and the experiences of those close to her are given full attention. Her work itself is discussed briefly; this is not a critical biography but a personal one.

CONSTANCE deMARKIEVICZ
1876–1927

A creator of the Irish Republic, first woman elected to the British Parliament, first minister of labor in the Irish Republic

Irish heiress Constance deMarkievicz enjoyed the privileges of her class until, at the age of forty, she became active in the fight for Irish independence. She joined the workers strike of 1913, worked towards the Easter Rebellion of 1916, and joined the freedom fighters of the Irish Republic in the 1920s. Through her efforts an organization was formed to train young rebels for the Irish volunteers, and she herself was a commissioned officer in the Citizen's Army.

Constance deMarkievicz was a firm believer in women's rights, and mistakenly believed that after independence, Irish women would obtain equal rights. She was the first woman elected to the British Parliament, and as the first minister of labor in the Irish Republic, she also was the first Western European woman to hold a cabinet position.

*** *Van Voris, Jacqueline*   CONSTANCE DEMARKIEVICZ   Illus. Feminist Pr., 1972. (grade 9 and up)
    Scholarly, well-documented biography is a straightforward feminist narrative with appeal to older, mature readers or students of history. Interesting and absorbing, the book records the life of Ms. deMarkievicz candidly and directly.

AGNES deMILLE
1908–

Dancer, choreographer, director of Broadway musicals and ballets

Although Agnes deMille was born into a distinguished theatrical family, she had to struggle to achieve success in the dance world. Her revolutionary use of American dance forms in her ballet *Rodeo* and her choreography of the musical *Oklahoma!* have directly influenced almost every musical produced since the 1940s. After those successes Ms. deMille went on to choreograph *Bloomer Girl, Carousel, Brigadoon, Gentlemen Prefer Blondes,* and several other shows.

Agnes deMille was the first woman to stage the book and

dance of an entire Broadway musical. She has performed with her own dance company, choreographed films, given a series of dance lecture programs on television, and has worked to improve basic minimum salaries and conditions for dancers.

Among the many honors bestowed on her are two Antoinette Perry (Tony) Awards and eleven honorary doctorate degrees. Ms. deMille has also written eight books, some autobiographical and some textbooks for dancers.

*** *deMille, Agnes* DANCE TO THE PIPER Illus. Little, 1952.
(grade 9 and up)
Extremely good personal account of the famous dancer and choreographer's life tells much about dancing as well as about other dancers. Of particular interest to those considering a career in the dance or theater, it also has wide general appeal.

BERNADETTE DEVLIN
1947–

Northern Ireland civil rights leader, member of British Parliament

Bernadette Devlin, who, at twenty-one, became the youngest member of the British House of Commons, sees the Irish struggle as one of class, rather than one of religion. She became one of Northern Ireland's twelve representatives to the British Parliament after helping to organize a student civil rights group, sit-ins, and the "long march" from Belfast to London in 1969.

Considered something of a folk heroine, she has frequently been dubbed the Irish "Joan of Arc." She became the youngest woman in history to serve as a member of Parliament, and broke tradition by delivering a speech only an hour after being sworn in. This was characteristic behavior for the forceful young champion of Northern Ireland's Catholic population.

*** *Devlin, Bernadette* PRICE OF MY SOUL Knopf, 1969. (grade 9 and up)
   Fascinating autobiography is dramatic and compelling. Gives a good picture of the political struggle in Ireland as well as the life story of the dynamic Ms. Devlin.

EMILY DICKINSON
1830–1886

American poet

Considered by many critics to be America's finest poet, Emily Dickinson spent most of her life in her parents' home in Amherst, Massachusetts. She attended Mt. Holyoke College for one year, but the strong evangelistic atmosphere proved too great an emotional strain for her.

Once thought rather social, she slowly withdrew from all contacts outside the family, and by the time she was in her thirties had become a veritable recluse. Few people knew she wrote poetry, and only a handful of her poems were published during her lifetime. She kept up extensive correspondence with some intellectuals who showed in-terest in her literary talents, but not until after her death and the discovery of 1,775 poems was the full extent of her poetic vision revealed. While her most recurrent themes are of death and faith, Ms. Dickinson can be appreciated by a wide audience for her concise, realistic style.

*** *Longsworth, Polly* EMILY DICKINSON: HER LETTER TO THE WORLD Crowell, 1965. (grade 7 and up)

Outstanding biography is a sensitive, well-rounded por-trayal of Emily Dickinson, and the people and places who helped influence her. Excerpts from her letters and poetry are judiciously combined with biography, resulting in a dra-matic and moving narrative.

*** *Wood, James Playsted* EMILY ELIZABETH DICKINSON: A PORTRAIT Nelson, 1972. (grade 7 and up)

Excellent biography is directed to serious, or more mature, students. Scholarly in its approach, it is also a warm personal portrait of the sensitive, brilliant poet.

** *Barth, Edna* I'M NOBODY! WHO ARE YOU? THE STORY OF EMILY DICKINSON Illus. Seabury, 1971. (grades 3-7)

Very good albeit brief biography of Emily Dickinson in-cludes thirty-five of her poems. Written for youngsters who may be too young to appreciate her poetry, the biography is quite readable and should act as a spur to understanding her work.

* *Benet, Laura* THE MYSTERY OF EMILY DICKINSON Illus. Dodd, 1974. (grades 5-9)

Somewhat flat, even superficial biography of Emily Dick-inson dwells on the "mysterious man" in her life. In the process, the author fails to convey sufficient warmth and sensitivity. Some of her poems and letters are included, and there is evidence of careful research.

DOROTHEA LYNDE DIX
1802–1887

Reformer and crusader for the mentally ill,
superintendent of army nurses during the Civil War

Dorothea Dix's life-long crusade for better treatment of the mentally ill took her across the country and abroad investigating the cruelty and abuses to which the insane were subjected. Presenting powerful arguments and evidence of the shocking neglect she found, she convinced legislators and philanthropists to build humane hospitals where the insane would no longer be chained and confined to stalls and filth. She was directly responsible for the founding of thirty-two state mental hospitals, and she inspired countless others.

During the Civil War, Dorothea Dix was appointed superintendent of the United States Army nurses. After the war she resumed her work for the mentally ill.

*** *Baker, Rachel* ANGEL OF MERCY: STORY OF DOROTHEA LYNDE DIX Messner, 1955. (grade 6 and up)

Outstanding, stirring, informal biography gives a warm, well-rounded portrait of the woman whose crusade for better treatment of the mentally ill had such a profound effect upon the world. The book is convincingly fictionalized, but accurate and informative.

** *Malone, Mary* DOROTHEA L. DIX: HOSPITAL FOUNDER Illus. Garrard, 1968. (grades 2-5)

Very good biography is readable, but lacks the spark displayed by the subject. Sympathetic and accurate, it is nevertheless somewhat dry.

* *Melin, Grace H.* DOROTHEA DIX: GIRL REFORMER Illus. Bobbs–
Merrill, 1963. (grades 3-7)

Mostly nonsexist, reasonably adequate biography is of
dubious accuracy and focusses on Dix's childhood rather than
on her adult accomplishments.

▶○━○◀

MARY MAPES DODGE
1831–1905
Author and editor

Young widowed Mary Mapes Dodge refused her parents'
economic aid and instead supported herself and her young
sons by working for a magazine and writing stories for
children. Encouraged by her publisher, she then wrote the
full-length book *Hans Brinker! or, the Silver Skates.* The
story, which is set in Holland, became an immediate success and continues to delight readers today.

As the first editor of the children's magazine *Saint
Nicholas*, Ms. Dodge assumed full charge of its policy and
content. Highly respected as an author and editor, she
persuaded many outstanding American and British writers
and artists to contribute to the magazine. Her standards
were high, and many books now considered children's
classics, as well as the works of talented youngsters who
became the leading writers of the following generation,
first appeared in *Saint Nicholas*.

†† *Mason, Miriam E.* MARY MAPES DODGE: JOLLY GIRL Bobbs–
Merrill, 1949. (grades 3-7)

Rather insipid, somewhat sexist biography of Mary Mapes
Dodge in no way conveys her abilities, accomplishments, or
adult personality. Focussing on her childhood, it is merely
a historical novel which uses the young Ms. Dodge as a central character. For a picture of the period it is reasonably
adequate; as biography it is unacceptable.

KATHERINE DUNHAM
1910–

Dancer, choreographer, and anthropologist

Katherine Dunham is generally considered the pioneer of
black dance art for she combined dance, music, and anthropology to create an accurate and beautiful new dance
form.

Despite financial and emotional hardships in her early
years, she graduated from college and was awarded a fellowship for dance research in the Caribbean Islands. She
employed anthropological methods to learn the island
dances and songs, and also acquired some of the natives'
unique musical instruments.

The influence of this study is seen in her dance form,
and led to her great success as a performer and choreographer throughout the world.

Katherine Dunham established her own school in New
York where students were instructed by drama directors
and the famed anthropologist Margaret Mead, as well as
by dancers.

*** *Bienmiller, Ruth* DANCE: THE STORY OF KATHERINE DUN-
HAM Illus. Doubleday, 1969. (grades 6-9)

Outstanding informal portrait of the famed dancer-choreographer is dramatic and inspiring. Of interest to older readers as well as those for whom the reading level is intended,
this is a fine, fast-moving, competently written biography.

** *Harnan, Terry* AFRICAN RHYTHM—AMERICAN DANCE: A
BIOGRAPHY OF KATHERINE DUNHAM Illus. Knopf, 1974.
(grades 5-9)

Good, extremely objective, occasionally dry biography
places great emphasis on Ms. Dunham's professional career,
detailing her techniques and style as well as discussing her
often strained relations with others. The book, aimed at elementary school readers, may serve well for reluctant or less
able readers who are interested in the dance, but is probably
of greater interest to young adults.

AMELIA EARHART
1898–1937

*First woman to fly the Atlantic Ocean alone, first person
to fly solo between Hawaii and California*

When pilot Amelia Earhart became the first woman to
cross the Atlantic by air as a passenger and log-keeper,
she became instantly famous. She continued to fly, lecture,
and write on her experiences, always working towards her
goals that women should have economic opportunities and
independence.

Amelia Earhart became the first woman pilot to fly the Atlantic alone as well as the first person to fly solo between Hawaii and California and nonstop between Mexico City and Newark, New Jersey. For her achievements she was awarded the Distinguished Flying Cross, the Cross of the French Legion of Honor, the Harmon International Trophy, and other awards and cash prizes. Purdue University appointed her to their faculty to advise young women on careers in new fields.

In 1937 Amelia Earhart and her copilot set off on a flight around the world. The plane disappeared in the Pacific and neither the plane nor its occupants has ever been found. While many theories have been advanced to explain the disappearance, none has been proved. In a letter to her husband, opened after her disappearance, she wrote, ". . . women must try to do things as men have tried. When they fail, their failure must be but a challenge to others." Amelia Earhart's courage, independence, achievements, and personality did much to further interest in aviation and to liberate women from traditional roles.

*** *Davis, Burke* AMELIA EARHART Putnam, 1972. (grade 6 and up)

Very fine biography is a substantial account of the adult motives, goals, and achievements of the aviator. Moving and dramatic, it is an informative narrative.

*** *Garst, Shannon* AMELIA EARHART: HEROINE OF THE SKIES Messner, 1947. (grade 7 and up)

Absorbing, exciting, vivid biography of Amelia Earhart is told with plausible fictionalized dialogue. The subject is introduced as a warm, ambitious, and dynamic woman; her story is competently told.

*** *Howe, Jane Moore* AMELIA EARHART: KANSAS GIRL Illus. Bobbs–Merrill, 1950. (grades 3-7)

Despite its emphasis on her childhood, this excellent biography clearly reveals the freedom Amelia Earhart was allowed in defying the prevailing stereotyped sex roles and customs of the day. Only one chapter deals with her adult life, but her childhood is accurately and perceptively portrayed in an exciting, readable manner.

*** *Mann, Peggy* AMELIA EARHART: FIRST LADY OF FLIGHT Illus. Coward, 1970. (grades 5-8)

Exceptionally lively and exciting, immensely readable biography also has appeal for older readers than those for whom it is intended. Simply written, it is a stirring, colorful portrait of Amelia Earhart.

*** *Parlin, John* AMELIA EARHART Dell, 1971. (grade 7 and up)

Vividly written, well-paced account of the life of the pioneer flier is dramatic, displaying clearly the color and excitement the subject showed in her life.

*** *Parlin, John* AMELIA EARHART: PIONEER IN THE SKY Illus. Garrard, 1962. (grades 2-5)

Excellent account of the life of the aviator is animatedly told, in depth yet with simplicity. Dramatic and inspiring, Earhart's efforts are shown to have challenged and helped other fliers, both men and women, to achieve greater successes.

*** *Ziefau, Lilee* AMELIA EARHART: LEADING LADY OF THE AIR AGE SamHar, 1972. (grades 7-10)

Brief, but very fine informative account of Amelia Earhart's life is told in a straightforward fashion, without resorting to fictionalization. Succinctly recreates all the known facts about her life in crisp, clear text.

** *Earhart, Amelia* LAST FLIGHT ed. George Putnam Harcourt, 1968. (reprint of 1937 edition) (grade 8 and up)

Fine personal narrative was edited and arranged by Amelia

Earhart's husband from material she sent back or left by way of dispatches, letters, diaries, and charts. The writing reveals much of her personality and is of particular interest to those readers who are already acquainted with one of her biographies and now wish to read an account in the flier's own words.

MARY BAKER EDDY
1821–1910

Founder of the Christian Science faith

Mary Baker Eddy, founder of the faith known as Christian Science, was cured of her own numerous, frequently debilitating ailments by a faith healer whose methods became the foundation of her religion, philosophy, and science of health. The only woman to establish a successful church in America, Ms. Eddy, with her writings and lectures, attracted thousands of students and converts, who subsequently spread her beliefs throughout the world.

Her belief that diseases and illnesses are illusions which can be overcome with faith and prayer is explained in her textbook *Science and Health,* which is used by practitioners and members in conjunction with the Bible.

By Ms. Eddy's completely nonsexist directive, Christian Science services are conducted by men and women, and God is referred to as "our divine Father and Mother." The home base for the church, situated in Boston, is called the "Mother Church."

Mary Baker Eddy was one of the most powerful and wealthy women in America and retained full control of the church until her death. More than three thousand branches of the Christian Science church are in existence today, and the newspaper she founded at the age of eighty-seven, *The Christian Science Monitor,* continues to be one of the world's leading daily newspapers.

* *Hay, Ella H.* CHILD'S LIFE OF MARY BAKER EDDY Illus. Christian Science Publishers, 1942. (grades 3-9)
   Nonsexist, but nonobjective, polemic biography lacks color and excitement but traces the life and career of Ms. Eddy with reasonable accuracy.

* *King, Marian* MARY BAKER EDDY: CHILD OF PROMISE Illus. Prentice-Hall, 1968. (grade 9 and up)
   Nonsexist, somewhat stylistically dull portrayal of the religious leader lacks balance and cohesion, but is faithful to her life.

GEORGE ELIOT
1819–1880
British novelist

Novelist George Eliot, who was recognized, even in her own time, as a writer of genius, chose a masculine pen name in order to be judged by tough literary standards rather than treated lightly as a woman writer.

Mary Ann Evans, as she was known in her personal life, was a brilliant student, whose facility with languages led to her great success as a translator. Although she was self-supporting and aided her widowed sister's six children, Ms. Evans's family considered her a failure for not marrying.

When she and George Henry Lewes, a philosopher and literary critic, met and fell in love they decided to live as husband and wife even though he was still married to a woman who had deserted him. With his encouragement, she began writing novels, and even those who criticized her way of life appreciated her enormous literary talent. *The Mill on the Floss*, one of her most famous novels, is based on her own life. Many of her other works, including *Adam Bede, Silas Marner,* and *Romola,* continue to be read and admired.

*** *Vipont, Elfrida* TOWARDS A HIGH ATTIC: THE EARLY LIFE OF GEORGE ELIOT Illus. Holt, 1971. (grade 7 and up)
   Very fine biography focuses on her earlier years but also discusses her novels and her life after she began writing them. A balanced, smoothly written biography, it gives an intimate and moving picture of the brilliant author.

QUEEN ELIZABETH I
1533–1603

Queen of England, 1558–1603

When Elizabeth Tudor ascended the British throne in 1558 she faced a nation with a dwindling treasury and a people torn by religious fears. Relying on her own intelligence and skillful leadership, as well as a wise selection of advisors, she used diplomacy rather than military might to keep England at peace and to maintain the European balance of power.

By founding the Church of England, Protestant Elizabeth I put an end to the age of persecutions of both Catholics and Protestants. She established colonies in America and other parts of the world, and built the British Navy to new and greater strengths. The defeat of the once mighty Spanish Armada during her reign clearly demonstrated the naval supremacy England had achieved.

Elizabeth's reign is further noted as a time of great contributions to the literary world. Among the English poets of the age, Ben Johnson, Christopher Marlowe, and of course William Shakespeare are outstanding.

Elizabeth chose never to marry, and during her forty-four-year reign remained popular with her subjects, making England a powerful and prosperous nation.

*** *Hanff, Helene* QUEEN OF ENGLAND: THE STORY OF ELIZABETH THE FIRST Illus. Doubleday, 1969. (grades 6-8)

Excellent biography is a good treatment for young or uninformed readers, for its clear, easy-to-understand narrative gives a good background on the Elizabethan era as well as portraying the queen as a strong, independent, and intelligent woman.

*** *Jenkins, Elizabeth* ELIZABETH THE GREAT Illus. Coward, 1959. (grade 9 and up)

An outstanding, soundly researched, well-documented biography of the queen which depicts her accurately with vigor and sensitivity. A fairly complete survey of her long life, this book is suitable for casual readers as well as serious students of history.

** *Bigland, Eileen* QUEEN ELIZABETH I Criterion, 1965. (grade 7 and up)

Very good, well-balanced account of Elizabeth's life assumes a certain knowledge of British history. Without this background the reader may have difficulty in following the biography.

QUEEN ELIZABETH II
1926–

Queen of the United Kingdom and the
Commonwealth of Nations, 1953–

Princess Elizabeth was only ten years old when her father became king of England. From that day on she was the heiress presumptive and she and her younger sister Margaret became the most photographed children in the world. Educated by private tutors, she joined the Girl Guides, and at fourteen, during the World War II Nazi air blitz of England, made her first public address over the radio.

In 1947 Princess Elizabeth married Prince Philip Mountbatten of Greece, who then became a British subject and was named duke of Edinburgh. In 1953 after the death of her father King George VI, Elizabeth was coronated Queen of the United Kingdom and the Commonwealth of Nations.

Her reign is notable for the large number of commonwealth nations that have gained independence. Elizabeth II has toured the British Commonwealth and made numerous other official visits throughout the world. The queen is a dedicated sovereign with enormous responsibilities and duties who still manages to spend a great deal of time with her four children and to enjoy her life-long interest in horseback riding. In recent years she has attempted to bring the monarchy closer to the everyday life of her subjects without sacrificing the pageantry and tradition that continue to have wide appeal.

* *Liversidge, Douglas* THE PICTURE LIFE OF ELIZABETH 2ND Illus. Watts, 1969. (grades K-3)

Impersonal but informative portrait tells more about the role of queen than the woman herself. Attractive in format, with numerous photographs, this probably should not really be classified as biography.

SAINT ELIZABETH OF HUNGARY
1207–1231

Princess who used royal revenues to help the poor

Elizabeth was criticized by her husband Louis, the landgrave of Thuringia, for giving so much of her royal revenue to the poor. The daughter of the king of Hungary, she was so devoted to religion and good works, that during a famine she fed nine hundred people at her palace gate, built a hospital, and cared for the sick. Many German legends and works of art depict the incident in which Elizabeth, concealing bread for the poor in her apron, was challenged by her husband. She let down the apron and instead of bread there appeared a mass of red roses. The miracle converted him and he no longer opposed her charities.

Widowed at twenty with four small children, she was literally thrown out of the palace by her brother-in-law, without even the barest necessities for herself and the children. Her son was later declared the heir to the estate and Elizabeth refused the regency in order to live the remainder of her short life quietly helping the poor and ill. Four years after her death she was canonized by Pope Gregory IX.

** *Harvis, Mary* ELIZABETH Sheed & Ward, 1961. (grades 1-4)
Brief, well-illustrated, good biography is a sympathetic and
thoughtful portrayal of the unselfish young princess.

CHRIS EVERT
1954–

Tennis champion

Chris Evert won her first tennis tournament when she was
eight years old, and by the time she was twenty she was
ranked first in the United States. Noted for her two-handed
backhand, classic forehand, intense concentration, and
great poise, she quickly became one of the biggest attrac-
tions in tennis.

When Chris Evert was only sixteen she won forty-six
consecutive matches against some of the leading players
in the world, was a member of the United States Wightman
Cup Team, reached the semifinals at Forest Hills, and
came in second for the Associated Press Female Athlete of
the Year Award. The following year, after she helped the
United States win the Wightman Cup from Great Britain,
the press chose her the most valuable player.

Chris Evert turned professional on her eighteenth birthday. In 1974, she won the women's singles championship
at Wimbledon, five out of eight tournaments on a spring
professional tour, the French and Italian championships,
and was ranked first in the United States.

In 1975, she was ranked number one in the country for
the second straight year and she won the women's singles
title at Wimbledon in 1976.

*** *Smith, Jay H.* CHRIS EVERT Illus. Creative Educ. Soc., 1975. (grades 3-7)

Attractive and colorfully illustrated with many action pictures, this text is a fast-paced, well-balanced portrait of the tennis star. Her techniques and personality are revealed and several of her important matches are excitingly described. Young tennis enthusiasts will find it interesting, and older less able readers will find it easy to read.

* *Jacobs, Linda* CHRIS EVERT, TENNIS PRO Illus. with photographs. EMC, 1974. (reading level, grades 4-6; interest level through high school)

Adulatory, somewhat gushy view of Chris Evert places more emphasis on her personality than on her tennis. Numerous photographs of her in action make the book extremely appealing, and the easy-to-read text and the discussion of her life off the court make it more suitable for older reluctant readers than younger elementary school youngsters.

ELEANOR FARJEON
1881–1965

British author of children's books

Books and writing were such an intrinsic part of Eleanor Farjeon's childhood that, under her father's tutelage, she could, by the time she was seven years old, type, correct proof, and read copy.

Her great gift for storytelling led to her writing many collections of short stories for children, as well as full-length children's novels and adult fantasies. Ms. Farjeon also wrote poetry, plays, and retold many historical and mythical tales for modern readers. She has won most of the distinguished book awards and her work remains popular with youngsters and adults.

Among her most popular titles are *Maria Lupin, Glass Slipper, Tales from Chaucer,* and her books of poems for children.

** *Colwell, Eileen* ELEANOR FARJEON Walck, 1962. (grade 10 and up)
Good, very brief profile is a literary, rather than personal, biography. Of particular interest to teachers, librarians, or those young readers who have enjoyed Ms. Farjeon's writings.

DOROTHY CANFIELD FISHER
1879–1958

Author

Dorothy Canfield Fisher's parents offered her every educational opportunity, and at a time when higher education for women was still a rarity, she earned a doctorate in literature. She was such a successful author of articles, short stories, and novels for children and adults that much of her work is still widely read. *Understood Betsy,* a novel for children, remains as popular today as when it was written.

She and her husband had a most unusual working partnership. He gave up his own writing ambitions to serve as her editor, critic, and business manager. He also made the children's clothes, tended the garden, and did much of the housework. Ms. Fisher's prodigious writings are a testimonial not only to her talent and ambition but also to the fact that she was free to devote all her time to her work.

When the Book-of-the-Month Club was formed, Dorothy Canfield Fisher became one of the first judges, and was instrumental in introducing new and established authors to the general public.

*** *Yates, Elizabeth* LADY FROM VERMONT: DOROTHY CAN-
FIELD FISHER'S LIFE AND WORLD (rev. ed. Original title, PEBBLE IN A POOL, now out of print but available.) Illus. Greene, 1971. (grade 8 and up)
Vividly written biography of the prolific author gives a good picture of the life of an educated woman who was able to realize her potential. As well as being a colorful biography, it provides interesting glimpses of city and country life in the early part of the century.

ALICE FITZGERALD
1874–1962

Nurse, teacher, and advisor in public health

Nursing was still not widely accepted as a respectable profession when Alice Fitzgerald announced to her wealthy, socialite family that she planned to become a nurse. She became an excellent student, a fine nurse, and an outstanding administrator and teacher. During World War I she travelled throughout Europe organizing hospitals, and served as chief nurse for the American Red Cross. Her work with the Public Health Nursing Service helped establish nursing schools in the Philippines and in the Far East.

105

She received honors, decorations, and medals from many countries, but with great humility announced that it was the nursing profession, more than herself, that had been so honored. When Alice Fitzgerald retired, at the age of seventy-four, she sent all the medals and decorations to her former school, Johns Hopkins School of Nursing.

*** *Noble, Iris* NURSE AROUND THE WORLD: ALICE FITZGERALD Messner, 1964. (grade 7 and up)
   Dramatic, inspiring profile of Ms. Fitzgerald is also the story of the nursing profession in its early days. Judicious use of dialogue adds warmth and reality, making this an unusually absorbing biography.

ROBERTA FLACK
1940–

Grammy Award winning singer, musician, composer

Roberta Flack's intellectual abilities were recognized early by her teachers, and when she was only fifteen she won a scholarship to Howard University. She became a teacher, and although she had been schooled in classical music, decided, in 1967, to begin a career in popular music.

After some success in a night club, she began recording, and within a few years had several successful albums, best-selling single records, two Grammy Awards, and was immensely successful as a concert performer. In 1971 she was named by *Downbeat* magazine as Female Vocalist of the Year.

106

She often accompanies herself on the piano; two of her most popular recordings, "The First Time Ever I Saw Your Face" and "Killing Me Softly With His Song," both won her several awards. She has had her own television specials, composed music for herself and others, and owns two music publishing firms.

Although Roberta Flack is black, she does not consider herself a soul singer, stating "there is no color in music." Her taste in music is varied, for she sings pop, blues, jazz, rock, spirituals, and European as well as American folk songs.

** *Jacobs, Linda* ROBERTA FLACK: SOUND OF VELVET MELTING Illus. EMC, 1975. (reading level, grades 4-6; interest level through high school)

Though occasionally gushy, a good portrait of the singer which clearly shows her intelligence and commitment to her work. An equal emphasis on her personal and professional life shows their interrelatedness.

** *Morse, Charles and Ann* ROBERTA FLACK Illus. Creative Educ. Soc., 1975. (grades 4-8)

Colorfully illustrated, occasionally glib biography is written in the colloquium of musical journalism. Based on interviews she has given to major newspapers and magazines, it constitutes good reporting and moves along quickly. Fans of the star, as well as other readers, will find it interesting.

PEGGY FLEMING
1948–

Olympic gold medal winning skater

Peggy Fleming began ice skating when she was nine years old and at age twelve won her first major competition. In the next few years she won five consecutive United States National Championship titles, three consecutive International Figure Skating titles, and, in 1968, was the only American to win an Olympic gold medal.

Peggy Fleming's skating style has been frequently likened to the ballet, for she is not only a superb athlete but magnificently graceful. In her free skating routines she dazzled judges and audiences alike.

After turning professional in 1968, Ms. Fleming appeared on her own television special and has skated as a guest star with the Ice Follies.

*** *Morse, Charles and Ann* PEGGY FLEMING Illus. Creative Educ. Soc., 1974. (grades 4-8)
  Fast-moving, attractively illustrated biography of the skating star also explains clearly and understandably the elements of skating that are considered in the competitive scoring. Ms. Fleming's talent and ambition are well portrayed in this account.

CHARLOTTE FORTEN
1838–1904
Teacher, author, and abolitionist

Charlotte Forten's wealthy, free black Philadelphia family was active in the antislavery movement and encouraged and appreciated her intellectual abilities. Her appointment as a teacher in Salem, Massachusetts, made her the first black teacher of white children.

Her abolitionist and educational activities led her to volunteer during the Civil War as a teacher in an experimental school for freed slaves in Port Royal, on the Sea Islands off South Carolina. After the war Charlotte Forten did some teaching, published articles, translated a book from the French, and held a position in the federal Treasury Department. She married Francis Grimké, a prominent pastor who was the son of a South Carolina planter and a slave woman and the nephew of the influential abolitionists and feminists Angelina and Sarah Grimké (page 132).

Charlotte Forten's *Journal*, a record of her life and an important addition to the history of slavery and abolition, was published after her death.

*** *Douty, Esther* CHARLOTTE FORTEN: FREE BLACK TEACHER
   Garrard, 1971. (grades 4-7)
   Very fine biography offers a dramatic, sensitive portrayal
of Charlotte Forten as well as recreating the period. Especially
useful for youngsters studying the Civil War period, this is
an absorbing, moving narrative.

*** *Longsworth, Polly* I, CHARLOTTE FORTEN, BLACK AND FREE
   Crowell, 1970. (grades 5-9)
   Excellent biography of the abolitionist, teacher, and author
is based on her own *Journal,* and is written as though it were
an autobiography. As biography it is unusually compelling,
and its value is increased by the inclusion of much material
on women's rights, other black leaders, and abolitionists.
Limited to the years between 1854-64, as was Ms. Forten's
Journal, this book has an epilogue which succinctly summarizes events and experiences after those years and a good
bibliography provides readers with information on how to
learn more about the period and people discussed.

ABIGAIL KELLEY FOSTER
1810–1887
Abolitionist, women's rights lecturer

Reared as a Quaker, Abigail Kelley Foster later rejected her
religion because it did not support her strong antislavery
beliefs.

She participated in the first women's antislavery convention, then gave up her job as a school teacher to devote
herself completely to this cause. She travelled, often without proper "chaperones," and lectured before public audiences of both men *and* women and, as a result, was subjected to severe critical abuse.

Abigail Kelley organized antislave societies, rallies, and fairs, and influenced many other women such as Susan B. Anthony (page 15) and Lucy Stone (page 270) to become active feminists and abolitionists. Many women learned their debating techniques from her.

After her marriage to Stephen Symonds Foster, she often toured and lectured with him and at one time refused to pay taxes on their farm, on the grounds that she was being taxed wtihout representation.

*** *Bacon, Margaret Hope* I SPEAK FOR MY SLAVE SISTER: THE LIFE OF ABBY KELLEY FOSTER Illus. Crowell, 1974. (grades 5-9)

Carefully researched and documented biography gives, with warmth and drama, an unvarnished picture of the abolitionist and feminist. Combining biography with a good picture of the period in which she lived, this is an intelligent, well-written portrait.

ANNE FRANK
1929–1945

World War II heroine, author

During World War II, from the time she was thirteen until she was fifteen, Anne Frank, an intelligent, gifted young Jewish girl, and her family hid from the Nazis. Crowded into an attic in Holland, isolated from the outside world, young Anne courageously matured from childhood to adolescence. The family was eventually captured by the Germans, and Anne died in a concentration camp.

111

After the war her father returned to the attic that had sheltered them and discovered, in its hiding place, the diary Anne had secretly kept. He allowed it to be published; it was translated into many languages, and was turned into a successful play and movie. Anne Frank's name has been given to villages and schools in Europe, and through her moving diary, she has become a symbol of the suffering inflicted by the Nazis.

*** *Frank, Anne* ANNE FRANK: DIARY OF A YOUNG GIRL Double-day, 1952, 1967. (grade 6 and up)

Touching, intimate view is offered in the now classic diary by young Anne Frank. It is a dramatic, emotional book that reveals the way a highly intelligent youngster gains courage and insights when placed in a most unusual situation.

*** *Steenmeijer, Anna G., ed.* A TRIBUTE TO ANNE FRANK Illus. Doubleday, 1970. (grade 7 and up)

Truly magnificent volume makes use of color and black-and-white photographs, documents, and previously unpublished material about and by Anne Frank to reveal not only the many dimensions of the young Nazi victim but the effect she has had on the post-World War II world. The beautiful book is really an anthology composed of introductory material, historical background, excerpts from the *Diary*, discussions of it and of Anne Frank herself, and excerpts from the prefaces to English and foreign editions. Included too is poetry written by youngsters and adults in reaction to the *Diary*, and a discussion of its influence on German, Israeli, and American children today. There are many photographs of Anne Frank, of busts, medallions, and other works of art of her, as well as photographs from the plays and the film of the *Diary*. This is an outstanding tribute.

** *Schnabel, Ernst* ANNE FRANK: A PORTRAIT IN COURAGE Illus. Harcourt, 1967. (grade 9 and up)

Very good, somewhat interesting portrait of Anne Frank

is less emotional and dramatic than her own diary. Based on interviews with many people who knew Anne, it provides a valuable supplement to the diary, revealing much additional information.

▶▸◂◂

ARETHA FRANKLIN
1942–

Grammy Award winning gospel and soul singer

The "queen of soul" or "lady soul," as Aretha Franklin is often called, began singing at local churches when she was only eight years old.

She had a lonely childhood for her mother left her and later died, and her father, a well-known prosperous minister, was often busy and away. However, their home was a mecca for some of the best black blues, gospel, and jazz musicians, and when Aretha was only a young teenager she was travelling and singing in gospel concerts. It was on these tours that she became acutely aware of racial discrimination, for although they could have afforded choice hotels and restaurants, they were often barred from them.

Aretha Franklin was well known to soul and gospel fans for a long time before winning five gold records in 1968. She has been chosen Female Vocalist of the Year twice by leading magazines, has won five Grammy Awards, and has starred in her own television specials. She often accompanies herself on the piano.

In addition to performing commercially, Aretha Franklin gives many benefits, has her own talent company with

113

a number of musical performers under contract, and with her sister has started her own record company.

*** *Olson, James T.* ARETHA FRANKLIN Illus. Creative Educ. Soc., 1975. (grades 4-8)
Vividly designed and illustrated biography of the successful singer shows her to be a sensitive, talented, and ambitious performer. Written in an easy-going and competent journalistic style, it is fast-moving with appeal for reluctant readers as well as all young fans of Aretha Franklin.

ELIZABETH "MUMBET" FREEMAN
1744–1829

First slave to win freedom in courts of Massachusetts

"Mumbet" Freeman was born a slave and remained one until, at thirty-seven, she became the first slave to achieve freedom in the courts of the state of Massachusetts. She then worked for a judge and his family, taking over the duties of an ill mother.

Her courage and wit saved the household when, during Shays's Rebellion, they were threatened with attack. Although Mumbet never learned to read or write, her intelligence and resourcefulness contributed to the support and education of grandchildren and great-grandchildren.

Mumbet Freeman was known and loved throughout her community, and when she died, the youngest of the grown children she had cared for composed the words on her tombstone. Although she was mourned by the family who loved her, she was not buried with them, but instead in the section of the cemetery reserved for blacks

*** *Felton, Harold W.* MUMBET: THE STORY OF ELIZABETH FREEMAN Illus. Dodd, 1970. (grades 3-7)

Compelling, fictionalized account of a little-known former slave provides an intimate, realistic glimpse into the life of a remarkable woman. Simply and briefly told, it is dramatic and exciting, and offers a good and accurate picture of the times. Despite a paucity of information available about Mumbet Freeman, the author has consulted all available sources, and cites them in the introduction.

JESSIE BENTON FREMONT
1824–1902

Author of travel articles, reminiscences, and reports

Jessie Benton Fremont's famous father, Senator Thomas Hart Benton of Missouri, appreciated her high spirits and encouraged her quick mind by giving her a fine education, much of which he personally supervised. In her teens she married John C. Fremont and accompanied him on a series of government expeditions to the West. She assumed the major responsibility for writing the reports of these expeditions. They were widely read by both the government and the general public and greatly influenced the settlement of the West.

All through Fremont's long career in the service of his country as an army officer and government official, she

115

travelled with him—often under hazardous conditions—gave birth to five children, and was significantly involved in many of his activities.

When great financial disasters reduced them to bankruptcy she supported her family with the writing and sale of numerous magazine articles. These reminiscences and travel sketches were enormously popular and she collected many of them into books. Jessie Benton compiled and edited her husband's own notes which were then published as his memoirs.

** *Randall, Ruth Painter* I, JESSIE: A BIOGRAPHY OF THE GIRL WHO MARRIED JOHN CHARLES FREMONT Illus. Little, 1963. (grade 7 and up)

Extremely well-written, mostly nonsexist biography moves quickly and dramatically, appealing to those interested in biography, history, and romance. Ms. Benton emerges as strong, courageous, and intelligent. However, the depiction of her in relation to her husband, rather than as an independent figure, detracts from this enormously absorbing and comprehensive biography.

* *Wagoner, Jean* JESSIE FREMONT: GIRL OF CAPITOL HILL Illus. Bobbs–Merrill, 1956. (grades 3–7)

Mostly nonsexist biography focusses on the subject's childhood, revealing her spunk and intelligence, but merely skimming over her adult accomplishments. Reasonably accurate, though over-fictionalized, it gives a fairly good picture of her early life and the era in which she lived.

WANDA GÁG
1893–1946

Artist and author of children's books

Wanda Gág, author and illustrator best known for her much loved picture books, *Millions of Cats, The Funny Thing, Snippy and Snappy, The A B C Bunny, Gone is Gone,* and *Nothing At All,* grew up in Minnesota where her artistic talents were early noticed. Her father died when she was fifteen, her mother was ill, so she became the head of the family. She sold drawings to newspapers, painted and sold greeting cards, gave art lessons to children, while simultaneously attending high school, caring for her five sisters and one brother, and running the household.

After high school she won numerous art scholarships in Minnesota and then went to New York to attend the Art Students League. There she worked as a commercial artist but it was her drawings, woodcuts, and lithographs which were featured in shows and won her several awards.

Wanda Gág had been a popular storyteller to the children of her many friends, and when she turned this talent into the writing and illustrating of children's books she met with great success. Her books have a folk-like simplicity that have endeared themselves to generations of children and continue to be enormously popular.

*** *Duin, Nancy E.* WANDA GÁG: AUTHOR AND ILLUSTRATOR OF
CHILDREN'S BOOKS SamHar, 1972. (grade 7 and up)
Unusually fine, warm, straightforward biography of the
artist-author-illustrator is short but captures her personality
and character as well as detailing her professional career.

●-0-●■●

INDIRA GANDHI
1917–

Prime minister of India, 1966–

Indira Gandhi, the prime minister of India, came from a
wealthy family dedicated to achieving the independence of
India. Her father, Jawaharal Nehru, became the first prime
minister of India and her aunt was Vijaha Pandit (page
220), the diplomat and ambassador.

Though education for women was a rarity in India,
Indira was educated both at Oxford and in India, and from
her earliest youth her intellectual abilities were encouraged
by her father. She always remained close to him and when
he was prime minister they travelled together on official
missions throughout the world. Her skills in dealing with
political and economic situations were put to good use at
home and on many trips of her own. She was the third
member of the Nehru family to serve as president of the
India National Congress, and also served as minister of
information and broadcasting. She was elected prime minister in 1966.

In the summer of 1975 a dark shadow was thrown over
Ms. Gandhi's regime when she responded to challenges to
her personal authority by declaring a state of emergency

in order to suppress effectively internal political opposition.

One of only a few women elected as a head of state, she has worked long and hard to further modernize India, to increase foreign trade, to urge women to go into professions, and to play an important role in India's affairs.

*** *Garnett, Emmeline* MADAME PRIME MINISTER: THE STORY OF INDIRA GANDHI Illus. Farrar, 1967. (grade 7 and up)
Very fine portrait of Indira Gandhi also provides a good account of the struggle for independence in India, as well as substantial information on the entire Nehru family. Nonetheless, it is her story, and it is told with warmth, understanding, and admiration resulting in good biography as well as history, past and current.

*** *Wilcoxen, Harriet* FIRST LADY OF INDIA: THE STORY OF INDIRA GANDHI Illus. Doubleday, 1969. (grades 4-7)
Very clear, easy-to-understand biography of Indira Gandhi also discusses India's independence. Concise, but fairly comprehensive, the biography is an inspiring narrative for young or less competent readers who are unacquainted with India's story.

SAINT GERMAINE
c. 1579–1601

Saint Germaine's farmer-laborer father paid little attention to her, and her stepmother physically abused her. In poor health from birth, she had a paralyzed hand and an unsightly skin condition. The stepmother, fearing contagion, refused to allow her in the house or near her other children, and so Germaine made her home in the adjacent stable and cared for the sheep.

She was known throughout the neighborhood for her efficiency, religious devotion, concern for young children and those even poorer than herself, and for a remarkable patience.

Germaine's neighbors associated her with miraculous happenings and the young girl startled even her stepmother when the crumbs she was carrying in her apron turned into beautiful flowers.

In 1601 she was found dead on her bed of straw. She was canonized in 1867.

* *Cantoni, Louise B.* THE GIRL IN THE STABLE Illus. Daughters of St. Paul, 1964. (grades 4-8)

Fast-moving biography of the self-sacrificing child closely follows her life as it has been recorded. Written with a strong religious focus, it nonetheless portrays a battered child who accepts her fate graciously and passively. The adult guiding a young reader must question whether this is a wise selection.

* *Cantoni, Louise* ST. GERMAINE AND HER GUARDIAN ANGEL Illus. Daughters of St. Paul, 1964. (grades 3-6)

Short, highly fictionalized biography of Germaine is an easy-to-read accurate portrayal but, like the above biography, should be evaluated on the basis of whether such young children should be exposed to a subject who passively and graciously accepts such a role.

ALTHEA GIBSON
1927–

Championship tennis player, professional golfer

Being born in South Carolina to poor black sharecroppers and growing up in the slums of New York's Harlem helped make Althea Gibson a tough fighter. Determined to find a way out of the misery that surrounded her, she started to play paddle tennis on a local street. At age twelve she won the New York paddle tennis championship. Seeing her potential as a tennis player, a wealthy southern black doctor offered her free tennis lessons and sponsored her general education.

After winning all the black tennis championships, Althea Gibson faced a difficult struggle to become the first black tennis player to break the color line and to play at Forest Hills. She then toured for the State Department, played in numerous biracial tournaments, and became a top-ranking international player.

In 1957 and again in 1958 Althea Gibson won the Wimbledon and United States nationals. After retiring from competitive amateur tennis, Ms. Gibson became a night-club singer, and then a professional golfer.

*** *Gibson, Althea, and Curtis, Richard* So MUCH TO LIVE FOR Putnam, 1968. (grade 7 and up)

Intimate story of Althea Gibson's career is directed not only to the athletically oriented reader but to anyone interested in warm, dramatic biography. Well-written, it is immensely readable, colorful, and dramatic.

121

* *Gibson, Althea* I ALWAYS WANTED TO BE SOMEBODY Harper, 1958. (grade 9 and up)

Despite a warm reception at its publication, this does not meet good literary standards. Furthermore, since it was written before the civil rights movement and heightened black consciousness, much of the biography is out of tune with today's sentiments and probably no longer reflects Ms. Gibson's own beliefs. However, it does provide a good picture of the tennis star's rise to fame, and clearly shows her struggles.

EMMA GOLDMAN
1869–1940

Anarchist, lecturer, feminist, and early advocate of birth control

Emma Goldman, cruelly oppressed by her family and school, also suffered the intense anti-Semitism of Czarist Russia. In Saint Petersburg, university students introduced her to radical ideas and she emigrated to the United States. Here she was disillusioned to note the exploitation of factory workers and was drawn to the anarchist movement. She embraced some of the violence the theorists espoused, but later rejected it as a necessary accompaniment to reform. Emma Goldman directed her public speaking and writing talents in support of birth control, antidraft measures, peace, and freedom of life-styles for women. For many years she was an editor of the radical magazine *Mother Earth.*

During the "red scare" of 1917, her advocacy of civil rights and liberties was seen by the United States government as dangerously subversive and "Red Emma," as she was called, was deprived of citizenship and deported to Russia.

Disillusioned by the totalitarianism of postrevolutionary Russia, Emma Goldman left to write, lecture, and travel in Sweden, Germany, England, and Canada. She published her autobiography, *Living My Life*, and actively supported the Spanish Civil War.

*** *Shulman, Alix* TO THE BARRICADES: THE ANARCHIST LIFE OF EMMA GOLDMAN Crowell, 1971. (grades 6-10)
Superb, feminist portrayal skillfully incorporates a good introduction to radicalism and anarchism. Few finer biographies of women exist for this age group, for it is sympathetic, yet objective and thoroughly researched but without scholarly pretensions. The author also relates Emma Goldman's life and work to the contemporary scene, increasing the value of the book for casual readers as well as students of history.

EVONNE GOOLAGONG
1951–

Australian tennis champion

Often described as the best mover in women's tennis, Wimbledon champion Evonne Goolagong seems to float on the court. A gifted, graceful athlete, she has been playing tennis since she was six years old.

Evonne Goolagong's family are aborigines, that is, descendents of the original, native Australians, and thus subjected to the same kind of discrimination and prejudices that American Indians and blacks face. Although her family is accepted in their own town, she has frequently been made uncomfortable because of her origins.

Her great aptitude for tennis was noticed early by Vic Edwards, one of Australia's best-known tennis coaches. He began coaching her when she was ten years old, and later became her legal guardian. By the time she was sixteen she had won all the junior titles in Australia and between 1968 and 1970 won forty-four singles tournaments and thirty-eight doubles.

In 1971 she became the fifth youngest Wimbledon singles champion. Since then, the dynamic young player has continued to play championship tennis, demonstrating always her aggressiveness and great speed on the court, and her cheerfulness and warmth off the court.

*** *Morse, Charles and Ann* EVONNE GOOLAGONG Illus. Creative Educ. Soc./Children's Pr., 1974. (grades 3-8)
　　Absorbing, exciting, and fast-moving like its subject, this biography is colorfully illustrated and appealing both to younger elementary school age children who are interested in tennis, and older reluctant readers. Although not completely up-to-date (always a problem with a contemporary sports figure), the book covers her career well, highlighting most of the important events.

** *Jacobs, Linda* EVONNE GOOLAGONG: SMILES AND SMASHES Illus. EMC, 1975. (reading level, grades 4-6; interest level through high school)
　　Readable, interesting, accurate biography is somewhat adulatory and old-fashioned in its gushy approach to viewing the tennis champion. Many photographs of her in action contribute a great deal to the book.

SHANE GOULD
1956–

Australian Olympic gold medal winning swimmer

When, in 1972, fifteen-year-old swimmer Shane Gould won three gold, one silver, and one bronze medal at the Olympics, she became the youngest Australian athlete ever to win an Olympic gold medal.

The champion began swimming when she was only three, at the advice of a physician, to help heal her skin after being burned in an accident. By the time she was nine years old she was swimming in school meets and starting to break records for her age group.

An outstanding student and avid reader, she still found time to swim three to four miles every day before and after school. At fourteen Shane set her first world record in the 400-meter freestyle and went on to break the 200- and the 100-meter freestyle records. Before her magnificent victory at Munich in 1972, she had won every freestyle record, and was the pride of Australia. After her great success in the Olympics she was named Australian of the Year.

Shane Gould continued winning meets, but lost much of her enthusiasm for competition and, in 1973, announced her retirement from competitive swimming.

*** *Jacobs, Linda* SHANE GOULD: OLYMPIC SWIMMER Illus. EMC, 1974. (reading level, grades 4-6; interest level through high school)

Excellent, exciting biography of the young Australian swimmer discusses both her family life and her training and achievements in swimming. Many photographs of her, some

with family and friends but most in action, contribute greatly
to this easy-to-read biography. Less able or reluctant readers
in junior high and high school will find this book interesting
as will younger readers.

MARTHA GRAHAM
1894–

Dancer and choreographer

In her long career as a dancer and choreographer, Martha
Graham has increasingly influenced the world of dance
and theater and has accumulated numerous honors attest-
ing to her ability.

As a youngster she studied under the famed dancer, Ruth
Saint Denis, and later taught at Denishawn, the school
Saint Denis and Ted Shawn founded. Ms. Graham also
taught at Rochester's Eastman School, established the
School of Modern Dance at Bennington College, and
started her own school, the Martha Graham School of Contemporary Dance. Her company performs regularly to enthusiastic audiences all over the world.

Martha Graham's choreography, unique and often experimental, draws its subjects from many human experiences such as history, the Bible, literature, and other cultures. Among the almost two hundred dances she has
created are *Frontier, Letter to the World* (based on the life
of Emily Dickinson), *Appalachian Spring, Clytemnestra,
Phaedra,* and *Triumph of Saint Joan.* For many of these

126

and other works, outstanding composers have written the music.

Her honors have been many. In 1932 she became the first dancer to win a Guggenheim Fellowship; her film *A Dancer's World* won awards at film festivals, and many of her world tours have been under the auspices of the State Department.

Petite, dynamic, and seemingly ageless, Ms. Graham in her eighth decade of life is still active as a producer, teacher, and lecturer.

*** *Terry, Walter* FRONTIERS OF DANCE: THE LIFE OF MARTHA GRAHAM Illus. Crowell, 1975. (grade 6 and up)

Splendidly told, nonadulatory biography of Martha Graham by the dance critic who has known her for a long time focusses on her career as a dancer and choreographer, although her personal life is also discussed. The author captures not only the personality and character of the subject, but also imparts, in an interesting manner, much material about modern dance and some of the other pioneers in the field. Of interest not only to those with knowledge of the dance, but to others as well.

ANNE MacVICAR GRANT
1755–1838
Author

Scottish-born Anne MacVicar Grant went to the New World with her mother to join her army officer father who was already there. She was taught to read by her mother who approved only of Bible reading, but through the interest of a neighbor, the distinguished Madame Schuyler, young Anne became acquainted with other academic and cultural pursuits. Anne MacVicar Grant later wrote a popular biography of her teacher, *Memoirs of an American Lady*.

During the American Revolution the young Scottish-American woman was torn between her friends who supported the Revolution and her own loyalty to the king. She returned to Scotland, where she spent the remainder of her long life. When her husband, a clergyman, died, she supported herself and her children with her writings.

*** *Bobbe, Dorothie* THE NEW WORLD JOURNEY OF ANNE MAC-
VICAR Putnam, 1971. (grades 7-9)

Very fine account of the life of young Anne MacVicar from the time she left Scotland until she returned as a young woman. Her intellectual and emotional development is traced in an engaging, fast-moving narrative which also offers a good, intimate view of the era in which she lived. The author, though not condoning slavery or some of the white-Indian relationships, explains them well in terms of the prevailing customs and beliefs. An appended bibliography includes Ms. Grant's own works as well as those about other people discussed in the biography.

JULIA GRANT
1826–1902

First Lady

Despite opposition from her well-to-do family, Julia Grant married young penniless army officer Ulysses S. Grant. Their early years, often marked by hardships and poverty, were spent on army posts and in various business pursuits. Julia Grant's presence and devotion to her husband and four children were a steadying influence on the hard-drinking Grant.

During the Civil War, his rise to fame and popularity as a general led him to politics and the presidency. Julia Grant, as First Lady, was an elaborate, somewhat ostentatious, but tasteful hostess.

After his presidential term, poor investments left them again in near poverty. The general, suffering from cancer, wrote his memoirs while Julia Grant nursed him and tried to make him comfortable with her usual encouragement and attention.

* *Fleming, Alice* GENERAL'S LADY: THE LIFE OF JULIA GRANT Lippincott, 1971. (grades 4-6)
    Despite being fairly well written and interesting, this biography is slightly sexist. Julia Grant emerges as the stereotyped young woman of her day, frivolous and superficial.

ROSE O'NEAL GREENHOW
1817–1864

Confederate spy

Prominent, popular, and influential Washington hostess Rose O'Neal Greenhow was a southern sympathizer and spy who operated quite openly from her home during the Civil War. Even the Union's famed detective Alan Pinkerton could not put an end to her espionage activities. Placed under arrest she continued to transmit messages, to confuse her guards, to wave a Confederate flag out of the window, and—with her young daughter—to create general confusion.

When Ms. Greenhow was offered parole on the condition that she cease her activities, she refused and was ordered south. Received there as a heroine, she published her memoirs and acted as an unofficial agent of the Confederacy in Europe. She was returning to discuss her trip with Jefferson Davis when her ship was beset by storms. Fearful of capture, she attempted to get ashore in a small boat. The heavy gold coins she was carrying so weighted her down that when the boat overturned, she sank and drowned. She was buried, with the honor befitting a heroine on a wartime mission, in a military funeral.

** *Faber, Doris* ROSE GREENHOW: SPY FOR THE CONFEDERACY
Illus. Putnam, 1968. (grades 5-7)
Good, though somewhat dry portrait of the Confederate spy gives an objective view of the Civil War, and depicts Greenhow as clever, manipulative, and competent.

LADY JANE GREY
1537–1554

Queen of England for nine days

Lady Jane Grey, the unwilling queen of England for only nine days, was something of a child prodigy. Though unhappy in her relationships with her parents, she found comfort in academic pursuits and became proficient in Greek and Latin, learned Hebrew, Arabic, French, and Italian, and studied philosophy, science, and the arts.

Her father-in-law, John Dudley, the duke of Northumberland, a power-hungry man eager to get the throne in his family, pursuaded King Edward VI to leave the crown to Lady Jane Grey's male heirs. He then changed the edict to read Lady Grey *and* her male heirs. After the king's death, when Lady Jane was only sixteen, she reluctantly permitted herself to be crowned queen.

Ten days later the legitimate heir Mary Tudor forced her from the throne. Though Mary was aware of Lady Jane's innocence, she was convicted of high treason and, with her husband, was beheaded in the Tower of London.

** *Malvern, Gladys* THE WORLD OF LADY JANE GREY Illus. Vanguard, 1964. (grade 9 and up)
Very well written, mostly nonsexist, romantic biography is smoothly fictionalized, placing the young queen in proper perspective in her historical setting. Those readers unacquainted with the period may not find this book sufficiently comprehensible.

GRIMKÉ SISTERS
Sarah M. Grimké 1792–1873
Angelina Grimké Weld 1805–1879

Southern abolitionists and feminists

Sarah and Angelina Grimké, reared on a typical southern slave-operated plantation, grew not only to despise the entire system but to work diligently to change it. They went north, became Quakers, and then active abolitionists and feminists. They were prolific writers and embarked on successful lecture tours of New England to be among the first women to speak before mixed audiences of men and women.

Their powerfully written antislavery and feminist pamphlets were often banned and burned in the South. They attracted considerable attention, not only for their pioneering well-articulated demands, but because they represented a small and unusual group—southern white women abolitionists.

When it was discovered that two young black men who bore the Grimké name were the sons of their brother and a slave woman, the sisters treated them as nephews and extended their hospitality and encouraged them in their academic pursuits. Both men achieved national prominence in their chosen vocations, the only male members of the large, otherwise white Grimké family to do so.

*** *Lerner, Gerda* GRIMKÉ SISTERS FROM SOUTH CAROLINA: PIONEERS FOR WOMEN'S RIGHTS AND ABOLITION Houghton Mifflin, 1967; pap. ed., Schocken, 1971. (Original title:

Grimké Sisters from South Carolina: rebels against slavery)

Adult biography is thoroughly researched and documented, offering a substantial, illuminating account of the Grimké sisters. Despite its scholarly approach, it is immensely readable, offering a colorful and elucidating account for older high school students.

** *Willimon, William and Patricia* Turning the World Upside Down Illus. Sandlapper Pr., 1972. (grade 6 and up)

Despite some minor literary flaws, a very fine, moving biography of two remarkable women. Providing an intimate and dramatic picture, it comprehensively and thoughtfully covers their lives in a fast-moving, easy-to-read style.

CONNIE GUION, M.D.
1882–

*First woman professor of clinical medicine
for whom a medical building is named*

Connie Guion deferred attending medical school in order to teach chemistry to women at Vassar College and to earn money for the education of her younger sisters. At the age of thirty-five she graduated from Cornell Medical School at the top of her class and began the career that led her to accumulate many honors and "firsts" as a woman physician.

She helped organize a clinic at New York Hospital, was later its chief, became the first woman member and first woman honorary member of the hospital's medical board, maintained a private practice, served on the board of numerous civic organizations, taught at Cornell Medical

School, and, in 1946, became the first woman in the country to be appointed a full professor of clinical medicine. In 1961 New York Hospital's "Doctor Connie Guion Building" was opened to patients, making her the first living woman doctor to have a building named after her.

Although Dr. Guion is regarded as the modern dean of women doctors, her warmth and personality, her lifetime involvements in behalf of humanity, her many outdoor interests, and her long-time hobby of stamp collecting make her more than just a physician with an impressive list of honors, degrees, and appointments.

*** *Campion, Nardi, and Stanton, Rosamond W.* LOOK TO THIS DAY: THE LIVELY EDUCATION OF A GREAT WOMAN DOCTOR, CONNIE GUION M.D. Illus. Little, 1965. (grade 7 and up)

Outstanding, warm, personal biography, based on first-hand interviews with the subject, gives a vivid, informal, and comprehensive portrait of the woman whose career was marked by many "firsts" for women.

SARAH HALE
1788–1879

Editor and author

Sarah Hale was educated at home, guided by her brother whose college syllabus she followed. When widowhood necessitated supporting herself and five young children she turned to writing. Among her first efforts was a book of nursery verse which included the well-known "Mary Had A Little Lamb."

As the first editor of the immensely popular magazine *Godey's Lady's Book,* Ms. Hale was influential in instituting reforms in women's education, health, dress, and career opportunities. Despite her tireless efforts on behalf of education for women, Sarah Hale did not embrace most of the demands of the feminist movement, nor did she advocate women suffrage.

An editor for forty years, she was responsible for the increased circulation of *Godey's Lady's Book,* and the many outstanding authors and poets represented on its pages. Sarah Hale was instrumental in the establishment of Thanksgiving Day as a national holiday and Mount Vernon as a national shrine. She authored and edited over fifty books.

*** *Burt, Olive* FIRST WOMAN EDITOR: SARAH J. HALE Messner, 1960. (grade 6 and up)

Enjoyably detailed portrayal of the famed editor concentrates on her achievements and, despite undistinguished writing, offers an engrossing and inspiring account.

*** *Fryatt, Norma R.* SARAH JOSEPHA HALE: THE LIFE AND TIMES OF A NINETEENTH CENTURY CAREER WOMAN Hawthorn, 1975. (grade 9 and up)

Nonfictionalized, straightforward account of this unusual woman is thoroughly researched and documented. Well-written, it is sometimes formal in tone, but still moves along at a fast pace.

FANNIE LOU HAMER
1917–

Civil rights worker

Even as a child, Fannie Lou Hamer worked hard picking cotton. The twentieth child of poor black sharecroppers in Mississippi, she noticed, as a youngster, that the dishonesty of white landowners kept her family in a constant state of poverty.

An early civil rights worker, Ms. Hamer was arrested and beaten during the 1962 Mississippi voter-registration drive. Although her husband lost his job and they lost their home, she still had hopes for a better future for the poor and hungry.

Fannie Lou Hamer lectured and travelled all over the country to raise funds for the Freedom Farm Collective, a 640-acre co-operative farm where people could work and benefit together.

*** *Jordan, June* FANNIE LOU HAMER Illus. Crowell, 1972. (grades 1-4)

Moving, emotional, and unusual treatment of the life of a woman whose earliest childhood was marked by great indignities, but who demonstrated courage and dignity throughout her life. Informal grammar and idiom of southern blacks is used successfully and adds authenticity to this easy-to-read biography. Written for early readers, it will be greatly appreciated by older children regardless of reading level, and by adults seeking material to read aloud to young children.

ALICE HAMILTON, M.D.
1869–1970

*Pathologist, first woman appointed to
Harvard University faculty*

Alice Hamilton, whose family stressed education and supported her intellectual interests, spent her professional
career after graduating medical school investigating diseases that developed as a result of a person's occupation.
Not merely content to discover their causes, she also
worked to change the conditions that led to these diseases
in the first place. The results of her long, careful studies
clearly showed the dangers of carbon monoxide, lead, and
mercury.

Dr. Hamilton was the first woman ever appointed to the
Harvard University faculty. She was professor of Industrial Medicine there, and wrote the first authoritative text
on industrial poisons.

Alice Hamilton spent much time as a Hull House resident. Her life-long association with Jane Addams (page
5) and her activities on behalf of peace indicate the wide
scope of her interests. Her sister, Edith, was a well known
author (see below).

*** *Grant, Madeline* ALICE HAMILTON: PIONEER DOCTOR IN IN-
DUSTRIAL MEDICINE Illus. Abelard–Schuman, 1967. (grade
7 and up)

Unusually fine and thorough examination of the life of
the woman who combined medicine with social reform. Dr.
Hamilton's early family influences are presented, but the
focus is on her long professional career. The author makes

clear the outstanding contributions of Alice Hamilton in a fluent, readable style which is not overburdened with details.

EDITH HAMILTON
1867–1963

Classicist, author, and authority on ancient Greeks

Edith Hamilton's parents encouraged her to learn modern and classical languages and to pursue any intellectual activities. Even as a child she was inspired and fascinated by tales of ancient Greece.

As the headmistress of Bryn Mawr School, the first strictly college preparatory school for girls in the United States, Edith Hamilton demanded of her students a deep dedication to academic excellence. Not until retiring from that position did she begin writing the books that brought her great fame. Her *The Greek Way,* published first in 1930 and still considered the standard work on ancient Greece, was followed by *The Roman Way, Mythology,* and several other acclaimed books on classical life.

Edith Hamilton, a modest woman despite her numerous honors and degrees, was honored just before her ninetieth birthday by the Greek government who declared her a citizen of Athens. She wrote two books after this, made a film for television, and was at work on another book when, at the age of ninety-six, she died. Her sister, Alice, was a famous pathologist (see above).

*** *Reid, Doris Fielding* EDITH HAMILTON: AN INTIMATE PORTRAIT Illus. Norton, 1967. (grade 9 and up)
   Outstanding, warm, and personal view of a remarkable

woman written by a close associate. Of particular interest to those who are familiar with Edith Hamilton's works, it also can spark the imagination and act as a spur to those who have not yet read any of her books. Ms. Hamilton emerges as the strong, hearty, and independent personality she was; her life, as well as this book, is a remarkable example of what a woman of any age can accomplish.

VALERIE HARPER
1940?–

Actress

Valerie Harper is known to television audiences as the fashionable, outspoken, and lovable "Rhoda." The show, which began in the fall of 1974, was an immediate hit. The program during which Rhoda got married has become one of the most popular television events since the birth of Lucille Ball's (page 21) baby on "I Love Lucy" more than twenty years before.

Valerie Harper, a former dancer and improvisational actress, had appeared in the chorus of several Broadway musicals and in many plays in California. For four years she played Rhoda on the "Mary Tyler Moore Show" and won three Emmys for best supporting actress before starring on her own show. In 1975 she won the Emmy Award for her own show. She also played a Mexican-American role in the film *Freebie and the Bean*.

Ms. Harper has been involved in several civil rights causes, including prison reform and farm and industrial labor disputes.

* *Jacobs, Linda* VALERIE HARPER: THE UNFORGETTABLE SNOW-
FLAKE Illus. with photographs. EMC, 1975. (reading level,
grades 4-6; interest level through high school)

Despite a fan-magazine style of writing, this is an absorbing, interesting biography that gives an accurate picture of
the professional and personal life of Ms. Harper. Excessive
adulation keeps the subject from seeming as real and human
as the rest of us. Photographs of Ms. Harper on and off the
television screen contribute to the book's value.

ESTHER HAUTZIG
1930–
Author, World War II exile

In 1941, ten-year-old Esther Hautzig and her family were
taken by the Russians from their wealthy home in Vilma,
Poland, and sent on cattle-trains to a forced-labor camp in
Siberia where they coped with extreme poverty, freezing
winters, and insufficient food. At the end of World War II,
the family was reunited in Poland and young Esther then
went to the United States where she completed her education. Ms. Hautzig is the author of books on education
and decorating, and wrote, at the urging of those who knew
her story, a memoir of her years in exile.

*** *Hautzig, Esther* THE ENDLESS STEPPE: GROWING UP IN SI-
BERIA Crowell, 1968. (grade 6 and up)

Outstanding, restrained but dramatic personal narrative of
childhood years spent in exile. Esther, her mother, and grandmother emerge as figures of great courage, for despite having
enjoyed the comforts of a wealthy life in Poland, coped with

140

the extreme hardships in Siberia. Other women, including a strong, kindly, Russian doctor and many Polish deportees, are also depicted as possessing unusual strength and fortitude. This personal memoir contains the elements of a classic and is actually for readers of all ages.

CAROL HEISS
1940–

Olympic gold medal winning ice skater

Carol Heiss's Olympic gold medal for ice-skating was the culmination of fourteen years of working six days a week, four-and-a-half hours a day. At ten, the New York-born skater became the youngest girl ever to win the National Junior Championship. By the time she was twelve she had won every other junior title and at thirteen finished fourth in the World Figure Skating Championship.

An accident causing a cut calf tendon resulted in a short setback, but she recovered to become the youngest female member of the 1956 United States Olympic skating team, and to win the world championship three times. She turned down many tempting offers to turn professional in order to remain eligible for her goal of winning an Olympic gold medal. Carol Heiss accomplished this in 1960, and soon after retired from competitive skating.

** *Parker, Robert* CAROL HEISS: OLYMPIC QUEEN Illus. Double-day, 1961. (grades 7-9)

Good and enjoyable biography of the Olympic ice skater might be particularly attractive to would-be skaters, but is

141

equally interesting to other readers. Simply written, light in tone, it appears to be directed to either younger readers or less able junior high readers.

SAINT HELENA
c.248–c.328

Roman empress, mother of Constantine

Helena, the mother of Constantine, was the first Christian empress dowager in history. After being converted to Christianity, she is said to have gone to Jerusalem to seek the True Cross. She found it, according to legend, indicating that Christianity would be spread throughout the world. Her royal position with its accompanying power and privileges was instrumental in furthering the cause of Christianity and she is probably the first woman to enshrine sites in the Holy Land.

Her son Constantine named the ancient city of Helenopolis for her and had gold medals struck in her likeness.

* *Daughters of St. Paul* NOBLE LADY: THE LIFE OF SAINT HELENA Illus. Daughters of St. Paul, 1966. (grades 5-9)
    Romantic, highly fictionalized portrait of Saint Helena is based on the facts of her life as far as they are known. She emerges as an independent young woman and a courageous older one.

* *Harris, Mary* HELENA Sheed & Ward, 1960. (grades 4-6)
    Brief portrait of Saint Helena is directed towards religious readers. The subject is depicted as warm, independent, and brave.

HANYA HOLM
1893–

Dancer, teacher, choreographer

German-born Hanya Holm has lived in the United States over forty years and has made numerous contributions to the world of dance and musical comedy.

Her early piano study and training which stressed the integration of music and body movement led Hanya Holm to believe that dancers ought to freely develop individual creative ability. She initiated the prestigious summer dance festivals at the University of Colorado where she has taught, performed, choreographed, and directed concerts, dances, and operas.

Hanya Holm's choreography of the Broadway musicals *My Fair Lady, Kiss Me Kate, Where's Charley?* and *Camelot* as well as her work in ballet, films, and television have brought her many honors and awards. She has won the New York Drama Critics Award, a Tony nomination, and an honorary doctorate from the City College of New York.

** *Sorell, Walter* HANYA HOLM: THE BIOGRAPHY OF AN ARTIST
    Wesleyan Univ. Pr., 1969. (grade 9 and up)
       Absorbing biography, written by an expert in the field, follows the development of the artist in terms that may be understood by those not familiar with the world of the dance. However, it is particularly recommended for those readers with an interest in dance, either as spectators or participants.

LOU HENRY HOOVER
1875–1944

First Lady, restorer of the White House, president of the Girl Scouts

Lou Henry was a young geology student at Stanford University when she met Herbert Hoover, a fledgling mining engineer. After she obtained her degree, they married and for many years travelled and lived with their young sons in different parts of the world. They eventually built a permanent home in California and a rustic summer camp in the Virginia mountains, both of which she helped design.

The Hoovers loved outdoor life and camping, and also shared many intellectual interests. The combination of his scientific background and her knowledge of German, French, and Latin made it possible for them to translate a lengthy Latin work which became a major contribution to science.

During World War I, Lou Hoover helped to organize the American Woman's Hospital in England. Throughout her life she took an active role in many civic associations and entertained extensively and tastefully. As First Lady she instituted and supervised restoration of parts of the White House and increased her long-time active participation in the Girl Scouts by serving as their national president.

* *Pryor, Helen R.* LOU HENRY HOOVER: GALLANT FIRST LADY
Illus. with photographs. Dodd, 1969. (grade 8 and up)
Informal, but stilted and somewhat dull biography carefully traces Ms. Hoover's life from childhood. She is portrayed

by the author (who knew her and utilizes her own recollections as well as outside sources) as a lively, intelligent, accomplished, and warm human being.

JULIA WARD HOWE
1819–1910

Suffragist, author of "Battle Hymn of the Republic"

Julia Ward Howe, best known as the author of the emotionally stirring Civil War poem "Battle Hymn of the Republic," was the first woman elected to the American Academy of Arts and Letters. Well-educated and socially prominent, she read Greek, Latin, and German as a youngster and enjoyed all intellectual pursuits.

Her husband, Samuel Gridley Howe, prominent as director of the Perkins Institute for the Blind, disapproved and tried to repress the interests and individualism which she so desired and valued. Despite his opposition, she continued her study of languages, religion, and philosophy and wrote poems and plays whose themes of violent, unfulfilled love and self-destruction angered her husband and puzzled her friends and critics.

The women's movement, in which she assumed leadership, afforded her relief from the personal alienation she felt, and after her husband's death she accelerated her activities. Ms. Howe was a founder of both the American Women's Suffrage Association and the New England Women's Club and was a prolific writer and a peace worker. She made several successful lecture tours and organized women's clubs throughout the nation.

Julia Ward Howe became an institution and when she died, at ninety-one, four thousand people sang her "Battle Hymn of the Republic" at the memorial service held in Boston's Symphony Hall.

†† *Wagoner, Jean B.* JULIA WARD HOWE: GIRL OF OLD NEW YORK
Illus. Bobbs–Merrill, 1945. (grades 3-7)
Rather insipid, somewhat sexist biography concentrates on the childhood of Julia Ward Howe and barely mentions her many accomplishments. Superficial and overfictionalized, this book is more a picture of a privileged and indulged youngster in nineteenth-century New York, than a real biography of Ms. Howe.

ANNE HUTCHINSON
1591–1643

*Colonial religious dissenter who attacked
Puritan orthodoxy*

Anne Hutchinson is best remembered as an early American religious dissenter who argued that neither men nor women ought to subordinate themselves to the doctrines and authority of the Puritan church and who was the first woman to preach to women. Her beliefs that salvation was possible despite earthly failings and that the spirit of God was in everyone challenged the rigid beliefs of Puritanism, but attracted many followers, some of whom were prominent and influential men.

Her opponents saw her as an anarchist who placed the

individual and his conscience above all conventional authority and she was brought to trial by both civil and ecclesiastical courts. Despite her sixteenth pregnancy, she was made to stand throughtout the trial, and was declared guilty of heresy.

Excommunicated and banished from the colony, the Hutchinsons, with thirty-five other families, moved to Rhode Island where people seemed more tolerant. They later settled in New York where Ms. Hutchinson was killed in an Indian raid.

*** *Faber, Doris* COLONY LEADER: ANNE HUTCHINSON Illus. Garrard, 1970. (grades 3-6)
    Outstanding, simply-told profile of Anne Hutchinson skillfully conveys her beliefs, activities, and the mood of the colonies. Ms. Hutchinson emerges as a strong, independent, and energetic woman in this sympathetic, warm biography.

QUEEN ISABELLA
1451–1504
Queen of Spain

Queen Isabella of Spain, known best to Americans as the financier of Columbus's expeditions to the New World, ruled jointly with her husband, Ferdinand II. Isabella became queen of Castille in 1474. In 1479, the union of Aragon and Castile brought about a strong central government despite the two states' differences in language, customs, and laws.

Queen Isabella's determination to unite Spain under Catholicism led to excesses of intolerance such as the Spanish Inquisition and the proscription of the Jews.

Highly intelligent, intensely patriotic, and in some ways extremely moral, she managed to raise the level of the court from its low moral stance to one of greater repute. Needless to say, her sponsorship of Columbus's voyage affected the course of history and changed the map of the world.

** *Noble, Iris* SPAIN'S GOLDEN QUEEN ISABELLA Messner, 1969. (grade 7 and up)

Well-written, satisfactory biography of Queen Isabella gives a good picture of her intelligence and determination and provides a good background for further study of the period. Interesting and well-paced, it employs much dialogue without overfictionalization.

MAHALIA JACKSON
1911–1972

Gospel singer and civil rights worker

Mahalia Jackson brought traditional Gospel singing from black churches to the entire world through personal appearances in concert halls, recordings, and performances on radio and television.

A woman devotedly faithful to God, Ms. Jackson refused to sing anywhere that liquor was served, and although she could easily have become a great blues performer, she preferred to sing "the glory of God."

She wholeheartedly embraced the civil rights movement and was, in recent years, one of its symbols. She performed at benefits for bus boycotts, sit-ins, and Martin Luther King's Southern Christian Leadership Conferences. One of her most memorable appearances was before 200,000 people at the Lincoln Memorial during the civil rights march on Washington in 1963. Ms. Jackson also performed at President Kennedy's inauguration in 1961, the Newport Jazz Festival, and in benefit performances throughout the world. Among her best known and loved songs are "He's Got The Whole World In His Hands," "I Can Put My Trust In Jesus," "I Believe," and "We Shall Overcome."

*** *Cornell, Jean Gay* MAHALIA JACKSON: QUEEN OF GOSPEL SONG Illus. Garrard, 1974. (grades 3-5)

Warm, tender biography moves quickly as it gives not only a good personal and professional account of the life of Ms. Jackson, but also describes the meaning of Gospel music and discusses the civil rights movement.

*** *Jackson, Jesse* MAKE A JOYFUL NOISE UNTO THE LORD: THE LIFE OF MAHALIA JACKSON, QUEEN OF GOSPEL SINGERS Illus. with photographs. Crowell, 1974. (grades 5-9)

Exceedingly good, dramatic, and compassionate biography of the Gospel singer also gives a substantial picture of Gospel music, and a perceptive, thoughtful portrait of segregation and the civil rights movement.

** *Dunham, Montrew* MAHALIA JACKSON: YOUNG GOSPEL SINGER Bobbs–Merrill, 1974. (grades 3-6)

Although highly fictionalized, this is an absorbing, sympathetic, and accurate picture of Mahalia Jackson's early life. There is emphasis on civil rights, religion, and family life. Although little of the book deals with her later success, it gives a vivid picture which captures the essence of her life.

RACHEL DONNELSON JACKSON
1767–1828

Frontierswoman, wife of a president

Rachel Jackson and her parents moved from colonial Virginia to Kentucky where she met and married a man whose constant, unprovoked violence led to their separation. When she and Andrew Jackson fell in love they married, mistakenly believing that her divorce had been granted. When they learned of the error, they had a second marriage ceremony.

The Hermitage, the large house which they built on their plantation, still stands. During the War of 1812 Rachel managed the plantation herself.

When Andrew Jackson became a presidential candidate, stories surrounding their marriage were distorted to make him sound like a home-breaker and her an adulteress. Although the rumors were later pronounced unfounded, they had taken their toll on the health of Rachel Jackson. She died of a heart attack just before he left for Washington.

* Govan, Christine RACHEL JACKSON: TENNESSEE GIRL Illus. Bobbs–Merrill, 1955. (grades 3-7)

   Limited, overly fictionalized, and somewhat sexist biography focusses on the childhood of Rachel Jackson, omitting most of the important details of her life. The book provides a good picture of pioneer life, and though the author portrays the subject as an active youngster, the story is rather insipid and tends to perpetuate stereotyped sex roles.

MARY JEMISON
1743–1833
Indian captive

Fourteen-year-old Mary Jemison who was born on a ship enroute from Ireland to America was captured by Indians and adopted by a Seneca family. She so thoroughly learned to consider herself an Indian that when given a chance to return to her own people she refused. She married first a Delaware Indian and, after his death, a Seneca warrior.

Mary Jemison became independently wealthy as a land- and cattle-owner and was known throughout the community for her hospitality and generosity to both Indians and whites. She became a legend in her own time when her life story, as she related it, was published.

*** *Lenski, Lois* INDIAN CAPTIVE: THE STORY OF MARY JEMISON Illus. by the author. Lippincott, 1941. (grades 7-9)

Excellent biography focusses on only a short period of Jemison's life but is based on careful and thorough research. Convincingly fictionalized and effectively illustrated, the book gives a good picture of the Seneca Indians as well as the story of Mary Jemison. Maps add to the understanding and value of the book.

** *Gardner, Jeanne* MARY JEMISON: SENECA CAPTIVE Illus. Harcourt, 1966. (grades 5-7)

Good account of Mary Jemison's entire life describes her changing attitudes as she assimilated into the Seneca community. Though simple and readable, it is at times a bit gory for the age group for which it is intended.

JOAN OF ARC
1412–1431
French heroine

According to legend, Joan of Arc was born at Domremy of a comfortable peasant family. At the age of thirteen she heard "voices"—first advising her to lead a holy life, later directing her to rally the French army behind her.

She led the army against the British and Burgundian forces, and was captured when she was only eighteen. The British turned her over to a French ecclesiastic court which accused her of heresy and witchcraft. Among the sins listed during her long, disgraceful, and unfair trial was one that she dressed like a boy.

Convicted and condemned to death, she was burned at the stake at the marketplace in Rouen. Her innocence was proclaimed in 1455, and Joan, known also as the Maid of Orleans, was beatified in 1909 and canonized in 1920.

*** *Churchill, Winston* JOAN OF ARC (Her life as told by Winston Churchill in A HISTORY OF THE ENGLISH-SPEAKING PEOPLES) Illus. Dodd, 1969. (grade 3 and up)

Beautiful illustrations by Larren Ford complement this dramatic story of Joan of Arc. Told with direct simplicity, this brief book is suitable for all ages.

*** *Fisher, Aileen* JEANNE D'ARC Illus. Crowell, 1970. (grades 3-6)

Excellent account of the life of the fifteenth-century heroine is enhanced by outstanding illustrations by Ati Forberg. Stirringly told, but lacking in some authenticity, this will also serve well as a read-aloud book for younger children.

*** *Paine, Albert Bigelow* GIRL IN WHITE ARMOR Illus. Macmillan, 1967. (grade 7 and up)

Abridged from author's full-length adult biography, *Joan of Arc: Maid of France*, this is a faithfully told, nonsexist account of the French heroine which gives a proper perspective in a historical setting. Maps, chronology, and a cast of characters and drawings contribute to make a truly distinctive biography.

*** *Ross, Nancy* JOAN OF ARC Illus. Random, 1953. (grades 6-9)

Worthwhile biography offers the dramatic story of Joan of Arc in a fast-paced, readable style. The subject moves realistically and historical background is skillfully woven into story.

*** *Williams, Jay, and Lightbody, Charles W.* JOAN OF ARC Illus. American Heritage, 1963. (grade 6 and up)

Outstanding story of Joan of Arc traces her heroic deeds in a scholarly fashion, yet retains appealing and sympathetic style. Illustrations, maps, paintings, and illuminations do not overshadow but aid in the flow of the text. Although directed to young readers, it is certainly of value to adults as well.

** *Struchen, Jeanette* JOAN OF ARC: MAID OF ORLEANS Watts, 1967. (grade 7 and up)

Good study of Joan of Arc is dramatic but unevenly told. Simple short sentences which utilize difficult vocabulary detract from an otherwise fine biography.

†† *Daughters of St. Paul* WIND AND SHADOWS Daughters of St. Paul, 1968. (grades 4-7)

Rather pedestrian, stylistically uneven, fictionalized biography of Saint Joan shows her to be merely an instrument of God, albeit a courageous one.

AMY JOHNSON
1903–1941

Pioneer British aviator

Amy Johnson's parents, despite some misgivings, encouraged her desire to become a pilot. At a time when women were barely accepted in the field of aviation, she met many obstacles but went on to set records and to win honors and awards.

She was the first woman to fly solo from London to Australia, the first woman to fly the Atlantic east to west, and she set a London to Cape Town record. Ms. Johnson was also a capable mechanic and became the first woman in the world to pass the test for the British Ground Engineers License.

Amy Johnson's achievements brought her much fame and she was in demand as a lecturer and newspaper writer. When World War II broke out she volunteered as a pilot, and drowned when bad weather forced her to land in the Thames estuary.

*** *Grey, Elizabeth* WINGED VICTORY Illus. Houghton Mifflin, 1966. (grades 7-10)
   Vivid profile of the English aviator is moving and dramatic. Ms. Johnson is depicted as the pioneering, brave, ambitious woman she was in this sometimes too admiring, but very well written and engrossing biography.

IRENE JOLIOT-CURIE
1897–1956

French scientist, winner of Nobel Prize in chemistry

Like her famous parents Marie and Pierre Curie, Irene Joliot-Curie became a scientist. During World War I, she and her mother established and supervised x-ray stations where the wounded could be immediately diagnosed and treated.

After the war, she worked with her mother at the Institute of Radium, and there she met Frédéric Joliot, another scientist. Their subsequent marriage was a complete partnership, and together they discovered artificial radioactivity. For this tremendous contribution to medicine and biochemistry they won the 1935 Nobel Prize in chemistry. Irene Joliot-Curie thus became the only woman besides her mother to achieve that award. Like her mother, too, she successfully integrated the roles of scientist, wife, and mother.

*** *McKowan, Robin* SHE LIVED FOR SCIENCE: IRENE JOLIOT-CURIE Messner, 1961 (grade 7 and up)

Outstanding biography is sometimes quite technical, thus limiting its appeal to those readers interested in science. Despite some complicated material, the book moves along quickly and covers aspects of Ms. Joliot-Curie's personal and professional life.

MARY HARRIS JONES
1830–1930
Labor agitator and leader

Mary Harris Jones helped organize and publicize every major labor struggle in this country for over fifty years. The Irish-born labor agitator first became involved in union activities after her husband and four small children died of yellow fever. "Mother" Jones, as she was known, was dubbed the "patron saint of the picket lines" for her work against low wages, long hours, and dangerous conditions. She inspired striking workers to remain loyal despite imprisonment and starvation, and when mine owners hired strike-breakers she led the workers' wives to disperse the scabs with mops and brooms.

Her life was in constant danger—she was beaten and jailed—but she courageously persisted in helping to organize the United Mine Workers and to participate in most major coal, rail, textile, copper, steel, garment, and transit strikes throughout the nation. She worked to end child labor, demonstrating its evils by leading a "children's crusade" of little Pennsylvania mill workers to the home of President Theodore Roosevelt in New York.

Mother Jones actively involved herself in class and labor struggles past her ninetieth birthday and, at age ninety-four, sat down long enough to dictate her autobiography.

*** *Jones, Mary* AUTOBIOGRAPHY OF MOTHER JONES Charles Kerr, 1925, reprint 1972 with a new introduction and bibliography. Original foreword by Clarence Darrow. (grade 8 and up)

Fast-moving autobiography is written in a clear, compelling style with dry humor, warmth, and drama. Although not written for young readers, it is immensely readable and fairly accurate.

*** *Werstein, Irving* LABOR'S DEFIANT LADY: THE STORY OF MOTHER JONES Crowell, 1969. (grades 5-9)

Superior biography of the dynamic labor leader is distinguished by its brisk narrative, balanced portrayal, and vivid picture of the subject and the issues in which she was involved. Thoroughly researched, it offers a good, thoughtful summary of her long life.

HELEN KELLER
1880–1968

Author and humanitarian

Helen Keller, deaf and blind from infancy, was at age seven an overindulged, unkept, and unmanageable youngster who seemed headed for oblivion. Then the gifted, perseverant, young teacher Anne Sullivan Macy (page 189) came into the household and eventually she and Helen were spelling words into each other's hands. Helen learned to read raised print with her fingers, to type, and to be self-reliant. Later she learned braille and oral communication.

Ms. Keller's unusually high intelligence and unending hard work led to her acceptance and graduation with honors from Radcliffe College and to the publication and enormous success of her autobiography, *Story of My Life*. With Ms. Macy, and later Polly Thomson as her "eyes and ears," Helen Keller wrote, lectured, and travelled on behalf of the handicapped, the women's suffrage movement, and the peace movement, and gained the admiration of the entire world.

Ms. Keller was a major influence in obtaining opportunities for the training and employment of the blind, and her life has inspired millions of other handicapped people to live creative and productive lives of their own.

*** *Bigland, Eileen* HELEN KELLER Illus. S. G. Phillips, 1967. (grades 7-10)
   Sensitive, dramatic biography gives a well-rounded portrait of Helen Keller. Anne Sullivan Macy's patience and skills are acknowledged, and the subject is seen from earliest childhood to her last years.

*** *Brown, Marion, and Crone, Ruth* SILENT STORM Illus. Abingdon, 1963. (grades 6-8)
   See Anne Sullivan Macy.

*** *Davidson, Margaret* HELEN KELLER Illus. Hastings, 1970; Scholastic Book Service, 1973. (grades 3-5)
   Stirring biography is clear, easy-to-read narrative prose, making use of fictionalization, but still remaining faithful to the truth. Vivid and intimate, it is colorful and absorbing.

*** *Gibson, William* THE MIRACLE WORKER Knopf, 1957. (grade 7 and up)
   See Anne Sullivan Macy.

*** *Graff, Stewart and Polly* HELEN KELLER Illus. Dell, 1965. (grades 2-7)
   Very fine, moving profile of Helen Keller is quietly compelling, highlighting the important events and experiences in her life.

*** *Graff, Stewart and Polly* HELEN KELLER: TOWARDS THE LIGHT Garrard, 1965. (grades 2-5)
   Excellent, simple profile of Helen Keller is a touching account of her life, showing her limitations, progress, and achievements.

*** *Keller, Helen* STORY OF MY LIFE Doubleday, 1954. (grade 7 and up)

Warm and dramatic autobiography was written by Ms. Keller when she was a student at Radcliffe. It is dignified, appealing, and inspiring and because it was written early in her life, it just tells her story up to that point. An appended account of her education incorporates letters and reports.

*** *Peare, Catherine O.* THE HELEN KELLER STORY Crowell, 1959. (grade 7 and up)

Very well written, perceptive profile provides a thoughtful examination of Helen Keller's life, paying full tribute to the efforts of her teacher, as well as her own achievements.

*** *Richards, N.* HELEN KELLER Illus. Children's Pr., 1968. (grade 6 and up)

Warm, dramatic biography is lavishly illustrated with drawings and photographs, adding to the interest and value of the book.

*** *Tibble, J. W. and Anne* HELEN KELLER Illus. Putnam, 1958. (grades 5-9)

Excellent, dramatic biography gives a vivid picture of the progress and achievements of Helen Keller.

*** *Waite, Helen E.* VALIANT COMPANIONS Macrae, 1959. (grade 7 and up)

See Anne Sullivan Macy.

** *Hickok, Lorena A.* THE STORY OF HELEN KELLER Illus. Grosset, 1958. (grades 4-6)

Despite excessive fictionalization, this is a good biography which captures the mood of Keller's life, and shows clearly the way in which she learned to communicate.

†† *Wilkie, Katherine E.* HELEN KELLER: HANDICAPPED GIRL Illus. Bobbs–Merrill, 1969. (grades 3-7)

Overfictionalized biography stereotypes black servants, making this otherwise mediocre book objectionable.

GRACE KELLY
1929–

Actress, princess of Monaco

Talented Grace Kelly of a socialite Philadelphia family was determined to become an actress. In New York, she studied drama, played roles on television, and then won a part on Broadway which led to a Hollywood contract. At only twenty-five she won the Academy Award for best actress for her performance in *The Country Girl*.

Her wedding in 1956 to the prince of Monaco was an event followed by people throughout the world. When she became Her Serene Highness, Princess Grace of Monaco, she retired from acting, appearing only occasionally for charitable events. Princess Grace has long been active in philanthropic work and considers herself a working woman as well as the mother of three children.

†† *Katz, Marjorie* Grace Kelly Coward, 1970. (grade 7 and up)
  Fast-moving, easy-to-read biography sounds like a fairy tale. It relates the story of a woman born to beauty and wealth who became an actress, won an Academy Award, married a handsome prince, lived happily ever after. The fault lies not with the facts but with the telling, for this biography dwells on all the stereotypes of sex and class and devotes only a few words to the princess's philanthropic work in Monaco. Reluctant readers may enjoy this book for its resemblance to fan-magazine stories, but it is a trivial, superficial biography.

FRANCES "FANNY" KEMBLE
1809–1893
Actress, abolitionist, author

On tour in America, British actress Fanny Kemble met and married a wealthy Philadelphian, Pierce Butler, who she later discovered was a slave-owner. A stay at his Georgia plantation reinforced her abolitionist beliefs and filled her with disgust and horror, especially when her humane recommendations were rejected by her husband.

She kept a detailed record of her life there: "Journal of A Residence on A Georgian Plantation" provides a unique contribution to the history of slavery.

Fanny Kemble's views of slavery, her independence, and her refusal to act the role of a dutiful, subjugated wife antagonized her husband who subsequently treated her as a prisoner in her own home. He deprived her of any jurisdiction over their two daughters and allowed her to see them only at prescribed hours. Finding this unbearable, she left him and eventually found personal and artistic satisfaction and success giving readings of Shakespeare in England and America, and writing poems, plays, criticism, and journals.

*** *Rushmore, Robert* FANNY KEMBLE Macmillan, 1970. (grade 7 and up)
  Excellent biography is analytical and well-researched. Lucidly and stirringly shows how an intelligent, well-educated nineteenth-century woman was cruelly oppressed.

*** *Scott, John Anthony* FANNY KEMBLE'S AMERICA Crowell, 1973. (grade 7 and up)

Superb biography gives a clear honest portrayal of Fanny Kemble's life in America and also gives an unusually fine picture of the period, revealing many facts of history which are not generally known to young readers. Intelligently written, this book evokes great emotion and shows the concepts of male/female and black/white equality as being closely related.

*** *Wise, Winifred E.* FANNY KEMBLE: ACTRESS, AUTHOR, ABOLITIONIST Illus. Putnam, 1966. (grades 7-10)
Excellent, competently researched biography describes Ms. Kemble's early professional career and her later conflicts concerning her marriage to a slave-owner. Vivid descriptions of slave life as described in Fanny Kemble's own journals are included.

** *Kerr, Laura* FOOTLIGHTS TO FAME: THE LIFE OF FANNY KEMBLE Illus. Funk & Wagnalls, 1962. (grades 7-11)
Fictionalized biography of Fanny Kemble is overly romantic and bland in the early chapters about her childhood and theatrical career. As the book and her life progress, Ms. Kemble's oppressive marriage is described and she emerges as an independent woman.

** *Wright, Constance* FANNY KEMBLE AND THE LOVELY LAND Illus. Dodd, 1972. (grade 9 and up)
This good adult biography is suitable for high school students. Well-documented with notes, comments, and a lengthy bibliography, the book depicts Fanny Kemble as intelligent and courageous. Although slow-moving at times, there is extensive use of extracts from letters and journals into the narrative and into conversations.

ROSE FITZGERALD KENNEDY
1890–

Civic leader, philanthropist, political campaigner, and mother of President John F. Kennedy

Rose Kennedy, a hard-working political campaigner, active philanthropist, and physical fitness enthusiast, had the unique ability to bring up sons and daughters who contributed much to their country. This, as well as her dignity, unswerving religious faith, energy, and self-discipline even in the face of great tragedy, combine to make her one of the most remarkable women of our time.

She purposefully and directly encouraged her children to be independent, competent, confident, competitive, and aware of current affairs. When her husband served as ambassador to Great Britain she assumed her role as hostess to world leaders with considerable success.

Her life has been marked by many tragic events. Her oldest son was killed during World War II, a daughter died in a plane crash, and another daughter is mentally retarded.

Her son John F. Kennedy, who became the thirty-fifth president of the United States, was assassinated in 1963, and only five years later his brother Senator Robert Kennedy was also assassinated.

Despite these great misfortunes she has managed to continue her activities in behalf of the Catholic church and mental retardation and takes great pride in her remaining son, Senator Edward Kennedy, and in her daughters and numerous grandchildren.

* *Eldred, Patricia Mulrooney* ROSE KENNEDY Illus. Creative Educ. Soc., 1974. (grades 4-8)

Rather prosaic, uninspiring, somewhat emotionless biography closely follows the facts of Rose Kennedy's life but fails to impart the spirit and warmth of the woman. The author reports the assassinations in the same matter-of-fact tone in which she reports other experiences in the subject's life.

* *Hawkes, Ann* ROSE KENNEDY Ilus. Putnam, 1975. (grades 2-4)

This accurate biography does not clearly depict the subject's strength, intelligence, religious devotion, or philanthropic activities. There is too much biographical material crammed into this short, easy-to-read volume without proper elaboration, which may result in leaving young readers somewhat puzzled.

BILLIE JEAN KING
1943–

Tennis champion, advocate of equal rights for women in tennis

Tennis champion Billie Jean King won her first tournament at age thirteen. At seventeen she won the women's doubles at Wimbledon and at eighteen was ranked fourth among Americans. In 1968, after three consecutive Wimbledon victories and wins in the United States Indoor, Easter Grass, and United States National, Ms. King was ranked first in the world.

During this time, Billie Jean King became infuriated by the fact that men's prize money so exceeded women's. In order to help women gain equal rights and equal prize money, she organized a boycott of women players against the official United States Lawn Tennis Association. (USLTA) tournaments. Ms. King also helped to establish the first independent women's tennis tour and a new magazine called *womanSport*.

On September 20, 1973, Billie Jean King beat the colorful male tennis star Bobby Riggs in a spectacular match watched by millions on television. She showed that women's tennis is as exciting as men's, and added another triumph to an already long list.

In 1975, after winning her fifth Wimbledon singles championship, she announced she would no longer play in major single competition but would continue in doubles and with the World Tennis Team.

*** *Baker, Jim* BILLIE JEAN KING Illus. with photographs. Grosset, 1974. (reading level, grades 4-6; interest level through high school)

Excellent, fast-moving biography of Billie Jean King is a balanced treatment, giving equal emphasis to her tennis playing and her involvement in the promotion of women's tennis and World Team Tennis. Many photographs of her on and off court enhance this biography which will be appealing to all her fans, but which is especially suitable for reluctant or less capable older readers. It is extremely easy to read, but also discusses issues that junior high and high school students will find of interest.

*** *Burchard, Marshall and Sue* SPORTS HERO: BILLIE JEAN KING Illus. Putnam, 1975. (grades 2-4)

Outstanding, dynamic portrait of the tennis champion explains the game as well as discussing her career. The role Ms. King played in promoting women's tennis is interestingly covered from a feminist perspective, and her famed match with Riggs is vividly and objectively described.

** *Olsen, James T.* BILLIE JEAN KING, LADY OF THE COURT Illus. Creative Educ. Soc./Children's Pr., 1974. (grades 4-7)

Illustrated with many colorful action drawings, this biography, though not quite up to date, is packed with information about the subject and shows her to be a talented, ambitious tennis player. However, it is stylistically uneven, and in an attempt to be journalistically informal it sometimes awkwardly misses its mark.

CORETTA SCOTT KING
1927–

Civil rights leader, peace advocate, singer

Although best known as the wife and then widow of civil rights leader Martin Luther King, Jr., Coretta King is very much a dynamic, talented person in her own right.

At both Antioch College and the New England Conservatory of Music where she was awarded scholarships, Ms. King received a thorough foundation in academic work and in singing. She put aside her immediate career goals when she married, deciding instead to work with her husband to try to achieve better relations between the races.

Despite increasing family responsibilities she took an active part in the Southern Christian Leadership Conference, frequently filling speaking engagements and giving benefit concerts. She also taught voice in a college music department in Atlanta, and was a Woman's Strike For Peace delegate at the International Disarmament Conference in Geneva in 1962.

When her husband was assassinated in 1968, Ms. King earned the respect of the world for her show of dignity and strength. She assumed many of his unfulfilled obligations in addition to those of her own and became the first woman to speak from the pulpit of Saint Paul's Cathedral in London.

Now president of the Martin Luther King, Jr. Center for Social Change in Atlanta, Georgia, she also holds important positions in many other organizations and has written a popular book about her life with her husband.

*** *Taylor, Paula* CORETTA SCOTT KING Illus. Creative Educ. Soc., 1975. (grades 3-7)

Very fine, readable biography examines Coretta King's commitment to the civil rights movement, and also shows her to be an intelligent, talented woman who did not really subordinate herself to her husband, but merely shifted her goals from a musical career to one dedicated to helping humanity. This profile illustrates how she used her own training and background appropriately towards this direction.

JILL KINMONT
1938–

Championship skier, educator

Jill Kinmont was trying out for the 1956 United States Olympic Ski team when she fell, broke her neck, and severed her spinal cord. Permanently paralyzed from the shoulders down, she was determined to make herself physically and financially independent. After years of unrelenting efforts she learned to write again, completed college, became a licensed teacher, and now supervises a school reading program in California.

Ms. Kinmont spends summers on a Paiute reservation teaching young Indian children a reading course she designed, and training Indian tutors. Successful as a fund-raiser for the reservation center, Jill Kinmont, surrounded by a warm and supportive family, has carved out a rich and useful life for herself at work and among her many friends.

*** *Valens, E. G.* LONG WAY UP: THE STORY OF JILL KINMONT
Illus. Harper, 1966. (grade 9 and up)
Deeply moving, dramatic account of a young woman who suffered a tragic accident. Of interest to all readers, it may hold a particular attraction for either skiing enthusiasts or as an inspiration for those with handicaps of their own. The subject is shown to be courageous and optimistic in this intimate and well-rounded biography.

KÄTHE KOLLWITZ
1867–1945
German graphic artist

Social injustices, peace, and brotherhood were themes running through the work of German graphic artist Käthe Kollwitz. Her works attempt to demonstrate the happiness and tragedies of the mother-child relationship and to portray the emotions attached to death. Her drawings, woodcuts, etchings, and sculpture were widely praised and she became the first woman member of the Prussian Academy of Art.

One of her two sons was killed in World War I, and though she loved her German homeland, she used her art as a protest against the rise of detested Nazism. She was forbidden to teach or exhibit her work because its social theme was considered "degenerate." Much of it was burned by the Nazis.

During the years following the war and just after her death, her work gradually reappeared and has again found enormous popularity both for its artistic merits and its relevance to contemporary social issues.

*** *Klein, Mina C. and H. Arthur* KATHE KOLLWITZ: LIFE IN ART Illus. Holt, 1972. (grade 9 and up)

Beautiful, touching, and sensitive book is a personal as well as artistic biography. Including more than one hundred reproductions of her drawings, woodcuts, etchings, and sculpture, this book is a delight to look at as well as read. The authors' distinguished writing, as well as Ms. Kollwitz's own work, clearly expresses the love she had for her work, husband, children, grandchildren, and her country, despite its actions.

OLGA KORBUT
1956–

Soviet Olympic gold medal winner in gymnastics

When four-foot, eleven-inch, eighty-four-pound Olga Korbut competed in the 1972 Olympics in Munich the sixteen-year-old gymnast not only won three gold medals but also stole the show for television viewers all over the world.

Under the Russian government's school sports system, she received training in gymnastics, and by her early teens was winning national and international awards. When she competed in the 1972 Olympics, she demonstrated the backward somersault on the uneven parallel bars and became the first person, male or female, to do so in competition. She is also the only female to do a back flip on the balance beam.

It was not only her disciplined gymnastic ability and her apparent fearlessness but her natural, often emotional personality that endeared her to audiences. When she toured the United States the following year she was greeted by enthusiastic capacity crowds. She received ABC's "Wide World of Sports" Athlete of the Year Award and the Associated Press's Babe Didrikson Zaharias Trophy for Female Athlete of the Year.

*** *Jacobs, Linda* OLGA KORBUT: GIRL OF TEARS AND TRIUMPH Illus. EMC, 1974. (reading level, grades 4-6; interest level through high school)

Well-balanced account of the gymnast's life focusses on her athletic career, but also discusses her personality and private life. Numerous photographs of her in action greatly enhance the easy-to-read text making the biography particularly appealing to older reluctant readers as well as younger children.

*** *Smith, Jay H.* OLGA KORBUT Illus. Creative Educ. Soc., 1974. (grades 4-8)

Colorfully illustrated, this nonadulatory biography depicts the popular young gymnast as a fearless, determined competitor who shows her emotions to her fans. The emphasis is on her athletic career, but her early life is also described.

** *Beecham, Justin* OLGA Illus. with photographs. Two Continents, 1974. (grade 7 and up)

Divided in its focus between a biography of Olga Korbut and an overview of gymnastics and the Olympic games, the book is enhanced by an abundance of candid and action photographs of the subject. The text, though lively and informal, lacks some cohesiveness and the transitions from biography to sports discussion are often abrupt and choppy.

** *Suponer, Michael* OLGA KORBUT: A BIOGRAPHICAL PORTRAIT Illus. Doubleday, 1975. (grade 6 and up)

Lavishly illustrated with black-and-white photographs of Olga Korbut in action, this profile of the gymnast offers few insights into her personality or private life. The book focusses on her training and achievements and on the style and technique of her trainer. It is essentially a portrait of the life of a Soviet gymnast, with Olga Korbut as an example of one of the most skilled. Somewhat dry and stiff (it is translated from the Russian), the book will still hold the interest of those who wish to know more about gymnastics. Illustrated instructions for the beginning gymnast are also included.

SUSETTE LA FLESCHE
1854–1903

Spokeswoman for Indian rights, author, lecturer, and artist

Susette La Flesche, an Omaha Indian, grew up on a reservation in Nebraska and attended a mission school, becoming fluent in French and English as well as her native language. Her quick mind and great thirst for knowledge came to the attention of her teacher, who arranged for her to attend an Eastern girls' seminary. Later she became a teacher on the Omaha reservation.

Ms. La Flesche, or Bright Eyes as she was also known, was imbued by her tribal leader father with a sense of responsibility to her people. She participated in many Indian reform movements, wrote articles for newspapers pleading their causes, and embarked on a lecture tour of the East with Thomas Tibbles, a white newspaperman; Standing Bear, an Indian Chief; and her brother. They were successful in making Americans aware of the grave injustices done to Indians and through their efforts an act was passed which allotted reservation land and citizenship rights to individual Indians.

After her marriage to Thomas Tibbles she continued to lecture in the United States and England, contributed additional articles and stories to magazines and newspapers, and illustrated a historical book about the origin of the Omahas.

*** *Crary, Margaret* SUSETTE LA FLESCHE: VOICE OF THE OMAHA INDIANS Illus. Hawthorn, 1973. (grades 7-10)

Very fine biography of the Indian spokeswoman also gives a good picture of the Omaha Indians and their fight for citizenship rights. Ms. La Flesche is depicted as an unusually intelligent, warm human being whose belief that Indians should be seen as people in the eyes of the law was a motivating force for her efforts to enlighten the public.

MARY ELIZABETH LEASE
1853–1933
Populist party speaker and agitator

Life as a Kansas farmer's wife and mother of four had been too confining for former teacher Mary Elizabeth Lease, so when her husband returned to his practice of pharmacy, she engaged herself in civic and social affairs and formed the Hypatia Society, a women's group for discussion of current issues.

As her interests widened she became actively involved in politics and her stirring, resonant voice and charismatic quality made her a successful public speaker on behalf of local groups. Ms. Lease also edited the *Union Labor Press*, founded a labor paper, and was elected president of a chapter of the Knights of Labor. She made a major contribution to the local and national scene as a speaker and agitator for the Farmer's Alliance and the Populist party, explaining to farmers in Kansas, Missouri, the far West, and the South how they were exploited by Eastern monopolies. Ms. Lease studied law and passed the Kansas bar examination; wrote for the New York *World;* published a book entitled *The Problem of Civilization Solved;* and was a continuous supporter of women's suffrage, prohibition, and birth control. She served as president of the National Society for Birth Control, and is remembered best as one of the first important women politicians in the nation.

*** *Stiller, Richard* QUEEN OF THE POPULISTS: THE STORY OF MARY ELIZABETH LEASE Illus. Crowell, 1970. (grades 6-9)
Outstanding, completely written biography traces the

173

Populist movement as well as giving a dramatic, perceptive portrait of the first important woman politician in America. The colorful personality of Ms. Lease emerges, and her important contributions are carefully noted in a vividly written book.

LOIS LENSKI
1893–

Author and illustrator of children's books

Popular author and illustrator of children's books, Lois Lenski began her professional career by illustrating books for other authors. The pictures she drew for her own son when he was young grew into the now classic picture books of the Mr. Small and Davy series. A thorough and exacting craftswoman, Ms. Lenski extensively researched lives and periods for *Indian Captive,* her biography of Mary Jemison (page 151), and for her historical novels *Blueberry Corners* and *Puritan Adventure.* For her regional books *Blue Ridge Billy, Prairie School Strawberry Girl, Judy's Journey,* and *Cotton in My Sack,* Ms. Lenski did not rely only on scholarly library research but went directly to the locations and gathered her background material firsthand.

Lois Lenski has won many of the major book awards for her work, much of which remains enormously popular with youngsters. Educators find Lenski's books to be good supplements to classroom assignments in social studies.

** *Lenski, Lois* JOURNEY INTO CHILDHOOD: THE AUTOBIOGRAPHY OF LOIS LENSKI Illus. Lippincott, 1972. (grade 9 and up)
 Fine autobiography considers Lenski's childhood, youth, and adulthood in informal, enjoyable detail. However, be-

cause this book is far less engaging than her books for young readers, it may be of greater interest to adults or those older readers with fond recollections of Lois Lenski's juvenile books.

MARGARET LESTER
1938–

Handicapped athlete, wife, and mother

Just before their marriage Australian Margaret Lester and her fiancé were in a car accident. He fully recovered from his injury but her spinal cord was so damaged that she was left paralyzed below her chest. Despite this disability, they married and had three children. Ms. Lester, with a resolute good-natured spirit, has done her own housework, cared for the children, completed college, and participates in many competitive sports including javelin and discus throwing, table tennis, and swimming. Her motto, "Anything can be done," is an essential part of the spirit and philosophy which has sustained her and allowed her to live a full and creative life.

*** *Epstein, June* MERMAID ON WHEELS: THE REMARKABLE STORY OF MARGARET LESTER Illus. with photographs. Taplinger, 1967. (grade 9 and up)
Inspiring biography of an intrepid, persevering young woman is written with feeling, intimacy, and intelligence. Dramatic and often humorous, it is a living tribute to the courage of one woman.

LILIUOKALANI
1838–1917

Last sovereign of Hawaii, songwriter

Liliuokalani, the last sovereign of Hawaii, was an accomplished songwriter whose "Aloha Oe" remains popular on the mainland as well as the islands. Educated in an American missionary school and married to a former Boston sea captain, she conscientiously prepared for her future role as sovereign by travelling throughout the islands, developing and supervising schools for boys and girls of Hawaiian blood, and by serving as regent during the king's absence. With her husband she paid a state visit to Queen Victoria and travelled across the United States where she was warmly received by the president.

In 1891 Liliuokalani succeeded to the throne. The crown had been consistently weakened by a constitution which gave increasing power to Americans, and she unsuccessfully tried to restore some of this power to the Hawaiians. Her attempt to proclaim a new constitution was truncated, for a time she was under arrest, and Hawaii was eventually annexed to the United States. The former queen, then widowed, continued to live in Honolulu in the home her husband had built and to receive a pension from the government and an income from her plantation. She became a symbol of the Hawaiian past, and prominent visitors to the island continued to pay their respects to her.

** *Malone, Mary* LILIUOKALANI: QUEEN OF HAWAII Illus. Garrard, 1975. (grades 3-5)

Good biography shows the queen as an intelligent, strong woman. In simple terms the author explains the final chapter in Hawaii's sovereignty; the politics are described clearly and accurately. The emphasis is on Liliuokalani's activities in her role as queen, but there is also an account of her carefree childhood.

** *Stone, Adrienne* HAWAII'S QUEEN: LILIUOKALANI Illus. Messner, 1949. (grades 6-9)

Smoothly written fictionalized biography moves along at a good pace, revealing the queen as a woman eager to play her role efficiently, and to do the best for her people.

** *Wilson, Hazel* LAST QUEEN OF HAWAII: LILIUOKALANI Illus. Knopf, 1963. (grades 6-9)

A good picture of the colonization of Hawaii and a sympathetic portrayal of the queen.

* *Newman, Shirlee P.* LILIUOKALANI: YOUNG HAWAIIAN QUEEN Illus. Bobbs–Merrill, 1960. (grades 3-6)

Mostly nonsexist, overly fictionalized biography of Liliuokalani concentrates on her childhood and youth, but gives a fairly good picture of life in Hawaii before Westernization.

MARY TODD LINCOLN
1818–1882

First Lady

Socially prominent Mary Todd Lincoln, a bright and enthusiastic student, grew into an attractive, warm, popular but somewhat temperamental and insecure young woman whose family did not approve of her marriage to Abraham

Lincoln. His long absences from their home in Springfield, Illinois, left her to take the major responsibility for their four sons and household which she managed, despite frequent illnesses.

Ms. Lincoln encouraged her husband in his quest for the presidency, but after becoming First Lady found the strain of war and criticism insurmountable. The South regarded the southern-born Mary Lincoln a traitor, the North questioned her loyalty; she was alternately considered ignorant of society and too extravagant in her entertainment. The death of her two sons, and the later assassination of her husband, almost destroyed her.

Lincoln's former law partner later spread false accounts of him which were given wide attention and served to exacerbate Mary Lincoln's distraught condition. Often behaving irrationally, and despite the false belief that she was in dire poverty, she remained a compulsive shopper and her son Robert, in an attempt to provide for proper medical care, requested a sanity trial. She was judged insane, placed in an asylum, but later declared sane. Mortified by this treatment, she left the country, returning only when she was gravely ill.

*** *Randall, Ruth Painter* I, MARY: A BIOGRAPHY OF THE GIRL WHO MARRIED ABRAHAM LINCOLN Illus. Little, 1959. (grade 8 and up)

Extremely good, well-balanced portrait of Mary Todd Lincoln is critical as well as sympathetic. The author, a fine writer and a renowned Mary Lincoln scholar, gives an unvarnished picture of her subject, presenting her in an interesting, thoughtful manner.

** *Anderson, La Vere* MARY TODD LINCOLN: PRESIDENT'S WIFE Illus. Garrard, 1975. (grades 2-4)

A good sympathetic portrait of Mary Todd Lincoln shows her to be strong-willed though somewhat dependent and unstable. A feeling for the period in general and the Civil War in particular is also conveyed.

* *Wilkie, Katherine E.* MARY TODD LINCOLN: GIRL OF THE BLUEGRASS Illus. Bobbs–Merrill, 1954. (grades 3-6)
   Mostly nonsexist, highly fictionalized biography focusses on the earlier years of Mary Lincoln's life. More historical fiction than biography, the book concentrates mainly on her adult life, and that part is superficial.

NANCY HANKS LINCOLN
1783?–1818

Pioneer wife, seamstress, mother of
President Abraham Lincoln

When Nancy Lincoln died at the age of thirty-five, her son Abraham Lincoln was only nine years old, but he remembered her well and said later, "she was highly intellectual by nature, had a strong memory, accurate judgment and was cool and heroic."

Others remembered her well too, and the picture which emerges is one of the hard-working pioneer wife who milked cows, churned butter, cooked, spun, and cared for her two children, Abraham and Sarah. Tall, slender, and dark, she was cheerful with a pleasant disposition, yet sometimes melancholy, and ambitious for her children. Greatly skilled at needlework, before her marriage to Thomas Lincoln she was employed by many prosperous families as a seamstress where she was treated as a social equal, although she came from "plain folk."

179

In 1818 the "milk sickness," a disease spread through cow's milk, reached epidemic proportions in the Lincolns' Indiana county. When Nancy contracted the dread disease there was no physician within thirty-five miles. Her children tried to care for her as best they could—as they had seen her care for others—but it was of no use. On the seventh day after becoming ill she died, but not without telling the children to "be good to one another."

** *LeSueur, Meridel* NANCY HANKS OF WILDERNESS ROAD: A STORY OF ABRAHAM LINCOLN'S MOTHER Illus. Knopf, 1949. (grades 3-7)

Beautifully written and illustrated portrait of Lincoln's mother relies on heavy fictionalization, but gives a good picture of the woman and her part in shaping Abraham Lincoln. Distinguished and dramatic prose is particularly suitable for reading aloud to young children.

* *Stevenson, Augusta* NANCY HANKS: KENTUCKY GIRL Illus. Bobbs–Merrill, 1954. (grades 3-7)

Mostly nonsexist, enjoyable profile of Nancy Hanks Lincoln emphasizes her childhood and is overfictionalized but gives a fairly good picture of frontier days, capturing the essence of Ms. Lincoln's life.

JENNY LIND
1820–1887

Swedish opera star

Sometimes referred to as the "Swedish nightingale," Jenny Lind was born in Sweden where she early began her studies of drama and music. At sixteen she made her opera debut and quickly climbed to stardom, becoming a favorite in her native Sweden as well as in Europe. A two-year tour of the United States under the auspices of P. T. Barnum brought her even greater prominence. She married while in the United States, and upon her return to England continued her successful appearances in oratorios and concerts. Always interested in helping other musicians to learn and attain excellence, she encouraged them in their musical studies and became a professor of singing at the Royal College of Music.

Jenny Lind's great success derived from her magnificent voice, her fine musicianship, and her great acting ability. Generous and philanthropic, she gave much of her earned fortunes to causes in which she believed.

** *Cavanah, Frances* JENNY LIND AND HER LISTENING CAT Illus. Vanguard, 1961. (grades 3-6)
Animated, fictionalized account of the childhood of Jenny Lind offers a delightful and tender portrait of the young girl whose talents were early nurtured.

* *Myers, Elisabeth* JENNY LIND: SONGBIRD FROM SWEDEN Illus. Garrard, 1968. (grades 4-7)
Somewhat sexist, but otherwise interesting and highly readable biography gives a lively account of Jenny Lind's life and career.

BELVA ANN LOCKWOOD
1830–1917

Attorney, advocate of women's rights, peace worker

Belva Ann Lockwood was solely responsible for getting Congress to allow women to practice law before the United States Supreme Court. Until she was in her eighties, she was active in civil rights for women and minorities, and in efforts towards world peace.

She left school at fifteen, but later as a young widow with a child to support became a teacher and continued her own education. She then decided to go to law school, but was rejected at several law schools in Washington, D.C. When she finally gained acceptance she was later refused her diploma until President Grant met her "demand" and ordered that it be given to her.

The Supreme Court refused to allow any woman to plead cases before it, but through Ms. Lockwood's lobbying efforts, Congress finally passed a bill that eliminated this barrier, and she became the first woman to practice before the nation's highest court.

A tireless worker for women's legal rights, she also represented the Eastern Cherokee Indians in their case against the United States and won for them an award of five million dollars. She also sponsored the first southern black man to practice before the Supreme Court.

Throughout her active professional life, Belva Ann Lockwood gave not only inspiration but also concrete help to many aspiring women attorneys.

*** *Dunnahoo, Terry* Before the Supreme Court: the story of belva ann lockwood Houghton Mifflin, 1974. (grade 6 and up)

Outstanding biography gives a strong impression of the subject's personality and accomplishments as well as describing the women's movement and the era with perception and inspiration. Discussions of law and politics are incorporated into this extremely readable biography.

** *Fox, Mary Virginia* Lady for the Defense Harcourt, 1975. (grades 6-9)

Good, objective, and accurate biography is stylistically inconsistent. At times the author employs much conversation, other times the narrative becomes quite formal. The accomplishments of the subject are clearly depicted, but the book lacks the excitement and inspiration that the subject herself displayed.

ESTHER POHL LOVEJOY, M.D.
1870–1967

Director and organizer of American Women's Hospital Service

Esther Pohl Lovejoy, one of the first women graduates of the University of Oregon medical school, became the first woman in America to hold the position of chairperson of the Board of Health in a major city. Dr. Lovejoy was an early advocate of community medicine and better sanitary conditions, the founder of a hospital in Alaska, and an active supporter of women's suffrage. She achieved recognition during World War I for her work with the Red Cross and as director and organizer of the American Women's

183

Hospital Service. Her help in developing orphanages, clinics, hospitals, and medical assistance to disaster victims and refugees in Europe and Asia won her many honorary degrees, decorations, and tributes from heads of state all over the world.

During World War II, Dr. Lovejoy helped the displaced and interned Japanese-Americans in this country, and aided in the selection of women doctors to serve in the Armed Forces. She worked tirelessly to achieve their equal status with male doctors in the services.

Dr. Esther Pohl Lovejoy did much to gain recognition for women in medicine. She wrote books about her own experiences and a history of women in medicine and served as the president of the American Medical Women's National Association.

** *Burt, Olive W.* PHYSICIAN TO THE WORLD: ESTHER POHL LOVEJOY Messner, 1973. (grade 7 and up)
   Lacking in distinctive literary style, this is nonetheless a dramatic, vivid account of a woman whose single-mindedness, persistence, boundless energy, and intelligence were determining factors in her great achievements.

JULIETTE GORDON LOW
1860–1927

Founder of the Girl Scouts of America

Juliette "Daisy" Gordon Low was, until the time she founded the Girl Scouts of America, a woman with few interests and ambitions. Known for her charm and good sense of humor, she had many artistic and creative talents but lived rather aimlessly as did many women of her high social position. At age fifty-one she met General Sir Robert Baden-Powell, founder of the Boy Scouts, and became interested in the Girl Guides, a similar organization for girls.

Ms. Low formed groups in Scotland and London and then returned to her native Savannah, Georgia, to organize units there. The first troop she organized in 1912 generated so much interest throughout the country that by 1915 Juliette Low had organized the Girl Scouts of America and was serving as their first president. During this early period she paid all the expenses herself and travelled throughout the country convincing, and sometimes coercing, prominent women to become leaders and organizers.

Girl scouting continued to grow during World War I. Ms. Low retired as president in 1920 but continued her active involvement as the founder. Despite a somewhat romantic, impractical nature, Juliette Low was a superb, intelligent organizer whose commitment to worldwide girl scouting was realized during her lifetime.

** *Radford, Ruby L.* JULIETTE LOW: GIRL SCOUT FOUNDER Garrard, 1965. (grades 2-5)

Very good, immensely readable profile of Juliette Low may be particularly attractive to young Brownies and Girl Scouts, but is of sufficient general interest to be enjoyed by others.

* *Higgins, Helen B.* JULIETTE LOW: GIRL SCOUT Illus. Bobbs–Merrill, 1951. (grades 3-7)

Adequate, highly fictionalized biography of Juliette Low emphasizes her childhood, devoting only minor attention to her later accomplishments.

JANET LYNN
1953–

Olympic figure skating champion

From the time Janet Lynn first put on a pair of ice skates at two-and-a-half, she showed the grace and superb balance that would later make her the first ranked amateur figure skater in the United States.

She reached the Nationals in 1963, the youngest skater ever to qualify, and at twelve she won the Junior Figure Skating Nationals. In 1968 she became the youngest skater ever to make the United States Olympic team and in 1969 she won her first Nationals Championship.

Free skating and jumping are her strong points; the mechanical exactness required for the compulsory school figures constitutes her weak area. Nevertheless, in 1971, Janet Lynn was ranked first in the United States and fourth in the world and won a bronze medal in the 1972 Olympics.

In 1973 after her fifth straight win in the Nationals, she decided to turn professional. She signed a contract with the Ice Follies for a great sum of money, much of which she has given to charity. In 1974 she won the first Professional Figure Skating Championship.

** *Jacobs, Linda* JANET LYNN: SUNSHINE ON ICE Illus. with photographs. EMC, 1974. (reading level, grades 4-6; interest level through high school)

Good, fast-moving, highly readable portrait of skater Janet Lynn describes her years of training and achievements, as well as her religious faith and commitment. At times overly laudatory, the author tends to depict Lynn as an almost story-book perfect individual. Many photographs of her on and off the ice are good contributions to the biography.

MARY LYON
1797–1849

Founder of Mount Holyoke College

Mary Lyon, the founder of Mount Holyoke College and a member of America's Hall of Fame, may be credited with opening the doors for women's higher education in the United States. Before opening Mount Holyoke, the first nonprofit, endowed institution of higher education for women, Ms. Lyon had already established a fine reputation launching schools and academies for young women. The college was conceived as an institution with academic standards equal to those at the finest men's colleges, and dedicated to Christian principles. Ms. Lyon placed all financial matters in the hands of trustees, to assure the college's continuity after her retirement.

In 1837 Mount Holyoke opened in South Hadley, Massachusetts with eighty students. Under Mary Lyon's capable administration, the enrollment rose, curriculum grew, and new methods of teaching were successfully introduced. The first principals of the later established Vassar and Wellesley colleges had been her students, as were the staffs of some of the finest schools throughout the nation. Many of Mount Holyoke's graduates, imbued with Ms. Lyon's evangelistic zeal, went into missionary work and community service. Today, Mount Holyoke is one of America's leading women's colleges.

*** *Banning, Evelyn I.* MARY LYON OF PUTNAM'S HILL Vanguard, 1965. (grades 5-8)
Excellent, warm picture of the founder of Mount Holyoke College traces Lyon's life from early childhood to her last years of great accomplishments. Written in an intelligent, but highly readable style, it may be of interest to readers older than those suggested by the publisher.

SHIRLEY MacLAINE
1934–

Actress, dancer, political activist

Shirley MacLaine, dancer and actress, has won three Academy Award nominations for her roles in films, but has made a greater contribution to society in her numerous other activities. As a philanthropist, she helps to support two Asian orphanages, and as an unpaid political worker she obtained an upper-level position in national politics. During 1972 she worked full time for presidential candidate George McGovern and was a delegate to the Democratic National Convention; she is a strong advocate of all legislation emphasizing women's rights. Shirley MacLaine has also worked and lived with blacks in Mississippi and the Masai tribe in East Africa, and has long been involved in civil rights.

*** *MacLaine Shirley* Don't Fall off the Mountain Norton, 1970. (grade 8 and up)

Excellent, well-rounded personal narrative of the subject's childhood and career will be of interest to all young readers. Ms. MacLaine emerges as a warm, very human, multidimensional woman in a vivid and fast-moving autobiography.

ANNE SULLIVAN MACY
1866–1936

Teacher to Helen Keller

Anne Sullivan Macy's tragic childhood was marked by near blindness, the death of her mother, desertion by her father, life in a public almshouse, and then the death of her beloved little brother. Surgery later restored much of her sight, and after her graduation from the Perkins Institute for the Blind she was offered a job teaching seven-year-old blind and deaf Helen Keller (page 157). Anne Sullivan Macy arrived at the Keller home to find an untutored, undisciplined but curious child. With determination, innovation, and insightful talent she soon had young Helen spelling words into her hands and behaving in a civilized manner.

When Helen Keller was later admitted to Radcliffe College, Ms. Macy attended classes with her, patiently spelling out the lectures and reading the course assignments to her. There she met young literary critic John Macy. They married, but eventually separated.

Anne Sullivan continued to live and travel with Helen

Keller, lecturing, demonstrating their teaching methods, and raising money for philanthropic causes. Not until her last few years did Ms. Macy receive the recognition she so richly deserved; for most people were unaware of the skill and years of unselfish dedication that preceded Helen Keller's great achievements. In 1955, Helen Keller wrote *Teacher*, a memoir and tribute to the remarkable woman who, though lacking social confidence and patience with her own handicaps, had taught those qualities to her student and brought her out of her darkness.

*** *Brown, Marion, and Crone, Ruth* THE SILENT STORM Illus. Abingdon, 1963. (grades 6-8)
   Extremely moving and dramatic account of Anne Sullivan Macy's life depicts her miserable childhood, her difficult youth, and her long-time relationship with Helen Keller.

*** *Davidson, Mickie* HELEN KELLER'S TEACHER Illus. Four Winds, 1965. (grades 3-7)
   Warm, intimate biography of Anne Sullivan Macy shows her grim childhood as well as her later achievements as teacher to young Helen Keller. Very readable, this book has enormous appeal.

*** *Gibson, William* THE MIRACLE WORKER Knopf, 1957. (grade 7 and up)
   Outstanding dramatic play about Anne Sullivan Macy and Helen Keeler which was presented on Broadway and then made into a motion picture is compelling and stirring both to read and to see.

*** *Malone, Mary* ANNIE SULLIVAN Illus. Putnam, 1971. (grades 2-4)
   Simplistic, but tender and perceptive biography is enhanced by Lydia Rosier's illustrations.

*** *Waite, Helen E.* VALIANT COMPANIONS Macrae, 1959. (grade 7 and up)

Extremely fine, substantial narrative examines the remarkable relationship between Helen Keller and Anne Sullivan Macy. Dramatic and emotional, it is written more from the perspective of Ms. Macy's life, but is both their stories.

DOLLEY MADISON
1768–1849

Washington hostess, First Lady

Popular, vibrant young widow Dolley Payne was living in Washington, D.C., when she met and married the brilliant congressional leader James Madison. A fine conversationalist with the rare gift of placing everyone at ease in all social situations, Dolley Madison soon became a prominent and successful Washington hostess. When James Madison served as Thomas Jefferson's secretary of state, Dolley was frequently called upon to act as unofficial First Lady.

During the War of 1812, when James Madison was president, the British burned the White House and Dolley Madison disregarded personal safety to salvage many important documents, including the famed Stuart portrait of George Washington.

After President Madison's retirement, they returned to their home in Virginia, Montpelier, where they continued their famed hospitality, receiving the public as well as dignitaries. When Dolley Madison returned to Washington as a widow, she retained her leading role in society. Her son's mismanagement of family funds placed her in a near state of poverty, but she was afforded some financial comfort when Congress, after years of deliberation, bought her husband's presidential papers from her.

** *Desmond, Alice Curtis* GLAMOUROUS DOLLEY MADISON Illus. Dodd, 1946. (grade 9 and up)
Extremely well-written and absorbing biography of Dolley Madison draws a well-rounded picture of the subject and offers a worthwhile view of the time in which she lived.

** *Grant, Matthew G.* DOLLEY MADISON Illus. Creative Educ. Soc./Children's Pr., 1974. (grades 2-4)
Lovely, abundant illustrations add to a warm, responsible biography of Dolley Madison. She is depicted as an intelligent, capable woman. Brief and easy to read, the biography also gives a good picture of the period.

** *Melick, Arden Davis* DOLLEY MADISON, FIRST LADY Putnam, 1970. (grades 4-6)
Somewhat uneven biography is a good portrayal of Ms. Madison. However, the format (short sentences, large print) indicates this is for very young readers, despite occasional difficult vocabulary.

** *Nolan, Jeannette* DOLLEY MADISON Messner, 1959. (grades 6-9)
Enjoyable biography of Dolley Madison introduces the subject as an intelligent, colorful woman in this convincingly fictionalized portrait.

** *Thane, Elswyth* DOLLEY MADISON: HER LIFE AND TIMES Macmillan, 1970. (grade 7 and up)
Substantial narrative is a somewhat detailed, scholarly account which combines history and biography with the life of Dolley Madison.

* *Davidson, Mary* DOLLY MADISON: FAMOUS FIRST LADY Illus. Garrard, 1966. (grades 2-5)
Simplistic, somewhat interesting, occasionally sexist but adequate biography of Dolley Madison.

* *Martin, Patricia Miles* DOLLEY MADISON Illus. Putnam, 1967. (grades 2-4)

Undistinguished, occasionally sexist portrait of Dolley Madison is oversimplistic and superficial, but acceptable.

†† *Monsell, Helen A.* DOLLY MADISON: QUAKER GIRL Illus. Bobbs–Merrill, 1953. (grades 3-6)

Overfictionalized, somewhat sexist biography offers few insights and lacks any substance. Focussing on Dolley Madison's childhood, the book notes little of her adult personality, character, or accomplishments.

MARIE ANTOINETTE
1755–1793

Queen of France

Marie Antoinette, queen of France during the revolution of 1789, was the daughter of the great Austrian ruler Maria Theresa. At age fifteen Marie married the heir to the French throne, Louis XVI.

Despite the economic hardships suffered by the French peasants and the growing movement in other countries towards more democratic institutions, Marie and Louis held to the old beliefs in royal supremacy. Her extravagant tastes led to even more taxes and burdens on the peasants, and even more than the king, Marie Antoinette became a symbol of the cause of French discontent.

In 1789 angry, hungry mobs stormed the Bastille prison and then the royal palace in Versailles and forced the royal family to return with them to Paris. There they were kept under house arrest in the Tuileries for nearly four years.

Throughout this period, Marie Antoinette displayed great personal courage.

In 1793, as the revolution fell into the hands of radicals, Louis XVI was beheaded and later that year, Marie Antoinette was tried and guillotined for encouraging civil war and betraying her country. Throughout the trial she maintained a conviction in the sanctity of the crown and remained calm and proud.

* *Komroff, Manuel and Odette* MARIE ANTOINETTE Messner, 1967. (grade 7 and up)
    Satisfactory biography gives a well-rounded picture of the queen as well as providing a good historical background.

SAINT LOUISE DE MARILLAC
1591–1660

A founder of the Sisters of Charity

After her husband died, Louise De Marillac, an upper-class French woman, dedicated her life to serving God and helping the sick and poor. A woman of high intelligence and courage, she was in poor health, yet managed to accomplish much.

Working closely with Saint Vincent de Paul, she helped to organize peasant women into caring for the neglected patients at the largest hospital in Paris, founded a home for foundlings, and even went out into the streets to nurse the victims of the plague.

Her own early desire had been to become a nun, and although this wish had been denied to her, the Sisters of Charity of which she was a founder was later declared a religious order. Its members took vows of poverty, chastity, and obedience.

In 1934, Louise De Marillac was canonized.

* *Dollen, Charles* MADEMOISELLE LOUISE: LIFE OF LOUISE DE MARILLAC Illus. Daughters of St. Paul, 1967. (grades 4-8)

   An absorbing biography that draws an accurate picture of the life of Louise, but lacks literary distinction. Written from a strongly religious perspective, this will probably be of interest only to readers seeking this focus.

MARIA MARTÍNEZ
1881–

Indian potter

By rediscovering pottery techniques which had been lost for centuries, Maria Martínez transformed the poor farming village of San Ildefonso into a prosperous place filled with successful artisans. She and her husband worked together, demonstrating and selling their finished and decorated pottery at fairs before gaining national recognition. They perfected an award-winning firing technique which resulted in black-on-black pottery. Maria's distinctively original work is done freehand, without the aid of a potter's wheel or closed kiln.

In more recent years Maria Martínez has worked with her son, artist Povov-Da, who decorates her pottery. An ex-

tremely clever businesswoman herself, she has encouraged
other Pueblo women to learn, thus giving them some of
the economic security she has enjoyed.

*** *Nelson, Mary Carroll* Maria Martinez Dillon, 1972.
(grades 5-9)
   Outstanding portrait incorporates cultural aspects of the
Pueblos with the life story of Maria Martínez, resulting in a
fine combination of anthropology and biography.

▶-◀●-◀

MARY
Mother of Jesus

Mary, the virgin mother of Jesus, has probably been artis-
tically portrayed more than any other woman in history.
Some of the world's greatest masterpieces are paintings
and statues of the Madonna and hymns to her are among
the world's most frequently sung. Cities, churches, innumerable geographical features, as well as baby girls have
been named for her throughout the world.
   According to tradition, she was the child of Joachim
and Anna. She married Joseph, and gave birth to Jesus in
a stable in Bethlehem. Jesus performed his first miracle
at the request of Mary, and when he was condemned to
die she stood beneath the cross.

** *Daughters of St. Paul* MARY QUEEN OF APOSTLES Illus. Daughters of St. Paul, 1955. (grades K-4)

Simple, well-written, attractively illustrated book of Mary follows her life as it is known. She is depicted as mother, teacher, and queen—a woman with strength and independence as well as goodness.

MARY II, QUEEN OF GREAT BRITAIN
1662–1694

Ruler of Great Britain, 1689–94

Mary Stuart, the daughter of James II and Anne Hyde, grew up in England and moved to Holland after marrying her Dutch cousin William of Orange. Although content with life in Holland, William and Mary, in what is known as the Glorious Revolution, assumed the English crown in order to prevent the establishment of Catholicism in England.

After Mary's death from smallpox, William reigned as sole sovereign until his death.

* *Kyle, Elisabeth* PRINCESS OF ORANGE Holt, 1966. (grades 7-10)

Romantic, well-written, highly fictionalized story of Mary II, Queen of Great Britain, covers her life only until she left Holland to return to England in 1686. Recreates fairly well the society of the time, but fails to give much illumination into the personality or character of Mary.

MARY, QUEEN OF SCOTS
1542–1587
Queen of France and Scotland

Mary, Queen of Scots, assumed the throne of Scotland when she was only a few days old. Raised in France by her mother, she became, by marriage, queen of France, but after the king's death went to live in Scotland.

Her royal position was difficult because she was a Roman Catholic, and Scotland, like England, was Protestant. Marriage to Lord Darnley afforded her little happiness and when he was murdered by the earl of Bothwell, whom she subsequently married, her subjects believed she was an accomplice. Forced to abdicate, she escaped to England only to be kept imprisoned for nineteen years by her cousin, Queen Elizabeth I.

Mary was constantly accused of conspiring to kill Elizabeth and to place herself on the throne. Seriously implicated in one such plot, she was tried and found guilty. Mary accepted the death sentence with great dignity and courage, and to the end declared her innocence.

** *Hahn, Emily* MARY, QUEEN OF SCOTS Illus. Random, 1953. (grades 7-9)
Good biography recreates the society in which Mary, Queen of Scots, lived in a well-balanced account of her life.

** *Plaidy, Jean* YOUNG MARY QUEEN OF SCOTS Illus. Roy, 1962. (grades 6-10)
Well-written and sympathetic, this book emphasizes

Mary's childhood and early years. A good picture of the times is drawn and the politics are carefully woven into the biography. A short concluding chapter discusses the queen's later years.

MARGARET MEAD
1901–

Anthropologist, author

For almost fifty years Margaret Mead has been a leading anthropologist. She was one of the first professionals to engage in field work, actually living among primitive cultures and learning their languages. Dr. Mead has lectured, taught at major universities, and written on subjects as varied as tribes in New Guinea, American Indians, world population, peace, family relationships, racial tensions, and careers for women. For many years a member of the Department of Anthropology at the American Museum of Natural History, and now curator of Ethnology there, Margaret Mead directed the new and outstanding permanent exhibit, Peoples of the Pacific.

During World War II when her visits to the Pacific were curtailed, Dr. Mead lectured, wrote, and directed studies for the Office of War Information and took care of her young daughter. Her books *Coming of Age in Samoa, Growing Up in New Guinea, Male and Female,* and *Sex and Temperament* have the dual distinction of being best sellers and of having gained high scholarly regard.

*** *Mead, Margaret* BLACKBERRY WINTER: MY EARLIER YEARS Illus. Morrow, 1972. (grade 9 and up)

Outstanding, feminist autobiography by Dr. Mead introduces the subject as youngster, student, mother, and grandmother as well as leading anthropologist. Fascinating and inspiring, it will motivate readers to learn more about her work, and perhaps to read her own writings based on field work.

*** *Morse, Ann and Charles* MARGARET MEAD Illus. Creative Educ. Soc., 1974. (grades 4-8)

Unusually fine biography of Margaret Mead explains the entire concept of anthropology in terms elementary school children can understand. At the same time the authors give a well-balanced, fairly full account of the subject's personal life as well as her work in the field, her writings, lectures, and philosophy.

GOLDA MEIR
1898–

Prime minister of Israel, 1969–74

Golda Meir's family left anti-Semitic Kiev to go to the United States when she was eight years old. Her great desire for higher education was discouraged by her traditional family who saw no need of it for women. Golda Meir was an independent, ambitious young woman whose Zionist beliefs were so strong that after she finally completed her education and married, she and her husband embarked in 1921 for Palestine. There they lived in a kibbutz and later in cities where their financial hardships were so great that at one time she washed clothing to help pay for their children's education.

Always active in civic and political work, Golda Meir became a member of the Israeli Knesset (Parliament) and during World War II served on the War Economy Advisory Council. She was instrumental in arranging many Jewish immigrations to Palestine and was one of the thirty-seven signers of Israel's declaration of independence. Ms. Meir became Israel's first ambassador to the Soviet Union, minister of labor, and foreign minister. As head of the Labor party she was chosen prime minister in 1969, thus becoming one of only three women so far elected as heads of state.

*** *Dobrin, Arnold* A LIFE FOR ISRAEL: THE STORY OF GOLDA MEIR Illus. Dial, 1974. (grades 3-6)

Outstanding biography gives a full picture of the life of Golda Meir and the growth of Israel. Without a textbook quality, the history of Israel is interestingly explained to young readers who may have no prior knowledge of it. The salient points of Ms. Meir's career are well told, with warmth, drama, and excitement.

*** *Mann, Peggy* GOLDA: THE STORY OF ISRAEL'S PRIME MINISTER Illus. Coward, 1971. (grade 9 and up)

Outstanding profile of Golda Meir is an immensely readable and substantial in-depth study of Israel's prime minister. Her life story is related against the background of the independence and growth of Israel.

*** *Morris, Terry* SHALOM, GOLDA Illus. Hawthorn, 1971. (grades 7-9)

Very fine, clear, and colorful biography gives an intimate personal view of Ms. Meir, at the same time drawing a good portrait of Israel.

*** *Noble, Iris* ISRAEL'S GOLDA MEIR: PIONEER TO PRIME MINISTER Messner, 1972; rev. ed. 1974. (grade 6 and up)

Excellent lively portrait of Golda Meir is clearly Israel's story as well. Informal, dramatic, and inspiring, it moves along quickly, bringing its subject to life. The revised edition is brought up to date with Ms. Meir's resignation.

*** Syrkin, Marie, ed. A LAND OF OUR OWN: AN ORAL AUTO-BIOGRAPHY BY GOLDA MEIR Putnam, 1973. (grade 9 and up)
Very well organized and intelligently selected interviews and material from published and unpublished statements by Ms. Meir comprise a warm, moving, and highly readable picture of the woman and her contributions to Israel and all of humanity.

*** Syrkin, Marie GOLDA MEIR, ISRAEL'S LEADER Putnam, 1969. (grade 9 and up)
Superb, authoritative biography of Golda Meir is a vividly written, absorbing, and comprehensive examination of her life and her contributions to Israel.

LISE MEITNER
1878–1968

Nuclear physicist, winner of Atomic Energy Commission Award

Lise Meitner, the Austrian-born physicist, and her long-time scientific partner, Nobel Prize winner Dr. Otto Hahn, lay much of the groundwork for the atomic bomb. Ms. Meitner was persistent in pointing out that she had nothing to do with the use made of their studies and felt that it was unfortunate that their discoveries had occurred during the war.

Her interest in atomic physics was initially fostered when, as a student, she read newspaper accounts of the Curies' work and, despite the lack of opportunities for women in science, chose this as her career.

In 1938 rising anti-Semitism forced this Jewish scientist to leave Austria for Sweden where she spent the next twenty years. Her departure from Dr. Hahn's lab was, she said, one of the great tragedies of her life.

With her nephew, Otto Frisch, she reported on the fission of uranium and thorium, and in 1966 she shared the Atomic Energy Commission's Enrico Fermi Award with Otto Hahn and Fritz Strassman. A proponent of greater participation of women in the professions and of the peaceful use of atomic energy, she lived long enough to see the beginnings of both.

*** *Crawford, Deborah* LISE MEITNER, ATOMIC PIONEER Crown, 1969. (grade 7 and up)

Very fine, somewhat technical biography is suitable more for the student of science than the casual reader. However, it is also a warm, dramatic profile of the brilliant and sensitive scientist, and combines not only science and biography but also recreates the climate and society in which Meitner lived and worked.

EDNA ST. VINCENT MILLAY
1892–1950

Pulitzer Prize winning poet

Edna St. Vincent Millay began writing verse as a youngster and at age fourteen had her first poem published in *Saint Nicholas* magazine. After graduation from high school she entered her poem "Renascence" into a national contest, won fourth prize, and garnered much critical attention and praise which in turn led to the award of a scholarship from Vassar College.

After graduation she moved to New York and took some minor writing jobs to help support herself. In 1923, *The Ballad of the Harp-Weaver and Other Books* won Millay the Pulitzer Prize, making her the first woman poet to be so honored. She won further acclaim for the libretto to Deems Taylor's opera *The King's Henchman.*

Millay's early work dealt with personal feelings, frequently employing themes of freedom and liberation of women. Her later work dealt with social problems and expressed her antiwar, antiisolationist attitudes. For many young people she symbolized the emancipation of the age in her famed lines: "My candle burns at both ends/It will not last the night;/But ah, my foes, and oh, my friends/It gives a lovely light!"

*** *Gurko, Miriam* RESTLESS SPIRIT: THE LIFE OF EDNA ST. VINCENT MILLAY Crowell, 1962. (grade 7 and up)
Outstanding, well-written biography of the poet discusses her personal life and work, clearly indicating her independence in both areas. Carefully researched and faithfully told, it is of interest to both those who know her poetry and those not yet well acquainted with it.

*** *Shafter, Toby* EDNA ST. VINCENT MILLAY: AMERICA'S BEST LOVED POET Messner, 1957. (grade 7 and up)
Very fine portrait of Ms. Millay covers aspects of both her personal life and her poetry, introducing her as a dynamic, multidimensional woman.

MARIA MITCHELL
1818–1889

Astronomer, discoverer of a comet

Maria Mitchell combined a distinctly Nantucket-woman self-reliance and an insatiable intellectual curiosity with her father's tutelage to become a skilled astronomer. She spent the time spared from her librarian duties reading scientific, classical, philosophical, and feminist works and gazing at the skies from the observatory her father had built for them.

In 1847 she discovered a new comet which was named for her. The king of Denmark awarded her a gold medal, she became the first woman elected to the American Academy of Arts and Sciences (an honor not bestowed upon another woman until 1943), was invited to join other prestigious organizations, and received wide acclaim both in Europe and the United States. She was later elected to the American Hall of Fame.

A member of Vassar's original faculty, she remained there for twenty-three years as one of the college's finest and best-known teachers. Instituting and insisting upon many unconventional teaching methods, she ignored the usual rote method and grading system and encouraged student participation in her own research. Maria Mitchell inspired many women students to follow in her footsteps and exerted great efforts to show that the sciences should include women on an equal basis with men.

*** *Baker, Rachel, and Merlen, Joanna B.* AMERICA'S FIRST WOMAN ASTRONOMER: MARIA MITCHELL Illus. Messner, 1960. (grade 6 and up)

Excellent, convincingly fictionalized biography of the astronomer shows the development of her scientific interests and traces her long and successful career. A warm, informal portrait avoids technical jargon and is thus of interest to casual readers as well as students of science.

*** *Wilkie, Katherine E.* MARIA MITCHELL: STARGAZER Illus. Garrard, 1966. (grades 2-5)

Despite its brevity and simplicity, this is a biography of unusual substance. The fast-paced narrative describes Mitchell's Nantucket childhood, interest in astronomy, and then her career as a professor at Vassar College.

** *Melin, Grace H.* MARIA MITCHELL: GIRL ASTRONOMER Illus. Bobbs–Merrill, 1964. (grades 3-7)

Good, highly fictionalized but accurate biography focusses on the childhood of Maria Mitchell. Because Ms. Mitchell's scientific and astronomical interests developed early, her childhood is a significant part of her life and worthy of discussion. The author offers good explanations of the elements of astronomy, comprehensible to very young readers, and devotes a small portion of the book to Mitchell's later achievements.

ANNE MOODY

1940–

Civil rights worker

Anne Moody's parents were poor black sharecroppers in Mississippi. They never had enough to wear or to eat, and even before Anne entered her teens she worked as a domestic for white families. With great determination, despite great odds, she graduated from high school and attended college where she became active in the civil rights movement, participating in demonstrations and working in voter registration drives in Mississippi. Like that of other members of the Congress of Racial Equality (CORE), Ms. Moody's life was often in danger, but she persisted, and after graduation from college continued her work in the movement. She has also served as coordinator of the civil rights training project of the School of Industrial and Labor Relations at Cornell University.

*** *Moody, Anne* COMING OF AGE IN MISSISSIPPI Dial, 1968. (grade 9 and up)

Absorbing, tender, and dramatic personal narrative for mature readers covers the early years of Ms. Moody's life and traces her development until she begins her higher education. A good picture is presented of her own life as well as life in the South for poor blacks before and at the beginning of the civil rights movement.

LOTTIE MOON
1840–1912

Southern Baptist missionary to China

One of the first southern women to receive a graduate degree, Lottie Moon taught at a college and directed a school for girls in Georgia. As a child she was disinterested in religion but later became suddenly converted at a revivalist meeting and dedicated her life to religion.

Volunteering for missionary work in China, she was chagrined to learn that southern Baptists would not send unmarried women. Later that policy was changed and Moon was appointed to China where she spent the rest of her life.

Known as the "patron saint" of southern Baptist missions, Lottie Moon trained newly arrived missionaries, did evangelistic work, founded a church, and focussed most of her teaching and attention on the girls and women of the interior Chinese villages. She was a frequent contributor to southern Baptist periodicals, and her efforts resulted in the formation of the Woman's Missionary Union.

During a famine in China when there was no relief money available, Lottie Moon donated her salary to feed local inhabitants. She actually starved herself, and died before arriving in the United States for medical care.

†† *Monsell, Helen A.* HER OWN WAY: THE STORY OF LOTTIE MOON Illus. Broadman, 1958. (grades 4-8)

Highly fictionalized biography is written from a religious perspective. The book deals mainly with Moon's childhood and fails to record or emphasize her many adult accomplishments. Slavery as practiced by her family is viewed as acceptable with no mention of its inherent evils.

†† *Summers, Jester* LOTTIE MOON OF CHINA Illus. Broadman, 1970. (grades 2-6)

Directed to religious readers, highly fictionalized, poorly written, flagrantly sexist biography gives only an adequate outline of Lottie Moon's career as a missionary. The author—as well as his subjects—treats blacks in a patronizing manner.

ANNE CARROLL MOORE
1871–1961

Pioneer in children's library work

The library profession was largely dominated by men when Anne Carroll Moore began her long career as a children's librarian. Ms. Moore truly loved children and books, and with her imagination and determinism, made children's literature an important part of the library system. She single-handedly shaped the present practices and philosophies of the New York Public Library children's rooms.

For ten years she was in charge of the children's room in the Pratt Free Library in Brooklyn, and for thirty-five years she administered the children's department of the New York Public Library. During this period her ideas and practices were widely emulated by libraries throughout the world. Even after her retirement she continued to lecture, write, and serve as a consultant to the world of children's books.

*** *Sayers, Frances Clark* ANNE CARROLL MOORE: A BIOGRAPHY Illus. with photographs. Atheneum, 1972. (grade 9 and up)

Fascinating, skillfully written biography incorporates excerpts from Anne Carroll Moore's writings and letters, offering a warm, informative view of her life. Young adults considering library work as a career or those attracted to children's literature will find this adult biography particularly interesting for it chronicles the history of children's libraries as well as telling the story of Ms. Moore's life—a wise approach, for it is impossible to separate the two.

ANNA MARY ROBERTSON MOSES
1860-1961
Landscape artist

If anyone could be considered a legend in her time, it would be "Grandma" Moses, one of the world's greatest landscape artists. As a child she drew pictures and maps, and later, as a young hired girl and mother and grandmother, she "painted" with needle and threads, making samplers and worsted pictures and occasionally little gifts and cards. Not until she was 75 did she cease using house paint and brushes to work with artists' oils and brushes.

A few of her paintings which were exhibited in a local drugstore came to the attention of a New York art collector. He encouraged her and she won wide acceptance with exhibits all over the world. When she was 89 years old she was invited to the White House to receive an award from President Truman, and later she and President Eisenhower corresponded and exchanged painted Christmas cards. She continued to paint almost to her death, at 101 years of age.

Grandma Moses's work, the result of exacting craftsmanship, has a simplicity and country quality about it that appeals to children, city and country dwellers, and sophisticated art critics. Her painting *July 4* hangs in the White House and is reprinted on a United States postage stamp.

*** *Graves, Charles* GRANDMA MOSES: FAVORITE PAINTER Illus. Garrard, 1969. (grades 3-5)

Necessarily simplified, but nonetheless superb biography of the artist includes many good black-and-white reproductions of her work, photographs of her family, and other illustrations. A warm, intelligent, and fast-moving biography depicts Grandma Moses as the highly independent, talented, and fascinating woman she was.

*** *Laing, Martha* GRANDMA MOSES: THE GRAND OLD LADY OF AMERICAN ART SamHar, 1972. (grade 7 and up)

Very fine, interesting, soundly researched, and well-documented account of the life of Grandma Moses is very brief (twenty-seven pages) but a substantial, straightforward narrative.

** *Armstrong, William* BAREFOOT IN THE GRASS: THE STORY OF GRANDMA MOSES Illus. Doubleday, 1970. (grade 5 and up)

Beautiful color reproductions of her work accompany a very good, though occasionally dry biography. Thoughtful and accurate, it gives a good, well-balanced account of the famed artist.

LUCRETIA MOTT
1793–1880

*Abolitionist, Quaker minister and preacher,
feminist leader*

Since Nantucket men were away months at a time on whaling ships, Nantucket women, like Lucretia Mott, were self-reliant and believed that women had the same abilities and rights as men. When Lucretia became a teacher and discovered salary discrepancies between men and women, her feminist consciousness was raised to even greater heights.

She and her husband were dedicated abolitionists who refused to use any product of slave labor and played leading roles in the movement. Ms. Mott, the mother of six children, was an outstanding Quaker minister and preacher who was chosen as a delegate to the World's Anti-Slavery Convention in London in 1840. Indignant that women were refused any part in the proceedings, she and Elizabeth Cady Stanton (page 266) planned a women's rights convention. Held in the summer of 1848 in Seneca Falls, New York, this historic meeting really began the American feminist and suffrage movement. Its participants issued a "Declaration of Sentiments" which, modelled after the Declaration of Independence, focussed on the issues that kept women subordinate to men.

For over fifty years Lucretia Mott, supported by her husband in her beliefs and causes, was a firm, determined, and highly respected leader in the many organizations dedicated to equality and freedom for blacks and for women.

*** *Faber, Doris* LUCRETIA MOTT: FOE OF SLAVERY Illus. Garrard, 1971. (grades 2-4)

Excellent biography of Lucretia Mott is simple, straightforward, and interesting. Despite its simplicity, it clearly shows the independence, accomplishments, and life-style of the abolitionist and feminist.

*** *Kurland, Gerald* LUCRETIA MOTT: EARLY LEADER OF THE WOMEN'S LIBERATION MOVEMENT SamHar, 1972. (grade 7 and up)

Excellent short biography of Ms. Mott gives an intelligent, straightforward account of her life. Her many accomplishments are interestingly detailed. Extremely well researched and documented.

* *Burnett, Constance* LUCRETIA MOTT: GIRL OF OLD NANTUCKET Illus. Bobbs–Merrill, 1963. (grades 3-7)

Satisfactory account of the childhood of Lucretia Mott gives a good picture of Nantucket and Quaker life. The opportunities for independence and equality for women are clearly indicated but her many contributions to abolition and women's rights are not.

ANNA CORA MOWATT
1819–1870

Actress and author

When socially prominent Anna Cora Mowatt and her husband suffered financial reverses she turned her interest in writing, amateur poetry readings, and dramatic acting into a professional career. One of her plays which satirized New York society was enthusiastically received. She then decided, despite the fact that it was considered unseeming for women of her class to perform on the public stage, to become an actress, and made her professional debut in a leading role.

Success came quickly to the attractive, dynamic, young woman whose intelligent interpretations were highly praised by critics. Between frequent bouts of illness and concern for her husband's chronic invalidism, she made successful tours of the United States and England, cared for three foster children, and wrote *Autobiography of an Actress,* still an important reference work on nineteenth-century theater.

One of the founders of the movement to make Mount Vernon a national shrine, she spent her last years, though quite ill, writing and publishing memoirs and novels.

213

* *Butler, Mildred* ACTRESS IN SPITE OF HERSELF: THE LIFE OF
ANNA CORA MOWATT Illus. Funk & Wagnalls, 1966. (grades
7-10)

   Bland, somewhat sexist biography tends to be moralistic
and stilted, incorporating obsolete views of women and phi-
lanthropy. The author does, however, give a reasonably accurate account of Ms. Mowatt's life and shows her many
accomplishments.

OLIVIA NEWTON-JOHN

Popular singer

British-born, Australian-reared Olivia Newton-John grew
up in an academic atmosphere. However, her interests
were in show business, and while a student she organized
a singing group. She won a singing contest in Australia,
and her prize, a trip to London, launched her on a successful career. She was a recording star in the United States
even before her arrival there.

   Olivia Newton-John's first record, "Let Me Be There,"
was a top country-western hit in the United States and won
her a Grammy Award. Her second hit, "If You Love Me
Let Me Know," was an even bigger success and "I Honestly
Love You" won her another Grammy. The winner of four
Grammys in 1975, as well as numerous other awards, she
now lives in California.

* *Jacobs, Linda* OLIVIA NEWTON-JOHN: SUNSHINE SUPERGIRL
Illus. with photographs. EMC, 1975. (reading level, grades
4-6; interest level through high school)

Interesting biography traces Ms. Newton-John's life from her early days in England and Australia and her career beginnings to her huge American success. The focus is evenly divided between her personal and professional life, and is at times too laudatory. Numerous photographs add to the book.

───

FLORENCE NIGHTINGALE
1820–1910

Reformer, organizer, and founder of the nursing profession

Florence Nightingale's wealthy, British, social family did not object to her attempts to alleviate suffering in family members, animals, or even close neighbors, but were horrified when she talked of making nursing her life's work. Hospitals were usually filthy and nurses were recruited from the lowest and most disreputable classes, but intelligent, well-educated Ms. Nightingale decided to obtain whatever training she could. She then took an unpaid position as supervisor of a nursing home where she immediately made efficient changes.

During the Crimean War, the secretary of war called upon her to organize and supervise nurses at the front. This was the first time a woman was asked to fill an official military mission and she was given full authority. Her radical changes reduced the death rate from 430 to 22 per 1,000.

She founded the Nightingale Training School for nurses, which soon served as a model for schools all over the world.

Though mainly an administrator, Florence Nightingale was keenly aware of the importance of bedside nursing. Her philosophy, practices, and dedication have given the profession of nursing the highly respected position it holds today.

*** *Colver, Anne* FLORENCE NIGHTINGALE: WAR NURSE Garrard, 1961. (grades 2-5)

Extremely moving, very simple, readable biography of Florence Nightingale succinctly summarizes her personal and professional life, skillfully conveying her motives as well as accomplishments.

*** *Harmelink, Barbara* FLORENCE NIGHTINGALE: FOUNDER OF MODERN NURSING Illus. Watts, 1969. (grade 7 and up)

Outstanding, well-balanced, straightforward account of Florence Nightingale's life clearly indicates that despite her own opposition to women's suffrage she was a strong supporter of the rights of nurses, and was single-handedly responsible for the elevation of nursing to professional status.

*** *Hume, Ruth F.* FLORENCE NIGHTINGALE Illus. Random, 1960. (grades 6-10)

Very fine, inspiring portrait of Ms. Nightingale also thoughtfully examines the society in which she lived.

*** *Nolan, Jeannette* FLORENCE NIGHTINGALE Illus. Messner, 1947. (grade 6 and up)

Dramatic picture of the pioneer nurse is convincingly fictionalized, affording an interesting and accurate picture of Ms. Nightingale, her work, and the times.

*** *Wyndham, Lee* THE LADY WITH THE LAMP: THE STORY OF FLORENCE NIGHTINGALE Scholastic Book Service, 1972. (grades 4-6)

Shorter version of the above, this is a fictionalized, fast-paced, tender account both readable and appealing.

ANNIE OAKLEY
1860–1926

Markswoman

The star of Buffalo Bill's Wild West show, Annie Oakley, known as the "girl of the Western plains," learned sharp-shooting as a child in the Ohio woods. There her earnings from the birds she shot helped support her family and paid off the mortgage on their farm. At sixteen she married Frank Butler, an expert marksman from whom she had won a match, and they toured vaudeville, eventually joining Buffalo Bill's Wild West show.

Small in stature, Annie Oakley could outshoot anyone, male or female, and developed an uncanny showmanship which made her a favorite with audiences. She was also popular with the cowboys and Indians in the show, and Sioux Chief Sitting Bull made her an adopted daughter, naming her "Little Sure Shot."

She made successful tours of the United States and Europe; was presented to Queen Victoria; performed for the Kaiser; and amassed numerous trophies, medals, honors and decorations. During World War I, though retired as a performer, Ms. Oakley toured army camps demonstrating marksmanship.

*** *Graves, C. P.* ANNIE OAKLEY: THE SHOOTING STAR Garrard, 1961. (grades 2-5)

  Anecdotal, engaging narrative traces her life in a log cabin in Ohio to stardom in Buffalo Bill's Wild West show to give a well-rounded though brief portrait of a fascinating woman.

*** *Wilson, Ellen* Annie Oakley: little sure shot Illus. Bobbs–Merrill, 1958. (grades 3-7)

Excellent biography of Annie Oakley emphasizes her childhood, and despite heavy fictionalization is quite faithful to her life. Ms. Oakley's childhood was an independent, achievement-oriented one, and thus concentration on that period does not lessen the value or interest of the biography.

━•━

JACQUELINE BOUVIER KENNEDY ONASSIS
1929–

First Lady, patron of the arts

Socialite Jacqueline Bouvier was a photographer for a newspaper when she met and married John Fitzgerald Kennedy, then the junior senator from Massachusetts. When she became the First Lady, she captured the imagination of the world with her linguistic ability; her plan to restore parts of the White House to museum elegance; her encouragement of the arts; and her own striking appearance, charm, and intelligence.

When President Kennedy was assassinated in 1963, the remarkable courage and dignity she showed during those tragic days won her the respect, admiration, and sympathy of a shocked world. Although she attempted to shield their children from the public eye, she found this was an impossible task.

Jacqueline Kennedy was married in 1968 to Aristotle Onassis, a Greek shipping magnate who died in 1975.

†† *Martin, Patricia Miles* Jacqueline Kennedy Onassis Illus. Putnam, 1969. (grades K-4)

A few sexist remarks make this entire brief biography un-acceptable. Unexplained descriptions of sexism in the White House, and the author's portrayal of Ms. Kennedy's behavior in handling them, are most objectionable.

ALICE FREEMAN PALMER
1855–1902

President of Wellesley College, pioneer educator

Though Alice Freeman Palmer's family respected and encouraged education, they wanted to use their limited funds to pay for her brother's college education. By promising to help educate him and her sisters she was able to persuade them to allow her to enroll in the University of Michigan, where she alternated work and study and earned undergraduate and graduate degrees in history.

Appointed first as head of the history department at the all-women's Wellesley College, Alice Freeman Palmer at the age of twenty-seven became president of the college. During her administration, scholastic standards were implemented and outstanding preparatory schools for Wellesley were initiated.

After her marriage she retired to concentrate her talent and energies on church and mission work, and to serve as a leader of numerous state and national committees for the education of women. She became a member of Wellesley's board of trustees, temporarily served as a dean at the University of Chicago, and helped Radcliffe achieve status as a college. A supporter of women's suffrage, Alice believed she best contributed to the cause by academically preparing women for citizenship and voting.

** *Fleming, Alice* ALICE FREEMAN PALMER: PIONEER COLLEGE
PRESIDENT Prentice-Hall, 1970. (grades 5-8)
   Very good biography of the woman who became one of
the first presidents of Wellesley College is dramatic and
warm, but lacks some of the spirit displayed by the subject.
Written for younger readers rather than those who might be
interested in learning about a college president, it is necessarily less than comprehensive and complete.

VIJAYA LAKSHMI PANDIT
1900–

*Ambassador, diplomat, and United Nations delegate
from India*

Madame Pandit, the first woman to address the United
Nations General Assembly, was one of the pioneers in
India's struggle for independence. Wealthy and cosmopol-
itan, her family supported Gandhi's nonviolent movement
and her brother Nehru later became India's first prime minister. Like her politically active mother and sisters, Mme.
Pandit was often arrested and spent her first prison term
in 1932 when the youngest of her three children was only
three years old. Her niece, Indiri Gandhi (page 118) became prime minister of India.

During World War II she lectured in the United States
on the Indian independence movement, and in 1945 she
was an observer at the United Nations. After India achieved
independence in 1947 she held many diplomatic positions.
Madame Pandit was a member of Parliament, minister of
health, and ambassador to Russia and to England. Later,

as the ambassador to both the United States and Mexico, she was the first woman to carry simultaneously two diplomatic posts.

As an author and the recipient of many honorary awards and degrees, Madame Pandit is one of the United Nations' most respected leaders. She received her widest recognition when she served as the president of the eighth General Assembly.

*** *Guthrie, Anne* MADAME AMBASSADOR: THE LIFE OF VIJAYA LAKSHMI PANDIT Illus. with photographs. Harcourt, 1962. (grade 9 and up)

Very fine, dramatic account of the life of Madame Pandit is told by a close friend, affording the reader an intimate though somewhat admiring view of the subject. The author tells not only the life story of Vijaya Pandit, but also the story of India and its independence in restrained but moving prose.

━━━━━━━━━━━━━━━━━━━━━━━━━━━━━━━━━━━

THE PANKHURSTS

Emmeline Pankhurst 1858–1928
Christabel Pankhurst 1880–1958
Sylvia Pankhurst 1882–1960
Adele Pankhurst 1885–

Militant suffragists and feminists

Emmeline Pankhurst was the founder of the Women's Political and Social Union, an organization whose initial function was to present petitions and quietly to try to influence Parliament to grant women the vote. As those methods proved futile, Emmeline and her group turned to mass demonstrations, arson, and actual fights with the police. When jailed, she went on hunger strikes, was brutally treated, and finally force-fed.

With her daughters, the widowed Ms. Pankhurst organized the militant British feminist movement and played an influential role in the final American struggle. Christabel, an attorney and the most intellectual of the daughters, saw suffrage as a major goal of the women's rights movement, while Adele and Sylvia concerned themselves with bringing the movement to the working-class woman. Sylvia was also involved in the pacifist movement.

In 1918 Emmeline Pankhurst saw the first results of her long years of struggle when women over thirty years of age were given the vote. Not until 1928, though, the year of her death, did younger British women gain enfranchisement.

*** *Noble, Iris* EMMELINE AND HER DAUGHTERS: THE PANKHURST SUFFRAGISTS Messner, 1971. (grade 7 and up)
Outstanding account of the life of feminist Emmeline Pankhurst and her daughters is written with feeling, drama, and vitality. Traces the entire suffragist movement in England, discussing the difficulties and concentrating on the courage, strength, and abilities of Emmeline Pankhurst.

ROSA PARKS
1913–

Civil rights worker, organizer of the Montgomery bus boycott

Rosa Parks, known as the "mother of the civil rights movement," had always suffered the humilities of black southerners. A quiet woman, she directed her resentments and energies into organizations like the National Association for the Advancement of Colored People, and into voter registration and education drives.

It was commonplace for a black person to be told by a bus driver in Montgomery, Alabama, to get up to give a white person a seat. On December 1, 1955, Rosa Parks, tired from a hard day of work, decided this time she would not relinquish her seat to a white man. Arrested and jailed, she was freed on bail and met with the black leaders of the city, including Martin Luther King. Together they organized the historic bus boycott of that city, during which no black person rode on a bus. The blacks of Montgomery walked miles to and from work, and though they were harassed and threatened, they held fast to their decision. Rosa Parks, the victim of many personal threats, took her case to the United States Supreme Court which handed down the decision that the bus company could no longer discriminate. The Montgomery bus company changed its rules and one year after Rosa Parks refused to give up her seat, no other black could be asked to do this.

*** *Greenfield, Eloise* Rosa Parks Illus. Crowell, 1973. (grades 1-4)

Outstanding book describes Rosa Parks's early experiences and feelings towards racial segregation, and clearly depicts her quiet heroism in defying the rules of her city. Her role in the Montgomery bus boycott is well described.

** *Meriwether, Louise* Don't Ride the Bus on Monday: the rosa parks story Illus. Prentice-Hall, 1973. (grades 3-5)

Faithful to Rosa Parks's life, this book also clearly describes the Montgomery bus boycott. However, the writing is somewhat dry, lacking spark and emotion. Although this is a picture book, it is really too difficult for very young readers to read or comprehend, but too immature in appearance for older readers.

ALICE PAUL
1885–

Suffragist, feminist, and social worker

Prior to receiving her doctorate in social work, American-born Alice Paul was studying slum conditions in London when she was drawn into the British women's struggle for suffrage. She learned the militant techniques of her British sisters, and on her return to the United States assumed the chairpersonship of the congressional committee of the national American Woman Suffrage Association. She organized a lobby to convince the president and Congress to pass the amendment giving women the vote. The suffrage parade she planned just before Woodrow Wilson's inauguration created a riot and led to her imprisonment. Harshly treated in the workhouse prison, she and other prominent women went on a hunger strike and were force-fed. Their cause attracted much attention and sympathy and the courts later refused to uphold the arrests.

Alice Paul founded the Congressional Union which later became the National Woman's Party whose single goal was the passage of the woman suffrage amendment. Their nonviolent but militant tactics served mostly to embarrass the president and other officials.

The work of Alice Paul and other early twentieth-century feminists and suffragists was a significant force in the final passage of the Nineteenth Amendment.

*** *Bratfisch, Virginia* THE NON-VIOLENT ALICE PAUL Illus. Women's Heritage Series, 1971. (grade 9 and up)

Brief but excellent profile of Alice Paul is devoted mostly to her life in the suffragist movement. Provides a good background to the history of the movement, incorporating lengthy quotations of Ms. Paul.

ANNA PAVLOVA
1881–1931
Russian prima ballerina

When the world-famous Russian ballerina Anna Pavlova was eight years old she attended a performance of the ballet *Sleeping Beauty* and decided to become a dancer. At ten she was admitted to the Imperial Ballet School in Saint Petersburg, where she underwent the most rigorous training available to young dancers. At seventeen, she made her debut, not as a member of the corps de ballet, as is the usual custom, but in a role. Within three years Pavlova had risen to the rank of prima ballerina of the Imperial Ballet, and although her position was secure there, she chose to form her own company to bring Russian ballet to the rest of the world.

Michel Fokine, the famed choreographer, created Pavlova's most famous role—the "swan" in *Swan Lake*. However, the dancer also scored great triumphs in *Les Papillons*, *Les Sylphides*, and *The Magic Flute*. Between her extensive tours throughout Europe and the United States, she made her home in England with her husband who served as her advisor and manager.

The phenomenal success of Pavlova was due to her great talent as well as her intensive discipline and devotion to her art. She refused to stop dancing, even when ill, and died while on tour.

*** *Malvern, Gladys* DANCING STAR: THE STORY OF ANNA PAV-LOVA Illus. Messner, 1942. (grade 6 and up)
Wonderfully moving, dramatic biography of the great Pavlova details her childhood, training, and sensational career providing a vivid picture of life in Russia and in ballet throughout the world. Not by any means limited to career-oriented readers, its appeal is much wider and is of interest to readers who are uninformed about ballet.

FRANCES PERKINS
1882–1965

Secretary of labor, first woman cabinet member

At a time when few women received a higher education, Frances Perkins attended Mount Holyoke College, where she became involved in crusades for social justice. Despite her father's conservative attitudes, she was determined to make social and labor reform her life's work, rather than teaching which her family considered more suitable.

Like many other young, idealistic college graduates of the day, she became closely allied with social reformer Jane Addams (page 5). She was a frequent resident at Hull House in Chicago, and then worked in Philadelphia and New York. In New York, Ms. Perkins entered government service as an aide to Alfred Smith and later to Franklin D. Roosevelt. When Roosevelt became president in 1932 he chose her to be his secretary of labor, the first woman to serve in a presidential cabinet. She remained throughout his terms and served also under President Harry Truman. Upon her resignation she wrote a book, *The Roosevelt I Knew*, contributed articles to magazines, and then returned to public life when President Truman appointed her as United States Civil Service Commissioner. Teaching, lecturing, and continued writing occupied her later years, and she was working on a book about Alfred Smith when, at eighty-four, she died suddenly.

*** *Myers, Elisabeth P.* MADAME SECRETARY: FRANCES PERKINS
  Messner, 1972. (grade 7 and up)
    Absorbing account of the life of the first woman cabinet member is smoothly written, gives a good picture of the early and mid-1900s in the United States, and makes clear Perkins's contributions and achievements in government.

MOLLY PITCHER
(Mary Ludwig Hays McCauley)
1754–1832

Revolutionary patriot

Separating the woman from the legend is often an impossible task, but much evidence points to Molly Pitcher being Mary Ludwig Hays McCauley, the wife of a Revolutionary soldier. Ms. McCauley did washing, cooking, and some nursing at her husband's camp. During the Battle of Monmouth she carried water to the thirsty soldiers who thus dubbed her Molly Pitcher. According to the legend, when her husband was wounded she took his place and continued to load the cannon, thereby contributing to the victorious battle.

After the war, she returned to domestic service, and was later given a payment and annuity for her service during the Battle of Monmouth. Records of this pension mentioned in a contemporary journal lend some authority to her story.

In 1876, the American centennial year, patriotic citizens suggested placing a tombstone over her grave. Later a monument to her was erected, helping to perpetuate her legend.

* Stevenson, Augusta MOLLY PITCHER: GIRL PATRIOT Bobbs–Merrill, 1952. (grades 3-7)
    Very highly fictionalized, but rather satisfactory profile of Molly Pitcher vividly conveys the time in which she lived.

POCAHONTAS
1595/96–1616/17

Legendary Indian heroine

Princess Pocahontas, daughter of the great chief Powhattan, intervened for the Jamestown colony leader Captain John Smith when her father was about to kill him. Though the story has been frequently wrapped in legend, Smith

228

himself has documented the incident as occurring when Pocahontas was only twelve or thirteen years old.

Her abilities as an emissary were acknowledged when she negotiated the release of Indian prisoners in Jamestown and generally fostered good will between Indians and settlers.

Her marriage to John Rolfe, a colonist, led to Pocahontas's acceptance of Christianity and the birth of a son, Thomas, whose many descendants in the United States can be traced back to the Indian princess. With her husband and child she went to England where she was presented to King James I and Queen Anne. Unaccustomed to the dampness and cold of England, Pocahontas took ill and died before her return. Over the years many romantic stories have grown around her and she has appeared, somewhat fictionalized, in the works of leading poets, playwrights, and novelists.

*** *Bulla, Clyde Robert* POCAHONTAS AND THE STRANGERS Illus. Crowell, 1971. (grades 4-7)

Distinguished writing and beautiful illustrations by Peter Burchard combine to create an outstanding, though somewhat fictionalized account of the legend of Pocahontas. Her conflicting loyalties are indicated, and she emerges as the real human being she was.

*** *D'Aulaire, Ingri, and Parin, Edgar* POCAHONTAS Illus. Doubleday, 1949. (picture book, reading level, grades 3-5)

Outstanding color illustrations and fine writing distinguish this picture book and early reader. Though fictionalized, it is faithful to the story of Pocahontas as it is known.

** *Wilkie, Katherine* POCAHONTAS: INDIAN PRINCESS Illus. Garrard, 1969. (grades 2-5)

Good account of Pocahontas is written with direct simplicity in a somewhat lively, narrative style.

* *Martin, Patricia* POCAHONTAS Illus. Putnam, 1964. (grades K-4)

Satisfactory biography of Pocahontas is simple and suitable for reading aloud, but lacks vigor and color.

* *Seymour, Flora* POCAHONTAS: BRAVE GIRL Illus. Bobbs–Merrill, 1961. (grades 3-7)

Highly fictionalized, somewhat patronizing biography of Pocahontas gives a reasonably adequate picture of Indian life but is more a novel than a biography.

†† *Wahl, Jan* POCAHONTAS IN LONDON Illus. Dell, 1967. (grades K-3)

Beautiful picture book illustrated by John Alcorm is untrue to the real or legendary Pocahontas. The publisher states that the authors have "recreated the beloved story of Pocahontas in London in a manner entirely their own." Pocahontas does not marry, does not have a child, nor does she die in this book, and in fact she looks and acts like a Disney character.

BEATRIX POTTER
1866–1943
Author and illustrator of children's books

Peter Rabbit, the best-known of Beatrix Potter's many books, is still loved by generations of children and parents. Throughout her lonely, though not unhappy childhood, she only had servants and animal pets as her friends, and drawing and nature were her greatest interests. Later Beatrix Potter wrote a series of letters to a young friend which developed into the little, pale-colored, illustrated books which are familiar to children throughout the world.

No commercial publisher was willing to publish her first book, *Peter Rabbit,* so she published it herself. Later it, like all her successive stories about animals, was published by Frederick Warne & Co., Inc., New York.

She and her husband lived on a farm in England where she wrote, became an active member of the neighboring community, and bought additional property with the intention of protecting areas of natural beauty.

*** *Aldis, Dorothy* NOTHING IS IMPOSSIBLE: THE STORY OF BEATRIX POTTER Illus. Atheneum, 1969. (grades 3-7)

Outstanding biography of Beatrix Potter discusses her lonely childhood, many interests and hobbies, and the development of her career. Warm and dramatic, it shows clearly her tremendous talents, success, and life-style. Of particular interest to devotees of her books, this biography has even wider attraction as a perceptive and inspiring study of an independent, imaginative woman.

** *Lane, Margaret* THE TALE OF BEATRIX POTTER: A BIOGRAPHY (2nd ed.) Illus. Warne, 1968. (grade 9 and up)

Full-length, adult biography is formally written, but is nevertheless a very fine, substantial evaluation of Ms. Potter's life and work. For mature readers particularly interested in an in-depth study.

** *Potter, Beatrix* LETTERS TO CHILDREN Harvard Univ. Pr., 1967. (grades 3-6)

Not really a biography, but a collection of reproductions of her letters to children in her own handwriting, as well as set in print for clarity. Complements other biographical studies of her life as well as the reading of her books.

* *Mayer, Ann Margaret* BEATRIX POTTER Illus. Creative Educ. Soc./Children's Pr., 1974. (grades 4-8)

Despite its carefully limited vocabulary, this interesting and easy-to-read biography moves quickly. The illustrations, while vivid and appealing to the television- and advertising-oriented youngster, seem grossly inappropriate in a biography of the woman whose own art was delicate, simple, and understated. The writing style lacks the delicacy and imagination the subject herself used, again making the book somewhat inappropriate and tasteless. However, it is a fairly accurate picture of Beatrix Potter's life, and although fictionalized, fairly responsible.

ANNEMARIE PROELL
1953–

Olympic ski champion

Annemarie Proell, a young Austrian skier, has earned more points and won more events than any skier in the world, male or female.

When Annemarie was only fifteen she became the youngest of eighteen women to belong to the Austrian National Ski Team. Her victories include the World Cup in 1971, 1972, 1973, and 1974, and the "Silver Jug" meet in 1972. In the 1972 winter Olympics she won two silver medals.

Sometimes considered difficult because of her short temper and air of overconfidence, she is, at the same time, a highly competitive, hard-working skier who is demanding of herself and is never satisfied unless she is number one.

*** *Jacobs, Linda* ANNEMARIE PROELL: QUEEN OF THE MOUNTAIN Illus. EMC, 1975. (reading level, grades 4-6; interest level through high school)

Well-balanced account of the life of the top skier is objective and nonadulatory. Emphasis is on her skiing career with a good deal of information about her personal life and personality. Further enhanced by numerous action photographs, the book gives the reader a good picture of the life of a champion skier.

MARTHA JEFFERSON RANDOLPH
1772–1836

Daughter and First Lady to Thomas Jefferson

Martha Jefferson Randolph, known as Patsy, was only ten when her mother died. However she never forgot the grief of her father, Thomas Jefferson, which perhaps accounts for the close bond that grew between them. She joined him in Philadelphia at the Continental Congress, and then went to Paris with him when he served as a minister to France. Here she became fluent in French, and under her father's guidance and interest studied the classics.

At eighteen, young Ms. Jefferson married a cousin and together they had twelve children. They lived near the Jefferson home, Monticello, and her father was always delighted to have her and the children near him. During Jefferson's presidency, Dolley Madison (page 191) and sometimes young Patsy Randolph acted as First Lady. Patsy's eighth child was born in the White House, the first baby to be born there.

* *Kelly, Regina Z.* MISS JEFFERSON IN PARIS Coward, 1971. (grades 4-7)

Acceptable, although somewhat sexist biography is a very well written story of the period during which Thomas Jefferson served as the American minister to France just before the 1789 revolution. Young Patsy never fully emerges as an individual with a personality of her own—a fault that may not lie with the author as much as with the subject.

VINNIE REAM
1847–1914
Sculptor

Vinnie Ream and her parents were living in Washington, D.C., when she happened to visit a prominent sculptor's studio. Only sixteen years old at the time, she decided to sculpt and her result so impressed the artist that he took her on as a pupil. She was soon making busts of congressmen, and did one of President Lincoln. After he was assassinated, Congress contracted with the eighteen-year-old artist to do a full-scale marble statue to stand in the Capitol.

With her parents, she went to Rome to turn the work into marble and in 1871 it was unveiled at the Capitol. Other commissions followed but when, at the age of thirty, Ms. Ream married an army engineer, she gave up her professional art career and instead devoted herself to various charities. Many years later, though quite ill, she returned briefly to sculpture and just before her death completed a commission of the Cherokee Indian, Sequoya.

** *Hall, Gordon* VINNIE REAM: THE STORY OF THE GIRL WHO SCULPTURED LINCOLN Holt, 1963. (grades 7-9)
Extremely well researched and documented biography gives a good picture of the life of Vinnie Ream, depicting her as a highly talented, clever young woman.

JOHANNA de LEEUW REISS
1932–

Author

When the Germans invaded Holland in 1940 many Jews thought they would be safe. Johanna de Leeuw Reiss's family thought so too, but two years later it was evident that this was not the case. Ten-year-old "Annie" and her sister left their parents to hide in an upstairs room of a farmhouse owned by sympathetic non-Jewish people. Until the war was over they stayed there, safe from the Germans but cut off from the rest of the world.

After the war she completed her education in Holland and became a teacher. After going to the United States she became an editor and then decided to write *The Upstairs Room* to answer her daughters' questions about her childhood. The book won several important American awards, and has been translated and published throughout Europe and in Japan. She was also awarded the Buxtehuder Bulle, one of western Europe's most prestigious book prizes, given to authors of children's books which promote peace. Reiss is the first American to win the prize and upon accepting it said, "I am glad that *The Upstairs Room*, which I wrote for my daughters, has been read by many more children. I hope they got from it that without hate, without bitterness, perhaps we can reach out to each other, just as we have done here today. That makes me have faith that there will never be a need again to write another 'Upstairs Room'."

*** *Reiss, Johanna* THE UPSTAIRS ROOM Crowell, 1972. (grade
   5 and up)
   Beautifully written, personal narrative is tender, moving,
and dramatic. Young "Annie" and her sister emerge as strong
and courageous as the couple who sheltered them.

●▬o▬o▬o▬o▬o▬o▬o▬o▬o▬o▬o▬o▬o▬o▬o▬o▬o▬o▬o▬o▬o▬o▬o▬o▬●

TERRY RENO

Model

Terry Reno, one of the most popular young American
models, has appeared on magazine covers and in advertisements in France, Britain, and Germany, as well as the
United States. She wisely obtained training in secretarial
skills, rather than depending on the often temporary success in the modelling field. Ms. Reno works hard and carefully observes and advocates good health habits, eating
intelligently, and scheduling plenty of rest.

** *Reno, Terry* THE MODEL (A Week With...Series) Illus.
   McGraw, 1967. (grade 7 and up)
   This career-oriented book is more than a biography, offering an objective, realistic view of the modelling profession.
Hard work, ambition, and talent, as well as physical attractiveness are shown to be necessary for success as a model in
this extremely readable, fast-moving portrait of Ms. Reno
and her work.

JOAN MOORE RICE
1954–

Olympic gymnast

Joan Moore Rice is a gymnast whose combined dancing and athletic ability result in beautiful ballet-like gymnastic routines.

She was an active and fearless youngster who began gymnastics when she was only six. Good training and coaching, as well as hard work and innate ability, enabled her to begin international competition by the time she was sixteen.

In 1971 and 1972 Joan Moore Rice tied for first place in the Elite Nationals. In the 1972 Olympics she tallied up a score high enough to rank twenty-first in the world. In both 1973 and 1974 she alone won the Elite Nationals, thus becoming the best amateur gymnast in the country.

In 1974 Ms. Rice retired from amateur gymnastics. Although this meant she would not be able to compete in the 1976 Olympics, it still enabled her to continue the work she enjoys. She and her husband, who is also a gymnast, opened a gymnastic school in Minneapolis. Here she has the opportunity to teach students the skills she has so beautifully mastered.

*** *Jacobs, Linda* JOAN MOORE RICE: THE OLYMPIC DREAM
   Illus. EMC. 1975. (reading level, grades 4-6; interest level through high school)
   Well-rounded, interesting account of the subject's life also gives a good picture of the life of a gymnast and the training needed to achieve success. The author includes an interesting informative discussion of the sport of gymnastics.

237

ELLEN SWALLOW RICHARDS
1842–1911

Chemist, pioneer in home economics

At twenty-five, Ellen Richards entered Vassar College where, influenced by Maria Mitchell (page 205), the astronomer, she decided to make science her life's work. She was accepted as a chemistry student at the Massachusetts Institute of Technology (MIT). Later she discovered that the reason she had not been charged any tuition was so that the school would not have a woman officially recorded as a student. She became the first woman to graduate with a degree in chemistry and was hired by MIT as an instructor and acting director of the first chemistry laboratory to study sanitation.

Ms. Richards was the first woman elected to the American Institute of Mining and Metallurgical Engineers, organized the science department of a large correspondence school, was a founder of the group that came to be called the American Association of University Women, and worked for the improvement of physical education in colleges.

An expert in food and nutrition, she served as a consultant to schools, hospitals, institutions, and the federal department of agriculture and almost single-handedly made home economics a profession. Her numerous articles, books, and lectures on home economics and other subjects, as well as her inexhaustible efforts to increase women's participation in the scientific professions, are just a few of Ellen Richards's many accomplishments.

*** *Douty, Esther* AMERICA'S FIRST WOMAN CHEMIST: ELLEN RICHARDS Messner, 1961. (grade 7 and up)

Outstanding biography is a warm, personal account of Ellen Richards's life. Nontechnical, it has appeal for all readers, but may be particularly attractive to those interested in science and home economics. Ms. Richards is introduced as a sensitive, diversified, and ambitious human being.

LINDA RICHARDS
1841–1930

Nursing educator who received first American nursing diploma

Linda Richards's interest in nursing was encouraged by a local Vermont doctor who relied on her assistance. When the first American school of nursing opened, she enrolled and became the first nurse to receive a diploma in the United States.

After graduation Ms. Richards helped develop educational programs in nursing and journeyed to England where she conferred with Florence Nightingale (page 215) and studied her methods of training nurses. Upon her return she worked despite the opposition of doctors who were satisfied with the poor care given by untrained nurses.

Linda Richards opened the first nursing school in Japan where she also engaged in evangelical work. After returning to the United States, she became a pioneer in the training of visiting nurses and worked to raise the standard of nursing care in mental hospitals.

239

Scholarships and awards are named in her honor, and in the New England Hospital for Women and Children there is a room dedicated to her containing mementos of her life.

*** *Baker, Rachel* AMERICA'S FIRST TRAINED NURSE: LINDA RICHARDS Messner, 1962. (grade 7 and up)
Unusually fine narrative biography of Linda Richards also covers the history of nursing in the late nineteenth and early twentieth century, as well as the development of new practices and methods. Directed to all readers, not just those interested in the career of nursing, it is a warm, dramatic, and stirring portrait of a dedicated woman of many accomplishments.

*** *Collins, David R.* LINDA RICHARDS: FIRST AMERICAN TRAINED NURSE Illus. Garrard, 1975. (grades 2-4)
Written with direct simplicity, a warm, inspiring, and lively account of the pioneer nurse draws a good picture of both her life, the early days of nursing, and the historical period in which she lived.

CATHY RIGBY
1952–

Olympic gymnast

At four feet, ten-and-a-half inches, eighty-nine pounds, Cathy Rigby was the smallest American on the 1968 Olympic gymnast team. Although she did not win any medals, her all-around scoring was the highest ever for an American gymnast.

Cathy Rigby, a premature baby, remained sickly for several years, but as she got older became an extremely active and physically daring child. At eleven she began intensive gymnastic training, and by the time she was fourteen, she was ready to compete in her first international meet.

In the 1970 World Games she took the silver medal for the balance beam competition, becoming the first American to win a medal in international gymnastics. The following year she became the first non-Russian to win a gold medal in competition held in the Soviet Union.

Outdoing all other Americans at the 1972 Olympics, she did not take any medals because the competition with the Russian and European gymnasts was too great.

Exhausted from years of hard work, the pressure of continuing the imposed "cute little girl" image, and the controlling influence of her coach, she decided to retire from gymnastic competition.

In 1974 she played the title role in a stage production of *Peter Pan,* and she continues occasionally to give exhibitions. Her success helped bring wide attention to gymnastics and has influenced many other young women to consider the sport for themselves.

* *Jacobs, Linda* CATHY RIGBY: ON THE BEAM Illus. with photographs. EMC, 1975. (reading level, grades 4-6; interest level through high school)

Interesting and readable but too laudatory in tone, the biography depicts Rigby and everyone else in her life as almost too good to be true. However, the photographs of her in action add considerably to the biography.

FELISA RINCÓN
1897–

Mayor of San Juan, Puerto Rico

Felisa Rincón was reared in a conservative middle-class Puerto Rican home. When her mother died, she was forced to quit high school to keep house and to care for her younger sisters and brothers. Not until 1932 did she take an active role outside the home. That year Puerto Rican women were first permitted to vote and, despite her father's initial objection, she went to the polls. Appalled to discover few other women had done so, she immediately became involved in Puerto Rican politics and set about urging women to exercise their right.

When appointed mayor of San Juan in 1946 to fill an unexpired term, Dona Felisa, as she was known to her constituents, became the first and only woman mayor of San Juan. Her reforms were immediate and she was reelected every four years, serving a total of twenty years.

Felisa Rincón's popularity rested not only on the close personal relationships and ready availability she maintained with the mostly impoverished residents of San Juan, but also on the improvements in housing, sanitation, health, and education she instituted. The development of a child care center was another one of her important contributions to San Juan.

A skilled politician, she worked closely with business and government officials on the mainland, bringing industry and other benefits to the island.

*** *Gruber, Ruth* FELISA RINCON DE GAUTIER: MAYOR OF SAN JUAN Illus. Crowell, 1972. (grades 5-8)

Superb, warm portrait of Felisa Rincón not only shows the development of her as a political figure, but also discusses the culture of Puerto Rico and male and female relationships as they exist there.

ELEANOR ROOSEVELT
1884–1962

Humanitarian, author, First Lady

Eleanor Roosevelt was a lonely youngster who overcame shyness and self-consciousness to become a woman of great influence in national and international affairs. As the wife of the thirty-second president of the United States, Franklin Delano Roosevelt, she chose not to be a social figure, but instead attended to more official business. She wrote newspaper and magazine columns and several books, lectured and toured the country, and during World War II visited army posts here and abroad. The press conferences for women reporters which she instituted comprised just one of her efforts to increase the participation of women at all levels of government and private industry. Placing particular emphasis on civil rights, she was a champion of all minority groups and resigned from the Daughters of the American Revolution when they refused the use of their concert hall to black singer Marian Anderson (page 10).

After her husband's death she was appointed a delegate to the first session of the United Nations, became the first chairperson of the United Nations' Human Rights Commission, and figured importantly in the Declaration of Human Rights. Her years of devotion to her own country and to all humanity earned her the title "First Lady of the world." Her death in 1962 was universally mourned.

*** *Blassingame, Wyatt* ELEANOR ROOSEVELT Illus. Putnam, 1964. (grades 2-4)
Crisp, clear, easy-to-read text is a faithful and warm but not sentimental account of the life of the great humanitarian. It captures the essence of Ms. Roosevelt and serves well as an introduction to her life for young readers.

*** *Davidson, Margaret* STORY OF ELEANOR ROOSEVELT Illus. with photographs. Four Winds, 1969. (grades 4-6)
Outstanding biography is accurate and well-written though very informal. Author brings the subject to life, clearly stating her many accomplishments and capturing her personality.

*** *Goodsell, Jane* ELEANOR ROOSEVELT Illus. Crowell, 1970. (grades 1-3)
Simple, but worthwhile biography is a stirring, thoughtful examination of Eleanor Roosevelt as youngster, wife, mother, and great humanitarian.

*** *Richards, Kenneth* ELEANOR ROOSEVELT Illus. Children's Pr., 1968. (grade 6 and up)
Very fine black-and-white photographs and illustrations compose the major part of this study of Eleanor Roosevelt. The text is also substantial, warm, dramatic, and informative.

*** *Roosevelt, Eleanor* THE AUTOBIOGRAPHY OF ELEANOR ROOSEVELT Harper, 1961. (grade 9 and up)
One-volume personal narrative consists of material selected from three volumes of memoirs of Eleanor Roosevelt. A final chapter which she added for this book tells of her activities through the 1960 elections. An outstanding book, it provides many warm, intimate glimpses of Ms. Roosevelt's life.

** *Gilbert, Miriam* SHY GIRL: THE STORY OF ELEANOR ROOSEVELT Doubleday, 1965. (grades 5-9)

A very readable, sympathetic account of Eleanor Roosevelt's unhappy childhood. Written at a very easy reading level, it should appeal to older less able readers, and may well spark their imagination to read a more complete biography of her.

** *Graves, Charles* ELEANOR ROOSEVELT: FIRST LADY OF THE LAND Illus. Garrard, 1965. (grades 2-5)

Good account of Eleanor Roosevelt is immensely readable but does not place sufficient emphasis on her role as an individual, although it does cite her accomplishments.

* *Weil, Ann* ELEANOR ROOSEVELT: COURAGEOUS GIRL Illus. Bobbs–Merrill, 1965. (grades 3-7)

This biography is filled with trivial accounts of Eleanor Roosevelt's childhood activities and only the final section deals with her adult life. Merely adequate, it really does not do justice to its subject.

ERNESTINE ROSE
1810–1892

Feminist, reformer

As the daughter of a rabbi, Ernestine Rose received more education and freedom than is usually afforded young girls in Russian Poland, but her rebellious spirit rallied against the subordination and inferiority of women taught in Jewish law. At age fourteen she completely disassociated herself from Judaism. Two years later, in objection to her widowed father's contractual agreement to marry her to an older man and to give her mother's inheritance to him as a dowry, she went to court and won back her rightful funds.

Ernestine Rose left Poland for England where she became acquainted with, and influenced by, social reformers, including Robert Owen. She married, and moved to New York, becoming active in the women's rights and free-thought movements. An immensely dramatic and strikingly attractive woman, she soon became known as the "queen of the platform" when she lectured on a wide range of subjects that included temperance, abolition, peace, the rights of women, and free thought. Her progressive ideas made her a controversial figure, even among supporters of women's rights, but she remained in close alliance with Susan B. Anthony (page 15) and Elizabeth Cady Stanton (page 266), and due to her dynamic personality and superior intelligence, influenced the reformers of her day.

*** *Suhl, Yuri* ELOQUENT CRUSADER: ERNESTINE ROSE Messner, 1970. (grade 7 and up)

Superior, well-written feminist biography is an outstanding, soundly researched examination of Ms. Rose's life as well as a good exploration of the reform movements of the day. The author is careful to paint an unvarnished, well-balanced account of the subject that is dramatic and colorful. As the only biography available of Ernestine Rose, it is recommended for older readers as well as the junior high and early high school ones for whom it was intended.

BETSY ROSS
1752–1836

Legendary maker of the first American flag

Quaker-born Betsy Ross ran an upholstery business with her husband, and after his death continued her skilled needlework, making flags for Pennsylvania and acquiring some property around the Philadelphia area. According to the well-known legend, George Washington, with a secret committee, visited her in her shop and commissioned her to design a flag for the new nation. She supposedly suggested a five-pointed star which could be cut with one scissor stroke. Some legends even say she was given an exclusive contract to manufacture the flags.

Her grandson first told the story of Betsy Ross and the first American flag at a historical meeting in 1870. The story, probably told to him by his mother, appealed to American patriotism and, despite lack of any documentation, was soon included in school textbooks.

A Betsy Ross Memorial Association was organized, funds were raised to make a national shrine of the house in which she supposedly made the flag, and her legend has been immortalized in stories and paintings.

** *Mayer, Jane* BETSY ROSS AND THE FLAG Random, 1952. (grades 4-6)
> Despite fictionalization and much invention of facts, this is a very good historical treatment, with Betsy Ross emerging as an independent, intelligent, and inspiring individual.

* *Weil, Ann* BETSY ROSS: GIRL OF OLD PHILADELPHIA Illus. Bobbs–Merrill, 1961. (grades 3-7)
> Overfictionalized story of Betsy Ross is a readable, satisfactory picture of early America but, from necessity, not really a biography of Betsy Ross.

HELENA RUBINSTEIN
1870?–1965

Founder of international beauty and cosmetic business

Helena Rubinstein, one of the wealthiest self-made women in the world, was, at fifteen, a bookkeeper for her father's small business in Poland. She then entered medical school, but decided not to complete the training, and went instead to Australia, where she opened a small shop in which she dispensed beauty advice along with cosmetics and creams she had brought from Europe. Immensely successful, she repeated this success in London and Paris, and at the start of World War I came to New York. Within a few years she had established salons across the country.

All her energies, thoughts, and time were concentrated on business and although she was a difficult taskmaster she was able to surround herself with competent, loyal people, many of whom were relatives. However, the success of her business was due almost in its entirety to the dedication, authority, and control which she exercised.

During World War II Helena Rubinstein helped innumerable Polish refugees find a welcome in the United States, and she did much to aid the war effort. The many foundations she created have given millions of dollars to charities, museums, and universities. Her private collection of paintings and jewelry contributed to the legend of beauty and opulence that surrounded her.

*** *Fabe, Maxene* BEAUTY MILLIONAIRE: THE LIFE OF HELENA RUBINSTEIN Illus. with photographs. Crowell, 1973. (grades 5-9)

Outstanding biography of the woman who made her fortune in the cosmetic business is a well-balanced, absorbing account clearly showing her abilities and energies and her commitment to business. Some of her personal failures are also dealt with.

WILMA RUDOLPH
1940–

Olympic track and field winner

That Wilma Rudolph ever learned to walk is something of a miracle. That she later became the first American woman to win three Olympic gold medals for track and field is not so much a miracle as it is the result of years of determination and hard work.

Illness had left Wilma, one of the youngest of nineteen children, badly crippled. The family worked together to follow medical rehabilitation instructions and by the time she was six years old she could walk.

From then on, nothing stopped her. In high school she played basketball and went out for track. At the age of sixteen, she became a member of the United States Olympic team, helping the women's team win a bronze medal. In 1960 she broke the Olympic record in the 200-meter dash, and along with her team mates set a 400-meter world record.

In 1961 Wilma Rudolph became the third woman ever to win the Sullivan Memorial Trophy for outstanding performance by an amateur athlete. She also was invited to race in the usually all-man Millrose Games held annually in New York's Madison Square Garden.

249

Wilma Rudolph has been busy since her days of competition, first as a junior high school teacher, now as director of the Youth Foundation in Chicago and coach of the women's track team. She is married and has four children, hosts television specials, did television commentary at the 1972 Olympics, and speaks before various groups.

In 1974 Wilma Rudolph was inducted into the new Black Athletes Hall of Fame. She is one of only three women included.

*** *Jacobs, Linda* WILMA RUDOLPH: RUN FOR GLORY Illus. with photographs. EMC, 1975. (reading level, grades 4-6; interest level through high school)

Inspiring, fast-moving biography of Wilma Rudolph traces her private life and career from sickly infancy through her Olympic achievements and her adult role as a coach, civic leader, television personality, and mother. Numerous photographs of her in action and with friends and family greatly enhance the easy-to-read text, as suitable for older reluctant readers as it is for elementary school youngsters.

FLORENCE SABIN, M.D.
1871–1953
Physician, scientist, researcher

Dr. Florence Sabin, who has been described as one of the foremost scientists of all times, specialized in the investigation of the lymphatic system, blood vessels, and the origin of red blood cells. Before receiving her medical degree from Johns Hopkins medical school, Florence Sabin made a three-dimensional model of the brain which led to a clearer understanding of its structure. Copies of it continue to be used in medical schools today and the textbook which she later published to accompany the model was long considered the finest one on the subject.

She was primarily a researcher and teacher. Her discoveries and many publications altered medical thinking, and brought her honors and awards. Yet even though she was next in line to be named head of the Department of Anatomy at Hopkins, a man was appointed in her stead. She did, however, become the first female full professor there, and later at the Rockefeller Institute set up the department of cellular studies and pioneered in the study of tuberculosis.

The first woman elected to life membership of the National Academy of Science and first woman president of the American Association of Anatomists, she "retired" at age seventy-three to move back to her home in Colorado. There she led an energetic crusade for health and sanitation improvements.

*** *Phelan, Mary Kay* PROBING THE UNKNOWN: THE STORY OF DR. FLORENCE SABIN Crowell, 1969. (grades 5-8)

Outstanding biography of the famed scientist is warm, dramatic, inspiring, and of particular interest to students of science, for some of it is slightly technical. The author writes with clarity, and explains scientific concepts and terms well, allowing uninformed readers to follow the text with ease.

SACAJAWEA
1787–1812

Indian interpreter for Lewis and Clark

Sacajawea, the captured and enslaved Indian wife of French-Canadian Toussaint Charbonneau, played a significant role in the famous Lewis and Clark expedition.

When Charbonneau was hired as an interpreter for Lewis and Clark, Sacajawea and their infant went along: their presence served as a signal that the expedition was not a warring party. Sacajawea's knowledge of several Indian languages and ability to speak with many tribes through a chain of interpreters contributed greatly to the expedition's progress. She helped cook, introduced the men to edible substances, saved valuable instruments and records from loss, and was instrumental in obtaining guidance and services from Indian tribes.

According to legend, she regularly served as a guide; though this information is undocumented, it is certain that she provided some vital direction on their return trip. Throughout the West, statues, monuments, streams, and mountain peaks are named for the young Indian woman whose important role in American history has largely gone unrecognized in textbooks.

*** *Blassingame, Wyatt* SACAGAWEA: INDIAN GUIDE Garrard, 1965. (grades 2-5)
   Simplistic but very fine story of Sacajawea gives a good picture of Indian life and culture while at the same time showing Sacajawea to be an unusually wise and independent young woman.

*** *Farnsworth, Frances* WINGED MOCASSINS: THE STORY OF SACAJAWEA Illus. Messner, 1954. (grade 6 and up)

Excellent biography of the Indian interpreter and guide moves with reality and warmth, emphasizing her intelligence, skills, and loyalty. Interesting and fast-moving, it also re-creates the Lewis and Clark expedition well.

** *Voight, Virginia* SACAJAWEA Illus. Putnam, 1967. (grades K-4)

Good, but not outstanding biography of the young Indian woman. Not especially dramatic, it is nonetheless an interesting tale, simply told.

* *Seibert, Jerry* SACAJAWEA: GUIDE TO LEWIS AND CLARK Houghton Mifflin, 1960. (grades 4-6)

The first section of this book is about Indian life in general; the second part deals with the Lewis and Clark expedition, describing Sacajawea's part in it. Not a true biography, it does, however, give a satisfactory account of some of Sacajawea's activities.

* *Seymour, Flora* SACAGAWEA: BIRD GIRL Illus. Bobbs–Merrill, 1945. (grades 3-7)

Highly fictionalized book describes Sacajawea's childhood, perhaps much as it might have been. The author fails to convince the reader of her true appreciation of Indian culture for there is something slightly condescending about her attitude towards it. A small portion of the book concentrates on Sacajawea's part in the Lewis and Clark expedition.

DEBORAH SAMPSON
1760–1827

Revolutionary soldier

Many women took over men's jobs during the American Revolution, but Deborah Sampson was one of only a few who actually served in the Continental Army. She disguised herself as a man and, using the name of Robert Shirtliff, enlisted with a Massachusetts regiment. She participated in several battles and when wounded, hid. Only when she was hospitalized with typhoid was her sex discovered, at which time she was discharged.

Deborah Sampson later married, had three children, and lectured on her experiences. She was eventually awarded a pension from the government for her services.

** *McGovern, Ann* DEBORAH SAMPSON GANNETT Four Winds, 1975. (grades 2-4)

Good, easy-to-read biography clearly states the limited options for women during the period in which Deborah lived. However, it does not fully capture the adventuresome spirit of the young revolutionary soldier.

MARGARET SANGER
1883–1966
Feminist, reformer, and advocate of birth control

Margaret Sanger was well convinced of the health risk associated with pregnancy. Her own mother had died young, worn out from successive childbearing and, as a nurse, Margaret Sanger saw firsthand the relationship of large families, poverty, illness, and misery and the often tragic results of self-induced abortions. She believed contraception was the cure. She studied European methods and despite laws which prohibited the dissemination of

254

such information, published a magazine, *The Woman Rebel;* wrote pamphlets and articles; and found printers willing to risk printing what were then defined as "obscene materials." She set up a clinic for dispensing contraceptive materials and coined the phrase "birth control." Constantly arrested and jailed, she refused to plead guilty claiming, "the law was wrong, not I." She fought a lonely crusade when even doctors were unwilling to support her and most feminists preferred to place priorities on women's suffrage.

Ms. Sanger lived to see her ideas gain respectability and to be hailed a heroine. She was a consultant for population control and family planning organizations throughout the world.

*** *Lader, Lawrence, and Meltzer, Milton* MARGARET SANGER: PIONEER OF BIRTH CONTROL Illus. Crowell, 1969. (grades 5-9)

Outstanding biography of the reformer shows her selflessness, conflicts about her own family, and determination to achieve her goals. Questions of sex and contraception are dealt with sensitively and tastefully in this extremely well written, moving, and stirring account.

*** *Sanger, Margaret* MARGARET SANGER: AN AUTOBIOGRAPHY Norton, 1938; repr. Dover, 1971. (grade 9 and up)

The reformer's own autobiography, written for adults, is an exciting, dramatic, and readable account of her life, clearly showing the forces that combined to propel her to the course she chose.

RUTH SAWYER
1880–

Children's author and literature specialist

Ruth Sawyer based *Roller Skates,* a prize-winning and long-time favorite children's novel, on her own life. She was an outstanding storyteller and lecturer, whose influence on schools of library science and rural libraries was tremendous. In her book *The Way of the Storyteller* she discusses her belief that storytelling is a living folk art.

Ms. Sawyer has served as a librarian, advisor to children's literature, and an author of numerous articles about children's books. Some of the books which she has written for children that have remained particularly popular with readers are *Enchanted School House, Journey Cake, Ho!,* and *The Long Christmas,* as well as other original stories and ancient retold tales.

** *Haviland, Virginia* RUTH SAWYER Walck, 1965. (grade 10 and up)

A very fine account of the life of Ruth Sawyer concentrates on her professional life, offering an interesting view. Students who enjoyed her books when they were younger and adults working in the field of children's literature will find this a worthwhile, enjoyable study.

CLARA WIECK SCHUMANN
1819–1896
Concert pianist

German-born Clara Wieck was a child prodigy who learned piano from her father, a demanding but skilled teacher. Before she had even entered her teens she gave recitals and concert tours and became acquainted with Robert Schumann, the composer who was a student of her father's. The two later fell in love, but her father strenuously objected to the marriage fearing that he would lose his selfish hold on her and that she would sacrifice her brilliant career.

Torn between love for them both, young Clara decided to defy her father and to marry Robert. She then combined marriage and motherhood with her career as a concert pianist, performing both classical works and helping to popularize her husband's work. Schumann, whose emotions had long been unstable, later became mentally ill and died in an asylum twelve years after their marriage. Clara Schumann continued to perform, but later, when the strain of touring became too difficult for her, limited herself to teaching others.

*** *Kyle, Elisabeth* DUET: THE STORY OF CLARA AND ROBERT SCHUMANN Holt, 1968. (grades 5-9)
Excellent, romantic story of Clara Schumann and her career, her love for her husband, and her relationships with her family. In this well-told and moving story, Clara is seen as a warm, sometimes ambivalent human being with a brilliant concert career of her own.

257

HANNAH SENESH
1921–1944
World War II heroine

A national heroine in Israel, Hannah Senesh was born and grew up in Hungary, but her interest in the Zionist movement grew and she decided in 1939 to emigrate to Palestine. Life there was difficult, and Hannah Senesh, despite her intellectualism, did the hard manual work expected of settlers.

During World War II she volunteered to join the parachute corps and, in 1944 when millions of Jews in Hungary and elsewhere were slated for certain death at the hands of the Nazis, she served in a relief mission to Hungary which attempted to thwart those plans. Hannah Senesh and five young men were the only Palestinians who parachuted down behind enemy lines in Hungary. It was a suicidal mission she knew, and she was captured and executed by the Nazis.

Hannah Senesh had kept a diary since she was thirteen, and through these memoirs, letters, her poetry which is read and learned by Israeli children today, and the recollections of those who knew her, she has become and remained a legend.

** *Masters, Anthony* THE SUMMER THAT BLED: THE BIOGRAPHY OF HANNAH SENESH Illus. Washington Square Pr., 1972. (grade 9 and up)

Primarily a biography of Hannah Senesh, this is also the story of prewar Hungary and Palestine and the attempt to rescue Hungarian Jews during World War II. The author recreates the events suspensefully, clearly, and dramatically to provide readers with a moving, warm account of the subject and of the times.

** *Senesh, Hannah* HANNAH SENESH: HER LIFE AND DIARY Schocken, 1972. (grade 9 and up)

Stirring, dramatic account of the life of Hannah Senesh is composed of her diary, memories of her childhood as told by her mother, letters, personal recollections of coparachutists, and translations of her poetry. The diary shows, in a warm and poignant style, her development from a young, almost carefree girl to a mature, committed young woman.

MARY WOLLSTONECRAFT GODWIN SHELLEY
1797–1851
Author

Mary Shelley's mother, the famed feminist author Mary Wollstonecraft (page 310), died in childbirth, leaving Mary to be brought up by her philosopher father, William Godwin.

She was only fifteen when she first met the twenty-year-old poet Percy Bysshe Shelley, and although he was already married the two began to live as husband and wife and later married. They were constantly moving and hounded by debts; two of their children died and then Shelley himself was drowned at twenty-nine.

Despite these trials, shy, intelligent Mary Shelley produced many lasting works of literature. She wrote six novels, several plays, short stories, two novellas, and several travel books. She completed her best-known work, *Frankenstein, or the Modern Prometheus,* before she was even twenty years old.

After her husband's death she published his *Posthumous Poems,* and edited and added notes to his *Poetical Works.* Her *Journal,* in addition to its own merit, forms the basis for all biographies of the poet.

* *Leighton, Margaret* SHELLEY'S MARY: A LIFE OF MARY GOD-
WIN SHELLEY Farrar, 1973. (grade 7 and up)
The biography focusses equally on Mary and Percy Shelley, only casually mentioning the writing and publication of her great novel, *Frankenstein.* Fairly well written, it follows the Shelleys' lives with reasonable accuracy but frequently sounds more like a travelogue than a biography.

SARAH KEMBLE SIDDONS
1755–1831

Actress

Sarah Kemble Siddons, raised in the theater, made her debut on the stage as a small child, and soon outshone the other members of her family. Her greatest success was in the Shakespearian role of Lady Macbeth, but her portrayals of Desdemona, Rosalind, Ophelia, and Queen Catherine were also memorable.

Her marriage was not a happy one, but she was a devoted mother, somehow managing to find time for career and family. A quiet, somewhat introspective, private individual, she nevertheless moved in a circle with prominent artists, writers, and government officials. Public opinion of her was mixed—she was loved by many, hated by others.

Celebrated in paintings by Gainsborough, Reynolds, and others, she had a dignity and warmth which was seldom equalled by other actresses.

*** *Jonson, Marion* A TROUBLED GRANDEUR: THE STORY OF ENGLAND'S GREAT ACTRESS, SARAH SIDDONS Illus. Little, 1972. (grade 7 and up)
Extremely well written biography of the famed British actress depicts her as a talented woman with great inner strengths, devoted to her family and able to support them emotionally and financially, and yet constantly developing as a performer.

CARLY SIMON
1943–

Folk singer, composer, Grammy Award winner

Folk singer Carly Simon discovered early that being the daughter of a famous, wealthy publisher was no guarantee of success and happiness. Although music was always an important part of her family life she did not start singing folk music seriously until college. At first she and her sister Lucy appeared together. Later Carly Simon decided to try going ahead on her own and began composing much of her own music and lyrics. Her own past and present experiences provide material for her songs, which give her a chance to express her thoughts and feelings.

In 1971 her first single, "That's The Way I've Always Heard It Should Be," won her a Grammy as the best new artist. Since then she has had several successful singles and albums and has performed many concerts.

In 1972 Carly Simon married singer-songwriter James Taylor and they now have a young daughter. The two have recorded some hit records together and occasionally perform a few songs together at the end of concerts.

** *Morse, Charles and Ann* CARLY SIMON Illus. Creative Educ. Soc., 1975. (grades 4-8)
    Colorfully and abundantly designed and illustrated, this good, well-paced biography of the folk singer-composer discusses both her private life and her musical career. At times it touches on complicated personal issues, and because of the brevity and superficiality of the treatment, may leave the reader a bit confused.

MARY SLESSOR
1848–1915

Missionary to Nigeria

Like many Scotch working-class girls of her day, Mary Slessor went to work in a factory at the age of eleven. She later became a missionary in Nigeria where, for thirty-nine years, she focussed on bringing industrial skills to the natives and building schools and churches. She moved beyond the scope of religious conversions and worked particularly hard in raising the status of African women.

Ms. Slessor established a home for girls where they learned such skills as basket-, bamboo-, and cane-weaving which enabled them to become somewhat economically independent. She personally cared for many homeless children, and for sick men, women, and children, and through her teachings and work helped improve vast areas of West Africa.

*** *Syme, Ronald* NIGERIAN PIONEER: THE STORY OF MARY SLESSOR Illus. Morrow, 1964. (grades 5-9)
    Very fine story of Mary Slessor shows her to be not only a missionary but also a woman of rare fortitude and administrative ability as well as of warmth, tenderness, and foresight.

BESSIE SMITH
1898–1937
Singer and songwriter

Bessie Smith, known as the "empress of the blues," was orphaned at age nine, won a prize in an amateur talent contest, and came under the wing of Ma Rainey, the outstanding blues singer of the time. By the time she was thirteen, Bessie Smith had become a seasoned professional and was on her way to becoming America's best loved blues singer. After World War I she went north, performed in clubs, and wrote and recorded blues music. She was popular and successful with both white and black audiences.

Ms. Smith's career and economic situation began to deteriorate during the depression. American interest in blues declined somewhat and she mismanaged her money and drank heavily. Just as life was beginning to look upward she was seriously injured in a car accident in Mississippi. Taken to the nearest hospital, she was refused admittance because she was black. By the time she reached a hospital that would accept her, the loss of blood was so great that she died.

*** *Moore, Carmen* SOMEBODY'S ANGEL CHILD: THE STORY OF BESSIE SMITH Illus. Crowell, 1970. (grades 5-8)
Beautiful, dramatic, and sad account of the life of the blues singer. Well-balanced and stirring, it traces her life from childhood to her untimely death.

➤●◀●➤●◀●➤●◀●➤●◀●➤●◀●➤●◀●➤●◀●➤●◀●➤●◀●➤●◀●➤●◀●➤●◀●➤●◀●➤●◀●➤●◀●➤●◀●➤●◀●➤●◀●➤●◀

MARGARET CHASE SMITH
1897–

Republican senator from Maine

Margaret Chase Smith had worked closely with her late husband, a congressman from Maine, when in 1940 she was elected to fill his unexpired term. Not satisfied just to serve in his stead, she worked hard, campaigned tirelessly, and in the next regular election polled three times the vote her husband had previously received.

The first woman to serve in both houses, Margaret Chase Smith was elected to four House of Representative terms, and four Senate terms, and held one of the best attendance records in Congress. She was the first senator openly to criticize McCarthyism, worked to raise the status of women in the armed forces, served on major congressional committees, and as the 1967 chairman of the Conference of All Republican Senators, was the first woman elected to such a leadership post.

In 1964 Senator Smith became the first woman to be nominated for the presidency of the United States at the national convention of a major political party, and made an impressively good showing. She is the recipient of fifty-two honorary degrees and numerous awards. Her global tours, national syndicated columns, and legislative efforts have made her known and respected throughout the world.

*** *Fleming, Alice* SENATOR FROM MAINE: MARGARET CHASE SMITH Crowell, 1969. (grades 5-8)
   Very fine, fast-moving account of the life of the senator covers her childhood in Maine through her remarkable career in Congress. One sees her as a young woman learning to be financially independent, and then as a senator's wife learning the ways of politics. The author gives a good picture of her life set against the politics and government of the last few decades.

MONICA SONE
1919–
Author

During World War II, President Franklin Roosevelt signed Executive Order 9066 which led to the evacuation and internship of more than 110,000 Japanese-American citizens and aliens living on the West Coast of the United States. Their property had to be sold or stored, for they could only bring what they could carry themselves. Monica Sone and her family were among these Japanese-Americans forced to move from their home to the relocation center. Monica had been born in Seattle, and her parents who had emigrated there from Japan brought her up to appreciate the cultures of both her own native land and theirs. She attended Japanese school as well as the local public schools, and even before the war began had known prejudice and discrimination.

Like many other American-born citizens of Japanese origin, she was later released from the center so that she could attend college.

** *Sone, Monica* Nisei Daughter Little, 1953. (grade 8 and up)

> Lively account is humorous and warm. Despite the great injustices imposed on Japanese-Americans during World War II when they were relocated in detention camps, Ms. Sone writes without bitterness, although critical of the government she had grown to love. She discusses her childhood in Seattle, a visit to Japan, and the hopes she had for carving out her future in America.

ELIZABETH CADY STANTON
1815–1902

Women's rights leader, author, lecturer

Elizabeth Cady Stanton, the daughter of a New York judge, learned early that laws prevented women from having any rights over their children and property. Despite the strain of running a household and raising seven children, she worked for the abolitionist movement, and then, with Lucretia Mott (page 211), organized the Seneca Falls Convention of 1848 from which the women's rights movement was born.

For over fifty years Ms. Stanton closely collaborated with Susan B. Anthony (page 15) to organize the movement, to publish a newspaper, and to lecture throughout the nation. She endorsed divorce, held liberal viewpoints on child rearing, wrote prolifically and eloquently on many subjects, but concentrated most of her efforts on suffrage and women's rights. With Ms. Anthony she wrote three volumes of *History of Woman Suffrage*, and in her *The Woman's Bible* she interpreted the Bible from a nonsexist point of view.

Though the name of Susan B. Anthony is the more famous, Elizabeth Cady Stanton's contributions to women's rights were even more diverse. Believing that suffrage, though a major goal, was only one way to free women from their narrow spheres, Ms. Stanton suggested other means for female liberation.

*** *Clarke, Mary Stetson* BLOOMERS AND BALLOTS: ELIZABETH CADY STANTON AND WOMEN'S RIGHTS Viking, 1972. (grade 6 and up)

Despite the somewhat frivolous title, this is a really superb, well-written, well-researched, accurate biography of Elizabeth Cady Stanton. The feminist movement is explained well, and Stanton's role in it clearly credited and defined.

*** *Csida, June Bundy* THE 19TH CENTURY RENAISSANCE WOMAN: ELIZABETH CADY STANTON Illus. Women's Heritage Series, 1971. (grade 9 and up)

Excellent though very brief booklet is an account of the role Elizabeth Cady Stanton played in the women's rights movement. Not by any means an in-depth picture of her personal life, it is nonetheless a very fine treatment of her work.

*** *Oakley, Mary Ann B.* ELIZABETH CADY STANTON Feminist Pr., 1972. (grade 9 and up)

Exceptionally fine, feminist biography of the great women's rights leader is an in-depth, well-researched, documented, and dramatic study of a brilliant, courageous, and determined woman. We see Elizabeth Cady Stanton as a human being blessed with unusual gifts and the willingness to use them, competently combining motherhood with her reform work.

*** *Salsine, Barbara* ELIZABETH STANTON: A LEADER OF THE WOMAN'S SUFFRAGE MOVEMENT SamHar, 1973. (grade 7 and up)

Brief but straightforward account of the life of Elizabeth Cady Stanton is accurate, interesting, and clearly states her motives and talents as well as her achievements.

*** *Stanton, Elizabeth Cady* EIGHTY YEARS AND MORE Illus. Schocken, 1971. (reprint of 1898 edition) (grade 9 and up)

Elizabeth Cady Stanton's own autobiography, written when she was past eighty, is extremely readable and serves as the source for many of the other biographies and profiles written by others about her. This new edition has an excellent introduction which provides additional perspective on the life of the great reformer.

** *Faber, Doris* OH, LIZZIE! THE LIFE OF ELIZABETH CADY STANTON Illus. Lothrop, 1972. (grades 5-9)

Good, lively biography treats Stanton with too much levity at times, not giving enough serious attention to her achievements and disappointments.

GERTRUDE STEIN
1874–1946

Author and patron of the arts

Wealthy, American-born, Harvard-educated Gertrude Stein and her brother Leo moved to Paris in 1903 where they encouraged new modern artists. There they began their famed collection which included the works of Matisse, Cezanne, Picasso, and others. Ms. Stein, who later achieved prominence as an author, was the outstanding champion and popularizer of abstract paintings.

Her early writings, dominated by the theory of "stream of consciousness," were difficult to understand and not well received by critics or the public. Success as an author finally came to her upon the publication of *The Autobiography of Alice B. Toklas*, in which she discussed life in Paris as shared with Ms. Toklas, her friend, confidante, and critic.

When Gertrude Stein made a trip back to the United States in 1934 she was treated as a major celebrity. The apartment in Paris in which she lived most of her life attracted artists, critics, writers, and musicians from Europe and the United States. A huge, imposing woman, Stein dominated not only the room in which she presided, but the entire world of the arts as well.

*** *Greenfeld, Howard* GERTRUDE STEIN: A BIOGRAPHY Illus. with photographs. Crown, 1973. (grade 8 and up)

Excellent, nonfictionalized biography of Gertrude Stein is enhanced by photographs and captures the spirit of the woman. For readers unacquainted with the work or life of Gertrude Stein, this is a fine introduction, not only to her but also to the many talented and brilliant people with whom she associated. Her relationship with Alice Toklas is described well, with warmth and good taste.

*** *Rogers, W. G.* GERTRUDE STEIN IS GERTRUDE STEIN IS GERTRUDE STEIN: HER LIFE AND WORK Illus. with photographs. Crowell, 1973. (grade 9 and up)

Outstanding biography of Gertrude Stein combines a study of both her personal life and her literary work. Of special interest to those who are acquainted with her work, it can also inspire others to read some of it. The talented and famous people who were so closely associated with Stein are described in the book, and her long-time companion Alice B. Toklas is prominently featured. Enhanced by many photographs and prints of her art collection as well as a good bibliography by and about her, this is a truly fine book.

*** *Wilson, Ellen* THEY NAMED ME GERTRUDE STEIN Illus. Farrar, 1973. (grade 9 and up)

Very readable and extremely warm account of the life of Gertrude Stein is more a personal biography than one that describes her work. It deals most honestly with her personal life-style and is well researched, containing a fine bibliography of books about and by her.*

* *Burnett, Avis* GERTRUDE STEIN Illus. Atheneum, 1972. (grade 6 and up)

In an attempt to be comprehensive, this biography fails to bring alive either Gertrude Stein or any of the other people discussed in the book. Uninformed readers might have trouble sorting out all the famous and talented people who appear in this book.

*These first three biographies do not duplicate each other as do most juvenile biographies about the same subject. For a reader with a particular interest in Gertrude Stein, therefore, all three should be considered for their different information, anecdotes, and perspectives.

LUCY STONE
1818–1893

Feminist, abolitionist, suffragist

Lucy Stone, a leading abolitionist and suffragist, would not subordinate herself to a man, so even after her marriage to abolitionist and feminist Henry Blackwell, she retained her maiden name.

As a young child Lucy Stone was disturbed at the hours of drudgery imposed on her mother, rejected the biblical stand that men should rule over women, and was determined to go to college.

At sixteen she began teaching and by twenty-five had saved enough money to enroll in coeducational Oberlin College, a school with a strong antislavery philosophy. The first Massachusetts woman to earn a college degree, Lucy Stone soon was hired as a lecturer for abolition and also became an effective crusader for the women's movement.

With Julia Ward Howe (page 145), she organized and led the American Woman Suffrage Association and after the Civil War worked for both black and female suffrage. With her husband she founded and largely financed a weekly newspaper, *Woman's Journal*, which she later edited. Considered the major voice of the feminist movement, the paper constituted an important chapter in the long history of women's rights.

*** *Blackwell, Alice Stone* Lucy Stone: pioneer of woman's rights Little, 1930. (Now out of print, but reproduced by both Krauss Reproductions and Gale, 1972.) (grade 9 and up)

Outstanding, definitive biography of Lucy Stone written by her daughter. Immensely readable, it is full of warm details and anecdotes as well as offering a good picture of the women's movement.

*** *Stapleton, Jean* Vanguard Suffragist: lucy stone Illus. Women's Heritage Series, 1971. (grade 7 and up)

A lovely biography of Lucy Stone is extremely brief, but vividly written, dramatic, and informative.

HARRIET BEECHER STOWE
1811–1896
Author

Harriet Beecher Stowe firmly believed that the evil of slavery lay in the system and that the North was as guilty as the South. Ms. Stowe saw herself as an instrument of God and her great antislavery novel, *Uncle Tom's Cabin,* more as a religious work than a novel. Its enormous success made her wealthy and famous, for it was translated into thirty languages, dramatized, and became a universal best seller. The moving story personalized slavery and stirred many people to action who had, until then, remained neutral.

Before the book's publication, Ms. Stowe cared for her large family and helped support them by writing for magazines and newspapers. Despite the enormous responsibility and interruptions of home and children, she became one of the most prolific writers of all time. She published more than thirty books and numerous essays and children's stories, many of which won critical acclaim.

*** *Rouverol, Jean* HARRIET BEECHER STOWE: WOMAN CRUSADER Illus. Putnam, 1968. (grades 3-6)
    Excellent account of the life of the great author is extremely simple, but clear in its explanations of her life and her achievements. Although readers of this book could not yet comprehend *Uncle Tom's Cabin,* the author has managed to make Ms. Stowe a meaningful subject.

* *Widdener, Mabel C.* HARRIET BEECHER STOWE: CONNECTICUT GIRL Illus. Bobbs–Merrill, 1949. (grades 3-7)

The emphasis on childhood in this biography is overfictionalized, only reasonably accurate, and not very interesting. Harriet Beecher Stowe's later writings and success as an author, as well as her influence on the nation's consciousness, receive only brief, superficial treatment.

ROSEMARY SUTCLIFF
1920–

Author of children's books

Almost each year for the last twenty has brought forth the publication of another one of Rosemary Sutcliff's widely praised books for children. Her historical novels are carefully researched, and her retelling of old legends and ballads is particularly appealing to the young.

Rosemary Sutcliff's father was a naval officer and she travelled quite a bit as a child, but an arthritic condition which has plagued her since childhood necessitated her being educated at home, a task her mother undertook. At one time Ms. Sutcliff considered becoming an artist but turned instead to writing. Among her books which have been most popular are *The Lantern Bearers, The Outcast, The Shield Ring, Warrior Scarlet,* and *Knights Fee.*

** *Meek, Margaret* ROSEMARY SUTCLIFF Walck, 1962. (grade 10 and up)

Good biography of the popular author emphasizes her professional career rather than her personal life, and is probably of interest mostly to librarians and others who work with children's literature.

BERTHA von SUTTNER
1843–1914

Austrian peace advocate, winner of Nobel Peace Prize

Baroness Bertha von Suttner, Austrian lecturer, organizer, and writer on peace, was a close friend of Alfred Nobel, the inventor of dynamite. She strengthened his interest in peace and is believed to have influenced him to establish the Nobel Peace Prize.

Her novel, *Die Waffen Nieder (Lay Down Your Arms)*, was a powerful plea for peace, and it met with great success. It was translated into more than a dozen languages and became known as one of the most important "novels of purpose" of all time.

As Bertha von Suttner's interest and involvement in the peace movement grew she wrote for peace magazines, founded the Austrian Peace Society, and worked tirelessly for the cause of peace. She was the only woman among ninety-six delegates from twenty-six countries at the 1899 Peace Conference at The Hague, and although the results of this conference were considerable, they did not go far enough to satisfy the firm believer in peace.

To further her beliefs that governments should employ arbitration before rather than after the use of force and should put an end to all fighting, she wrote and lectured extensively. In 1905 her efforts were rewarded when she was awarded the Nobel Peace Prize. She continued her work almost until her death, travelling throughout the world to lecture, reaping honors from other peace lovers and abuse from the militaristic.

*** *Lengyel, Emil* AND ALL HER PATHS WERE PEACE: THE LIFE OF BERTHA VON SUTTNER Nelson, n.d. (grade 8 and up)

Extremely well written, nonfictionalized biography of the highly gifted and influential Nobel Peace Prize winner is both interesting and inspirational. The author places equal emphasis on the subject's personal life and her work, achieving a fine balance.

HENRIETTA SZOLD
1860–1945
Founder of Hadassah, Zionist leader, educator

Henrietta Szold, the founder of Hadassah, a women's Zionist organization, was born in Baltimore, Maryland. The first of eight daughters of a rabbi, she received the education usually reserved for a Jewish firstborn son, and she became fluent in German, French, and Hebrew. She taught high school and religious school, and organized the first night school in the United States where adult immigrants could learn America's history, customs, and language. Henrietta Szold also contributed articles to Jewish periodicals, translated and edited Jewish literature into English, and was editor of the American Jewish Year Book.

A visit to Palestine in 1910 strengthened her growing interest in Zionism, a cause to which she devoted the remainder of her life. She founded Hadassah and became the first director of Youth Aliyah, which began bringing Jewish youngsters from Germany into Palestine during the 1930s.

The recipient of many honors, she was the first woman to receive the honorary degree of Doctor of Hebrew Letters, conferred on her by the Jewish Institute of Religion, and was known as the "Mother of the Yishuv," the Jewish settlement in Palestine.

* *Cone, Molly* HURRY HENRIETTA Illus. Houghton Mifflin, 1966. (grades 5-8)

Disappointing, highly fictionalized account of the early life of Henrietta Szold places too much emphasis on personal details of her family and too little on her accomplishments. In a brief postscript the author admits she has not really written a biography, merely a story.

SHIZUYE TAKASHIMA

1928–

Artist and author

Like many Americans of Japanese descent, Canadian-born Shizuye Takashima was interned during World War II. She looks back at the four years she spent in a prison camp for Japanese-Canadians with sadness rather than bitterness and hatred.

After the war she studied at the Ontario College of Art and has since become a successful painter. Her work has been exhibited in galleries in the United States and Canada, and she has won several honors and awards.

Her personal memoirs, *A Child in Prison Camp,* won her

the award for the best illustrated book in Canada. It has been translated into Japanese, and both film and radio adaptations are planned.

** *Takashima, Shizuye* A CHILD IN PRISON CAMP Illus. Morrow, 1974. (grade 5 and up)
In a touching personal memoir, the Japanese-Canadian artist describes her life as a child in an internment camp during World War II. Simply written in the present tense, it has a dignified, distinguished style that extends its appeal to older readers as well as young ones. The beautiful full-color illustrations by the artist are an important component to the book.

MARIA TALLCHIEF
1925–

Prima ballerina

The daughter of an Osage Indian father and Scotch-Irish-Dutch mother, Maria Tallchief is a true American. She began studying ballet at age four and at eighteen made her New York debut in a leading role. Here she worked under the brilliant, famed choreographer George Balanchine, who created several ballets for her. One of her most notable roles was the sugar plum fairy in *The Nutcracker*.

Although she grew up without any particular Indian consciousness or culture, Maria Tallchief says she is proud of her Indian heritage and when the Osage Tribal Council held ceremonies in her honor, she was declared a princess.

*** *Gridley, Marion E.* MARIA TALLCHIEF: THE STORY OF AN AMERICAN INDIAN Dillon, 1973. (grades 5-9)

Especially fine biography of the prima ballerina chronicles her childhood, youth, career, and activities since retirement in a warm, fast-moving text. The author shares her wide knowledge of Indian life with the reader by first telling the history of the Osages, and then moving on to the life of Maria Tallchief.

** *DeLeeuw, Adele* MARIA TALLCHIEF: AMERICAN BALLERINA Illus. Garrard, 1971. (grades 4-7)

Lively biography chronicles Maria Tallchief's career and describes her retirement from dancing as an intelligent, considered decision. Of particular interest to would-be dancers, this is a good career-oriented biography.

†† *Tobias, Tobi* MARIA TALLCHIEF Illus. Crowell, 1970. (grades 2-5)

This brief biography, while lively and colorful, is extremely sexist. Clearly implied is that a career and home life are incompatible and that society values a homemaker more than a career woman.

IDA TARBELL
1857–1944

Journalist, historian, muckraker, and lecturer

Ida Tarbell's early interest in the women's rights movement led her to see education as a means to achieve freedom. After graduating from college she went to Paris to study the role of women in the French Revolution, and while there began her career as a journalist and historian, contributing to prominent American periodicals.

In 1904, after two years of extensive research, Ida Tarbell published *The History of the Standard Oil Company*, which revealed the unscrupulous methods the Rockefeller-owned company used to force smaller rival companies out of business. Her exposé resulted in lawsuits, new antitrust laws, and the landmark United States Supreme Court decision that forced Standard Oil to break up into smaller, separate companies. For this pioneer muckraking work, she won national acclaim and the nickname "terror of the trusts."

Throughout her long career, Ida Tarbell published and edited a national magazine, researched and wrote extensively on Lincoln, wrote biographies of business leaders, lectured, served on advisory committees to the government, taught at many colleges, and, at eighty-two, published her autobiography.

*** *Fleming, Alice* IDA TARBELL: FIRST OF THE MUCKRAKERS Crowell, 1971. (grades 5-8)

Very fine, intelligent biography of Ida Tarbell discusses her personal life as well as her crusading efforts and exposé of the trusts. Warm, dramatic, and vigorous, this book captures the many dimensions of Ms. Tarbell.

** *Conn, Frances G.* IDA TARBELL, MUCKRAKER Nelson, 1972. (grades 4-7)

Good biography of Ms. Tarbell clearly indicates her ability, intelligence, and accomplishments, but lacks excitement and color.

SUSIE KING TAYLOR
1848–1912

Teacher, nurse

Her grandmother taught her to read, even though it was illegal, and when she was only fourteen, slave Susie King Taylor escaped to freedom. She married a liberated slave, and when he joined the Union's First South Carolina Volunteers she became the regimental laundress. She also served as nurse and teacher to these first black soldiers and, after the war, taught at a freedmen's school in Savannah. Later, when she moved north, she became a founder of the Boston branch of the Women's Relief Auxiliary of the GAR (Grand Army of the Republic) and served as the president of the group that aided veterans of the war and their dependents.

*** *Booker, Simeon* SUSIE KING TAYLOR, CIVIL WAR NURSE McGraw, 1969. (grades 4-9)

    Based on her own diary, this biography gives a fine picture of the intrepid young woman who was laundress, teacher, and nurse to a group of black Union soldiers. Simply written, it is directed to older reluctant readers as well as enthusiastic younger ones. The author does a good job of combining history and biography.

SAINT TERESA OF AVILA
1515–1582

Spanish-born Saint Teresa joined the Carmelite Order at a time when discipline had been greatly relaxed. Wishing to change this, she spent her last years founding convents which restored the former discipline and observance.

Teresa was a great mystical writer and her autobiography and letters, marked by forthrightness, realism, humor, and kindliness, have resulted in her being among the most appreciated women of religion. Although not officially so designated, she is popularly known by the title "doctor of the church." She was canonized in 1622.

* *Discalced Carmelite Nuns of Buffalo* A DAUGHTER OF THE
    CHURCH: LIFE OF THE GREAT SAINT TERESA OF AVILA Illus.
    Daughters of St. Paul, 1964. (grades 3-5)
    Simply written, delicately illustrated life story of Teresa captures her essence. Written from a strong religious perspective, it is probably limited in its appeal and interest.

VALENTINA TERESHKOVA
1937–

Soviet cosmonaut, first woman in space

History was made on June 16, 1963, when a former Soviet amateur parachutist, Valentina Tereshkova, became the first woman in space. Her spaceship Vostok V1 returned to earth after 48 orbits and 1.2 million miles in 70 hours, 50 minutes.

After Soviet Cosmonaut Yuri Gagarin became the first man to orbit the earth, Ms. Tereshkova, an active member of Jomsomol (Young Communist League), wrote to the authorities volunteering herself as a cosmonaut. She was accepted, but only after proving that her physical endurance and stamina matched that of the male cosmonauts.

In preparation for her historical flight she underwent arduous technical and physical training.

After her return to earth Premier Khrushchev commented upon the West's "bourgeois" notion that woman is the weaker sex, reminding the world that Tereshkova was in flight longer than all four American astronauts combined.

Valentina Tereshkova received her country's greatest honor when she was named a hero of the Soviet Union. She has also received the Order of Lenin and the Gold Star Medal, as well as honors and tributes from other nations.

She continued her training and now is an aerospace engineer in the Soviet space program. She is married to a fellow cosmonaut and they have a young daughter.

** *Sharpe, Mitchell* "IT IS I, SEA GULL": VALENTINA TERESHKOVA, FIRST WOMAN IN SPACE Illus. with photographs. Crowell, 1974. (grade 7 and up)
    A good account of the life of the Soviet cosmonaut is mostly scientific, space-oriented in its focus, but occasionally shifts to the romantic. Sometimes self-conscious in its feminist perspective, it succeeds best when it is a straightforward narrative, emphasizing the scientific aspects of her work. Although it may appeal to the general reader, it will probably be of special interest to those eager to learn more about space.

ELLEN TERRY
1848–1928

British actress

At age nine Ellen Terry, the child of successful British touring actors, made her theatrical debut. She became one of England's greatest performers, and continued to perform almost until her death. She was married a few times, but was greatly devoted to two children she had with a man to whom she was not married.

Both a comic and tragic performer, Ellen Terry scored one of her greatest triumphs as Portia in Shakespeare's *Twelfth Night*. She also appeared in plays of George Bernard Shaw, with whom she maintained a lengthy correspondence. For twenty-five years she was a leading lady to the famed Sir Henry Irving, touring with their successful company in England, the United States, and Canada.

In her later years Ms. Terry lectured and gave readings in England, the United States, and Australia on the works of Shakespeare. In 1925 she received the Grand Cross of the Order of the British Empire.

** *Fecher, Constance* BRIGHT STAR: A PORTRAIT OF ELLEN TERRY
Illus. Farrar, 1970. (grade 7 and up)
    Extremely well written story of the actress discusses her personal life as well as the roles she played. The great actor Sir Henry Irving plays a prominent role in the book, as he did in her professional life, affording the reader an interesting perspective on nineteenth-century British theater.

TITUBA
c.1692–?

Slave, suspected witch

Tituba grew up as a slave in the West Indies where the practices of herbal medicine, card reading, and spells and magic were common. She was forced to come as a slave to the cold bleak New England village of Salem during a period in which its citizens were accusing women of witch-craft. Tituba's native customs naturally made her an early suspect.

When brought to trial she pleaded guilty, for this was her only chance to avoid death by hanging, drowning, or burning. Her tales of the witchcraft she and others "practiced" surpassed even the wildest imaginations of the citizens of Salem.

Eventually Tituba was released, but still she remained a slave. She was sold for her jail fees to a weaver who then purchased her husband. Tituba lived long enough to see the hysteria surrounding the Salem witch trials come to an end.

*** Petry, Ann TITUBA OF SALEM VILLAGE Crowell, 1964. (grade 5 and up)

Beautifully written, dramatic, and highly fictionalized story of Tituba is based on thorough research, but reads more like a story than a biography. The character of Tituba—independent, bright, and resourceful—emerges distinctly and colorfully, and the reader is swept along by events. This is a book that lends itself beautifully to reading aloud to family or classroom—the author has employed outstanding literary skill. *Tituba* is as suitable for adults as it is for elementary school children.

SOJOURNER TRUTH
c.1797–1883

Abolitionist, reformer, feminist, preacher

"Sojourner Truth," as Isabella Baumfree was known, was born a slave in New York, survived the cruelties of several owners, saw all her brothers and sisters and children sold and separated, but won a legal case against her son being sold south.

After obtaining her freedom she worked as a domestic. Mystical visions told her to become a preacher. Though illiterate, she knew the Bible well, and her powerful stirring voice and manner attracted listeners in churches, highways, and streets. In her travels she crossed paths with abolitionist and women's rights leaders, and in embracing these causes became the first black woman to give antislave and feminist lectures in America.

During the Civil War Sojourner Truth raised funds for black volunteer regiments, was received in the White House by President Lincoln, and after emancipation worked with freed blacks and in hospitals. At her urging many blacks migrated west.

Her speech at a women's rights convention has been recorded as one of the most stirring polemics for equal rights, and she is remembered today as the symbol of the oppression of black women.

*** *Ortiz, Victoria* Sojourner Truth: a self-made woman Illus. with old prints and photographs. Lippincott, 1974. (grade 6 and up)

Well-researched and based on facts as far as they are presently known, this very fine, warm, and human biography combines a carefully drawn portrait of Sojourner Truth with a good description of the feminist and abolitionist movement. The split that often existed between the two groups is discussed here, and Sojourner Truth's role in both is clearly established.

*** *Pauli, Hertha* Her Name Was Sojourner Truth Avon, 1971. (grade 7 and up)

Unusually fine, thoroughly researched, stirring account of

the life of Sojourner Truth also gives a good picture of the times. Author draws parallels between her life and the current civil rights movement, adding to the interest and value of the book.

*** *Peterson, Helen* SOJOURNER TRUTH: FEARLESS CRUSADER Illus. Garrard, 1972. (grades 3-6)
 Brief, simple but nonetheless superb and dramatic account of Sojourner Truth explains the principles by which she lived, and clearly shows the unusual determination and courage she demonstrated, as well as the inherent evils of slavery.

HARRIET TUBMAN
1820–1913

Fugitive slave, rescuer of slaves, Civil War spy and nurse

Known as the "Moses" of her people, fugitive slave Harriet Tubman, in the ten years preceding the Civil War, courageously and cleverly delivered three hundred southern slaves to freedom in the North. She herself was born a slave, worked as a field hand while still a child, and at thirteen was struck over the head by an overseer with a two-pound weight, the effects from which she never fully recovered.

Harriet Tubman worked closely with the Underground Railroad and spoke at many abolitionist meetings. After escaping from Maryland to Philadelphia she returned to guide safely all the members of her family to freedom, and then became so successful a "conductor" that she boasted that in her nineteen trips she "never lost a passenger." At one time rewards for her capture were as high as $40,000.

During the Civil War she was a cook and nurse and the

only black woman to serve as a Union scout and spy. After emancipation she worked at a freedmen's hospital, established a home for poor aged blacks, and, though illiterate herself, worked to establish southern black schools. Harriet Tubman was a firm supporter of the suffrage movement, and also helped to establish the African Methodist Episcopal Church in New York state.

*** *Conrad, Earl* HARRIET TUBMAN: NEGRO SOLDIER AND ABOLITIONIST International Publishers, 1942. (grade 9 and up)
Brief, extremely good, straightforward account is well researched, accurate, and informative. Nonfictionalized, it is moving and dramatic.

*** *Epstein, Sam and Beryl* HARRIET TUBMAN: GUIDE TO FREEDOM Illus. Garrard, 1968. (grades 3-6)
Simple early reader, or read aloud book, is a stirring account of the rescuer of Tubman's people. Vivid and colorful, this is a story of the times as well as of the life of Harriet Tubman.

*** *Lawrence, Jacob* HARRIET AND THE PROMISED LAND Illus. Simon & Schuster, 1968. (preschool and up)
Beautifully written and illustrated picture book offers an unsentimental but immensely dramatic picture of Harriet Tubman and her successful efforts on behalf of other slaves.

*** *McGovern, Ann* RUNAWAY SLAVE: THE STORY OF HARRIET TUBMAN Four Winds, 1965. (grades 2-4)
Excellent biography of Harriet Tubman gives an intimate, colorful, and compelling picture of her goals, activities, and accomplishments.

*** *Petry, Ann* HARRIET TUBMAN: CONDUCTOR ON THE UNDERGROUND RAILWAY Crowell, 1955. (grade 7 and up)
Truly superb study is an outstanding example of biography. Written with realism and warmth, it gives a dramatic picture of a remarkable woman.

*** *Sterling, Dorothy* FREEDOM TRAIN Illus. Doubleday, 1954. (grade 6 and up)

Exciting, fast-moving account of Harriet Tubman's activities is competently told. Perceptive and intimate, it offers a warm picture of her life.

** *Grant, Matthew G.* HARRIET TUBMAN Illus. Creative Educ. Soc., 1974. (grades 3-5)

Graphically illustrated, this simple biography lacks the fire and spirit displayed by the subject. Older reluctant readers will find it attractive and easygoing, without being too immature in approach.

** *Humphreville, Frances* HARRIET TUBMAN: FLAME OF FREEDOM Houghton Mifflin, 1966. (grades 4-6)

Satisfactory biography lacks literary distinction but gives a good, highly fictionalized account of Harriet Tubman's life. Author focusses on Tubman's childhood, but also gives a good summary of her adult activities.

** *Winders, Gertrude* HARRIET TUBMAN: FREEDOM GIRL Bobbs–Merrill, 1969. (grades 3-7)

Despite concentration on her childhood and youth, a good biography of Harriet Tubman. The author vividly describes family slave life, and Ms. Tubman's personality from childhood emerges consistently independent and resourceful. A small part of the book describes her adult life competently and dramatically.

* *Swift, Hildegarde* RAILROAD TO FREEDOM Illus. Harcourt, 1932. (grade 9 and up)

Highly fictionalized account of the Underground Railroad tells much of Harriet Tubman's part in it. Attitudes towards women in general are somewhat sexist, and excessive use of southern black dialect detracts from the book's impact. Nonetheless, this is a satisfactory survey of the movement and Harriet Tubman's part therein.

ELIZABETH VAN LEW
1818–1900
Southern spy for the Union

Socially prominent Elizabeth Van Lew was known in Richmond, Virginia, to be an abolitionist even before the Civil War. She and her wealthy mother had freed not only their own slaves, but purchased other slaves and freed them too. She openly supported the Union during the Civil War, bringing supplies to federal officers who were imprisoned in the South. She helped many escape, and obtained vital military information for transmission to the North.

Because of her high social position, Ms. Van Lew was able to engage in her espionage activities with little interference, and when the Union Army reached Richmond she maintained five relay stations between the city and their headquarters. So as not to arouse suspicion, she affected a peculiar dress and behavior, earning the name "Crazy Bet."

After the war Elizabeth Van Lew, who had spent her fortune on war activities, was appointed postmistress of Richmond by President Grant. Despite the hostility of her neighbors and the scorn of Richmond society, she carried on her duties admirably. During her last years she fought for women's rights, protesting against taxation without representation.

*** *Nolan, Jeannette C.* YANKEE SPY: ELIZABETH VAN LEW
    Messner, 1970. (grade 7 and up)
    Very good, convincingly fictionalized account of the espionage activities of Elizabeth Van Lew shows her as a woman unwilling to compromise her beliefs for the sake of society's acceptance. Fast-moving and dramatic, it also offers a good picture of the Civil War period and life in the South.

PABLITA VELARDE
1918–

Artist

In the Indian school near Santa Fe, New Mexico, Pablita
Velarde was first introduced to various art forms and was
encouraged to express herself within the traditions and culture of her native Pueblo Indians. Somewhat defiant of
society, Pablita Velarde decided to become a painter even
though, in her pueblo, painting was considered men's work.
Instead of marrying like her sisters when she completed
school, she took various jobs, many of which consisted of
routine decorative painting. She did, however, sell many of
her paintings which, like her life, are a mixture of Indian
and non-Indian culture. In her desire to portray Indian life
she reproduced many scenes and subjects and also wrote
down many of the old Indian tales with which she had become familiar as a child, illustrated them, and published
them in book form.

Ms. Velarde has won many awards and is now a very
successful painter, as is her daughter, Helen Hardin.

*** *Nelson, Mary Carroll* PABLITA VELARDE Dillon, 1971.
(grade 5 and up)

Extremely fine account of the life of the Indian artist discusses in depth the culture from which she sprung, as well as
her private and professional life. Immensely readable, this
book is very appropriate for older reluctant readers as well as
elementary and junior high readers.

QUEEN VICTORIA
1819–1901

Queen of England, 1837–1901

Victoria, who was to become queen of England during one of its most glorious periods, spent a most unhappy and lonely childhood. Her father died before she was one year old and she and her mother lived in seclusion and relative poverty. She succeeded to the British throne shortly after her eighteenth birthday and was delighted to gain quickly the love of her subjects. Her happiness grew during her courtship and marriage to her intelligent and handsome cousin, Prince Albert.

The queen relied heavily on Albert's recommendations concerning Parliamentary affairs, and although she personally opposed many reform proposals, she followed Albert's advice and publicly supported the government in most of its endeavors. Victoria took her position as head of the army seriously; during the Crimean War she established England's highest war decoration, the Victoria Cross, and later the Regiment of the Royal Irish Guards.

After her beloved Albert's death in 1861, Victoria stepped out of public life. Finally, as her popularity declined, she became a more active regent and regained the public's esteem. In 1874 Parliament bestowed the title of empress of India upon Victoria in recognition of her strong support of the imperialist policy. In 1887 her fiftieth year as queen was celebrated by an elegant jubilee. The pageantry was repeated ten years later when delegates from throughout the world came to London to honor Queen Victoria.

When Victoria died in 1901 after reigning sixty-four

years (the longest reign in English history), she left thirty-one grandchildren and thirty-seven great grandchildren, many of whom were crowned rulers of Europe.

** *Glendinning, Sally* QUEEN VICTORIA: ENGLISH EMPRESS Illus. Garrard, 1970. (grades 4-8)
    Well-done, interesting, though brief and simple biography of Queen Victoria offers a good picture of her life and times. Vivid and colorful writing brings the subject to life with warmth and style.

** *Grant, Neil* VICTORIA: QUEEN AND EMPRESS Illus. Watts, 1970. (grade 7 and up)
    Good, though somewhat textbookish portrait of Queen Victoria is especially useful as an aid to social studies, for it describes her life against the historical period in which she lived. Depicting her strengths and weaknesses, it offers a well-rounded study of her as an individual, too.

** *Haycraft, Molly Costain* QUEEN VICTORIA Messner, 1956. (grades 6-10)
    Author paints a vivid picture of Queen Victoria, showing her as a real living woman in this warm, personal biography. Emphasis is on her as an individual, rather than on the period in which she reigned.

LILLIAN WALD
1867–1940

Public health nurse, social worker, and reformer

After graduating from the New York Hospital training school for nurses, Lillian Wald went to medical school, but while teaching health and nursing care to tenement dwellers in New York's Lower East Side decided to give up medicine in order to devote her energies to public health nursing. She obtained financial backing from wealthy Jewish philanthropists to set up a program which she later developed into the Visiting Nurse Service and the Henry Street Settlement House, a neighborhood center for civic, education, and social work.

Lillian Wald was instrumental in creating the first public school nursing program in the nation, worked for legislation to end child labor, was active in the peace movement, mobilized nurses for emergencies during World War I, worked for political candidates, supported women's suffrage, wrote two autobiographies, and was an enormously successful fundraiser. Her importance in the field of social work was great, but it is for her contributions to the profession of public health nursing that she is best remembered.

*** *Block, Irvin* NEIGHBOR TO THE WORLD: THE STORY OF LILLIAN WALD Crowell, 1969. (grades 5-9)
   Outstanding straightforward account of the life of Lillian Wald depicts her as a woman who devoted her life to helping the poor of New York's Lower East Side, and having a profound effect on many other social issues of her day. Warm, dramatic, and stirringly told.

*** *Williams, Beryl, and Epstein, Samuel* LILLIAN WALD: ANGEL OF HENRY STREET Messner, 1948. (grade 6 and up)
   Very fine, convincingly fictionalized biography of Lillian Wald moves along at a dramatic pace and offers insights into the woman whose entire life was one of service to others, and whose abilities were used to obtain many needed reforms.

MARY EDWARDS WALKER, M.D.
1832–1919
Civil War physician, dress reformer

During the Civil War Mary Edwards Walker, who had long practiced medicine, worked as an unpaid volunteer in hospitals, helped organize the Women's Relief Association, and was appointed a Union Army surgeon. She was captured and imprisoned for several months and later served as a supervisor of a hospital for women prisoners and headed an orphanage. Dr. Walker was awarded the Congressional Medal of Honor for Meritorious Service, but later suffered the indignity of having it withdrawn.

After the war she lectured in the United States and abroad, became involved in the women's rights movement, published pamphlets and books, and was elected president of the National Dress Reform Association. Dr. Walker, who had opposed women's confining attire, adopted the bloomer outfit. During the war she wore the same uniform as male officers; later she dressed exclusively in male clothing.

Dr. Walker was a Civil War celebrity who later lost much of her influence. She was attacked for the tactlessness and eccentricities which alienated her not only from the suffragists she supported, but also from her relatives and friends.

†† *Hall, Marjory* QUITE CONTRARY: DR. MARY EDWARDS WALKER
Funk & Wagnalls, 1970. (grades 7-11)
Highly fictionalized yet somewhat accurate account of Mary Walker is a critical, negative account of her controversial life. Not a particularly sympathetic view, the book clearly

brings to light her various idiosyncrasies. In fact, the reader may question why the author chose to write a biography of Dr. Walker, since she seems so unenthused about her subject and writes such an unbalanced account.

NANCY WARD
1738–1822

Cherokee leader, peace advocate

Nancy Ward long held the most honored office in the Cherokee nation, that of "Beloved Woman." She first earned it as a teenager when she replaced her husband as war chief, after he was killed in battle. She retained her influential role with her people until the end of her long life.

During the Revolutionary War, Nancy Ward worked for peace by discouraging Cherokee involvement with either side. By warning Americans of impending raids she often saved lives on both sides. She helped negotiate treaties between the Cherokees and Americans, but found they were often later broken.

As owner of one of the first cattle herds in the Cherokee nation, she introduced dairying and taught her people to make butter and cheese. She also fought hard against American attempts to seize Cherokee lands. As a result of all her efforts on their behalf, and not because of her inherited position, the Cherokee people sought Nancy Ward's advice on all matters. She is sometimes called the "Pocahontas of the West;" her wisdom and leadership were acknowledged not only by the Cherokee nation, but also by surrounding white settlers and traders.

295

*** Felton, Harold NANCY WARD, CHEROKEE Illus. Dodd, 1975. (grades 4-8)

Highly fictionalized, historically accurate, beautifully written text embodies the spirit of the woman, her culture, and her work in behalf of her people. The author does not spare America guilt in the treatment of the Cherokees and shows that although the subject's influence on her people was great, she was unable to halt many of their mistakes and others' injustices. By refraining from eulogizing her, the author brings Nancy Ward to life as a warm human being.

MARTHA DANDRIDGE CUSTIS WASHINGTON
1732–1802

First Lady

Martha Washington's education in Virginia stressed domestic arts rather than academic ones. First married at eighteen, she was widowed at twenty-six and was a wealthy young mother of two when she met and was courted by George Washington, plantation owner and commander of the Virginia forces. After their marriage she took full charge of their home in Mount Vernon, managing both the household and domestic servants, and making the plantation famous for its warmth and gracious hospitality.

During the American Revolution, when her husband was the commander of the American forces, she spent winters at his headquarters, giving encouragement to him and his men.

Although her primary interests were family and friends, she capably dispatched the many social demands made upon her as the nation's first First Lady.

* *Anderson, La Vere* MARTHA WASHINGTON: FIRST LADY OF THE LAND Illus. Garrard, 1973. (grades 2-4)

Simple, brief biography focusses on Martha Washington's role as mother, wife, and gracious hostess, so that she emerges as a woman willing to assume any duties expected of her.

* *Vance, Marguerite* MARTHA, DAUGHTER OF VIRGINIA Illus. Dutton, 1947. (grade 5 and up)

Despite good literary style, a somewhat sexist biography depicts Martha Washington only in relationship to her husband, and slavery as an acceptable institution.

†† *Wagoner, Jean* MARTHA WASHINGTON: GIRL OF OLD VIRGINIA Illus. Bobbs–Merrill, 1949. (grades 3-7)

Somewhat sexist, rather insipid, and overfictionalized biography of Martha Washington concentrates on her childhood giving only a fair portrait of the society in which she lived.

ANNIE DODGE WAUNEKA
1912–

Navajo Indian leader, winner of Medal of Freedom Award

Annie Dodge Wauneka's father, a highly respected traditional Navajo Indian leader, encouraged her and other young Indians to become educated. He often depended on her for assistance in serving their people. She was particularly helpful as an interpreter and later followed in his footsteps to become a member of the Tribal Council, the first woman to hold such a position.

Her particular interest was better health and sanitation, and as head of the Health Commission she worked to eradicate tuberculosis among the Navajos, to improve maternal and child health services, and to encourage education.

In 1963 Ms. Wauneka was awarded the Medal of Freedom Award for her long crusade to improve health services. She has served as an advisor to the United States Surgeon General and is active in the Girl Scouts of America and the Head Start program. Two of her daughters have also become public health workers, following their mother and grandfather in their dedication to the Navajo nation.

*** *Nelson, Mary Carroll* ANNIE WAUNEKA Dillon, 1972. (grade 5 and up)

Highly inspirational, dramatic portrait of Annie Dodge Wauneka is also a vivid picture of the Navajo culture. Good, readable text is suitable for older less able readers as well as elementary and junior high students.

IDA WELLS-BARNETT
1862–1931

Journalist, lecturer, and reformer

Ida Wells-Barnett's parents were slaves, and she too was born to slavery. She was educated at a freedmen's school and at fourteen became the head of her family when her parents and three of their eight children died of yellow fever. To support them she became a teacher, continued her own education, and occasionally wrote articles for a local newspaper. Eventually she became half-owner of the *Memphis Free Speech.*

In 1892 three black male friends were lynched. She used her paper to attack the crime, and began investigating and publishing the facts about other lynchings. The paper was mobbed and destroyed and Ms. Wells subsequently became totally committed to a zealous crusade against lynching. She wrote, lectured, organized antilynching societies and black women's clubs, founded the first black women's suffrage society, and tirelessly worked for other civil rights. She continued this work after her marriage to a prominent black attorney and the birth of their four children.

Although Ida Wells-Barnett worked closely with white women in the feminist movement, and with Jane Addams in a successful struggle to prevent segregated schools in Chicago, she was philosophically a black militant. She did not want or trust the help of whites in black causes, and after she helped organize the National Association for the Advancement of Colored People was disappointed to find it committed to accommodation and compromise.

*** *Wells, Ida B.* CRUSADE FOR JUSTICE: THE AUTOBIOGRAPHY OF IDA B. WELLS ed. Alfreda M. Duster. Illus. Univ. of Chicago Pr., 1970. (grade 9 and up)
  Autobiography of Ida B. Wells-Barnett, edited and introduced by her daughter, is a moving dramatic story of her life and the causes she espoused. Written clearly, in a straightforward manner, it is vivid and inspiring.

EDITH WHARTON
1862–1937
Author

Edith Wharton's father taught her to read as a youngster and encouraged her love for books. At sixteen she wrote and published a volume of poetry, and much later sold some verses and stories to magazines. Her first major work, coauthored with an architect, was *The Decoration of Houses,* a defense of the classical style in interior decoration. Collections of short stories followed, and when she was forty she published her first novel, *The Valley of Decision.* Her 1905 novel *The House of Mirth* dealt with the contemporary New York social scene and received critical and popular acclaim. Other "novels of manners" included the famed *Ethan Frome* and her Pulitzer Prize winning *The Age of Innocence.*

Ms. Wharton lived most of her life in Europe where she travelled, enjoyed gardening, continued to write, and moved in literary circles. She received awards from France and Belgium for her work with refugees and the wounded during World War I. She returned to the United States in 1923 to receive an honorary degree from Yale University, and later was made a member of the National Institute of Arts and Letters and the American Academy of Arts and Letters.

** *Coolidge, Olivia* EDITH WHARTON Scribner, 1964. (grade 9 and up)

Well-written biography of the life of Edith Wharton discusses her work, the society in which she lived, and her personal relationships with other literary figures. Her life is treated somewhat superficially, but for those familiar or interested in her writing, this is a good nonfictionalized account.

PHILLIS WHEATLEY
c.1753–1784
Poet

African-born Phillis Wheatley was only seven or eight when she landed in America. The wealthy Bostonians who purchased her were so impressed with her intelligence that they taught her to speak and read English. Within a little more than a year, she had achieved the literacy level of an adult.

Young Phillis's poetry brought her to the attention of many prominent Boston citizens who invited her to their homes and requested her to write poems for specific people and occasions. When a poem she wrote to George Washington was published, the general invited her to visit his military headquarters. During a visit to England, Phillis Wheatley was entertained by nobility, and plans were made to publish a book of her poetry.

Phillis Wheatley's accomplishments helped dispel the beliefs that blacks could not benefit from education and that intelligence and talent were restricted to whites. Years after she and her young children had died in poverty, the abolitionists brought her work to the attention of the public, and today it is included in many anthologies.

*** *Fuller, Miriam* PHILLIS WHEATLEY: AMERICA'S FIRST BLACK POETESS Illus. Garrard, 1971. (grades 3-6)
Despite its brevity and simplicity, this a very fine, tender, sympathetic biography of the young poet. She emerges as a gentle, bright, and talented young woman.

*** *Graham, Shirley* STORY OF PHILLIS WHEATLEY Illus. Messner, 1949. (grades 6-10)

Convincingly fictionalized, apparently well researched biography of Phillis Wheatley is a sad story, for despite her talent and early opportunities, her life ended in poverty and early death.

* *Borland, Kathryn K., and Speicher, Helen R.* PHILLIS WHEATLEY: YOUNG COLONIAL POET Illus. Bobbs–Merrill, 1968. (grades 3-6)

Overly fictionalized but somewhat interesting account of the life of the young poet offers a view of the period and some insights into her personality and intelligence.

NARCISSA PRENTISS WHITMAN
1808–1847

Missionary

New York-born Narcissa Whitman was a religious child who dreamed of a missionary career even before she met and married physician and missionary Dr. Marcus Whitman. They accepted a commission in Oregon, and made the long and rugged trip there. She and the other woman in their party became the first white women to cross the Continental Divide.

Once in the Northwest the Whitmans established their mission among the treacherous Cayuse Indians. Narcissa Whitman taught in the school, and when Dr. Whitman had to go east managed the mission. She helped administer medical services to the Indians and settlers who came through their area, and attempted to establish peaceful relations with the Cayuse. Her only child was accidentally drowned, but over the years she cared for eleven foster children, for seven of whom she and her husband became the legal guardians.

In 1847 a measle epidemic carried by settlers from the East hit the community. Because the Indians had no immunity to the disease it had a devastating effect on them. While white children responded to medical care, the Indians did not, and great numbers of the children died. The Indians attributed this to witchcraft and retaliated in a raid, killing Marcus and Narcissa Whitman and fourteen others.

*** *Eaton, Jeannette* NARCISSA WHITMAN: PIONEER OF OREGON Illus. Harcourt, 1941. (grade 7 and up)

Very fine, fictionalized account of the life of Narcissa Whitman shows her as a true pioneer, a woman of remarkable intelligence, courage, and warmth. Absorbing and dramatic, it is history as well as biography.

** *Place, Marian T.* MARCUS AND NARCISSA WHITMAN, OREGON PIONEERS Illus. Garrard, 1967. (grades 2-5)

Very good, well-told account of the lives of the Whitmans is more his story, for her role is somewhat minimized. Exciting and dramatic, this is a touching and vivid story which depicts them both as dedicated, perseverant human beings.

** *Cranston, Paul* TO HEAVEN ON HORSEBACK: THE ROMANTIC STORY OF NARCISSA WHITMAN Messner, 1952. (grade 7 and up)

A beautiful love story which depicts Narcissa Whitman as a woman who went west more from duty and love for her husband than from any inner drive or motivation of her own.

* *Warner, Ann S.* NARCISSA WHITMAN: PIONEER GIRL Illus. Bobbs–Merrill, 1953. (grades 3-7)

Overly fictionalized account of the childhood of Narcissa Whitman is nevertheless fairly accurate, gives a good picture of the times, and demonstrates her early purposefulness and intelligence. Her later life is summarized in the final portion of the book.

303

KATHY WHITWORTH
1939–

Professional golfer

When professional golfer Kathy Whitworth was named woman athlete of the year in 1965 and 1966, it was hard to believe that this tall, well-built athlete had weighed two hundred pounds when she was only thirteen years old.

Young Kathy discovered golf when she was fourteen and promptly fell in love with the game. She entered her first big tournament after graduating from high school and won it. In 1959 she turned professional and after one year was ranked number twenty-six. At this time she began steadily to lose weight.

Her marvelous long drive was beginning to be matched by increased skill in her putting and chip shots. By 1962 she was winning tournament after tournament, and finished second among professional women golfers in earnings. In 1965, Ms. Whitworth won the first of six awards which are given to the woman who wins the most tournaments in a year.

Kathy Whitworth has served as president of the Ladies Professional Golf Association (LPGA), has been named LPGA Player of the Year seven times, and is the all-time big money winner of LPGA.

** *Eldred, Patricia Mulrooney* KATHY WHITWORTH Illus. Creative Educ. Soc., 1975. (grades 4-8)
Good, colorfully illustrated biography of the golfer discusses her athletic career in detail and describes her role in

fostering new interest in woman's golf which has purposefully coincided with the increase in prize money given to women players. Lacking somewhat in drama and excitement, it is nonetheless a more than adequate portrayal of Ms. Whitworth.

KATE DOUGLAS WIGGIN
1856–1923
Author and kindergarten educator

Kate Douglas Wiggin's family fostered her love for reading and books. Despite an erratic early education, she turned to writing and had some stories accepted for publication. When a school for training kindergarten teachers opened in California, she was one of the first students, and her warmth and talent with children and in the arts flourished. She headed the first free kindergarten in California and later opened a school for training other teachers.

A natural writer, Ms. Wiggin wrote a book based on her own experiences, collections of short stories, and explanations of kindergarten principles. Among her most popular books for young people were *The Birds' Christmas Carol* and *Mother Carey's Chickens*, and the classic *Rebecca of Sunnybrook Farm* which has been made into a play and a movie, and is still enjoyed by children.

*** *Mason, Miriam* YOURS WITH LOVE, KATE Illus. Houghton Mifflin, 1952. (grade 7 and up)
   Very well written, faithful account of the author and edu-

cator shows her as an active, assertive little girl grown into an active, accomplished, and very personable woman.

** *Mason, Miriam E.* KATE DOUGLAS WIGGIN: THE LITTLE SCHOOLTEACHER Illus. Bobbs–Merrill, 1957. (grades 3-7)
Good though highly fictionalized account of the life of Kate Wiggin emphasizes her childhood, but shows the personality, determinism, and assertiveness that eventually culminated in outstanding achievements.

LAURA INGALLS WILDER
1867–1957
Author of children's books

Laura Wilder's career as author of the beloved Little House series of children's books began in 1932 when she was sixty-five. She had published several farming articles before beginning the semiautobiographical series on American pioneer life. The books were enormously popular with young readers and literary critics alike. Included in the series, which was written to be on a progressively more advanced reading level, are *Little House in the Big Woods, Little House on the Prairie, On the Banks of Plum Creek, By the Shores of Silver Lake, Little Town on the Prairie, The Long Winter, These Happy Golden Years*, and *Farmer Boy*.

Laura Wilder won many awards and honors, her books were translated into twenty-six languages, a library was named after her, and the Children's Library Association established an award in her name to be given once every five years for a lasting contribution to literature for children. She was the award's first recipient.

** *Wilder, Laura* ON THE WAY HOME ed. Rose Lane. Harper, 1962. (grade 7 and up)

Interesting journal of Laura Ingalls Wilder covers the period of her journey from South Dakota to Mississippi in 1894. Her daughter Rose Wilder Lane, then seven years old, accompanied her parents and has edited this journal and added a "setting" of her own. Although not truly biography, it is a personal narrative of interest to adults working with children's literature, and those readers young and old who have never really outgrown Laura Wilder's Little House books. Although the Little House books are essentially biographical, libraries do not shelve them with biographies, and so they have not been evaluated as such here. They do, however, offer fine pictures of young Ms. Wilder from childhood to maturity, as well as vivid portraits of pioneer life.

** *Wilder, Laura Ingalls* WEST FROM HOME: LETTERS OF LAURA INGALLS WILDER, SAN FRANCISCO ed. Roger L. MacBride. Harper, 1950. (grade 6 and up)

This collection of letters which Laura wrote to her husband describes her trip from Mansfield, Missouri, to San Francisco during the 1915 Panama Pacific Exposition. Interesting and lively, the letters form an account and memoir of the trip which may loosely be termed biography. For those Wilder devotees who wish to know more about her life following her early Little House books, this is a welcome addition.

FRANCES WILLARD
1839–1898

Temperance leader, feminist

New York state-born, Wisconsin-reared Frances Willard enjoyed the same interests and outdoor games as her brothers and also wanted to share their opportunities. Her father objected to her desires for an education, but she did manage to get some schooling and a degree from a Methodist institution. It was enough to enable her to become a teacher, and she soon became a well-recognized educator and dean of women at Northwestern University.

In 1873 a group of church women who were organizing a temperance crusade asked Frances Willard to become their leader. She accepted, and thus began her life-long struggle as a leader of the movement. A founder of the national Woman's Christian Temperance Union (WCTU), she became its president and also a promoter of other causes which would advance and aid the status of women. Among these were labor, health, prison reform, peace, and women's suffrage. She set up groups abroad to fight alcohol and narcotic abuse and tried to pressure politicians. Mainly because she stressed themes of home and family, her huge following was composed mostly of basically conservative women whose only real concern was temperance. Frances Willard, however, widened their interests and was able to involve many of them in other major social issues.

*** *Mason, Miriam E.* FRANCES WILLARD: GIRL CRUSADER Illus. Bobbs–Merrill, 1961. (grades 3-7)

Despite the emphasis and focus on her childhood, this is a very fine biography of the temperance leader and reformer which gives more than satisfactory attention to her adult accomplishments, as well as a good portrait of her childhood. Ms. Willard emerges as a strong, purposeful leader in this readable and fast-moving account.

MAIA WOJCIECHOWSKA
1927–

Children's author

Maia Wojciechowska's family escaped from Poland at the start of the German invasion. They lived in various parts of France during World War II, and moved first to London and then to the United States. She and her older brother, loyal to their beloved Poland and scornful of the French who collaborated with the Nazis, spent most of their time in France committing acts of sabotage against the Nazis. Maia vowed never to speak to the Germans or the French for the duration of the war, a vow which created great difficulties in and out of school.

Today Ms. Wojciechowska is a very successful author of twelve books for young readers. *Shadow of a Bull* won the 1965 Newberry Medal; *Odyssey of Courage* is the biography of Cabeza da Vaca, the Spanish explorer.

*** *Wojciechowska, Maia* TILL THE BREAK OF DAY Harcourt, 1972. (grade 6 and up)

Very moving, dramatic autobiography shows the subject's rejection of values of her elders and of her attempt to reconcile her own conflicts and ambivalences. Of interest to adults as well as young readers because of its psychological insights and fine writing.

MARY WOLLSTONECRAFT
1759–1797
Feminist, critic, author

Mary Wollstonecraft, the author of *A Vindication of the Rights of Women*, is the earliest feminist writer. The book, like many of her other writings, is a persuasive argument for education, job opportunities, and legal rights for women. She was a journalist and critic of note and was the only woman in a London circle of intellectuals that included Thomas Paine and William Blake.

She argued that women's wasted lives were a result of men's tyranny and though *A Vindication of the Rights of Women* brought her fame, it was widely attacked by contemporary critics. Feminists a century later were greatly influenced by it and the work has long been considered a classic in the women's rights movement.

Wollstonecraft's childhood was filled with the misery of poverty and violence and an unhappy love affair when she was thirty resulted in the birth of a daughter. She later fell in love with the famed freethinker William Godwin, whom she married. At thirty-eight, Mary Wollstonecraft gave birth to another daughter and died four days later. The child grew up to become Mary Shelley (page 259), the author of *Frankenstein,* and wife of the poet Percy Bysshe Shelley.

*** *Flexner, Eleanor* MARY WOLLSTONECRAFT Coward, 1972.
  (grade 9 and up)

Outstanding, scholarly, completely feminist adult biography is highly suitable for mature teenagers. Despite being scholarly, it is an immensely readable, interesting, fast-moving, and touching account. Psychologically oriented, the author attempts successfully to explain much of the thought and behavior of the subject, evoking much sympathy for the remarkably intelligent woman who suffered so enormously and died so tragically.

DOROTHY WORDSWORTH
1771–1855

Diarist, writer of descriptive prose, critic, and poet

Although Dorothy Wordsworth was not the gifted or prolific poet her brother William Wordsworth was, she had an unsurpassed talent for describing ordinary things in a most extraordinary way. Her brother frequently relied on these descriptions to provide material for his poems.

William and Dorothy Wordsworth shared a love of nature, and she served as both his inspiration and critic. They had a life-long friendship with Samuel Taylor Coleridge, and he too made use of her phrases and descriptions in such major works as "The Rime of the Ancient Mariner" and "Christabel."

Dorothy Wordsworth did not write for the public, but kept diaries and journals which were published after her death. This work provides a guide to the dates when Wordsworth's poems were written and reveals the extent of her genius for description.

** *Manley, Seon* Dorothy and William Wordsworth: the heart of a circle of friends Illus. Vanguard, 1974. (grade 8 and up)

Beautifully written book captures the spirit and mood of the Wordsworths and their surroundings. Mostly a biography of the poet William Wordsworth, it is also the story of her life, and a portrait of their dear friend, poet Samuel Taylor Coleridge. Ms. Wordsworth is depicted as far more than her brother's inspiration but as a writer, critic, and poet herself. Some of William's poetry is appropriately woven into the text, and the book is greatly enhanced by the inclusion (in an appendix) of excerpts from Dorothy Wordsworth's journal, a few of her poems, and a selection of William's poetry.

FRANCES WRIGHT
1795–1852
Author, reformer, feminist

Frances Wright was a wealthy, brilliant, well-educated young Scotch woman who wrote a popular, enthusiastic travel memoir of her American visit. Attracted to many radical causes, she later moved to the United States where she established a commune which was intended to give slaves a chance to work, eventually earning their freedom. The experiment proved a failure and cost Ms. Wright half of her fortune as well as her popularity.

She became one of the first women to advocate publicly such social issues as birth control; free public education for all; equal rights for women; liberal divorce laws; and an end to organized religion, segregated schools, and capital punishment. She was sharply criticized for her own lifestyle, that of her close associates, and for the causes she pleaded in her lectures and in the newspaper that she published. Only her belief in free education received wide support.

Frances Wright was a freethinker and reformer who opposed marriage but eventually married. She financially supported her husband for the fifteen years of their marriage, but after their divorce, he was awarded all her property.

*** *Stiller, Richard* COMMUNE ON THE FRONTIER: STORY OF FRANCES WRIGHT Illus. Crowell, 1972. (grades 6-10)
    Very well written, stirring account is well balanced, showing Ms. Wright's weaknesses as well as strengths, her failures as well as achievements, and depicting her also as an inspirational, exciting, sympathetic human being.

►-●==0-●==●-●==●-●==●-●==0-●==0-●==0-●==●-●==0-●==0-●==0-●==●-●==0-●==0-●==0-●==0-●==●-●==●-●==●-◄

MILDRED "BABE" DIDRIKSON ZAHARIAS
1913–1956

Athlete

"Babe" Didrikson's athletic accomplishments seem not to have been exceeded by anyone, male or female. She won almost every honor and award given to athletes, including ninety-two medals for sports feats. As a teenager, she set national records in basketball and became known as a one-woman track team by setting records in several different events. She won two Olympic gold medals, and every title in amateur and professional golf.

Babe excelled in every sport she tried, including javelin

313

throwing, the hurdle race, high jump, shot put, discus throw, tennis, billiards,. diving, skating, and lacrosse. She also sewed many of her own clothes, cooked, and was an expert typist.

Even after cancer surgery, Babe Didrikson continued to win golf tournaments. When illness finally forced her to stop competing, she made personal appearances to aid cancer fund-raising and dictated her autobiography. She and her husband, wrestler George Zaharias, established a fund in her name to support cancer clinics, and also established a trophy to be awarded annually to the leading amateur woman athlete in the United States.

*** *De Grummond, Lena Y., and Delaune, Lynn D.* BABE DIDRIKSON: GIRL ATHLETE Bobbs–Merrill, 1963. (grades 3-7)

Excellent biography of Babe Didrikson emphasizes her childhood and youth, but gives a good capsule view of her adult achievements. From her earliest years she was an unusual athlete and a remarkable individual, and the authors have skillfully conveyed this, her personality, and achievements.

*** *Zaharias, Babe Didrikson* THIS LIFE I'VE LED: AN AUTOBIOGRAPHY, as told to Harry Paxton. Illus. with photographs. Barnes, 1955. (grade 7 and up)

Very fine personal narrative by the subject while she was in the terminal stages of her illness is unusually warm, colorful, and never morbid. Written for adults, it is immensely readable, and is further enlivened by numerous photographs.

Collective
Biographies

** *Abdul, Raoul* FAMOUS BLACK ENTERTAINERS OF TODAY Illus. with photographs. Dodd, 1974. (grades 6-9)

Profiles of Aretha Franklin, soul singer; Martina Arroyo, opera singer; Micki Grant, composer, lyricist, and performer; Diana Ross, singer-actress; and Cicely Tyson, actress, are, for the most part, interesting and readable. Some are written as interviews; others are narratives. Stylistically uneven, the biographies are somewhat lacking in the vitality displayed by the subjects themselves.

** *Adams, Russell L.* GREAT NEGROES, PAST AND PRESENT Illus. Afro-American, 1969. (grade 6 and up)

Attractively designed collection gives brief, informal studies of blacks in sciences, business, religion, education, literature, theater, music, and art. Arranged by historical periods and by subject, these nonfictionalized profiles are readable and informal. Useful for reference but also suitable for browsing, they have appeal to junior high and high school students, and adults. Half-page illustrations by Eugene Winslow contribute greatly to the text. Included are singers Marian Anderson and Leontyne Price; educators Mary McLeod Bethune and Mary Church Terrell; dancer Katherine Dunham; journalist-reformer Ida Wells-Barnett; sculptor Edmonia Lewis; abolitionists Sojourner Truth and Harriet Tubman; banker Maggie Lena Walker; cosmetician and businesswoman Sarah Breedlove Walker (known as Madame C. J. Walker); actress and singer Ethel Waters; slave poet Phillis Wheatley; and Pulitzer Prize winning poet Gwendolyn Brooks.

317

*** *Alexander, Rae Pace* YOUNG AND BLACK IN AMERICA Illus. Random, 1970. (grade 6 and up)

Eight black individuals describe their youth in this book. A brief overview precedes long, well-chosen excerpts from Anne Moody's *Coming of Age in Mississippi* and Daisy Bates's *Long Shadow of Little Rock*. Both selections are good representations of young black womanhood and, although the extracts stand well by themselves, they should also act as a spur to reading the complete autobiographies.

*** *Archer, Jules* FAMOUS YOUNG REBELS Messner, 1973. (grade 8 and up)

Outstanding, nonfictionalized, and brisk in-depth narratives of the lives of twelve people who rebelled against society. Objective, well-balanced, and thoroughly researched accounts of birth control advocate Margaret Sanger; feminist and suffragist Elizabeth Cady Stanton; and socialist labor reformer Elizabeth Gurley Flynn have a feminist focus and highlight the women's accomplishments at the same time depicting them as unique human beings.

** *Atkinson, Margaret F., and Hillman, May* DANCERS OF THE BALLET Illus. with photographs. Knopf, 1962. (grades 7-9)

Attractively arranged profiles of ballet dancers are preceded by an overview of the ballet field. The training of dancers, traditions and techniques of ballet, as well as the work of those who are not seen onstage are told clearly and precisely, and terms used in the ballet are explained. The profiles of the dancers give career highlights as well as information about personal lives. Though not a current book, much of it is still of interest, particularly to would-be dancers.

Included are Diana Adams, Alicia Alonso, Ruthanna Boris, Leslie Caron, Yvette Chauviré, Yvonne Chouteau, Alexandra Danilova, Elaine Fifield, Margot Fonteyn, Beryl Grey, Rosella Hightower, Renée Jeanmarie, Nora Kaye, Tanaquil LeClerq, Colette Marchand, Alicia Markova, Mary Ellen Moylan, Nina Novak, Janet Reed, Tatiana Riabouchinska, Moira Shearer, Mia Slavenska, Maria Tallchief, Marjorie Tallchief, Tamara Toumanova, Jocelyn Vollmar.

*** *Bearden, Romare, and Henderson, Harry* SIX BLACK MASTERS OF AMERICAN ART Illus. Doubleday, 1972. (grade 7 and up)

Outstanding profile of Augusta Savage is distinguished for its simple but stirring narrative which gives a vivid picture of the life of the black sculptor. Ms. Savage's work was exhibited widely, but she made her most enduring mark in the art world as the teacher and mentor of many younger artists. This profile details her early personal and later professional life, clearly stating the prejudices and the obstacles she faced because she was a black woman. Photographs of her and of her work enhance the material.

* *Benet, Laura* FAMOUS AMERICAN POETS Illus. Dodd, 1950. (grades 7-9)

Profiles of Emily Dickinson, Laura E. Richards, Mary Carolyn Davies, and Celia Thaxter are brief and rather superficial. The literary style is rather flowery and old-fashioned and, although informative, lacks sufficient appeal for today's readers.

** ——— FAMOUS NEW ENGLAND AUTHORS Illus. Dodd, 1970. (grade 7 and up)

Intelligent profiles of Harriet Beecher Stowe, Emily Dickinson, Mary Eleanor Wilkins Freeman, Amy Lowell, Edna St. Vincent Millay, Louisa May Alcott, and Sarah Orne Jewett have a textbook quality but are clearly written and most informative. For those readers who want their facts without any garnishment, this is a welcome volume.

** ——— FAMOUS POETS FOR YOUNG PEOPLE Illus. with photographs. Dodd, 1964. (grades 7-9)

Author has interwoven their poetry into these brief, lively, and thoughtful profiles of Rosemary Carr Benet, Emily Dickinson, Rachel Field, Eleanor Farjeon, Jane Taylor, Ann Taylor, Christina Rossetti, and Laura E. Richards.

** ——— FAMOUS STORY TELLERS FOR YOUNG PEOPLE Illus. with photographs. Dodd, 1968. (grades 7-9)

Objective, utilitarian, clear if sometimes dry profiles of

Frances Hodgson Burnett, Mary Mapes Dodge, Lucretia Peabody Hale, Margaret Sidney, Kate Wiggin, Edith Nesbit, Juliana Horatia Ewing, Charlotte Mary Yonge, Dinah Maria Murlock Craik, and Mary L. S. Molewsworth provide good accounts of their lives.

*** *Bennett, Lerone, Jr.* PIONEERS IN PROTEST Johnson, 1968. (grade 9 and up)
Outstanding profiles of Sojourner Truth and Harriet Tubman are included in a collective of those who pioneered in the black protest and civil rights movements. These colorful and elucidating accounts offer warm, human, and intimate views of the lives of two early fighters for black freedom.

*** *Bliven, Bruce* A MIRROR FOR GREATNESS: SIX AMERICANS McGraw, 1975. (grade 7 and up)
Vivid, compelling narrative provides a substantial portrait of abolitionist and feminist Sojourner Truth which will interest competent readers in elementary school as well as young adults.

* *Bolton, Sarah K.* FAMOUS AMERICAN AUTHORS Crowell, 1954. (grade 7 and up)
Rather ordinary collection is reprinted and partly revised from the original book written in 1905. The writing style appears uneven, the flowery phrases are unappealing to young readers, and material is too superficial for older readers. Undocumented, it nevertheless offers accurate information on the lives of Louisa May Alcott, Harriet Beecher Stowe, Edith Wharton, and Willa Cather.

** ——— LIVES OF GIRLS WHO BECAME FAMOUS Illus. Crowell, 1949. (grades 7-10)
This is a revision of a 1914 publication, which explains why the literary style and treatment are outdated. However, the readable profiles are still interesting and valuable. Included are social reformer Jane Addams; authors Louisa May Alcott, Julia Ward Howe, Harriet Beecher Stowe, and Margaret Fuller; singer Marian Anderson; feminist Susan B. Anthony; American Red Cross founder, Clara Barton; actresses Ethel Barrymore and Katharine Cornell; scientist Marie Curie;

aviator Amelia Earhart; educator Mary Lyon; painter Rosa Bonheur; poet Elizabeth Barrett Browning; handicapped humanitarian Helen Keller; nurse Elizabeth Kenny; singer Jenny Lind; cabinet member Frances Perkins; humanitarian Eleanor Roosevelt; pioneer nurse Florence Nightingale; and French author Madame de Staël.

*** *Bontemps, Arna* FAMOUS NEGRO ATHLETES Dodd, 1964. (grades 7-9)
Fast-moving, enthusiastic profile catches the spirit of champion tennis player Althea Gibson. Substantial in length, this is an appealing, warm study.

** ——— WE HAVE TOMORROW Houghton Mifflin, 1945. (grades 7-10)
Somewhat laudatory and old-fashioned in tone, the profiles of Mildred Blount, hat designer; Hazel Scott, pianist; and Beatrice Johnson Trammell, nurse, are good. Only the very early career of Scott is discussed; the profile of Blount is highly fictionalized, but satisfactory; and the sketch of Trammell is quite interesting.

*** *Boynick, David King* WOMEN WHO LED THE WAY: EIGHT PIONEERS FOR EQUAL RIGHTS Crowell, 1972. (grade 7 and up)
Originally entitled *Pioneers in Petticoats*, this new edition consists of the same thoroughly researched, lively profiles of educator Mary Lyon; feminist Susan B. Anthony; attorney Belva Ann Lockwood; feminist and minister Antoinette Brown; physician Alice Hamilton; industrial engineer Lillian Gilbreth; aviator Amelia Earhart; and department store executive Dorothy Shaver. Each woman emerges as a persistent, determined, and highly individualistic person who has made important contributions to society.

*** *Brimberg, Stanlee* BLACK STARS Illus. with photographs. Dodd, 1974. (grades 4-7)
Very fine, anecdotal, but not overly fictionalized accounts of the lives of Harriet Tubman and singer Billie Holiday bring the women to life in a realistic and very readable style.

*** *Bruner, Richard W.* BLACK POLITICIANS McKay, 1971. (grades 6-8)

Outstanding profile of Congresswoman Shirley Chisholm is simply but perceptively written, making good use of quotations from her autobiography and other published material.

*** *Buckmaster, Henrietta* WOMEN WHO SHAPED HISTORY Illus. with photographs. Macmillan, 1966. (grade 7 and up)

Interestingly detailed profiles of women whose lives were characterized by a dedication to an idea or principle and who have influenced history are included in this collection. Non-fictionalized, interesting, and accurate, the portraits are long enough to capture the personalities of the subjects, but short enough for those merely wishing reference material. A commendable selection of women, many of whom worked for equal rights for women and blacks. Included are mental health reformer Dorothea Lynde Dix; educator and abolitionist Prudence Crandall; feminist Elizabeth Cady Stanton; physician Elizabeth Blackwell; abolitionist Harriet Tubman; founder of the Christian Science church, Mary Baker Eddy.

*** *Burgess, Mary W.* CONTRIBUTIONS OF WOMEN: EDUCATION Dillon, 1975. (grades 6-10)

Fictionalized (but not overly so), comprehensive profiles cover all salient details of the lives of six prominent educators in an informal, interesting manner. The author gives a strong impression of personality as well as of the accomplishments of each woman in a style that will have appeal to older reluctant readers as well as to younger competent ones. Included are profiles of Emma Hart Willard, a pioneer in secondary education for girls; Mary Lyon, the founder of Mount Holyoke College; Martha Berry, founder of schools in the Appalachians; Patty Smith Hill, a pioneer of modern kindergartens; Florence Sabin, physician, scientist, researcher, and teacher; and Mary McLeod Bethune, black educator and founder of a college.

*** *Burnett, Constance B.* FIVE FOR FREEDOM Greenwood Pr., 1968 (repr. of 1953 ed.) (grade 9 and up)

A truly distinguished and competently researched work which traces the individual lives of Lucretia Mott, Elizabeth

322

Cady Stanton, Susan B. Anthony, and Lucy Stone, pioneers in the women's rights movement; and Carrie Chapman Catt, whose strong leadership led to the final passage of the Nineteenth Amendment. An adult, but readable and stirring account of their lives is told against the background of the fight for women's rights, and the transitions from one profile to the next are adroitly handled to show that the five women's lives were interwoven. Stylistically smooth, this book combines fine literary prose and good character insights with clearly stated facts, providing fascinating and inspiring reading for high school students.

** *Burt, Olive W.* BLACK WOMEN OF VALOR Illus. Messner, 1974. (grades 4-8)

Fictionalized profiles of social worker and humanitarian Juliette Derricotte, banker Maggie Walker, journalist Ida Wells-Barnett, and educator Septima Poinsette Clark are good, but lack drama, warmth, and vitality. Somewhat self-consciously nonsexist and nonracist, a certain spontaneity and spark appear to be missing. However, the author throws interesting light on the accomplishments of the women, and stresses the roles they played in working towards helping others and achieving success themselves.

* ——— NEGROES IN THE EARLY WEST Illus. Messner, 1969. (grades 4-7)

A short chapter on women includes an adequate study of businesswoman Mammy Pleasant and rather sketchy, superficial profiles of businesswoman Biddy Mason and pioneer Mary Fields.

*** *Butler, Hal* SPORTS HEROES WHO WOULDN'T QUIT Messner, 1973. (grade 6 and up)

Lively, warm, informal profile clearly depicts swimmer Gertrude Ederle to be a sports personality "who wouldn't quit" when the nineteen-year-old woman became the first woman and the sixth person to swim the English Channel.

* *Butwin, Miriam, and Chaffin, Lillie* AMERICA'S FIRST LADIES 1789-1865; AMERICA'S FIRST LADIES 1865-PRESENT Illus. Lerner, 1969. (reading level, grades 4-6; interest level through high school)

323

Some sexism is present in this two-volume set which focusses more on the presidents' achievements than on the personalities and accomplishments of the First Ladies. Directed to slow or reluctant readers, the profiles offer brief, undistinguished summaries of the lives of the women. Photographs and paintings of the First Ladies and their families somewhat perk up this only adequate book. Volume 1 includes Martha Washington through Mary Todd Lincoln. Volume 2 includes Eliza Johnson through Pat Nixon.

*** *Cavanah, Frances* WE CAME TO AMERICA Macrae, 1954. (grades 7-11)

Mostly personal accounts, these profiles include Anna Howard Shaw, a minister and feminist from England; Princess Ileana of Romania; Mary Antin, author from Russia; Lily Dache, hat designer from France; and Phillis Wheatley, young black poet from Africa. Other firsthand accounts by women immigrants from Ireland, Mexico, Holland, Poland, Sweden, and Switzerland are of women who are not prominent. Their stories are moving and recreate their era well. Each chapter in this fine book is excerpted from other works; complete citations are included. A brief but good introduction precedes the accounts, and suggested readings further enhance the value of the book.

*** ——— WE WANTED TO BE FREE Macrae, 1971. (grade 7 and up)

Warm, human, and moving stories by twentieth-century refugees are richly varied by national origin and by mood and tempo. Some describe conditions in their native country; others tell of the earliest experiences as refugees. Maria Trapp, Austrian singer, relates an amusing story; Helen Vlachos, Greek newspaper publisher, tells a suspenseful one. Others are touching or anecdotal, all are good. Also included are memoirs by Mary Antin, Russian-born author; Laura Fermi, Italian-born author; and Sigrid Undset, Norwegian winner of the Nobel Prize in literature.

*** *Chamberlin, Hope* A MINORITY OF MEMBERS: WOMEN IN THE U.S. CONGRESS Praeger, 1973. Illus. (grade 9 and up)

Very fine feminist, adult book which will be of interest and use to high school students for reading and research. Profiles of varying lengths focus on the political and professional careers of the women who have served in the United States Congress in an interesting, polished journalistic style that is forthright, perceptive, and lively. Included are Jeannette Rankin, Rebecca Latimer Felton, Alice M. Robertson, Winifred Mason Huck, Mae Ella Nolan, Florence P. Kahn, Mary T. Norton, Edith Nourse Rogers, Katherine Langley, Pearl Peden Oldfield, Ruth Hanna McCormick, Ruth Bryan Owen, Ruth Baker Pratt, Effiegene L. Wingo, Willa B. Eslick, Hattie W. Caraway, Virginia Ellis Jenckes, Kathryn O'Loughlin McCarthy, Marian Williams Clarke, Isabella Greenway, Caroline O'Day, Nan Wood Honeyman, Elizabeth Hawley Gasque, Rose McConnell Long, Dixie Bibb Graves, Gladys Pyle, Frances P. Bolton, Margaret Chase Smith, Jessie Sumner, Clara G. McMillan, Florence Reville Gibbs, Katherine Edgar Byron, Veronica B. Boland, Winifred C. Stanley, Willa L. Fulmer, Clare Boothe Luce, Emily Taft Douglas, Helen Gahagan Douglas, Chase Going Woodhouse, Helen Douglas Mankin, (Eliza) Jane Pratt, Vera C. Bushfield, Georgia L. Lusk, Katherine St. George, Reva Beck Bosone, Cecil M. Harden, Edna F. Kelly, Marguerite Stitt Church, Ruth Thompson, Elizabeth Kee, Vera D. Buchanan, Gracie Pfost, Leonor K. Sullivan, Eva Bowring, Hazel H. Abel, Iris F. Blitch, Edith Green, Martha W. Griffiths, Coya Knutson, Kathryn E. Granahan, Florence P. Dwyer, Catherine May, Edna Simpson, Jessica McCullough Weis, Julia Butler Hansen, Catherine D. Norrell, Louise Goff Reece, Corinne Boyd Riley, Maurine B. Neuberger, Charlotte T. Reid, Irene Bailey Baker, Patsy T. Mink, Lera M. Thomas, Margaret M. Heckler, Shirley Chisholm, Bella S. Abzug, Ella T. Grasso, Louise Day Hicks, Elizabeth B. Andrews, Elaine S. Edwards, Yvonne Brathwaite Burke, Marjorie Holt, Elizabeth Holtzman, Barbara Jordan, Patricia Schroeder.

** *Chapin, Victor* GIANTS OF THE KEYBOARD Illus. Lippincott, 1967. (grade 8 and up)

Good straightforward discussions of the lives of German pianist Clara Schumann and Venezuelan pianist Teresa Carreño are factual but somewhat dry. Of interest chiefly to readers with a knowledge of music, the biography emphasizes the subjects' professional lives, with some attention given to their contemporaries.

*** *Chittenden, Elizabeth* PROFILES IN BLACK AND WHITE: MEN AND WOMEN WHO FOUGHT AGAINST SLAVERY Illus. with photographs and engravings. Scribner, 1973. (grade 6 and up)

Anecdotal profiles are interestingly written, appealing to younger or unenthusiastic readers as well as mature, eager ones. Graphically attractive collection includes profiles of Prudence Crandall, white educator of blacks; Ann Wood, teenage slave who led others to freedom; Ellen Craft, fugitive slave and educator; Charlotte Forten, free black educator; Sarah Dickey, white educator of blacks.

*** *Chu, Daniel* AMERICA'S HALL OF FAME Four Winds, 1972. (grade 7 and up)

Concise biographies of Mary Lyon and Emma Hart Willard, pioneers in education for women, are accurate and interesting and should be a spur to further reading.

** *Churchill, Winston* HEROES OF HISTORY: A SELECTION OF CHURCHILL'S FAVORITE HISTORICAL CHARACTERS Illus. Dodd, 1968. (grade 9 and up)

Very well written profiles of Joan of Arc, Queen Elizabeth I, and Queen Victoria are adapted from Churchill's *History of the English-Speaking Peoples*. An attractive book, it provides good reading and the personalities and characters of the subjects emerge reasonably well.

* *Coates, Ruth Allison* GREAT AMERICAN NATURALISTS Illus. Lerner, 1974. (reading level, grades 4-6; interest level, grade 7 and up)

Somewhat pedestrian, but adequate profile of Rachel Carson, marine biologist and conservationist, lacks drama and warmth and tries to credit Ms. Carson with all environmental reforms, rather than just the ones for which she is responsible. However, her accomplishments are clearly stated, and the biography is fairly interesting, although the style is hampered by the demands of writing for reluctant readers.

*** *Cook, Fred J.* THE MUCKRAKERS: CRUSADING JOURNALISTS WHO CHANGED AMERICA Doubleday, 1972. (grade 9 and up)

Overall picture of early crusading journalists includes an outstanding chapter on Ida Tarbell, the woman who exposed the Standard Oil trust, which is extensive in coverage. The author painstakingly explains muckraking and gives a substantial portrait of Ms. Tarbell's pioneering contributions.

*** *Coolidge, Olivia* WOMEN'S RIGHTS: THE SUFFRAGE MOVEMENT IN AMERICA 1848-1920 Illus. with photographs and old prints. Dutton, 1966. (grade 6 and up)

Excellent feminist history of the women's suffrage movement highlights the major events in the lives of individual feminists, and clearly depicts their contributions. Included are early suffragists and feminists Susan B. Anthony, Elizabeth Cady Stanton, Lucy Stone, Lucretia Mott, and latter-day suffragists Alice Paul and Carrie Chapman Catt.

** *Cooper, Alice C., and Palmer, Charles* TWENTY MODERN AMERICANS Illus. Harcourt, 1942. (grades 6-9)

Lively, informal biographies of aviator Amelia Earhart, sculptor Malvina Hoffman, tennis champion Helen Wills, author Pearl Buck, and social worker Jane Addams are written in polished prose style. Appropriately anecdotal, yet straightforward, they are flawed only by a somewhat parochial attitude towards other nationalities, a rather widespread attitude at the time this collective was written. For example, Indians and Africans are called primitives in the profile of Malvina Hoffman; dialects are unnecessarily used in the profile of Jane Addams. However, these are minor points.

*** *Crane, Louise* Ms. AFRICA: PROFILES OF MODERN AFRICAN WOMEN Illus. Lippincott, 1973. (grade 7 and up)

Good introduction is followed by straightforward, nonfictionalized profiles of African women of achievement. Arranged by country of origin, the book includes profiles of Annie Jiagge, Court of Appeals judge from Ghana (with shorter profiles on her mother and grandmother); Angie Brooks, first African woman president of the United Nations, from Liberia; Irene Ighodaro, doctor from Sierra Leone, from Nigeria; Margaret Kenyatta, mayor of Nairobi, from Zambia;

327

Rahantavololona Andriamanjato, first African woman engineer, from Madagascar; Joyce Sikhakane and Winnie Mandela, prisoners of apartheid; Brigalia Bam, churchwoman, active in the World Council of Churches; and Miriam Makeba, singer from South Africa. This intelligent, well-written book is further enhanced by attractive photographs.

*** *Crawford, Deborah* FOUR WOMEN IN A VIOLENT TIME Crown, 1970. (grade 7 and up)

Fast-moving narrative tells the stories of four women who went to America to escape religious perscution but found they still had to fight for freedom of worship. The women are Anne Hutchinson, Mary Dyer, Lady Deborah Moody, and Penelope Stout. Their lives are not told in individual profiles but are intertwined in this very readable book.

*** *Darling, Edward* WHEN SPARKS FLY UPWARD Washburn, 1970. (grades 6-10)

In a fine introduction to this excellent collection the author states he has written profiles of people who "set out to do their own thing." Chatty profiles of Eleanor Roosevelt and Susan B. Anthony are informal but respectful, and anecdotes are used to draw parallels to other more current events which may be more familiar to young readers.

*** *Daugherty, Sonia* TEN BRAVE WOMEN Illus. Lippincott, 1953. (grades 7-9)

Excellent profiles are written from the perspective of one important date in the life of each woman. The author employs the use of flashbacks to give the reader a complete picture of each of these women: religious liberal Anne Hutchinson; feminist and First Lady Abigail Adams; First Lady Dolley Madison; pioneer and missionary Narcissa Whitman; educator Mary Lyon; mental health reformer Dorothea Dix; feminist and author Julia Ward Howe; feminist Susan B. Anthony; historian, journalist, and muckraker Ida Tarbell; humanitarian and First Lady Eleanor Roosevelt.

* *Daughters of St. Paul* 57 STORIES OF SAINTS FOR BOYS AND GIRLS Illus. Daughters of St. Paul, 1963.

Readable, fictionalized profiles of twenty-eight canonized women tend to emphasize their sacrifices and to give scant attention to their self-reliance and independence. Portrayed mostly as instruments of the Lord, the women do not emerge as full-dimensional. However, it must be realized that this is how these saints have long been portrayed in history and in authenticated sources.

*** *David, Jay, ed.* BLACK DEFIANCE: BLACK PROFILES IN COURAGE Morrow, 1972. (grade 7 and up)

Very fine profiles of Sojourner Truth, black abolitionist and feminist; Harriet Tubman, black abolitionist; and Fannie B. Williams, an organizer of women's clubs and author, are preceded by a very brief, succinct summary of their lives. The profiles themselves focus on the role of the subject in defying society and are well selected for their content and style. The treatments of Sojourner Truth and Harriet Tubman are excerpted from longer biographies; the material on Fannie B. Williams is autobiographical.

*** ——— GROWING UP BLACK Morrow, 1968. (grade 7 and up)

An outstanding, thought-provoking collection of personal narratives offers insights into various experiences of "growing up black." Selections by civil rights worker Daisy Bates, author Elizabeth Adams, and entertainer Ethel Waters are well chosen for their impact and clear picture of the psychological and physical difficulties of being a black child in America. The editor's brief introduction to each selection offers enough background to make the excerpt from the longer work understandable and more meaningful. The selections themselves are emotional and shocking, and serve as a spur to reading the complete biography.

*** ——— GROWING UP JEWISH Morrow, 1969. (grade 7 and up)

Twenty-five Jewish writers recollect incidents from their youth in a well-organized, well-chosen collection. The editor briefly introduces each selection, giving some background of the subject. The biographical narratives of Glueckel of Hamelin; Rebekah Kohut, educator and social worker; Edna Ferber, novelist; Edna Sheklow, playwright; Gertrude Berg, writer, actress, and producer; and Elsa Rosenberg, Canadian author, are all written from the perspective of the adult looking back at her Jewish childhood. The long excerpt from Anne Frank's diary was written by her when she was only fourteen and hiding from the Nazis. The general introduction and the briefer ones to each selection are informative and tie the collection together. The selections themselves are admirable and diversified, yet show some of the common links that exist among Jewish people of all nations and times.

* *David, Jay, and Crane, Elaine* LIVING BLACK IN WHITE AMERICA Morrow, 1971. (grade 8 and up)

A variety of profiles about individual blacks and their experiences in society. Interesting selections from their own adult recollections by Elizabeth Keckley, who served as confidante and dressmaker to Mary Lincoln; Mary Church Terrell, feminist, educator, and author; and Billie Holiday, singer, are included. A longer, particularly dramatic and moving excerpt from author Ellen Tarry's own autobiography, *The Third Door*, is included as well as portions of the autobiographical books by Anne Moody (*Coming of Age in Mississippi*) and Daisy Bates (*Long Shadow of Little Rock*). [Note: These last two are not the same selections included above in *Growing Up Black* by Jay David.] Each selection in this collection is preceded by a very brief, well-written capsule summary of the subject's life, particularly in relation to the profile that is included in the book.

* *Davis, Mac* ONE HUNDRED GREATEST SPORTS FEATS Illus. Grosset, 1964. (grades 6-9)

Excellent, fast-moving accounts of the lives and sports accomplishments of Gertrude Ederle, swimmer; Marion Laedwig, bowler; Sonja Henie, ice skater; Patricia McCormick, diver; "Babe" Didrikson Zaharias, all-around athlete; Fanny Blankers-Koen, track star; Wilma Rudolph, track and field star; Althea Gibson, tennis champion; Nancy Vanderheide, archer; and Stella Walsh, track star.

*** ——— ONE HUNDRED GREATEST SPORTS HEROES Illus. Grosset, 1958. (grades 6-9)

Brief profiles of swimmers Gertrude Ederle and Florence Chadwick; tennis champions Suzanne Lenglen, Maureen Connolly, and Helen Wills; all-around athlete "Babe" Didrikson Zaharias; ice skater Sonja Henie; markswoman Annie Oakley; and track star Stella Walsh are written in crisp, journalistic style and arranged in an attractive, appealing format. The illustrations are worthwhile additions to this attractive volume.

** *Davis, Mary L.* WOMEN WHO CHANGED HISTORY: FIVE FAMOUS QUEENS OF EUROPE Illus. Lerner, 1975. (grade 7 and up)

Informal, objective biographies of Eleanor of Aquitaine, queen of France and England; Queen Isabella of Spain; Queen Elizabeth I of England; Marie Antoinette of France; and Catherine the Great of Russia portray the queens as independent, intelligent women. Although not outstanding in literary style, the material is interesting and readable.

*** *Dekle, Bernard* PROFILES OF MODERN AMERICAN AUTHORS Tuttle, 1969. (grade 9 and up)

Pearl Buck is succinctly portrayed in a precise, well-written profile in this collection of twenty-nine modern American authors. Not a critical essay, but a good summary of Ms. Buck's personal life and her works, this enjoyable as well as utilitarian short profile is a good introduction to her writing.

** *Delderfield, Eric R.* KINGS AND QUEENS OF ENGLAND Illus. Stein & Day, 1972. rev. ed.

Fine reference book is enhanced by reprints of portraits, genealogical trees, and illustrations of coats and arms. Good clear profiles provide utilitarian accounts in readable form. This is a revised but similar edition to a 1966 book (Taplinger) which may still be available in libraries.

*** *Deur, Lynne* DOERS AND DREAMERS: SOCIAL REFORMERS OF THE 19TH CENTURY Illus. Lerner, 1972. (reading level, grades 4-6; interest level through high school)

Unusually fine profiles are informative and accurate yet simple enough to be understood by less able readers. Included are feminists Susan B. Anthony, Elizabeth Cady Stanton, and Lucy Stone; mental health reformer Dorothea Dix; feminist and journalist Amelia Jenks Bloomer; author and feminist Julia Ward Howe; and social reformer Jane Addams. The lively text is greatly enhanced by the inclusion of many photographs, some quite rare.

*** *Devaney, John* GREAT OLYMPIC CHAMPIONS Illus. with photographs. Putnam, 1967. (grades 5-9)
Top-notch profiles of "Babe" Didrikson Zaharias and Carol Heiss convey their championship qualities. Adding to the value of this informative, lively book is an appendix which, arranged by events, lists in chronological order all the Olympic champions, their records, and their nationalities.

*** *Dobler, Lavinia, and Toppin, Edgar A.* PIONEERS AND PATRIOTS: THE LIVES OF SIX NEGROES OF THE REVOLUTIONARY ERA Doubleday, 1965. (grades 4-8)
Good illustrations and reproductions of a page from a handwritten manuscript enhance the profile of poet Phillis Wheatley. The informally drawn portrait of the poet is sympathetic and appealing.

** *Dobrin, Arnold* VOICES OF JOY, VOICES OF FREEDOM Illus. Coward, 1972. (grade 5 and up)
Good profiles of black singers Ethel Waters, Marian Anderson, and Lena Horne are written from the perspective of how they met racial prejudice. These fairly accurate accounts are somewhat pedestrian and lack the spark that the subjects themselves displayed.

*** *Drotning, Phillip T., and Smith, Wesley W.* UP FROM THE GHETTO Cowles, 1971. (grade 7 and up)
Very fine profiles of Anna Langford, attorney; Shirley Chisholm, congresswoman from New York; and Gwendolyn Brooks, prize-winning poet, are included here. All black women, they came from humble roots and moved to the top of their professions. The authors dramatically and inspirationally make clear the routes the women took to achieving success.

*** *Epstein, Beryl and Samuel* WHO SAYS YOU CAN'T? Coward, 1969. (grade 7 and up)

Substantial, well-written chapter discusses the contributions of doctors Frances Kelsey and Helen Taussig, who were responsible for averting the tragedy that would have occurred if thalidomide (the drug that caused birth defects when taken by women during pregnancy) had been permitted to be manufactured and sold in the United States. The chapter focusses mostly on their role in this medical research, but also gives a good portrait of each woman as an individual.

*** *Epstein, Perle* INDIVIDUALS ALL Macmillan, 1972. (grade 8 and up)

Excellent accounts of the lives of Americans who defied established customs and laws. The profile of poet Emily Dickinson offers some good insights and incorporates her poetry into the text. The treatment of modern dancer Isadora Duncan is objective and gives an excellent, well-balanced portrait. A chapter about the Brook Farm commune, a nineteenth-century attempt to create an ideal, completely self-sufficient community, discusses Sophia Ripley and Margaret Fuller.

*** *Eunson, Roby* THE SOONG SISTERS Illus. with photographs. Watts, 1975. (grade 7 and up)

An unusually fine biography of three Chinese women who have helped to shape their country's history. All three women were educated in the United States and after returning to their native land married three of the most prominent men of China.

The oldest sister, Ch'ing-ling, married Dr. Sun Yat-sen, the revolutionary leader. Although she has been widowed for more than fifty years, she has remained consistently active in the revolutionary and Communist movements. Today she resides in Peking and serves as the vice premier of the People's Republic of China.

Ai-ling, the middle sister, married H. H. Kung, one of the most successful businessmen of China. She herself was a shrewd businesswoman and acquired much property in her own name. She taught at the college her husband founded and her philanthropic and war work during World War II was noteworthy.

The youngest sister, Mei-ling, became the most famous and most controversial of the three sisters. Married to President Chiang Kai-shek, she was not only a First Lady, but also an extremely important Chinese leader. Among her most important achievements during World War II were her efforts to interpret for the Western world China's position and needs. A frequent visitor to the United States, she was largely responsible for that country's strong endorsement of her husband's government, during and after World War II.

This biography moves along at a brisk pace, interestingly tracing the lives of the women, and also giving a good picture of the political history of modern China. Objective in style and tone, the author depicts both the personal and political strengths and weaknesses of each woman and her husband. The political and ideological rift between Mei-ling Chiang and Ch'ing-ling Sun is clear, and yet the reader learns of the personal loyalties that long existed among the Soong family.

** *Evans, I. O.* BENEFACTORS OF THE WORLD Illus. Warne, 1968. (grades 5-9)

An accurate portrayal of the life of Helen Keller is stylistically somewhat stiff, thus lacking a certain amount of warmth and spirit. Despite this blandness, it is well written, and readers who like facts without emotion will find it most satisfactory.

*** *Faber, Doris* PETTICOAT POLITICS: HOW AMERICAN WOMEN WON THE RIGHT TO VOTE Illus. with photographs, old prints, and cartoons. Lothrop, 1967. (grades 7-10)

Despite a flippant title, this is a serious, thoughtful narrative of the struggle for women's rights. Profiles of Susan B. Anthony, Lucy Stone, Elizabeth Cady Stanton, Lucretia Mott, Alice Paul, Carrie Chapman Catt, and the Pankhursts are given within the context of the feminist and suffragist movement. Good bibliography and appendix consisting of the text of the Declaration of Sentiments issued at the 1848 Women's Rights Convention at Seneca Falls add immeasurably to the value of this fine text.

*** *Faber, Harold and Doris* AMERICAN HEROES OF THE 20TH
CENTURY Illus. Random, 1967. (grades 5-9)
Especially attractive, readable collection of profiles is en-
hanced by numerous photographs. Lively, vivid profiles of
singer Marian Anderson; handicapped humanitarian Helen
Keller; photographer Margaret Bourke-White; aviator Amelia
Earhart; and suffragist and peace worker Carrie Chapman
Catt are included.

** *Farmer, Lydia H.* BOOK OF FAMOUS QUEENS Crowell, 1964.
(grade 7 and up)
Profiles of Neferteti, Cleopatra, Zenobia, Isabella of Spain,
Catherine de Medici, Elizabeth I, Mary Queen of Scots, Maria
Theresa, Catherine II of Russia, Marie Antoinette, Josephine,
Victoria, Tzu Hsi, Wilhelmina, Juliana, and Elizabeth II are
well balanced, readable accounts. Useful for reference or
reading, they highlight important events in the life of each
woman.

*** *Fax, Elton C.* CONTEMPORARY BLACK LEADERS Illus. with
photographs. Dodd, 1970. (grade 7 and up)
Outstanding, fast-moving narratives pay tribute to the
courageous efforts of black civil rights workers Coretta Scott
King, Fannie Lou Hamer, and Ruby Dee. The book offers insights into the character of each woman, and the superficiality often common to collections is artfully avoided.

*** ——— SEVENTEEN BLACK ARTISTS Illus. with photographs. Dodd, 1971. (grade 9 and up)
Excellent, well-rounded portraits of black artists discussing their black experiences as well as their artistic ones in a
warm, informal manner, without resorting to chattiness or
fictionalization. Women included are Elizabeth Catlett, Faith
Ringgold, Norma Morgan, and Charlotte Amévor.

*** *Feurlicht, Roberta* IN SEARCH OF PEACE: THE STORY OF
FOUR AMERICANS WHO WON THE NOBEL PEACE PRIZE Illus.
Messner, 1970.
Excellent profile of Jane Addams is enhanced by many photographs which complement the text and help make her
seem alive to contemporary readers. The text focusses equally
on Ms. Addams's efforts for peace and her settlement work.

*** *Fleming, Alice* PIONEERS IN PRINT: ADVENTURES IN COUR-
AGE Reilly & Lee, 1971. (grade 6 and up)

Dramatic, moving profile of Lorraine Hansberry, the black
playwright and author of *Raisin in the Sun,* discusses her
early life, professional career, marriage, and early death
from cancer.

*** ——— REPORTERS AT WAR Illus. Regnery, 1970. (grades
5-9)

Marguerite Higgins, World War II and Korean War correspondent, is profiled in a brisk, candid narrative. Told with
sympathy and dignity, the account reflects the courage and
determination displayed by Ms. Higgins.

*** *Flynn, James* NEGROES OF ACHIEVEMENT IN MODERN
AMERICA Dodd, 1970. (grade 7 and up)

Straightforward narratives are interesting, informative
portrayals of children's librarian Augusta Baker, Congresswoman Shirley Chisholm, educator Mary McLeod Bethune,
singer Marian Anderson, and jurist Constance Baker Motley.

* *Foley, Rae* FAMOUS AMERICAN SPIES Dodd, 1962. (grade 7
and up)

Interesting profiles of Emma Edmonds (known more au-
thoritatively as Sarah Emma Edmonds), Rose O'Neal Greenhow, Elizabeth Van Lew, and Belle Boyd are overly fictionalized and lack proper documentation. Edmonds's profile is
based on her own fictionalized account rather than on the
authoritative sources.

*** *Foster, G. Allen* VOTES FOR WOMEN Illus. Criterion, 1966.
(grade 8 and up)

An outstanding overview of the struggle for women's
rights as well as of the right to vote. Well-researched, documented, and dramatically interesting, this book is written
from a feminist perspective. Included is much biographical
material on feminists and suffragists Lucy Stone, Lucretia
Mott, Susan B. Anthony, Elizabeth Cady Stanton, Carrie
Chapman Catt, Victoria Woodhull (first woman candidate
for president), and Anna Ella Carroll (Civil War military
strategist). A fine book which can be considered a collective

biography, will serve as a spur to further reading of individual biographies.

*** *Freedman, Russell* TEENAGERS WHO MADE HISTORY Illus. Holiday, 1961. (grade 8 and up)

Very fine, energetic biographies of athlete "Babe" Didrikson Zaharias and poet Edna St. Vincent Millay focus on the years before they were twenty, but also briefly discuss later events. Intimate and vivid accounts provide good inspiration for young readers. Selections from Millay's poetry as well as suggested readings contribute to the value of this collection.

*** *Garfinkel, Bernard* THEY CHANGED THE WORLD: THE LIVES OF 44 GREAT MEN AND WOMEN Illus. Platt & Munk, 1973. (grades 4-9)

Exceptionally attractive collection contains full-page color portraits and small black-and-white photographs, enhancing the excellent, succinct profiles of the following women: Queen Elizabeth I of England, scientist Marie Curie, founder of the nursing profession Florence Nightingale, handicapped humanitarian Helen Keller, and scientist-author Rachel Carson. Despite the brevity, each profile captures something of the subject's personality and discusses her most salient characteristics and important accomplishments.

*** *Gelfand, Ravina, and Patterson, Letha* THEY WOULDN'T QUIT: STORIES OF HANDICAPPED PEOPLE Illus. Lerner, 1962. (reading level, grades 4-6; interest level, grades 4-12)

Inspiring profiles of track and field star Wilma Rudolph, who was lame as a child; medical scientist Dr. Florence Seibert, who was a polio victim; and singer Kate Smith, who faced a serious weight problem. Intended for all readers, but will have special meaning to those who have limitations or handicaps of their own.

** *Gelman, Steve* YOUNG OLYMPIC CHAMPIONS Illus. with photographs. Grosset, rev. 1973. (grades 6-10)

Good informative profiles employ overly informal journalistic style but give good accounts of the lives of all-around athlete "Babe" Didrikson Zaharias, track star Wilma Rudolph,

337

ice skater Sonja Henie, and swimmer Chris Von Saltza. A long appendix lists Olympic winners in individual and team events, adding considerable value to this readable volume.

*** *Genett, Ann* CONTRIBUTIONS OF WOMEN: AVIATION Illus. with photographs. Dillon, 1975. (grades 5-8)

Absorbing, well-organized, nonfictionalized profiles offer substantial, well-rounded views of six women in aviation. Written in a lively style and employing appropriate anecdotes, the profiles are immensely readable and are suitable for older, less capable readers as well as elementary school youngsters. Included here are Amelia Earhart and Jacqueline Cochran, pioneer award-winning aviators; Anne Morrow Lindberg, navigator and pilot; Jerrie Mock, first woman to fly solo around the world; Geraldyn Cobb, first woman to pass the astronaut testing program; and Emily Howell, the first woman pilot for a United States scheduled airline. A final chapter contains very brief profiles on other women in aviation.

*** *Gilfond, Henry* HEROINES OF AMERICA Illus. with photographs. Fleet, 1970. (grades 8-10)

Excellent, easy-to-read profiles give enough details to draw well-balanced, sympathetic portrayals of these women: social reformer Jane Addams; founder of Visiting Nurses Service, Lillian Wald; pioneer physician Elizabeth Blackwell; athlete "Babe" Didrikson Zaharias; United States Senator Margaret Chase Smith; Congresswoman Shirley Chisholm; handicapped humanitarian Helen Keller; humanitarian and First Lady Eleanor Roosevelt; singer Marian Anderson; painter Georgia O'Keefe; photographer Margaret Bourke-White; astronomer Maria Mitchell; civil rights leader Coretta Scott King; colonial journalist Anna Zenger; young slave poet Phillis Wheatley; author Harriet Beecher Stowe; poet Edna St. Vincent Millay; author Pearl Buck; author and scientist Rachel Carson; actresses Maude Adams, Ethel Barrymore, Helen Hayes, Katharine Cornell, and Minnie Maddern Fiske.

*** *Gleasner, Diana* WOMEN IN SPORTS: SWIMMING Illus. with photographs. Harvey House, 1975. (grade 5 and up)

Fast-moving, extremely easy-to-read profiles of diver Christine Loock, speed swimmer Kathy Heddy, synchronized swimmer Gail Johnson Buzonas, marathon swimmer Diana Nyad, and speed swimmer Shirley Babashoff will interest older less capable readers as well as younger competent ones. The author focusses on both the careers and the personal lives of the swimmers from a feminist perspective.

*** *Gridley, Marion E.* AMERICAN INDIAN WOMEN Illus. Hawthorn, 1974. (grades 7-10)

Inspiring, extremely well-told profiles of Indian women are competently researched and give much information on the history and culture of each tribe, as well as telling of the individual lives and careers of the women. Writing with candor, the author provides an objective view of several issues and disputes. Included are Wetamoo, Pocasset chief; Pocahontas, Indian princess; Mary Musgrove Bosomworth, Creek leader; Nancy Ward, Cherokee leader; Sacajawea, interpreter and guide to Lewis and Clark; Winema, Modoc princess and peacemaker; E. Pauline Johnson, Canadian Mohawk poet; Susan La Flesche Picotte, Omaha physician; Gertrude Simmons Bonnin, Sioux educator; Roberta C. Lawson, community leader; Pablita Velarde, Pueblo painter; Maria Martínez, Pueblo potter; Annie Dodge Wauneka, Navajo leader; Esther Burnette Horne, educator; Maria and Marjorie Tallchief, Osage prima ballerinas; Wilma L. Victor, Choctaw educator and government official; Elaine Abraham Ramos, Tlingit college educator; Milly Hadjo Francis, Creek Indian; and Sarah Winnemucca, Paiute Indian teacher and interpreter.

** ——— CONTEMPORARY AMERICAN LEADERS Illus. with photographs. Dodd, 1972. (grades 5-8)

Accurate portrayals of several Indian leaders are somewhat dry as they attempt to crowd too many details into easy-to-read, simplistic profiles for young readers. The author clearly stands in admiration of the individual subjects as well as the of Indian tribes, and although the profiles are not as lively as readers might desire, they offer useful information about the leaders and about the customs and history of Indians. Women included are educator LaDonna Harris, potter Maria Martínez, and advisors to the government Annie Dodge Wauneka and Helen L. Peterson.

339

*** *Grimsley, Will, and Associated Press, eds.* THE SPORTS IM-
MORTALS Illus. with photographs. Prentice–Hall, 1972.
(grade 7 and up)

First-rate, journalistically informal biographies not only
let the records speak for themselves, but also provide engaging realistic glimpses of the private lives of each sports figure.
Adults as well as young readers will enjoy the profiles of all-
around athlete "Babe" Didrikson Zaharias, skater Sonja
Henie, and tennis champion Helen Wills.

*** *Gurko, Miriam* THE LADIES OF SENECA FALLS: THE BIRTH
OF THE WOMEN'S RIGHTS MOVEMENT Illus. Macmillan, 1974.
(grade 9 and up)

This extraordinary well-written and interesting book is not
technically biography. It is, rather, a well researched, vigorous
history of the early feminist movement in the United States.
The sympathetic author has integrated substantial unvarnished portraits of those women whose involvement with the
movement really *was* the movement. Included here are Elizabeth Cady Stanton, Mary Wollstonecraft (although not an
American, her influence was considerable), Fanny Wright,
Sarah and Angeline Grimké, Lucretia Mott, Margaret Fuller,
Susan B. Anthony, and Lucy Stone. The text of the Declaration of Sentiments and Resolutions, as issued at Seneca Falls
in 1848, is included as well as many old prints and photographs, all of which enhance this particularly valuable book.

** *Halacy, Daniel S.* MASTER SPY Illus. McGraw, 1968. (grades
5-8)

Readable, crisp profiles of Rose O'Neal Greenhow, American Confederate spy; Mary Louvestre, former slave and
Union spy; and Mata Hari, World War I spy for the Germans,
are fast-moving and appealing.

*** *Hays, H. R.* EXPLORERS OF MAN: FIVE PIONEERS IN ANTHRO-
POLOGY Illus. Macmillan, 1971. (grade 9 and up)

An outstanding profile of anthropologist Margaret Mead
focusses on her early career and the professional aspects of
her life. Not a personal sketch, it gives a good interpretation

of her work, explaining it and serving to act as a spur to reading some of her own books. Good bibliography is included.

* *Heath, Monroe* GREAT AMERICAN AUTHORS Illus. Pacific Coast Publications, 1962. (grades 6-9)

Oversized paperback allots one page to each author. The brief summaries of each subject's life are almost subordinate to the half-page pencil portraits. The sketches themselves, bland and rigidly patterned, fail to convey more than some essential and accurate facts of each author's life. Strictly utilitarian, this may serve as a reference source. Included are Harriet Beecher Stowe, Emily Dickinson, Edith Wharton, and Willa Cather.

* ——— GREAT AMERICAN WOMEN AT A GLANCE Illus. Pacific Coast Publications, 1957. (grades 9-12)

Oversized paperback book allots one page to each woman. Half of each page consists of a large pencil portrait as well as a few small drawings, all of which tend to overshadow the brief, biographical summaries. Somewhat dry, though reasonably accurate, the sketches do not capture the spirit of these remarkable women but are useful perhaps for reference.

Included are educators Emma Hart Willard, Mary Lyon; authors Edith Wharton, Willa Cather, Harriet Beecher Stowe, Pearl Buck; poets Emily Dickinson, Edna St. Vincent Millay; reformers and feminists Lucretia Mott, Dorothea Dix, Margaret Fuller, Elizabeth Cady Stanton, Susan B. Anthony, Julia Ward Howe, Carrie Chapman Catt, Jane Addams; astronomer Maria Mitchell; American Red Cross founder, Clara Barton; artist Mary Cassatt; pioneer physician Elizabeth Blackwell; Christian Science founder, Mary Baker Eddy; Girl Scout founder, Juliette Gordon Low; handicapped, philanthropist Helen Keller; aviator Amelia Earhart; sculptor Malvina Hoffman; and First Lady and humanitarian Eleanor Roosevelt.

** *Heiderstadt, Dorothy* BOOK OF HEROES Bobbs–Merrill, 1954. (grades 4-7)

Biographies, which are more like stories, of Saint Elizabeth of Hungary and Joan of Arc are well written and touching, but rather eulogistic and fictionalized.

** —————— More Indian Friends and Foes Illus. McKay, 1963. (grade 3-7)

Good profiles of Kateri Terakwitha, a Canadian Indian who became a nun, and Pasquala, an Indian who warned a mission of an impending attack, are well told but lack distinction and excitement.

** *Higdon, Hal* Champions of the Tennis Court Illus. Prentice–Hall, 1972. (grades 5-9)

Very good, brief, but somewhat superficial profiles of Suzanne Lenglen, Helen Wills, Maureen Connolly, and Billie Jean King tell a bit about their personal lives as well as about their tennis careers. Simply written, the profiles do not really capture the personalities of the women too well, but are interesting and will appeal to young elementary school tennis enthusiasts as well as older, less able readers.

*** *Hirsch, Carl S.* Guardians of Tomorrow: pioneers in ecology Illus. Viking, 1971. (grade 6 and up)

In an extremely well written, thoughtfully organized book, one chapter ("Something in the Wind") discusses Rachel Carson's contributions to ecology. This is not a personal biography; the entire focus is on her work and writing. It clearly reveals the extent of Ms. Carson's foresight, brilliance, and concerns for the environment.

** *Hoff, Rhoda* Four American Poets: why they wrote Walck, 1969. (grade 7 and up)

Thoughtful, but somewhat prosaic profile of Emily Dickinson is followed by a good selection of her poetry. Attractively designed book is appealing, and though the subject moves with some reality and warmth, the profile lacks distinction.

*** *Hollander, Phyllis* American Women in Sports Illus. Grosset, 1972. (grade 5 and up)

Fascinating survey of women who have achieved fame and distinction in the sports world. Well-organized by sport, chapters cover horseback riders, swimmers, runners, tennis players, ice skaters, golfers, skiers, and bowlers as well as one chapter devoted exclusively to all-around athlete "Babe" Didrikson Zaharias.

A fine introduction briefly summarizes the role women have played as spectators and as participants, and an epilogue reflects on the progress women have made and are continuing to make in the male-dominated field of sports. The profiles are written in a breezy style, and fortunately do not rely on the clichés often employed in the past by juvenile sports writers.

Included are horseback riders Eleanor Sears, Kathy Kusner; swimmers Gertrude Ederle, Florence Chadwick, Patricia McCormick, Chris Von Saltza; track and field athletes Stella Walsh, Olga Connolly, Wilma Rudolph, Wyomia Tyus Simburg; tennis players Helen Wills, Helen Hull Jacobs, Alice Marble, Maureen Connolly, Althea Gibson, Billie Jean King; ice skaters Theresa Weld, Tenley Albright, Carol Heiss, Laurence Owen, Peggy Fleming; golfers Glenna Collett, Patty Berg, Mickey Wright, Kathy Whitworth; skiers Gretchen Fraser, Andrea Mead Lawrence, Penny Pitou, Marilyn Cochran; bowlers Floretta McCutcheon, Marion Laedwig, Sylvia Wene Martin.

*** *Hollander, Phyllis and Zander* IT'S THE FINAL SCORE THAT COUNTS Illus. Grosset, 1973. (grade 6 and up)

In this collective biography of people who have achieved success in life after first becoming prominent as athletes, there is a chapter, written in a brisk, narrative style, on Tenley Albright, Olympic gold medal figure skating champion, who is now a surgeon practicing in Boston. We are introduced to the subject as a young girl who, although dedicated to skating, is equally devoted to her studies and graduates from Radcliffe College and Harvard Medical School; becomes a surgeon; marries; and raises a family.

*** ———, *ed.* THEY DARED TO LEAD: AMERICA'S BLACK ATHLETES Illus. Grosset, 1972. (grade 5 and up)

A vividly written profile of Althea Gibson, championship tennis player, is exciting and offers much inspiration.

*** *Hood, Robert E.* TWELVE AT WAR: GREAT PHOTOGRAPHERS UNDER FIRE Illus. with photographs. Putnam, 1967. (grades 6-10)

Outstanding, nonfictionalized profile of Margaret Bourke-

343

White traces her professional career, briefly touching on her personal life. Her courage, single-mindedness, and personality are skillfully captured without the book being sentimental.

*** *Hopkins, Lee B.* BOOKS ARE BY PEOPLE: INTERVIEWS WITH 104 AUTHORS AND ILLUSTRATORS OF BOOKS FOR YOUNG PEOPLE Illus. with photographs. Citation, 1969. (grade 6 and up)

These short, extremely lively, and well-written profiles are suitable for both young readers and adults. Each profile is about three pages, and in anecdotal fashion tells something of the personal and professional life of the author and/or illustrator. Included are authors Pura Belpré, Claire Huchet Bishop, Sonia Bleeker, Sara W. Brewton, Beatrice Schenk de Regniers, Aileen Fisher, Lou Ann Gaeddart, May Garelick, Virginia Kahl, Ruth Krauss, Joan Lexau, Myra Cohn Livingston, Phyllis McGinley, Ann McGovern, May McNeer, Eve Merriam, Elsa Holmelund Minarik, Lilian Moore, Lillian Morrison, Tillie S. Pine, Mariana Prieto, Ann Herbert Scott, Millicent E. Selsam, Ruth A. Sonneborn, Ellen Tarry, Blanche Jennings Thompson, Janice May Udry, Sandol Stoddard Warburg, Julia Wilson, Rose Wyler, Margaret B. Young, Charlotte Zolotow; illustrators Adrienne Adams, Ann Grifalconi, Nonny Hogrogian; author-illustrators Jeanne Bendick, Marcia Brown, Barbara Cooney, Ingri d'Aulaire, Barbara Emberley, Marie Hall Ets, Louise Fatio, Berta Hader, Dahlov Ipcar, Dorothy Lathrop, Lois Lenski, Anita Lobel, Winifred Lubell, Katherine Milhous, Evaline Ness, Maud Petersham, Ellen Raskin, Margret Rey.

*** ———— MORE BOOKS BY MORE PEOPLE: INTERVIEWS WITH 65 AUTHORS OF BOOKS FOR CHILDREN Illus. with photographs. Citation, 1974. (grade 6 and up)

Similar to the above book by Hopkins, these profiles of authors and illustrators for older children are equally informal and informative and will appeal both to young readers and adults.

Included are authors Natalie Babbitt (who also illustrates books), Carol Ryrie Brink, Betsy Byars, Natalie Savage Carl-

344

son, Ann Nolan Clark, Beverly Cleary, Elizabeth Coatsworth, Hila Colman, Julia Cunningham, Marguerite Lofft deAngeli (who also illustrates her books), Elizabeth Borton de Treviño, Lavinia Dobler, Julie Edwards (known also as actress-singer Julie Andrews), Eleanor Estes, Jean Fitz, Genevieve Foster, Jean Craighead George, Shirley Glubok, Virginia Hamilton, Esther Hautzig, Carolyn Haywood, Irene Hunt, Elaine L. Konigsburg, Nancy Larrick, Jean Lee Latham, Madeleine L'Engle, Jean Merrill, Emily Cheney Neville, Barbara Rinkoff, Charlemae Hill Rollins, Louisa Shotwell, Zilpha Keatley Snyder, Virginia Sorensen, Elizabeth George Speare, Dorothy Sterling, Mary Stolz, Sydney Taylor, Pamela Travers, Mary Hays Weik, Sister Noemi Weygant (who is also a photographer), Maia Wojciechowska, and Elizabeth Yates.

*** *Hughes, Langston* FAMOUS AMERICAN NEGROES Illus. Dodd, 1954. (grade 7 and up)

Truly outstanding, beautifully written profiles of poet Phillis Wheatley, abolitionist and slave Harriet Tubman, and singer Marian Anderson are accurate, sensitive, and touching accounts.

*** ——— FAMOUS NEGRO HEROES OF AMERICA Illus. Dodd, 1958. (grade 7 and up)

Brief profiles of abolitionist Harriet Tubman and journalist Ida Wells-Barnett are dramatic and stirring accounts, clearly revealing the subjects' contributions to history.

*** ——— FAMOUS NEGRO MUSIC MAKERS Illus. with photographs. Dodd, 1955. (grade 5 and up)

Stirring profiles of singers Bessie Smith, Ethel Waters, Marian Anderson, Mahalia Jackson, and Lena Horne make liberal use of quotations and anecdotes. The dignified informality contributes to the flow of the text and helps dramatize the lives of the women.

*** *Hume, Ruth* GREAT WOMEN OF MEDICINE Illus. Random, 1964. (grades 7-11)

Excellent, informal biographies are lively, readable, and accurate and are further enhanced by photographs and old prints. Included are inspirational profiles of women who

345

pioneered in the health fields: Florence Nightingale, nurse; Elizabeth Blackwell and Mary Putnam Jacobi, American physicians; Elizabeth Garrett-Anderson and Sophia Jex-Blake, British physicians; and Marie Curie, Nobel Prize winning French scientist. There is also a chapter on more contemporary women.

*** *Ingraham, Leonard and Claire* AN ALBUM OF WOMEN IN AMERICAN HISTORY Illus. Watts, 1972. (grade 5 and up)

Attractive, well-organized book offers a fairly comprehensive study of American women throughout history. The focus is on their struggle for equality, with an emphasis on their difficulties and accomplishments. As biography, the sketches are brief and superficial, but as resource material or for general background reading this volume is excellent. Only the implication that women have been easily won over to feminist causes, a statement which history does not substantiate, detracts from the outstanding qualities of this valuable book. The illustrations and photographs add considerably to the effectiveness of this oversized volume.

** *Jacobs, Helen Hull* FAMOUS MODERN AMERICAN WOMEN ATHLETES Illus. with photographs. Dodd, 1975. (grade 7 and up)

Tennis player-author Jacobs's collection includes extremely informative accounts of the athletic careers of bowler Judy Cook Souta, skater Janet Lynn, skier Cindy Nelson, swimmer Shirley Babashoff, tennis player Billie Jean King, and track star Francie Larrieu. The profiles contain a number of personal quotations that well complement the detailed stories of each athlete's rise to stardom. However, despite the author's firsthand contact and personal relationship with the women, the narrative is rather impersonal and fails to convey the vigor and excitement displayed by the stars themselves.

* *Jakes, John* GREAT WOMEN REPORTERS Illus. Putnam, 1969. (grade 7 and up)

Included here are superficial, although entertaining profiles of ten women reporters: Jane Grey Swisshelm, aboli-

346

tionist, feminist, and pioneer journalist and editor; Nellie Bly, pioneer reporter and reformer; Winifred Black, who first used stunts to get stories and later became known as a "sob sister" (a woman reporter who wrote emotional reports of tragedies and disasters); Nixola Greeley-Smith, interviewer and journalist; Rheta Childe Door, feminist and journalist; Irene Kuhn, reporter in China and the United States; Dorothy Thompson, one of the best-known and highest paid newspaper writers in the world; Dorothy Kilgallen, famous feature writer, "sob sister," and long-time television panelist; Adela Rogers St. Johns, novelist, short story and newspaper writer; and Marguerite Higgins, Pulitzer Prize winning war correspondent. These women are profiled in a journalistic style which is appropriate but whose content perpetuates stereotypes of sex and nationality. Though the achievements of each woman are reported, the implication is that they arrived at their goals by employing "feminine wiles" and that each woman constituted an exception to a rule of "feminine behavior."

*** *Johnston, Johanna* THE INDIANS AND THE STRANGERS Illus. Dodd, 1972. (grades 2-5)

Twelve beautifully written short stories in blank verse about Indians include an excellent profile of Sacajawea, the Indian interpreter to Lewis and Clark. Based on the known facts of her life, the compelling narrative is dignified without being sentimental. Excellent woodcuts by Rocco Negri are effective and contribute greatly to the book.

*** ——— A SPECIAL BRAVERY Illus. Dodd, 1967. (grades 2-5)

Unusually fine book is designed for young readers or for reading aloud. Literary style is somewhat like free verse, warmly and dramatically highlighting and conveying the ideas and deeds of singer Marian Anderson, educator Mary McLeod Bethune, and abolitionist Harriet Tubman. Important details and facts are included in a brief appendix, rather than allowing them to interfere with the flow of the text. Illustrations by Ann Grifalconi are beautiful, and they share equal importance with the text in this rather unique book.

*** ——— Women Themselves Illus. Dodd, 1973. (grades 3-6)

Extraordinarily fine book richly combines the best in literature, biography, and feminism. The author introduces the book with an overview of women and how they have been limited in their opportunities, and she ends with a fine discussion on where women are presently and what the future holds. In between are superb, though brief, blank verse profiles of fifteen women. Each portrait gives a general overview of the woman, but focusses on the salient point of her career and shows clearly the uniqueness of her accomplishments, particularly so in the context of the way women were viewed during the subject's lifetime. Strongly feminist, the author is never self-consciously or militantly so, instead gently but firmly reminding the reader either of the discrimination the subject faced, or what her deeds meant to other women. Included are Anne Hutchinson, colonial religious leader and dissenter; Anne Bradstreet, colonial poet; Deborah Moody, landowner and builder; Phillis Wheatley, black colonial poet; Abigail Adams, colonial feminist; Emma Willard, pioneer educator; Ernestine Rose, feminist and reformer; Elizabeth Blackwell, pioneer woman physician; Elizabeth Cady Stanton, feminist and abolitionist; Harriet Beecher Stowe, abolitionist author; Clara Barton, founder of the American Red Cross; Victoria Woodhull, feminist and presidential candidate; Nellie Bly, pioneer woman reporter; Carrie Chapman Catt, feminist and suffragist.

*** *Jones, Hettie* Big Star Fallin' Mama: five women in black music Illus. with photographs and old prints. Viking, 1974. (grade 7 and up)

Outstanding collection is distinguished by its insightful views of the subject as well as by a literary style that captures the mood of the women and their lives. The interesting, informative first chapter deals with the origins of the "blues," and is followed by substantial, in-depth chapters on each of the five women. Included are blues singers Ma Rainey, Bessie Smith, Billie Holiday, and Aretha Franklin, and gospel singer Mahalia Jackson. Candid in the appraisal of each woman,

348

never eulogistic in tone, the author also conveys a good picture of the racial discrimination that the women faced in both their careers and personal lives.

** *Kelen, Emery* FIFTY VOICES OF THE TWENTIETH CENTURY Lothrop, 1970. (grade 7 and up)
Very brief profiles provide only a summary of each life, but are followed by a good selection of quoted statements made by each subject. Despite excessive brevity, the biographical information is well presented, and the format and content of the book provide a good reference source. The women included are singer Marian Anderson; anthropologist Margaret Mead; former prime minister of Israel, Golda Meir; poet Marianne Moore; and Indian diplomat Vijaya Pandit.

** *Kirk, Rhina* CIRCUS HEROES AND HEROINES Illus. Hammond, 1972. (grade 6 and up)
In an attractively designed, well-organized history of the circus are profiles of Mollie Bailey, circus owner; Annie Oakley, markswoman; Lillian Leitzel, aerialist; May Wirth, bareback rider; Antoinette Concello, trapeze artist; and the family of Wallendas, high wire artists. The competent narratives give good accounts of the lives of these performers against a background of circus life, but lack the vitality that the subjects themselves displayed. Accompanying photographs and illustrations in color and black-and-white add considerably to the total enjoyment of this book.

* *Knight, Frank* STORIES OF FAMOUS EXPLORERS BY LAND Illus. Westminster, 1966. (grades 4-6)
Adequate profile of Mary Kingsley, African explorer, is somewhat dry, offering a sketchy view of her accomplishments. Clearly indicated is her initiative, resourcefulness, and courage, and it is apparent that Ms. Kingsley felt great respect for the Africans. The author, however, does not seem fully to share that veiw, for he describes native Africans as "savage."

*** *Lavine, Sigmund* FAMOUS MERCHANTS Illus. Dodd, 1965. (grade 7 and up)
Excellent profiles focus on the professional rather than on the personal lives of Elizabeth Arden, cosmetician and found-

er of a huge beauty business; and Margaret Fogharty Rudkin, founder of Pepperidge Farm bread. Interesting, fast-moving accounts comprehensively cover the women's achievements.

*** *Lawson, Don* TEN FIGHTERS FOR PEACE: AN ANTHOLOGY Lothrop, 1971. (grade 7 and up)

A very fine anthology of articles written by those who have worked for peace includes an article by Jeannette Rankin— who has worked all her long life for peace and who was the first woman elected to the United States House of Representatives—and a selection from *Daybreak,* the autobiography of Joan Baez, folk singer and peace worker.

* *Leipold, L. Edmond* AMERICA BECOMES FREE Illus. Denison, 1972. (grades 3-5)

Profile adequately relates the legend of Molly Pitcher but lacks spirit and imagination.

* ———— FAMOUS AMERICAN ARTISTS Denison, 1969. (grades 5-9)

Poorly written, dull portrait of artist Mary Cassatt does not capture the spirit or talent of the gifted woman.

* ———— FAMOUS AMERICAN ATHLETES Denison, 1969. (grades 5-9)

Dull biographies of ice skater Carol Heiss and bowler Shirley Rudolph Garms do not capture their personalities though their lives are accurately traced.

†† ———— FAMOUS AMERICAN DOCTORS Illus. Denison, 1969. (grades 5-9)

Profiles of Karen Horney and Marie Zakrzewska are not sexist, but are without any literary merit. The author, in reference to immigrants, implicitly states that poverty is due to lack of ambition and capabilities, an attitude to be avoided in books for young readers.

* ———— FAMOUS AMERICAN ENGINEERS Denison, 1972. (grades 5-9)

Despite an emphasis on her talents and abilities to be successful, there is a note of sexism in this profile of Lillian Gilbreth. She is described as completely subordinate to her husband, and in widowhood as having lost the head of her household.

* ——— FAMOUS AMERICAN FICTION WRITERS Denison, 1972. (grades 5-9)
Superficial account of the life of Pearl Buck is little more than a catalogue of facts, informally and accurately stated. The profile is neither critical nor personal and offers no insights into her life.

†† ——— FAMOUS AMERICAN INDIANS Illus. Denison, 1967. (grades 5-9)
Patronizing and anthropologically unsound profiles of potter Maria Martínez and Indian princess and heroine Pocahontas are dull, dry, and pedestrian.

†† ——— FAMOUS AMERICAN MUSICIANS Denison, n.d. (grades 5-9)
Extremely dull, pedantic profiles of two black singers, Lena Horne and Marian Anderson. The introduction to the book offers an uncomfortable racial stereotype and the profiles fail to produce any spark of excitement, are unrealistic in attitudes to society, and are thus totally unacceptable.

* ——— FAMOUS AMERICAN NEGROES Illus. Denison, 1967. (grades 5-9)
This biography of Marian Anderson lacks warmth and barely touches on the discrimination the singer faced in her personal life and career.

* ——— FAMOUS AMERICAN POETS Illus. Denison, 1969. (grades 5-9)
Although rather mediocre in style, these profiles do give interesting facts about the poets. Included are Phillis Wheatley and Edna St. Vincent Millay.

* ——— FAMOUS AMERICAN TEACHERS Denison, n.d. (grades 5-9)

Plodding, somewhat sexist profiles of Emma Hart Willard and Mary Lyon, pioneer educators of women; Martha Berry and Mary McLeod Bethune, founders of schools and a college; and Annie Sullivan Macy, teacher of deaf and blind Helen Keller. These intrepid women are the subjects of a group of uninspired though reasonably well-researched biographies.

†† ——— FAMOUS AMERICAN WOMEN Illus. Denison, 1967. (grades 5-9)

Poorly written, distorted interpretations of a remarkable group of women are sexist and patronizing. Some of the most important accomplishments of the women are not discussed, and the writing is dull and textbookish. Included are profiles of feminist Susan B. Anthony; poets Emily Dickinson and Emma Lazarus; aviator Amelia Earhart; revolutionary heroine Molly Pitcher; educator Elizabeth Peabody; Indian interpreter for Lewis and Clark, Sacajawea; Washington hostess and First Lady, Dolley Madison; author Willa Cather; and the first First Lady, Martha Washington.

* ——— GREAT AMERICAN POETS Illus. Denison, n.d. (grades 4-5)

Reasonably accurate but superficial profile of Edna St. Vincent Millay gives no hint of her work but simply chronicles her life in a straightforward, factual way.

* ——— HEROES OF A DIFFERENT KIND Illus. Denison, n.d. (grades 4-5)

Poorly written, although nonsexist, profile of black poet Phillis Wheatley fails to draw a sympathetic, realistic, personal, or professional portrait.

* ——— MAKERS OF A BETTER AMERICA Denison, n.d. (grades 3-5)

Reasonably accurate nonfictionalized account of the life of Clara Barton is rather insipid and fails to bring alive that vital woman.

* ——— WHEN OUR COUNTRY WAS YOUNG Illus. Denison, n.d. (grades 3-5)

Brightly, but unimaginatively illustrated legend of Pocahontas is adequate but lacks fire and vitality.

*** *Lerner, Gerda* THE WOMAN IN AMERICAN HISTORY Addison–Wesley, 1971. (grade 9 and up)

This unusually superb book for adults is an ambitious, objective survey of the roles and contributions of individual women and groups of women in the history of the United States. Some women are identified by a sentence or two; others are discussed in detail—therefore, the book cannot be considered true biography. The author, a noted scholar and historian, writes in a clear, readable, well-paced style and this book could be used as a text, as an introduction to further study, or as simply background information.

** *Levinger, Elma E.* GREAT JEWISH WOMEN Behrman, 1940. (grades 3-7)

Extremely well written profiles are short on facts, but provide very worthwhile views of biblical women and ten modern women. The essence of each woman is captured, and though not useful for reference purposes, these are thought-provoking accounts which will inspire young readers to delve further. Included are many biblical women as well as these women of more recent times: actress Elisa-Rachel Felix (known as Rachel); writer Grace Aguilar; philanthropists Judith Montefiore, Clara de Hirsch, Sophie Irene Loeb, and Lina Strauss; educator Rebecca Gratz; poets Penina Moise and Emma Lazarus; and heroine Sarah Chizick.

** *Levy, Elizabeth* BYLINES: PROFILES IN INVESTIGATIVE JOURNALISM Four Winds, 1975. (grade 7 and up)

Not really biographies, but interestingly written profiles of reporters which discuss their techniques and motives as well as some of their most important stories. Included are Oriani Fallaci, an Italian reporter who employs feelings and emotion as well as facts in her writing, and Gail Sheehy, who combines the dramatic techniques of fiction writing with probing, investigative reporting, which gives the reader a sense of the story as well as of the facts.

** ——— LAWYERS FOR THE PEOPLE: A NEW BREED OF DE-
FENDERS AND THEIR WORK Knopf, 1974. (grade 8 and up)
Though not a biography in the true sense, each of these
profiles discusses a lawyer and her work, giving a good picture
of the focus of her practice, her clients, and something about
her own background. Informally written in a facile, lively,
journalistic style, it is also a good introduction to the profession of law. Included among those attorneys who have worked
for various causes are Linda Huber, a public defender who
defends juveniles and has worked to establish children's rights
in courts; Fay Stender, an expert on prison reform; Carol
Libow, a member of an all-women law firm; and Eleanor
Holmes Norton, a black civil liberties lawyer and New York
City's commissioner of Human Rights.

*** *Lieberman, Mark* THE PACIFISTS: SOLDIERS WITHOUT GUNS
Praeger, 1972. (grades 7-10)
In an excellent and thoughtful profile of Jane Addams, social worker and Nobel Peace Prize winner, her life and social
work activities are summarized, but the focus is on her pacifist beliefs and her efforts to avert war and to insure peace
after World War I. The author also discusses the harsh treaty
of World War I (which Jane Addams had opposed) as a factor contributing to the onset of World War II.

* *Life International* NINE WHO CHOSE AMERICA Illus. Dutton,
1957. (grade 8 and up)
Stilted, rather mediocre profile of successful businesswoman Helena Rubinstein clearly indicates her ability, but has
some sexist overtones, not in relation to the subject but to
women in general. However, the profile gives a reasonably
accurate picture of Rubinstein's career and touches briefly
on her personal life.

*** *Lorimer, Lawrence, ed.* BREAKING IN: NINE FIRST-PERSON
ACCOUNTS ABOUT BECOMING AN ATHLETE Random, 1974.
(grade 7 and up)
One very well selected chapter is adapted and abridged
from Althea Gibson's book *I Always Wanted to Be Somebody*.
This excerpt tells of her beginning tennis career at fourteen.

354

A brief but good introduction and afterword by the editor bring Gibson's own words into context and remind readers of her inspiration to women and blacks.

*** *Lutzker, Edythe* WOMEN GAIN A PLACE IN MEDICINE Illus. McGraw, 1969. (grade 8 and up)

An excellent, factual, and inspirational discussion of the first British women doctors, with a focus on the careers of pioneers Sophia Jex-Blake, Edith Pechey, Isabel Thorne, Matilda Chaplin, and Helen Evans. Elizabeth Blackwell and Elizabeth Garrett-Anderson, whose careers preceded the aforementioned, are also discussed, as well as the men and women who encouraged, discouraged, and strongly opposed them. The author has done her research well, and she combines the history of medical treatment for women with biography, doing both competently. Throughout the book, the discrimination women doctors faced is stressed, and the final chapter reminds readers that women still face discrimination in medicine as well as in other fields.

** *McAdam, Robert* PLAY THE GAME SERIES Illus. Bowmar, 1971. (grades 3-8) *Forty for Sixty* includes profile on Wilma Rudolph, Olympic sprinter; *Chief Cloud of Dust* includes profile on Peggy Fleming, Olympic ice skater; *Bull on Ice* includes profile on "Babe" Didrikson Zaharias, all-around athlete.

All three books, available singly or in series, are very attractively illustrated by Pete Bentovja, but the text lacks the excitement the subjects displayed in their lives. Simply written, it may serve well for less able older readers, or for very young sports-oriented youngsters. The titles are taken from the first story in each book (none of which are about women), so they do not indicate the remaining subjects to be found in the text.

** *McConnell, Jane and Burt* OUR FIRST LADIES: FROM MARTHA WASHINGTON TO PAT RYAN NIXON Crowell, 1969. (grade 6 and up) (rev. eds. of this book are issued as each new First Lady is added)

Warm, informal portraits of each First Lady are moderately fictionalized, each biography being liberally sprinkled with pertinent anecdotes which reveal the characters of the women and help place them in the proper historic periods. Some profiles, the one on Abigail Adams in particular, are exceptionally fine; others are rather pedestrian. Few political or important historical facts emerge from this enjoyable, satisfactory volume written without scholarly pretensions.

*** *McKown, Robin* HEROIC NURSES Illus. Putnam, 1966. (grades 5-9)

Unusually fine collection of profiles of nurses is not directed only to the career-minded reader. Well-documented, the book serves as a reference as well as a source of inspiration for any young reader. Included is a chapter on the earliest nurses followed by profiles of Jeanne Mance, a seventeenth-century French-Canadian nurse; Florence Nightingale, pioneer nurse; Mary Bickerdyke, Civil War nurse; Clara Barton, founder of the American Red Cross; Rose Hawthorne Lathrop, nurse for the incurably ill; Edith Cavell, nurse and spy; Mary Breckinridge, frontier nurse; Sister Elizabeth Kenny, polio nurse; and Princess Tsahai Haile Selassie.

*** *McNeer, May* ARMED WITH COURAGE Illus. Abingdon, 1957. (grades 4-9)

Handsome, extremely readable profiles of Florence Nightingale, pioneer in nursing, and Jane Addams, social reformer and winner of Nobel Peace Prize, stress their roles as crusaders. Partially fictionalized text is enhanced by Lynd Ward's outstanding illustrations. These biographies are as suitable for reading aloud as they are for older, independent readers.

*** ——— GIVE ME FREEDOM Illus. Abingdon, 1964. (grades 4-9)

Simply written, beautifully told and illustrated biographies of black singer Marian Anderson and feminist Elizabeth Cady Stanton emphasize their courage and determination in the face of opposition. The illustrations by Lynd Ward add immeasurably to the semifictionalized text. Although directed to older elementary and junior high students, these biographies are also recommended for reading aloud to younger children.

356

*** *Malvern, Gladys* THE SIX WIVES OF HENRY VIII Illus. Vanguard, 1972. (grade 7 and up)

Extremely well-written, absorbing, balanced account of the lives of the women who married King Henry VIII of England. The queens—Catherine of Aragon, Anne Boleyn, Jane Seymour, Anne of Cleves, Catherine Howard, and Catherine Parr—emerge as distinct personalities. Although each profile can stand by itself, the book is best read as a continuing saga. Other important people of the period are discussed and the society in which they lived is clearly explained so that readers with little or no knowledge of the history will find the book completely understandable.

*** *Marks, Geoffrey, and Beatty, William K.* WOMEN IN WHITE Illus. Scribner, 1972. (grade 9 and up)

Outstanding history of women in medicine thoroughly researches and documents their contribution since antiquity. The role of women in the science of midwifery is reviewed and the struggle to win a place in modern medicine is fully discussed with the focus on pioneer physicians Elizabeth Blackwell, Elizabeth Garrett-Anderson, Sophia Jex-Blake, Mary Putnam Jacobi, Emily Dunning Barringer, and Alice Hamilton. Women in related fields are considered too, and there are good portraits of Florence Nightingale, founder of the profession of nursing; Dorothea Lynde Dix, crusader for humane treatment of the mentally ill; Jane Addams, in whose settlement house preventive medicine was practiced; and Marie Curie, the discoverer of radium. A final chapter summarizes the outstanding work of contemporary women. Crisp, clear, readable text is geared to the serious high school reader.

* *Martin, Mabelle E.* EARLY YEARS OF SOME GREAT MEN AND WOMEN Illus. Highlights, 1964. (grades 2-6)

Bland profiles of social reformer Jane Addams; feminist and First Lady Abigail Adams; handicapped, philanthropist Helen Keller; and young black poet Phillis Wheatley stress their early lives and briefly summarize their later achievements. Mediocre in style, these biographies are fairly accurate but lack spirit and character insights.

** *Martin, Mabelle, et al.* BIOGRAPHIES OF BLACK AMERICANS
FOR ALL AMERICANS Illus. Highlights, 1971. (grades 2-6)

Good, informal profiles of tennis champion Althea Gibson,
singer Marian Anderson, educator Mary McLeod Bethune,
former slave and successful dressmaker Elizabeth Keckley
are undistinguished, but readable and appealing to young or
reluctant readers.

*** *Maynard, Olga* AMERICAN MODERN DANCERS: THE PIO-
NEERS Illus. Little, 1965. (grade 7 and up)

Good introduction to modern dance told through the biographies of Mary Wigman, Isadora Duncan, Ruth St. Denis,
Martha Graham, Hanya Holm, and Tamaris. The emphasis
on the professional lives of the women is sometimes technical
but not difficult to understand, and is of particular interest
to youngsters attracted to the art of dance.

*** *Meade, Marion* WOMEN IN SPORTS: TENNIS Illus. with photographs. Harvey House, 1975. (grade 5 and up)

Highly readable profiles of tennis stars Billie Jean King,
Rosemary Casals, Chris Evert, Evonne Goolagong, and Margaret Court give equal emphasis to their careers and their
personal lives. Clearly feminist in perspective, the biographies will be of interest to older reluctant readers as well as
to younger enthusiastic ones.

** *Melick, Arden Davis* WIVES OF THE PRESIDENTS Illus. Hammond, 1972. (grade 6 and up)

Attractive collection of profiles is a readable, thoughtful
examination of the lives of the thirty-eight First Ladies of the
United States. Of historical as well as biographical interest,
the book may serve best for reference, for it chronicles details
of the lives of the women that are often omitted from such
collections. At all times, the focus is on the subject, not on
her husband.

*** *Merriam, Eve* INDEPENDENT VOICES Illus. Atheneum, 1968.
(grades 4-6)

Outstanding biographies in verse of Elizabeth Blackwell,
pioneer American physician; Ida Wells-Barnett, black journalist; and Lucretia Mott, feminist and abolitionist. Good for

reading aloud, these are recommended by the author for school assemblies, and indeed they serve many purposes. The profiles capture the personalities and accomplishments of the women, without being too factual in approach.

*** ——— GROWING UP FEMALE IN AMERICA Illus. Doubleday, 1971. (grade 9 and up)

Really superb, feminist book includes a brief biographical sketch of ten women, followed by stories told in their own words taken from letters, diaries, or other writings. The editor has chosen her subjects well, and has constructed an interesting, moving picture of what it has been like for these and other similar women to grow up in America. Included are Eliza Southgate, an eighteenth-century New England schoolgirl; Elizabeth Cady Stanton, feminist; Maria Mitchell, astronomer; Mary Ann Webster Loughborough, wife of a Confederate officer; Arvazine Angeline Cooper, pioneer; Dr. Anna Howard Shaw, minister; Susie King Taylor, black Civil War nurse; "Mother" Mary Harris Jones, labor reformer and organizer; Elizabeth Gertrude Stern, social worker and writer; Mountain Wolf Woman, a Winnebago Indian.

*** *Mersand, Joseph, ed.* GREAT AMERICAN SHORT BIOGRAPHIES Dell, 1966. (grade 7 and up)

Reprinted in this well-edited collection are profiles of poet Emily Dickinson, dancer-choreographer Agnes deMille, and singer Marian Anderson. The profiles are reprinted from other sources. Louis Untermeyer's short biography of Emily Dickinson is an exquisitely written, perceptive picture, which discusses her life within the context of her work. The fast-moving, exciting profile of Agnes deMille by Eleanor Clymer and Lillian Erlich gives an intimate view of the woman who contributed so much to the world of ballet and show business. Ruth Woodbury Sedwick's beautifully written profile of Marian Anderson first appeared in 1940 and, as stated in a brief afterword by the editor, represents her career up to that time; the reader is brought up to date by the editor but the profile is timeless because it so warmly captures the essence of the woman.

*** *Meyer, Edith Patterson* CHAMPIONS OF FOUR FREEDOMS Little, 1966. (grade 7 and up)

Clearly written, well-researched profiles of Julia Lathrop, a pioneer in establishing juvenile courts and who later became first chief of the United States Children's Bureau; and Eleanor Roosevelt, First Lady, humanitarian, and United Nations delegate are included among a series of biographies of people and institutions who worked to establish and continue freedom of speech and of religion and freedom from want and from fear. Appendixes containing President Roosevelt's 1941 speech which outlined the four freedoms and the preamble to the Charter of the United Nations add to the value of this fine book.

*** *Nathan, Dorothy* WOMEN OF COURAGE Random, 1964. (grade 6 and up)

Top-notch biographies of Susan B. Anthony, Mary McLeod Bethune, Amelia Earhart, and Margaret Mead move quickly and dramatically. Immensely readable, these lively biographies give full portraits of the subjects, allowing the reader to see the women as warm and accomplished individuals.

* *Needham, Irene B., and Young, Irene H.* BIOGRAPHIES OF GREAT COMPOSERS Illus. Highlights, 1964. (grades 2-6)

An undistinguished profile of Cecile Chaminade, the French composer and pianist of serious and light music, is included here. It lacks depth and excitement, despite its informality.

*** *Neilson, Frances and Winthrop* SEVEN WOMEN: GREAT PAINTERS Illus. Chilton, 1968. (grade 7 and up)

Splendid personal and critical profiles of seven women artists are distinguished by insights into their lives and work, with careful mention of the special problems they encountered because of their gender. Each profile is accompanied by several black-and-white and at least one color reproduction of the artist's work. The vivid portrayals of each painter are further enhanced by careful, well-organized documentation, and an appendix offers a partial but substantial listing of museums and galleries with representative works by the artists. The readable narration makes the book suitable for

360

young readers, but it is of equal interest and use to adults. The seven painters included are Swiss-born Angelica Kauffman; Elizabeth Louise Vigee-Librun, Berthe Morisot, and Marie Laurencin of France; and Americans Cecilia Beaux, Mary Cassatt, and Georgia O'Keefe.

*** *Newlon, Clarke* FAMOUS PUERTO RICANS Illus. with photographs. Dodd, 1975. (grade 7 and up)

A fine introduction to Puerto Rican history and culture is followed by profiles of varying lengths. Included in this collection are excellent biographies of Carmen Maymi, director of the Women's Bureau of the United States Department of Labor; Miriam Colón, actress-founder of the Puerto Rican National Theatre; Cóncha Meléndez, writer and critic; Lupe Anguiano, educator; and Vikki Carr, singer. The profiles are clearly feminist and focus equally on the women's careers and their Puerto Rican identity.

** *Perham, Margery, ed.* TEN AFRICANS: A COLLECTION OF LIFE STORIES Illus. with photographs. Northwestern Univ. Pr., 1964. (grade 9 and up)

These life stories of Africans were collected and recorded before 1936 and contain much of anthropological and historical interest. The histories lack excitement, but are informative accounts of the lives of those who tell them, and are good supplements to a study of Africa under colonial rule. Included here are the stories of Nosente, a Bantu woman born in mid-nineteenth century, and Kofoworola Aina Moore, a Nigerian woman who was educated at Oxford University in England.

* *Pessin, Deborah* GIANTS ON THE EARTH: STORIES OF GREAT JEWISH MEN AND WOMEN FROM THE TIME OF THE DISCOVERY OF AMERICA TO THE PRESENT Behrman, 1946. (grades 3-6)

Somewhat sexist, exceedingly brief, fictionalized biographies of author Grace Aguilar, actress Elisa-Rachel Felix (known as Rachel), philanthropist Rebecca Gratz, and poet Emma Lazarus. Some insights and personal glimpses into their lives are provided, but little information is revealed. The women are viewed as adjuncts to the men, indicating few of their real strengths.

361

** *Peters, Margaret* THE EBONY BOOK OF BLACK ACHIEVEMENT Illus. Johnson, 1970. (grade 6 and up)

Good, brief, factual but informal profiles of journalist Ida Wells-Barnett and educator Mary McLeod Bethune. Although no attempt is made to capture their personalities or to give an intimate view of their lives, the book serves well for reference purposes.

*** *Petry, Ann* LEGENDS OF THE SAINTS Illus. Crowell, 1970. (grades 1-4)

Outstanding book includes beautiful color illustrations by Anne Rockwell and contains the stories of St. Catherine of Alexandria and Joan of Arc. The literary style is exceptionally fine, and is touching and dignified without being morbid or overly sentimental.

* *Phillips, Julien* STARS OF THE ZIEGFELD FOLLIES Illus. Lerner, 1972. (reading level, grades 4-6; interest level, grade 9 and up)

Exceedingly superficial, easy-to-read profiles of Fanny Brice, Marilyn Miller, and Anna Held are written in fan-magazine style and are directed towards reluctant or less able readers. Although it may capture the interest of such readers, the lack of depth and warmth means the profiles offer little of value in inspiration or information.

** *Pilarski, Laura* THEY CAME FROM POLAND: THE STORIES OF FAMOUS POLISH-AMERICANS Dodd, 1969. (grade 8 and up)

Good but ordinary profile of the Polish-born actress Helena Modjeska is informal but factual, relating the events of both her personal and professional lives.

** *Polatnick, Florence T., and Saletan, Alberta L.* SHAPERS OF AFRICA Illus. Messner, 1969. (grade 6 and up)

Good, readable profile of Queen Nzinga, who fought against the Portuguese conquest of Angola in the early seventeenth century, is included in this collection. Nonfictionalized, the account gives a good historical view, serving well for reference purposes.

*** *Poole, Lynn and Gray* SCIENTISTS WHO WORK OUTDOORS Illus. Dodd, 1963. (grade 8 and up)

Very fine biographies focus on the professional careers of marine biologist Dixy Lee Ray, and anthropologists Margaret Mead and Betty Jane Meggers, discussing their education and early training as well as some of their accomplishments. Highly readable, these biographies are of particular value to those wishing to know more about the professions of the subjects.

* *Prindville, Kathleen* First Ladies Macmillan, 1964. (grades 4-8)

Interesting profiles of First Ladies place unnecessary emphasis on them as adjuncts rather than as individuals with accomplishments of their own.

*** *Reeder, Red* Bold Leaders of the Revolutionary War Little, 1973. (grades 7-10)

Short biographies of Margaret Corbin, a woman who filled her husband's place in battle when he was killed, and Deborah Gannett Sampson, who, disguised as a man, enlisted and fought in the Revolutionary War, are well researched and documented and provide absorbing and lively reading. The emphasis is on their role in the Revolutionary War, but other material about their lives is also included.

** *Reidman, Sarah R.* Men and Women Behind the Atom Abelard–Schuman, 1958. (grade 7 and up)

Very good though rather technical biographies of Marie Curie, Nobel Prize winning scientist; her daughter Irene Joliot-Curie, also a Nobel Prize winning scientist; and information on Lise Meitner, a pioneer in work on the splitting of the atom. The book provides good background information for further study and for reading of individual biographies by the science student or enthusiast.

** *Rice, Tamara Talbot* Czars and Czarinas of Russia Illus. Lothrop, 1968. (grade 7 and up)

Good profiles are straightforward, interesting narratives of Elizabeth Petrovna and Catherine the Great. Provides useful background for further reading or studying, and captures the personalities of the women.

*** *Richardson, Ben* GREAT AMERICAN NEGROES Illus. Crowell, 1956. (grade 7 and up)

Very fine, warm, and informative biographies trace the entire lives of singer Marian Anderson, educator Mary McLeod Bethune, dancer and anthropologist Katherine Dunham, and author Ann Petry.

** *Rittenhouse, Mignon* SEVEN WOMEN EXPLORERS Lippincott, 1964. (grades 7-9)

Clearly written, factual biographies of seven women who had an urge to learn of new lands and who were willing to travel hazardous roads. The seven women, some of whom were single and others who were married to explorers, all made individual contributions to knowledge and these profiles give good, unemotional accounts of this and also discuss some aspects of their private lives. The women are Alexine Tinnè, Florence von Sass Baker, and Delia J. Denning Akeley, explorers of Africa; Fanny Bullock Workman, explorer of the Himalayas in India; Kathleen M. Kenyon, who worked in the Near East; Louise Arner Boyd, an Arctic explorer; and Isabella Lucy Bird Bishop, who explored Asia.

*** *Rollins, Charlmae* FAMOUS AMERICAN NEGRO POETS Illus. Dodd, 1965. (grades 6-9)

Especially good, brief, readable, and dramatic profiles of poets Frances Harper, Effie Lee Newsome, Margaret Walker, Phillis Wheatley, and Gwendolyn Brooks. The author skillfully has interwoven examples of their poetry into the biographies, which are suitable for reference and background material as well as for casual reading.

** ——— FAMOUS NEGRO ENTERTAINERS OF STAGE, SCREEN AND TV Dodd, 1967. (grade 7 and up)

Good but sometimes dry profiles of singers Marian Anderson, Josephine Baker, Lena Horne, Eartha Kitt, and Leontyne Price are readable and useful for reference. Lacking vitality and style, they serve best for background information.

** ——— THEY SHOWED THE WAY: FORTY AMERICAN NEGRO LEADERS Crowell, 1964. (grade 4 and up)

Brief but very fine biographies of Ida Wells-Barnett, reformer and journalist; Mary McLeod Bethune, educator; Frances

Ellen Watkins Harper, abolitionist and poet; Edmonia Lewis, sculptor; Harriet Tubman, abolitionist; Phillis Wheatley, poet; and Maggie Lena Walker, banker. Also included is a profile of Deborah Gannet (also known as Deborah Gannet Sampson) which lacks proper documentation. (According to most authoritative sources, Ms. Sampson is descended from Governor William Bradford, Miles Standish, and John Alden and there is no indication that she was not white.)

*** *Rosenblum, Morris* HEROES OF ISRAEL Illus. Fleet, 1972. (grades 7-10)

Very well-written narratives, despite their brevity, are broad in scope as they trace the lives of Israeli heroines Hannah Senesh and former Prime Minister Golda Meir. The emphasis is on their contributions to Israel, and their stories are told with dignity and drama.

*** *Ross, Nancy* HEROINES OF THE EARLY WEST Random, 1960. (grades 7-11)

Remarkably good book deals with many underlying feminist issues. Profiles of Abigail Scott Duniway, feminist and pioneer of the West; Sacajawea, interpreter to Lewis and Clark; Narcissa Whitman, missionary; Mary Richardson Walker and Sister Mary Loyola, missionaries, are vivid, exciting, and dramatic. An introductory chapter discusses pioneer women in general, illuminating the impact they had on the recorded history of this nation.

*** *Ross, Pat, comp.* YOUNG AND FEMALE: TURNING POINTS IN THE LIVES OF EIGHT AMERICAN WOMEN Random, 1972. (grade 7 and up)

Well-chosen selections from the autobiographies of eight American women are compiled in this brief collection. The editor has chosen women whose backgrounds and areas of achievement vary, but she has neatly coordinated the material to show that each woman, at some point in her youth, made a decision that helped her find direction. An excellent feminist foreword discusses the pressure to conform to stereotypic sex roles that faced these young women, and the determination and intelligence which enabled them to become successful, well-rounded human beings. Each selection is

365

introduced with a brief overview of the subject's life, emphasizing her spirit and uniqueness. Included are actress, feminist, and political worker Shirley MacLaine; black Congresswoman Shirley Chisholm; feminist, reformer, and journalist Dorothy Day; engineer and author Emily Hahn; birth control advocate Margaret Sanger; black tennis champion Althea Gibson; reporter and author Edna Ferber; and photo-journalist Margaret Bourke-White.

*** *Ryan, Joan* CONTRIBUTIONS OF WOMEN: SPORTS Illus. Dillon, 1975. (grade 6 and up)

Very fine, lively profiles of all-around athlete "Babe" Didrikson Zaharias, Olympic equestrienne and jockey Kathy Kusner, track athlete Wilma Rudolph, tennis player Billie Jean King, ice skater Peggy Fleming, and swimmer Melissa Belote are told from a feminist perspective, showing the women's unique contributions to sports and focussing on the increasing recognition given to women in sports. Each chapter highlights the woman's athletic career, but attention is also given to her personal life.

*** *Sabin, Francene* WOMEN WHO WIN Illus. with photographs. Random, 1975. (grades 5-8)

A very fine feminist introduction discusses the obstacles that have stood in the way of women entering and rising to the top of the sports world. The informal, narrative profiles themselves are also written from a feminist perspective, giving well-balanced accounts of the personal and professional life of each woman. The author explains many important points about each sport, enhancing the profiles, but also making them more comprehensible to those who are not sports-oriented. Included are tennis champion Billie Jean King; figure skater Janet Lynn; Olympic track star Cheryl Toussaint; swimmers Jenny Bartz, Lynn Genesko, Nina MacInnis, and Sharon Berg; bowler Paula Sperber; gymnast Cathy Rigby; skiers Marilyn, Barbara, and Lindy Cochran; diver Micki King; and golfer Kathy Whitworth.

*** *Schwartz, Bert* GREAT BLACK ATHLETES Pendulum Pr., 1971. (grade 8 and up)

366

Outstanding profile of Althea Gibson focusses on her tennis career from its beginnings until her championships at Wimbledon and Forest Hills in 1957. There is little discussion of her personal life: the emphasis is on her tennis game and on her status as the first black tennis player to compete at Forest Hills.

*** *Severn, Bill* FREE BUT NOT EQUAL: HOW WOMEN WON THE RIGHT TO VOTE Illus. Messner, 1967. (grade 7 and up)

Feminist book follows the development of the suffrage movement in America, providing a dramatic and inspiring overview. Although not really a collective biography, there is a great deal of information on the lives of feminists and suffragists Victoria Woodhull, Susan B. Anthony, Elizabeth Cady Stanton, Lucy Stone, Lucretia Mott, Harriet Stanton Blatch (daughter of Elizabeth Cady Stanton, and latter-day suffragist), Alice Paul, Carrie Chapman Catt, and Anna Howard Shaw. Particularly suitable for background information before reading the lengthier individual biographies of these women.

*** *Shevey, Sandra* LADIES OF POP-ROCK Illus. with photographs. Scholastic Book Service, 1972. (grades 7-12)

Journalistically sophisticated profiles of popular contemporary singers Buffy Sainte-Marie, Janis Ian, Melanie, Joni Mitchell, Tina Turner, Bonnie Bramlett, Grace Slick, Cass Elliot, Marilyn McCoo Davis, Florence La Rue Gordon, Roslyn Kind. Well-written sketches which discuss the singers' personal philosophies and significant aspects of their public and private lives are preceded by a general overview of the women and their challenges in the popular music field. The women are depicted as being concerned about society and committed to making changes in it.

** *Silverman, Al* MORE SPORT TITANS OF THE TWENTIETH CENTURY Illus. Putnam, 1969. (grade 5 and up)

A profile of Helen Wills, one of the first American women tennis champions, offers good insights into the role of a woman in the world of sports. The journalistic style is appealing but ordinary.

*** ——— SPORTS TITANS OF THE TWENTIETH CENTURY Illus. Putnam, 1968. (grade 5 and up)

Fast-moving, dramatic profile of all-around athlete "Babe" Didrikson Zaharias is written in journalistic style, adding excitement and vitality to an already inspiring story.

*** *Smaridge, Morah* FAMOUS AUTHOR-ILLUSTRATORS FOR YOUNG PEOPLE Dodd, 1973. (grade 7 and up)

Informative short biographies of author-illustrators Kate Greenaway, Beatrix Potter, Wanda Gág, Lois Lenski, Marie Hall Ets, Marcia Brown, and Joan Walsh Anglund are extremely well written and interesting. Nonanecdotal, straightforward narratives discuss the achievements, literary and artistic style, and personal lives of each subject. Valuable to adults interested in children's literature as well as to young readers.

** ——— FAMOUS BRITISH WOMEN NOVELISTS Illus. Dodd, 1967. (grades 7-10)

Short, interesting, and sometimes anecdotal profiles of British novelists Jane Austen; Anne, Charlotte, and Emily Brontë; Fanny Burney; Agatha Christie; George Eliot; Rumer Godden; Sheila Kaye-Smith; Victoria Sackville-West; Dorothy Sayers; Mary Stewart; Mary Webb; and Virginia Woolf provide good background for further study or the reading of their works.

*** ——— FAMOUS MODERN STORYTELLERS FOR YOUNG PEOPLE Illus. Dodd, 1969. (grades 7-9)

Excellent profiles of Laura Wilder, Eleanor Farjeon, Mary Norton, Claire Huchet Bishop, Elizabeth Enright, Marguerite deAngeli, Carol Ryrie Brink, Elizabeth Coatsworth, Rumer Godden, P. L. Travers, Astrid Lindgren, and Marguerite Henry offer good insights into the personalities of these writers who are familiar to young readers. The style is lively and readable, without resorting to fictionalization.

*** ——— TRAILBLAZERS IN AMERICAN ARTS Illus. Messner, 1971. (grades 3-6)

Attractive book contains a profile of Marian Anderson which highlights the important events in her life in an immensely readable, dramatic style.

*** *Smith, Margaret Chase, and Jeffers, Paul H.* GALLANT WOMEN McGraw, 1968. (grades 4-8)

Senator Margaret Chase Smith has written fine introductions to short, partially fictionalized biographies of ten courageous and determined American women who overcame obstacles to reach a goal. The collection includes a good cross-section of American women, and each biography offers insights into why the subject has chosen her particular route to self-fulfillment and achievement, clearly outlining her contributions to society. Despite the informality and simplicity of style, the biographies focus on important aspects of the women's lives and reflect sound research. The biography of Dolley Madison places too much emphasis on her role as an adjunct though it clearly reports her heroism in saving important documents; but the other biographies are extremely well balanced treatments. They include colonial religious leader Anne Hutchinson; black abolitionist Harriet Tubman; author Harriet Beecher Stowe; founder of the American Red Cross, Clara Barton; pioneer physician Elizabeth Blackwell; feminist Susan B. Anthony; teacher of Helen Keller, Annie Sullivan (Macy); aviator Amelia Earhart; black tennis champion Althea Gibson; cabinet member Francis Perkins; humanitarian, First Lady, and United Nations delegate, Eleanor Roosevelt.

*** *Squire, C. B.* HEROES OF CONSERVATION Illus. Fleet, 1974. (grades 7-10)

Outstanding, short, but reasonably thorough summary of the adult and professional life of Rachel Carson clearly shows her sense of responsibility, her foresight, and the criticism to which she was subjected. Woven into the narrative are quotations from her writings which may act as a spur to reading her own works.

*** *Squire, Elizabeth D.* HEROES OF JOURNALISM Fleet, 1974. (grades 7-10)

Straightforward narrative focusses on the journalistic career of pioneer newspaper reporter Nellie Bly and photojournalist Margaret Bourke-White. Although fairly brief, the profiles are somewhat comprehensive and the crisp, clear, nonfictionalized text introduces subjects vigorously and succinctly.

*** *Stambler, Irwin* WOMEN IN SPORTS Illus. with photographs. Doubleday, 1975. (grade 7 and up)

A very fine introduction discusses the role of women in sports. With a strongly feminist focus, it points out that women have not had equal opportunities but are now approaching more equity in both status and money. Substantial profiles emphasize the athletic careers but also give nonvarnished, objective views of the personal lives of twelve women in different sports. These colorful and elucidating accounts should appeal even to those who are not especially knowledgeable or enthusiastic about sports. Included are profiles of "Babe" Didrikson Zaharias, all-around athlete; Cathy Rigby, gymnast; Billie Jean King, tennis champion; Anne Henning, speed skater; Robyn Smith, jockey; Mary Decker and Wyomia Tyus Simburg, track champions; Shirley Muldowney, drag racer; Barbara Ann Cochran, skier; Micki King, diver; and Theresa Shank, basketball player.

** *Stein, M. L.* BLACKS IN COMMUNICATIONS: JOURNALISM, PUBLIC RELATIONS AND ADVERTISING Illus. with photographs. Messner, 1972. (grade 6 and up)

Although this is more a career book and history of blacks in communications than a collective biography, profiles of women appear in a chapter entitled "Ladies of the Press" and are interspersed through other chapters. Lively and anecdotal, they are brief and focus mainly on the professional rather than on the personal lives of the subjects. Included are journalists Audreen Ballard, Charlayne Hunter, Betty Washington, Marilyn I. Duncan, Angela Parker, Nancy Hicks, Jean Perry, Jeannye Thornton, Almena Lomax, Barbara Campbell, and Ruth N. Ross. Television newscasters Melba Tolliver, Lucille Rich, Edith Huggins, Barbara J. Caffie, Carol Jenkins, Valerie Coleman, Joan Murray, and Belva Davis are also profiled.

*** *Sterling, Dorothy, and Quarles, Benjamin* LIFT EVERY VOICE Doubleday, 1965. (grades 5-9)

Very fine profile of Mary Church Terrell, black educator, is a substantial, straightforward account. Informal in style, it nevertheless recreates in detail the accomplishments of Ms. Terrell, who was the first black woman to serve on a school board in the United States.

*** *Sterling, Philip, and Logan, Rayford* FOUR TOOK FREEDOM Doubleday, 1967. (grades 7-10)

Harriet Tubman is one of the four blacks profiled in this excellent collective volume. This accurate and thoughtful portrayal of the remarkable abolitionist who escaped from slavery and helped others to do likewise is movingly told.

*** *Sterne, Emma Gelders* I HAVE A DREAM Illus. Knopf, 1965. (grade 5 and up)

Skillfully written account of the black struggle in America includes brief portraits of Daisy Bates, leader in school integration; Marian Anderson, singer and civil rights worker; and Rosa Parks, who led the way to the end of bus segregation. Very readable, the information imparted is considerable and suggested readings contribute to the value of the book.

*** ——— THEY TOOK THEIR STAND Illus. Macmillan, 1968. (grades 7-12)

Informative account of the abolition and civil rights movements as told through the lives of southern white people includes sensitive, appealing portraits of Sophia Auld, first teacher of slave and abolitionist Frederick Douglas; Angelina Grimké, abolitionist and feminist; and Anne Braden, daughter of a contemporary segregationist family who became active as a civil rights worker. History and biography are interwoven to provide an immensely readable and thoughtful book.

*** *Stevenson, Janet* WOMEN'S RIGHTS Illus. Watts, 1972. (grade 5 and up)

Included in this superb feminist history of women's rights are brief profiles and photographs of Lucretia Mott, Elizabeth Cady Stanton, Lucy Stone, Susan B. Anthony, and Anna Howard Shaw, all early feminists, as well as Stanton's daughter Harriet Stanton Blatch and Carrie Chapman Catt, latterday suffragists. Discussed also, but in less detail, are Angelina and Sarah Grimké, abolitionists and feminists, and Alice

Paul, feminist and suffragist. A graphically attractive and immensely readable volume, this book provides a colorful and elucidating account of the important events and themes in the struggle for women's rights. Suitable for browsing, reading, or reference, this volume is a fine accompaniment to other more detailed biographies.

*** *Stiller, Richard* THE SPY, THE LADY, THE CAPTAIN AND THE COLONEL Illus. Scholastic Book Service, n.d. (grades 4-8)

Good, easy-to-read account of Elizabeth Keckley will interest reluctant as well as enthusiastic readers. The profile chronicles Ms. Keckley's life from her early days as a slave to her success as a dressmaker and confidante to First Lady Mary Lincoln.

*** *Stirling, Nora* WHO WROTE THE CLASSICS? vol. 1. Day, 1965. (grade 8 and up)

Very fine profiles of Jane Austen and the Brontës are included here. The chapter on the Brontës treats them as individuals and is perceptive and interesting; the one on Jane Austen gives a personal as well as critical view of her work. These nonfictional narratives are warm and appealing.

*** ——— WHO WROTE THE CLASSICS? vol. 2. Day, 1969. (grade 8 and up)

An excellent profile of Edith Wharton is brief but animated, and describes the effects of the author's personality on her writing.

*** ——— WHO WROTE THE MODERN CLASSICS? Illus. Day, 1970. (grade 9 and up)

Beautifully written, informative biography of Willa Cather is substantial in length and depth. Her life, personality, and works are discussed, and this book provides good background for the reading of Cather's works.

*** *Stoddard, Hope* FAMOUS AMERICAN WOMEN Illus. Crowell, 1970. (grade 7 and up)

These superb collective biographies of modern women who have been successful in their endeavors are extremely valuable. Accurate and informative, the biographies offer engrossing, intimate views of each woman and provide considerable information about their personal lives and achievements. The author highlights experiences of childhood, youth, and adulthood to show the complete personalities and characters of each subject. Informal and extremely readable, the biographies provide good reading as well as useful reference material. Included are social reformers Jane Addams, Dorothea Dix, Margaret Sanger; photographer Dorothea Lange; dancers Agnes deMille, Isadora Duncan, Martha Graham; philosopher Susanne Langer; singers Rosa Ponselle, Marian Anderson; authors Louisa May Alcott, Willa Cather, Gertrude Stein, Harriet Beecher Stowe, Edith Hamilton; feminists Susan B. Anthony, Margaret Fuller, Lucretia Mott; actress Ethel Barrymore; artist Mary Cassatt; educators Mary McLeod Bethune, Mary Lyon; aviator Amelia Earhart; humanitarian and First Lady Eleanor Roosevelt; poets Emily Dickinson, Edna St. Vincent Millay, Harriet Monroe; cabinet member Oveta Culp Hobby; sculptor Malvina Hoffman; anthropologist Margaret Mead; astronomer Maria Mitchell; jurist Constance Baker Motley; scientist Florence Sabin; Senator Margaret Chase Smith; abolitionist and slave Harriet Tubman; athlete "Babe" Didrikson Zaharias; industrial engineer Lillian Gilbreth; founder of Christian Science church, Mary Baker Eddy; religious leader Sister Frances Xavier Cabrini; and handicapped humanitarian Helen Keller.

*** *Sullivan, George* QUEENS OF THE COURT Illus. with photographs. Dodd, 1974. (grades 5-9)

Substantial, lively portraits of tennis champions Margaret Court, Billie Jean King, Chris Evert, Evonne Goolagong, Rosemary Casals, and Virginia Wade focus on their professional lives. The author also incorporates explanations of the game which will aid those who do not know much about tennis to enjoy the profiles more, but will not bore those who are already knowledgeable about tennis. An introduction discusses some of the advances and changes made in women's tennis today, and a concluding chapter discusses some of the outstanding women of the past. A glossary of tennis terms and many good action photographs further enhance the text.

* *Surge, Frank* FAMOUS SPIES Illus. Lerner, 1969. (reading level, grades 4-6; interest level, grade 7 and up)

Mediocre, sketchy views of spies Delilah, Mata Hari, Belle Boyd, Emma Edmonds, Rose O'Neal Greenhow, and Elizabeth Van Lew are somewhat enlivened by good photographs. In an obvious attempt to entice reluctant readers, the author treats a subject with wide appeal oversimplistically and not too successfully.

** ———— SINGERS OF THE BLUES Illus. Lerner, 1969. (reading level, grades 4-6; interest level through high school)

Despite some literary flaws, these are fairly good profiles of Billie Holiday and Bessie Smith. A profile of Ma Rainey is too brief to be of much value.

*** *Taylor, Kathryn* GENERATIONS OF DENIAL: SEVENTY-FIVE SHORT BIOGRAPHIES OF WOMEN IN HISTORY Illus. Time-Change Pr., 1971. (grade 9 and up)

Brief but excellent feminist profiles of seventy-five women —some famous, some obscure—who have made important contributions to society. Included in the sixty-five-page pamphlet are suffragists, feminists, military leaders, queens, witches, reformers, revolutionaries, educators, scientists, inventors, writers, entertainers, explorers, and artists. Bibliographies follow each profile and a more complete bibliography is also included. An excellent and handy little reference work, this is interesting as well as utilitarian.

*** *Teitz, Joyce* WHAT'S A NICE GIRL LIKE YOU DOING IN A PLACE LIKE THIS? Illus. with photographs. Coward, 1972. (grade 9 and up)

Feminist book is directed towards young women looking for good role-models in different professional careers. The author, herself a graduate of Harvard Law School, provides a superb introduction and conclusion which reveals her own feminist values and beliefs. The eleven inspirational profiles are written in a lively, journalistic style. Included are chapters on journalist Ann Zill, attorney Marion Wright Edelman, physician Marjorie Nelson, oceanographer Sylvia A. Earle, physicist Devrie S. Intriligator, company president Jane Evans, campaign committee chairperson Marion Edney, economist Gail Pierson, foreign service officer Eleanor Hicks, systems analyst Margaret Hamilton, and writer Susan Edmiston.

*** *Terkel, Studs* GIANTS OF JAZZ Illus. Crowell, 1957. (grade 7 and up)

Warm, informal profiles of Bessie Smith and Billie Holiday are brief, but cover the important events of their professional lives in a lively, dramatic style.

** *Tharp, Edgar* GIANTS OF SPACE Illus. Grosset, 1970. (grades 5-9)

Accurate, brief profile of the Russian cosmonaut Valentina Tereshkova gives equal emphasis to her personal life as well as to her contributions to space exploration. Somewhat superficial, it is nevertheless a good introduction to her accomplishments.

*** *Trease, Geoffrey* SEVEN STAGES Vanguard, 1965. (grades 7-10)

Very fine profiles of actress Sarah Siddons, singer Jenny Lind, and dancer Anna Pavlova are included in this collection of people prominent in the theatrical fields. Good straightforward narratives reveal the motivations and the accomplishments of the three women, and comprehensively cover the highlights of their lives and careers.

** ——— SEVEN SOVEREIGN QUEENS Illus. Vanguard, 1971. (grade 7 and up)

Well-written, interesting biographies of Cleopatra, Boudicca, Galla Placida, Isabella, Christina, Maria Theresa, and Catherine the Great combine history and biography, doing justice to both.

** ——— SEVEN QUEENS OF ENGLAND Vanguard, 1953. (grade 6 and up)

Warm, informal portraits of Maud, Mary, Elizabeth I, Mary II, Anne, Victoria, and Elizabeth II are interesting and well written, suitable for reading as well as for reference.

*** *Untermeyer, Louis* THE PATHS OF POETRY: TWENTY-FOUR POETS AND THEIR POEMS Illus. Delacorte, 1966. (grades 6-10)

Twenty-five poets and their poems are discussed in this unusually well-written collection. Included are extremely perceptive profiles of Elizabeth Barrett Browning and Emily Dickinson which weave their poetry into the text. Dignified writing brings out the drama of their lives, and uses biography to help interpret their work.

*** *Walker, Greta* WOMEN TODAY: TEN PROFILES Hawthorn, 1975. (grade 7 and up)

An outstanding, briskly written collection includes many women of whom little or nothing has been published for young readers. A very fine feminist introduction precedes portraits of women who have carved out successful careers for themselves, and who have shown evidence of struggling to get what they want out of life. However, the emphasis is not so much on career guidance or modelling, but on seeing the women as people who have set forth goals, and followed the appropriate routes to getting there. Included in these journalistically informal, highly readable profiles are Betty Friedan, feminist writer and lecturer; Dorothy Pitman Hughes, day care center advocate; Marketa Kimbrell, actress and street theater organizer; Eleanor Holmes Norton, attorney and New York City commissioner of Human Rights; Eve Queler, pianist and conductor; Lola Redford, cofounder of Consumer Action Now; Marlene Sanders, television producer; Gertrude Schimmel, police inspector; Gloria Steinem, feminist, writer, publisher; and Marcia Storch, physician. Young adult and adult readers will also find this book interesting and worthwhile; junior high readers will not find it too difficult.

*** *Wayne, Bennett, ed.* BLACK CRUSADERS FOR FREEDOM Illus. Garrard, 1974. (reading level, grades 3-4; interest level through high school)

The outstanding Discovery biographies of Harriet Tubman, the rescuer of other slaves, and Sojourner Truth, abolitionist and feminist, originally written for early elementary school readers, have been combined with other biographies in this one volume and reset with smaller print and with photographs and old prints rather than line drawings, making them more appealing to older readers. The result is an outstanding book for older reluctant readers, easy to read, but nonetheless dramatic and stirring.

*** ———— FOUR WOMEN OF COURAGE Illus. Garrard, 1975. (reading level, grades 3-4; interest level through high school)

Four Discovery books for early elementary school readers have been combined in this one volume, reset with smaller print and with photographs rather than line drawings, thus making it more suitable in format for older readers. The biographies of aviator Jacqueline Cochran, pioneer nurse Linda Richards, and humanitarian Helen Keller are fast-moving, warm, and interesting and should be of great interest to older readers despite the limited vocabulary and shorter-than-usual sentences. The biography of Dorothea Dix is also good, but is somewhat dry and not quite as good as the others. Generally, though, this is an outstanding book for reluctant readers.

*** ———— WOMEN WHO DARED TO BE DIFFERENT Illus. with photographs. Garrard, 1973. (reading level, grades 3-4; interest level, grades 3-12)

The editor has chosen four women who achieved success in fields which excluded women, and reprinted individual biographies of them which Garrard published in an easy-to-read format for younger children. Incorporating the theme of women who dared to be different, highlighted by photographs, the book is further enhanced by the inclusion of brief notes and photographs of contemporary women who have been successful in related fields. The women whose lives are told in simple, but detailed narrative are Annie Oakley, markswoman; Maria Mitchell, astronomer; Nellie Bly, reporter; and Amelia Earhart, aviator. Extremely well organized, neither the text nor the format is so juvenile as to "embarrass" the older reader. Both the content and format have interest and appeal to older readers, and because it is career-oriented as well as being good biography, this is a collection of unusual merit and one of the very few for reluctant readers.

*** ———— WOMEN WITH A CAUSE Illus. Garrard, 1975. (reading level, grades 3-4; interest level through high school)

Four individual Discovery biographies of Anne Hutchinson, colonial religious dissenter; Lucretia Mott and Susan B. Anthony, feminists and abolitionists; and Eleanor Roosevelt, humanitarian, are combined in a format more suitable for

377

older reluctant readers. Reset in smaller type, and old prints and photographs substituted for line drawings, they are warm and inspiring and although easy to read are not too childish for older readers. The biography of Susan B. Anthony is slightly stilted, but nonetheless good, and the ones of the other women are truly excellent.

*** *Weinberg, Arthur and Lila* SOME DISSENTING VOICES world, 1970. (grade 7 and up)

A very fine profile of Jane Addams is included in this collective of six American dissenters. Equal emphasis is given to her activities and work among the poor surrounding Hull House and her efforts in behalf of peace. The authors show both crusades as reflective of Ms. Addams's great interest in humanity and her willingness to go against the main stream of prevailing beliefs. Her achievements as well as her unfulfilled dreams are described vividly in this well-balanced account of her life.

** *Werner, Vivian* SCIENTIST VERSUS SOCIETY Hawthorn, 1975. (grade 9 and up)

The author has included well-written accounts of the lives of seven scientists who were surrounded by controversy during their lifetime because their work opposed prevailing societal beliefs. Included in this collection is a profile of Ada Augusta, the countess of Lovelace. The daughter of the poet Lord Byron, she was a mathematical genius who was prevented from developing and making use of her abilities because of her sex. There is more emphasis on her personal life than on her actual mathematical prowess, but this is a warm, interesting profile that clearly shows the limitations imposed on women in the nineteenth century.

** *Wheeler, Thomas, ed.* THE IMMIGRANT EXPERIENCE: THE ANGUISH OF BECOMING AMERICAN Dial, 1971. (grade 8 and up)

Each chapter is a contribution from someone who immigrated to the United States. Jade Snow Wong, a Chinese immigrant and the author of *Fifth Chinese Daughter*, has written one of the excerpts. Ms. Wong is now a ceramist. The

378

substantial chapter gives a good picture of a Chinese-American woman and a family that valued education and opportunity. The author herself, in this selection, holds many traditional views of sex roles, but the chapter cannot really be termed sexist.

*** *Williams, Eric, ed.* THE WILL TO BE FREE: GREAT ESCAPE STORIES Nelson, 1970. (grade 6 and up)

Dramatic escape stories tell, in individual chapters, the experiences of Mme. Anne Brusselman, a Belgium woman who hid and passed on to safety Allied soldiers during World War II, and Christine Arnothy, a teenage girl who escaped from Hungary when the Russians took over the country. Told in the words of the subjects, the book is exciting and well organized

*** *Wintterle, John, and Cramer, Richard S.* PORTRAITS OF NOBEL LAUREATES IN PEACE Abelard–Schuman, 1971. (grade 7 and up)

Very fine, vivid studies of Bertha von Suttner, Jane Addams, and Emily Greene Balch are included here. Ms. von Suttner, the author who worked for peace and helped to inspire Alfred Nobel to create the award, received it herself in 1905. Jane Addams, social reformer and peace advocate, was awarded her prize in 1931. Ms. Balch, economist and sociologist and international secretary and honorary president of the Women's International League for Peace, received the award in 1946. Well-researched, straightforward narratives bring each woman to life clearly, but place the emphasis on her work rather than on her personal life.

*** *Wright, Helen, and Rapport, Samuel* GREAT ADVENTURES IN NURSING Harper, 1960. (grade 7 and up)

Excellent book directed to the career-oriented young woman gives a dramatic, vivid picture of nursing. Composed of reprints of articles and biographical sketches, this volume gives a general approach to nursing and also presents the personal and professional life stories of individual nurses. Included are Sister Elizabeth Kenny, polio nurse; Princess

Ileana of Romania; Mary Breckinridge, frontier nurse; Lillian Wald, founder of the Visiting Nurses Service; Florence Nightingale, pioneer nurse; Mother Bickerdyke, Civil War nurse; and Edith Cavell, World War I nurse and spy.

*** *Yolen, Jane* PIRATES IN PETTICOATS Illus. McKay, 1963. (grades 7-9)

Lively profiles of women who ventured into what is usually thought of as a male-dominated profession—the ingenuous, courageous world of piracy! Carefully researched and well-documented, these fanciful stories sound like pure fiction, but are not. The author does not preach at her young readers, but still makes it clear that illegal excitement and adventure are not acceptable substitutes for the law.

*** *Young, Margaret* BLACK AMERICAN LEADERS Illus. Watts, 1969. (grade 7 and up)

Despite their brevity, these profiles are useful for reference and as a spur to further reading. Thirty-six different black leaders are grouped into four categories: civil rights, government, international, and political leaders. Included are abolitionists Harriet Tubman; educator Mary McLeod Bethune; jurist Constance Baker Motley; state official Ersa Hines Poston; attorney Patricia Roberts Harris; Congresswomen Shirley Chisholm and Barbara Jordan (at the time of publication, a state senator from Texas); and city official Vel Phillips. The book is attractively designed with vital statistics preceding the brief capsule summaries of the life of each subject, and the photographs contribute to the book's value.

Appendixes

A

Women Classified
by Nationalities

African

Andriamanjato,
   Rahantavololona
Bam, Brigalia
Brooks, Angie
Ighodaro, Irene
Jiagge, Annie
Kenyatta, Margaret

Makeba, Miriam
Mandela, Winnie
Moore, Kofoworola Aina
Nosente
Nzinga
Sikhakane, Joyce

American*

Abel, Hazel
Abzug, Bella
Adams, Abigail Smith
Adams, Adrienne
Adams, Diana
Adams, Elizabeth
Adams, Louisa Johnson
Adams, Maude
Addams, Jane

Akeley, Delia J. Denning
Albright, Tenley
Alcott, Louisa May
Amévor, Charlotte
Anderson, Marian
Andrews, Elizabeth
Angelou, Maya
Anglund, Joan Walsh
Anthony, Susan Brownell

*Individuals listed under American Indian and Black American
are also listed here.

383

Antin, Mary
Arden, Elizabeth
Arnold, Margaret Shippen
Auld, Sophia

Babashoff, Shirley
Babbitt, Natalie
Bailey, Mollie
Bailey, Pearl
Baker, Augusta
Baker, Irene Bailey
Baker, Josephine
Balch, Emily Green
Ball, Lucille
Ballard, Audreen
Barringer, Emily Dunning, M.D.
Barrymore, Ethel
Barton, Clara
Bartz, Jenny
Bates, Daisy
Bates, Katherine Lee
Baugh, Laura
Beaux, Cecilia
Belote, Melissa
Belpré, Pura
Bendick, Jeanne
Benet, Rosemary Carr
Berg, Gertrude
Berg, Patty
Berg, Sharon
Berry, Martha

Bethune, Mary McLeod
Bickerdyke, Mary Ann
Bishop, Claire Huchet
Black, Winifred
Blackwell, Elizabeth, M.D.
Blatch, Harriet Stanton
Bleeker, Sonia
Blitch, Iris
Bloomer, Amelia Jenks
Blount, Mildred E.
Bly, Nellie
Boland, Veronica
Bolton, Frances P.
Bonaparte, Elizabeth Patterson
Bonnin, Gertrude Simmons
Bono, Cher
Boone, Rebecca
Boris, Ruthanna
Bosomsworth, Mary Musgrove
Bosone, Reva Beck
Bourke-White, Margaret
Bowring, Eva
Boyd, Belle
Boyd, Louise Arner
Braden, Anne
Bradstreet, Anne Dudley
Bramlett, Bonnie
Breckinridge, Mary
Brewton, Sara W.
Brice, Fanny

Bridgman, Laura
Brink, Carol Ryrie
Brooks, Gwendolyn
Brown, Antoinette
Brown, Marcia
Buchanan, Vera
Buck, Pearl
Burgess, Abbie
Burke, Yvonne Braithwaite
Burnett, Frances Hodgson
Bushfield, Vera
Buzonas, Gail Johnson
Byars, Betsy
Byron, Katherine Edgar

Cabrini, Sister Frances Xavier
Caffie, Barbara J.
Campbell, Barbara
Caraway, Hattie W.
Carlson, Natalie Savage
Carroll, Anna Ella
Carson, Rachel
Casals, Rosemary
Cassatt, Mary
Cather, Willa
Catlett, Elizabeth
Catt, Carrie Chapman
Chadwick, Florence
Child, Lydia Maria
Chisholm, Shirley
Chouteau, Yvonne
Church, Marguerite Stitt

Clark, Ann Nolan
Clark, Eugenie
Clark, Septima Poinsette
Clarke, Marian Williams
Cleary, Beverly
Coatsworth, Elizabeth
Cobb, Geraldyn
Cochran, Barbara Ann
Cochran, Jacqueline
Cochran, Linda (Lindy)
Cochran, Marilyn
Coleman, Valerie
Collett, Glenna
Colman, Hila
Concello, Antoinette
Connolly, Maureen
Connolly, Olga Fikotova
Cooney, Barbara
Cooper, Arvazine Angeline
Corbin, Margaret
Cornell, Katharine
Crabtree, Lotta
Craft, Ellen
Crandall, Prudence
Cunningham, Julia
Custer, Elizabeth

Dare, Virginia
Dat-So-La-Lee
d'Aulaire, Ingri
Davies, Mary Carolyn
Davis, Angela

Freeman, Elizabeth
   "Mumbet"
Freeman, Mary Eleanor
   Wilkins
Fremont, Jessie Benton
Friedan, Betty
Fuller, Margaret
Fulmer, Willa L.

Gaeddart, Lou Ann
Gág, Wanda
Garelick, May
Garms, Shirley Rudolph
Gasque, Elizabeth Hawley
Genesko, Lynn
George, Jean Craighead
Gibbs, Florence R.
Gibson, Althea
Gilbreth, Lillian
Glubok, Shirley
Goldman, Emma
Gordon, Florence La Rue
Graham, Martha
Granahan, Kathryn E.
Grant, Julia
Grant, Micki
Grasso, Ella T.
Gratz, Rebecca
Graves, Dixie Bibb
Greeley-Smith, Nixola
Green, Edith
Greenhow, Rose O'Neal

Greenway, Isabella
Grifalconi, Ann
Griffiths, Martha
Grimké, Angelina
Grimké, Sarah
Guion, Connie, M.D.

Hader, Berta
Hahn, Emily
Hale, Lucretia Peabody
Hale, Sarah
Hamer, Fannie Lou
Hamilton, Alice, M.D.
Hamilton, Edith
Hamilton, Margaret
Hamilton, Virginia
Hansberry, Lorraine
Hansen, Julia Butler
Harden, Cecil M.
Harper, Frances Ellen
   Watkins
Harper, Valerie
Harris, LaDonna
Harris, Patricia
Hautzig, Esther
Hayes, Helen
Haywood, Carolyn
Heckler, Margaret M.
Heddy, Kathy
Heiss, Carol
Held, Anna
Henning, Anne

Kohut, Rebekah
Konigsburg, Elaine L.
Krauss, Ruth
Kuhn, Irene
Kusner, Kathy

Laedwig, Marion
La Flesche, Susette
Lange, Dorothea
Langer, Susanne
Langford, Anna Riggs
Langley, Katherine
Larrick, Nancy
Larrieu, Francie
Latham, Jean Lee
Lathrop, Dorothy
Lathrop, Julia
Lathrop, Rose Hawthorne
    (Mother Mary Alphonse)
Laurencin, Marie
Lawrence, Andrea Mead
Lawson, Roberta C.
Lazarus, Emma
Lease, Mary Elizabeth
Leitzel, Lillian
L'Engle, Madeleine
Lenski, Lois
Lewis, Edmonia
Lexau, Joan
Libow, Carol
Liliuokalani
Lincoln, Mary Todd

Lincoln, Nancy Hanks
Lindberg, Anne Morrow
Livingston, Myra Cohn
Lobel, Anita
Lockwood, Belva Ann
Loeb, Sophie
Lomax, Almena
Long, Rose McConnell
Loock, Christine
Loughborough, Mary Ann
    Webster
Louvestre, Mary
Lovejoy, Esther Pohl, M.D.
Low, Juliette Gordon
Lowell, Amy
Loyola, Sister Mary
Lubell, Winifred
Luce, Clare Boothe
Lusk, Georgia L.
Lynn, Janet
Lyon, Mary

McCarthy, Kathryn
    O'Loughlin
McCormick, Patricia
McCormick, Ruth Hanna
McCutcheon, Floretta
McGinley, Phyllis
McGovern, Ann
MacInnis, Nina
MacLaine, Shirley
McMillan, Clara G.

Parks, Rosa Lee
Pasquala
Paul, Alice
Peabody, Elizabeth Palmer
Perkins, Frances
Perry, Jean
Petersham, Maud
Peterson, Helen
Petry, Ann
Pfost, Gracie
Phillips, Vel
Picotte, Susan La Flesche
Pierson, Gail
Pine, Tillie S.
Pitcher, Molly
Pitou, Penny
Pleasant, Mary Ellen
  "Mammy"
Pocahontas
Ponselle, Rosa
Poston, Ersa Hines
Pratt, (Eliza) Jane
Pratt, Ruth Baker
Price, Leontyne
Prieto, Mariana
Pyle, Gladys

Rainey, Ma
Ramos, Elaine Abraham
Randolph, Martha Jefferson
Rankin, Jeannette
Raskin, Ellen
Ray, Dixy Lee

Ream, Vinnie
Redford, Lola
Reece, Louise Goff
Reed, Janet
Reid, Charlotte
Reiss, Joanna de Leeuw
Reno, Terry
Rey, Margret
Rice, Joan Moore
Rich, Lucille
Richards, Ellen Swallow
Richards, Laura E.
Richards, Linda
Rigby, Cathy
Riley, Corinne Boyd
Rincón, Felisa
Ringgold, Faith
Rinkoff, Barbara
Ripley, Sophia
Robertson, Alice M.
Rogers, Edith Nourse
Rollins, Charlemae Hill
Roosevelt, Eleanor
Rose, Ernestine
Ross, Betsy
Ross, Diana
Ross, Ruth N.
Rubinstein, Helena
Rudkin, Margaret Fogharty
Rudolph, Wilma

Sabin, Florence, M.D.
Sacajawea

St. Denis, Ruth
St. George, Katherine
St. Johns, Adela Rogers
Sainte-Marie, Buffy
Sampson, Deborah
Sanders, Marlene
Sanger, Margaret
Savage, Augusta
Sawyer, Ruth
Schimmel, Gertrude
Schroeder, Patricia
Scott, Ann Herbert
Scott, Hazel
Sears, Eleanor
Seibert, Florence
Selsam, Millicent E.
Shank, Theresa
Shaver, Dorothy
Shaw, Anna Howard
Sheehy, Gail
Sheklow, Edna
Shotwell, Louisa
Sidney, Margaret (pseud.)
Simburg, Wyomia Tyus
Simon, Carly
Simpson, Edna
Slick, Grace
Smith, Bessie
Smith, Kate
Smith, Margaret Chase
Smith, Robyn
Snyder, Zilpha Keatley

Sone, Monica
Sonneborn, Ruth A.
Sorensen, Virginia
Souta, Judy Cook
Southgate, Eliza
Speare, Elizabeth George
Sperber, Paula
Stanley, Winifred C.
Stanton, Elizabeth Cady
Stein, Gertrude
Steinem, Gloria
Stender, Fay
Sterling, Dorothy
Stern, Elizabeth G.
Stolz, Mary
Stone, Lucy
Storch, Marcia, M.D.
Stout, Penelope
Stowe, Harriet Beecher
Strauss, Lina
Sullivan, Leonor K.
Sumner, Jessie
Sutcliff, Rosemary
Swisshelm, Jane Grey

Tallchief, Maria
Tallchief, Marjorie
Tamaris
Tarbell, Ida
Tarry, Ellen
Taussig, Helen, M.D.
Taylor, Susie King

Wojciechowska, Maia
Wong, Jade Snow
Wood, Ann
Woodhouse, Chase Going
Woodhull, Victoria
Workman, Fanny Bullock
Wright, Frances (Fanny)
Wright, Mickey
Wyler, Rose

Yates, Elizabeth
Young, Margaret B.

Zaharias, Mildred "Babe"
  Didrikson
Zakrzewska, Marie
  Elizabeth, M.D.
Zenger, Anna
Zill, Ann
Zolotow, Charlotte

American Indian

Bonnin, Gertrude Simmons
Bosomsworth, Mary
  Musgrove
Chouteau, Yvonne
Francis, Milly Hadjo
Harris, LaDonna
Hightower, Rosella
Horne, Esther Burnett
Johnson, E. Pauline
La Flesche, Susette
Lawson, Roberta C.
Lewis, Edmonia
Martínez, Maria
Mountain Wolf Woman
Pasquala

Peterson, Helen L.
Picotte, Susan La Flesche
Pocahontas
Ramos, Elaine Abraham
Sacajawea
Tallchief, Maria
Tallchief, Marjorie
Tekakwitha, Kateri
Velarde, Pablita
Victor, Wilma L.
Ward, Nancy
Wauneka, Annie Dodge
Wetamoo
Winema
Winnemucca, Sarah

Australian

Court, Margaret
Fifield, Elaine
Goolagong, Evonne
Gould, Shane

Kenny, Elizabeth
Lester, Margaret
Wirth, May

Austrian

Maria Theresa
Meitner, Lise
Proell, Annemarie

Suttner, Bertha von
Trapp, Maria

Belgian

Brusselman, Anne

Hirsch, Clara de

Black American

Adams, Elizabeth
Amévor, Charlotte
Anderson, Marian
Angelou, Maya
Arroyo, Martina

Bailey, Pearl
Baker, Augusta
Baker, Josephine
Ballard, Audreen
Bates, Daisy
Bethune, Mary McLeod
Blount, Mildred E.
Brooks, Gwendolyn
Burke, Yvonne Braithwaite

Caffie, Barbara J.
Campbell, Barbara
Catlett, Elizabeth
Chisholm, Shirley

Clark, Septima Poinsette
Coleman, Valerie
Craft, Ellen

Davis, Angela
Davis, Belva
Davis, Francis Reed Elliot
Dee, Ruby
Dunham, Katherine

Fields, Mary
Flack, Roberta
Forten, Charlotte
Franklin, Aretha
Freeman, Elizabeth
    "Mumbet"

Gibson, Althea
Grant, Micki

Hamer, Fannie Lou

Hansberry, Lorraine
Harper, Frances Ellen
   Watkins
Harris, Patricia
Holiday, Billie
Horne, Lena
Huggins, Edith
Hughes, Dorothy Pitman
Hunter, Charlayne

Jackson, Mahalia
Jenkins, Carol
Jordan, Barbara

Keckley, Elizabeth
King, Coretta Scott
Kitt, Eartha

Langford, Anna Riggs
Lewis, Edmonia
Lomax, Almena
Louvestre, Mary

McCollough, Geraldine
Mason, Biddy
Moody, Anne
Morgan, Norma
Motley, Constance Baker

Newsome, Effie Lee
Norton, Eleanor Holmes

Parker, Angela

Parks, Rosa Lee
Perry, Jean
Petry, Ann
Phillips, Vel
Pleasant, Mary Ellen
   "Mammy"
Poston, Ersa Hines
Price, Leontyne

Rainey, Ma
Rich, Lucille
Ringgold, Faith
Ross, Diana
Ross, Ruth N.

Savage, Augusta
Scott, Hazel
Smith, Bessie

Tarry, Ellen
Taylor, Susie King
Terrell, Mary Church
Thornton, Jeannye
Tituba
Tolliver, Melba
Toussaint, Cheryl
Trammell, Beatrice Johnson
Truth, Sojourner
Tubman, Harriet
Tyson, Cicely

Walker, Maggie Lena

Walker, Margaret
Walker, Sarah Breedlove
Washington, Betty
Waters, Ethel
Wells-Barnett, Ida

Wheatley, Phillis
Williams, Fannie B.
Wood, Ann

Young, Margaret B.

British

Aguilar, Grace
Anne, Queen of England
Anne of Cleves
Anning, Mary
Augusta, Ada
Austen, Jane

Baker, Florence von Sass
Bell, Gertrude
Bird, Isabella Lucy
Boleyn, Anne
Booth, Evangeline
Boudicca
Brontë, Anne
Brontë, Charlotte
Brontë, Emily
Browning, Elizabeth Barrett
Burney, Fanny

Catherine of Aragon
Cavell, Edith
Chaplin, Mathilda, M.D.
Christie, Agatha
Craik, Dinah Mulock

Edwards, Julie
Eleanor of Aquitaine
Eliot, George
Elizabeth I
Elizabeth II
Evans, Helen, M.D.
Ewing, Juliana

Farjeon, Eleanor
Fonteyn, Margot

Garrett-Anderson, Elizabeth,
    M.D.
Godden, Rumer
Greenaway, Kate
Grey, Beryl
Grey, Lady Jane

Howard, Catherine

Jex-Blake, Sophia, M.D.
Johnson, Amy

Kaye-Smith, Sheila
Kemble, Frances (Fanny)

Kenyon, Kathleen
Kingsley, Mary

Markova, Alicia
Mary I
Mary II
Maud

Nesbit, Edith
Newton-John, Olivia
Nightingale, Florence
Norton, Mary

Pankhurst, Adele
Pankhurst, Christabel
Pankhurst, Emmeline
Pankhurst, Sylvia
Parr, Catherine
Pechey, Edith, M.D.
Potter, Beatrix

Rossetti, Christina

Sackville-West, Victoria
Sayers, Dorothy
Seymour, Jane
Shelley, Mary Godwin
    Wollstonecraft
Siddons, Sarah Kemble
Stewart, Mary
Sutcliff, Rosemary

Taylor, Ann
Taylor, Jane
Terry, Ellen
Thorne, Isabel, M.D.
Travers, P.L.

Victoria

Webb, Mary
Wollstonecraft, Mary
Woolf, Virginia
Wordsworth, Dorothy

Yonge, Charlotte Mary

Canadian

Johnson, E. Pauline
Rosenberg, Elsa

Takashima, Shizuye

Chinese

Chiang, Mei-ling Sung
Kung, Ai-ling Sung
Sun, Ch'ing-ling Sung

Tzu Hsi
Wong, Jade Snow

Cuban

Alonso, Alicia

Dutch

Blankers-Koen, Fanny
Hari, Mata
Juliana

Reiss, Joanna
Tinnè, Alexine
Wilhelmina

Egyptian

Catherine of Alexandria,
  Saint

Cleopatra
Nefertiti

Ethiopian

Haile Selassie, Tsahai

French

Angouleme, Marie Therese
  Charlotte
Auriol, Jacqueline
Bernadette of Lourdes, Saint
Bernhardt, Sarah
Bonaparte, Josephine
Bonheur, Rosa
Caron, Leslie
Chaminade, Cecile
Chauviré, Yvonne
Curie, Marie

Dache, Lily
Germaine, Saint
Jeanmarie, Renée
Joan of Arc
Joliot-Curie, Irene
Josephine
Laurencin, Marie
Le Clerq, Tanquil
Lenglen, Suzanne
Mance, Jeanne
Marchand, Colette

Marie Antoinette
Marillac, Saint Louise de
Morisot, Berthe
Rachel

Staël, Madame de
Vigee-Librun, Elizabeth
  Louise

German

Frank, Anne
Glueckel of Hamlin
Holm, Hanya

Kollwitz, Käthe
Schumann, Clara Wieck

Greek

Vlachos, Helen

Hungarian

Arnothy, Christine

Elizabeth, Saint

Indian

Gandhi, Indira

Pandit, Vijaya Lakshmi

Irish

deMarkievicz, Constance

Devlin, Bernadette

Israeli

Chizick, Sarah
Meir, Golda

Senesh, Hannah
Szold, Henrietta

Italian

Agnes, Saint (Roman)
Catherine de Medici
Deledda, Grazia

Fallaci, Oriana
Fermi, Laura
Galla Placida (Roman)

Japanese

Takashima, Shizuye

Mexican-American

Anguiano, Lupe

Carr, Vicki

Norwegian

Henie, Sonja

Undset, Sigrid

Polish

Hautzig, Esther
Modjeska, Helen
Novak, Nina

Rose, Ernestine
Rubinstein, Helena
Wojciechowska, Maia

Puerto Rican

Colón, Miriam
Maymi, Carmen

Meléndez, Cóncha

Romanian

Ileana

Russian

Catherine the Great
Danilova, Alexandra
Elizabeth Petrovna
Korbut, Olga

Pavlova, Anna
Riabouchinska, Tatiana
Tereshkova, Valentina
Toumanova, Tamara

Scottish

Grant, Ann MacVicar
Mary, Queen of Scots
Molewsworth, Mary

Shearer, Moira
Slessor, Mary

Spanish

Isabella

Teresa of Avila, Saint

Swedish

Christina
Lind, Jenny

Lindgren, Astrid
Meitner, Lise

Swiss

Kauffman, Angelica

Syrian

Zenobia

Venezuelan

Carreño, Teresa

Yugoslav

Slavenska, Mia

B

Classified List
of Selected Biographical Subjects

Abolitionists

Anthony, Susan Brownell
Child, Lydia Maria
Craft, Ellen
Crandall, Prudence
Forten, Charlotte
Foster, Abigail Kelley
Grimké, Angelina
Grimké, Sarah
Harper, Frances Ellen
    Watkins

Kemble, Frances (Fanny)
Mott, Lucretia
Stanton, Elizabeth Cady
Stone, Lucy
Stowe, Harriet Beecher
Truth, Sojourner
Tubman, Harriet
Wright, Frances (Fanny)

Actresses

Adams, Maude
Angelou, Maya
Bailey, Pearl
Ball, Lucille
Barrymore, Ethel
Berg, Gertrude
Bernhardt, Sarah
Bono, Cher

Brice, Fanny
Caron, Leslie
Colón, Miriam
Cornell, Katharine
Crabtree, Lotta
Dee, Ruby
Fiske, Minnie Maddern
Harper, Valerie

Hayes, Helen

Held, Anna

Henie, Sonja

Kelly, Grace

Kemble, Frances (Fanny)

Kimbrell, Marketa

Luce, Clare Boothe

MacLaine, Shirley

Miller, Marilyn

Modjeska, Helen

Mowatt, Anna Cora

Rachel

Ross, Diana

Siddons, Sarah Kemble

Tyson, Cicely

Waters, Ethel

American Civil Rights Workers (contemporary)

Anderson, Marian

Bates, Daisy

Braden, Anne

Chisholm, Shirley

Dee, Ruby

Hamer, Fannie Lou

Jackson, Mahalia

King, Coretta Scott

MacLaine, Shirley

Moody, Anne

Parks, Rosa

American Civil War Figures

Barton, Clara

Bickerdyke, Mary Ann

Boyd, Belle

Carroll, Anna Ella

Dix, Dorothea Lynde

Edmonds, Sarah Emma

Forten, Charlotte

Grant, Julia

Greenhow, Rose O'Neal

Loughborough, Ann W.

Truth, Sojourner

Tubman, Harriet

Van Lew, Elizabeth

Walker, Mary Edwards, M.D.

American Colonial Figures

Bradstreet, Anne Dudley

Dare, Virginia

Dyer, Mary

Hutchinson, Anne

Moody, Lady Deborah

Pocahontas

Tituba

Zenger, Anna

American Revolutionary Figures

Adams, Abigail Smith
Arnold, Margaret Shippen
Corbin, Margaret
Pitcher, Molly
Ross, Betsy

Sampson, Deborah
Ward, Nancy
Washington, Martha
    Dandridge Custis

Anthropologists

Mead, Margaret

Meggers, Betty Jane

Artists and Illustrators

Adams, Adrienne
Amévor, Charlotte
Anglund, Joan Walsh
Babbitt, Natalie
Bendick, Jeanne
Bonheur, Rosa
Brown, Marcia
Cassatt, Mary
Catlett, Elizabeth
Cooney, Barbara
D'Aulaire, Ingri
deAngeli, Marguerite
Emberley, Barbara
Ets, Marie Hall
Fatio, Louise
Gág, Wanda
Greenaway, Kate
Grifalconi, Ann
Hader, Berta

Hoffman, Malvina
Hogrogian, Nonny
Ipcar, Dahlov
Kauffman, Angelica
Kollwitz, Käthe
Lathrop, Dorothy
Laurencin, Marie
Lenski, Lois
Lobel, Anita
Lubell, Winifred
Martínez, Maria
Milhous, Katherine
Morgan, Norma
Moses, Anna Mary Robertson
    (Grandma Moses)
Ness, Evaline
O'Keefe, Georgia
Petersham, Maud
Potter, Beatrix

Raskin, Ellen
Ream, Vinnie
Rey, Margret
Ringgold, Faith
Savage, Augusta

Takashima, Shizuye
Velarde, Pablita
Vigee-Librun, Elizabeth
    Louise

Athletes

Albright, Tenley, *ice skater*
Babashoff, Shirley, *swimmer*
Bartz, Jenny, *swimmer*
Baugh, Laura, *golfer*
Berg, Patty, *golfer*
Berg, Sharon, *swimmer*
Blankers-Koen, Fanny, *track and field*
Belote, Melissa, *swimmer*
Buzonas, Gail Johnson, *swimmer*
Casals, Rosemary, *tennis player*
Chadwick, Florence, *swimmer*
Cochran, Barbara Ann, *skier*
Cochran, Lindy, *skier*
Cochran, Marilyn, *skier*
Collett, Glenna, *golfer*
Connolly, Maureen, *tennis player*
Connolly, Olga Fikotova, *track and field*
Court, Margaret, *tennis player*

Decker, Mary, *track and field*
Ederle, Gertrude, *swimmer*
Evert, Chris, *tennis player*
Fleming, Peggy, *ice skater*
Fraser, Gretchen, *skier*
Garms, Shirley Rudolph, *bowler*
Genesko, Lynn, *swimmer*
Gibson, Althea, *tennis player*
Goolagong, Evonne, *tennis player*
Gould, Shane, *swimmer*
Heddy, Kathy, *swimmer*
Heiss, Carol, *ice skater*
Henie, Sonja, *ice skater*
Henning, Anne, *ice skater*
Jacobs, Helen Hull, *tennis player*
King, Billie Jean, *tennis player*
King, Micki, *swimmer*
Kinmont, Jill, *skier*
Korbut, Olga, *gymnast*
Kusner, Kathy, *horsewoman*

Laedwig, Marion, *bowler*

Larrieu, Francie, *track and field*

Lenglen, Suzanne, *tennis player*

Loock, Christine, *swimmer*

Lynn, Janet, *ice skater*

McCormick, Pat, *swimmer*

McCutcheon, Floretta, *bowler*

MacInnis, Nina, *swimmer*

Marble, Alice, *tennis player*

Muldowney, Shirley, *drag racer*

Nelson, Cindy, *skier*

Nyad, Diana, *swimmer*

Owen, Laurence, *ice skater*

Proell, Annemarie, *skier*

Rice, Joan Moore, *gymnast*

Rigby, Cathy, *gymnast*

Rudolph, Wilma, *track and field*

Shank, Theresa, *basketball player*

Simburg, Wyomia Tyus, *track and field*

Smith, Robyn, *horseracing jockey*

Souta, Judy Cook, *bowler*

Sperber, Paula, *bowler*

Vanderheide, Nancy, *archer*

Von Saltza, Susan Christina, *swimmer*

Wade, Virginia, *tennis player*

Walsh, Stella, *track and field*

Weld, Theresa, *ice skater*

Whitworth, Kathy, *golfer*

Wills, Helen, *tennis player*

Wright, Mickey, *golfer*

Zaharias, Mildred "Babe" Didrikson, *golfer, track and field*

Attorneys
(not serving as Congresswomen or senators)

Edelman, Marion Wright

Harris, Patricia

Huber, Linda

Langford, Anna Riggs

Lease, Mary Elizabeth

Libow, Carol

Lockwood, Belva Ann

Motley, Constance Baker

Norton, Eleanor Holmes

Poston, Ersa Hines

Stender, Fay

Authors

Adams, Elizabeth
Aguilar, Grace
Alcott, Louisa May
Angelou, Maya
Anglund, Joan Walsh
Antin, Mary
Austen, Jane
Babbitt, Natalie
Bell, Gertrude
Belpré, Pura
Bendick, Jeanne
Bishop, Claire Huchet
Bleeker, Sonia
Brewton, Sara W.
Brink, Carol Ryrie
Brontë, Anne
Brontë, Charlotte
Brontë, Emily
Brown, Marcia
Buck, Pearl
Burnett, Frances Hodgson
Burney, Fanny
Byars, Betsy
Carlson, Natalie Savage
Carson, Rachel
Cather, Willa
Christie, Agatha
Clark, Ann Nolan
Cleary, Beverly
Coatsworth, Elizabeth

Colman, Hila
Cooney, Barbara
Craik, Dinah Mulock
Cunningham, Julia
Custer, Elizabeth
d'Aulaire, Ingri
de Angeli, Marguerite Lofft
Deledda, Grazia
de Regniers, Beatrice Schenk
de Treviño, Elizabeth Borton
Dobler, Lavinia
Dodge, Mary Mapes
Edwards, Julie
Eliot, George
Emberley, Barbara
Enright, Elizabeth
Estes, Eleanor
Ets, Marie Hall
Ewing, Juliana
Farjeon, Eleanor
Fatio, Louise
Ferber, Edna
Fisher, Aileen
Fisher, Dorothy Canfield
Fitz, Jean
Foster, Genevieve
Freeman, Mary Eleanor
    Wilkins
Fremont, Jessie Benton
Fuller, Margaret

Gaeddart, Lou Ann
Garelick, May
George, Jean Craighead
Glubok, Shirley
Glueckel of Hamlin
Godden, Rumer
Grant, Anne MacVicar
Greenaway, Kate
Hader, Berta
Hahn, Emily
Hale, Lucretia Peabody
Hale, Sarah
Hamilton, Edith
Hamilton, Virginia
Hautzig, Esther
Haywood, Carolyn
Henry, Marguerite
Hunt, Irene
Ipcar, Dahlov
Jewett, Sarah Orne
Kahl, Virginia
Konigsburg, Elaine L.
Krauss, Ruth
Larrick, Nancy
Latham, Jean Lee
Lathrop, Dorothy
L'Engle, Madeleine
Lenski, Lois
Lexau, Joan
Lindgren, Astrid
Livingston, Myra Cohn
Lobel, Anita

Lubell, Winifred
McGinley, Phyllis
McGovern, Ann
McNeer, May
Meléndez, Cóncha
Merriam, Eve
Merrill, Jean
Milhous, Katherine
Minarik, Elsa Holmelund
Molewsworth, Mary
Moore, Lilian
Morrison, Lillian
Nesbit, Edith
Ness, Evaline
Neville, Emily Cheney
Norton, Mary
Petersham, Maud
Petry, Ann
Pine, Tillie S.
Potter, Beatrix
Prieto, Mariana
Raskin, Ellen
Rey, Margret
Rinkoff, Barbara
Rollins, Charlemae Hill
Sackville-West, Victoria
Sawyer, Ruth
Sayers, Dorothy
Scott, Ann Herbert
Selsam, Millicent E.
Sheklow, Edna

Shelley, Mary Godwin
   Wollstonecraft
Shotwell, Louisa
Sidney, Margaret (pseud.)
Snyder, Zilpha Keatley
Sone, Monica
Sonneborn, Ruth A.
Sorensen, Virginia
Speare, Elizabeth George
Staël, Madame de
Stanton, Elizabeth Cady
Stein, Gertrude
Sterling, Dorothy
Stolz, Mary
Stowe, Harriet Beecher
Sutcliff, Rosemary
Takashima, Shizuye
Tarbell, Ida
Tarry, Ellen
Taylor, Sydney

Thompson, Blanche Jennings
Travers, P.L.
Udry, Janice May
Undset, Sigrid
Warburg, Sandol Stoddard
Weik, Mary Hays
Weygant, Sister Noemi
Wiggin, Kate Douglas
Wilder, Laura Ingalls
Wilson, Julia
Wojciechowska, Maia
Wollstonecraft, Mary
Woolf, Virginia
Wordsworth, Dorothy
Wright, Frances (Fanny)
Wyler, Rose
Yates, Elizabeth
Yonge, Charlotte Mary
Young, Margaret B.
Zolotow, Charlotte

Aviators

Auriol, Jacqueline
Cobb, Geraldyn
Cochran, Jacqueline
Earhart, Amelia

Howell, Emily
Johnson, Amy
Lindberg, Anne Morrow
Mock, Jerrie

Businesswomen and Entrepreneurs

Arden, Elizabeth
Cochran, Jacqueline

Dache, Lily
Evans, Jane

Laurencin, Marie
Mason, Biddy
Pleasant, Mary Ellen
    "Mammy"
Rubinstein, Helena

Rudkin, Margaret Fogharty
Shaver, Dorothy
Walker, Maggie Lena
Walker, Sarah Breedlove
Wells, Mary K.

Circus Personalities

Bailey, Mollie
Concello, Antoinette
Leitzel, Lillian

Oakley, Annie
Wirth, May

Congresswomen

Abel, Hazel
Abzug, Bella
Andrews, Elizabeth
Baker, Irene Bailey
Blitch, Iris
Boland, Veronica
Bolton, Frances P.
Bosone, Reva Beck
Bowring, Eva
Buchanan, Vera
Burke, Yvonne Braithwaite
Bushfield, Vera
Byron, Katherine Edgar
Caraway, Hattie W.
Chisholm, Shirley
Church, Marguerite Stitt
Clarke, Marion Williams
Douglas, Emily Taft

Douglas, Helen Gahagan
Dwyer, Florence P.
Edwards, Elaine
Eslick, Willa B.
Felton, Rebecca Latimer
Fulmer, Willa L.
Gasque, Elizabeth Hawley
Gibbs, Florence R.
Granahan, Kathryn E.
Grasso, Ella T.
Graves, Dixie Bibb
Green, Edith
Greenway, Isabella
Griffiths, Martha
Hansen, Julia Butler
Harden, Cecil M.
Heckler, Margaret M.
Hicks, Louise Day

411

Holt, Marjorie
Holtzman, Elizabeth
Honeyman, Nan Wood
Huck, Winnifred Sprague
   Mason
Jenckes, Virginia Ellis
Jordan, Barbara
Kahn, Florence P.
Kee, Elizabeth
Kelly, Edna F.
Knutson, Coya
Langley, Katherine
Luce, Clare Boothe
Lusk, Georgia L.
McCarthy, Kathryn
   O'Loughlin
McCormick, Ruth Hanna
McMillan, Clara G.
Mankin, Helen Douglas
May, Catherine
Mink, Patsy T.
Nolan, Mae Ella
Norrell, Catherine D.
Norton, Mary T.

O'Day, Caroline
Oldfield, Pearl
Owen, Ruth Bryan
Pfost, Gracie
Pratt, (Eliza) Jane
Pratt, Ruth Baker
Rankin, Jeannette
Reece, Louise Goff
Reid, Charlotte T.
Riley, Corinne Boyd
Robertson, Alice M.
Rogers, Edith Nourse
St. George, Katherine
Schroeder, Patricia
Simpson, Edna
Smith, Margaret Chase
Stanley, Winifred C.
Sullivan, Leonor K.
Sumner, Jessie
Thomas, Lera M.
Thompson, Ruth
Weis, Jessica McCullough
Wingo, Effiegene
Woodhouse, Chase Going

Dancers

Adams, Diana
Alonso, Alicia
Boris, Ruthanna
Caron, Leslie
Chauviré, Yvette

Chouteau, Yvonne
Danilova, Alexandra
deMille, Agnes
Duncan, Isadora
Dunham, Katherine

412

Fifield, Elaine
Fonteyn, Margot
Graham, Martha
Grey, Beryl
Hightower, Rosella
Holm, Hanya
Jeanmarie, Renée
Kaye, Nora
Le Clerq, Tanquil
Marchand, Colette
Markova, Alicia
Moylan, Mary Ellen

Novak, Nina
Pavlova, Anna
Reed, Janet
Riabouchinska, Tatiana
Shearer, Moira
Slavenska, Mia
Tallchief, Maria
Tallchief, Marjorie
Tamaris
Toumanova, Tamara
Vollmar, Jocelyn

Educators

Anguiano, Lupe
Berry, Martha
Bethune, Mary McLeod
Blackwell, Elizabeth
Bonnin, Gertrude Simmons
Clark, Septima Poinsette
Crandall, Prudence
Dickey, Sarah
Forten, Charlotte
Gratz, Rebecca
Hamilton, Edith
Harris, LaDonna
Harris, Patricia
Kohut, Rebekah
Lyon, Mary

Macy, Anne Sullivan
Mitchell, Maria
Moise, Penina
Moore, Anne Carroll
Palmer, Alice Freeman
Peabody, Elizabeth Palmer
Ramos, Elaine Abraham
Richards, Ellen Swallow
Sabin, Florence
Szold, Henrietta
Taylor, Susie King
Terrell, Mary Church
Wiggin, Kate Douglas
Willard, Emma Hart

Explorers

Akeley, Delia J. Denning
Baker, Florence von Sass
Bird, Isabella Lucy Bishop
Boyd, Louise Arner

Kenyon, Kathleen
Kingsley, Mary
Tinnè, Alexine
Workman, Fanny Bullock

Feminists and Suffragists (noncontemporary)

Adams, Abigail
Anthony, Susan Brownell
Blatch, Harriet Stanton
Bloomer, Amelia Jenks
Catt, Carrie Chapman
Child, Lydia Maria
Day, Dorothy
Door, Rheta Childe
Duniway, Abigail Scott
Foster, Abigail Kelley
Fuller, Margaret
Goldman, Emma
Grimké, Angelina
Grimké, Sarah
Hale, Sarah
Howe, Julia Ward
Jacobi, Mary Putnam
Lockwood, Belva Ann

Mott, Lucretia
Owens-Adair, Bethenia
Pankhurst, Adele
Pankhurst, Christabel
Pankhurst, Emmeline
Pankhurst, Sylvia
Paul, Alice
Rankin, Jeannette
Rose, Ernestine
Stanton, Elizabeth Cady
Stone, Lucy
Walker, Mary Edwards
Wells-Barnett, Ida
Willard, Frances
Wollstonecraft, Mary
Woodhull, Victoria
Wright, Frances (Fanny)

Handicapped

Bridgman, Laura
Keller, Helen
Kinmont, Jill

Lester, Margaret
Rudolph, Wilma
Seibert, Florence

Journalists and Newscasters

Ballard, Audreen
Bloomer, Amelia Jenks
Bly, Nellie
Caffie, Barbara J.
Campbell, Barbara
Coleman, Valerie
Davis, Belva
Day, Dorothy
Door, Rheta Childe
Duncan, Marilyn I.
Edmiston, Susan
Fallaci, Oriana
Greeley-Smith, Nixola
Hicks, Nancy
Higgins, Marguerite
Huggins, Edith
Hunter, Charlayne
Jenkins, Carol
Kilgallen, Dorothy

Kuhn, Irene
Lomax, Almena
Murray, Joan
Parker, Angela
Perry, Jean
Ross, Ruth N.
St. Johns, Adela Rogers
Sheehy, Gail
Steinem, Gloria
Swisshelm, Jane Grey
Tarbell, Ida
Thompson, Dorothy
Thornton, Jeannye
Vlachos, Helen
Washington, Betty
Wells-Barnett, Ida
Zenger, Anna
Zill, Ann

Legendary Heroines and Figures

Dare, Virginia
Joan of Arc
Pitcher, Molly

Pocahontas
Ross, Betsy
Sacajawea

Librarians

Baker, Augusta

Moore, Anne Carroll

Missionaries

Loyola, Sister Mary
Moon, Lottie
Slessor, Mary

Swain, Clara A.
Walker, Mary Richardson
Whitman, Narcissa Prentiss

Musicians

Carreño, Teresa
Chaminade, Cecile
Flack, Roberta
Franklin, Aretha
Grant, Micki

Queler, Eve
Schumann, Clara
Scott, Hazel
Simon, Carly

Nurses

Barton, Clara
Bickerdyke, Mary Ann
Breckenridge, Mary
Cavell, Edith
Davis, Frances Reed Elliott
Edmonds, Sarah Emma
Fitzgerald, Alice
Haile Selassie, Tsahai
Kenny, Elizabeth

Lathrop, Rose Hawthorne
   (Mother Mary Alphonsa)
Mance, Jeanne
Nightingale, Florence
Richards, Linda
Sanger, Margaret
Taylor, Susie King
Trammell, Beatrice Johnson
Wald, Lillian

Peace Advocates

Abzug, Bella
Addams, Jane
Baez, Joan
Balch, Emily Greene

Lockwood, Belva Ann
Rankin, Jeannette
Suttner, Bertha von

Philanthropists

Gratz, Rebecca
Hirsch, Clara de

Montefiore, Judith
Strauss, Lina

Physicians

Albright, Tenley
Barringer, Emily Dunning
Blackwell, Elizabeth
Chaplin, Matilda
Evans, Helen
Garrett-Anderson, Elizabeth
Guion, Connie
Hamilton, Alice
Horney, Karen
Ighodaro, Irene
Jacobi, Mary Putnam

Jex-Blake, Sophia
Kelsey, Frances
Lovejoy, Esther Pohl
Nelson, Marjorie
Pechey, Edith
Picotte, Susan La Flesche
Storch, Marcia
Taussig, Helen
Thorne, Isabel
Walker, Mary Edwards
Zakrzewska, Marie Elizabeth

Pioneers

Boone, Rebecca
Cooper, Arvazine Angeline
Dare, Virginia
Duniway, Abigail Scott

Fields, Mary
Walker, Mary Richardson
Whitman, Narcissa Prentiss
Wilder, Laura Ingalls

Poets

Bates, Katherine Lee
Benet, Rosemary Carr
Bradstreet, Anne
Brooks, Gwendolyn
Browning, Elizabeth Barrett

Davies, Mary Carolyn
Dickinson, Emily
Field, Rachel
Harper, Frances Ellen
    Watkins

417

Johnson, E. Pauline
Lazarus, Emma
Lowell, Amy
Merriam, Eve
Millay, Edna St. Vincent
Monroe, Harriet
Moore, Marianne
Newsome, Effie Lee

Petry, Ann
Richards, Laura E.
Rossetti, Christina
Taylor, Ann
Taylor, Jane
Thaxter, Celia
Walker, Margaret
Wheatley, Phillis

Relatives of Famous People*

Adams, Abigail
Adams, Louisa Johnson
Arnold, Margaret Shippen
Bonaparte, Elizabeth
   Patterson
Boone, Rebecca
Custer, Elizabeth
Fremont, Jessie Benton
Grant, Julia
Hoover, Lou Henry
Jackson, Rachel Donnelson

Kennedy, Rose Fitzgerald
King, Coretta Scott
Lincoln, Mary Todd
Lincoln, Nancy Hanks
Madison, Dolley
Onassis, Jacqueline Bouvier
   Kennedy
Randolph, Martha Jefferson
Roosevelt, Eleanor
Washington, Martha
   Dandridge Custis

Religious Leaders

Brown, Antoinette
Cabrini, Sister Frances
   Xavier
Dyer, Mary
Eddy, Mary Baker
Hutchinson, Anne

Lathrop, Rose Hawthorne
   (Mother Mary Alphonsa)
Moody, Deborah
Shaw, Anna Howard
Tekakwitha, Kateri

*Collective biographies of American First Ladies may be found
   on pages 323, 324, 355, 358, and 363.

Royalty

Angouleme, Marie Therese
    Charlotte
Anne, Queen of England
Anne of Cleves
Boleyn, Anne
Bonaparte, Josephine
Catherine of Aragon
Catherine the Great
Catherine de Medici
Christina
Cleopatra
Eleanor of Aquitaine
Elizabeth I
Elizabeth II
Elizabeth Petrovna
Elizabeth, Saint
Galla Placida
Grey, Lady Jane
Haile Selassie, Tsahai

Howard, Catherine
Ileana
Isabella
Juliana
Liliuokalani
Maria Theresa
Marie Antoinette
Mary I
Mary II
Mary, Queen of Scots
Maud
Nefertiti
Nzinga
Parr, Catherine
Seymour, Jane
Tzu Hsi
Victoria
Wilhelmina
Zenobia

Saints

Agnes
Cabrini, Sister Frances
    Xavier
Catherine of Alexandria
Elizabeth

Germaine
Helena
Joan of Arc
Marillac, Louise de
Teresa of Avila

Scientists

Augusta, Ada

Carson, Rachel

419

Clark, Eugenie
Curie, Marie
Earle, Sylvia
Hamilton, Margaret
Intriligator, Devrie S.
Joliot-Curie, Irene
Kelsey, Frances

Mead, Margaret
Meggers, Betty Jane
Meitner, Lise
Ray, Dixy Lee
Richards, Ellen Swallow
Sabin, Florence
Seibert, Florence

Singers

Anderson, Marian
Arroyo, Martini
Bailey, Pearl
Baker, Josephine
Bono, Cher
Bramlett, Bonnie
Brice, Fanny
Carr, Vicki
Crabtree, Lotta
Davis, Marilyn McCoo
Dee, Ruby
Elliot, Cass
Flack, Roberta
Franklin, Aretha
Gordon, Florence La Rue
Grant, Micki
Holiday, Billie
Horne, Lena
Ian, Janis
Jackson, Mahalia

Kind, Roslyn
Kitt, Eartha
Lind, Jenny
Makeba, Miriam
Melanie
Mitchell, Joni
Newton-John, Olivia
Ponselle, Rosa
Price, Leontyne
Rainey, Ma
Ross, Diana
Sainte-Marie, Buffy
Simon, Carly
Slick, Grace
Smith, Bessie
Smith, Kate
Trapp, Maria
Turner, Tina
Waters, Ethel

Slaves

Craft, Ellen
Freeman, Elizabeth
   "Mumbet"
Keckley, Elizabeth
Louvestre, Mary

Tituba
Truth, Sojourner
Tubman, Harriet
Wheatley, Phillis

Social and Welfare Workers, Reformers

Addams, Jane
Blackwell, Elizabeth
Bloomer, Amelia
Bly, Nellie
Booth, Evangeline
Breckinridge, Mary
Buck, Pearl
Derricotte, Juliette
Dix, Dorothea Lynde
Flynn, Elizabeth Gurley
Goldman, Emma
Gratz, Rebecca
Hamilton, Alice
Hughes, Dorothy Pitman
Jones, Mary Harris
La Flesche, Susette
Lathrop, Julia

Lathrop, Rose Hawthorne
   (Mother Mary Alphonsa)
Loeb, Sophie
Low, Juliette Gordon
Maymi, Carmen
Nightingale, Florence
Perkins, Frances
Rose, Ernestine
Sanger, Margaret
Szold, Henrietta
Tarbell, Ida
Truth, Sojourner
Wald, Lillian
Wauneka, Annie Dodge
Wells-Barnett, Ida
Willard, Frances
Wright, Frances (Fanny)

Spies

Boyd, Belle
Cavell, Edith
Delilah
Edmonds, Sarah Emma
Greenhow, Rose O'Neal

Hari, Mata
Louvestre, Mary
Tubman, Harriet
Van Lew, Elizabeth

World War II Figures

Arnothy, Christine
Brusselman, Anne
Frank, Anne
Hautzig, Esther

Kollwitz, Käthe
Reiss, Joanna de Leeuw
Senesh, Hannah
Wojciechowska, Maia

Index

Index of Women Included in Individual and Collective Biographies
(American unless otherwise indicated)

425

433

THE COMPLETE BOOK OF MENOPAUSE

Every Woman's Guide to Good Health

Carol Landau, Ph.D.,
Michele G. Cyr, M.D.,
and Anne W. Moulton, M.D.

A Perigee Book

This book is meant to educate and should not be used as an alternative to appropriate medical care. The authors have made every effort to ensure that the information presented is accurate. In the light of ongoing research, however, it is possible that new findings may invalidate some of the data presented here.

A Perigee Book
Published by The Berkley Publishing Group
200 Madison Avenue
New York, NY 10016

The authors gratefully acknowledge permission to reprint material from the following: American Psychiatric Association: *Diagnostic and Statistical Manual of Mental Disorders, Third Edition, Revised,* Washington, DC, American Psychiatric Association, 1987.

Grosset/Putnam edition: April 1994
First Perigee edition: March 1995
Perigee ISBN: 0-399-51906-8
Published simultaneously in Canada.

The Library of Congress has cataloged the Grosset/Putnam edition as follows:

Landau, Carol.
    The complete book of menopause : every woman's guide to good health / Carol Landau, Michele G. Cyr, Anne W. Moulton.
      p.   cm.
    "A Grosset/Putnam book."
    Includes bibliographical references and index.
    ISBN 0-399-13946-X (alk.paper)
    1. Menopause—Popular works. I. Cyr, Michele G. II. Moulton, Anne W. III. Title.
    [DNLM: 1. Menopause—popular works. 2. Women's Health—popular works. WP 580 L2528c 1994]
    RG186.L36 1994
    612.6'65—dc20   93-38651 CIP
    DNLM/DLC

Printed in the United States of America

10 9 8 7 6 5 4 3 2 1

This book is printed on acid-free paper.

❧ ACKNOWLEDGMENTS

SOMETIMES YOU GET LUCKY. WE GOT LUCKY IN 1992. FIRST, COLLEEN Mohyde of The Doe Coover Agency telephoned us. Colleen had read our letter to the editor of *Vanity Fair,* in response to an article pointing out that menopause was not such a negative and symptomatic time for most women. One thing led to another. Colleen encouraged us to write a book and off we went. Colleen's editorial advice and guidance, as well as Doe's encouragement, have been invaluable.

Four months later, we got lucky again. A woman who was working part-time in our division offered to be our research assistant for the rapidly expanding book. Kathleen Jenkins is a junior at Brown University, as well as an accomplished playwright. She is a most talented writer, a diligent research assistant, and the voice of common sense. Kay has typed, annotated, edited and deciphered, and we are indebted to her.

As soon as we spoke to Jane Isay at Putnam's, we knew we were in good hands. Jane has been an enthusiastic, insightful and supportive editor. She has helped us maintain a positive outlook throughout the project and working with her has been a pleasure.

We would like to thank our consultants, Elizabeth Buechler,

M.D., Dorothy Bianco, Ph.D., Belinda Johnson, Ph.D., Douglas Kiel, M.D., Jacqueline Puhl, Ph.D., and Iris Shuey, M.D.

Steven A. Wartman, M.D., brought the three of us together when he was the Chief of the Division of General Internal Medicine at Rhode Island Hospital. We would like to thank all of the members of the division. Albert Most, M.D., our Chief of Medicine, has also been most supportive.

Laura Wald also helped us with research. Brenda Manchester and Helen O'Connor helped to type the manuscript.

We would also like to thank our colleagues at Women's Health Associates: Elaine Carlson, M.D., Sherri Fitts, Ph.D., Felise Milan, M.D., Karyn Montgomery, M.D., Laura Nevel, M.D., Karen Pevin, Norma Schorr, Jody Spencer, Ph.D., Mary-Anne Spizzirri, and Flora Treger, M.D.

Thank you to the staff of the Brown University Sciences Library, and to the Rhode Island Hospital Pharmacy Drug Information Service.

Other helpful colleagues and friends: David Abrams, Sally Ashworth, Kelly Brownell, Laura Brady, Richard Bump, Karen Carlson, Kenneth Coté, Elda Dawber, John DiOrio, Jr., Betty Fielder, Betty Wasielewski Harrington, Marcia Lawler, Jeannette Maynard, Barbara McCrady, Stephanie McKenna, Betsy Meyer, Bill Norman, Michael Norman, Patricia O'Sullivan, Olive Osborn, Lee Quattrucci, Judy Quattrucci, Melinda Small, Mark Smith, Michael Stein, Dominick Tammaro and Marion Wachtenheim.

The Wayland Collegium of Brown University provided initial support for our work. Professors Lucile Newman and Sally Zierler were especially helpful.

Ocean Coffee Roasters has been a relaxing "second office" for many of our meetings. We would like to thank Carol Grande in particular.

We thank our families, to whom this book is dedicated.

We have changed the names and identifying data of our patients; we would like to thank them, as well as other women who have shared their stories with us.

◆ CONTENTS

❧ PREFACE

"WOMEN BEWARE! IF YOU'RE NOT MENOPAUSAL NOW, YOU WILL BE someday and you're sure to hate it!" This is the message that the three of us were hearing in 1992, and it motivated us to write this book. In numerous books, magazines, medical journals and conferences, we were being told that menopause is a difficult time and one to be feared. But this message did not match our experiences. Seven years ago, the three of us founded a women's health practice, Women's Health Associates, in conjunction with the Brown University School of Medicine's Department of General Internal Medicine at Rhode Island Hospital. We see adult women of all ages in our practice and have come to quite a different conclusion. Menopausal women may have special needs, but we are more impressed by their resourcefulness and strength. We do not see menopause as any type of pathology, but instead, as another creative stage of women's lives.

We created Women's Health Associates in response to the needs of many of our patients that we were seeing from other practices. We knew that women needed a place to come for their primary medical care. We knew that women today are among the most sophisticated health care consumers, who want to make their own decisions based on up-to-date information. We also knew that women needed comprehensive care to talk over concerns, be heard, and make informed treatment decisions. And we knew that women wanted to be able to come to a comfortable setting, where they would be free to focus on issues of prevention. Women want to maintain health, as well as to have a place to go when suffering from an illness.

We created an environment not only where women would be free to ask questions about their health, but where we would encourage their questions. We created an environment where primary care internists work side by side with clinical psychologists, gynecologists, nurse practitioners and nutritionists. We all work together and refuse to parcel out a woman's health by her organs. Our interest, then, is in the overall lives of women, not in their bodies alone. Our top priority at Women's Health is to maintain a setting where clinicians and patients can listen to each other and learn from each other. We have developed long-term relationships with many of our patients over the years, and they have shared their experiences with us, as well as their medical concerns.

When it comes to menopause, we have learned the most from our patients. Previously we had not known how frightened women are about menopause. When we started teaching and writing about menopause, many women who were *pre*menopausal would grimace and say, "Oh yuck!" Yet *post*menopausal women would often shrug and say, "No big deal." Since we have seen hundreds of women between the ages of forty-five and fifty-five, we have come to appreciate the individuality of each woman's experience, and we have come to understand the resourcefulness that women share.

Our primary goal is to share this philosophy—that each woman has an individualized experience at menopause, but shares many commonalities with other women. Women do not need a simplistic approach to their health care at menopause or at any other time of life. What they do need is the maximum amount of information and freedom to make these important health care decisions.

So we wrote this book because we had the opposite point of view from that which drums up fears about menopause. It is time to present a more comprehensive approach, one that emphasizes the power of women. Writing this book has been an education in itself. One of our first projects was to give seminars about menopause in a variety of community settings. Each time we offered a seminar, it would quickly become filled to capacity. At first, each of us would give a twenty-minute presentation and leave time for questions. However, after the first two sessions, we found that we could never leave the auditorium because we were surrounded by women asking more and more questions. Finally we came up with the concept of "menopause town meetings." In these sessions, we condensed our introductory remarks to a total of a half hour, and just let women ask questions. And did we get questions! We heard hours and hours of questions and shared experiences. These town meetings have been exciting and empowering experiences for all of us. We have enjoyed them so much, in part because they have provided us with a wealth of new stories about women's lives. We have recorded all these questions and included them for you in the back of the book as a second appendix. This allows you to find information quickly.

We have also included a glossary at the back of this book that explains medical and psychological terms. We believe that definitions are important so that we can share a vocabulary. In this book, we will use language that is easy to understand. Frequently, the three of us challenge one another to "Speak English!" when one of us becomes too technical. Learning a new vocabulary is important because it helps us counter the prevailing prejudices about menopause in our society. By being as specific as possible, we can regain access to the information ourselves and form more educated decisions about the next phase of our lives.

✦ How to Use This Book

The Complete Book of Menopause is your comprehensive guide providing the most recent information. Armed with this knowledge, you can defeat the fear factor and make your own decisions. In each chapter, we will provide you with the information about the changes associated with the menopausal years.

We see menopause as a natural series of gradual changes. We know that by providing information, most women will be reassured. This information can fall into three categories: the biological, the psychological and the social. All too often, there has been an overemphasis on the biological aspects of menopause. We see the three areas as interconnected. In addition, the misinformation about women's biology has then been incorrectly attached to misinformation about psychology and women's social lives as well. The changes we describe will use the biopsychosocial model. This comprehensive approach has been used to teach medical students for over forty years but is still sometimes neglected. It is hard to imagine a woman's life that is affected by biology alone, psychology alone, or social factors alone. The comprehensive approach is more accurate and more powerful.

The three areas are interconnected. Bill Moyers's recent public television series and book, *Healing and the Mind*, highlighted this comprehensive approach (Moyers, 1993). Visits to doctors often involve psychological issues. Menopause has medical and psychological components and they should be treated together. A woman does not need to be suffering from symptoms or an illness in order to benefit from seeing a physician. She does not need to have a diagnosable psychiatric disorder in order to benefit from seeing a psychologist, or other mental health professional. By viewing the biological and psychological factors together, and by learning how to modify them during menopause, a woman can take charge of her own health care.

We need to look at social issues as well. There is a hefty amount of prejudice against women, especially aging women, in many of the writings on menopause. We plan to correct that. This prejudice has led to an unfortunate negative attitude toward menopause. It is internalized by too many of us and can lead to unnecessary anxiety. A second result of social forces is the polarization of women into two camps. The hormone replacement therapy (HRT) camp essentially portrays menopausal women as deficient and needing to have their hormones replaced. Many of these writings also prescribe estrogen for symptoms that have been shown not to be related to a lack of estrogen. The other camp, the anti-estrogen camp, sees estrogen as an evil medication, promoted by some larger medical and economic forces that exploit women. We see both of these views as limited. The question of HRT is only one of many issues that we need to explore during menopause, but it is a critical one. There are arguments to be made on both sides of the HRT issue, but this is not a war; this is your *life*. So polarization is not the answer.

Our belief is that each woman needs to make her own decisions in a comfortable and anxiety-free environment. We want women to participate actively in their health care during each crucial stage of life. As women facing menopause today, we have a variety of choices, and we want to help you make these choices.

The choices you make should be based on the information we provide, as well as your own individual symptoms, values and common sense. We believe that the best way for you to make these decisions is to be an active reader. Take the material provided here and apply it to your own life. We have found that the best way to learn is through this interaction. We have provided self-assessments and guided questionnaires that can help you assess your own needs during the menopausal years. By participating in these exercises, you can begin to make some tentative choices about your health care.

In each chapter, we also want to empower you to be able to communicate better with your health care professional. Each chapter will provide new communication strategies for interacting with your health care provider in an assertive and clear fashion. You can take your newfound information, your tentative choices, and talk them over. Most women want and need to form a partnership with their physicians and health care professionals.

Through our teaching at the Brown University School of Medicine, we have learned that communication is key. We have learned that women in particular value this communication and want to maximize each visit with their physicians. Many menopausal women visit their doctors primarily because they do not know what to expect during the menopausal years, not because they are suffering from any symptom. We want to respond to this concern. We understand this concern as well, because all of us are patients, as well as doctors. We know how it feels to be concerned about our health and to need information. We know that you are reading this book not only to learn about your own menopause but to learn how to deal with doctors, and we plan to help you do just that.

One study on doctor-patient communication revealed that over half of patients' complaints were not elicited by physicians, so we can't count on physicians to help us bring up our most pressing concerns (Todd, 1989). We have to identify them ahead of time. These communication issues are unfortunate. The three of us spend much of our time as faculty working with physicians during their medical residency, in order to improve their communication skills. We supervise these young doctors to help them become better listeners and to help them identify with patients' concerns. But in this book, we use similar strategies, and provide you, the patient, with a way to communicate better with your doctor. We know that being a patient can make you feel powerless and anxious at times. The suggestions in each chapter can help you regain feelings of control and competence about your own health care decisions.

Dr. Sherrie Kaplan at the New England Medical Center found that although women ask questions more often than men, the average patient asks less than four questions during a fifteen-minute office visit. Dr. Kaplan suggests that we prepare for the office visit by thinking through our concerns (Stark, 1992). Yet the anxiety-provoking nature of these doctor-patient encounters makes it difficult to process complicated information. Numerous researchers have written about the "data overload" that you get during an appointment. It is most important then to go to your appointment with a specific list of information and questions that you would like addressed. There is nothing wrong with taking notes before your visit and using them if you need to during the visit in order to talk with your clinician. In fact, many women use the list just as a "prompt" immediately before the appointment. Another way of coping with this data overload is to bring a friend or family member with you to the visit as some of our patients do. This is completely appropriate and quite common, especially if you are concerned about a specific problem that causes you significant anxiety.

As patients, we can try to approach the encounter with as much clarity as possible. Dr. Howard Beckman of Wayne State University studied over seventy patients and found that the beginning of the visit was a key time. When the doctor asked the patient, "What can I do for you?" Beckman's research found that the patient was interrupted on the average only eighteen seconds into the interview! (Beckman, 1984). No wonder patients might ask only four questions. We are amazed that they can manage to question that much after having been interrupted so early in the conversation. From this research we can learn two things: First, we should make our most important concerns known immediately. Second, we might need to be assertive in order to avoid being interrupted. It is a good idea, however, to try to be as succinct and clear as possible by thinking through your concerns ahead of time. Health care professionals, too, are under pressure. As health care providers we know that often we cannot share with patients the reasons for our pressure. The patient before you may have been twenty minutes late. Early in the day there may have been an emergency. This does not excuse clinicians who are routinely late, or excuse at all those who might be rude. But it is important to remember that health care professionals do have stresses outside of the examining room.

We know that as women you are aware of some of these issues. Patients are often concerned about their doctor's feelings. As women we've been taught our whole lives to be worried about the other person's feelings. Yet, if we do so in the doctor-patient interaction, we are often likely to become disappointed and perhaps resentful because our needs have not been met. Physicians have their own issues and may well be doing their best in communicating with us, but may not be answering our specific questions, or meeting our needs of that particular visit. In our residency training program, we focus on teaching physicians to be sensitive and to try to address the patient's agenda directly. However, many physicians have not been trained in this way and have a wide range of communication styles. Many are skilled interviewers and kind listeners; others can be abrupt and dismissive.

If the problem is embarrassing, it is important to address it anyway. We all feel vulnerable during the doctor-patient interaction, and when we are sick, it is extremely difficult to be "assertive." But it is possible to try and be clear. For example, an overweight woman might be afraid to talk to her doctor about chest pain, fearing that she will get a lecture about her weight. Nonetheless, that symptom is important and the doctor really does want to know about it.

It is also important to remember that you and your physician are only two members of the health care team. You may not be seeing a physician as your primary care provider but may be seeing a physician's assistant or a nurse practitioner. There is almost always a nurse or physician's assistant in the physician's office and she or he can answer your questions if you need to call back to get clarification. Health maintenance organizations offer many educational programs about specific problems like menopause. Many group practices also have clinical psychologists and other mental health professionals. Pharmacists can answer your questions about medication.

Another emphasis in the book is communication with families, so each chapter also contains a section on how to communicate about specific issues with family members. Problems in communications are the most frequent complaints presented to marital and family psychotherapists. The typical dynamic experienced by women is that their husbands don't listen to them and do not share feelings. However, their husbands often respond by saying something like, "I don't understand. I talk to her more than anyone else and she is my best friend." A man may feel most in touch when he is giving advice, while what his wife really wants is for him to listen and be empathic. Menopause can exacerbate this dynamic because many women feel particularly vulnerable and in need of support. At the same time, men are often going through their own transitions and are confused by their wives' concerns.

Similar types of communications problems exist in other communications patterns, between a woman and her lover, her friends and her children. We do not make the erroneous assumption that many books make, addressing women as if everyone is white, heterosexual and married for the first time. The present American experience is much more diverse. We find that all women can feel more connected to their friends and families when they can clearly identify their needs. We make specific suggestions for how to talk to spouses, partners, family members and friends about menopausal symptoms and midlife issues.

Communicating with other women about menopause is another crucial support system. Self-help groups and other resources are available to women. Often, just by acknowledging that hot flashes are driving you crazy, you will feel better. You will know that it might be time to take a walk with a friend who is a good listener. Or, your concerns about sexuality might be a signal that you need to discuss them with your partner or spouse. One of the gifts we have received from our patients is the knowledge that as women we have tremendous strength in our ability to change. Perhaps because we focus on relationships and put concerns for others first, we usually manage to go through life and make successful choices. Our strengths as women have led us to share problem-solving techniques and feelings with one another. It is important to remember that as women, we have long been experts at providing information for our family and providing support for one another.

The last part of the communications section in each chapter deals with resources. You will be amazed at how many resources there are for menopausal women. Pamphlets and educational materials are published by numerous foundations and self-help groups and are usually easy to read and free of charge. Menopause newsletters can put you in touch with a network of women who are eager to share information and support.

While we are on the subject of resources, let's remember that we all have many internal resources, as well as resources that we share with other women. We cannot let women be denied the opportunity that men have—that is, to approach our middle years with dignity and optimism. We can learn from lives of other women. Each chapter of this book will tell you the stories of many women—women from our practice, women who are our friends and colleagues, and women in literature and biography. We will mention only two for now. Janet Reno was named Attorney General of the United States while we were writing this book. A prosecutor in Dade County, Florida, for many years, Reno has led an active and exciting life. Prior to her accepting the nomination as attorney general, she had taken care of her mother who was in failing health and whom Reno describes as her best friend. This remarkable woman speaks passionately about the needs of women and children in her new role as attorney general. When the major networks complained because of her lack of makeup, Reno responded, "Like I can't go on their T.V. network unless I look good?" (Perspectives, 1993). Finally, a woman has enough power to challenge unreasonable expectations and to speak up! Janet Reno is clearly thriving at the age of fifty-three.

Also remember Margaret Sanger, one of the founders and leaders of the birth control movement in the United States. She was tireless in her work. When she was in her fifties, she was smuggling European-made diaphragms into the United States. This came after a career that had already spanned twenty years, and after she had launched a radical newspaper called *The Women Rebel* (Conway, 1992).

Yes, our lives change during our menopausal years, but there is nothing wrong with change. Change can bring new freedom and new power. Our work as founders of one of the nation's first women's health practices has taught us to value the lives of midlife women. Their stories are sometimes difficult, always moving and, ultimately, profoundly optimistic in their demonstration of the strengths of the female experience. We have developed a point of view best expressed by Ursula LeGuin:

> "It seems a pity to have a built-in rite of passage and to dodge it, evade it and pretend nothing has changed. That is to dodge and evade one's womanhood, to pretend one's like a man. Men, once initiated, never get the second chance. They never change again. That's their loss, not ours. Why borrow poverty?" (LeGuin, 1976)

THE
COMPLETE
BOOK OF
MENOPAUSE

CHAPTER ONE

The Natural History of Menopause

MENOPAUSE. IF YOU ARE LIKE MOST AMERICAN WOMEN, THE WORD fills your heart with dread. You don't know what to expect. You are worried—worried about hot flashes and disabling symptoms, worried about your sex life and worried about the rest of your life. Most of all, you are confused about whether or not to take hormone replacement therapy. But here is the good news: The negative aspects of menopause have been overstated dramatically, while the positive aspects have been virtually ignored. As you read on, you will find that the more you learn about the real facts concerning menopause, the better you will feel. And you will realize that with our comprehensive medical-psychological approach, you will be able to make good decisions about your health and you will enjoy the next ten years and more.

The next *ten* years? This phrase may strike you as odd since many women see menopause as some single threshold that we cross over. You don't just wake up one morning and become menopausal. Menopause is a natural, normal, developmental phase of a woman's life. Menopause is *not* a disease. It is the third major biological change in a woman's life, the last of the naturally occurring transitions. It is also the transition for which we receive little preparation. First, at menarche, or the onset of the menstrual cycle, we were given a pink pamphlet. It had floral borders and was titled something like "What Every Girl Must Know." The pamphlet introduced us to our reproductive system by providing a diagram of the uterus and ovaries and explaining the menstrual cycle. Later in our lives, books on pregnancy and childbirth provided a tremendous amount of information regarding the changes of the second transition many women experience as mothers. Until recently, there has been little written about menopause, the third transition. By helping you understand the natural course of menopause, you will be able to know what to expect and more importantly, what you don't need to worry about.

For most women the menopausal years are composed of three parts over about ten years. Figure 1-1 shows you the phases of the menopausal years. The perimenopause usually begins in the mid-forties. Menstrual periods become irregular, often closer together. At this time, many women begin to have hot flashes. This phase usually lasts about four years. We believe that the perimenopausal period deserves more attention. The onset of hot flashes can be extremely disturbing to some women, especially before they realize that the transition has begun. Some of the research about menopause suggests that some women begin to have problems with mood swings during this period. Most women are greatly relieved when they find that they have begun the perimenopausal period and that there is nothing else wrong with them.

Menopause itself is actually defined as the permanent end of menstrual periods which occurs when the ovaries stop producing hormones. Only in retrospect can anyone be certain that menstrual periods have permanently ended, since they may become very infrequent before they completely stop. Menopause is a gradual, natural process. Even if a woman's periods do end suddenly, without any warning (and this happens to 10 percent of women), the process leading to this has been a gradual reduction of the hormones produced by the ovaries. Previously, physicians diagnosed menopause if a woman had had no menstrual periods for twelve months, was not pregnant and was of the appropriate age, typically between forty-eight to fifty-five years. The lack of menstruation does not precisely define the change in hormone levels, and for that reason it is important that hormonal levels be tested. More recently, physicians have considered the diagnosis of menopause after there have been no menstrual periods for only six months. The average age of menopause is fifty-one.

Women are considered postmenopausal after the menopausal transition has occurred. We find postmenopausal women to be ex-

FIGURE 1-1
THE MENOPAUSAL YEARS

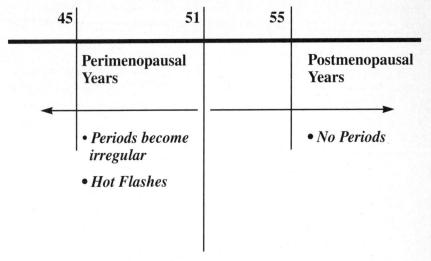

45		51	55
Perimenopausal Years			Postmenopausal Years
• *Periods become irregular*			• *No Periods*
• *Hot Flashes*			

Average Age of Menopause
Periods Stop

tremely generous in helping younger women understand menopause. When one of our wise postmenopausal friends heard that a younger woman expressed anxiety about menopause, she replied, "Menopause should be the worst thing that happens to us!" Here is another well-kept secret. Postmenopausal women are often like midlife men in one key way—they have more power! Many are free of family responsibilities for the first time in many years. Other women continue to cope with multiple family responsibilities but feel a new sense of energy during midlife. Whatever the situation, postmenopausal women can come into their own. We need only to think of Sandra Day O'Connor, Maya Angelou and Beverly Sills, just to name a few—not to mention Margaret Mead, who first coined the term "postmenopausal zest,"—to know that the postmenopausal years can be a time when we can be free at last.

These are the stages for women who experience menopause naturally. Hysterectomy and oophorectomy, or the removal of the uterus and the removal of the ovaries, brings on a sudden and dramatic change in hormone levels. Women who have had hysterectomies and oophorectomies, then, go through quite a different set of changes. Many articles about menopause confuse symptoms of natural menopause with those of oophorectomy. It is important to know that they are different. We discuss those differences in Chapter Nine, "Hysterectomy."

The contrast in attitudes between women who are premenopausal and those who are postmenopausal lead us to believe that what we see here is fear, not only a fear of menopause, but a fear of the aging process itself. As doctors involved with women's health for over fifteen years, we know that the dangerous combination of a fear of aging and a lack of information is causing needless anxiety. Most women will sail through menopause. We know that menopause, like other periods of human development, is unique for each individual. A woman needs to make her own decisions. We do not believe in prescribing estrogen wholesale as a miracle cure for what has been portrayed as a newly discovered disease. We want women to participate actively in their health care during each crucial stage of life. As women facing menopause today, we have a variety of choices, and we want to help you make those choices by providing unbiased and empowering information.

Although we can't tell you exactly what your menopause will be like, our experience has helped us understand what natural menopause will bring for most women. Since we founded a health care practice for women, we have treated hundreds of women using a medical-psychological team approach. Based on our work and combined research, we have come to understand the menopausal years. Our principal message to you is this: Do not expect major debilitating problems. It is going to be okay and you are going to be fine. It's just like our patients tell us: most women thrive during the menopausal years. The apprehension of this natural period in your life will most likely outweigh any real discomfort you will actually experience. So the tremendous fear and anxiety are unnecessary. The road to overcoming these fears and anxieties is to understand fully what menopause signifies. By doing so, you will dispel the many myths of menopause that have affected all of us. In fact, contrary to the stereotype, only 10 percent of all menopausal women find it to be a major disruption to their lives. Most everyone else finds it troubling at times, but certainly not a major problem. You may well have some symptoms, but they can be treated. Here is what will happen.

✦ WHAT WILL HAPPEN BIOLOGICALLY DURING MENOPAUSE?

The definitive study of the natural history of menopause has been conducted by epidemiologist Sonja McKinlay and sociologist William

McKinlay and their associates at the American Institute for Research. Their Massachusetts Women's Health Study followed 2,500 women ages forty-five to fifty-five for a ten-year period. Overall, they found that menopause was not a particularly problematic time for most women. One of their intriguing findings was that most women have neutral or negative feelings *before* menopause, but that feelings become more positive as women actually experience menopause (McKinlay and others, 1987). The first step toward developing a positive and more realistic attitude toward menopause is to understand our biology.

The change in our menstrual cycle occurs because of a decline in one of our female hormones, estrogen. Estrogen is produced by our ovaries. The ovaries gradually stop producing estrogen as our egg supply dwindles. The female baby begins life with approximately 400,000 eggs in her ovaries (they are *very* small). After the onset of menstruation, each month, approximately 1,000 eggs will try to develop but only one per month will be successful. Over a lifetime, about 400 eggs will be released to the tubes for possible fertilization. And sometime between the ages of forty-five and fifty-five, the eggs will be gone.

But the demise of these eggs is not a big deal. Unfortunately, all too often the medical profession, by continuing to use negative terminology about menopause, suggests that this biological change is, by necessity, a loss. A lecture at a major medical school included the sentence, "The ovary is the most precisely doomed organ in the human body." Menopausal women are accused of experiencing "ovarian failure." But rather than focusing on menopause as a negative, we can see it as a positive. Thus, we should not be talking about "ovarian failure" when we mean natural menopause. The ethicist Mary Mahowald has reviewed the overly negative vocabulary about menopause and points out that an organ is only doomed for a woman who has experienced herself primarily as a reproductive entity. If she has no interest in children in the first place, or if she has raised her children, then the lack of ovarian functioning should not be called ovarian failure but rather, "ovarian fulfillment," or perhaps "ovarian success" (Mahowald, 1992). It is important for all of us to counter this bleak outlook by expressing ourselves in more accurate and often humorous phrases.

✦ WHAT SYMPTOMS ARE COMMON?

We can certainly expect some hot flashes. Hot flashes begin before menopause, during the perimenopausal phase. Estimates vary, but anywhere between 30 percent to 80 percent of menopausal women will have a hot flash. This symptom is a sudden sensation of heat rising to the top of one's head and the upper part of the body. When the hot flash is over, a woman may begin to shiver. Most women who experience hot flashes are upset by the unpredictable and uncontrollable nature of them. The sweating and sudden temperature changes can also be disruptive to sleep patterns and some women visit their physicians for the related problem of insomnia.

One fact is clear: The hot flash is the hallmark of the menopausal experience. Interestingly, there are some cross-cultural differences in the experience of these symptoms. It is not clear that women in all cultures are plagued by the experience of hot flashes. Studies vary, but one compared Japanese and Canadian women. In this study, only 20 percent of Japanese women, in contrast to over 60 percent of Canadian women, reported hot flashes (Lock, 1991). These results could be explained by differences in diet and the use of naturally occurring estrogens like ginseng. It is also possible that Japanese women may be reticent about reporting such a symptom, or that Japanese women did not perceive the hot flash itself as negative. The same article suggested that many Japanese people believe that menopausal women should not be working outside of the home, so that they can take care of their aging parents. Some Japanese women, therefore, might believe they were self-indulgent even to discuss their hot flashes (Lock, 1991). In some cultures where older women are revered and have a special place in the society, menopausal symptoms are reported less often. So cultural differences are one of the many sociological factors that can affect symptoms at menopause.

The precise reason and physiological mechanism for hot flashes is unclear and we explore the possibilities in Chapter Two. Hot flashes may last for a period of months or up to a period of seven years. When they are severe and frequent they can be difficult. The most effective treatment for hot flashes is short-term hormone replacement therapy (HRT) described in great detail in chapters Two and Six. There are some other treatments as well. On the other hand, many women find hot flashes to be minimal, time-limited and thus are not an issue of great concern. If we were to wager on one symptom that you would have during menopause, it would be hot flashes.

A second common concern of menopausal women is vaginal dryness. Vaginal dryness is a gradual change that can be treated either with estrogen replacement therapy or with topical lubricants, and for most women is not a serious problem. It is a symptom that may occur suddenly in the case of surgical removal of the ovaries, but for those experiencing natural menopause it usually takes years to become noticeable. Vaginal dryness can be more of a problem to postmenopausal women who do not take hormone replacement therapy or use lubricants and who are not sexually active. Vaginal dryness can be uncomfortable, but it is not traumatic and should not be used as evidence of some dreaded "sexual decline." Some psychoanalytic authors have done women a tremendous disservice in not only emphasizing the problem of vaginal dryness but also in linking the biological changes of the reproductive system with psychological changes. The psychoanalyst Helene Deutsch and her views on the psychology of women have had devastating effects on midlife women. She connected the supposed physical decline of women in their forties and fifties to a lack of emotional warmth. Her words are frightening: ". . . everything she acquired during puberty is now lost piece by piece, and with the lapse of reproductive services, her beauty vanishes and usually the warm vital flow of feminine emotional life as well" (Deutsch, 1945, p. 461). There is no truth to this notion, but unfortunately, such prejudices remain throughout the medical care system and in American culture as well.

The last category of symptoms is called miscellaneous because there is a variety of symptoms that can occur in addition to hot flashes and changes in sexuality. We caution you here that although it is important to list some of these symptoms, you should not *expect* them to occur. The danger here is that any symptom can be connected to menopause when it may well be a random event or simply the result of the aging process. The fact is that many women go to physicians at the time of menopause rather than at earlier stages in their lives, and thus their symptoms, which may be long-standing, may be identified at this time. Some of the symptoms include headaches, mood changes, joint pain and fatigue. There are other changes in women that are associated with the aging process including hair changes, skin changes and a change in muscle tone. To some extent, these changes are affected by estrogen decline at menopause, but they are more often a result of the natural aging process. Yet what is important to remember is that this multiplicity of symptoms tends to be much less frequent and much less severe than either hot flashes or vaginal dryness. The most important consistent symptom is the hot flash. For this reason, one menopause newsletter is aptly named *Flash*.

✦ WHAT WILL HAPPEN PSYCHOLOGICALLY?

Psychological changes at menopause are usually based on our previous choices and our present relationships, and have little to do with hormones. Contrary to the popular stereotype of being "finished at forty or fifty," there is little evidence that midlife as defined as the forties or the fifties is necessarily a period of true crisis for men or women. In addition, many of the books on "life span" have assumed that women's development is just like men's. These theorists tend not to take into account that women make many specific choices that focus more on family issues and relationship issues. Given this family orientation, women may experience *more* freedom at the time of menopause, after their children have grown, rather than experiencing any sense of decline. In fact, studies of marriage reveal that the forties and fifties are the period of the second-highest level of satisfaction in marriages (the highest level is the prechildren era).

Some women, especially during the perimenopausal period, have sudden mood changes. We see this as some possible psychological vulnerability to the changes that women are beginning to experience. This fluctuation is similar to premenstrual syndrome (PMS). There are some anecdotal reports that suggest that women who have had difficulty with PMS also have difficulty with mood swings during menopause (Sherwin, 1993). However, mood swings do not constitute a serious clinical depression. The mood swings associated with perimenopause tend to be sudden but minor, and can be handled.

Depression, on the other hand, is a serious, psychological problem distinct from menopause that will often require psychological treatment. We discuss depression at length in Chapter Seven. There is no such thing as a menopausal depression, but the erroneous belief that hormonal changes cause depression persists. Many women believe that menopause causes some horrendous sudden depression. This may be a problem of definition, because of the mood swings associated with the perimenopause. True clinical depression is something else. It involves a more overwhelming and persistent feeling of sadness, combined with other symptoms such as weight loss, sleep disturbance, and difficulties in concentration. When we look at true clinical depression, there is no increased risk at the time of menopause. In fact, younger women are at greater risk for depression.

For the menopausal women who do become depressed, there is no evidence that changes in hormones cause the depression. Studies of women who have become depressed during their menopausal years have found a link with such social stressors as unhappy relationships and coping with aging parents. These women, as studied by the McKinlays, had multiple sources of worry. These worries and social factors, not differences in hormones, seemed to be directly related to the depression (McKinlay and others, 1987).

We do not underestimate the problem of depression in American women in today's society. Many women are depressed during their menopausal years, just as many women are depressed in any point in the life cycle. We outline treatments for depression in Chapter Seven, but you should not approach menopause with the view that the hormonal changes at that time cause clinical depression.

✦ WHAT WILL HAPPEN SEXUALLY?

Sexuality depends on the quality of your relationship, the stress in your life, your health and your attitudes toward sex in general. Obviously there is tremendous variability in these factors in the lives of menopausal women. Some women have been in sexual relationships with men for over thirty years when they reach menopause. Others are beginning to date again. Some are relating sexually to women, either for the first time, or in long-term relationships. So it is difficult to say what will happen to women sexually during menopause. There are a few reports of women who reported a decrease in their sexual interest, or their libido, during the menopausal years, but overall, this is not true for most women. There are some biological changes, though, during menopause that may impact on the sexual relationship.

The first issue is that vaginal dryness can cause discomfort during intercourse. This can be a definite problem sexually but can be treated with topical lubricants or hormone replacement therapy. However, some of the reports that we have read written by men, insisting that women be placed on estrogen because of this problem alone, strike us as being overly phallocentric in their concerns. We believe that vaginal dryness, with respect to sexuality, should not be categorized as the woman's problem, but that it should be seen in the context of a relationship. For example, many women are in long-term marriages to men and the men are having sexual changes as well. One male change is that the hormones are no longer sent out in pulses rising and falling in a daily rhythm, but become more consistent. The concentration of testosterone remains the same all day long rather than peaking early in the morning and subsiding later in the day. At the same time, men's sexual responses slow down and it takes longer for them to attain an erection and longer to reach climax. For some couples, this change can be positive, especially in the case when the man has had previous problems with premature ejaculation.

Thus, rather than identifying women as suffering from menopausal deficiency, it is more important to view men and women alike within the context of aging. Adaptation to these changes in sexuality can often be associated with very positive changes in a relationship. Some of the biological changes in menopause can actually force couples to communicate. An informal study of lesbian women also suggests that the ability to share feelings about sexuality, and the ability to communicate, may be more important than any biological changes.

One woman told us that she did not have time to worry about sexuality at menopause because she had just fallen in love with a younger man and had a great sex life. Isabel Allende tells us, "My husband and I got together very late in our lives and we discovered a passionate love affair. There is passion for older women in midlife. Absolutely!" (Rountree, 1993, p. 157).

So, the reports of the death of the libido at menopause have been greatly exaggerated. This is not a common symptom, but even for women who do have a decrease in sexual interest, there are many treatment options. We discuss them in Chapter Three.

It is true that hormone replacement therapy and/or topical lubricants will treat the problem of vaginal dryness that occurs during menopause. Other studies suggest the "use it or lose it" phenomenon. That is to say that continued sexual functioning can, in and of itself, help the sexual adjustment during menopause. Some women, when faced with some minor sexual problems, withdraw from sexuality and this can be a serious problem. In contrast, by continuing to remain sexually active, not surprisingly, sexual adjustment can be positive.

By now you are probably worried about what you can do about all this. The answer is, in short, a lot! The menopausal years provide us with many choices and opportunities to change and improve our health.

Although estrogen has been promoted as the cure to the "menopausal disease," it is only one option for treating some of the symptoms of menopause. This book will help you decide whether or not you want to proceed with hormone replacement therapy. Too many books on menopause emphasize the issue of hormone replacement therapy alone, as if that alone will keep us young and prevent osteoporosis, coronary artery disease and hot flashes. Indeed, as described in Chapter Six, hormone replacement therapy can be beneficial for many women, but it is only one of many issues that should engage us. Equally important are our attitudes toward menopause and life changes, our overall health and our health care.

✦ MAINTAIN A POSITIVE ATTITUDE

There are many choices and challenges that we face in the menopausal years. Overall, the most important coping strategy is to maintain a positive attitude. By the time we are menopausal, we have been inundated with negative stereotypes from many sources. We all understand why any woman may come to menopause with a negative attitude. Until recently, we've seen little in the popular culture about menopause. Older women are virtually absent from television news programs and other types of entertainment. In the popular media, women are rarely seen in advertisements after the age of thirty-five, with the exception of advertisements for hair coloring products, diet programs, support bras, laxatives, denture cleaners, sleep preparations, and a sundry of other problem solving products. Interestingly, older women, such as in the popular television series *Murder She Wrote* with Angela Lansbury and the *Golden Girls,* have gained attention in the past few years, but middle-aged women in their late forties and fifties continue to be absent. This tells us something about our fears about this transitional period.

In the 1990s, menopause has become a hot topic on television. We did suffer through Edith Bunker's menopause in the 1970s, only to see her become "even more crazy" in dealing with her husband's verbal abuse. By the 1990s Julia Sugarbaker was allowed to go through menopause with humor on the television program *Designing Women.* Yet the negativism remains. In the television program *Sisters,* Teddy, a fashion designer in her late thirties, is distraught by the way she is being unjustly criticized by an older critic. Her response to this is to call a press conference where she sympathizes with the woman for having "such a difficult menopause." Now that menopause is in the public domain, it unfortunately serves as the brunt for hostility that is especially troubling when it is between women.

Even two recent books about menopause have had negative undercurrents. Gail Sheehy's book *The Silent Passage* brought the subject of menopause out into the open. But Sheehy overestimates the power of estrogen. "Within days the blue-meanie moods lifted, I was able to write for twelve hours straight on deadline . . . I was staggered by the potency of the female hormone" (Sheehy, 1992 p. 19). In addition, Sheehy's description of a group of women in Beverly Hills is strikingly lacking in empathy and by its detailed description of each woman physically, only emphasizes the myth that as women we must define ourselves either through our reproductive organs or through physical youth and beauty. She writes, "Surely what they all wanted to hear from me and Doctor Allen was that some magic regimen—yoga and yogurt, or yams and ginseng and green leafy vegetables—would allow them to remain as middle-aged women exactly as they had been: youthful wives, sexually appealing and responsive lovers, efficient career builders. They were not ready to consider a new self-definition" (Sheehy, 1991 p. 48). This "I am more self-aware than you are" approach, only feeds into our fear of aging rather than casts it aside. Although *The Silent Passage* ends with exhortations for a new life and growth, the overall tone of the book up until that chapter is so strikingly negative that it is hard for the reader to recover. When we recently discussed this book with one of our patients, we pointed out that the last chapter is positive and she replied, "Are you kidding? I quit reading long before then."

In Germaine Greer's *The Change*, the author contends that sexuality will probably end for most women and that our best bet is to retire to our herb garden, read books and become "crones" (Greer, 1992, p. 362). There are many problems with this analysis. The first is that Greer assumes that menopause must be a crisis. This is not the case, as documented by numerous longitudinal studies of women. The second problem is that Greer, although provocative and entertaining, has always been overly fixated on sexuality and has paid less attention to other aspects of women's development (Greer, 1970).

Although Greer is correct in noting that estrogen has a strong placebo factor, it has been shown to be more effective for stopping hot flashes than anything else. Since hot flashes are the most prevalent and the most troubling symptoms to many women, this is an important consideration, and Greer is doing us a disservice by overestimating the risks of hormone replacement therapy while also misjudging the use of natural substances. Greer is also in danger of becoming the Martha Stewart of menopause when she suggests that we should grow, collect *and* prepare our own herbs since, "Most dried herbs sold in commerce are not only old and valueless but can be contaminated" (Greer, 1992, p. 231).

So is it any wonder that we approach menopause with such negative beliefs? We have been taught that our ovaries are shrinking, our eggs are dying, we are going to become psychotically depressed and that our only hope is to take estrogen or become a crone and, let's face it, we *are* getting old! It does not matter that most of this is nonsense and that our alternative to becoming old is to die young. Given this choice, we should approach menopause with a sense of humor and with a commitment to maintain our health. Perhaps rather than bemoaning our fate, we should continue to enjoy life.

One way to not only enjoy the menopausal years but to rejoice in them is to read other women's stories. If we do so, we will learn that each of us is unique and that menopause may well be easier than other stages of life! Three books that have helped us listen to women are *Women of the Fourteenth Moon,* edited by Dena Taylor and Amber Coverdale Sumrall (Taylor and Sumrall, 1991), *Written By Herself,* edited by Jill Ker Conway (Conway, 1992) and *On Women Turning Fifty,* by Cathleen Rountree (Rountree, 1993). We learn, for example, from Cathleen Rountree's interview with the lawyer Gloria Allred who says, "I like being in my fifties. I don't think it's anything to be ashamed of. We should get medals for having survived what women have to go through to reach the age of fifty and the obstacles they face. It's a real test of survival" (Rountree, 1993, p. 63).

Changing our beliefs about menopause is critically important, for our physical, as well as our psychological well-being. A study by Dr. Myra Hunter in Great Britain reveals that a woman's belief in the negative stereotypes about menopause can be linked to depression (Hunter, 1990). Other studies have also documented this correlation: Women who fear menopause and have negative beliefs about it may well do worse than women who have an optimistic attitude. So it is our attitude and our outlook toward midlife and not our hormones that can lead us to sadness, depression and preoccupation with physical symptoms.

✦ PAY ATTENTION TO HEALTH, NOT ILLNESS

Menopause is a time when we need to pay attention to our overall health. For many women, menopause may be the first stage of life when there is enough leisure time to even consider sports and physical activity as part of a regular routine. For others, the beginning rumblings of our body, such as the beginnings of arthritis or a lack of energy, pinpoint that it is now time to pay attention. Exercise is a key factor in the prevention of osteoporosis and heart disease and in creating a feeling of general well-being. In fact, there is a strong interaction between physical and psychological health. People who are in good physical health are reporting the fewest psychological symptoms. A study of the readers of the journal *Melpomene: A Journal for Women's Health Research* revealed that these women found exercise to be an important source of satisfaction. In contrast to the average American woman, only 15 percent of these women said they were on a special diet, 9 percent in order to lose weight and 5.5 percent for other health reasons. This is in contrast to somewhere between at least 40 and 50 percent of the more general population of American women. The Melpomene women, to a large degree used physical activity as well as talking and individual time for themselves as a way to cope with stress (Lutter, 1992).

Our chapter on healthy bodies (Chapter Ten) emphasizes the need to pay attention to nutrition, exercise and to avoid substance abuse. We have no interest in becoming the "health police," to overburden you with too many prescriptions for a variety of health maintenance and exercise regimens. On the other hand, if you can find a specific physical activity that you enjoy, this can probably be one of the most important health decisions of your life.

Another way to focus on health is to accept that we do change as we grow older. Another story from *Women Turning Fifty* can help us here. Dolores Huerta is one of the founders of the United Farm Workers and has led an amazing life. As a young mother, she took her children with her when she worked with migrant farm workers. Now that Huerta is older she says, "I know that I will have to slow down some day, because I've seen it happen to other people. When I do reach that point, I'll be able to read books and do a different kind of activity" (Rountree, 1993, p. 133). She's not slowing down yet, though. When she was in her fifties, Dolores Huerta was beaten unconscious in a demonstration against George Bush in San Francisco. She survived.

✦ TAKE CHARGE OF YOUR HEALTH CARE

We have learned a lot from our menopausal patients. We have learned that women want information. They want a physician who will listen to them. They want access to other health care professionals as well. They want to be actively involved in choices regarding their own health. We will help you create your own Women's Health team in the last chapter of this book. For now, there are some general communications strategies that you can use to take charge of your health.

The typical physician-patient interaction puts the patient at a terrible disadvantage in communication. Many courses on effective communication emphasize nonverbal aspects including: eye contact, posture, gestures, dress, voice and natural expression. Now consider the typical doctor-patient interaction. In many cases a woman is seeing her male primary care physician. All too often she may be sitting at the edge of an examining table wearing a hospital johnny, feeling either too cold or too hot and is anxiously awaiting information about her health. The physician may be standing, fully clothed, looking down at the patient and is acting hurried. Even the best of communicators would find this situation untenable. The power dynamics are such that the woman patient is at an incredible disadvantage. The problems in doctor-patient, male-female communication can become so difficult that one study was aptly titled, "Intimate Adversaries" (Todd, 1989).

What to do? As a patient you have several choices. We suggest that you make an appointment specifically to talk to your physician. Many primary care physicians now schedule time with the patient (fully clothed!) for a consultation in the office. If this is not the normal procedure in the practice you go to, you have the opportunity and right to schedule such a visit. Another possibility is to specifically ask the physician to sit down after the physical exam is over. You can state that you would like to discuss some concerns and need a few minutes of his or her time. Not many physicians would say no to this request.

Remember the other members of the health care team—nurse practitioners, mental health professionals, physician assistants and pharmacists. All too often a woman is given a prescription being told, "take this for your blood pressure." One of the most important problems as we get older is that medications interact with one another, and can cause unexpected side effects. So you have the right to know the precise details of a medication plan, or regimen. Your physician should give you these details. If for some reason that does not happen, don't forget your pharmacist. Most pharmacists are very comfortable and eager to discuss the issues of medication with you. Some of the questions you might want to ask include: What will this medication treat? How should I take it? How many times a day? With food, or on an empty stomach? With water, or is water not important? If I decide to stop the medication, can I stop suddenly, or should I taper off? What will happen if I stop the medication? Are there other medications that I should not take while taking this one? Are there foods and beverages that I should avoid? Can I be exposed to the sun while taking this medication?

Studies have shown that over 50 percent of prescriptions filled each year are not always taken properly. Another study found that 50 percent of people on medications for a long period of time stopped taking their medication before they should have. Finally, 20 percent of prescriptions are never even filled (Katz, 1992). It is important then to know why and how to take the medication. If you have any reservations, it is much better to discuss them with your doctor, nurse or pharmacist than to become quiet and not let the physician know of your concerns.

By communicating clearly, setting your priorities for each appointment, and asking questions, you can take charge of your health care. You *can* take the power. In fact, many women come to our practice because they "just couldn't take it anymore," and were fed up with the previous health care system. Creating a new health care team with a new attitude can help you through this developmental period and can be one of your strongest support systems.

✦ Learning from the Experience of Women

So you want to know what your menopause will be like. What *can* you expect? We wish we could tell you exactly what your menopause would be like, because we know that you feel anxiety and that you would feel better if you could prepare. However, menopause is much more variable than other women's transitions like menarche or pregnancy. Each woman brings her own genetic background, her psychological issues and her social context to menopause. Her overall physical health is another issue. If you are like most women, you will be just fine, and you will experience a few hot flashes. You may have some other symptoms but the changes will be gradual, not dramatic and can be treated. To help you appreciate the variety in the menopausal experience, here are the short stories of four women who represent some of the possibilities during menopause.

• Allison is a forty-nine-year-old divorced woman who has returned to Brown University in the Resumed Undergraduate Education program. We have seen her on our way to meetings on campus, sitting on the Green, wearing a baseball cap, a comfortable sweatshirt and blue jeans, running shoes and obviously enjoying her studies in American History. She and her husband have been divorced for ten years, and her two children are grown and doing well.

Allison came to us originally because she was concerned about her blood pressure, which was at one time 160 over 116. She had had very few hot flashes and they were fleeting and not debilitating. Allison had not had a period in about six months. Allison was slightly overweight and there was no history of osteoporosis in her family. She did not smoke or drink. She was concerned about hormone replacement therapy because there was a family history of breast cancer in her mother and her aunt. Although Allison was doing quite well overall, she was terrified that menopause would cause her health to deteriorate. She came to us with a high level of anxiety.

We met with Allison in order to discuss her concerns. We reassured her that menopause, in and of itself, would not make her health deteriorate. Allison had believed many of the myths that we have discussed previously, and now experienced a great feeling of relief. We did share our concerns with Allison about her blood pressure. She was surprised to learn that it is heart disease that is the most significant cause of death for women over the age of fifty. Allison, upon hearing this news, became highly motivated to lower her blood pressure, and reduce any other risk factors for heart disease. She worked with our nutritionist to lower her fat intake and began a walking program. She was a woman who had never engaged in any physical activity and had little interest in aerobics or any activity that was strenuous. But she learned to enjoy walking and we now see Allison walking on a local boulevard two miles a day, three or four times a week.

Allison also appreciated the opportunity to think through the issues about hormone replacement therapy that we detail in Chapter Six. After thinking things over, and given her family history, she decided not to take hormone replacement therapy. Allison returns to see us now on a yearly basis, and is approaching her menopausal years with a new sense of optimism and commitment to her health.

• Gladys is an African-American woman who lives with her husband, three dogs and several cats. She and her husband are both retired from jobs in accounting firms. They had no children and are devoted to one another. Although they are not wealthy, they had saved quite a bit of money and enjoy traveling. Gladys, at age fifty, had serious problems with hot flashes. Her sleep was becoming disrupted, and she was feeling fatigued and out of sorts, something extremely unusual for her. Her husband came with her to her appointment and, after discussing the issues of hormone replacement therapy, Gladys decided to begin treatment. Her hot flashes stopped almost immediately and she was greatly relieved. Gladys is an example of a woman who benefited tremendously from hormone replacement therapy.

• Sarah is a forty-nine-year-old lesbian woman who is an advertising executive. She came to see us because she has begun to wake up sweating at night. Sarah has a history of panic attacks and is concerned that the stress of her high-powered job is affecting her mental health. We have seen Sarah for several medical and psychological sessions and have ascertained that she is generally in good health. But Sarah is a good example of someone who needs to work on problematic behaviors in order to preserve her health. Sarah smokes two packs of cigarettes a day. She functions well at work, and is content in her relationship of ten years. Her FSH (follicle-stimulating hormone) level is 42 MIU/ml, indicating that Sarah may be entering menopause. We explained to her that smokers tend to have earlier menopause and that nicotine does not help at all with anxiety. Although Sarah uses smoking to cope with stress, she has agreed to consider a smoking-cessation program. We've worked with her to set a quit date and to explore a stress management program. Sarah does not wish to consider HRT at this time.

• June came to see us originally because of her concern for her twenty-one-year-old daughter. Her daughter had been a victim of date rape and was having terrible difficulty going back to college. We saw her daughter for a few sessions of psychotherapy and referred her to a psychotherapist located near her college. After her daughter returned to college, June talked more with us about her health and her concerns. Although June has been troubled by hot flashes, she has become increasingly depressed at the same time. Not only is she concerned about her younger daughter, but her older daughter is having difficulty in her marriage. June exemplifies some women who do become depressed during menopause. Although her hot flashes were one issue, another issue was June's multiple sources of worry. She was worried about both of her daughters, her husband's response to his unemployment and financial worries. We worked with June for several months, focusing on these issues. First, we taught her relaxation exercises to help deal with the hot flashes. In addition, she learned to dress in layers of clothing and to carry a fan with her. In order to help June develop more social support, we encouraged her to reach out to a neighbor who had been interested in establishing a deeper friendship with her. June and her neighbor now "walk and talk" every morning and have developed a close friendship. We helped her husband find career counseling, but he continued to have difficulty securing employment. June still has many difficulties but is coping better now through the techniques she has learned and through the social support she now enjoys.

These four women, from different lifestyles and backgrounds, all have some things in common. First, they all were eager to discuss the issue of menopause and to get as much information as possible. Each of them wanted to make the decision about hormone replacement therapy for herself. All of them benefited from relationships that they found supportive and felt great relief in talking about their problems with a friend or family member. These women viewed menopause not as a crisis but as a new phase in their lives. You will hear the stories of other women's lives as we go through each chapter.

We cannot forget Rae, who comes to see us for health care on an annual basis. She is enjoying menopause just as she has enjoyed other stages of her life. She loves working as a newspaper editor, she has a wide network of friends, and she is active in local politics. When we specifically ask her about menopause she looks puzzled, then smiles and responds, "No periods, remember?" Rae is having a great time. She reminds us that menopause is just part of life.

You will be able to think through the issues for maintaining your health as you read through each chapter of this book. But we have to remember to look at the big picture: as women, we have coped through earlier stages of life and we will cope and thrive during menopause as well. You have already met some of the women from our practice, and you know many menopausal women who are thriving. The fact is that we can rejoice in our menopausal years, enjoy life to its fullest and reach new heights. Our philosophy is that if we provide women with a comfortable health care environment, and with a maximum of information, women can use their resources to make important decisions. We can take charge of our health care in order to get relief from any menopausal symptoms. We can all use our internal and external resources to maintain our health and prevent health problems.

So now you know. Menopause brings a certain number of changes and in some cases, difficult symptoms. None of them are debilitating and most of them are not serious, but they can trouble you. As you read on, you will learn about each category of symptoms, and other issues that should concern us at midlife. You will learn that midlife brings with it a set of choices and that each of us can deal with these choices with help from our physicians, family and friends. Ultimately, we have as much control over menopause as we do over any other phase of our lives, and maybe even more. Read on.

CHAPTER TWO

Hot Flash!

DEATH, TAXES, AND NOW HOT FLASHES? WHILE IT IS TRUE THAT most menopausal women will experience hot flashes, we can be reassured that they are neither as inevitable as death, nor as bad as taxes. The only guaranteed consequence of menopause is the usually welcomed end of menstrual periods. Hot flashes are the second most predictable consequence of menopause but get more press because they are much more newsworthy than the last period. In fact, hot flashes are so common in the menopausal years that some have called them the calling card of menopause.

What is truly remarkable about menopausal hot flashes is the tremendous woman-to-woman variation. While Ethel, who is now ten years postmenopausal, concedes that she had years of hot flashes, she scoffs at their significance in her day-to-day existence. On the other hand, Victoria has been having hot flashes now for six years with only recent relief after doubling the dose of her estrogen patch. Pam was in the enviable position of experiencing not one hot flash in the eight years since she stopped menstruating, even without hormone replacement therapy.

We learn from these varied experiences that there is, in fact, no consistent pattern to menopausal hot flashes or any woman's reaction to them. One woman's "symptom" is a passing "sensation" to another. Unfortunately, this variability in the frequency and experience of hot flashes has created yet another opportunity to blame the victim. Women who do have debilitating hot flashes are often chided by their physician or family members for their poor tolerance, exaggeration of symptoms and inability to cope. Compounding the problem of individual variability in experience of hot flashes is the scientific community's poor understanding of them.

Not unlike premenstrual syndrome, hot flashes are poorly understood and are often discounted as yet another "female problem." Unlike premenstrual syndrome, however, there is a highly effective treatment which many physicians eagerly prescribe. While hormone treatment may be appropriate for many women, for many others it is unnecessary. What women really need is adequate information to make an informed decision about hormone replacement therapy and alternative methods of treatment rather than a prescription completed hastily as if to write off the entire problem. This chapter will give you the facts about hot flashes, including the lingo used to describe them, the likelihood that any woman will experience them, the consequences, the proposed causes and available treatments.

Despite the fact that hot flashes are so common, many women continue to be embarrassed by them. We prefer the approach of one of our patients, Kai, who is a professor at a small college. She dealt with her hot flashes with humor. When she began to sweat and turn red during a lecture she'd say to her students, "Let's take a break." She would then remove one of her carefully planned layers of clothing and her students would joke with her, calling these episodes "Flash Alerts."

* FLASHES, FLUSHES AND NIGHT SWEATS

The medical terminology that describes hot flashes is confusing, since the physicians who initially wrote about hot flashes chose to divide them into the subjective feelings of the patient, versus the objective measurable physiological changes. No other medical condition is so strictly divided into its subjective and objective aspects. Logically, the entire event could be designated as a *hot flash* and it is obscure why it is not. The experience of a heart attack is not divided into the subjective pain versus the objective electrocardiogram changes. Since you're reading this chapter, you might want to know how the medical profession describes hot flashes.

Hot *flash* refers to the subjective experience that precedes any measurable physiologic changes. Although there is considerable variability in the experience, most women first notice an intense feeling of warmth throughout the upper body. Some women additionally note an aura and state that they "just don't feel normal" prior to the onset of the actual warmth. These feelings may be accompanied by rapid or irregular heartbeats, headache, weakness, faintness, anxiety or dizziness. Most often, the entire episode ends with significant sweating and a cold clammy, chilled feeling.

In contrast, the hot *flush* constitutes the objective changes that occur during the episodes. In most cases, the hot flash precedes the hot flush. During the flush, there is visible redness of the upper chest, neck, face, followed by perspiration in the same areas. There is a measurable increase in skin temperature, blood flow and heart rate. Finger temperature increases as much as 6 degrees Centigrade during an episode. The skin temperature drops at sites where sweating occurs. (That is the whole point of sweating, after all.)

Now that you are familiar with the lingo, you may appreciate a story retold in *Women of the Fourteenth Moon*. It seems that a male gynecologist corrected a woman's use of the term "hot flash" saying, "No, dear, they are called hot flushes" to which she replied, "Well, dear, when *you* get one you can call it anything you want" (Parke, 1991, p. 7). You may want to use this line if you find yourself in a similar situation, then change doctors.

Night sweats are the nocturnal form of hot flashes. Most women who experience night sweats complain about them more bitterly than daytime flashes. Hot flashes are more frequent at night and may awaken women from sleep. This disturbance of sleep can, in turn, cause severe daytime fatigue, irritability, inability to concentrate and impaired memory. In 1981, Dr. Erlik and associates demonstrated that nighttime hot flushes, measured by increased skin temperature, are clearly associated with episodes of waking. The authors conclude that "the occurrence of waking episodes with hot flushes contributes to the insomnia seen in older women. This chronic sleep disturbance could alter psychological function." They add that estrogen probably improves mood and cognitive functions by eliminating night flushes (Erlik and others, 1981, p. 1744). We know that many women who have hot flashes at night complain of sleep disruption. They may awaken drenched in perspiration and be forced to get out of bed to change their clothes.

In their study of menopausal hot flushes and waking episodes, the same researchers found that women were awakened before any changes in skin temperature occurred (Erlik and others, 1981). These findings suggest that the subjective hot flash, rather than the discomfort associated with flushing and sweating, causes the sleep disruption. Many women can sleep through the hot flash experience, especially when they are in a cold room. This seems logical enough.

Vasomotor symptoms refer to the whole array of subjective and objective events that constitute hot flash, flush and night sweats. These refer to changes that occur in the circulation, including increased blood flow, temperature and heart rate.

◆ THE NUMBERS

Although almost 75 percent of menopausal women in the United States experience hot flashes, only 10 to 15 percent of women have symptoms that are severe enough to cause them to consult a physician (Kronenberg, 1993). Interestingly, there is tremendous cultural variation in the report of hot flashes among women, ranging from 25 to 85 percent. Japanese women report hot flashes much less frequently than women from Western cultures (Lock, 1991). Many now feel that the Japanese diet, high in naturally occurring plant estrogens, may account for these differences.

The occurrence of hot flashes is highest during the first two years after menopause and lessens with increasing years from the last menstrual period. Of the women who experience hot flashes, 85 percent will have them for more than one year and 20 to 50 percent for up to five years. Women who have surgical menopause (oophorectomy) often have frequent and severe hot flashes soon after their ovaries are removed (Kronenberg, 1990).

Hot flashes are not limited to perimenopausal or postmenopausal women. Guess what? Men can have hot flashes too. According to Drs. Isaac Schiff and Brian Walsh, hot flashes are a result of the sudden withdrawal of estrogen (Schiff and Walsh, 1989). Men often have hot flashes when they experience a sudden withdrawal of the male sex hormone, testosterone. One study found that 73 percent of men have hot flashes after the removal of their testicles to treat prostate cancer. Also, men who have other types of testicular insufficiency have also reported hot flashes. As many as two-thirds of premenopausal women may also experience hot flashes (Kronenberg, 1990). Many women have their first hot flashes after childbirth, presumably related again to the sudden drop in estrogen levels. When hot flashes occur before the end of menstrual periods, they signify that estrogen levels produced by the ovaries are reduced, but not enough to stop menstruation. Women who experience hot flashes while still menstruating need to have other causes of these symptoms, like hyperthyroidism, evaluated. Your health care professional can order a blood sample of hormone levels in order to diagnose menopause.

The good news is that hot flashes improve with time. Most women will be completely hot-flash free within five years of the last menstrual period. However, for some they can last for five years or more. There is little to predict which women will experience prolonged hot flashes. We do know that women who have surgical menopause when both ovaries are removed may experience more severe hot flashes for a longer period of time. So far, there has been no clear relationship established between the occurrence of hot flashes and a woman's menstrual history, including the age of her first period, the age of menopause or the number of pregnancies. Neither do a woman's employment status, social class, age, marital status nor workload predict hot flashes (Kronenberg, 1993). Even today, prejudices flourish, with hot flashes and other menopausal symptoms being seen as the self-indulgence of middle- or upper-class women. Women who experience hot flashes tend to weigh less than women who do not (Kronenberg, 1990). Since estrogen is stored in fat, women who have a higher percentage of body fat are likely to have a less dramatic decline in their estrogen levels at menopause. At last, the corpulent get revenge on the emaciated!

✦ ANATOMY OF A HOT FLASH

Hot flashes can occur any time during the day but seem to be most frequent from six A.M. to eight A.M. and six P.M. to ten P.M. This may be good news for the women who work outside their homes from nine A.M. to five P.M. and fear that hot flashes will interfere with their work (Doress and others, 1987). The frequency of hot flashes varies considerably from woman to woman, from day to day, from year to year. It appears that almost half of women in the forty- to sixty-year-age group report hot flashes on a daily basis. Far fewer report multiple hot flashes in a day, or as few as one hot flash per week (Kronenberg, 1990).

Researchers have tried to identify the factors that precipitate hot flashes. Stress usually leads the list of possible triggers of hot flashes, but this is still controversial (Kronenberg, 1993). One study was completed to specifically answer the question, "Does stress actually trigger

TABLE 2-1

If you have never had a hot flash, this is what it is like:

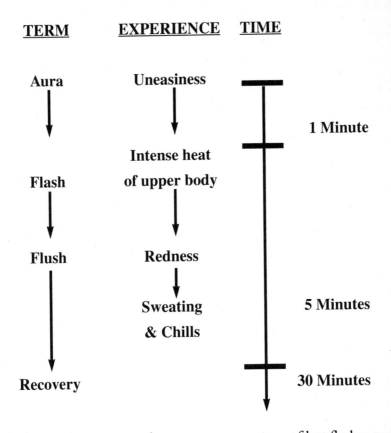

TERM	EXPERIENCE	TIME
Aura	Uneasiness	
		1 Minute
Flash	Intense heat of upper body	
Flush	Redness	
	Sweating & Chills	5 Minutes
Recovery		30 Minutes

hot flashes or does stress make women more aware of hot flashes and, therefore, more likely to report them?" The authors found that stress does not make women report more hot flashes but probably does cause a specific physiologic change that triggers them (Swartzman and others, 1990). Warm weather also triggers hot flashes and worsens both their intensity and frequency. Ethel recalls that she really didn't have time for hot flashes while caring for her failing father-in-law, but she did acknowledge fairly predictable hot flashes in the late afternoons of one summer. She recalls that it was "no big deal" and would get in her car, roll the windows down and go for a ride when she felt an impending flash. Ethel's story emphasizes that anything that can raise the normal body temperature can trigger hot flashes, including hot weather, hot drinks, rooms, beds, foods and alcohol.

The typical hot flash may begin with an aura—an initial sensation of uneasiness. Some women also report palpitations, headaches or dizziness. Many women are relieved when they learn that this experience is a prelude to a hot flash, not an anxiety attack. The aura is followed by a sensation of heat across the upper chest, neck, face and head. This sensation usually precedes the flush by less than a minute. The flush is heralded by redness in the same distribution that lasts for several minutes. Sweating, accompanied by chills, often follows. The total duration of a typical hot flash and flush is five minutes. Although dramatic flashes and flushes last only five minutes, it may take a woman approximately thirty minutes to return to normal (Budoff, 1983).

While there is a fair amount of uniformity in the experience of an individual hot flash and flush, there is very little consistency in the frequency, intensity and duration of hot flashes for women. Our experience with our patients has shown us the variety of women's experiences. Whereas Sue is completely thrown by her night sweats, Jenna uses them as a time to get up, stretch for a while and then return to bed. One difference between these women is that Jenna can make her own hours and Sue has an eight-thirty to five job.

✦ THE MYSTERY OF HOT FLASHES

It is quite remarkable that as late as 1978 investigators wrote, "Rather surprisingly, the flush has received very little scientific investigation. The rationale for estrogen treatment has been questioned with some justification" (Sturdee and others, 1978, p. 79). Alas, the specific biochemical cause of hot flashes and flushes remains elusive even now. Certainly the slow start to investigate the basis of hot flashes has contributed to this problem, and we have made relatively little progress even with the intensified study in the 1980s.

It was initially assumed that a lack of estrogen was solely responsible for hot flashes. Yet women who have had no estrogen production from birth do *not* suffer from hot flashes. It has become clear that it is the relative drop in estrogen levels that causes hot flashes. As with other substances that cause symptoms, when they are withdrawn, the body becomes accustomed to the presence of estrogen and its disappearance causes a disequilibrium.

More specifically, the levels of female hormones are regulated very carefully by the feedback loop between the blood and two sensing areas of the brain known as the pituitary gland and hypothalamus. Both areas respond to low levels of estrogen by increasing the hormones that they produce. The pituitary gland produces luteinizing hormone (LH) and follicle-stimulating hormones (FSH), which are the hormones typically measured to diagnose menopause. The hypothalamus produces gonadotropin-releasing hormone (GRH), which acts on the pituitary gland to produce FSH and LH in response to low estrogen levels. Initially, researchers believed that the elevated levels of FSH and LH were the sole cause of menopausal hot flashes, but this turns out to be untrue.

Although scientists have explored a number of theories, currently the most promising explanation for menopausal hot flashes lies in the hypothalamus. Although we don't know the exact biochemical cause of hot flashes, it does seem that it is related to the hypothalamus' role as the body's temperature regulation center. The hormone (GRH) produced in the hypothalamus in response to lowered estrogen levels seems not to be the sole cause of hot flashes, but is likely to be a major player in the reaction.

We do know that the substances responsible for revving up the body's nervous system increase during hot flashes. Specifically epinephrine (adrenaline) rises during hot flashes and may be responsible for the increased heart rate, increased blood flow through the circulation and increased temperature. It may also explain the subjective feelings of anxiety or dread that many women experience preceding and during hot flashes. It is unclear what causes the surge of adrenaline during a hot flash, but it may be a response to an event in the hypothalamus. Although estrogen withdrawal and the body's reaction to it are the underlying causes of hot flashes, the specific symptoms and physiologic changes observed are likely to be caused by the effects of epinephrine on the nervous system. This becomes important when treatment options are considered. Although estrogen replacement is the most logical choice for treatment, there may be alternative approaches that prevent or lessen the severity of hot flashes by other means.

✦ THERAPY FOR HOT FLASHES

As with any treatment decision, the first step is to evaluate the severity of the symptoms you are experiencing. We have included a hot flash diary for you to review and complete. By filling it out, you can get a true picture of how much hot flashes are interfering with your life. Also, you may be able to pinpoint some triggers such as stress or caffeine. This will help you develop a plan for preventing hot flashes that can be monitored by continuing the diary. In addition, you can use this diary to assess your response to any specific treatment that you are trying.

HORMONES

Estrogen withdrawal, unquestionably, sets off the cascade of events that lead to hot flashes. Estrogen is a highly successful treatment for hot flashes. Estrogen is over 90 percent effective in relieving hot flashes; an impressive statistic for any therapy. If you have no major reason to avoid estrogen, then remember that estrogen is truly the "flash blaster." In many cases, hot flashes can be treated with as little as .3 milligram (mg) of conjugated estrogen but may require up to 1.25 mg per day. We discuss the dosages of estrogen in detail in Chapter Six. The estrogen patches are equally successful in treatment at doses of .05 mg to .1 mg (Ravnikar, 1990). Symptom relief with estrogen is not immediate, however, and it may take up to four weeks of therapy to assess effectiveness. This is important to remember when your doctor suggests an increased dose of estrogen before the completion of a full four-week trial on the lower dose.

If an adequate trial of estrogen therapy at the higher dose fails to eliminate hot flashes, then there are several other possible causes. Common conditions that can mimic menopausal hot flashes include hyperthyroidism, alcoholism and diabetes. Carcinoid syndrome, a rare condition of an excess of the chemical serotonin, can also cause episodic flushing.

Because most women's hot flashes dissipate after three to five years from the last menstrual period, treatment with estrogen may be time-limited if it was started only for hot flashes. If, on the other hand, hormone replacement therapy is also being used to prevent the long-term consequences of menopause like vaginal dryness, osteoporosis and coronary artery disease, then therapy may be continued for many years. Women who have successfully been treated with hormone replacement therapy and wish to discontinue this therapy may choose to try a period off hormone replacement therapy on a yearly basis. Beware that if estrogen is stopped abruptly, hot flashes will return, and probably in a big way! If, however, the estrogen is tapered over weeks to months, then the body has an opportunity to reequilibrate, and it is possible that hot flashes will not recur once the medication is stopped completely. An older regimen of hormone replacement therapy involved daily estrogen doses for three out of four weeks of any month. Many women experienced hot flashes during the one week off estrogen, thereby demonstrating the importance of tapering the dose of estrogen rather than abruptly stopping it.

Table 2-2

HOT FLASH DIARY

Date	Day	Time	Food	Stress	Flash	Severity (1–5)	Notes
2/1	MONDAY	6:00 A.M.			√	4	Awakened from sleep
		7:00 A.M.	Muffin Coffee		√	5	On way to work
		Noon	Tuna Sandwich Diet Coke Brownie				
		1:30 P.M.			√	3	Sitting at desk
		3:00 P.M.		Argument with co-worker			

- After two full weeks, count the number of hot flashes per day and average.
- After two full weeks, average the severity of hot flashes experienced.
- Look for any patterns in flashes—food, caffeine, stress, days of week, times of day.

Alternative forms of hormone therapy have been investigated because so many women are unable to take estrogen and many women prefer not to take it. The use of the other major female hormone, progesterone, has been investigated thoroughly. Hot flashes can be reduced by 70 to 90 percent with medroxyprogesterone alone (Schiff and others, 1980). It is intriguing that women who were treated with placebo consistently showed a rather significant decrease in hot flashes (as much as 25 percent in women receiving placebo alone) (Albrecht and others, 1980; Bullock and others, 1975). There is no clear explanation for this response to a supposedly ineffective substance. Perhaps the expectation of a response to treatment increases a brain substance that can by itself decrease the frequency of hot flashes. This is not evidence that women who respond to placebo are exaggerating their symptoms. This phenomenon of placebo response is seen to some extent in all treatment studies of females and males. What it does mean is that any therapeutic response must be compared to response that is seen with placebo alone. If, for example, a therapy is touted as effective but only reduces hot flash frequency by 25 percent, then it is not better than placebo. Medroxyprogesterone is not without side effects but it may be an alternative therapy for women who are not candidates for estrogen therapy but have severe frequent hot flashes for which they desire treatment.

Nonhormonal Drug Therapy

A number of nonhormonal drugs have also been used in the treatment of hot flashes with variable success. Many of the drugs found to be effective in treating hot flashes were developed to treat high blood pressure. Their success with hot flashes probably relates to their effects in the circulatory system.

The most promising medication to date has been the blood pressure medicine Clonidine. Clonidine has also been used in the treatment of nicotine, alcohol and heroin withdrawal. This is not to imply that hot flashes are analogous to heroin withdrawal! Clonidine acts in all these situations to modify the overdrive of the circulatory system. It has no effect on hormones and does not treat the other symptoms or consequences of menopause. In one study, Clonidine doses lower than those used for high blood pressure reduced the number of hot flashes and their severity significantly when compared to placebo (Clayden and others, 1974). A similar medication, Lofexidine, can also decrease the number of hot flashes (Jones and others, 1985). The beta-blockers, another class of blood pressure medication, have had some promise as well. Sotalol has been found to decrease hot flashes by 62 percent

(Young and others, 1990). For many of these medications, there may be side effects related to lowering blood pressure. Some women may experience light-headedness and fatigue when begun on any of these drugs, depending on the dose.

Another class of drugs has been somewhat successful in the treatment of hot flashes. Veralipride is a medication that acts on yet another substance produced in the brain called serotonin. Total elimination of hot flashes has been found in 60 to 80 percent of women. After the medication was stopped, hot flashes were eliminated for three months, but returned in six months. The medication is also associated with breast tenderness and some production of milk by the breast that disappears rapidly after the medication is discontinued (Young and others, 1990).

While many of these medications hold promise in decreasing the frequency and severity of hot flashes, none of them are as effective as hormone therapy. Additionally, none of them treat the other symptoms of menopause or prevent the long-term consequences. For women who cannot take or choose not to take hormones, these may be reasonable alternatives when hot flashes cannot be managed otherwise.

NONPRESCRIPTION REMEDIES FOR HOT FLASHES

There have been a number of substances that have been suggested as effective in treating hot flashes. Most of these have not been studied rigorously. In the case of hot flashes, this is particularly important since the response to placebo is so high. As is true with prescription drugs, a woman needs to consider the potential side effects, complications and financial cost compared to its benefits in treating the symptom. We wish there were more studies about the effectiveness of nonmedical approaches to hot flashes. The truth is, though, that as little as women's health has been studied, nonmedical treatments of symptoms have been studied even less. We are delighted that the National Institute of Health finally established the Office of Alternative Medicine, because that means that new research will be forthcoming. But here is some of what we do know:

Vitamin E appears in many lists of treatment for hot flashes, but much of the information we have about it is anecdotal at best. Vitamin E occurs in a number of food substances, including wheat and rice germ, legumes, corn, almonds and egg yolks. It can also be taken as a vitamin supplement beginning at 100 international units a day and increasing to 400 international units a day. Although vitamin E is a relatively safe vitamin, if you have heart disease, hypertension or diabetes, you should consult your physician before starting to take it (Dukes, 1992). Vitamin E is a vitamin that can be stored in the body's fat and it is important that doses be kept at no more than 400 international units per day to avoid toxic effects. For some women, vitamin E may completely relieve hot flashes. Up to two-thirds of women may experience relief from hot flashes with daily vitamin E.

Vitamin B complex is important for the normal functioning of the nervous system and some women have reported help with hot flashes and the daytime consequences of night sweats.

Ginseng is an herbal source of estrogen and is available as a tea. Although ginseng is available in health food stores it is, nonetheless, a form of hormone therapy. It can be effective in treating hot flashes as well as the other symptoms of menopause but it carries the same risks as estrogen replacement therapy. The dose of estrogen taken is very difficult to estimate and, therefore the effects are difficult to predict. It is also very expensive.

Many other *herbs* have been used in the treatment of menopause and are highly recommended by many women, including Germaine Greer. Again, there have not been many studies of most of these substances and some, including black cohosh, contain estrogen. Most of the herbs used in the treatment of hot flashes and menopausal symptoms are available in a dried form for tea but may also be available in capsules and as powder. It is important that herbal therapy be used cautiously and based on a clear understanding of the active substance. Herbs that contain estrogen carry the same potential for complications as hormone replacement therapy and need to be considered in the same context. Some women have used these "natural" substances and have experienced unpredictable bleeding, so, even "natural" products may have very significant side effects. Some of the herbs used in the treatment of menopausal symptoms include dong quai, damiana, cramp bark, golden seal, licorice root, oil of primrose, red raspberry leaves, sarsaparilla and spearmint.

We do not want to leave you with the impression that we are against the use of herbs and alternative treatments. The problem is that there has not been enough research to evaluate their effectiveness. In general, we feel that if they are safe and work for you, by all means, try them.

OTHER STRATEGIES TO DEAL WITH HOT FLASHES

A number of other techniques have been used in the management of hot flashes. Relaxation techniques, biofeedback, visualization, hypnosis, meditation and massage have all been used with some success. Because each woman's experience with hot flashes is so different, it is impossible to predict her response to the many forms of treatment. You may want to try some of these methods. All of these behavioral treatments are essentially educational. They involve skills that require practice. As you practice these and become comfortable with them, they can be easily and quickly used to deal with any stress, including hot flashes.

Paced respirations or controlled breathing has been shown to be more effective than either relaxation or biofeedback in dealing with hot flashes. The same principles apply here as they did to labor or childbirth. You need to focus consistent breathing in order to relax, rather than "fight" the flash. Relaxation techniques may be particularly effective in women who do experience more hot flashes when stressed. When increased stress is recognized, relaxation techniques may actually be used to avert hot flashes. When hot flashes begin, many women also find relaxation techniques helpful to lessen the severity of the attack and avoid the escalation that can occur during the episode.

Amy, a sales representative for a computer software company, found paced respirations and relaxation techniques very effective. She was having relatively infrequent hot flashes but they occurred at the most inopportune times. It seemed that anytime she was about to give a major presentation, she would experience a flash. This is completely understandable, since stress can increase the occurrence of hot flashes. Amy did not want to take HRT. She was able to learn relaxation techniques and practiced them before major presentations in order to decrease her anxiety and thereby avoid her dreaded hot-flash trigger.

Biofeedback would seem to be an ideal technique since it capitalizes on an individual's ability to monitor and alter involuntary functions. Because subjective symptoms of hot flashes are so dramatic this would seem to be a perfect opportunity to alter the body's response. Biofeedback teaches the techniques of changing muscle tension, lowering blood pressure and heart rate, as well as temperature. Specifically in the case of hot flashes, the woman is instructed to think of increased blood flow in her hands that may allow a diversion of blood from the head and upper chest to the extremities.

Visualization is another mind-body technique. It builds on relaxation techniques. During the hot flash, the woman is instructed to imagine herself in cold water or snow that will allow the mental removal of the sensation of heat from the body. Similarly, self-hypnosis creates a mental and physical state of relaxation. While in this state, a woman can suggest methods of dealing with symptoms such as hot flashes by establishing a detailed image that can be called upon during subsequent episodes. In the case of a hot flash, this image may be one of cooling and can be called up during each episode. Meditation has been shown to lower heart rate and blood pressure and may ease the discomfort associated with the hot flashes in this way.

One study found that acupuncture reduced the frequency of hot flashes. This is an area that needs more attention.

Hot Flash Prevention

A number of substances can precipitate hot flashes. Included among the lists are hot drinks, hot rooms, hot beds, hot foods, alcohol, and stress. If these substances do trigger hot flashes even if only in some women, avoidance is a logical first step if hot flashes are bothersome. Some of the behavioral techniques outlined above may have a role in prevention if stress is a major contributor to the episode.

Nutrition may play a role in prevention as well. We know that women who are underweight are likely to experience more severe symptoms of menopause because of the relative lack of estrogen stored in their body fat. For this reason, it is advisable that women not be significantly underweight. A diet supplemented with plant estrogens, that is soy flower and linseed, may benefit women with hot flashes as well. This could, in part, explain the lower occurrence of hot flashes among Asian women who consume a large proportion of their calories from foods high in plant estrogens. If caffeine, alcohol, sugar and spicy foods are possible triggers of hot flashes, then they should be avoided. The most sensible dietary approach is to eat a balanced variety of foods that are nutritious and to avoid any foods that may precipitate hot flashes.

Exercise has a significant beneficial effect on menopausal symptoms as it does with premenstrual symptoms. Regular exercise probably decreases FSH and LH and in this way decreases some of the symptoms of menopause. Exercise increases the natural endorphins, or opiate-like substances produced by the brain, and these may have a beneficial effect on menopausal symptoms and stress as well. If you are going to start an exercise program, you should check with your doctor and you may want to also consult an exercise physiologist in order to achieve aerobic effects. (See Chapter Ten, "Promoting a Healthy Lifestyle.") It is best to exercise three to four times per week. Yoga may be used also or as additional exercise and may achieve the same beneficial effects.

✦ COMMUNICATION

COMMUNICATING WITH YOUR
HEALTH CARE PROFESSIONAL

We have found that hot flashes are often the symptoms that bring menopausal patients to our practice. Therefore, hot flashes often begin the conversation with your health care professional. This interaction is a critical part of your health care. In each chapter, we will be reviewing different communication strategies specific to the topic covered. Remember, in general, you should expect this communication to be part of your office visit. Do not be afraid to ask questions. You should ask follow-up questions if you don't understand the answers. It is our hope that by the end of this book, you will have an ample repertoire of communication strategies.

To begin your conversation regarding hot flashes, you may wish to review, with your health care professional, your hot-flash diary. Make a special effort to communicate to your health care professional the disruptiveness of your hot flashes. Even if your hot flashes are infrequent but debilitating, you might consider some form of treatment. Together, you may identify specific triggers and try some prevention strategies before considering other treatment. Clearly communicate what types of treatment you would and would not consider. You may wish to review the treatments presented in this chapter and rate them as *yes, no,* and *possibly.* This designation will help you plan a strategy of treatment. It may be that if all else fails, you would be willing to try HRT, but that you'd rather use prevention and behavioral techniques first.

If you do decide to try medication, remember that you have not failed. Many of us learned this lesson anticipating our pregnancies and deliveries. After all, this is not a competition to see who can tolerate the most pain and suffering. Even if you are one of those die-hard natural childbirth types, remember that hot flashes can give you as many sleepless nights as newborns, without the irresistibly cute faces to greet you. If you are feeling pressured by others in either direction, toward or away from treatment, express your concerns about this with them. This includes your doctor. Many physicians have strong opinions about hormone replacement therapy. Most of them (but not all) are pro-HRT. You need to be clear that you value your physician's advice but that the decision must ultimately be your own. Do not be discouraged if your physician only recommends hormone replacement therapy for your hot flashes. Persevere and ask follow-up questions such as: Can you recommend any other forms of treatment? We have found that these follow-up questions are as important as the initial questions for women to ask. The issue of hot flashes is just one part of the HRT decision, but a crucial part since HRT can be so effective. You will weigh other factors as we progress through this book.

COMMUNICATING WITH FRIENDS AND FAMILY

Family and friends can be very helpful if you share your symptoms and decision making with them. They may be in a good position to help you assess how hot flashes have affected you and your interactions with others. They may also be willing to help with solutions. Amy's family was willing to keep the temperature lower in their house after they realized that the hot rooms triggered her hot flashes in the evening and during the night. Amy's husband and children layered on extra clothing to help keep her hot flash–free.

To summarize, hot flashes are very common among menopausal women but are not usually severe enough to warrant medical treatment. It is important for each woman to assess how bothersome they are in order to make decisions about treatment. Severity is not just frequency. Hot flashes may be relatively infrequent but very disruptive. Remember that hot flashes do not last forever nor do the treatments. For many women, controlling hot flashes, rather than being controlled by them, is critical to improvement. This philosophy of taking charge of your health is at the core of the women's health movement.

Our patient Kai ran into a perimenopausal friend, Donna, who was just beginning to experience her first flashes. Kai shared her humorous approach to hot flashes with Donna who responded, "That's great! But haven't you heard? They're called power surges now!"

RESOURCES

Women's best resources for dealing with hot flashes are other women. Newsletters about menopause are multiplying like rabbits! Here are three:

A Friend Indeed
Box 515, Place du Parc Station
Montreal, Canada H2W 2P1

Published by Janine O'Leary Cobb, "A Friend Indeed" is the grandmother of them all. It is especially intriguing because it contains

*both comments from Canadian and American women. It provides
information on recent research, a forum to exchange experiences and
support for the woman approaching or experiencing menopause. It
reviews almost all of the books that deal with the various aspects of
menopause. It comes out ten times a year and a subscription is $30.*

Hot Flash: Newsletter for Midlife and Older Women
Dr. Jane Porcini
National Action Forum for Mid-life and Older Women
Box 816
Stony Brook, NY 11790-0609
(212) 725-8627

*This quarterly newsletter gives information on political and social issues
related to the physiology and psychology of menopause, and resources.
$25 a year with a membership.*

Menopause News
2074 Union St.
San Francisco, CA 94123
(415) 567-2368

*"Menopause News" is published six times a year by Judith S. Askew. It
provides medical and psychological information, publishes letters and
reviews books and videotapes. The cost is $24 a year.*

*If all else fails . . . consider a portable fan. One of our favorites is called
the "Tiny Tornado," available from the Solutions Catalogue (P.O.
Box 6878, Portland, Oregon, 97228).*

❦ CHAPTER THREE

Sexuality

"WHY DO WOMEN FAKE ORGASMS? . . . BECAUSE MEN FAKE FOREPLAY!" This is one of the best jokes of Miriam, our fifty-five-year-old patient who regales us with funny stories whenever we see her. Miriam went through menopause four years prior to our meeting her. She comes to see us every year for her annual physical, Pap smear, to have her blood pressure checked and to schedule her mammogram. Over the years we have enjoyed our relationship with Miriam and she has taken advantage of the abundance of information and resources available through our practice. Most recently, we provided a referral for infertility evaluation because her thirty-two-year-old daughter and husband had not been able to conceive.

Miriam worked as a secretary full-time, but recently reduced her hours to part-time. She is bright, engaging and articulate. Her husband Tom is a journalist, a quiet and wryly humorous man. He and Miriam have been married for thirty-three years and have three children, who are now in their late twenties and early thirties. When asked about her own sex life Miriam replied, "Now that's foreplay! We take longer than we used to and I love it." Miriam was eager to share her story with other women. Miriam and Tom have always communicated well, partially because they have so much in common. They are both active in their church and enjoy hiking, camping and other outdoor activities. She told us that she and Tom have always enjoyed sex but that their patterns had changed with time. Originally slaves to the missionary position, Miriam read Masters and Johnson in the early seventies, and she and Tom began to be more sexually adventurous, exploring different positions and incorporating more romance into their lovemaking. Now that they were in their fifties, they had intercourse somewhat less often, but still enjoyed themselves and were both orgasmic. Miriam often was on top during sexual intercourse. This helped when she had some problems with vaginal dryness, in that she could control the pace and the positions during intercourse. She added that, "Tom just turned sixty and his back hurts now and then, so this position is great for both of us." When we commented on the couple's ability to communicate well about sex, she retorted, "After three children and thirty-three years of marriage, if we can't talk about sex, what's it all about?"

Miriam is an especially open and humorous woman, but her story is not all that unusual. Most menopausal women enjoy their sexuality and adjust quite well to the biological changes associated with menopause. This may surprise you, if you've believed the stereotypes of frustrated, sex-starved menopausal women. There is a long history of viewing older women primarily as asexual. Other popular myths have portrayed older women as sexually depraved and voracious. We see little about well-adjusted, mature women. Even as recently as 1992, Germaine Greer was exhorting menopausal women to give up sex and men and retire to their gardens, because she believes that sexuality is a useless endeavor (Greer, 1992). These antiquated myths and this unsound advice do a disservice to the millions of sexually active menopausal couples.

✦ SEXUAL ADJUSTMENT: PSYCHOLOGICAL ISSUES

Entirely too much of what we have read and seen about menopause has focused exclusively on the female biological changes. This is problematic for two reasons. First, biology is *not* our destiny, especially with regard to sex. Second, sex occurs in the context of a relationship and therefore, partners bring issues to the sexual encounter as well. So if you are in a hurry to get to the biological changes, you can skip ahead a few pages. Otherwise, settle back and read on—we have some unlearning to do!

The brain is the most important of all the sexual organs, when we are younger, and as we age. Most sex therapists find that concern and worry about sex are usually more problematic than any physical or sexual changes themselves. It is almost impossible to enjoy sex if you are worried or anxious about it. Whatever the biological problem, when it comes to sex, your attitude will be the most important determinant of how well you cope.

Women who have enjoyed healthy sex earlier in their lives are exceptionally able to maintain their sexuality at midlife. (So, if you're reading this when you're perimenopausal and not enjoying sex, get going!) This is probably true because these women have seen sex as an integral, enjoyable part of life and have learned to value communication with their partners about sex. Couples who are affectionate physically tend to feel connected sexually as well. This connection leads to a well-established pattern of sexuality and can be easy to maintain, despite any biological changes associated with menopause. If sex has never been enjoyable for a woman, the additional stresses of menopause may be more difficult to overcome. One author has suggested that some menopausal women use "the change" as an excuse for avoiding sex that has never been fulfilling throughout the marriage (Hallstrom, 1977). In our experience, it is not that women in this situation purposefully lie to their husbands, but that menopausal symptoms may be "the last straw" in a marriage that has a marginal sexual adjustment. If you add vaginal dryness and the possibility of painful intercourse to a sexual relationship that has not been fulfilling, you can see how that relationship could deteriorate. Yet, even for these women, if menopause becomes the time when they finally address the sexual problems with their partners, they can learn to communicate directly and openly with their partners. Then the next phase of their sexual life can be vastly improved.

This brings us to the "use it or lose it" phenomenon. Good sex at menopause breeds more good sex (without breeding babies!). An intriguing study conducted by Drs. Gloria Bachmann and Susan Leiblum found that postmenopausal women who are more sexually active have fewer problems with lubricating and vaginal changes than other women. They reported higher levels of sexual desire, greater sexual satisfaction and more comfort expressing sexual preferences (Bachmann and Leiblum, 1991)—proof again that it is the interpersonal, not just the hormonal changes associated with menopause that determine adjustment. We emphasize the interpersonal aspects of your life because you can have a lot of control over the them. We don't want you to see menopause as a menacing hormonal event that happens *to you*. Rather, the entire menopausal transition is just another phase of life that you have the power and resources to deal with.

Sexuality is also part of a woman's more general physical sense of self. Women who are physically active feel better overall, and therefore can be more active sexually. The nature of physical activity doesn't need to be strenuous or intensive. You do not need to go to the gym on a daily basis to maintain a feeling of physical activity. But getting some movement into your life will preserve your health and maintain your activity level. Walking, swimming, dancing, gardening or any movement that you enjoy can be a regular pleasure in your life. We discuss this more in our chapters on stress and promoting a healthy lifestyle, because feeling physically fit can improve our sense of self-worth. Since all of us have internalized negative attitudes toward aging, it is important to feel good about ourselves physically. Any effort we take to improve our lifestyle in the area of physical activity relates directly to feeling better psychologically at midlife. It is also clear that in addition to releasing tension, exercise and physical activity can increase sexual energy.

Sexuality is only one part of the general area of sensuality. Sex does not just mean intercourse, but can involve a deep emotional attachment and a wide variety of sensual and enjoyable activities. For some couples, if the man has truly been faking foreplay, as Miriam jokes, then the woman may become resentful. One of the most common problems in long-term relationships is that the partners lapse into routinized, predictable, nonromantic sex. Each member of the couple can foresee exactly what will happen next. We have actually had some women tell us that they work on their grocery lists in their mind during these boring sexual encounters. In the case where a menopausal woman has been with her partner for many years, it may be difficult for the couple to find themselves sexually attracted to one another if there has been little intimacy or physical affection.

However, many couples use their time at midlife to rekindle their relationships. With the children out of the house (or at least out of diapers), or with the extra time gained from reduced work pressures, couples can turn to one another and start again. This involves a renewed commitment from each member of the couple, but many couples find that midlife can be an extremely happy period where sex is just one of many activities they share together. Other couples like Miriam and Tom have always worked together well and also see that sex can change over a lifetime. They can remain intimate and are not limited by some specific sexual routine. We have found that couples who are maintaining a physically active and intimate relationship are the same couples who continue to value their sexual intimacy and self-expression. These fortunate couples who value communication continue to share their feelings about sex, as well as other aspects of their lives.

◆ BEWARE OF STEREOTYPES

We need to look at some of the social stereotypes of sexuality and menopause. Do not believe them! The most destructive myth of "finished at fifty" is just a new spin on "finished at forty." Both medical materials and popular press articles have overplayed sexual problems at menopause. This exaggeration was not always the case. An analysis of articles appearing in the popular media found that prior to 1950, menopause was seen as both positive and negative. Often it was portrayed as a serene period in women's lives. But by 1960, the view that menopause meant a loss of sexuality and youth grew substantially. Interestingly, prior to 1960, HRT was recommended for severe symptoms only, but after that date it was being promoted as a cure for a wide variety of mild and cosmetic as well as severe symptoms (Bell, 1990). Of course, the 1960s were the height of Robert Wilson's *Feminine Forever* propaganda. This book claimed estrogen to be a treatment for every older woman's symptoms and neglected to mention the author's ties to pharmaceutical companies (Wilson, 1966). The promises of this book were seen in a different light once the increased risk of uterine cancer was later linked to unopposed estrogen.

An additional stereotype of the menopausal women was provided by the infiltration of orthodox psychoanalytic theory into the popular culture. Freud's original theories, after all, really did women a tremendous disservice. Much of Freudian or psychoanalytic theory focuses only on the reproductive aspects of a woman's life. Thus, menopause was seen as the end of the road for women. Helene Deutsch, one of Freud's students, was a notable psychoanalyst but did terrible damage to women's views of midlife. Her comments on sexual changes can be summed up in one word—"horrifying." Her words were, "Everything she acquired during puberty is now lost piece by piece." If one were to point out that most menopausal women were quite active and happy, Dr. Deutsch had this response, "She herself has the feeling of heightened vitality. . . . She becomes enthusiastic about abstract ideas, changes her attitude toward her family, leaves her home from the same motives as in her adolescence . . . narcissistic self-delusion makes her painted face appear youthful to her in the mirror" (Deutsch, 1945, p. 462). So Dr. Deutsch promulgated three myths. First, we lose all of our sexuality. Second, we lose our psychology of being female as well. Finally, to add insult to injury, any sign of vitality at midlife is seen only as a form of narcissism. Unfortunately, the views of Dr. Deutsch and other psychoanalysts have permeated society for a long time, despite the fact that they were never supported by any data. Combine them with the mass media emphasis on youth, and the prescribed form of female beauty, and it is no wonder that a woman over fifty is bound to be worried about her appeal.

American women see middle age as an unattractive physical stage of life for women. But not so for men. Although we can hope that times have changed, evidence proves much the contrary. The Disney company, for example, continues to elaborate their portrayal of sex-starved, unsightly and even monstrous female villains that helps to shape the way society views the sensual nature of middle-aged women. Powerful images of women at midlife struggling to repossess their youth are prominent throughout folklore—from the old Russian tale of the "Baba Yaga," where a middle-aged homely witch attempts to destroy and consume youthful innocence by breakfasting on the lovely heroine; to Ursula the Sea Witch in Disney's recent movie *The Little Mermaid*. Ursula, through trickery and sorcery, steals the sweet, cherished voice and youthful appearance of the heroine, Ariel, to seduce her handsome prince. Ursula takes her place following earlier Disney villainesses envious of youth and beauty including the Wicked Step-mother in *Cinderella,* the Evil Queen in *Snow White* and Maleficent in *Sleeping Beauty.* These films, already etched in the memories of today's menopausal women, are now made readily available on videocassette and are greatly contributing to how children view aging women. We should not be surprised when they grow up thinking that older women are witches, hags and just plain nasty.

We are making some progress in the war against the stereotypical aging female as women gain power in all areas—business, arts and entertainment, industry and even the medical profession. But these stereotypes do remain. It is only recently that we are beginning to have role models of women who are over the age of fifty and are still active in all areas of life. From women like Joanne Woodward to Rita Moreno to Tina Turner, things are changing. We are slowly but surely shedding old stereotypes and accepting women as competent, powerful and yes, even sexual role models.

Hasn't sexuality for women always been about relationships? As women, we know this, even though advertising has tried its best to convince us otherwise by emphasizing physical attractiveness alone. There is no reason to assume that the relationships themselves will deteriorate at menopause. In fact, sex and relationships often improve with age. Women who go to marital therapy, for example, usually complain about the lack of intimacy with their husbands. Many midlife men though, are reevaluating their lives and taking more time to develop relationships. Therefore, midlife becomes a developmental period when men and women often have time to improve their long-standing relationships. Many midlife women who are lesbian have a heightened sense of sharing because they go through the menopausal experience together. We have also found that lesbian women are not as burdened by the socially restrictive view of sexuality as young and physically attractive in a prescribed way. Many lesbians have been able to escape the stereotypes of midlife women by recognizing and battling them together. It is clear that sexuality, when seen in the context of a relationship, does not need to change in a negative way at the time of menopause.

Two of our recent cases make this clear. Both of them experienced sexual reawakenings in their late forties and early fifties. Maria is a forty-nine-year-old lesbian woman who works as a computer programmer. She came to see us originally for numerous complaints, including concerns about her adjustment to perimenopause. She was able to work with many issues in individual therapy. However, she also wanted to talk about her sexual adjustment. Maria had been in psychotherapy ten years previously for an extended period of time. At that time, she experienced the loss of her grandmother, "my role model for female strength," and her sister, who died of cancer in her twenties. She knew that she was lesbian from an early age, but never felt comfortable acting on this feeling. During her earlier psychotherapy, she worked on issues of how it felt to be a gay adolescent in a traditional family in conservative Boston. Maria is a strong and courageous woman who also has a deep commitment to psychotherapy as a process. In individual therapy and in group therapy she was able to work through many issues, including her sexuality and sexual orientation. Over the past ten years, Maria had been involved with several women but never felt that she was in an intimate relationship or one that felt right to her.

Maria describes herself as a "late bloomer," and so she knew that she needed more work in order to develop an intimate relationship. In her second phase of psychotherapy, she felt like she was coming together psychologically and sexually. Previously Maria was involved in relationships that were limited by their very nature: either women who were involved with someone else, or were unavailable psychologically. As she continued to work in psychotherapy, however, Maria realized that by allowing herself to become involved in an intimate relationship with another woman, she would take the final step toward accepting her sexuality and improving her life. Over time, Maria became involved with Liz, another woman who worked in the same company. They developed an intense and close relationship based on equality and commitment. Maria shared her previous feelings of loneliness and isolation while Liz talked about years in an unhappy marriage.

Together, they worked on similar concerns and were able to support and help one another. They have an active sexual life, and Maria felt that her sexuality had finally begun to flourish in midlife. She and Liz spend time traveling, enjoy hot tubs and women's folk music, and feel relaxed in their new-found sexual life together. Maria and Liz now share their home with one of Liz's daughters who is in college. Maria and Liz tend to their garden, work on joint political projects and are quite contented.

When Maria began to have hot flashes, she asked Liz about it, since Liz was fifty-three. Liz told her that her own hot flashes had not been severe, but that she had been troubled by a few months of night sweats. Maria is keeping track of her hot flashes with her hot-flash diary, and how much they interfere with her life, while considering the information about estrogen, osteoporosis and heart-disease prevention before making her decision.

Many lesbian women who come from extremely traditional backgrounds find that midlife can be a time of integration. Freed from the pressures of needing their parents' approval and often secure in their careers, they can become completely comfortable with their sexuality. For these women, midlife can be a time of deep sexual satisfaction. Positive sexuality for Maria and Liz came to them late in life. Other lesbian couples who have been together for many years may have problems similar to those of some heterosexual couples. Janet and Bob present a frequent pattern. Janet, one of our fifty-six-year-old patients, came to us with the most common sexual complaints of midlife heterosexual couples. As she described a typical day of established routine, we began to see how her sexual problems had become serious.

Janet awoke on a Friday morning at 7:30 a.m., just as she did every week-day morning. On weekends, she and her husband of twenty-five years, Bob, allowed themselves to sleep until 9:00, but no later, as their cocker spaniel, Bessy, demanded that their schedule be pushed no further. At 7:30, Janet was the first in the family to rise. She made her way to the kitchen, awakening her sixteen-year-old son along the way, and then pushed the button on the automatic coffeemaker (which she prepared religiously the night before). After fixing her family breakfast, she waved them off with the customary exchanges, "Have a good day." Janet was then left standing alone in her bathrobe to begin her typical Friday chores. Bathroom cleaning and laundry were at the top of the list. Later in the day, she found a spare moment for a walk to the park with her neighbor Julie, a chance to chat with her friend and walk Bessy at the same time. At 2:00 p.m., she did her usual Friday marketing for the weekend meals. At 3:30 p.m., she picked up her son from a friend's house across town and then wrote a letter to her daughter at college. By the time Bob arrived home, she had dinner on the table. After eating, Janet's son left almost immediately for a date.

Left alone, she and Bob did what they did almost every other night. Bob helped clear the dishes and then Janet washed them while they both watched *Wheel of Fortune*. After cleaning up, they sat together on the couch while Bob flipped through the channels to see what movie or television show they would choose for the evening. Janet found her mind wandering that night, watching her husband watch the television and wondering why it was she could not bring herself to reach out and touch him. When she thought of asking him to make love, she was discomforted by the question and forecasted the same predictable preparations for sex. She would go to the bedroom first. He would follow five minutes later when he knew that she had undressed and washed, and then they would both lie on the bed. He would kiss her gently, only a few times, and then he would touch her to see if she was lubricated. If all went well, Bob would reach climax in five minutes, tell her that he loved her, and then they would both return to witness the outcome of the sitcom that had been interrupted.

On that particular Friday night, Janet did not ask Bob to make love to her. She was frustrated by the fact that they were not able to spend a longer time loving each other and she felt there was little hope of ever changing their dull sex life. What Janet did not know as she sat on the couch with her husband was that Bob, too, was feeling a need for greater companionship and heightened sexual experience. Because of their well-established lack of communication, they had no idea that what they shared most was a deeply felt need for one another.

Although this pattern had existed for most of their marriage, as Janet reached her postmenopausal years she began to blame herself. She felt that because she was lubricating less and had been experiencing some pain during intercourse, that it was her fault that she had no desire for her husband. This self-blame is what lead her to visit our practice, and prompted her decision to change a marriage lacking in communication and sensuality. We referred Janet and Bob for sex therapy. Although Bob was nervous, he was anxious to cooperate. During sex therapy, they uncovered that Janet and Bob had enjoyed intercourse when they were first married. But, neither of them had talked much about individual sexual needs. Janet had always deferred to Bob sexually, but she was unclear which parts of the sexual experience he enjoyed most. This lack of communication had not allowed their sexual experiences any room for growth or exploration.

During therapy, it was also discovered that they had avoided experimentation with foreplay and had a relationship that otherwise did not include a lot of affection or sensuality. Even though Janet and Bob had been uneasy about accepting the referral to sex therapy, they were quickly amazed at how they were able to learn new communication patterns and sexual skills. After a relatively short period of sex therapy, Janet and Bob were able to articulate their needs and listen well. They discovered a whole new experience involving the nonintercourse parts of the sexual encounter. In addition, Janet and Bob felt comfortable using a lubricant like Astroglide when necessary. In their fifties, they are finally enjoying sex as equal partners. Now a typical Friday night is far from typical. They make a point of getting out of the house, seeing a movie, or sampling different restaurants. Even if it is only for a long walk (holding hands!), they have shared something by relaxing with each other. These days, when Janet and Bob awaken on a Saturday morning, it is their son who takes Bessy for her morning stroll through the park. There's no need for them to rush.

The stories of Maria and Janet illustrate only two of the many women we have seen who indeed experienced some biological changes at the time of menopause. But like all women, their lives were affected by psychological and sociological factors as well. Sexuality is a complex and delicate issue, and improving your sexuality at midlife can involve numerous biological, psychological and social changes.

✦ THE BIOLOGY OF SEX AT MENOPAUSE

Fear not! This is not meant to be affirmation of all of your worst fears about menopause. If we are completely honest, our greatest dread is that at the time of menopause our sexual organs will, at best, dry up and, at worst, fall out. Thankfully, this is far from the truth. There are several biological changes that are associated with menopause. However, most of them do not occur until five years after the final menstrual period. In addition, we know that women's lives are extremely variable, so that not every woman will have difficulty with these changes. Some of the changes that do occur in menopause are difficult to separate completely from changes that would occur with aging alone.

Whatever the cause, the specific biologic changes that are experienced can be divided into two large categories: those that relate to anatomy and those that relate to physiology. In other words, there are changes that occur in the actual sexual organs as well as changes in the sexual response. First, let's look at the normal step choreography of the sexual response.

In order to understand menopausal sex fully, let's review the basics. The fulfilling sexual encounter is preceded by sexual interest. The physiological stages of sexual response were popularized by Virginia Masters and William Johnson. These stages are excitement, plateau, orgasm and resolution (Masters and others, 1970). During the excitement stage of sexual interaction, the vagina is lubricated by secretions that are released from the vaginal walls and there is an increase of muscle tension. During the plateau phase, there is some local constriction in the outer one-third of the vagina and the clitoris becomes elevated somewhat. The orgasm stage is the peak of sexual response, the most enjoyable moment. Physiologically, the outer one-half of the vagina, as well as the uterus, contract in a rhythmic way. During the resolution phase, there is a decrease in vasocongestion and the muscle tension disappears. If orgasm has occurred, then the resolution stage for women is quite quick, but if it has not, then the resolution stage takes a longer amount of time.

It is true that with aging, sexual arousal takes longer for both men and women. One view of this is that women are slower to arouse with age. Another view, however, is that women do not get enough stimulation to become aroused. The net result is that it takes longer for women to become lubricated during foreplay. The explanations for these changes are numerous, including decreased blood flow to the vagina, which makes it less sensitive to stimulation; a change in the neurologic connections, which causes relative numbness; and decreased vaginal lubrication related to estrogen levels.

There is some evidence that there may be a change in the experience of orgasm and a decrease in the frequency of orgasm after menopause. But in fact, the frequency of orgasm has been studied less than the frequency of sexual intercourse. Even Miriam admits to some changes in her orgasms. But as she has said to us, "They may have changed a little, but I'm certainly not going to give them away!"

This change in orgasmic intensity and frequency may be related to the accompanying changes with aging, including the slower ascent to the excitement phase as well as the anatomical changes that are presented in more detail below. Additionally, the uterine contractions which occur with orgasm may be less intense for postmenopausal women. For those women who have experienced hysterectomy, many report a change in the sensation of orgasm related to the complete absence of these uterine contractions.

The anatomical changes that occur with menopause are integrally related to the physiologic changes in sexual response. It is clear that the female sexual organs depend, in part, on estrogen to maintain their anatomy and function. This is not to say that the decrease in estrogen levels at the time of menopause leads to irreparable, inevitable or disastrous changes. Above all, we should take heart in the fact that the only predictable change at menopause is the end of menstrual periods and with it the end of fertility. For many women, this freedom from concerns about pregnancy and female sanitary products is a welcomed change.

The most frequent symptom of sexual changes at menopause is vaginal dryness. Yet, only 25 percent of women actually experience vaginal dryness five years after the last menstrual period. This percentage increases as women get older. But, far fewer women complain of vaginal dryness than hot flashes. Women who become menopausal because of surgery will experience symptoms of vaginal dryness much earlier than women who have natural menopause, whose symptoms may be delayed ten to fifteen years (Nachtigall and Heilman, 1991). Unlike hot flashes, vaginal symptoms may worsen, and not improve with time. Do not despair, however, because there are many good treatments for these symptoms.

The specific changes that occur in the vagina include thinning of the tissue lining called the vaginal epithelium. In premenopausal women, there may be forty to fifty layers of these epithelial cells, but in postmenopausal women, these may be reduced to four or five layers (Sachs, 1991). The end result of this loss of protective coating is that the vagina may become irritated or inflamed more readily. This may be experienced as bleeding or pain at the time of intercourse and burning which can be severe with urination. The medical term used to classify these changes is "atrophic vaginitis." This implies that the vagina is inflamed (itis) and that the lining has thinned (atrophic). The changes that are seen with the lining are attributed to a decrease in estrogen levels. Although estrogen replacement is an effective cure for this condition, it is not the only treatment available. We have also learned from the many women who do not experience these vaginal symptoms that there may be ways to prevent their occurrence.

The vagina also becomes shorter and narrower at the time of menopause. The vagina's elasticity is also reduced as is the fatty tissue in the labia surrounding the vagina. These changes may or may not be bothersome to any individual woman. The specific anatomical changes that occur in the vagina can lead to discomfort with intercourse, known as dyspareunia. This, in particular, is compounded by vaginal dryness. Some women who anticipate painful penetration at the time of intercourse may actually have involuntary spasms at the vaginal opening known as vaginismus.

We often joke among ourselves that the list of gynecological complaints are somewhat "phallocentric." That is to say that many of the anatomical complaints are problematic particularly for male/female intercourse. It is important for a woman to first identify what problems are physically uncomfortable for her alone. After establishing that, she can then understand better what other issues may be particularly difficult with respect to sexual intercourse. Sexual problems among menopausal lesbian women have been detailed less often than those of heterosexual women. However, this may be because lesbian women have been studied even less than heterosexual women at midlife.

✦ URINARY SYMPTOMS

More women than ever before are becoming aware of the possibility of urinary incontinence now that protective shields are routinely advertised on television and radio. The message in these advertisements is that the problem is nearly unique to older women. While it is true that more older women than older men experience incontinence, it is by no means a problem unique to older women. Basically incontinence is the involuntary loss of urine. In general, incontinence is classified into two types. The first is stress incontinence which is the loss of urine, which occurs with anything that can increase abdominal pressure on the bladder including laughing, coughing or bearing down to lift something. This type of incontinence does tend to get worse with age unless preventive measures are taken. The cause of stress incontinence is the weakening and relaxation of the muscles and the ligaments which hold the pelvic organs in place. Like any muscle or ligament, these can weaken with time unless strengthened with exercise. It is also true that estrogen maintains their elasticity and strength. Women who are most prone to this type of incontinence are those who have had multiple pregnancies which can stretch and weaken some of the connecting structures of the pelvic organs.

The second type of incontinence is urge incontinence. This is experienced as an inability to hold the urine when the urge to urinate is felt. Women who have experienced this type of incontinence need to urinate as soon as the urge is felt. Urge incontinence seems to be related to a weakening of the muscle which holds the urine in the bladder or increased tone of the detrusser muscle.

Both the prevention and treatment of incontinence involves specific exercises for the weakened muscles. Like any muscles which may lose strength because of disuse, or in this case because of hormonal changes, this repeated exercise can increase their size and strength. While many of the ligaments and muscles of the urinary tract are not easily exercised, there are specific muscles which can be exercised to control the flow of urine. A simple way to identify the muscles involved in stopping the flow of urine is to voluntarily stop urinating midstream. Once the action that tenses these muscles is identified in this way, the exercise can be repeated at other times. These exercises, called Kegel's, in honor of the surgeon who invented them, are described further in a later section (Kegel, 1951).

The tissue in the bladder and urethra also become thinner during the postmenopausal period. Therefore, they can become irritated more often and open to infections. Symptoms of urinary tract infections (UTIs) are burning with urination, frequent urinating of small amounts and urgency. In the postmenopausal period, it can be difficult to distinguish burning due to infection because of bacteria, from that caused by vaginal atrophy and irritation.

These postmenopausal UTIs can be treated by antibiotics, as we detail in a bit. They can be prevented in a number of ways, including frequent urination to avoid holding urine in the bladder for long periods, drinking plenty of fluids, wiping from front to back, and urinating before and after intercourse.

✦ CHANGES IN THE MALE AT MIDLIFE

We see sexuality as part of the intricate relationships between couples. Janet and Bob's ability to improve their sex life would not have been possible if both of them had not been ready to change. Problems in sexuality at midlife are usually related to both male and female changes. It is important to remember that most menopausal women are married to men who are several years older. One of the changes is that older men take longer to arouse and therefore have erections more slowly. At the same time, their levels of testosterone are lower as well and the daily changes with a peak of testosterone in the morning are less dramatic. This change in testosterone levels may alter the length and desire of a man's sexual experience.

Some authors believe that the changes in sexual experience at midlife have more to do with the fact that men, not women, are less interested in sex. This is based on studies that show that most sexual encounters in male/female couples are determined by male initiation.

Thus if the male loses interest in sex and initiates less often, the couple will have fewer sexual experiences (Blumstein and Schwartz, 1985). So maybe women are reflecting changes in male biology rather than the other way around.

Certain medical conditions in older men also affect sexual behavior. Men who are diabetic often have problems with sexual arousal, as do men who are on medication for hypertension or heart disease. In addition, sexual dysfunction can occur in men who have had prostate surgery. In summary, any assessment of sexual changes in midlife for heterosexual women should look at the male/female biological, as well as psychological and social issues.

◆ HOW TO DEAL WITH ALL THIS

KEEP AT IT

In our menopause town meetings, most women want to know, "What can I do about sexual changes?" Our best advice is that practice may not make perfect, but it is important for women who want to maintain their sexuality. Masters and Johnson recommended sex one to two times a week for a continued active sex life. So, if you are in a sexual relationship and it is enjoyable, just keep doing what you have been doing. Use the muscles involved in sexual activity, enjoy intercourse, experience orgasms. All this helps—biologically, psychologically, and interpersonally! If you and your partner have some sexual concerns, try to talk about them, experiment, and share.

MASTURBATION

Some menopausal women report that partner availability is a major problem. This is often true for women and is a source of sadness for many. But with respect to sexuality, it is important to remember that intercourse is not the only answer. Masturbation can be helpful and can keep you in shape sexually whether or not you have a partner. If you are like our patient Corinne, you might involuntarily flinch or even say "Shh!," upon hearing or reading the word "masturbation." Corinne is a forty-nine-year-old bookkeeper who finds herself in the single world again after twenty-five years of marriage. After working through her feelings about her divorce, she now thinks ahead to the idea of dating. Part of her sexual reawakening was that she wanted to reclaim her sexuality. Given her family history, having been brought up in an Irish, Roman Catholic family, similar to those spoofed in the play *Sister Mary Ignatius Explains It All*, it took us many weeks to even talk to Corinne about masturbation as part of actual conditioning. She had difficulty with the concept because at the age of forty-nine, she had never spoken the word, nor had any of her family members. Corinne is like many women who have been socialized to believe that masturbation is dirty, or even sinful. The truth is that there is nothing wrong with masturbation, and it is helpful in maintaining sexual functioning. Women lubricate during masturbation and use many of the same muscles as they do in other sexual encounters. Masturbation can also reduce tension.

KEGEL EXERCISES

Kegel's exercise can not only improve sexual functioning, but also decrease urinary incontinence. Developed by a surgeon, Dr. Arnold Kegel, in the 1950s, these exercises increase muscle tone in the vaginal area (Kegel, 1951). They involve tensing and relaxing the pubococcygeal muscles around the area of the urethra, vagina and anus. In order to identify these muscles, you can do one of two things. One is to begin to urinate and then stop. The same muscle you use to control urination is the muscle that you will contract then relax during the Kegel exercises. You can also locate and use this muscle by inserting a tampon and squeezing around it. You should hold this muscle for at least five to ten seconds and then release it slowly. After mastering the slow Kegel exercise, you should also do a series of rapid ones. They should be repeated ten to fifteen times, and the whole session should be repeated three to five times per day. Maureen, one of our patients, was delighted to learn these very specific instructions. Previously, she had only heard the part about stopping the flow of urine. She thought that that was the only way to do Kegel's exercise and soon found it to be too difficult and quit. Actually, you can do them anytime you feel like it, anywhere.

There are numerous advantages to the Kegel exercises. First, by developing the muscles around the vaginal area, the woman can have more control and pleasure during the sexual encounter. Second, Kegel exercises can tone up muscles and stop incontinence. Finally, they can build up the muscles in order to counteract any muscle loosening that occurs as a result of menopause. Kegel exercises can be done at any time of the day since they are invisible to the observer. We have read frequently that women can integrate Kegel exercise into any part of their daily routine—like when you are on the elevator, or driving. We have chuckled when we imagine all the women stopped in their cars at various stoplights doing their ten Kegel exercises, and wondered how many minor traffic accidents have resulted! In all seriousness, repetition is important and many women have found that these exercises have had a positive impact on their sex life.

HRT

Many women seriously consider starting HRT because of vaginal dryness. The specifics of HRT are covered in detail in Chapter Six. Estrogen can reverse atrophic vaginitis and this improvement removes a major barrier to satisfying sex. Progesterone, while medically necessary for women with uteri, seems to have no effect on sexual functioning. On the other hand, androgens, the male hormones, seem to affect lipids and sexual responsiveness. There is some evidence that this is particularly true for women who have had surgical menopause (Walling and others, 1990). The use of androgens or testosterone is becoming more common in the U.S. and has been used more extensively in England. Testosterone is sometimes prescribed to treat loss of libido. This positive effect needs to be considered with the potential negative side effects, including facial hair growth, mood changes and acne. Because of this, the dosage needs to be monitored very carefully. Germaine Greer, in her usually provocative fashion, describes feeling overwhelmed by impulses of aggression after taking testosterone, but it is clear that this use of androgens is an area to watch for the future (Greer, 1991).

Because estrogen also reverses the thinning of the area around the bladder, it has been suggested that taking estrogen will reduce the incidence of urinary tract infections. However one recent study suggested that women who take estrogen had a higher rate of urinary tract infections. It is clear that estrogen does reduce painful intercourse, or dyspareunia, because of better lubrication and less irritation.

Many women wish to reverse vaginal dryness but would prefer not to take oral estrogen or use the patch. Vaginal estrogen creams are available and are effective in treating atrophic vaginitis. Even though it is applied locally, the estrogen is still absorbed into the system and carries the same risks as estrogen taken in pill form. The amount absorbed will be relatively low, however, if the cream is used infrequently (two or three times per week) or for short periods of time. There is evidence that at low doses, as little as one-eighth of that usually recommended for vaginal dryness, the estrogen cream can be effective. For women using estrogen cream who have not had a hysterectomy, progesterone may still be necessary to cause menstrual bleeding and prevent uterine cancer.

There are also a number of nonmedicated lubricants including KY jelly, Replense and Astroglide. Some actually work to "plump up" the cells lining the vagina and can work for up to three days, eliminating the need to apply these right before intercourse. Do not use petroleum jelly because it can build up in the vagina and may disguise early symptoms of infection; it has also been reported as a cause of condom breakage. Some women have used vitamin E as a cream or a suppository vaginally.

Many women find the messiness of the cream relatively unacceptable. It is not meant to be used prior to intercourse since it is likely that your partner will absorb the cream as well. The side effects of estrogen are even more unwelcome for men! If added lubricant is needed, then any of the nonmedicated lubricants can be used. For women who cannot use estrogen, there are vaginal creams with 1 to 2 percent testosterone that are also effective in treating atrophic vaginitis (Greenwood, 1984).

Vaginal infections may also develop in the post menopausal period. The symptoms of vaginal infection are easily confused with one of those of atrophic vaginitis, which is characterized by irritation, itching, and discharge. It is important that these symptoms be evaluated so that appropriate treatment can be started. Many vaginal infections—yeast infections are the most common type—can be treated topically with antifungal creams. Some require antibiotics taken orally. Infections can be discouraged by altering the vaginal PH with vinegar and water douches, aci-gel or Astroglide. Advice to wear cotton underwear and avoid tight-fitting pants is not a plot to keep you from being sexy but is a way of discouraging yeast overgrowth in the vagina.

CONTRACEPTION

It is true that even in the perimenopausal and early postmenopausal period, the occasional egg can be produced by the ovaries, making birth control a necessary evil for those at potential risk of an unwanted pregnancy. Women should continue to use contraception for a full year after the last menstrual period. The form of contraception really depends on personal preference and medical considerations. Many women and doctors avoid birth control pills in older women (everyone's definition of older is different). It is clearly true that the risks are higher for women who smoke. Barrier methods (diaphragm and condoms) can be very effective when used with spermicidal creams, jellies or foams. IUDs may be more of an option for women who are not worried about future fertility, although they are relatively less favored than other methods. Finally, sterilization is a frequently chosen method for women (tubal ligation) or their partners (vasectomy). For all intents and purposes, these must be considered permanent and irreversible.

SEXUALLY TRANSMITTED DISEASES

We had a lot of fun with our patient Corinne when she went on her first date as a divorced "older" woman. Like many women, when we broached the issue of sexual behavior, her first words were, "I absolutely, positively cannot do this. I was not good at it when I was seventeen and I'm not good at it now!" But after a few sessions of rehearsal, we helped Corinne understand that as a mature woman, she could approach her dating world with much more judgment and maturity and with less to risk. But the world of sexually transmitted diseases and HIV has made the sexual arena a dangerous place. And so we needed to deal with the issues of STDs with Corrine.

The most common diseases of concern include HIV, herpes and genital warts. All of these are caused by viruses and are relatively incurable infections. HIV infection is obviously the worst of the three. A basic rule is that condoms are dress code for all heterosexual encounters. Spermicidal creams, jellies or foams may be partially effective in preventing transmission of HIV and other viruses. Diaphragms may provide yet another barrier to infection. It is here that communication with your partner is critical. Do not allow yourself to be convinced that protection is unnecessary for any reason. Once you have established a long-term monogamous relationship with an individual, this may be an option but not before.

ABSTINENCE

We have met women in our practice who have chosen to give up sexual relationships. This is, of course, a personal choice, and when both parties of a relationship are comfortable with it, it seems to have no ill effects. However, problems can arise for women who have chosen not to engage in sexual activity for many years and who then begin again. The women who have not had hormone replacement therapy or have taken no other preventive actions may meet with some difficulty.

✦ DEALING WITH LOSS OF SEXUAL INTEREST

Sexual interest is a complex topic. Many of the women who complain of this loss also complain of unpleasant symptoms like vaginal dryness and dyspareunia. It seems clear that when sex becomes uncomfortable or even painful, a woman would lose interest. So the first step is often to deal with these anatomic or physiological changes. Some women choose to use hormone replacement therapy, or nonmedicated creams to treat the anatomic changes first. Estrogen does significantly improve these gynecological changes, but as we mentioned earlier, progesterone shows no benefit in this area. The most recent area of development is that of using the male hormones, androgens, to increase sexual interest. But many women find some of the side effects of the androgens to be unpleasant.

A second area of concern is communicating with your partner. Loss of sexual interest may well be interpersonal as well as physiological. So after the anatomic symptoms have been treated, if sexual interest continues to be a problem, you need to discuss this with your partner. Sometimes it is the result of relationship issues that are stressful. Other times a loss of sexual interest can be a result of what some call "habituation," that is, the result of a long-term sexual relationship that can sometimes lead to less variability and ultimately a decrease in sexual interest. Many women and their partners find that when this issue is directly addressed, partners can share their concerns and develop new sexual patterns that are more enjoyable for both of them.

Finally, it is important to note that loss of sexual interest can be a symptom of several psychological problems. Loss of sexual interest is also a symptom of depression. A history of sexual abuse may also be an issue. Other symptoms are detailed in our chapters on stress and depression. If you find that you have some of these symptoms, it is important to get psychological help. Psychological problems can be treated effectively and the sooner you get help the better.

✦ FOCUS ON SENSUALITY

As we discussed earlier, sexual behavior is just part of a sensual relationship. If a relationship has become boring, then of course it is difficult to rekindle sexual interest. Given the fact that many people have more time to share with their partner at menopause, a new sensuality can flourish. Many couples at this point in life take the time to help one another relax by using massage, or taking a bath together. Physical activities like running, golf or playing tennis can bring a couple closer together. Exercise, then, can serve two purposes, keeping a couple physically fit while enhancing their sensuality. Being affectionate, touching, and sharing emotions and experiences are often characteristics which most women associate with a positive sex life.

During the pre-children era, many couples had infinite time to explore their sensuality. When children come along many couples make a point to set aside one night a week to be alone, but even that one night is often sacrificed if another family responsibility arises. All too often this becomes a pattern, where the couple's romance and sensuality is put on hold. If the couple is fortunate enough to reach midlife intact, they can reclaim their romance and sensuality together. Janet and Bob were still watching *Wheel of Fortune,* even though their children were out of the house and they had the opportunity to do just about anything they wanted together.

✦ COMMUNICATION

COMMUNICATING ABOUT SEXUALITY WITH YOUR PARTNER

Many women find this to be extremely difficult. Despite the sexual revolution of the sixties and seventies, sex remains a taboo topic of conversation for many couples, even when they are sexually active. If a couple can be specific and nonjudgmental with one another, they can make sexual changes. For many women the first step is to express their unhappiness to their partner. Many women feel protective of the husband's sexual ego. Janet was afraid of hurting Bob's feelings and making him feel like a bad lover. She actually believed that Bob could become impotent if she were critical of him in any way. Yet this is the very first step in repairing a sexual relationship. Janet and Bob decided to seek sex therapy, but that is often unnecessary if you can learn to communicate as a couple.

Here are some basic communication strategies for approaching this subject with your partner. First, think through what you would like to say. Be specific and practical. Most women do not have difficulty identifying the problem to themselves. You need to directly approach your partner and say that you would like to discuss your sex life. This may not be easy. Other women have had, like Corinne, negative responses to the words penis, vagina, orgasm, masturbation, intercourse, clitoris, and so on. We all need to overcome this early conditioning that makes sex a taboo topic.

Second, identify the problem as a joint venture. This way your partner should not feel criticized and you can create an attitude of sharing and cooperation. For example, Janet could have said, "We enjoyed sex so much in our twenties, I want us to try and make it better now." This would be more effective than by saying "You don't kiss me enough during sex" at the beginning of the conversation. Although your partner may express some initial resistance, you should not give up. You need to ask about your partner's feelings, and most women are experts at doing this.

Third, try to be specific and nonjudgmental. By using sentences that begin "I feel . . ." rather than "You should . . . ," your partner will have the most positive response. For some couples, the husband is less eager and perhaps less able to express his feelings about this subject. For that reason, it is important not to give up easily.

In addition to communication problems, sexual anxiety can make things worse at first. Once you become aware of a sexual problem, anxiety can increase during a sexual encounter. This then leads to a negative experience and therefore the cycle continues. Masters and Johnson refer to this as being a spectator during sex (Masters and others, 1970). A Victoria's Secret negligee may look appealing on the rack but seem ridiculous when you put it on for a sexual encounter. By observing yourself, while at the same time engaging in sex, the pressure to perform is difficult and counterproductive. This is all the more reason to approach your partner and try to deal with sex with a spirit of adventure and a sense of humor.

Some women find romantic and erotic movies to be helpful in getting aroused, or to break out of old routines. Please know that we do not mean common pornography, which is dehumanizing and objectifying to women. If books and videos do not work in helping you to get aroused, you might try inviting Jeff Bridges, Denzel Washington, or k.d. lang over to your house for the afternoon. Seriously, it is important to note whether you cannot get aroused with your partner specifically or by fantasy or if you can feel aroused at all. You also need to be sure that any medical symptoms, like painful intercourse, are being treated properly. If they have been treated successfully and the sexual problems remain, then it is probably time to get help. If the problem is primarily sexual, then sex therapy is in order.

COMMUNICATING WITH YOUR CLINICIAN

Just as sex is a taboo topic in society, and just as sex might be difficult to talk about with your partner, it is often awkward to address with your physician. Yet most clinicians are very comfortable talking about the specific gynecological changes at menopause. After identifying the

problem specifically, you can talk it over with your primary care professional. This is one of those times when you will need to talk to your
doctor in some depth, rather than asking a few questions after you have
had your Pap smear. It is important to set your priorities about what
issues you want to discuss, and to do this ahead of time. You might
choose to jot them down on a notepad that you can look at before
talking to the physician. If your doctor recommends hormone replacement therapy, you should make that decision after reading some of the
next few chapters.

Your gynecologist or internist will be able to help you identify the
physical problems that are contributing to your problems in sexuality.
If your primary problem is lack of sexual interest, or if you feel that it is
a relationship problem, then you may also ask your physician for a
referral to a psychologist or other mental health professional.

We found that Corinne, who entered the dating world after many
years, soon overcame her insecurities. The same woman who had come
to our office whispering the word "masturbation," and doubting
whether she could go through with a "first date," became a confident,
happy, sexually active woman. Corinne developed an openness and
willingness to communicate with her doctors and her newfound partner. Corinne had met David, a caring, forty-five-year-old lawyer (and
"a younger man!") who interested her in new hobbies like tennis and
photography while at the same time accompanying her to her favorite
place, the theater. Ultimately, Corinne became more alive sexually at
midlife than she would have ever dared to think of before. When Corinne visits us now, she is full of stories about previously uncharted
territories and a newfound self-confidence. Descriptions and concerns
regarding her sex life are no longer inaudible, we hear her loud and
clear.

Talking about sex is often especially difficult for a woman if her
clinician is a man. It may make you feel ashamed or vulnerable. This is
a natural response to what is a taboo and emotional topic. Try to remember that listening to you talk about sexual issues is a part of your
doctor's job and chances are, he has heard it all before. Even if your
doctor is a woman, you may be reluctant to discuss sexual problems
because you may feel like you are betraying your partner. Your partner
will feel better, too, if you both get help. And your clinician is in the
best position to get you that help.

Although most clinicians are comfortable in talking about sex,
you may be unlucky and have a negative experience. One possibility is
that you feel brushed off, that your doctor minimizes your concern. If
so, you should restate your concerns clearly. Another possibility is that
your doctor strongly recommends HRT, and if you decide against it,

he or she may become impatient with your complaints. In that case you should specifically ask, "Are there any other remedies for vaginal dryness?" Or, you may choose to ask about something else that we have recommended in this book.

A less common but more troubling problem is if your doctor seems unusually interested in your sex life. If a doctor, or any other health care professional is making you feel uncomfortable, you should speak up immediately. In some instances, doctors have made sexual advances to patients, or touched their patients inappropriately. If this happens to you, you should terminate your relationship immediately and report the incident to your state Health Department Board of Medical Review. Do not worry about your clinician's feelings and do not blame yourself. It is not your fault, and if the individual acted inappropriately with you, you are probably not the first to experience this clearly unethical behavior.

✦ WHEN TO GET HELP: SEX THERAPY

No matter how many changes you make, it is sometimes necessary to get outside help with a sexual problem. This is as true for menopausal women as it is for women at earlier points and later points in the life cycle.

Sex therapy is a specific and structured approach to treatment and requires specialized education. Most sex therapists are licensed psychologists, social workers or psychiatrists. Beware of self-promoting "sexperts" and be sure the person has the appropriate licensing and credentials.

If the therapist focuses solely on you and the woman's role in appearance and improving her appeal, then you are in the wrong place. Sex therapy, by definition, defines sex as a couple's issue. Sex therapists are usually comfortable working with lesbians as well as heterosexual couples, but you should ask your friends about their reputation in this area. If communication in general is more of a problem, or if you are having too many arguments about other topics, then marital therapy is indicated. Marital therapy is a more general type of therapy that we discuss in our section on depression. Many couples who have sexual problems feel the need to work on the more general marital issues first. So in discussing this resource with your partner, you might try to identify which problem is interfering more in the marriage. Do the sexual problems lead to communication problems, or do they reflect the existing marital problems? If you are unable to make these decisions, you may go see a psychological consultant who can help you sort this out.

We hope you will not do what many couples do; that is, they hope the problems will disappear if they ignore them. Not talking about a problem only makes it worse, it doesn't make it go away. This is particularly true in the area of sexuality, since postmenopausal women who have problems with vaginal dryness and muscle changes tend to get worse over time if they do not get help. Remember, through the eyes of Miriam, "At twenty-five, sex was new and exciting, but let's face it, I didn't have a clue. Now, thirty-three years later, I'm *hot*—pun intended!"

RESOURCES

BOOKS

The field of sex therapy virtually exploded in the late 1960s and 1970s. Consequently, there are many good books that can help you.

For Each Other: Sharing Sexual Intimacy, by Lonnie Barbach, Ph.D. (New York: Signet Penguin Books, 1984), is an excellent and detailed book. Dr. Barbach has also made a videotape titled "Sex After 50: A Guide to Lifelong Sexual Pleasure," available from The Institute for Health and Aging (1-800-866-1000).

Women on Top, by Nancy Friday. This sequel to *My Secret Garden* details women's sexual fantasies (New York: Pocket Books, a Division of Simon & Schuster, 1991).

Intimate Partners: Patterns in Love and Marriage, by Maggie Scarf (New York: Random House, 1987).

The Time of Our Lives: Women Write on Sex After Forty, by Dena Taylor and Amber Coverdale Sumrall. This is an edited book of a variety of women's writings on their sexual experiences after the age of forty (Freedom, CA: Crossing Press, 1993).

ASSOCIATIONS

American Association of Sex Educators, Counselors and Therapists
435 N. Michigan Ave, Suite 1717
Chicago, IL 60611
(312) 644–0828

The American Association of Sex Educators, Counselors and Therapists (AASECT) can help you find a reputable sex therapist: it is a referral service. It also publishes a National Register of Certified Sex Educators and Sex Therapists.

Eve's Garden
119 W. 57th St, #420
NY, NY 10019
(212) 757-8651

A women's erotic mail-order catalog available for $1.

CHAPTER FOUR

Maintaining Our Health: Strong Bones

WE KNOW FROM OUR MENOPAUSE TOWN MEETINGS THAT YOU ARE RE-ally worried about osteoporosis and the possibility of fractures, as well as the dowager's hump. Too many advertisements for estrogen have pictures of that hump! Don't worry, we are not going to include one. You know what it looks like and you don't need more anxiety. High anxiety does not help people change. What you do need is a clear head to process all the new information about preventing osteoporosis. Besides, women entering the menopausal years today have a great opportunity to plan to maintain healthy bones. We can now make changes in our lifestyle that will lead to healthier and happier menopausal years and beyond. Until recently, osteoporosis was another excellent example of a health problem which, having a particular significance for women, had escaped the notice of medical researchers. We now know that this process of bone weakening causes substantial health problems, and can even lead to death for older women. But with appropriate guidance, women now have access to new treatments and preventions that will help avoid many of the heartaches and difficulties suffered by previous generations.

A woman in her menopausal years is likely to carry the responsibility for the care and well-being of elderly members of her family. Quite often, our patients have come to us concerned about the condition of their mothers, having watched them develop back pain or suffer hip fractures. These women begin to see their own future in the suffering of their parents. There can be no greater influence than viewing our parents suffer to make us question our own vulnerabilities. So many of our patients have come to us eager to learn what they can do to prevent it from happening to them. Elaine, a forty-nine-year-old interior decorator is one of those women.

Elaine first came to us because she was experiencing insomnia, headaches and what she thought were hot flashes. After a full evaluation, we learned that she was entering the menopause phase. She was also experiencing tension headaches and was under considerable stress. Elaine is an excellent example of the new generation of women. She came to us not only to address her present problems, but to plan the next phase of her life so that she could maintain her health. Elaine is a competent and self-educated woman in the area of health, the type of woman who listens eagerly to the Thursday morning news on the radio in order to find out what the *New England Journal* had published that week.

As a single parent of two adolescent girls, Elaine was more than busy as she worked full-time in her successful design practice. Elaine's "take charge" attitude had helped her raise her two daughters, since their father had moved to the West Coast and saw them only sporadically. Her divorce had left Elaine somewhat bitter, but over time, those negative feelings had mellowed to a humorous skepticism. Elaine was able to detect phoniness and sentimentality, and able to cut through to the heart of the matter quickly.

Her previously active, seventy-three-year-old mother, Kristina, was always close to Elaine and her family, providing advice and support. She lived nearby in an apartment building and, until recently, had an active and independent life filled with other friends and travel. But recently, Kristina had fallen on the ice and broken her hip. After one complication after another, Kristina had never been able to return to independent living and she had moved into Elaine's house. Although the family was coping, it was not what anyone wanted and was therefore somewhat stressful.

Having witnessed Kristina's condition and inability to care for herself, Elaine was now incredibly motivated. She was particularly dedicated to preventing the development of osteoporosis in herself and had read everything she could find on the subject. We enjoyed meeting with Elaine, but always knew that the sessions with her would be lengthy and detailed. If we had missed anything in the popular press, Elaine could fill us in. She was also worried because she had been told by a previous physician that she had osteoarthritis. She wanted to know if this was related to osteoporosis.

✦ WHAT IS OSTEOPOROSIS?

Osteoporosis is a chronic decrease in bone mass to the point that specific parts of the skeleton are so fragile that they are at great risk of fracturing. Osteoporosis is a significant problem for certain women, primarily white and Asian. For African-American and possibly Hispanic women, the good news is that they develop osteoporosis less frequently. African-American women, in general, attain greater spinal-bone mass than white women and have a lower fracture rate. The major cause of osteoporosis is the decline of estrogen, produced by the ovaries, after menopause. By the time a woman has reached eighty, she may have lost up to 40 percent of her bone substance (Cutler and Garcia, 1992). After menopause, she can lose 1 percent to 3 percent of bone mass per year (Cutler and Garcia, 1992a). The greatest decline in bone mass occurs between the ages of forty-five and seventy (Cutler and Garcia, 1992a). Not surprisingly, as the bone becomes thinner, more and more fractures can occur and many woman are unaware of small fractures that occur in the spine.

Osteoporosis literally means, porous bone. *Osteo-* for bone, and *porosis-* for porous. It is one of the most disabling and common bone disorders. The process of osteoporosis is somewhat complex. The decade of research on osteoporosis shows that osteoporosis is not simply a disease caused by a calcium imbalance. Many other factors are involved, including: genetics, exercise, body frame, and lifestyle, including nutritional issues and other related medical problems. There are two types of bone—cortical and trabecular. Cortical bone is the hard compact *outer* layer of bones (see Figure 4-1). About 80 percent of our skeletal mass is cortical bone. Trabecular bone refers to the spongy, more porous *interior* meshwork of bones that looks a bit like a honeycomb. Trabecular bone accounts for the remaining 20 percent of our bone mass. Each bone has an outer shell of dense cortical bone and a central cavity containing a varying amount of trabecular bone. One study found that if estrogen therapy is begun within the first three years of menopause, an actual modest increase in bone mineral density can be observed within a two-year period (Ettinger and others, 1987).

FIGURE 4-1

Although estrogen may protect the skeleton at whatever age it is begun, most experts believe that early therapy (within a few years of menopause) produces the greatest benefit. The loss of estrogen that occurs with menopause affects trabecular bone first, causing vertebral and wrist fractures.

While vertebral bone loss actually begins to occur earlier in women, it is significantly increased in perimenopausal and in early postmenopausal women who have rising FSH (follicle-stimulating hormone) and decreasing estrogen levels. Bone loss from the wrist also

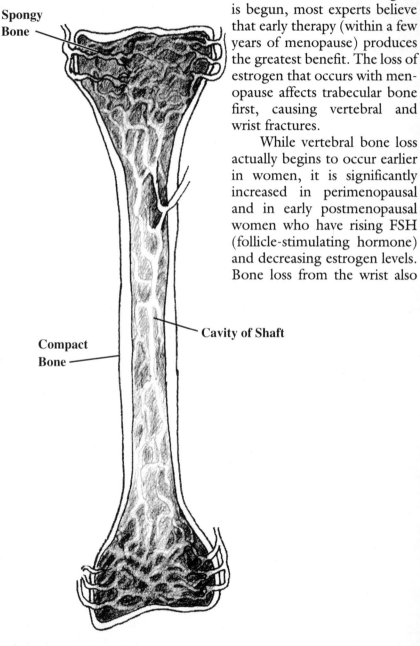

Spongy Bone

Cavity of Shaft

Compact Bone

Bone Structure

increases after menopause. Cortical bone loss occurs at a slower rate throughout postmenopausal life. Cortical bone loss, which occurs later, has even more serious consequences since it contributes to the 40 percent of white women who will have sustained hip fractures by age eighty.

Bone is actually a very active organ system. Osteoclasts are the cells that break down old bones, while osteoblasts build the new bone. Following this process, the new bone is toughened through a process of depositing phosphate and a special calcium. A continuous renovation process with bone being dissolved and reformed is called bone remodeling. The amount of bone in the body at any point in time reflects the balance of these remodeling forces. Dr. Kenneth Cooper refers to these forces as "the demolition squads and the builders." (Cooper, 1989, p. 20) Both processes are affected by many different factors, like a decrease in calcium intake or certain medications.

Osteoarthritis (degenerative arthritis) is another chronic process that wears away the cartilage (protective layer of connecting material) between the bones and leads to joint stiffness and pain. Although osteoporosis and osteoarthritis are both common in women, they are not related. So the presence of one does not mean the existence of the other. Elaine had been alarmed unnecessarily—she had no signs of osteoarthritis or osteoporosis.

✦ THE CONSEQUENCES OF OSTEOPOROSIS

Hip fractures are the most significant consequence of osteoporosis in women. Annually, 250,000 hip fractures occur in the United States (Fleming, 1992). The rate of hip fractures increases dramatically with age in white women, and 80 percent of all hip fractures are associated with osteoporosis. White women have a 15 percent lifetime risk of having a hip fracture (Byyny and Speroff, 1990). These fractures are a particularly significant source of suffering, loss of functioning and even mortality in older women. Surprisingly, between 12 to 20 percent of patients with hip fractures die due to the fracture or its complications within three months (U.S. Congress, 1992). This is because of complications that are life-threatening such as blood clots, pneumonias or heart problems. Of those who survive, many are disabled and may become permanent invalids, like Kristina. According to the National Osteoporosis Foundation, the cost related to hip fractures caused by osteoporosis exceeded seven billion dollars per year in 1990, and these costs are projected to increase to more than thirty billion by the year

2020. All the more reason for all of us to take appropriate precautions and lifestyle changes to promote bone health.

FRACTURES

Fractures of the spine can cause significant back pain. The most common sites for vertebral fractures are in the upper and middle back. The pain with the fracture can be intense but short-lived, decreasing over the following few months. In some cases, it can linger as chronic back pain, due to many factors, including an increasing shift in the spine orientation (thoracic kyphosis). This condition can usually be treated with nonsteroidal anti-inflammatory drugs (NSAIDs) or aspirin and by exercise. On the other hand, many women don't know they have these fractures because they either never experienced symptoms, or did not have symptoms severe enough to cause them to see a physician. They usually find out about their fractures because they are seen on X rays that have been done for other purposes.

Fractures of the forearm bone (the radius) occur earlier in the postmenopausal period than do hip fractures. This risk increases tenfold in white women between the ages of thirty-five and sixty. A white woman has approximately a 15 percent lifetime risk of a wrist fracture, referred to as a Colles' fracture. This is the most common fracture among white women, until age seventy-five, when hip fractures become more common.

Another of Elaine's concerns was her height: her mother had lost several inches and now had the infamous dowager's hump, a permanent curvature of her upper spine. Approximately 50 percent of women over the age of sixty-five will have spinal compression fractures, which cause this shrinking process.

All of us, men and women alike, lose height as we age. This is a result of several factors, including poor posture, some shrinkage of the discs between the bones of our spine and osteoporosis. But remember, most women don't need to worry about actually developing a dowager's hump, but may experience some normal loss of height.

✦ RISK FACTORS FOR OSTEOPOROSIS

Elaine was worried about her personal history as compared to her mother's. There are various factors, including medications and nutritional deficiencies that are risks for osteoporosis. Elaine was right to be concerned about her menopause affecting her risk. By far, the most important risk factor for the development of osteoporosis is loss of estrogen. Seventy-five percent or more of bone loss which occurs in women during the first twenty years after menopause is attributed to estrogen deficiency, rather than to the aging process itself. The risk of having osteoporosis actually depends on two factors—the bone mass that has been achieved prior to menopause (an important point for early prevention) and the subsequent rate of bone loss.

Women who are overweight actually have a decreased risk of developing osteoporosis. This effect is believed to be secondary to the stress that increased weight puts on bones, causing them to remodel rapidly. Maureen, one of our patients who has been struggling with diets all of her life, was delighted to hear this news and said, "Finally, revenge over Nancy Reagan and her size four dresses!"

There are some risk factors that we have no control over such as our sex, family history and ethnic background. That does not mean that we cannot do anything to counterbalance these risks. Elaine was worried because she had a Scandinavian background, as did her mother, Kristina, but, unlike her mother, she was of medium build and slightly overweight. Her mother had also had a hysterectomy at the age of forty, had never been on HRT and had not been a physically active woman. Elaine's lifestyle was far different from her mother's. Her mother had been generally active with her volunteer activities, card games and outings to museums, whereas Elaine's generation had focused a bit more on physical activity. Elaine enjoyed skiing, sailing and jogging, and used physical activity as part of her daily routine throughout the year. In fact, Elaine was sailing so often that we needed to talk to her about over exposure to the sun with respect to skin cancer. On the other hand, her exposure to the sun made it likely that she was getting enough vitamin D, one of the necessary ingredients for bone health. Elaine's physical activity lowered her overall risk a bit. We have more control over some of the risk factors for osteoporosis. And the perimenopausal years are a good time to make some critical changes.

Smoking may be an important risk factor for the development of osteoporosis and it can diminish the effects of any other positive measures that are taken (e.g., hormone replacement therapy or exercise) to prevent osteoporosis. We know that early calcium intake contributes to peak bone mass in young women but for most of us this information comes too late. The good news is that we can still affect our bones with an adequate calcium intake later in life as we will describe in a bit.

Consumption of excessive caffeine and alcohol deplete calcium from our bones and are important risk factors for osteoporosis and fractures. Certain medications can also contribute to osteoporosis, including certain antacids (not calcium carbonate-based), too much thyroid hormone, corticosteroids and antiseizure therapy. But even if you do need to be on these medications, there are ways to minimize these effects.

✦ EVALUATION FOR OSTEOPOROSIS

None of the experts in osteoporosis have suggested that we should screen *all* perimenopausal women in an attempt to select a group of women who are at particularly high risk. This is due to several factors. There is an enormous individual variation in the ability of the body to maintain its bone density. Although measurements of bone mass at different sites of the body may vary, any significant bone loss at any site in the body is important information regarding future risk of fractures. Unfortunately, not all of the equipment at various medical facilities is "state of the art." However, this should not discourage you from getting bone densitometry if your primary care professional suggests it. It is important to check the reputation of the center you are going to.

In the end, about half of menopausal women do not experience any ill effects of menopause on their bones. The ultimate question then becomes: How do we predict the ones that will develop osteoporosis and who should we be testing?

Most experts feel that the additional information that screening will provide is indicated in the following situations. First, it is indicated in any postmenopausal woman whose decision to commit to lifelong HRT will be strongly influenced by the determination of low bone mass. Elaine expressed interest to us regarding HRT therapy because of her risk of developing osteoporosis. Second, testing should be done in any woman with evidence of vertebral compression fractures or thinning of the bones on plain X-ray films. Third, any woman who must receive six months or more of steroid therapy for other medical conditions should have testing.

There are several new procedures that have been developed to measure the density of the bone. The diagnosis of osteoporosis cannot be made by plain X-ray films, unless the osteoporosis is quite advanced. Be wary of any physician who informs you that he or she can tell that you have osteoporosis by looking at a regular chest X ray or hip film. A regular X ray is not an accurate way to assess osteoporosis. At least 30 to 40 percent of bone mineral must be lost before the diagnosis of osteoporosis can be made on X ray. Advances in the assessment of osteoporosis are now happening rapidly. At the present time there are four other methods that are helpful in the diagnosis: Single-photon absorptiometry (SPA), Dual-photon absorptiometry (DPA), Dual-energy X-ray absorptiometry (DEXA) and CT scan. Most centers have been using the DPA and measure the bone mineral density of the lumbar spine, proximal femur and total body to assess the degree of osteoporosis. DEXA is the newest and most common technique. It is faster and has a clearer resolution than the DPA.

Any woman who has apparent osteoporosis should be screened for other conditions that might be causing this process. Some women can develop primary hyperparathyroidism (overactive parathyroid gland), an exaggerated response of one of the glands in the body which produces an elevation in serum parathyroid hormone (PTH). The PTH, in turn, causes release of calcium from the bones. In this case, checking certain blood levels (parathyroid hormone, calcium, phosphorous, and alkaline phosphatase) may be helpful. Thyroid function tests are important as well, since hyperthyroidism is associated with osteoporosis. Assessment of kidney function is important for a so-called secondary hyperparathyroidism that occurs with kidney failure. Blood counts may be ordered, looking for a particular type blood cell malignancy (multiple myeloma) that is associated with some weakness of the bone. Do not be worried about this list of complicated sounding and perhaps frightening diseases. Most women who have osteoporosis are suffering from an unfortunately common disorder that is not caused by any of these conditions, but you should be checked out anyway.

✦ PREVENTING OSTEOPOROSIS

Figure 4-2 is our plan for the prevention of osteoporosis. There is no doubt that exercise and diet have very important effects on bone strength. The earlier in life a woman adopts a nutritional plan to prevent osteoporosis, the greater her chances are of averting the disease. The most essential dietary requirement is adequate daily amounts of calcium. Calcium intake has been shown to be low in both males and females who go on to develop hip fractures. Women with higher calcium diets have lower rates of hip fracture than women with diets that lack adequate calcium.

Individual calcium requirements vary among women due to a variety of factors, including age, dietary habits, drug use, diseases and hormonal status. Rates of calcium absorption can vary as well. Women

FIGURE 4-2

PRESCRIPTION FOR HEALTHY BONES PREVENTION OF OSTEOPOROSIS

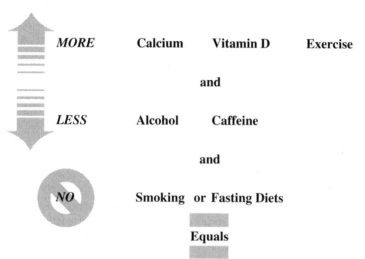

MORE Calcium Vitamin D Exercise

and

LESS Alcohol Caffeine

and

NO Smoking or Fasting Diets

Equals

PREVENTING OSTEOPOROSIS

who eat a reasonable diet can expect to absorb approximately 30 to 40 percent of their dietary calcium, but this declines with age. We recommend an intake of 1,000 mg for perimenopausal women, to 1,500 mg per day for postmenopausal women. Unfortunately, this means that a substantial percentage of women in this country are not eating enough calcium. Because of concern about calories and cholesterol, many women have actually conscientiously restricted dairy products from their diet. This may not be a good choice since excessive thinness is associated with an increased risk of osteoporosis. In addition, a woman's risk of osteoporosis may be greater than her risk of developing heart disease from an elevated cholesterol. So a good solution to this dilemma is to eat low-fat dairy products.

There are many foods, including dairy products, sardines, tofu and certain vegetables, like broccoli and collard greens, that are important sources of absorbable dietary calcium. We have found that increasing calcium is one of the easiest and single most important changes that we can make in our lives to prevent osteoporosis. It is shocking that the average amount of calcium taken in by most American women is closer to 450–550 mg a day (Cooper, 1989). By using the list of calcium-rich foods, daily intake can be increased substantially (see Table 4-1). But here is the bind: most women are worried about their calories as well. It seems unlikely to us that women who have avoided dairy products for one reason or another will change their lives by drinking four glasses of skim milk per day. One or two glasses seems possible.

Also, certain women may have lactose (contained in dairy products) intolerance. This occurs because the enzyme that breaks down lactose (lactase) is diminished. They can also eat other foods that are supplemented with calcium. Products like Lactaid may help reduce the gastrointestinal symptoms, or they can eat nondairy foods high in calcium. Calcium supplements are likely to be necessary if this condition is present.

At the same time, calcium supplements can be extremely helpful. In looking at calcium supplements, it is important to consider not only the dosage, but also the amount of calcium that's immediately available to the body. Calcium carbonate appears to deliver the largest percentage of calcium to the body. Over-the-counter antacids are also usually composed of calcium carbonate alone. They contain 250 mg of elemental calcium per tablet. So, two to four tablets a day can increase intake by 500–1000 mg. In general, calcium tablets should be taken with meals and doses above 500 mg should be divided. This process will improve our ability to absorb the calcium. The only contraindication to taking calcium is a personal history of calcium kidney stones. There are, however, some side effects from taking calcium supplements which include bloating and constipation, but these conditions can usually be avoided by increasing fluid intake, dietary fiber, and maintaining regular exercise. The food industry has now made it easier to have a calcium rich diet by supplementing many basic foods such as fruit juices, cereals and breads.

Here is a way to test your calcium supplement. Take a glass and fill it up half with water and half with vinegar. Drop in your supplement and wait a half an hour. At the end of that time, the supplement should be completely dissolved. If it is not, the supplement is not providing your body with the calcium that it needs. This experiment simulates what happens in your stomach. An undissolved tablet will not be absorbed into your bloodstream.

Vitamin D is necessary for us to absorb calcium efficiently. Therefore if we have a deficiency in vitamin D, we will not be able to absorb

Table 4–1

CALCIUM CONTENT IN VARIOUS FOODS

Food Item	Serving Size	Calcium Content (mg)	Calories
Milk			
Whole	8 oz	291	150
Skim	8 oz	302	85
Yogurt (with added milk solids)			
Plain, low-fat	8 oz	415	145
Fruit, low-fat	8 oz	343	230
Frozen, fruit	8 oz	240	223
Frozen, chocolate	8 oz	160	220
Cheese			
Mozzarella, part skim	1 oz	207	80
Muenster	1 oz	203	105
Cheddar	1 oz	204	115
Riccotta, part skim	4 oz	335	190
Cottage, low-fat (2%)	4 oz	78	103
Ice Cream, Vanilla (11% fat)			
Hard	1 cup	176	270
Soft serve	1 cup	236	375
Ice Milk, Vanilla			
Hard (4% fat)	1 cup	176	185
Soft Serve (3% fat)	1 cup	274	225
Fish and Shellfish			
Oysters, raw (13–19 med.)	1 cup	226	160
Sardines, canned in oil drained, including bones	3 oz	372	175
Salmon, pink, canned, including bones	3 oz	167	120
Shrimp, canned, drained	3 oz	98	100
Vegetables			
Bok Choy, raw	1 cup	74	9
Broccoli, cooked, drained, from raw	1 cup	136	40
Soybeans, cooked, drained, from raw	1 cup	131	235
Collards, cooked, drained, from raw	1 cup	357	65
Turnip greens, cooked drained, from raw	1 cup	252	30
Tofu	4 oz	108	85
Almonds	1 oz	75	165

*Adapted from National Osteoporosis Foundation, 1992

calcium well. Vitamin D is generated by exposure of the skin to the sun and a well-balanced diet. We need fifteen minutes per day of sunshine to get enough vitamin D. Therefore, it is possible that some women are not getting enough sunshine on a daily basis. In addition, milk is the only dairy product that is fortified with vitamin D. So you should not believe that you are getting vitamin D by eating cheeses or yogurt that has not been fortified. Finally, there is tremendous variability in the amount of vitamin D fortification in milk. Tests from various dairies found that some milk has too little and other milk has too much vitamin D. Attempts are now being made to standardize this process. If you have health problems that leave you housebound, you may need supplements of between 400 to 800 units of vitamins per day. Anyone with severe liver or kidney impairment may also have a decreased ability to metabolize vitamin D, and may need supplements as well. You should not take vitamin D and calcium supplements without checking with your doctor. This is a situation where the amount of calcium absorbed into your bloodstream could be excessive and dangerous.

If you want to prevent osteoporosis, please try to stop smoking! This is also true if you wish to prevent heart attacks, stroke, lung cancer, wrinkles, early menopause and early aging. We continue this discussion in many of our other chapters.

Moderate alcohol consumption may increase the risk of the development of osteoporosis, and is another compelling reason to restrict alcohol intake. Alcohol works as a diuretic and causes an increase in the loss of calcium from bone. Too much alcohol can also interfere with calcium absorption in the stomach. Women who drink more than one drink per day are at increased risk for the development of osteoporosis. While learning more about Elaine and her daily habits, we discovered that she had one to two glasses of wine at night to relax while she unwound from her busy day. Quite often, she would begin her relaxation with a gin and tonic while fixing dinner, and admitted that her alcohol consumption had risen since her mother moved in. Elaine is not alone. We see many women who use alcohol to cope with stress. We talked with Elaine about her feeling that she deserved some reward at the end of a hard day. Elaine began to understand that alcohol could do more harm than good, especially if her intake increased. We discussed other outlets for relaxation, including a short walk, an herbal bath, or a cup of tea with a good book. In the end, she decided to buy a microwave oven and encouraged her mother to use it to help prepare dinner. This way, Kristina had an activity that made her feel more like a contributing member of the family, and Elaine could pick up that mystery novel that she had been meaning to finish. As Kristina increased her ability to get around, she was able to alternate cooking dinner with Elaine and her two daughters. And, as Elaine cut back on alcohol and the family began to share more of the chores, her headaches began to diminish. This did not surprise us, as headaches are often related to stress and substance abuse. We discuss headaches, as well as stress, in greater detail in Chapter Eight.

Caffeine is also known to act as a diuretic and increases the loss of calcium through the urine so that it is wise to restrict caffeine-containing beverages to one to two per day. There are certain other foods that can affect the absorption of calcium, such as oatmeal and bran. Ironically, high-fiber diets that are seen as healthy to reduce fat and increase bulk can actually interfere with calcium absorption, because they increase the rate at which food is passed through the gastrointestinal tract. Obviously, you don't want to eliminate any of these foods from your diet, as they play an important role in other aspects of prevention. You can maximize your calcium intake by not eating these foods at the same meal as the foods that you take to ensure an adequate supply of calcium.

✦ WHAT ABOUT EXERCISE? IT WORKS!

We need to deal with this exercise issue again. We are surprised that so few women at our town meetings ask about exercise. Then again, why should we be? It turns out that only 22 percent of Americans engage in thirty or more minutes of even light to moderate physical activity five or more times per week. But this is a key issue in maintaining our health, especially our bones.

You have probably noticed that we are referring to "physical activity" and "exercise." Physical activity is any movement resulting in energy expenditure. Exercise, on the other hand, is a leisure-time physical activity that is structured and designed to improve physical fitness. If you are not interested in regular exercise, at least try to be more physically active: It can pay off. Physical inactivity, or a sedentary lifestyle is a health risk for high blood pressure, elevated fats and obesity. In contrast, physical activity is positively related to a longer and healthier life (Blair, 1989).

So, if we know these facts about exercise, why aren't we doing more? There are plenty of reasons. First, it is hard to get going! In addition, most women in the menopausal years grew up with little exposure to enjoyable physical activity or sports. The dreaded gym class in school was the little we got, and it was often combined with "hygiene" (those famous "What every girl should know" pamphlets again). Few of us received any encouragement to explore the role of physical activity, sports or exercise. Many of us felt like klutzes.

Then there is the role of the "cosmetic body." Having little education on the positive aspects of physical activity in our teens, we were then confronted with the demands of "looking right." We spent years feeling inadequate, not thin enough, or buxom enough, or whatever enough. Then came the aerobics movement. We know as many women who were turned off by Jane Fonda's videotape as those who began aerobics. Let's face it: Most of us are not born with a tall and lean body composition like Jane Fonda in the first place.

So what did many of us do? We continued to repress the physical aspects of our lives. We dieted, or did nothing. Why enter a losing battle? Why begin a new activity that will bring back bad memories?

It is time to change all of that. We are women now, not the young girls thrown into gym classes in those awful blue suits. First and foremost, physical activity and exercise is no longer a cosmetic *or* a competitive issue: it is a critical health issue. We do not need to be "good" at it; we do not need to be "attractive"; we just need to do it. This is especially true with respect to bone health.

Weight-bearing exercise, even as little as thirty minutes a day about three times a week, will help. You may well ask: what is a weight-bearing exercise? A weight-bearing activity is one where our bodies must be supported. This would include walking, jogging and many sports activities listed in Table 4-2. Non–weight-bearing activities are those like bike riding, where a bicycle seat supports our body, or swimming, where we are partially supported by the water. As we will describe in our health promotion chapter, an exercise program does not need to be extreme for us to gain health benefits. Table 4-2 also details an exercise program where the target is better bone health. The principle here is to put stress on the bones in a consistent fashion in order to strengthen them. We need to focus exercise on certain areas of the body. Exercises like running or jogging, aerobics, stair climbing and dancing are beneficial for the leg, hip and spine.

Remember that we have arms as well as legs. Since women tend to suffer fractures in the upper arm as well as in the forearm at the wrist, it is important to exercise the upper body as well. These activities would include racket sports, weight training and rowing. (Try some push-ups if you are really tough!) Aerobics classes, of course, can exercise all areas of the body, depending on the specific exercises that are included.

One problem here is that many women enjoy walking and yet

walking apparently does not provide as much stress on the bones and therefore does not harden them as much as jogging. Using the principle of slow but steady change, why not alternate jogging with walking? You are probably walking because you enjoy it and are comfortable, but by increasing the amount of jogging you do, you can also improve your bone health.

The studies that evaluate the effectiveness of exercise on osteoporosis suggest that the exercise needs to be at least *thirty* minutes of duration. Weight training, of course, will vary, depending on the individual's abilities and strengths. With respect to frequency, as little as three days a week can be beneficial.

BEGINNING AN EXERCISE PROGRAM

The first step is to decide that it is important. You and your clinician can work out why you are exercising. Are you exercising primarily to build up your bone strength, or are you interested in maximal cardiovascular fitness? After you have decided your goal, you can choose an exercise plan and setting, as we describe in our chapters on heart health and/or promoting a healthy lifestyle.

The next step is to allot a specific amount of time necessary to accomplish your goals. You might also decide whether you are a solitary exerciser or a social exerciser. The buddy or partner system is often extremely helpful to a woman, as you will learn in a bit. It provides social connection as well as extra motivation. We have also met women who are very active socially and who work long hours who would prefer to use their exercise routine as a private meditation time. So structure your exercise routine according to your individual situation.

There are many barriers to exercise including the weather, being overweight, lack of time, and sometimes the lack of funds to participate in the type of exercise we enjoy most. Time is a difficult issue for menopausal women with multiple roles. That is one of the reasons that we have suggested that exercising with a friend can have multiple benefits. It is also important to know that this might be one of the most important health decisions of your life, for improved bone health, improved cardiovascular fitness and an overall sense of physical well-being.

Women who live in the city face additional problems since they may be worried about safety. Fortunately, many suburban malls now offer mall walking and early-morning exercise programs. Exercise videotapes can also be helpful.

Finances can be a difficult problem. The only real equipment you need for exercise is a good pair of shoes for the appropriate activity or a bicycle if you prefer. Layers of clothing can be developed from your existing wardrobe. Jogging and bike paths are becoming more and more a part of the American landscape and are always available.

Table 4-2 depicts an exercise program for healthy bones. Exercise has to be fun. It has to be a chance to socialize or spend precious time alone, wear comfortable clothes, and do something physical. We can overcome the old ghosts of gym class and the new ghosts of mirrored aerobic classes with youngsters wearing Spandex. The first step is to move exercise to the top of your priority list.

Two other areas related to bone health are often ignored. They

---

Table 4–2

FIT PROGRAM FOR
HEALTHY BONES

Purpose: Maintain Bone Health

Frequency:	2–3 times per week
Intensity:	Moderate
Time:	20–30 minutes
Types:	Weight-bearing exercise
	Against gravity
	Increased resistance
	Examples: Weight training
	Rowing
	Stair climbing
	Step machine
	Racquet sports
	Jogging
	Step aerobics

Note: Activities of limited benefit: walking, swimming

are good posture and prevention. It is clear that by straightening our posture, our height can be affected. If we sit up and stand straight (mother was right), we will look taller. In addition, pulling our shoulders back and pulling in our abdominal muscles will improve our posture and bone health and make us feel better overall.

For those of you who have already developed osteoporosis, your first step is to maintain the bone density that you still have. The advantage of early detection, or secondary prevention, is that you can make changes. Your choices here include HRT, calcium-rich diet and some of the medications we have recommended. In addition, if you are beginning to experience pain, it is important to develop a regimen that addresses that pain effectively. Your physician can prescribe nonsteroidal anti-inflammatory drugs like ibuprofen to treat your pain. It is important, also, to maintain your exercise, despite some minimal pain. Try to begin any exercise program with slow stretching in order to warm up and to minimize the actual possibility of injury. If you find an exercise program, whether it be walking, tennis, bicycling or aerobics, it is a good idea to find a partner. It is important to choose someone whose skills and whose health are at about your level. It is unlikely that you will both feel down on the same day and therefore, if one of you has the motivation to keep going, you can help the other. Your partner may also suffer from some of the same problems with osteoporosis, therefore, you can share with her your feelings about this difficult problem. Sharing your feelings with a person who has a similar type of problem is one of the most therapeutic activities. You will feel better, she will feel better and so it goes. Osteoporosis may be a part of aging for many of us, but we can prevent much of it and we can cope with it if we continue an active lifestyle, maintain our bone density, and develop a support system.

Prevention of fractures involves many changes. As we get older, whether we have osteoporosis or not, it is important to reduce our chance of accidents. Here are some suggestions to help prevent injuries and falls: Bend your knees when picking anything up, and avoid lifting heavy objects whenever possible. Women who are beginning to suffer from osteoporosis can organize their household to minimize the possibility of accidents and resulting fractures. Objects that are used frequently should be placed in higher places. Slippery floors and loose floor rugs are also to be avoided, and stairways should include good strong railings. Be especially careful climbing and descending stairs. Stairs and hallways should be properly lit. We should be careful to remove loose wires and cords from the floor. The prevention of falls is yet another good reason to avoid high-heeled shoes.

How Estrogen Can Help

Appropriate estrogen replacement therapy can have a major impact on the risk of osteoporosis with a 50 to 60 percent decrease in fractures in the arm and hip (Lindsay, 1991). Estrogen improves calcium absorption and makes it possible to utilize supplemental calcium in lower doses, reducing the side effects associated with higher doses, such as constipation and flatulence. Estrogen probably has a direct protective mechanism on bone in addition to increasing the absorption of calcium. Estrogen receptors have been isolated in bone cells, suggesting that estrogen directly stimulates bone formation.

This decision about estrogen includes consideration of many risks and benefits for each woman, as we describe in our chapter on hormone replacement therapy. The literature on HRT and osteoporosis is reasonably clear: HRT does reduce the risk of weakening of the bones and subsequent fractures. Elaine was anxious to take HRT because of her experience with her mother. She was also having hot flashes at the time and some sleep disturbances as well, so it was not a difficult decision for her. In contrast, Lauranne, a fifty-one-year-old teacher, whose mother had osteoporosis, also had a sister who was diagnosed with breast cancer at age forty-five. Most experts would agree that the decision to take HRT on a long-term basis should be weighed against the possible increased risk of breast cancer with long-term therapy. We describe this further in the chapter on HRT.

Other Medications

Many women will choose not to take estrogen if they are at risk for breast cancer or for other reasons. Not all these women will, in fact, experience osteoporosis. Good nutrition and weight bearing exercise are the basics here. In addition, there are several other medications that have been investigated. Calcitonin is another substance in the body which stimulates the uptake of calcium by the bone. It has been used either as an injection or as a nasal spray, and both forms can reduce bone loss. Although the nasal spray is not yet approved by the FDA, it may be available in a few years.

We are all familiar with fluoride and its miraculous effect on the decline of dental cavities in this country. There were initial hopes that it would be an effective therapy for osteoporosis. It is a potent stimulator of bone formation, particularly trabecular (spongy) bone, but it appears to decrease cortical (compact) bone and therefore increases fractures. Finally, there is promising data on another medication, etidronate disodium, which has been used, to date, only in clinical studies. It appears to reduce bone weakening and the rate of new vertebral fractures in postmenopausal women, but additional studies are needed.

✦ COMMUNICATION

In choosing a primary care professional, you need to find someone who emphasizes prevention. A primary care physician is, by definition, an internist or a family practitioner who is trained in comprehensive care and prevention. Both fields require board exams. Some gynecologists practice primary care as well. Many primary care offices and group practices have nurse practitioners and physicians assistants who may serve as your primary clinician. These health care professionals are well trained and licensed and some of them may have more interest in and knowledge about preventive care than some physicians. Hospitals can provide you with a list of general internists, family practitioners or general gynecologists who admit to their institution. Such issues as type of insurance accepted, age or gender of the practitioner may be important to you.

Your particular concerns about osteoporosis should be part of any discussion you have with your health care provider about prevention, menopausal symptoms or treatment with HRT. You will want to discuss this subject with the primary care professional who will be following you long-term, making recommendations about diet and exercise, in addition to monitoring any therapy. Many different physicians may have expertise in the area of osteoporosis and can be used as consultants. These include gynecologists, reproductive endocrinologists (a gynecologic subspecialty) and endocrinologists (a subspecialty of internal medicine).

A thorough office visit about prevention of osteoporosis is a good idea. Any discussion with your clinician that is extensive may require extra time. It is a good idea to let the secretary or office manager know that you wish to have a more extensive discussion with your physician at the time of scheduling the appointment. On the day of the appointment, you may choose to call ahead to see if the physician is running on time, so that you can plan your schedule accordingly. By this time you have set up essentially a contract with the office where you know that this will be an extended office visit.

If you are in good health during your menopausal years, then the goal is to maintain your health. If you are concerned about osteoporosis, the first step is obviously to discuss it with your clinician and to work on a prevention plan together. If you find that you are in a very high-risk group, then you might consider the bone densitometry measurements we have suggested. Remember that screening for osteoporosis is not recommended for all menopausal women. Third-party reimbursement may be limited to women who are high-risk when it comes to screening for osteoporosis. This is important because the cost of any bone densitometry can range between $80 and $400, so you should check with your health insurance plan.

If your physician does not take your concerns seriously, your first step is to restate your concerns carefully and clearly and to mention your risk factors. The questionnaire can help you evaluate your risk for osteoporosis. As we mentioned earlier, if your physician recommends a routine X ray, this is not sufficient. You can also ask for a recommendation to an osteoporosis specialist. Most generalists are quite comfortable getting a second opinion. The National Osteoporosis Foundation can also be helpful in providing you with the name of a specialist in your area.

COMMUNICATION WITH YOUR FAMILY

Your prevention program may well require changes in the entire family system. This is true because most women are in charge of the food preparation in families, as unfair as this may be. For example, Barbara, a fifty-three-year-old mother of five, was the energetic hub of her large and active family. Although she had enjoyed sports as a young woman, her family's needs had swallowed up her time and after her hysterectomy, ten years ago, she had gained thirty pounds. She had spent the last twenty years driving her five sons to and from various sporting events and attending as many as she could. This year she created her prevention program and decided to cut down on red meat, increase calcium and ask for a NordicTrack machine for Christmas. Twenty-five years ago, Barbara would serve her family steak and potatoes for dinner. Ten years ago, she focused more on chicken and rice with added vegetables. This year, after meeting with our nutritionist, she carefully prepared a dinner of stir-fried tofu and broccoli in a soy/peanut sauce. She met with mass rebellion. Her five sons, as well as her husband taunted her saying, "Mom's gone veggie!"—as if it were some leftover disease from the sixties—"Tofu, you've got to be kidding!"

Barbara met with our psychologist, as well as our nutritionist, and together they all decided that this was insensitivity and resistance to change, rather than any major family problem. The psychologist sug-

EVALUATING YOUR RISK
FOR OSTEOPOROSIS

Do you have these risk factors?

		YES	NO
A.	White or Asian	_____	_____
	Family history of osteoporosis	_____	_____
	Slim	_____	_____
	Small-framed	_____	_____
	Early menopause (Before age 40)	_____	_____
	Very fair skin	_____	_____
B.	Smoking	_____	_____
	Alcohol intake of more than five ounces per day	_____	_____
	Low level of exercise	_____	_____
	Diet low in calcium	_____	_____
C.	Medications for		
	Thyroid replacement	_____	_____
	Seizures	_____	_____
	Blood clots	_____	_____
	or		
	Any steroid	_____	_____

SCORING: Count each YES answer. A higher score indicates an increased risk for osteoporosis. (Adapted from National Osteoporosis Foundation, 1991.)

gested that Barbara's husband, William, come with her to the next session. There, they could discuss as a family the importance of Barbara changing her habits in order to lose weight and become more physically active. Just this session alone impressed upon William the seriousness of Barbara's commitment. He agreed that if he and the boys did not like her menu planning, they would do their own. At first the family developed a two-tiered system, with Barbara eating more calcium and vegetables in her diet and William and the boys ordering out for pizza. Over time, however, Barbara would sneak in different forms of tofu and the family grew to accept certain of her menus. (Yes, we did suggest that William or the boys do the cooking, but change sometimes takes time!) Most importantly, she uses the NordicTrack machine every evening, and has enjoyed proving them all wrong about her commitment to change. Barbara had not always been comfortable with regular exercise after her hysterectomy, and given the intense demands of her family. When her sons began to see how much happier and alive she seemed, they began to encourage her and of course, ultimately they had to all take turns on the track, with Barbara having first choice.

Barbara's family benefited from her changes in that they began to eat a more healthy diet and began to exercise more too. But Elaine was in the interesting situation of being the mother of teenage daughters and was concerned about their bone health as well as her own. Mia and Karen, age fifteen and seventeen, were typical teenagers. Both were physically active but their diet seemed to fluctuate between fast food, heavy on the grease, to restriction of calories in order to control their weight. Yet we know that peak bone mass is reached between the relatively young ages of twenty-five and thirty-five. So, a teenage girl who has begun to avoid dairy products without replacing them with other sources of calcium is setting up a lifetime habit that can have long-term negative consequences. One study of girls between the ages of fifteen to nineteen found that they only consume about 600 mg of calcium per day (Cooper, 1989). That is considerably less than the 1000–1500 mg that most people recommend. Even the presently recommended daily allowance (RDA) is 800 mg and thus, these teenagers were not even reaching that minimal amount.

The good news is that the younger girls apparently retain more calcium, but still the two girls were setting up bad habits in their teenage years. If you add to that the habits that develop in the late teens and twenties of consuming a lot of caffeine, and drinking perhaps too much alcohol, then the patterns become even worse. Elaine tried to talk to her daughters about these issues and at first, they were reluctant to change. Over time, especially with the example of their grandmother, with whom they were both close, they began to see the necessity to change also. They added some frozen yogurt to their diet and would drink skim milk from time to time. Their mother shared with them the list of calcium-rich foods, including sardines or salmon with the bones left in. They laughed and exclaimed to their mother, "Yeah, right. No way are we gonna munch salmon between meals."

We hope, as time goes on, that Elaine will minimize her risk for osteoporosis and Mia and Karen will build up their bone mass and that her mother, Kristina, will have some alleviation of her suffering.

R E S O U R C E S

National Osteoporosis Foundation
1150 17th Street, NW, Suite 500
Washington, DC 20036
(202) 223-2226

The foundation publishes books and pamphlets on osteoporosis, and puts out a catalog of patient-education materials, including readings and other resources. A $25 membership gets you the quarterly newsletter, "The Osteoporosis Report," with articles on research, medical advances, prevention and treatment. They distribute pamphlets with respect to prevention of osteoporosis and could direct you to your closest treatment center. The National Osteoporosis Foundation publishes one of the best books on osteoporosis called Boning Up on Osteoporosis: A Guide to Prevention and Treatment. *This readable book tells us about risk factors, prevention of osteoporosis and exercise training.*

Ourselves Getting Older *has a chapter on osteoporosis. This book is published by the Boston Women's Health Collective, and it is quite detailed and easy to read. Just as many publications published by the pharmaceutical industry are very pro-hormone replacement therapy, some parts of this book are extremely antihormone replacement therapy. As long as you are aware of this point of view, this chapter can be extremely helpful.*

❖ RESOURCES FOR EXERCISE

With respect to exercise and osteoporosis, we discuss accessing resources in great detail in our final chapter. However, it is important to note that almost any part of the country has either a YWCA or a Jewish Community Center nearby. These types of centers tend to offer low-cost programs in contrast to some of the fancier health clubs and gymnasiums. Many of them also have exercise physiologists who can help you in developing a personalized exercise program. But if all else fails, remember that walking is one of the first steps to maintaining your bones at the menopausal period.

CHAPTER FIVE

Maintaining Our Health: Healthy Hearts

IF YOU ARE LIKE MOST WOMEN, YOU ARE WONDERING, "WHY SHOULD I be concerned about heart disease?" Yet there are several good reasons for you to become knowledgeable about your heart. Cardiovascular disease, which includes heart disease and stroke, is the number one cause of death in all U.S. women over the age of forty. Surprised, are you? It's not cancer, but heart disease that claims more women's lives! African-American women are particularly vulnerable, since their rates of heart disease and stroke are one and a half times greater than those of white women. In all, an estimated 250,000 American women die from heart disease each year (Wenger and others, 1993). Heart disease is an area where health promotion can really pay off. And the menopausal years are ideal for developing a healthier lifestyle.

This chapter will outline for you the most recent information regarding women and the development of cardiovascular disease. Until recently, the risk of cardiovascular disease in women received little attention. A prime example: The Oregon affiliate of the American Heart Association (AHA) organized the first women's health conference on coronary heart disease twenty-five years ago entitled *Hearts and Hus-*

bands. This conference had, as its sole purpose, the education of women concerning the risks of heart disease in their spouses (American Heart Association, 1989). It took that same organization more than twenty years to hold their first conference on women and coronary disease. In contrast to the tremendous amount of attention paid to men and cardiovascular disease, information on the development of coronary disease in women is very limited.

This gender bias in the medical understanding of heart disease has very deep roots. The best known studies of heart disease prevention are the Multiple Risk Factor Intervention Trial (the famous MR FIT study)(Neaton and others, 1984), and the Lipid Research Clinic's Coronary Primary Prevention Trial (LRC-CPPT)(Program, 1984). These two studies are the sources for the belief that if a person lowers his cholesterol by 1 percent, his risk of developing cardiovascular disease is decreased by 2 percent. You can probably guess why we are using the word "his": they only studied men.

While most experts agree that the so-called "traditional risk factors for heart disease" (that is, those identified for men) play a role in the development of heart disease in women, there is still a lot to learn about heart disease in women. Two pioneer studies, The Framingham Heart Study (Eaker and Castelli, 1987) and The Nurses' Health Study (Stampfer and others, 1987) have given us much of the important information available about women and their risk factors for the development of coronary disease. Women lag approximately seven to ten years behind men in the development of coronary artery disease. Some of this discrimination in the research and treatment of women's cardiovascular disease may be due to the way in which our society has valued aging women. Men who have heart attacks are more likely to be perceived as being in their "prime" (midlife), while typically women with heart disease are in their sixties and seventies and, therefore, considered less valuable, economically and otherwise.

We met Ellen in our practice several years ago. She was a respected cardiac care nurse who had quit her job at age fifty-four because of burnout. Ellen had been active in training young nurses for over twenty-five years. Her work on the cardiac unit had always been challenging, but over the previous few years she had found the intense environment less satisfying. She wanted to spend more time pursuing new interests. As a single woman, she also valued her independence. Ellen felt that by taking so much of the job home with her, it was difficult to concentrate on anything else. One day it occurred to her that she could do something else.

She came to us because she discovered that she could not get her own physician to take her newly developed chest pain seriously. She found this particularly infuriating as she had cared for the same physician's patients in the hospital and knew that he had special respect for her clinical judgment. Ellen realized that she needed to take charge of her own health care. She was interested in knowing her own risk of cardiovascular disease and taking steps to maintain her health.

This chapter will help you, like Ellen, assess your own risks for cardiovascular disease. Read the information we have provided and fill out the questionnaire on healthy hearts. This will facilitate conversation between you and your health care provider. The menopausal years are an excellent time to make important changes in lifestyle that can reduce the chance of heart disease later on in life.

✦ WHAT IS ATHEROSCLEROSIS AND CORONARY ARTERY DISEASE?

Coronary heart disease or coronary artery disease (CAD) is defined as the narrowing of one or more of the blood vessels that supply blood flow to the heart. As we age, these arteries accumulate material in a process called atherosclerosis, which decreases the diameter of the vessels supplying blood to the heart. Figure 5-1 depicts a normal and a diseased artery. This narrowing in the diameter of the blood vessels to the heart causes a decrease in the blood flow to the heart muscle. The heart is not able to pump effectively, which causes symptoms such as chest pain or shortness of breath. If a woman develops significant narrowing in the blood vessels that feed her heart, she may experience chest pain from a decreased blood supply of the heart (the technical term is *angina pectoris*). A heart attack occurs when the blood supply to the heart is severely reduced and is called a myocardial infarction. If the heart fails to pump effectively, fluid backs up into the lungs and this is called congestive heart failure. From now on we will refer to coronary heart disease or coronary artery disease as "heart disease," for simplicity.

The obvious question regarding women and heart disease is why are we relatively protected from heart disease before menopause? Why do women, on average, develop significant heart disease a decade later than men do? We know that there are many factors that could account for this sex difference. According to several studies, estrogen has a beneficial effect on serum cholesterol. Estrogen therapy reduces low-density lipoprotein (LDL) cholesterol or the bad cholesterol and increases serum high-density (HDL) cholesterol, or the good

FIGURE 5-1

ATHEROSCLEROSIS — HARDENING OF THE ARTERIES

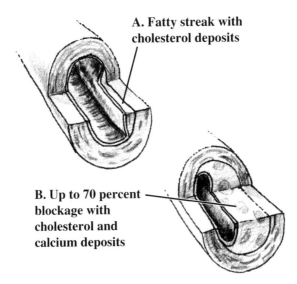

A. Fatty streak with cholesterol deposits

B. Up to 70 percent blockage with cholesterol and calcium deposits

cholesterol (Barrett-Connor and Bush, 1991). There are also theories for why women who take hormones might have less heart disease. There are estrogen receptors in the walls of the arteries, suggesting that estrogen might also have a direct positive effect on the arteries (McGill, 1989). Additionally, estrogen may decrease the formation of harmful clots in the arteries (Ylikorkala and others, 1987).

Another hypothesis for the protective effect of the female gender is that before menopause, women who are premenopausal have lower red blood cell (hematocrit) levels because they are menstruating regularly and, perhaps, lower blood cell count enables better flow through the coronary vessels. Men with high serum iron levels seem to have higher rates of coronary heart disease (Salonen and others, 1992). Maybe the opposite is true, and premenopausal women who are menstruating and have lower serum iron levels than males have decreased rates of coronary heart disease on that basis. Does this mean we should be avoiding vitamins that contain iron? If you are being treated for anemia, it is probably wise to take the iron as prescribed. For women without anemia, whose iron is part of a vitamin supplement, the dose is probably low enough to be harmless. To be on the "safe" side however, ask your health care professional.

One thing is clear: We need much more information about

women and heart disease. We do have enough information now to know that the menopausal years provide us with the ideal time to make changes necessary to prevent heart disease.

✦ RISK FACTORS

Although we know less about women than we do about men, there are many identifiable risk factors for coronary artery disease. It is important to know your specific risks so that you can share them with your physician and more importantly, so you can begin to change the risk factors that you can control.

BIOLOGICAL FACTORS

Biological risk factors for heart disease in women fall into two main groups: The first category is nonhormone related factors, such as diabetes, hypertension, elevated cholesterol and smoking. The second category includes hormonal factors. Even when a man and woman with the same number of risk factors are compared, the man will still have three and a half times the rate of developing heart disease. Clearly, just being male is a risk factor for heart disease. Some biological influence appears to be protecting women as compared to men. Unfortunately, this changes for women as we age.

The presence of *diabetes mellitus* is one of the most significant factors in the development of heart disease in women. Diabetes is a disease that occurs when the body cannot make effective use of insulin, a hormone that processes sugar. This leads to the sugar levels in the blood becoming too high, which has several short- and long-term effects on the body. Diabetes occurs more in women than it does in men, and the presence of diabetes appears to cancel any female advantage in the development of heart disease. Women with even mild diabetes, or what is termed glucose intolerance, have an increased risk of developing heart disease. Diabetes appears to speed up the process of atherosclerosis in the heart. If you have a family history of diabetes or heart disease, a personal history of other cardiac risk factors or symptoms of diabetes (excessive thirst, excessive urination, weight loss or persistent vaginal yeast infections) then you should be screened for diabetes. There are blood and urine tests for diabetes, but the urine tests tend to be much less precise. The diagnosis of diabetes is made in anyone who has one or more fasting blood sugars greater than or equal to 140 mg/dl or anyone who demonstrates sustained blood sugar levels greater than 200 mg/dl during an oral glucose tolerance test.

Hypertension, another risk factor for heart disease, is an elevation of the blood pressure. The development of high blood pressure is a complicated process. Your health care professional measures your blood pressure by two numbers; the higher of which is called the systolic blood pressure and the lower of which is called the diastolic pressure. Normal blood pressure is considered any blood pressure under 140/90 in people under the age of sixty, or 160/90 in people older than sixty. Borderline hypertension is defined as blood pressure 140/90–105, and high blood pressure is when the measure is more than 140/105. Blood pressure should be measured on at least three different office visits to make the diagnosis correctly.

Hypertension is the most common of all cardiac risk factors occurring in up to 20 percent of the entire population. It occurs more in African-Americans and more often in men (both African-American and white) until the age around menopause at which point it starts to be more common in women. Blood pressure can be elevated by even moderate chronic alcohol consumption as well as certain drugs. It frequently occurs with other cardiac risk factors, including obesity and diabetes. In most cases, it can be effectively treated with diet, exercise, and medication.

An elevated *cholesterol* is a common risk factor for the development of coronary heart disease. Cholesterol is divided into two broad classes, high-density lipoprotein (HDL cholesterol) and low-density lipoprotein (LDL cholesterol). HDL, the so called "good cholesterol," removes cholesterol out of the bloodstream, and LDL, the "bad cholesterol," carries cholesterol to the bloodstream.

Younger women have lower total cholesterol levels than men of the same age. This difference is thought to be due to higher estrogen levels. Between the ages of twenty and fifty, a woman's total cholesterol levels and LDL levels are lower than they are in men. But things change after menopause: women develop increasing levels of total serum cholesterol with increases in LDL, the bad cholesterol, and decreases in HDL, the good cholesterol. The higher your HDL cholesterol, the lower your risk of developing heart disease.

Cholesterol values are now frequently obtained as part of routine blood tests. Cholesterol values can vary by as much as 30–50 points for a variety of reasons. Certain factors are known to affect the accuracy of the cholesterol measurement including: recent illness, surgery or heart attack, pregnancy, recent weight gain or loss, new (within four to eight weeks) use of postmenopausal hormones or oral contraceptives and different phases of the menstrual cycle. The quality of the test is important too. Remember that getting tested at your local mall is not as reliable as going to a reputable laboratory.

If your initial cholesterol is found to be elevated, you will probably be asked to give a fasting specimen. This involves fasting for sixteen hours overnight and then having your total cholesterol, HDL-cholesterol, and triglyceride levels measured. Your LDL-cholesterol can be calculated based on these values. Treatment recommendations from your health care professional should always be based on the cholesterol values from this full fasting panel and not on an elevated value for one random (i.e., nonfasting) total cholesterol. This is because it is necessary to know your HDL-cholesterol, LDL-cholesterol and triglycerides before any decisions can be made regarding treatment.

Smoking is probably the most significant risk factor for the development of coronary artery disease in young women (under age forty), and it plays an important role in the development of heart disease in older women as well. It is a disgrace that women were targeted in the 1970s during a period of increased political action for women, in marketing campaigns for cigarettes. Most of you remember "You've come a long way baby," the advertisement that attempted to link political freedom in women with smoking. What they forgot to tell us was that on the way you could get heart disease, lung disease, cancer, earlier menopause and wrinkles! In addition, if you already have a risk of cardiovascular disease due to additional risk factors, smoking will only compound it.

Once you quit smoking, within three to four years, your risk of coronary disease goes back to the same risk as you would have had if you had never smoked. However, if you cut back your smoking to even the lightest amount, one to four cigarettes per day, you would still have a significantly increased of risk of coronary disease. While rates of smoking have dropped in the U.S., this decline has been seen more in males than females. This is most likely because women have different reasons for smoking than men, and therefore varying quit rates. For instance, women are more likely to smoke to relieve stress, to reduce unpleasant feelings and to suppress appetite (Orlandi, 1987). It is only recently that smoking cessation programs have attempted to take these gender differences into account in designing programs for women.

✦ THE GREAT WEIGHT DEBATE

Obesity contributes to the development of coronary disease, but some of its impact may be due to concurrent hypertension, diabetes, or elevated cholesterol (Bush, 1991). (Note: Technically a person can be overweight without being obese. Being overweight is just weighing more than desirable; whereas being obese means an excess of body fat. Some athletes are overweight without being obese. Thus the scale weight does not necessarily reflect being "over-fat." Midlife women who are overweight usually do have an excess of body fat. Nonetheless, we are using the word "overweight" because the word "obese" is almost always used in a pejorative fashion.) Most women who are overweight will develop one or more other factors, including hypertension, diabetes or an elevated cholesterol.

It gets even more difficult to avoid weight gain as we get older because of metabolic changes. Our body metabolism slows down and we need fewer calories to maintain our present weight. Also, as we age, a larger proportion of our weight becomes fat rather than muscle tissue. This is a definite problem, and one that each woman needs to face individually.

The medical attitude toward dieting changes regularly. We know that extra weight is a risk factor for heart disease, but there is little evidence that we can help people lose large amounts of weight. For moderately overweight women, "yo-yo dieting" may be more dangerous than maintaining their present weight. A recent analysis of one study found that people who continue to gain and lose weight more than ten pounds at a time over twenty years (yo-yo dieters), had a higher rate of heart attacks than those whose weight remained constant (Stampfer and others, 1987). So, in addition to our having trouble losing weight, it is clear that the yo-yo dieting problem remains. Psychologist Kelly Brownell of Yale University, a leading obesity researcher, has suggested an approach that we support. He suggests, "I propose that smaller but well-maintained weight losses may well be more beneficial than larger but poorly maintained weight losses" (Keeping Your Weight, 1993). His conclusion is based on decades of research in this area as well as a study of the MR. FIT program, which analyzed over 12,000 men. Many of these men were at risk for heart attacks because they were overweight. Those men whose weight remained constant over time had a lower rate of heart disease than those who lost weight only to regain it. So weight is a complicated health problem.

It is not just what you weigh, but the shape of your body that is important with respect to heart disease. Women who have "pear-shaped," or female-pattern obesity, are less likely to develop high blood pressure, elevated insulin levels and early diabetes than overweight women who are "apple-shaped," or have so-called male-pattern obesity.

Our patient, Ellen, had taught her patients how to follow cardiac diets for twenty years and yet when it came to her own dieting, like many of us, she had really struggled. By the time she had quit her job, she was about twenty to twenty-five pounds overweight. She had been through the hospital-sponsored liquid-diet program twice, regained all of the weight, and became discouraged. She knew that she had a strong family history of diabetes, as well as heart disease, and was determined not to fall into those patterns.

A family history of heart disease predicts heart disease in women as well as men. Having a parent with a history of a heart attack before age sixty increases the risk of heart attack or angina for women. This effect is significant whether the parent is a mother or a father. We do not know if this risk is due to a familial clustering of specific risk factors like hypertension or diabetes, or to some, as yet unidentified, genetic factors. Although we can do nothing about our genetic heritage, we can minimize our other risk factors. For example, Ellen's father died of a heart attack at age forty-six, another reason that her symptoms of chest pain were of such concern to her and why she was so motivated to make changes. We worked with Ellen to cut the fat in her diet, rather than to dramatically cut calories, and this plan of action seemed to work for her.

There has been some research done on the relationship between various *hormonal factors* and the development of heart disease in women. There appears to be no association between age of menstruation, number of pregnancies, age at first pregnancy and the risk of developing heart disease. There is also no evidence that *natural menopause* per se increases a women's risk of heart disease. In other words, in the immediate period after natural menopause there is no abrupt change in the risk of developing heart disease. The risk of heart disease increases gradually with age in the years after menopause.

In contrast, we know there is an association between *early surgical menopause* and risk of heart disease. Early surgical menopause is defined as the removal of the uterus and ovaries prior to the expected age of natural menopause. Because the increased risk of heart disease is well documented in women with early surgical menopause, most physicians agree that they should be on HRT. Most doctors also favor the use of HRT in women who experience early menopause for other reasons like chemotherapy for cancer, or primary ovarian failure.

Should all postmenopausal women be put on *hormone replacement* for this reason? Most of the studies that were done in the 1970s and 1980s placed women on estrogen (ERT) alone, which was the standard of care at that time, not on HRT which combines estrogen with progesterone, so we know little about progesterone's effects. While there have been quite a few studies to date on the subject of ERT, most have been so small and lasted such a short period of time that it has been difficult to draw definite conclusions. *Nonetheless, the majority of studies support the conclusion that there is a reduction in the risk of coronary disease with ERT.*

There has been concern that the addition of progesterone to estrogen therapy would reduce the positive effects of estrogen alone on the heart. This is why most experts advise that the dose of progesterone should be as low as possible to still prevent endometrial cancer while maximizing the positive effects of estrogen on the heart (U.S. Congress, 1992). To the surprise of many, the most recent information suggests that estrogen and progesterone combined may be even more protective than estrogen alone (Nabulsi and others, 1993).

Are you confused? You are not alone. The fact is that this is a key issue in women's health that deserves attention. The good news is that there are several long-term studies underway to further evaluate this. The Women's Health Initiative, a large study of 160,000 women which was started in the fall of 1993, will follow women between the ages of fifty to seventy-nine for twelve years looking for the development of specific types of cancer and cardiovascular disease (Associated Press, 1993). There will also be a smaller group of women within the study who will be treated with different hormone regimens, calcium and vitamin D, as well as a low-fat diet, and followed for changes in their cholesterol, heart disease, cancer rates and osteoporosis.

✦ PSYCHOLOGICAL FACTORS

There has been a great interest in the psychological and social factors that affect the development of coronary heart disease in males. Much has been written about the development of a Type A personality, classically portrayed as the hard-driving individual. First identified in 1959, by Drs. Friedman and Ronsenman, the Type A personality was noted to be frenetic, impatient, high-achieving and competitive. These authors suggested that people with Type A personalities needed to learn to relax and become calmer in order to lower the risks for cardiovascular disease (Friedman and Rosenman, 1974).

Since that time, the relationship between Type A behaviors and risk of heart attacks has been examined. As is frequently the case in behavioral science research, there are problems with the measurements used and the global generalizations that are drawn from the studies. It is the *hostility* of the Type A personality that is most associated with cardiovascular disease. Others hypothesize that it is not Type A behavior, but the personality traits of freneticism and authoritarianism that are the culprits. So, although the Type A question is still somewhat controversial, there is evidence that being hostile is not healthy for our hearts!

Of course, there is another problem with the original research regarding psychological and social factors and coronary heart disease: it was—*surprise!*—limited primarily to white male patients. Now there is a growing body of research on women and minorities with Type A behaviors. Type A behaviors have been associated with stress in African-American men and women. One study of employed white women found that Type A's were less satisfied with their work, worked longer hours, and had been in their current jobs for a shorter time than the Type Bs. In addition, the Type As reported more nervousness in all situations than did the Type Bs. A study of employed African-American women revealed that Type A women were more likely to have higher blood pressure, higher cholesterol and lower coping scores than were Type B.

Some new intriguing studies of sex differences in anger and hostility are now emerging. It seems that men and women experience similar levels of anger, but that men express anger in a more aggressive manner. Women tend to express anger within an interpersonal context, with an emphasis on the specific relationship. Men tend to add the hostility factor. Clearly, this is a new and growing area of research.

✦ SOCIAL FACTORS

Given the acceptance that Type As have more cardiovascular risk, there was concern that as women entered the work force in large numbers there would be increasing numbers of women with heart disease. As women, we were warned against working full-time or pursuing high-powered careers. This fear has been unfounded. In fact, working outside the home *per se* has no effect on the likelihood of developing heart disease, but there are certain characteristics of the work situation which do appear to be important in its development. The clerical, or "pink-collar" workers who have unsupportive bosses, suppressed hostility and decreased job mobility have been shown to have a higher rate of heart disease than other women. It seems that these women are stressed by their lack of control, high level of responsibility and the underutilization of their skills. The group of women at highest risk for heart disease are clerical women who have three or more children and who are married to blue-collar men (Haynes, Feinleib & Kannel, 1980). Their rates of heart disease were as high as those for men in white-collar jobs—the highest-risk occupational group. Perhaps we should worry more about the hostility of some Type A men and how they treat their secretaries than we should about women becoming executives.

Stress itself can cause physiological changes in heart functioning. One study of Swedish women found that women whose jobs were both hectic and monotonous had one and a half times greater risk of developing coronary artery disease over a ten-year period. If you are one of the many women whose jobs are stressful, hectic or monotonous, this is not meant to frighten you. Your feelings should be validated by this knowledge because you already know that stress isn't good for you. Many women feel trapped by their jobs, especially when they're given little credit for their tremendous efforts.

It is not particularly helpful for us to tell you that if you have a difficult job situation, you are more likely to have heart disease, without making some additional suggestions. Once again, we don't want our advice to add stress to your life. So you will see in the following section ways in which you can do the best to change your occupational situation. Many women have found that they have more power than they know, and we want to help you gain access to that power.

✦ PREVENTING THE DEVELOPMENT OF HEART DISEASE

Now is the time to make changes in your habits and health care that can decrease your chance of heart disease.

SMOKING CESSATION

If you smoke, you should now know that stopping is critical to improved heart health. It is absolutely clear that smoking will damage your cardiovascular system; can cause cancers of the head and neck and lungs; and harms those around you who are exposed to your second-hand smoke. We know from our patients who smoke that quitting can be excruciatingly difficult. There is hope, however, as the science of smoking cessation improves. Remember that your risk of heart disease will decline within one to five years of quitting to where it would have been *if you had never smoked*.

There are many programs available. The local chapters of the American Lung Association and the American Heart Association, or your state health department should have listings of these for you. Many hospitals and work sites now run cessation programs. You should try to find out who runs the programs and whether their effectiveness has been evaluated. For example, what are the quit rates of smokers in these programs. Medication, including the nicotine patch or nicotine gum, can be prescribed by your health care professional or as part of the program you join. The best approach is to combine the use of nicotine gum or the transdermal nicotine patch with counseling. Most insurance programs will pay for the gum and at least one trial of the patch. Remember that the goal is to quit. Women are not as successful at quitting as men, but there are several important lessons we can learn from this difference. Because women are more likely to use smoking to control weight or to make them feel better in stressful situations, it is critical to their success that weight control and stress reduction are handled simultaneously. Do not be discouraged if it takes many attempts. As you will see in our chapter on healthy aging, the science of changing behavior is developing rapidly and can help you attack this difficult problem.

COPING WITH JOB STRESS

Problems at work can be a chronic stress on our health. Extremely difficult careers, like Ellen's, can lead to repressed anger or hostility that we know is a risk factor for heart disease. So it's a good idea to develop coping skills for dealing with job stress.

Ellen had left her stressful job behind, but she had a lot of good advice for younger nurses and other women who worked in stressful occupations. One of the best ways Ellen had of coping with her stresses in the cardiac care unit was her involvement with her social network of other nurses and staff members at the hospital.

Ellen and her colleagues at the hospital had developed educational programs for their patients, and eventually for themselves. One of the patient education programs was about the stress of cardiac procedures. In the process of preparing this program, Ellen and her colleagues realized they could also benefit from their own training session in stress management. They asked the hospital's health psychologist to teach them relaxation techniques. They also learned that they could make some small changes to reduce stress and prevent burnout. For example, they helped one another take "time-out" if one of them had a challenging patient or a stressful care situation.

Informal organizations of one or two women can be helpful in providing the social support that we have discussed. By talking about the common problems of the job, women can work together to take control of their own abilities to change. This can be a small step, like better exercise facilities on the job. Women can also organize in order to make more significant changes within their workplace. Ellen helped the younger nurses establish twelve-hour shifts so that they could spend more time with their young families, working fewer days per week. Most women are concerned about greater flexibility and the possibility of family-leave time. Some women employ job sharing for this reason.

Ellen felt "burnt out" by the age of fifty-four, despite all she had been able to accomplish at work. She found it to be extremely helpful to consider her alternatives. She had a partial pension but felt that it was not adequate. She began to think of a way she could work half-time in order to support herself. In addition, this would help her maintain some health insurance benefits, as well as some retirement benefits. For now, she works "per diem," or paid on a daily basis, in a variety of hospital settings. This variety has allowed her to use her substantial skills, meet new people, and view nursing as a profession from a more optimistic and powerful perspective.

PHYSICAL ACTIVITY

For many of us, a lifestyle that included physical activity was not fostered at an early age, but what we may learn is that a daily routine filled with physical activity can be quite pleasurable. You will note that we are not using the word "exercise" at this point. That is because, although exercise, structured and routine physical activity, is important, so is general lifestyle change. Consider this: you can get a lot of benefit for your heart just by beginning to incorporate some modest *physical activity*. Even small amounts of physical activity cannot only be beneficial, but actually fun. Several studies, once again conducted only on men, unfortunately, find that you can reduce the risk of heart attacks by up to 20 percent just by such activities as a fifteen-minute walk each day. There are numerous small changes you can make in your lifestyle as well—taking the stairs instead of the elevator, not looking for the parking place closest to the store, walking rather than driving short distances and so on. For most women we find that this is a basic change in attitude, part of a commitment to become physically active.

In general, women *exercise* much less than men, so it's not surprising that there are fewer studies looking at the role of exercise in the prevention of heart disease in women. At least one study though, suggests that regular exercise may prevent coronary heart disease in women (Douglas and others, 1992). Exercise has a favorable effect on cholesterol, but for women, moderate to intensive efforts may be necessary to produce significant improvements in this area. There also may be some benefit for women who have already had a heart attack.

Maximal cardiovascular fitness requires regular moderate aerobic activity. This can be done, for example, by walking twenty-five to thirty minutes a day or sixty minutes three times a week at 3 to 3.5 miles an hour. Table 5-1 depicts an exercise program for heart health. Other examples of aerobic exercise include low-impact or step aerobics, bicycling, using a stationary bicycle or treadmill. Begin any exercise with a five-minute warm-up time to stretch and limber up to prevent any injuries.

Most importantly, before starting an exercise program, you should consult with your physician. The benefits of exercise for women extend beyond the risk of heart disease. Many women have found that exercise (particularly enjoyable exercise) is also a major stress management tool. Identifying and maintaining an exercise plan is one of the most beneficial decisions that we can make during our menopausal years.

HEART-HEALTHY NUTRITION

When considering a healthy diet to prevent heart disease, as with all diets, we feel that the basic tenets of common sense combined with sensitivity should prevail.

When we talked with Ellen regarding her diet, we concentrated on her concerns to prevent heart disease rather than just focusing on calories alone. We suggested that she try to cut down her total fat intake, specifically saturated fat intake. Saturated fat comes from meat, dairy and certain fish products as well as from vegetable sources including palm oil and coconuts. Saturated fat actually interferes with the body's ability to remove excess cholesterol. Polyunsaturated fats, which include corn, safflower, sunflower and soybean oils, can help the body to remove excess cholesterol.

When Ellen came to see us, she had routine blood work that showed an elevated LDL level. This put her at additional risk for the development of heart disease and really motivated her to develop a diet and exercise program. Specific changes in diet should be considered for any woman with an elevated LDL cholesterol. No restrictions should be recommended without knowledge of the woman's HDL

Table 5–1

FIT PROGRAM FOR
HEALTHY HEARTS

Purpose: Maximum cardiovascular fitness

Frequency: Start: 2–3 times per week
Goal: 3–4 times per week

Intensity: Start: moderate—about 65% maximum
heart rate
Goal: more vigorous 70–80% maximum
heart rate

Time: Start: 2–5 minutes, repeat 2–3 times
Increase about every 2 weeks by 5 minutes
8–10 minutes, repeat 2–3 times
Gradually increase.
Goal: 20–30 minutes continuous activity
per session

Types: Large muscles, continuous repetitive
motion.
Examples: Walking, Biking, Swimming
Low- or high-impact aerobics
Step aerobics
Jogging (after 1–2 months)
Racketball

and LDL cholesterol. Many women, even after menopause, will have high HDL (the good) cholesterol levels, which will increase their total cholesterol levels. Your physician's recommendation should be specially tailored to you and your health needs, and not based on some generalizations about ideal body weight or cholesterol values for men.

Ellen was relieved when we did not lecture her about her weight. We shared with her our philosophy that women should not be ashamed of the natural change in their bodies over time. We helped Ellen see that she would do much better at controlling her weight if she focused on physical activity and a low-fat diet, not caloric intake. As women, we have all been conditioned to be preoccupied with our caloric intake while at the same time serving as the main cooks for our families and friends. Men, on the other hand, are less likely to be involved in food preparation and tend to have incorporated exercise into their lifestyle. If, for example, we choose to watch our weight during menopause, we need to focus more on weight-bearing exercises and building muscle mass. These activities may help to get us out of the kitchen, and allow us to worry less about the number of calories consumed. If we continue to exercise and focus on our health, we will not only be in better physical shape, but our psychological attitude toward aging will improve as well.

Ellen was like most people in this country, consuming a diet containing 35 to 42 percent fat. The Surgeon General recommends diets containing less than 30 percent fat with 10 percent from saturated fat and 20 percent from unsaturated fat (Consumer Reports, 1992). However, many experts feel that the percent of fat should be even lower. There are several different nutritional plans to choose from including one from the American Heart Association.

For example, one simple change that Ellen made was to change her snack foods. Ellen tended to munch on potato chips. This is problematic since potato chips have ten times as much fat as pretzels. So, just by switching to pretzels, Ellen reduced her fat intake. Ellen was also surprised to learn that not all pizza is created equal when it comes to fat. For example, one frozen pizza brand contains 50 percent of its calories from fat, and another only 12 percent. All the more reason to read the labels! (Friedman, 1993).

For those of us who are watching our weight, it is important to remember to "let the buyer beware." The diet industry in the United States is a profit-oriented business, and we are likely to be lured by false advertising. A recent study by the New York State Consumer Protection Board found that of five products labeled as "diet" foods, all of them had at least 20 percent more calories than the amount specified. Of twenty products analyzed, sixteen exceeded by anywhere from 2 to 49 percent. This is true despite a federal law prohibiting such deception (Gershoff, 1992). The dramatic "before and after" photos in many television advertisements for diet programs may well be one or two women in a program of one hundred. The diet industry routinely exploits women by making false promises of quick success. A review of all the major diet programs by *Consumer Reports* found very few differences in how much weight people lost, so there's no need to spend a lot of money, in the hopes of a miracle cure (Losing Weight, 1993).

Some notions about nutrition are changing. We now know that sodium restriction is not necessary for everyone. While it is true that women with high blood pressure should restrict salt intake, salt restriction does not maintain heart health for all women. So if you do not have high blood pressure, you do not need to worry that much about restricting your salt intake.

Recent reports from the Nurses' Health Study suggest that adequate vitamin E in your diet may reduce your risk of cardiovascular disease (Stampfer and others, 1993). For this reason, some physicians recommend taking 400 International Units of vitamin E daily.

Moderate alcohol consumption has been found to have a beneficial effect on cholesterol, specifically by raising the HDL cholesterol. There are several reasons for women to be cautious about this information. Most of the earlier data to support this is derived from male populations. So-called "moderate" drinking is also different for males and females. Women cannot drink as much as men; they develop more serious consequences from drinking smaller amounts for shorter periods of time than men do. The evidence that moderate alcohol consumption increases HDL cholesterol in women is actually limited. Beware of advice to drink one to two glasses of wine per day to increase your HDL, because the risks greatly outweigh the potential benefits for women.

✦ When Is Medication Indicated?

Treating *hypertension* in women has not been evaluated in depth and may involve some racial differences. It is clear that antihypertensive medication benefits black women with high blood pressure, but it is not clear if white women receive the same benefit from treatment of borderline high blood pressure. Clearly, there is a need for new long-term studies of women with hypertension, using some of the newer blood-pressure agents before we can draw meaningful conclusions about medication for hypertension. In the meantime, blood pressure should be treated on an individual basis with diet, exercise and a reduction of alcohol intake. Medication should be discussed with your primary care professional.

Treatment of *diabetes* begins again with diet and exercise. The majority of women who develop diabetes in their forties and fifties have type II diabetes, once called adult onset diabetes, which tends to develop gradually. It is especially responsive to diet and exercise. In some cases, a medication may be added, and less often a woman will need to be treated with insulin.

Most clinicians feel that a total *cholesterol* above 260–300 should be treated. Diet is always the first line of therapy. If diet is not successful in lowering cholesterol in six to nine months, drug therapy should be considered. Further information about the type of medications used is available from the American Heart Association brochures or from your physician.

Studies in men suggest that *aspirin* is an effective medication to prevent heart attacks. It makes sense that aspirin might have this effect since it makes platelets (clotting cells) less likely to form clots. In a Nurses' Health Study report, it was suggested that women who took one to six aspirin per week were less likely to have a fatal heart attack than those who took no aspirin (Manson and others, 1991). However, taking more than seven aspirin per week had no benefit. You should talk this over with your primary care professional to consider your own risks and benefits.

At menopause, *hormone replacement therapy* can be considered to prevent heart disease. The risks and benefits of HRT must be carefully weighed, as we detail in Chapter Six, "Hormone Replacement Therapy." The type of HRT is important when considering heart disease prevention. Much of the information on the beneficial effect of HRT on heart disease is based on studies of estrogen alone. The information on progesterone is conflicting, as we discussed (Grady and others, 1992).

✦ COMMUNICATION

Perhaps Ellen's greatest frustration came when her physician colleague did not take her symptoms seriously. This example is the most ironic, but many women with concerns about cardiovascular disease are faced with the problem of being dismissed when they try to communicate with their health care professional. One way to deal with the situation is to develop a specific and assertive approach.

For their annual visits, many women in their thirties and forties choose to see only an obstetrician/gynecologist who is focused on gynecological problems and prevention of breast and gynecological cancer. As we age, our needs for screening become more complex. If you have not already done so, you should identify a primary care professional who will emphasize prevention, help you to assess your personal risks and determine the lifestyle changes that will be most beneficial to your health.

Most women between the ages of forty-five and fifty-five do not have heart problems, so prevention is the most important aspect of the menopausal years. However, some women do experience chest pain. This symptom may or may not represent serious cardiac disease. For example, palpitations and chest discomfort may occur as part of menopausal symptoms. Your symptoms may be caused by one of the numerous non–heart-related chest-pain syndromes. Whatever the cause, these symptoms can be quite frightening and need to be taken seriously. The first step to getting some answers is to identify an appropriate primary care professional.

Once you have identified a primary care professional whom you trust, you need to consider how to maximize communication. Many features of the current health care system work against this. There is relatively little time scheduled for each patient so you need to come into the office armed with your questions and concerns. You may want to anticipate the answers and be ready with the next level of questions.

In order to prepare yourself for conversation with your clinician, consider the following scenarios:

> Your clinician says something like, "I don't think you are at increased risk for heart disease."
> You may ask, "Why not?"
> He/she says, "Women are less likely to have heart disease."
> You may ask, "What about the role of [any risk factor you have] and my increasing risk of heart disease with age?"

If you need a workup for heart disease, you might consider your needs for medical information. For example, there are two major categories of patients: repressors and sensitizers. Repressors (avoiders) tend to cope with stress by not thinking about it or distracting themselves. These patients do not appear to be anxious. Sensitizers, on the other hand, are anxious and handle the anxiety by gathering information and by paying careful attention to details. You probably already know if you are a sensitizer or a repressor. If you are a repressor, you might want a small amount of general information, and if you are a sensitizer, you'll want more detail. Be sure to let your physician and the rest of the staff know your needs in this area. Medical tests and procedures like cardiac-stress testing can be stressful—psychologically. But the tests are meant to evaluate your cardiovascular system—not stress your psyche! Hospital environments can be intimidating and the high-tech equipment can look and sound frightening. Sometimes health care professionals have grown so accustomed to the environment, that they forget that it is foreign to most other people. We have found that it is important to discuss these tests and procedures in some detail. As a patient, you have a right to know the answers to these questions: What does the test involve? Is it painful? Is it uncomfortable? What will the results mean? What is the cost? Will insurance cover it? When and how will I learn the results? What is the next step if the test is positive? Most studies have found that patients feel less anxious when provided with this information. But others have found that it depends on the needs and personality styles of the individual.

Over time, you will get a sense of whether your physician is taking your symptoms or health concerns seriously. We have found that many of our patients have changed their doctors over the issue of evaluation and treatment of chest pain and even known coronary disease. Ellen had always had a good relationship with her clinician and even worked side by side with him in the coronary care unit, but she came to us thoroughly annoyed when he dismissed her symptoms of chest pain.

COMMUNICATING WITH YOUR FAMILY

Women function as the caretakers of the entire family—the cook, the pill dispenser, the one who finds the health care and the one who remembers the appointments. They often admit to us that they neglect their own health concerns because they feel they already have too much to worry about. Many women in their fifties are experiencing the refilled nest (i.e., their children are moving back in the house again for financial reasons). In some cases, their children are dependent on them for care of the grandchildren. For many reasons family members may not be sensitive to the perimenopausal woman's health and other needs.

Marjorie and her husband sold their profitable gourmet food shop and were fortunate to be able to retire in their early fifties. Marjorie and Jim had been good partners in their business, enjoyed working together and deeply respected one another. When their two children were young, Marjorie had worked in the shop less. Like most women, she took the larger share of family and household responsibilities. Now, she was looking forward to early retirement and the time it would allow her to take off twenty pounds, start exercising regularly and get her blood pressure under control. When Marjorie came back to see us three months after she retired, she was five pounds heavier and her blood pressure was even higher. She told us at that time that she was off to help one of her children paint a new house. When we discussed exercise in order to help her with her weight, as well as her blood pressure, she burst into tears and confessed that she had even less time for herself than she did when she was working! She and her husband had used their savings to help one child start a business and another buy a house, instead of buying the RV they wanted. Although her husband was enjoying golf four times a week, Marjorie found that somehow she had no time to exercise and was eating more. She was frustrated and sad.

When we examined the family dynamics, we all realized that Marjorie and the whole family had raised their expectations of her. Jim was viewed as the "retired exec." who had earned his leisure, whereas Marjorie had become the suddenly available grandmother. She and her children now believed that she should help out with the grandchildren, run errands and be generally available. She felt this way because both her daughter and her daughter-in-law were working full-time in jobs that did not offer as much flexibility as Marjorie had had in the shop. Marjorie, like many women, used food as a quick pick-me-up when she was overcommitted and tired. And we can understand that tendency. Food is tasty, available and a deep part of our female culture. Yet, in this case, it was becoming dangerous to Marjorie's health.

We worked with Marjorie to help her change the family dynamics. We pointed out that her children were now twenty-five and twenty-seven years old and fully able to manage their family lives without so much help from Mom. She could still enjoy being helpful to her two children and their families, without doing quite so much. We then pointed out that the problems needed to be reframed. It was not that her daughter and daughter-in-law worked outside of the home but that *both parents* worked, and therefore both parents needed to look at the responsibilities of the family. We discuss the problems of employed women in our chapter on stress. Besides, Jim was retired now, too, and therefore could be more available. (A little consciousness-raising for two generations at a time!)

We helped Marjorie find a way to explain this to her children. We then encouraged Marjorie to use the same problem-solving skills that she and Jim had used in the business with her weight and exercise concerns. She tried it this way: "Jim, remember how when we expanded the shop, we developed a plan? Well, I need your help now in creating a plan for me to have more time to exercise." This began the conversation. Marjorie was not interested in joining Jim on the golf course. ("Boring!") Marjorie joined the Jewish Community Center where she could swim—an activity she enjoyed as a young adult. (We needed to do a quick session on overcoming exposed-thigh anxiety). Jim cut back his golf to three times a week so he could help more with the house and be available for any grandparenting duties. Marjorie, having met some young mothers at the pool, came home one day and said, "Jim, we didn't co-parent, but we can certainly co-grandparent!"

Now, it wasn't quite that easy all the time. Everyone in the family system, and indeed, all of us expect a lot from mothers and grandmothers. We are particularly busy helping women set limits around the holiday seasons. ("You are the *only one* who can bake the Christmas cookies?" or "You have to do *all* of Passover alone?" You get the picture.) Yet there are many possible ways to change the family dynamics. You need to remember first that you have responded to the needs of your family members and should not feel uncomfortable asking for the same consideration. This is an ideal time in your life to make some changes in your habits and in your family role, but it is not always easy. Family dynamics *can* shift even in the menopausal years. You may well meet some resistance, but push through your initial avoidance of conflict. Changing doesn't mean rejecting your family, it just means changing.

If the direct approach with your family does not work, you can also try asking a family member to come to the physician's office with you. Hearing from your physician or health care provider that changes in the family's schedules, meals or physical activity are *necessary* for your health may make an impact on your spouse or child. If none of these approaches work, you might want to try family counseling, which we describe more in chapters on stress and depression. The menopausal years are a time when it is necessary to make these changes. There is a lot of time left to live, and we need to take some for ourselves in order to maintain and improve our health.

RESOURCES

There are numerous and growing resources for women who have concerns about coronary-artery disease. Additional resources for smoking cessation, nutrition and exercise are listed in the prevention section.

THE FEDERAL GOVERNMENT

National Heart, Lung and Blood Institute (NHLBI)
Information Center
P.O. Box 30105
Bethesda, MD 20824-0105
(301) 951-3260

The NHLBI Information Center provides education materials on high blood pressure, cholesterol, smoking, obesity and heart disease. It publishes an excellent handbook for women on heart disease entitled The Healthy Heart Handbook for Women *as well as many different brochures on risk factors for heart disease. A directory of publications is available.*

Food and Drug Administration (FDA)
Office of Consumer Affairs, HFE-88
5600 Fishers Lane
Rockville, MD 20857
(301) 443-3170

The FDA publishes on diverse topics, including general drug information, medical devices, and food-related subjects, including fiber, fats, sodium, and cholesterol. Their newsletter, FDA Consumer, *has covered such relevant topics as: heart bypass surgery, balloon angioplasty, dieting and nutrition for women. Subscriptions can be ordered through a Consumer Information Center (CIC) catalogue. Educational brochures are also available through the CIC catalog. A free copy of the catalog can be obtained by writing the* **Consumer Information Center, Pueblo, CO 81009.**

Food and Nutrition Information Center (FNIC)
National Agricultural Library
10301 Baltimore Avenue, Room 304
Beltsville, MD 20705-2351
(301) 504-5719

The FNIC answers questions concerning nutrition, foods, and food labeling. They provide bibliographies and resource guides on a wide variety of food and nutrition topics.

Human Nutrition Information Service (HNIS)
Department of Agriculture
6505 Belcrest Road
Room 328A
Hyattsville, MD 20782
(301) 436-8617

HNIS reports results of research on food consumption and dietary guidance in popular publications. A list of DEA publications is available.

Office on Smoking and Health (OSH)
Center for Chronic Disease Prevention and Health Promotion
Mail Stop K-50
Centers for Disease Control
1600 Clifton Road, NE
Atlanta, Georgia 30333
(404) 488-5705

This office provides information and brochures on smoking cessation free of charge to the public.

ASSOCIATIONS

American Heart Association (AHA)
National Center
7320 Greenville Avenue
Dallas, TX 75231
(214) 373-6300

The AHA is probably the most available and well known of all resources. It provides pamphlets and other educational materials not only on heart disease but also on prevention, smoking, nutrition and exercise. In 1989 the AHA held a national meeting in Washington on Women and Coronary Artery Disease which resulted in new educational materials, including a videotape and a brochure entitled Women and Heart Disease: The Silent Epidemic. *Most local offices of the AHA now have a task force on women and heart disease, which, among other activities, will provide speakers on the subject to community groups. Local offices of the AHA offer support groups, classes in CPR, and all of the brochures are free to the individual. This is an important resource for anyone concerned with cardiovascular disease.*

American Lung Association
1740 Broadway
New York, NY 10019-4374
212-315-8700

Local offices of the lung association are an excellent resource for smoking programs that are available in the community as well as for educational materials—videos, manuals and brochures on smoking cessation. You can reach your local office by dialing 1-800-586-4872.

American Diabetes Association
1660 Duke Street
Alexandria, VA 22314
(800) 232-3472; (703)5549-1500

The ADA offers programs and information about diabetes prevention and treatment. Local chapters provide patient and family education activities as well as patient education publications. There is a catalog of publications and products. Membership, which includes a monthly newsletter, "Diabetes Forecast," is $24.

The Women's Health Initiative *is looking for women between the ages of fifty and seventy-nine. This study of 160,00 women is the largest women's health study to date. If you are interested in participating, you can call 301-402-2900 and this office will send you a brief summary of the study and a list of the participating centers. The study, which began in September 1993, will be recruiting patients until late 1995.*

BOOKS

1. *Lowfat Low Cholesterol Cookbook* edited by Scott Grundy, M.D., and Mary Winston, Ed.D. (American Heart Association) (New York: Random House, 1989).

   This book provides creative low-fat recipes, as well as nutritional information.

   2. *Women and Heart Disease:* What You Can Do to Stop the Number One Killer of Women by Edward B. Dietrich and Carol Cohan (New York: Random House, 1992).

   This is a good overview of the subject.

   3. *Our Bodies, Getting Older,* and *Our Bodies, Ourselves,* both published by the Boston Women's Health Book Collective (New York: Simon and Schuster, 1976).

   Both books have chapters on healthy lifestyles. These are two of the best books we know for helping women take charge of their health.

MAGAZINES

Prevention Magazine
Customer Communications
Rodale Press
33 E. Minor St.
Emmaus, PA 18098
(215) 967-5171

PHARMACEUTICAL COMPANY PUBLICATION

CardiSense
P.O. Box 549158
Miami, FL 33054-9875

CardiSense is a free quarterly newsletter published by Marion Merrill Dow, Inc. It includes information about exercise and health promotion.

SELF-HELP GROUPS

Most general medical hospitals with cardiac units provide support groups and educational programs for patients with heart disease and their families. Local chapters of the American Heart Association also sponsor support groups for people who have had heart attacks and their families. We have devoted attention to support groups for exercise and other lifestyle changes in our chapter on promoting a healthy lifestyle (Chapter Ten).

CHAPTER SIX

Hormone Replacement Therapy

Isn't it ironic that for most of our lives hormones have been blamed for any number of behavioral and mood impairments and are now being touted as the cure-all for what ails us at menopause? It is no wonder that we are a bit leery about estrogen. After all, many of us are the survivors of birth control pills, which initially were promoted as the answer to all of our contraceptive prayers, but later were linked to heart attacks, blood clots and cancer. Nonetheless, for most women who are approaching menopause one of the most significant decisions they will make is whether or not to take estrogen. For some women, the decision is made deliberately after careful consideration of the information available. For others, it is made based on a philosophical stance against tampering with natural events. For still others, it is made by default when the issue is not addressed specifically. Each of these positions has merit, but it is important for everyone to have access to the facts about hormone replacement therapy (HRT). We have found at our menopause town meetings that the question of hormone replacement therapy is at the top of everyone's list. This chapter provides a framework of knowledge for women who are considering HRT.

✦ HORMONAL CHANGES

During the time around menopause, our ovaries' production of the hormone estrogen begins to gradually decline. Estrogen is produced predominantly by the ovaries although it is also produced in smaller amounts by fat tissue and the adrenal glands. When the ovaries are surgically removed, as is often done with hysterectomy, the decline in estrogen is abrupt and complete. The majority of us will experience a gradual decline as we follow the course of natural menopause. As the blood levels of estrogen produced by the ovaries begin to decrease, the brain's pituitary gland senses the lowered levels. In essence, our pituitary gland functions as a thermostat for estrogen, as well as other hormones. When the levels of estrogen fall below the present normal level, the pituitary gland responds by producing stimulating hormones to increase the ovaries' estrogen production.

As the ovaries' ability to produce estrogen continues to diminish, the pituitary gland increases its production of stimulating hormones to stoke the fires of the ovaries. These stimulating hormones are called FSH (follicle-stimulating hormone) and LH (luteinizing hormone). FSH and LH can be measured by a simple blood test. When the level of FSH rises above 40 MIU/ml, this is considered diagnostic of menopause. It may not be entirely obvious to you why FSH and LH are measured to diagnose menopause when the primary problem is decreasing estrogen levels. The reason is that the normal cyclic changes in estrogen levels and the tremendous individual variation make the interpretation of testing estrogen directly difficult. The stimulating hormones give information about the adequacy of estrogen levels for each individual woman as detected by her own pituitary gland. If the estrogen levels are too low, the stimulating hormones will be high, and conversely if estrogen levels are normal, the stimulating hormones will be unusually low.

✦ WHAT IS HORMONE REPLACEMENT THERAPY?

Hormone replacement therapy implies that hormones are being replaced to a level that is considered currently or previously normal. For menopause, the normal levels refer to premenopausal hormone levels. This is extremely important since many of the symptoms of menopause are directly attributable to the lower levels of estrogen produced by the ovaries as compared to the premenopausal levels. Estrogen is the specific hormone which is replaced to a premenopausal level when HRT is used.

Although birth control pills are considered hormone therapy, they do not represent hormone replacement therapy since they are being added to already normal levels of estrogen. Many comparisons have been made between birth control pills and estrogen used for menopausal symptoms, but there is the important distinction between *replacement* in the case of menopause and *addition* in the case of birth control pills. This distinction becomes particularly important when the side effects of estrogen are considered. Menopausal women who are treated with estrogen have blood levels of estrogen at the low-end of normal, in contrast to younger women who are being treated with birth control pills and who have high levels of estrogen. In fact, menopausal women taking the usual dose of estrogen replacement therapy have estrogen levels that would be considered very low for premenopausal women.

The major hormone player in menopause is estrogen. Estrogen has been shown to be highly effective when used for a number of symptoms associated with menopause. This information has led scientists to conclude that conditions such as hot flashes, vaginal dryness and osteoporosis are directly or indirectly related to the extremely low levels of estrogen associated with menopause.

The additional hormone often included in hormone replacement therapy is progesterone. Progesterone is not specifically responsible for the conditions associated with menopause, but is added to estrogen therapy to prevent some of the complications which occur when estrogen is used alone. In the normal premenopausal menstrual cycle, estrogen is the hormone which allows the lining of the uterus to build up in preparation for a potential pregnancy. If the egg does not become fertilized and mature, then progesterone levels increase and cause the shedding of the built-up uterine lining (endometrium), causing menstrual bleeding. In this way, progesterone stops the buildup of the uterine lining, which would otherwise continue if estrogen were the only hormone available.

In the case of hormone replacement with both estrogen and progesterone, it is the estrogen which treats the conditions associated with low estrogen levels, and it is progesterone which prevents the continued buildup of the endometrium. The accumulation of the uterine lining puts women at a greater risk for endometrial cancer. For a woman who has no uterus (i.e., who has had a hysterectomy), the addition of progesterone is unnecessary.

✦ PILLS, POTIONS, PATCHES, PELLETS AND PLANTS

Carolyn is a fifty-year-old waitress who had a hysterectomy at age forty-five for severe bleeding from uterine fibroid tumors. She did not have her ovaries removed at the time of her hysterectomy. Several months before her annual appointment, she had begun to experience hot flashes and was wondering whether she was going through menopause. Carolyn is like almost 30 percent of American women who, because they have no uterus, do not have the usual marker of the absence of their menstrual periods. This makes diagnosing menopause more difficult than it is for a woman who does have her uterus. Carolyn had blood tests drawn, including an FSH and LH. Menopause was diagnosed when Carolyn's FSH returned at 60 MIU/ml. (anything above 40 is consistent with menopause). Carolyn decided that her hot flashes were beginning to interfere with her work and chose to begin therapy with the estrogen patch. She felt that she would probably continue estrogen therapy indefinitely because she was very concerned about osteoporosis, since she had been told on numerous occasions that she was at high risk because she was extremely small, had never consumed adequate amounts of calcium, and did not exercise beyond that which she did at work.

As is often the case, we needed to tinker a bit with her treatment to minimize problems. When Carolyn developed local skin irritation at the site of the patch, we advised her to wave the patch in the air to remove some of the alcohol prior to applying it and to apply it to her buttocks. These simple maneuvers relieved the problem and she continues to use the patch twice weekly.

We can see from Carolyn's example that the manner in which women take the estrogen portion of their hormone replacement therapy can vary. The most well-studied form of estrogen has been estrogen tablets taken by mouth. The estrogen available in these tablets is called conjugated estrogen and the most frequently prescribed form is derived from *pre*gnant *mare*s' ur*ine* and is called Premarin. The dose of conjugated estrogen necessary to control the symptoms of menopause is usually in the range of 0.625 mg per day to 1.25 mg per day. Some women get relief of hot flashes, specifically, with as little as 0.3 mg per day, but the dose needed to prevent osteoporosis is 0.625 mg per day.

Vaginal estrogen creams have also been used for some time to control vaginal dryness. The creams provide estrogen directly to the area that is symptomatic. We now know that there is also absorption of the estrogen hormone through the vaginal lining into the blood-stream. In this way, women who use vaginal creams absorb estrogen as if they were taking it as a pill. The difference between vaginal creams and pills or patches is that the amounts of estrogen absorbed using the cream are generally lower, but less predictable and more erratic. It is also clear that vaginal estrogen creams have some of the same side effects and complications as oral estrogen taken alone.

The newer form of estrogen is the estrogen transdermal patch which has gained a great deal of popularity. The estrogen patch allows a woman to receive estrogen replacement therapy through the skin. The usual dose of estrogen required by patch is 0.05 mg or 0.10 mg, replaced twice a week. Initially, it was feared that some of the cardio-vascular benefits of estrogen taken orally would be lost if the patch were used instead. This has not been proven in further study. It was, additionally, an early concern that the patch may not have the same beneficial effect on osteoporosis since all of the studies of osteoporosis had been done with estrogen taken orally. Not surprisingly, it is now known that estrogen which enters the body through the skin has an equivalent protective effect against osteoporosis.

There are many new forms of estrogen being developed. Estrogen pellets are implanted below the skin and release estrogen continuously, thereby eliminating the need to take a pill every day. However, women who have not had hysterectomies still require progesterone. In very rare circumstances estrogen is injected into the muscle. In Europe, estrogen is now available in a gel which is applied to the abdomen. Soon to be approved is an estrogen tablet which is absorbed through the lining of the cheek into the bloodstream (like smokeless tobacco).

Estrogen also occurs "naturally" in some plants. Ginseng con-tains estrogen and has been promoted as a natural method of treating hot flashes. If this constitutes "natural" or implied "safe" treatment, then estrogen derived from pregnant mare's urine (Premarin) should probably be given the same distinction. Seriously, estrogen from any source carries the same risks and benefits and should be taken as a medication in the proper dose and with appropriate medical evaluation and follow-up.

✦ THE TIMING OF HORMONE REPLACEMENT

Many women begin to think through their own HRT decision well before they are menopausal. Harriet is a forty-six-year-old bookstore salesclerk who was still having regular menstrual periods but wanted to consider the decision about hormone replacement therapy before her periods stopped. She came to us to explore her options. She had a history of debilitating premenstrual symptoms for years, which improved with exercise and diet manipulations. She did not want to experience similarly severe symptoms of menopause if these could be prevented.

Harriet appreciated the opportunity to review in detail her family history and the possible risks and benefits of HRT. A careful review of her history revealed that she was at great risk for having heart disease because she smoked for fifteen years, had a moderately elevated cholesterol, and a mother who had several heart attacks beginning in her fifties. She was also at significant risk for osteoporosis because of her small body frame, her history of smoking, and her mother's history of severe osteoporosis with fractures. There was very little on the downside of taking hormone replacement therapy for Harriet, as she had no family history of cancer and she was not resistant to the idea of continued periods. She decided to begin hormone replacement therapy at menopause.

Menopause typically occurs between the ages of forty-eight and fifty-five, with an average age of approximately fifty-one years. The exact age that any given woman will experience menopause depends on heredity (when her mother and grandmother experienced menopause) and environment (smoking and living at high altitudes lowers the age of menopause). Only 1 percent of women experience premature menopause which is menopause that occurs before the age of forty.

Menopause can occur prematurely if the ovaries are removed (oophorectomy), usually at the time of a hysterectomy (removal of the uterus). In this case, the sudden depletion of estrogen can cause very significant, dramatic symptoms, including severe hot flashes and vaginal dryness. When compared to naturally occurring menopause, surgical menopause produces symptoms that are far more troubling. Many women report similar "estrogen withdrawal" symptoms after childbirth when estrogen levels plummet from the very high levels during pregnancy. Many of our patients can give dramatic descriptions of hot flashes and night sweats, which compounded the sleep deprivation during the early days of motherhood.

The natural history of menopause is that menstrual periods may change in frequency and duration years before the complete cessation of periods. Fertility begins to decline at age thirty but may be present until the last menstrual period when ovarian function has ceased. This is important information for women who would not welcome a "change of life" pregnancy. Indeed, women can experience hot flashes while they are still menstruating, and it is presumed that this represents an early symptom of menopause.

The medical community is divided about the advisability of beginning estrogen therapy while a woman is still having periods but suffering from hot flashes. We tend toward the position of Lila Nachtigall, M.D., as presented in her book *Estrogen: The Facts That Can Change Your Life*. She takes a firm stand against HRT before the very last period. We also know and understand the special circumstances when a woman may be very disabled by menopausal symptoms, and if properly evaluated might be placed on a brief course of therapy (Nachtigall and Heilman, 1991). Others advocate the use of an estrogen-progesterone regimen in women who are still menstruating but who have symptoms of menopause.

✦ THE GOOD NEWS ABOUT HRT

TREATMENT OF SYMPTOMS

HOT FLASHES

Let's start with the good news about hormone replacement therapy. First and foremost, estrogen is effective in the treatment of hot flashes. Approximately 98 percent of women experience complete resolution of hot flashes when they take estrogen. For most women, hot flashes are not disabling and may or may not cause enough discomfort to warrant therapy. For those women who do experience severe and unpleasant hot flashes or have significant disruption of their sleep, estrogen therapy represents a welcomed relief.

The dose of estrogen necessary to eliminate hot flashes varies from woman to woman. Some women experience complete resolution of their hot flashes on as little as .3 mg per day of conjugated estrogens, whereas others may need as much as 1.25 mg per day.

As you recall, Carolyn diagnosed her own menopause because she was having severe hot flashes. In fact, her hot flashes had become so disruptive, that her generally sunny disposition had turned to overcast, with threats of storms. In her opinion, her irritability and less-than-pleasant treatment of customers was leading to fewer tips and a major decline in income. Carolyn was inclined to take HRT for the long haul because of her concern about osteoporosis, but many other women choose to replace hormones for a brief time for the treatment of hot flashes only. In this situation, these women can take the lowest possible dose that treats the hot flashes. In general we start Premarin at .3 mg per day in such circumstances. Because hot flashes occur for an indefinite but limited period of time after menopause, the duration of estrogen therapy will also vary from woman to woman. Many physicians attempt to taper the estrogen therapy after six months to a year to determine whether hot flashes will recur. Two things need to be considered in this situation. The first is that once estrogen therapy has been instituted, it is important that it not be stopped suddenly. If this is done, then the symptoms resulting from the sudden drop in blood estrogen levels can be more devastating than the symptoms which prompted the therapy in the first place. More specifically, hot flashes are likely to be much more severe when estrogen is stopped suddenly than when the level of estrogen gradually declines as it does with spontaneous menopause. An analogous situation is the sudden decrease in estrogen levels seen with surgical removal of the ovaries. Some of our patients have unfortunately learned this themselves when they decided to stop their HRT cold turkey.

The second important point is that hormone replacement therapy may be started for one or more reasons. If the sole reason for instituting treatment with estrogen is the relief of hot flashes, then it makes sense to consider stopping the medication once the hot flashes have dissipated and no longer require treatment. On the other hand, as in Carolyn's situation, if therapy was begun for relief of hot flashes as well as the long-term prevention of osteoporosis or heart disease, then treatment—if well tolerated—may be continued indefinitely.

VAGINAL DRYNESS

Another specific symptom which may prompt a woman to consider estrogen replacement therapy is vaginal dryness. This symptom most often becomes noticeable several *years after* the onset of menopause unless, as in the case of surgical menopause, the decrease in estrogen was sudden and complete.

Linda, a bank teller, had a hysterectomy and oophorectomy at age thirty-six because both her mother and grandmother had ovarian cancer and she was estimated to have a fifty-fifty chance of ovarian cancer. After her surgery, she was started on estrogen patches twice weekly. She had no hot flashes but had severe vaginal irritation that did not respond to any of the usual treatments for vaginal inflammation. She was getting discouraged. After some time, we determined that Linda was suffering from estrogen-related vaginal dryness. Her symptoms completely disappeared after a few weeks when her dose of estrogen was doubled.

Linda's case points out the problems of hysterectomy and oophorectomy at a young age. For most women experiencing natural meno-pause, vaginal dryness does not tend to become noticeable until about five years after the last menstrual period. Vaginal dryness may be a problem only during intercourse, in which case lubricants may be used and completely remedy the situation. Many women also suffer from the associated symptoms of vaginal dryness, including irritation of the vaginal lining, which can cause burning and itching. The linings of the urethra (the outlet from the bladder) and bladder can be affected and cause urinary symptoms, including burning, frequent urination, pres-sure to urinate, and ultimately, urinary tract infections. Because these changes are caused by low levels of estrogen, estrogen replacement therapy is highly effective in preventing and reversing them. Estrogen might also be helpful in preventing urinary tract infections, since it restores the bacteria that normally live in the vagina (Byyny and Sper-off, 1990). There is one recent study, however, which contradicts this and suggests that elderly women taking estrogen are actually more prone to urinary tract infections (Orlander and others, 1992). There is, to date, no confirmation of, or explanation for this finding. It could be that women treated with estrogen are more sexually active, and as a result are more susceptible to urinary tract infections.

If estrogen therapy is begun prior to the onset of the symptoms of vaginal dryness and irritation, then it will prevent their occurrence as long as it is continued. If, however, estrogen therapy is begun to treat established symptoms, then it may take months for these to reverse completely. It is important to remember that although symptoms may persist for months after estrogen is begun, in most cases if therapy continues, the symptoms will improve.

Linda chose to take oral estrogen because she was at serious risk of the complications of early surgical menopause and was not solely treat-ing vaginal dryness. Many women opt for vaginal cream to treat the local symptoms of vaginal dryness and irritation. Vaginal estrogen cream constitutes hormone replacement therapy. Even though it is applied locally, it is absorbed into the bloodstream as is the estrogen in tablets or patches. Because of this absorption, vaginal creams carry the same risks as other forms of estrogen therapy and should only be used with a complete understanding of the risks and benefits.

PREVENTION OF THE LONG-TERM COMPLICATIONS OF MENOPAUSE

It is relatively easy for women who are suffering from severe hot flashes or vaginal irritation to see the potential benefit of estrogen therapy. It is much more difficult for women who are having no symptoms related to menopause to see the advantages of beginning therapy. Both osteoporosis and heart disease represent significant health risks for most menopausal women and are not symptomatic until advanced. The greatest benefit to be derived from estrogen therapy, with respect to osteoporosis and heart disease, is when therapy is instituted close to the onset of menopause. This means that women who are feeling well otherwise may want to consider the long-range possibilities of osteoporosis and heart disease and to begin therapy early in order to accrue the greatest benefit. This is not to say that treatment with estrogen therapy years after menopause is without benefit, but rather that the effect is dampened with time. Both osteoporosis and heart disease are described in far more detail in Chapters Four and Five.

Estrogen replacement therapy decreases osteoporotic bone fractures by about 50–60 percent (Lindsay, 1991; U.S. Congress, 1992). Exercise and calcium also have important roles in reducing osteoporosis, but they are less effective than estrogen replacement therapy in improving bone strength.

The more important good news from a public health standpoint is estrogen's protective effect against heart disease. Women who take estrogen have a lower rate of heart disease when compared to those who do not. The combined results of over twenty studies revealed a 44 percent reduction in heart disease with estrogen therapy (U.S. Congress, 1992). These results have been repeatedly challenged by those who claim that the women who are placed on estrogen therapy are most likely to have a lower risk of heart disease, based on the absence of other risk factors. More specifically, it has been claimed that women who smoke and have high blood pressure are less likely to be treated with estrogen than those who do not have these risks.

Perhaps the most compelling data is from the Nurses' Health Study, which has reported a 50 percent reduction in heart disease among the women taking estrogen replacement therapy (Stampfer, 1991). This study is a long-term study which also accounts for all other known risk factors that might influence the development of heart disease.

The way in which estrogen therapy can reduce the occurrence of heart disease is at least partly due to a favorable effect on cholesterol. Estrogen has been consistently shown to increase HDL cholesterol (the good cholesterol) and to lower LDL cholesterol (the bad cholesterol). This change in the ratio of good and bad cholesterol tips the balance to a more favorable ratio which decreases the likelihood that heart disease will develop.

OTHER EFFECTS

Many promoters of estrogen therapy as the miracle cure for aging would have us believe that it will reverse any number of unwanted changes in skin, hair, muscle and energy. The information related to these changes is much scarcer than that related to the clear biological events of heart attacks and osteoporotic fractures and the easily monitored symptoms of hot flashes and vaginal dryness.

There is some evidence that estrogen may improve the ability of the skin to maintain moisture. It is not at all clear that estrogen therapy slows down the skin's natural aging process which results in wrinkles. There are similar claims, which may or may not be true, that estrogen therapy will improve the appearance of the hair.

What we do know is that there is a strong placebo effect of estrogen on some of the symptoms associated with menopause. Any drug, even sugar pills, can reduce a symptom by 10 to 40 percent. It is, therefore, no surprise that estrogen therapy should have a similar beneficial effect on the treatment of menopausal symptoms, particularly since the women who take the therapy have usually been convinced that it will change their lives. This strong placebo effect, however, makes it difficult to assess symptoms such as fatigue, lassitude and irritability, which may be very responsive to the power of suggestion.

To summarize, then, estrogen is extremely effective in treating the most prominent symptoms of menopause, which are hot flashes and vaginal dryness. Estrogen is also highly effective in reducing the risk of osteoporosis, with its associated fractures and complications, as well as reducing the risk of heart disease. There are very few drugs which are as effective as estrogen. Indeed, if there were not side effects or complications of estrogen use, it would be a nearly perfect treatment.

✦ THE BAD NEWS ABOUT HRT

You may ask, Who in their right mind would take a medication which has been clearly associated with cancer to treat a natural physiological event? The answer to this all-important question lies in the real story linking hormone replacement therapy to cancer. During the 1960s and early 1970s, many menopausal women began estrogen treatment for symptoms of menopause. This was coincident with the release of the extremely popular book *Feminine Forever,* by Robert Wilson,

M.D., which extolled the positive effects of HRT. The bubble burst in 1975 when two important studies that linked estrogen therapy with endometrial cancer were reported. In fact, women taking estrogen were four to seven times more likely to develop the cancer than women not taking estrogen therapy (Ernster, 1988). As a result of this information, estrogen use by menopausal women dropped by nearly 30 percent. Much more is now known about the true increased risk of uterine cancer associated with hormone replacement therapy.

It is known definitely that if cancer of the uterus (endometrial cancer) is present at the time estrogen is started, it will respond to the estrogen therapy by enlarging. This reaction to estrogen places endometrial cancer in a category termed "estrogen-responsive tumors." Breast cancer is also considered an estrogen responsive cancer. The symptoms of endometrial cancer include, predominantly, irregularities of menstruation. Irregular periods (usually bleeding between periods) and changes in menstrual blood flow (usually heavier) may be signs of endometrial cancer. At the time of menopause, these changes are very common and can create uncertainty on the part of the physician as to whether the patient is experiencing symptoms of endometrial cancer or normal menopause. When there is sufficient doubt, the physician may recommend an endometrial biopsy. This involves the removal of a small amount of the uterine lining with a small plastic catheter inserted into the cervix. The procedure can be done in the office without general anesthesia. It may be associated with some discomfort when the small plastic catheter is inserted and some crampy abdominal pain thereafter. Many physicians recommend an endometrial biopsy when they initially prescribe estrogen therapy if they have any concern that the patient may have an early endometrial cancer. Endometrial biopsies are not routinely recommended for all women prior to starting hormone replacement therapy. In the circumstance when estrogen alone is used in a menopausal woman who has not had a hysterectomy, then initial and yearly endometrial biopsies are currently recommended.

If hormone replacement therapy is begun and there is preexisting endometrial cancer which has not been detected, there will often be symptoms that should prompt the patient and the physician to consider endometrial biopsy. These include irregular menstrual bleeding at a time not anticipated by the hormone replacement therapy schedule (see Figure 6-1 on p. 159). It is imperative that these abnormalities of menstrual bleeding be reported to the physician so that the appropriate evaluation can be instituted. In fact, many physicians request that patients keep a diary of their hormone replacement therapy schedule with the days of bleeding so that this can be reviewed during office visits.

The only good news about endometrial cancer is that it is a relatively slow-growing cancer which normally causes symptoms before becoming advanced. It is also a relatively rare tumor. Most women who have endometrial cancer can be completely cured with hysterectomy.

Estrogen therapy is also capable of promoting new cases of uterine cancer when none existed before therapy. We now know that estrogen causes a buildup of the lining of the uterus, which in the normal woman would be followed by monthly shedding and menstrual bleeding. When the lining is allowed to continue to build up without being shed, the stage is set for a cancer to develop. The addition of a progestin can completely eliminate the increased risk of uterine cancer associated with estrogen. Progesterone is the hormone that increases in the second half of the menstrual cycle and causes menstrual bleeding. It is also well-known that the addition of progesterone ten days per month will decrease nearly all of the risk of endometrial cancer, and an addition of progesterone for twelve days per month will eliminate all of the additional risk of endometrial cancer that could be conferred by estrogen.

Many women have difficulty getting beyond the word "cancer" in the discussion of potential complications of hormone replacement therapy. Here it is extremely important to recognize that, indeed, estrogen alone has been associated with uterine cancer. It can cause new cancers and increase the growth of preexisting cancers. However, abnormalities of menstrual bleeding will raise suspicion of a preexisting cancer in a woman on hormone replacement therapy, and these cancers can be detected by endometrial biopsy. They are, furthermore, highly treatable tumors which are nearly always curable. Although estrogen can also cause new cancers, this additional risk can be completely eliminated by the use of a progestational agent. So the news is not so bad after all, and needs to be considered carefully by the woman who has concerns about menopausal symptoms or the long-term conditions associated with menopause.

THE BREAST CANCER CONTROVERSY

If the threat of endometrial cancer didn't drive you away from hormone replacement therapy, then brace yourself for the breast cancer story. Breast cancer is now the second-leading cause of death for women with cancer. The lifetime risk of this cancer for United States women is estimated to be one in nine (Henderson and Wender, 1991). It is this alarmingly high rate of breast cancer which has caused such concern over any factor which could raise the risk even slightly. Although this figure has received a lot of attention we must remember that "lifetime" risk refers to a woman's chance of dying at age eighty-five! During the menopausal years, the risk of breast cancer is less. Still, we worry.

Paula's story makes this point particularly well. She was a forty-nine-year-old woman who had breast cancer that was treated with mastectomy and chemotherapy at age forty-eight. Her last menstrual period was shortly after chemotherapy treatment began. Paula married her second husband, Greg, when she was in her early forties. Paula had worked as a volunteer fund-raiser for nonprofit agencies and Greg, who was sixty, was a retired businessman and avid hiker. Both had been unhappily married before, and were cautious about marrying a second time, yet were excited that they each had found someone with whom to share their life. Their relationship became a source of great joy for both of them, and they spent the first seven years of their marriage almost carefree. When Paula discovered that she had cancer, she and Greg were able to work through the issues of her illness and surgery.

If Paula had come to us before her breast cancer, we might have advised against HRT because of her family history of breast cancer. Paula's mother had had breast cancer. This recommendation is somewhat controversial within the medical community, as is the relationship between breast cancer and hormones. Many studies have been done to specifically address the question "Does noncontraceptive estrogen use increase the risk of breast cancer in women?" The results vary widely, from suggesting that estrogen actually reduces the risk of breast cancer to demonstrating that estrogen increases the risk of breast cancer. The study reporting the most dramatic increase in breast cancer risk suggests that women who ever used estrogen are 1.7 times more likely to develop breast cancer than women who have not used estrogen (Mills and others, 1989).

Some studies indicate that there is a trend toward an increased risk of breast cancer with longer duration of estrogen use and with higher doses. Findings have been very inconsistent with regard to the type of estrogen taken (i.e., conjugated versus unconjugated estrogens) and the comparative risk of estrogen used alone versus estrogen used with progestins.

In October 1992, a study was published to help make some sense out of the morass of information currently available. Specifically, the authors combined the results of all of the studies which have been done focusing on postmenopausal estrogen use and breast cancer. The author concludes "there is no compelling evidence that, overall, women who have ever used postmenopausal estrogens are at increased risk of breast cancer" (Henrich, 1992, p. 1902). There were inconsistent and inconclusive findings across the studies, regarding an increased risk of breast cancer in women who had experienced surgical menopause, benign breast disease, family history of breast cancer or had used estrogens for prolonged periods of time. Prior reports had suggested that there was a significant increase in the risk of breast cancer after five years of estrogen use, the highest risk being experienced in women who had used estrogens for at least fifteen years.

For women like Paula, with a family history of breast cancer, the situation is different. It has been demonstrated that there is a significant increase in the risk of breast cancer among women with a family history of breast cancer. Women who have a family history of breast cancer may experience the greatest increase in risk from estrogen use, although this finding has been inconsistent as well. In fact, one review suggests that the risk of breast cancer for women who have taken estrogens and have a family history of breast cancer is three times that of women with a family history of breast cancer who have not taken estrogens. Several studies also suggest that while there may be a slight increase risk of breast cancer among current users of estrogen therapy, that the type of tumors found are less advanced tumors and that, in fact, the women on estrogen replacement therapy experience a lower death rate from breast cancer than those women not on estrogen therapy. It is completely plausible that women who are taking estrogen replacement therapy are more likely to get yearly mammograms and be evaluated for anything suspicious of breast cancer. This increased vigilance in screening for breast cancer could lead to the detection of earlier breast cancers and better outcomes.

So the major problem with estrogen use and breast cancer appears to be if *too much* has been taken for *too long* by someone with a *family history* of breast cancer. Based on what can be gleaned from studies available to us now, we must conclude that there is no clear evidence that postmenopausal estrogen use, in general, increases the risk of breast cancer. There may be a small increased risk of breast cancer for women who have used higher-dosed estrogens (greater than 1.25 mg of conjugated estrogens daily) and for those women who have used estrogens for longer periods of time (greater than fifteen years).

Many breast cancers will grow more rapidly in the presence of estrogen. This is similar to the situation with endometrial cancer and makes it absolutely imperative that all women who are considering beginning estrogen replacement therapy have a breast exam and a mammogram to ensure that no early cancers are present. Thereafter, it is important to continue with yearly mammograms and breast exams in the event that a very early cancer was not detected with mammography. Breast self-examination is recommended monthly and any suspicious changes should be reported immediately to a physician for further evaluation.

Women like Paula, who have had breast cancer prior to menopause, cannot take estrogen replacement therapy. Even if the cancer is completely cured, as we hope it was for Paula, estrogen therapy should not be prescribed. For these women, there continues to be a much greater chance of developing a second breast cancer and any remaining cancer cells could be stimulated to grow with estrogen. Breast cancer is considered an "absolute contraindication" to estrogen replacement therapy. In medicine, however, nothing is really absolute and there are some physicians who feel that for women who have had breast cancer, short-term (one to two years) estrogen therapy is reasonable to treat hot flashes or vaginal dryness. Yearly endometrial biopsies are recommended rather than adding progesterone to the regimen. This is still very controversial, but we tend to take the cautious approach and advise patients with symptoms to try all possible alternative therapies as we will describe later.

As if this were not complicated enough, now we must consider progestin's effect on breast cancer. There is still insufficient evidence to make any conclusions regarding the role of progestins and breast cancer. There has been one study which showed a greatly increased risk of breast cancer in women who use combined estrogen and progestin therapy (Bergkvist and others, 1989). However, there were problems with this study which have made the medical community unwilling to accept these results without confirmation. What is very clear is that we need more information about the use of estrogen and progestin and the occurrence of breast cancer.

If you are concerned about using estrogen replacement therapy, the current information available suggests that:

• if you have had diagnosis of breast cancer, you should not take estrogen (there may be exceptions);
• if you have a family history of breast cancer (in particular in a sister or mother), then you may opt against hormone replacement therapy;
• if you have decided to take hormone replacement therapy, doses of conjugated estrogens in excess of .625 mg per day should be used with caution;

• the potential risk of hormone replacement therapy used for longer than fifteen years needs to be weighed against the potential benefits; and

• if you take hormone replacement therapy, you should be screened for breast cancer on a yearly basis, and any new or suspicious lumps detected from breast self-exams should be reported immediately.

CLOTS

Birth control pills, which have much higher doses of estrogens, have been clearly associated with the development of blood clots. The most frequent site for this type of clotting is in the veins of the leg. These clots in the deep veins of the calf and thigh (deep venous thrombosis) can break off and travel to the lungs (pulmonary embolism). Pulmonary emboli can be fatal and are the basis of the major concern about deep venous thrombosis.

There have been no studies that show that postmenopausal estrogen replacement therapy is associated with an increased risk of this type of clot formation. However, estrogen therapy should be considered potentially risky in women who have had blood clots while on birth control pills or during pregnancy. These women may have underlying conditions which cause them to form clots when estrogen is taken for therapy or when estrogen levels rise during pregnancy. Women who have had deep venous thrombosis with pregnancy or birth control pills in the past are said to have a "relative contraindication" to estrogen replacement therapy. In essence, this suggests that caution must be used in these situations and that potential risk of clot formation needs to be weighed against the potential benefits of treatment.

LIVER AND GALLBLADDER DISEASE

Another potential complication of estrogen therapy relates to the liver and gallbladder. Estrogens which are taken by mouth are absorbed through the intestine and pass into the liver, where they are broken down before entering into the bloodstream. Because of this, estrogen should not be taken by women with active liver disease. This constitutes another "absolute contraindication" to estrogen use.

Women who take estrogen therapy appear to have approximately twice as much gallbladder disease as women who do not (Petitti and others, 1988). It is plausible, but not yet proven, that estrogen therapy which does not require breakdown by the liver (i.e., therapy with patches, pellets or creams) may cause no increase in gallbladder disease. This benefit of alternative forms of estrogen therapy is theoretical and needs to be proven in practice. If women who may be predisposed to gallbladder disease (women who are overweight, have a family history of gallstones, or a prior history of gallstone or gallbladder disease) choose to take estrogen therapy, they may opt for one of the non-oral forms of therapy.

FIBROIDS

Fibroid tumors are benign tumors of the lining of the uterus. They often cause no symptoms whatsoever and may only be detected during an examination of the uterus during an internal or pelvic exam. They may alternatively cause symptoms of lower-abdominal fullness or may cause irregular or heavy menstrual bleeding. Nearly all fibroid tumors can be detected by pelvic ultrasound, but they may need to be distinguished from endometrial cancer, or other causes of bleeding, by an endometrial biopsy. Irregularities of bleeding cannot be assumed to be caused by fibroids until endometrial cancer is excluded as the cause. Estrogen replacement therapy can cause some fibroid tumors to increase in size and cause symptoms where none existed previously.

Women who are known to have fibroid tumors are often cautioned against beginning hormone replacement therapy because the diagnosis of fibroid tumors constitutes a "relative contraindication" to estrogen treatment. As is the case with all relative contraindications, each woman needs to carefully weigh potential benefits of treatment against the possible complications of treatment related to her situation. If fibroids are detected while you are taking hormone replacement therapy and they are causing more symptoms, it may be wise to stop therapy. If the fibroid tumors shrink, it suggests that the estrogen therapy was causing them to increase in size. The plans for continued treatment will need to be carefully considered in light of all of the pros and cons of treatment.

MIGRAINES

Migraine headaches are listed in many references as a relative contraindication to estrogen treatment. Migraine headaches can worsen when women with a history of migraines are started on estrogen replacement therapy. On the other hand, many women's migraine headaches improve at the time of menopause and do not worsen with hormone replacement therapy! As with all of the potential complications of treatment, each individual woman should discuss this with her health care provider and decide for herself.

PERIODS . . .

This may not represent a life-threatening complication of therapy, but it is most certainly an unwanted side effect of cyclic combined therapy with estrogen and progestin. Many women may view this as a cruel plot concocted by male gynecologists or possibly a strategy of the sanitary products companies to improve sales (to the best of our knowledge, neither of these suspicions has foundation). What is clear is that few, if any, women are sad to lose their periods at the time of menopause. The idea of resuming menstruation is particularly unappealing to women who are, frankly, delighted to be freed from monthly menstrual periods. One of our patients summarized her feelings about the options well when she said "I had really been looking forward to menopause and no periods. My daughter even said, 'So menopause means no periods? That sounds great!' So, why on earth would I want to take medication that would guarantee me monthly periods indefinitely. What a stupid idea!" This is, indeed, the sentiment of many women who are faced with the information about hormone replacement therapy. This is not an issue for women who have had their uteri surgically removed.

For those women who do have their uteri, the options are relatively limited. To eliminate the increased risk of uterine cancer, a progestin needs to be added to the estrogen. There is, however, an option to take estrogen alone, but regular endometrial biopsies are essential to find early treatable cancers. In the most traditional method, estrogen and progesterone are cycled to simulate a premenopausal menstrual cycle. This causes shedding of the uterine lining at the end of the twelve day therapy with progestin. This monthly bleeding which, for most women, lasts about four days is usually lighter than premenopausal menstrual periods. The good news is that monthly bleeding will not continue forever with hormone replacement therapy. After some years of therapy, the uterine lining becomes nonfunctioning and thereby fails to build up to a point where it can shed. It can be anticipated that after a few years of therapy, monthly bleeding will stop.

Because so many women opt against hormone replacement therapy based on their unwillingness to continue menstrual periods, alternative methods of combining estrogen and progestins have been introduced. This has the advantage of eliminating the risk of endometrial cancer and yet does not cause monthly menstrual bleeding. Estrogen and progestin are given continuously throughout the month. Progestin is given in much lower doses (e.g., Provera 1–2.5 mg per day) than the dose given for only twelve days out of the month. (e.g.,

Provera 10 mg per day). The daily dose of progestin prevents the uterine lining from building up throughout the month and thereby not only reduces the risk of endometrial cancer but also fails to cause menstrual bleeding. Many women experience irregular spotty bleeding during the first three months of therapy and even thereafter one-third to one-half of women still experience some bleeding. However, the good news is that after one year of therapy, nearly all women are free of any bleeding at all. Still a number of women completely stop treatment prior to this time because of the nuisance of unpredictable spotty bleeding. Because of this unpredictable bleeding, other regimens of HRT are being developed.

So the news is not all bad after all. For women who have had a hysterectomy this is not an issue. For those women who do have uteri, the choices are to grin and bear monthly menstrual bleeding with a combined cyclic therapy for several years, to opt for combined continuous therapy and grin and bear spotty bleeding for three months up to one year, or to take estrogen alone and have yearly endometrial biopsies. The risk of endometrial cancer narrows the choices, but women can still exercise their preferences between bleeding and biopsies.

OTHER SIDE EFFECTS

Women who opt for hormone replacement therapy and fill their prescriptions for estrogen and progestin will certainly take pause when they open the package insert and are faced with the impressive list of complications and side effects of these drugs. Although this is the exact list provided for birth control pills, it is likely that far fewer women who take birth control pills actually read or react to the package insert. It is our suspicion that younger women, feeling far less mortal, adopt a "not me" reaction to this information. As we shall discuss in Chapter Eight, our chapter on midlife and stress, during the menopausal years, we view medical complications and risks in a more serious fashion. What is interesting, of course, is that the warnings are much more pertinent to birth control pills than they are to postmenopausal hormone replacement therapy. This is because the doses of hormones in replacement therapy are far less than those in contraceptive therapy, and they are being given to patients who are hormone-deficient as opposed to premenopausal women who have normal hormone levels. Nonetheless, there are side effects which may be experienced by women taking hormone replacement therapy. Since the occurrence of any side effect associated with estrogen and progestin is very unpredictable, it would be unwise for women who would otherwise take hormone replacement therapy to discount it on the basis of the threat of a particular side effect.

Fluid retention is the most commonly reported side effect of women taking hormone replacement therapy that includes progesterone. In most circumstances, this lasts only a few weeks. If the symptoms of fluid retention continue, a reduction in dietary salt intake may be warranted. Approximately 2 percent of women consider this side effect problematic enough to stop therapy.

Breast tenderness is reported by a number of women, but is nearly always temporary. For those women who continue to be troubled by this, changes in the progestin may help relieve the breast tenderness. The combined continuous form of therapy may be less likely to cause breast tenderness and should be considered as an option for women who find this intolerable.

PMS-like symptoms have been reported in some women during the time that they are taking progesterone in the combined cyclic form of therapy. Women like Harriet who have had severe PMS may be particularly concerned about this possibility. Anxiety, irritability and depressed mood may all be experienced. For many women, these associated symptoms resolve completely after several months of therapy but for some, they may continue to be unbearable. The combined continuous form of therapy may eliminate these symptoms because of the lower dose of progesterone prescribed. Harriet had already decided that at the first sign of problems, she would try the combined continuous schedule.

Some women taking hormone replacement therapy report *weight gain* as an unpleasant side effect. This weight gain may be related to the fluid retention experienced early in the course of hormone replacement therapy. Some of it may be related to the normal decline in metabolism which causes women to gain weight after menopause. Estrogen may also increase the proportion of the body's fat tissue as is does during pregnancy. These effects of estrogen can be reasonably controlled by increasing exercise and decreasing salt in the diet.

A number of *other symptoms* are less frequently reported by women but are, nonetheless, bothersome in any individual woman who experiences them. Nausea, headaches and increased vaginal discharge have all been associated with hormone replacement therapy. Many of these symptoms are fleeting and will disappear completely despite continuation of therapy. Others may need to be controlled in alternative ways or may lead to discontinuation of the treatment if they remain unacceptable.

In all circumstances, it is crucial that a record of symptoms be kept and that these be discussed with the physician prescribing the medications. The list of symptoms associated with hormone replacement therapy presented here is not all inclusive and any symptom which develops in the course of therapy with hormones should be reported. Women who are taking hormone replacement and are experiencing symptoms early in the course of treatment should, in most cases, be encouraged to continue therapy since the odds that the symptom will disappear completely are good.

✦ HORMONE TREATMENT SCHEDULES

Despite the apparent complexity of hormone replacement therapy schedules, there are relatively few methods being used currently. There may be some subtle variations in treatment schedules, but the principles of each method are distinct. Figure 6-1 summarizes the three major hormone replacement schedules.

UNOPPOSED ESTROGEN THERAPY

For women like Carolyn and Linda who have had a hysterectomy, estrogen can be taken alone without the addition of a progestin. Since their uteri have been removed, there is no risk of uterine cancer. This form of therapy is called unopposed estrogen. In the past, it was felt that there may be some rationale to discontinuing estrogen therapy for one week per month. For the most part, this practice has been discontinued since there is no evidence of benefit and many women actually experience hot flashes during the week off estrogen therapy.

For women who still have a uterus, unopposed estrogen therapy without endometrial biopsies is not usually recommended because of the increased risk of endometrial cancer. Some women are so opposed to continued periods and have such potential benefit to be gained by estrogen therapy that they agree to regular endometrial biopsies to detect uterine cancer. All women who have a uterus and are started on unopposed estrogen therapy should have a pretreatment endometrial biopsy and yearly biopsies thereafter while on treatment. There are even some who would advocate biopsies every six months. Any bleeding that is experienced should be reported immediately and should prompt additional endometrial biopsies.

Figure 6–1

SUMMARY OF
HORMONE REPLACEMENT SCHEDULES

Unopposed Estrogen

Day of Months 1 2 3 4 5 6 7 8 9 10 11 12 13 14 15 16 17 18 19 20 21 22 23 24 25 26 27 28 29 30

Estrogen   ->

Progesterone   none

Bleeding   none

Cyclic Combined

Day of Months 1 2 3 4 5 6 7 8 9 10 11 12 13 14 15 16 17 18 19 20 21 22 23 24 25 26 27 28 29 30

Estrogen   ->

Progesterone - - - - - - - - - - - - - - - |

Bleeding | - - - - - - - - - |

Continuous Combined

Day of Months 1 2 3 4 5 6 7 8 9 10 11 12 13 14 15 16 17 18 19 20 21 22 23 24 25 26 27 28 29 30

Estrogen   ->

Progesterone ->

Bleeding   spotting possible for up to one year

    The form of estrogen taken should be based on the patient's preference for route of administration and consideration of the conditions that may favor one form of therapy over another. A woman with a family history of gallbladder disease may opt for estrogen patches as opposed to estrogen pills to decrease the potential of this complication. Many women prefer patches despite the increased cost because they can be used twice weekly, rather than pills which need to be taken on a daily basis. As discussed earlier in this chapter, vaginal creams may have somewhat erratic absorption into the bloodstream and may be less desirable because of this.

✦ CYCLIC COMBINATION THERAPY

The method of combining both estrogen and progestin in a cyclic fashion to simulate the premenopausal menstrual cycle is the most frequently used method of hormone replacement. There is absolutely no reason to prescribe hormone replacement in this method to women who have had hysterectomy, because the major reason for using this method is to reduce the risk of endometrial cancer.

Although there are subtle variations in technique, the basic premise in this form of therapy is that estrogen and progestin are combined and the progestin is given for a sufficient number of days during the month to reduce the risk of endometrial cancer. In light of this underlying principle, there are two major ways of dosing the hormone therapy. The first is to prescribe estrogen continuously throughout the month and to add the progestin for the first twelve days of the month. Bleeding which occurs on day twelve of progestin therapy or later is considered normal and requires no further evaluation. If bleeding occurs on day eleven or before, endometrial biopsy is recommended. Likewise, if there is any breakthrough bleeding or heavy withdrawal bleeding, further evaluations should proceed with an endometrial biopsy.

Another method of prescribing cyclic combination therapy is to prescribe the estrogen therapy during days one through twenty-five of the month and the progestin on days fourteen through twenty-five. There is one week per month during which time no hormone replacement therapy is prescribed. With this method, it can be anticipated that menstrual bleeding should begin approximately on day twenty-five and if it begins on day twenty four or before, then endometrial biopsy may be recommended (some physicians biopsy only when bleeding occurs before day twenty-three). Currently, we see no clear reason to discontinue estrogen therapy for one week per month. There is a chance that hot flashes will recur because of the sudden withdrawal of estrogen. Many physicians, however, continue to prescribe hormone replacement therapy in this method based on previous theoretical concerns about continuous estrogen therapy. We did not include this schedule since we do not use it in our practice.

The dose of progesterone prescribed in the cyclic combination therapy method should be high enough to cause menstrual bleeding. In general, medroxyprogesterone is given at a dose of 10 mg per day during the twelve days of treatment. For women who experience unpleasant side effects from progesterone, the trend is toward decreasing the dose to 5 mg per day and continue at that level if monthly menstrual bleeding still occurs. The estrogen portion of hormone replacement therapy can be taken as pills or patches. Pellets have also been used in Europe for this purpose. Vaginal creams are rarely used in combination with progesterone since the absorbed estrogen is unpredictable and would not be consistent enough or sufficient to cause a buildup of the uterine lining.

The cyclic combined form of therapy has been the most widely used and for many women, is very acceptable. It does require that a close record be kept of the timing of menstrual bleeding in order that early bleeding can be investigated further with endometrial biopsy.

✦ CONTINUOUS COMBINED THERAPY

For most of you who abhor the idea of continued menstrual periods, this form of therapy may be appealing. Additionally, women who experience unpleasant side effects from the higher doses of progesterone used with cyclic combined therapy may find this more tolerable. The method of therapy is quite simple and consists of continuous estrogen and progesterone therapy throughout the month. The dose of progesterone is significantly lower than those used in the cyclic combined method: medroxyprogesterone 2.5 mg per day as opposed to medroxyprogesterone 10 mg per day. Since this regimen is a relatively recent development, the optimal dose requires further study.

Although the major benefit of this form of therapy is that it does not cause monthly menstrual bleeding, it is frequently associated with irregular bleeding in the first several months. Most women who can continue to take the therapy for one year can expect that all bleeding will stop. Biopsies should be performed for any irregular bleeding during the course of therapy, so most women will get one or more.

As with the other types of treatment, estrogen can be taken in the form of pills, patches or pellets. Careful records should be kept of any bleeding which is experienced during the treatment and reported to the prescribing physician. Some women do experience side effects from the progesterone throughout the month and these symptoms should be reported as well.

✦ ALTERNATIVES TO HORMONE REPLACEMENT THERAPY

There are a number of nonhormonal and nondrug treatments for the symptoms and long-term complications of menopause. Rather than present a shopping list of possible prevention and treatment options here, these alternatives are presented in the individual chapters to which they apply. It is important, however, to recognize that hormone replacement therapy is not the only way to treat and prevent menopausal symptoms and associated conditions.

Paula survived breast cancer and began having hot flashes shortly after her chemotherapy. Because of her breast cancer, she was not a candidate for hormone replacement therapy, but desperately needed relief from her unremitting hot flashes. We met with Paula and worked out a behavioral and non-hormonal plan to deal with her hot flashes. We spoke with her about a comprehensive non-hormonal treatment plan that included self-monitoring triggers, paced respirations, vitamin E and increased physical activity. She did get some relief from our suggestions, and commented on the added benefits she gained with the exercise and physical activity program regarding weight loss and an increase of energy. In fact, Paula told us that she felt that she and Greg had grown even closer since they had worked on the problem together and she expressed an interest in joining him on the hiking trails.

We have been touched by the stories of women who have had the courage to cope with breast cancer, only to face difficult symptoms of menopause. We always wish that we had more to offer, but we are hopeful that new non-hormonal treatment strategies will be developed. Survivors of breast cancer are now taking an active role in making this happen. If you are facing a situation similar to Paula's, you may find helpful *The Menopause Self-Help Book* by Susan M. Lark. This illustrated book focuses on treatments for menopause that are non-hormonal. Dr. Lark is a physician whose book focuses on a healthy diet, vitamins and minerals for menopause, stress reduction, as well as acupuncture and yoga. Although many of the vitamins she recommends have not been tested, most of her advice is practical and sound.

✦ THE BIG PICTURE

There is no "one size fits all" formula to answer the question, "Should I take hormone replacement therapy at menopause?" For any individual woman a particular risk or benefit may take on more importance than all the others. It is well known that each individual places very different values on the consequences of taking or not taking the medication. In the case of hormone replacement therapy, some women have no interest in hearing about the benefit in preventing heart disease once they have heard that they will continue to have menstrual periods. For other women who have experienced the pain and suffering of a relative with osteoporotic bone fractures, the nuisance of menstrual periods may seem very insignificant. As women making this very important decision it is important that we take personal inventory of all of the pros and cons of taking hormone replacement therapy. By necessity, this inventory will need to acknowledge our individual risk for developing the conditions that might be prevented or caused by hormone replacement therapy and set priorities accordingly. Likewise, we will need to specifically assess the consequences of taking or not taking hormone replacement therapy based on our attitudes and past experiences.

It is difficult to determine even the approximate number of women who are currently taking hormone replacement therapy. The Massachusetts Women's Health Study found that 9.2 percent of the women surveyed were being treated with hormone replacement therapy (Avis and McKinlay, 1990). This is in contrast to a survey of women in a California community which demonstrated that 32 percent of the women between ages fifty and sixty-five reported estrogen use with 6 percent reporting progestin use as well (Harris and others, 1990).

Also from the Massachusetts Women's Health Survey, we know that 20–30 percent of women never fill their prescriptions for hormone replacement therapy (Ravnikar, 1987). It is particularly interesting that surveys have shown that nearly all gynecologists would prescribe estrogen therapy for most of their patients (U.S. Congress, 1992). If in fact only between 9 and 30 percent of women actually take hormone replacement therapy, we must assume that the majority of patients for whom hormone replacement therapy is recommended opt against it either before having the prescription written out or filled, or after beginning therapy. Other women may not be able to afford health care or medications. Many women may not be seeking medical attention.

It is also possible that more women are taking hormone replacement therapy, but only for a short time to treat menopausal symptoms. This is supported by a study that looked at women's decision making around the choice of hormone replacement therapy. The authors found that the women studied gave the highest priority to the impact that hormone replacement replacement therapy would have on their lives in the short term as opposed to the impact it would have on their long-term risk of morbidity and mortality. It is particularly disturbing that the women who were surveyed in this study felt that they had inadequate information to make a decision about hormone replacement therapy and that their health care providers did not listen to them (Rothert, 1991).

If you are in the category of women who can consider HRT, you should review your symptoms of hot flashes, vaginal dryness, and your risks of osteoporosis and heart disease. If your symptoms are severe and you are at risk of developing osteoporosis and heart disease, you might seriously consider HRT. This is something to discuss with your health-care professional in depth.

To see how much women can differ, let's take our last look at Pam, a fifty-six-year-old high school guidance counselor who opted against hormone replacement therapy when she suddenly stopped menstruating at age forty-eight. It was Pam's good fortune that she never had a hot flash, nor any vaginal dryness. She had sailed through menopause. When asked to what she attributed her incredibly uneventful passage through menopause, she said, "I exercise religiously, I eat and sleep well, and I may be a little bizarre, since I never had a single labor pain with either of my two children."

✦ COMMUNICATION

Now that you have reviewed the choices about hormone replacement therapy, you might be feeling overwhelmed. "How in the world am I going to make this decision—one of the most important health care decisions of my life? First of all, don't be intimidated! By now we have explored the various issues with you and we have confidence that you will be able to make this decision. After all, you have probably made numerous other decisions with respect to your own health care, and that of your family members. You have probably, in the past, decided what kind of birth control to use and some of you who are mothers may have made decisions about childbirth and delivery. Any of you who have had surgery for sports injuries know that you had to make that decision and weigh it against other alternative treatment approaches. You will be better able to make this decision by reviewing your risk of heart disease and osteoporosis, and your symptoms like hot flashes and vaginal dryness, and if you follow the strategy that we outline below. You may notice that we did not include symptoms of stress or depression. This is because hormone replacement therapy is not an appropriate treatment for those problems. We discuss this further in those chapters.

Some of you may be wishing for the good old days, when a benevolent and paternalistic male physician would take you aside and say, "Dear, just do this." (One of us was actually patted on the head once when she was in her twenties and trying to decide about birth control. Her paternalistic but well-meaning obstetrician/gynecologist told her that she should just get pregnant because he really preferred to deliver babies.) If you have a trusting relationship with your health care professional and feel comfortable with her or his judgment, you may wish to ask what they would do in similar circumstances.

We suggest that you try to take an open-minded approach to this decision. It is important to go into the decision without being encumbered with political or philosophical beliefs. As you know by now, we see estrogen neither as a miracle wonder drug, nor as a dangerous external "chemical" substance. We have tried to present the evidence objectively and we hope that you will be able to utilize it objectively as well.

After reviewing your symptoms and risks, you may want to discuss it with your partner. A person who lives with you can provide a second opinion about the effect of your symptoms on your daily life. Sometimes family members can remember additional details of family history that could be helpful. If your mother, grandmother, or any of your aunts are interested, you might discuss the issue of estrogen with them. Similarly, by talking to sisters and friends, you can get a sense of how estrogen has affected women who have decided to take it. By talking to women who have chosen not to use hormone replacement therapy, you can understand their perspective as well. So by now you should have a sense of your own symptoms and your health needs. In addition, you have gotten some helpful information from women who have made different decisions about estrogen.

It is helpful not to look at this decision as forever. You need not be married to treatment and divorce is always an option. You can make a tentative decision to try hormone replacement therapy and evaluate the consequences. One way to evaluate the effects of hormone replacement therapy is to monitor your symptoms after a trial of several months of hormone replacement therapy. For hot flashes, it may take up to four weeks to assess the effectiveness of treatment and for vaginal dryness it can require months. It is also useful to ask your clinician about the hows and whys of taking hormone replacement therapy, just as you would with any other medication.

Once you start taking HRT, if you have unpleasant side effects, such as bloating or mood changes, you might be inclined to stop hormone replacement therapy. But if you have made the decision to try it in the first place, a better alternative is to discuss the situation with your physician like Carolyn did when she was having difficulties with the patch. Often, she or he can lower the doses of the medication or change the schedule, and the side effects can be managed. It is important to talk it over before making your next decision.

Finally, if your side effects cannot be managed, or if you cannot take hormone replacement therapy because you have a history of breast cancer, or if you choose not to take it in the first place, please remember that you have many alternatives. In every section of this book we have discussed alternative methods that do not involve hormone replacement therapy to cope with symptoms. For example, many women who have hot flashes learn to do paced breathing exercises and relaxation procedures which help them manage. Other women have found that changes in their diet can be helpful. Similarly, topical lubricants can be used to cope with vaginal dryness. It is important for all of us to remember that hormone replacement therapy, albeit an important decision, is not the only choice to improve our health during menopause.

✦ RESOURCES

Communicating with your family members and friends is one way to help you make the hormone replacement therapy decision. A continuing process of communication with your health care provider about hormone replacement therapy is also critical to your health care during the menopausal period. There are numerous other resources that might be useful in this process. First, one of the best uses of our federal tax dollars is *The Menopause: Hormone Therapy Replacement and Women's Health*. This book, although somewhat technically written, is an excellent overview of the pros and cons of hormone replacement therapy. It was written by a consensus panel of leaders in the field and it summarizes what was known in 1992 when it was published. Many of the conclusions are similar to ours. But, you might chose to look at it and to even look at some of the original articles that it references. It is available through the U.S. Bureau of Public Documents.

BOOKS

Many women find the book we discussed earlier helpful—Lila Nachtigall's *Estrogen: The Facts Can Change Your Life*. Another helpful book is Janine O'Leary Cobb's *Understanding Menopause* (New York: A Plume Book, The Penguin Group, 1993).

SELF-HELP

Self-help groups can be extremely beneficial in coping with the decision about hormone replacement therapy. For example, you may not have friends who are struggling with the question to the same extent that you are and by joining a self-help group you can find women with similar concerns. Many of the self-help groups have women who have gone through the menopausal transition and can serve as role models for women who have chosen to take hormone replacement therapy and those who have not. Self-help groups can be extremely powerful because of the intimacy and solidarity that usually develops. If you do not know of a self-help group in your area, you may turn to Chapter Eleven, "Resources," which details your possibilities. Many women's health practices and women's hospitals can be helpful if you call their department of public relations.

PHARMACEUTICAL COMPANIES' PUBLICATIONS

Wyeth-Ayerst Laboratories
P.O. Box 9251
Garden City, NY 11530-9836

Publishes a series of pamphlets called "Life after 45" on menopause, aging, and related issues, with a bias for estrogen therapy. Also Seasons Magazine, *with articles on menopause, health, aging, keeping fit, which is free.*

CIBA Pharmaceutical Company
Division of CIBA-GEIGY Corporation
5566 Morris Avenue
Summit, NJ 07901

Publishes an eight-page booklet on menopause: "Midlife: No Crisis" including definitions, symptoms and treatment, focusing on estrogen therapy.

Mead Johnson Laboratories
Bristol Myers Squibb Company
P.O. Box 4000
Princeton, NJ 08543-4000

Publishes "For the woman approaching menopause," a synopsis of biological and psychological issues.

➤ CHAPTER SEVEN

Myths of Depression

LET'S GET ONE THING STRAIGHT: NATURAL MENOPAUSE IN AND OF IT-self does not cause depression. This may come as a surprise to you because almost everything we read about menopause associates it with depression. As early as 1945, the psychoanalytic view of the menopausal woman was reflected in the work of Helene Deutsch who wrote, "With the cessation of this function, she ends her service to the species, her genital organs become atrophied and the rest of the body gradually shows symptoms of aging" (Deutsch, 1945). This dated theory of the menopausal stage of life has permeated our culture and continues into the 1990s. Articles over the past several years have managed to emphasize this point by consistently describing depression almost exclusively as a problem of midlife women and linking it to a hormonal deficiency.

Certainly when we read these articles we *could become* depressed, but there is one major problem with them. There is no evidence that they are true. Never has a scientific study indicated that menopause alone is a cause of depression. In fact, younger American women tend to have higher rates of depression than older women. Specifically, young women with children under the age of five at home, who are divorced or not getting along with their partner/spouse, are at the greatest risk of depression. Although these factors make a lot of sense, unfortunately we read very little about these women.

The Massachusetts Women's Health Study found that there is no evidence of a menopausal depression when menopause is natural (McKinlay and others, 1987). This study was not limited to women who seek medical attention, but rather included women from the larger community. Menopausal women did not experience depression at the time of menopause any more often than did younger women. The McKinlays found rather consistent rates of depression hovering between 5 and 10 percent for premenopausal, perimenopausal and postmenopausal women, with a slight increase at the perimenopausal period. This group of perimenopausal women may represent women who are experiencing numerous medical symptoms, as we will discuss in a bit.

In this same study, women who had undergone hysterectomies and oophorectomies, on the other hand, had a rate of depression closer to 18 percent. The high rate of depression in this group may have been in response to the *dramatic* drop in hormone production experienced with surgical menopause. In addition, hysterectomy and oophorectomy require major abdominal surgery and a long recovery period. The McKinlays and their associates also suggest that women who are depressed are more likely to suffer from more gynecological symptoms. These women, therefore, might have hysterectomies and oophorectomies more often than nondepressed women (McKinlay and others, 1987). We discuss this in greater detail in Chapter Nine, "Hysterectomy."

Despite these efforts of prominent social scientists to dispel the myth of the menopausal depression, it still flourishes in medical articles and in the popular media. For the most part, the television screen avoids the faces of women in the menopause years. The few women over the age of forty that we see on television on a regular basis are women in their sixties, like Angela Lansbury in *Murder She Wrote*. It was not until recently that we could see Blanche, the youngest member of *The Golden Girls*, and Julia Sugarbaker on *Designing Women* deal with their characters' journey through menopause.

Hollywood, too, has contributed to the myths of menopause that American women absorb. Even the moving film, based on Fannie Flagg's novel *Fried Green Tomatoes at the Whistle Stop Café*, gives an inaccurate message with regard to Evelyn's depression. Evelyn is discouraged and sad, turning only to candy bars and television, when she meets Mrs. Threadgoode. When she describes some of her symptoms,

Mrs. Threadgoode turns to her and says, "Girl, you've got to get your-self some hormones!" The film illustrates that a woman during her menopausal years can develop a more fulfilling and enriching phase of her life. Indeed, the character Evelyn does get those hormones and gets over her "depression." But Evelyn obviously has other stressors in her life that have nothing to do with hormones, including an unin-volved husband, no job or hobbies, a lack of family and social support systems, and practically no physical activity. In fact, she is not only dissatisfied with her situation, but inquisitive and thirsty for a better life. During the film, we watch her break out of old habits and establish a close relationship with a new friend. She begins to exercise regularly, take up new interests and stop asking her husband for permission. It is her exercise regimen, new healthy eating habits and a fulfilling friend-ship that warrant credit for her escape from "depression," not the hor-mones alone. One of our favorite and somewhat bizarre examples of television's view of psychological problems during menopause is from the series *Picket Fences,* where they devoted an episode to a woman who became psychotic because of her menopause and ran over her husband with a steamroller! Alas, her insanity defense was not success-ful. In reality, we haven't come across too many menopausal steam-roller operators, and there is no actual increased risk of depression or psychosis at this time of life.

The truth is that even though menopause does not cause depres-sion, depression can still affect many women at menopause. Why? Be-cause depression is the most common mental health problem shared by all American women. It strikes up to one out of ten American women at any point in time. So even though menopause does not cause depression, just this baseline statistic means that many of you are depressed at this moment. Depression is so common in women that it is often called "the common cold" of female psychological problems. The reason that it is so important to make the distinction that some menopausal women are depressed, but that menopause does not cause depression, is that by blaming depression on menopause alone, many women will not get the adequate care they need. The danger here is that serious cases of depression may be dismissed and misdiagnosed as a natural part of menopause. This is particularly troubling since there are now numerous effective treatments for depression.

A tragic result of this misdiagnosis was reported in *New York* mag-azine in October 1992 (Wolfe, 1992). Theodora Sklover, a former New York City executive, suffered from long-term depression and had experienced many financial reversals. Her friends knew that she was depressed, as she did herself, but ". . . she'd read that menopause could cause depression, and instead of seeking out a psychiatrist for treatment, she went to a physician who gave her estrogen-replacement pills" (Wolfe, 1992, p. 54). The HRT may have helped some of her symptoms of menopause, but it didn't treat her serious case of depression. Theodora Sklover's condition deteriorated, and she eventually jumped to her death from the window of her tenth-story apartment in Manhattan.

Had Sklover had access to more accurate information, she would have known that HRT is not a cure for depression, but that there are many other effective treatments, including antidepressant medication and psychotherapy. It is not hard to understand how women today in Sklover's position may well assume that the symptoms and treatments for depression and menopause are one and the same. HRT for these women is seen as a convenient way to cure depression, more so than beginning psychotherapy. How can we blame menopausal women for this view?

Theodora Sklover's case is just the most dramatic example. The response of Sklover's friends is indicative of the fears that could well continue to fuel the menopause anxiety: "Others panicked. They felt frightened because her death seemed to say something to them about the plight of aging, unattached, professional women in New York" (Wolfe, 1992, p. 47). Sklover's was not a tragedy of aging, menopause or a psychological disease of professional women. Her tragedy was a result of misinformation. Despite the fact that hormones alone do not cause a menopausal depression, millions of women suffering from clinical depression will continue to blame it on this "hormonal imbalance" and not receive the treatment they so desperately need.

A more common case of misinformation regarding the hormone-depression connection is exemplified by Rose, one of our patients. Rose came to see us because of what she described as a "hormonal problem." She was a fifty-two-year-old woman who had worked in a small jewelry factory for the past twenty-five years. Her husband, Ed, was a recovering alcoholic who had been sober for the past ten years. Her three children were grown and lived in nearby communities with their families. Rose was a very funny and insightful woman who was able to cut through to the heart of most matters. She was treasured by her family and at work, for her problem-solving abilities. She also served as a resource in her Baptist church. But something had changed in the way Rose saw the world over the past several years. Ed was a stable and caring man who worked as an accountant and was active in AA. He also tended to spend a lot of time on carpentry, a hobby he loved. Rose's three children relied on her for periodic baby-sitting and were still extremely dependent on her. She was especially close to her thirty-year-old daughter Cathy. Rose had continued to work because she knew the owners well and was able to change her hours to meet her family needs over the years. She was clearly underemployed, even though she recently had been promoted to supervisor.

Rose came to us because her periods were irregular and she had been having severe hot flashes for several years. She was tired, irritable and sad. When we evaluated Rose, we found that she was still perimenopausal since her periods were sporadic and had not stopped completely. Rose represents a category of women who need further attention. Rose, at the age of fifty-two, had experienced a prolonged and difficult perimenopausal period. Although her periods had started to become irregular at the age of forty-eight, they continued. Drs. Peter J. Schmidt and David Rubinow at the National Institute of Mental Health have suggested that this *peri*menopausal period may represent a high-risk time for depression, rather than the *post*menopausal period that has received previous attention (Schmidt and Rubinow, 1991). This would also fit with the Massachusetts Women's Health Study that there was an increase in the rate of depression during the perimenopause (McKinlay and others, 1987). We have found that women whose perimenopausal period is both long and symptomatic may be at risk for depression. This makes perfect sense because difficult symptoms can cause sleep disturbances and a disruption in daily life, which can increase stress. Rose was troubled by her hot flashes, but afraid of HRT because of a family history of cancer.

When we talked with Rose at length, we found that the history of cancer in her family was that of pancreatic cancer. Rose was not aware that the reasons not to take HRT are related to breast or uterine cancer. We discuss this in detail in Chapter Six, "Hormone Replacement Therapy." When Rose started HRT, her hot flashes vanished within weeks and she was greatly relieved.

However, Rose still struggled with her sadness. She had also learned recently that her daughter Cathy was going to be moving out of state. Rose, like many women, remained close to all of her grown children and found that she enjoyed relating to these adults she and Ed had raised. The extended perimenopause was an additional stress, but not the only cause of her symptoms. Since Cathy had been her main support over the past ten years, her moving was potentially a major loss to Rose.

It became apparent to us that Rose had struggled with dysthymia for many years. She was always somewhat pessimistic, expected little from life, and had grown accustomed to the role of being everyone's caretaker. During a course of short-term psychotherapy, we helped

Rose expand her network of friends. We also watched her discover different expectations from her relationship, including more reciprocity. She developed a friendship with a woman at work and initiated more shared activities with Ed.

Rose's story helps us understand that depression during the menopausal years is complicated. Psychological problems, like life, are not that simple. One of the primary reasons we wrote this book was our outrage at the dangerous persistence of both popular and the medical media to portray depression in women as primarily a hormonal problem of midlife women. McKinlay, McKinlay and Brambilla conclude that "menopause as a physiologic process provides a single convenient potentially treatable cause, which is attractive to the busy clinician and avoids the need to consider other, more complex and probably less treatable explanations" (McKinlay and others, 1987, p. 360). It is easier to dismiss menopausal women as suffering from hormonal changes, rather than to examine their complex, social and physical problems.

✦ WHAT IS DEPRESSION?

The epidemiologist Dr. Myrna Weissman suggests that we can view depression as a mood state, a symptom or a syndrome (Weissman, 1980). Depression can also be seen as a continuum of severity, ranging from a "bad day" on the far left of the continuum to a major depressive episode on the far right. Men and women alike have bad days where they feel sad and irritable, and frequently we use the expression "I'm depressed today." But clinical depression is more than fleeting sadness. Depression as a psychological disorder has been studied in great depth. The American Psychiatric Association's *Diagnosis and Statistical Manual, Third Edition Revised,* is a book that describes all major psychiatric problems. There are many different forms of depression. Sometimes a loss, like a divorce, or being fired from a job can precipitate a depressive episode. These reactions to painful or stressful situations are usually called "adjustment reactions." These are usually short-term. To be depressed, of course, is also part of a normal grieving process. One category, "dysthymic disorder," is characterized by at least two years of feelings of low self-esteem, hopelessness, worthlessness, negativism and sadness. This is a long-term problem, and many women may continue to function quite well, despite their personal pain. You can look at Table 7-1 to see whether you might have symptoms of dysthymic disorder (American Psychiatric Association, 1987).

As we move further to the right on the scale, we encounter the

Table 7–1

SYMPTOMS OF
DYSTHYMIC DISORDER

1. Have you had a depressed mood for most of the day, more days than not, for at least two years?

2. Do you have, when you are depressed, at least *two of* the following?
   1. poor appetite or overeating
   2. insomnia or hypersomnia
   3. low energy or fatigue
   4. low self-esteem
   5. poor concentration or difficulty making decisions
   6. feelings of hopelessness

3. Have you ever had a manic episode—overly high amounts of energy, poor judgment. If so, you may have a bipolar disorder.

4. Are you taking medications that can cause depression? If so, check with your primary-care doctor.

•If you have answered YES to questions 1 & 2, and NO to 3 & 4, you may have dysthymia.

Adapted from the *Diagnostic and Statistical Manual of Mental Disorders, Third Edition*, Revised (Washington, DC: American Psychiatric Association, 1987).

more intense and disruptive types of depression. At the far right we find a major depressive episode (as you can see in Table 7-2). A Major Depressive Episode involves frequent and daily symptoms including frequent crying, sadness, loss of interest, inability to concentrate, weight changes, a loss of interest in sex, and may include suicidal plans and suicidal feelings (American Psychiatric Association, 1987). Some women who are already dysthymic may develop more severe symptoms and progress to a Major Depressive Episode also. If suicidal plans become a part of your symptoms, it is crucial to get professional help as soon as possible. Many people have fleeting thoughts of suicide when they are mildly depressed or under severe stress, but when these feelings turn into specific ideas of action or actual impulses toward suicide, it is important to respond immediately. Remember that these feelings can be treated successfully by a mental health professional.

There are several other psychological problems that include depressive symptoms. These include a bipolar disorder or what was once called manic depressive disorder. The essential feature here is that, in addition to episodes of major depression, there are also episodes of manic or extremely active behavior and sometimes euphoric times when the person shows impaired judgment.

✦ Women's Depression: The Psychological Common Cold

Women are much more likely than men to suffer from depression. Two to three times as many women suffer from depression than do men (Weissman and Klerman, 1985). This stark statistic is almost completely ignored in medical school and psychological training programs and is also overlooked in the ample self-help literature on depression. Not surprisingly, formal psychological treatments for depression have often underplayed women's issues as well. It is possible for us as women to get adequate treatment for depression if we approach the situation with care and with the maximum amount of information.

✦ A Comprehensive Approach to Depression

Biological Changes

The best way to understand depression and why women suffer from it so often is to use a comprehensive approach. Let's look first at the possible biological factors affecting depression. We have just outlined the hormonal change associated with menopause. Another biological factor is heredity. There does seem to be a tendency for major depression to occur in families, generation after generation. If you have a biological relative, such as a mother, father, grandparent, sister or brother, who has been diagnosed as depressed, then you have a greater risk for depression. This does not necessarily mean that you *will* suffer from depression. Yet this is important information for your health care

Table 7-2

THE DEPRESSION CONTINUUM

Increasing Severity →

"Bad Day"	"Blues" "Moodiness"	Long-term sadness Negativism Low self-esteem	Sadness Tearfulness Feelings of loss in response to a specific stressor Time limited	Frequent Daily *Symptoms* Tearfulness Loss of interest
TRANSIENT FEELINGS	PERSISTENT MOODINESS	DYSTHYMIC DISORDER	ADJUSTMENT OR GRIEF REACTION	MAJOR DEPRESSIVE EPISODE

Table 7-3

SYMPTOMS OF
MAJOR DEPRESSIVE EPISODE

Have you had at least *five* of the following symptoms during the same two-week period, and is this a *change* from your usual functioning?

1. depressed mood most of the day, nearly every day.

-or-

2. markedly diminished interest or pleasure in all, or almost all, activities most of the day, nearly every day.

-and-

3. significant weight loss or weight gain when not dieting (e.g., more than 5 percent of body weight in a month), or decrease or increase in appetite nearly every day.

4. insomnia or hypersomnia nearly every day.

5. psychomotor agitation or retardation nearly every day.

6. fatigue or loss of energy nearly every day.

7. feelings of worthlessness or excessive or inappropriate guilt nearly every day.

8. diminished ability to think or concentrate, or indecisiveness, nearly every day.

9. recurrent thoughts of death (not just fear of dying), recurrent suicidal ideation without a specific plan, or a suicide attempt or a specific plan.

•If you answered YES to 1 or 2 and YES to four items from 3–9, you may be suffering from a major depressive episode.

•Adapted from *The Diagnostic and Statistical Manual of Mental Disorders, Third Edition Rev.* 1987.

provider to have, especially when talking about possible symptoms of mood changes.

A third and important biological change is the experience of hot flashes and other vasomotor symptoms during menopause. When hot flashes or night sweats disrupt a woman's sleep, she can become sleep deprived. This sleep deprivation can lead to a vulnerability to psychological problems like depression. This has been called the "domino effect" of hot flashes (Sherwin, 1993). This domino effect was a problem for Rose and for another of our patients, Joan. Joan was experiencing symptoms of menopause when she came to see us. In addition, she complained of low energy, fatigue and a loss of the ability to concentrate. Because Joan was an accomplished painter and had been very productive, her loss of creative energy was very disturbing to her. At the same time, she informed us that she was experiencing night sweats that would awaken her in the middle of the night. Quite often she found it difficult to return to sleep. The sleep deprivation led to loss of concentration which in turn made Joan feel mildly irritable and frustrated. This indirect result of a biological change associated with menopause is worth exploring further so that it can be clarified.

Joan also felt like she had a "hell of a case of PMS." This is a description that many of our patients use to describe their mood changes during the menopausal years. In fact, if you have suffered from PMS, you may be more likely to have similar symptoms at menopause. What makes Joan's experience and that of other women who feel like they have PMS is that the feelings are usually transient, sometimes cyclical, and more in the category of moodiness or the blues—on the left end of our continuum.

In contrast, women suffering from a major depressive episode like Theodora Sklover tend to feel depressed and sad most of the day, every day for a longer period of time. Depressed women often describe a feeling that they just cannot function anymore. It is important to distinguish the transient PMS-like symptoms from a major depressive episode or dysthymia, because the treatments are quite different.

Joan, for example, decided not to take hormone replacement therapy. She believed that she was at low risk for cardiovascular disease and osteoporosis. Joan benefited from a nonmedical approach to dealing with her hot flashes. She began to wear layers of cotton clothing—and learned paced-breathing exercises. She also reported that taking 400 units of vitamin E was helpful to her. She carried a small fan with her, and soon began to feel better. Joan, a creative woman all the way, decided that she would just get up when she experienced night sweats and do some painting at that time. Joan was fortunate in that she did not have a structured job during the day and could nap when she chose to do so.

Too many other women, like Rose, suffer in silence. They approach their symptoms and sometimes their lives with a quiet sadness. They view menopausal symptoms and even depression as something to live through. We believe that women need to know all their options, from HRT to nonmedical approaches to alleviate hot flashes. They also need to know the different approaches to treating depression. These choices can improve physical and psychological functioning and help women gain control of their lives.

PSYCHOLOGICAL CHANGES

We have seen that many of the psychological changes are positive. Women who tend toward depression, however, often have problems with self-esteem. Self-esteem is defined as the general feeling of worth and importance, separate from the present situation. Thus self-esteem is something we each carry within us as individuals. Although much has been written about self-esteem and depression in general, less attention has been paid to how women specifically define our self-esteem. We still psychologically *organize* our lives around family and relationship issues. Alexandra Kaplan and others at the Stone Center at Wellesley College have developed new literature looking at women's psychological development. These scholars suggest that the best way to understand women's adult development is through a *self-in-relationship model*. Unlike models of male development, a female model of development postulates that women define themselves *primarily* through relationships with others—family members, friends, lovers, children. Thus, any attempt to understand women's development, and especially depression, must place relationship issues at the *center* (Kaplan, 1986).

One of our patients, Rebecca, was a fifty-year-old woman who came to see us because of a difficult divorce. Rebecca's divorce had been traumatic; she discovered that her husband had been in an extramarital affair for many years. She had raised her fifteen-year-old daughter essentially alone because her husband had always traveled extensively on business. However, during the divorce, her husband suddenly filed for sole custody, and therefore suggested that he should keep the family home. When this strategy failed, he filed for bankruptcy during the divorce itself, only to reemerge two years later doing quite well. Rebecca, however, took on private tutoring in addition to her teaching, and managed to provide well for herself and her daughter, although they had a modest lifestyle.

Rebecca had always worked as a reading specialist in a school and was very invested in her career. Nevertheless, she always felt that it was not very worthwhile, because she made so much less money than did her financially successful husband. Rebecca's family history only bolstered her view that a woman's importance was related to her marriage alone. Her father was also a successful businessman and was devoted to her mother. Her mother, however, was very protective of her father and insisted that Rebecca and her younger sister be extremely quiet when their father was around so they wouldn't bother him. She painted an image of two little girls playing in their room with dolls while the mother and father talked quietly over cocktails in the living room. Thus, "being quiet and dutiful" was an important part of Rebecca's self-esteem. We also discovered through our work together that Rebecca's mother had abused alcohol for many years and essentially had anesthetized herself into a quiet and subservient position. After a course of psychotherapy, it became clear to Rebecca that she would live through her traumatic divorce.

SOCIAL CHANGES

In the past, most of the writing about menopause emphasized one sociological factor labeled, "the empty-nest syndrome." The empty-nest syndrome was defined as women feeling sad and a sense of loss when their children moved out of the home. Although the empty nest has received a tremendous amount of attention, it may or may not affect menopausal women. This becomes clear when we trace the history of the use of the term "empty-nest syndrome."

The "empty-nest syndrome" was first used in a study in 1966 in the *American Journal of Psychiatry* (Deykin, 1966). The study, rather than examining large numbers of women in American society, looked at eleven women in a psychiatric hospital in Boston, who were suffering from major depressive episodes. Among these eleven women, nine were found to have had conflicted relationships with their adult children (Deykin, 1966, p. 1422). Hence the empty-nest syndrome was hatched! There are several problems with this simplistic analysis. One of the most destructive effects of the popularization of psychology is that frequently people generalize from a very small group to a large group. The very fact that these women were hospitalized sets them apart from the majority of women at midlife, and yet the empty nest has been generalized as a syndrome for most midlife women. If they had examined a more representative group of women in midlife who had children, they would have found that these women may or may not have had primarily sad feelings about their children moving out. We discuss this more in Chapter Eight, "Realities of Stress." Whether or not the empty-nest syndrome exists, it certainly would not affect all women at menopause. Some women bear children in their early twenties, and their children have been out of the home for ten years before they reach menopause. Other women have teenagers still at home. The empty-nest syndrome serves as an example of how all midlife women have been lumped together in one handy waste-basket category.

Another problem with emphasis on the empty-nest syndrome is that women now work outside of the home in record numbers. Our sources of satisfaction are not as restricted as they once were. One study found, not surprisingly, that the lowest rates of depression occurred in women who were both employed and had low employment strain as well as low strain in their marriage. Conversely, the highest level of depression occurred in women who had only one source of gratification, that is women who were not employed outside of the home and who were also experiencing a high level of stress in their marriage (Aneshensel, 1986).

RACIAL ISSUES

Minority women have higher rates of depression too, with one study finding that African-American women had 42 percent higher rates of depression than white women (Russo and Olmedo, 1983). Latin women and Asian-American women also suffer from depression more than men (Loo, 1988). Native American women have rates of suicide twice as high as other American women, and their rate of death from alcoholism is six times as high. Most importantly, their rate of treatment for these problems is lower than that of other groups (U.S. Department, 1988). This is undoubtedly a result of less access to mental health services. These increased rates do not surprise us because depression in menopausal women has been linked to multiple sources of worry, and being a member of a minority group can add another level of concerns, from discrimination to harassment.

A related sociological issue for depression is that of poverty. The economic struggles for women in the 1980s worsened the situation dramatically. Most people on welfare in the United States are mothers and their children. Many of them receive virtually no financial support for these children from the fathers. The skyrocketing divorce rate has also left additional women in a state of poverty, creating a new term, "the feminization of poverty." Others have pointed out that many women are just "one divorce away from poverty." In addition, many married women have husbands who have been either laid off from their jobs, or whose financial situation did not develop as the family had hoped. These economic losses become an additional reason for some women to work outside of the home. And remember, women still suffer from unequal pay for equal work. It is clear that poverty and its associated stress is a risk factor for depression as well as numerous other mental health problems. For any woman, menopausal or not, these economic stresses can precipitate depressions.

The severity of pain from relationships can also be seen in the divorce rate of 40 to 50 percent of all American marriages; and divorce during midlife can be a powerful trigger for depression. Pressures relating to extramarital affairs, as in the case of Rebecca, are common when divorce occurs during the menopausal years. The breakup of a long-term relationship may be particularly threatening to a woman struggling with issues of aging and a heightened awareness of potential loss. For many midlife women like Rebecca, betrayal comes as a sudden and traumatic shock, profoundly threatening self-esteem.

The Massachusetts Women's Health Study documents that these social changes at midlife are powerful among women who do become depressed. There was an association between depression and *multiple sources of worry*. Another important factor was the actual number of people who were worrying the depressed woman. Women who were worried about someone, usually a member of their family, were *three times* more likely to be depressed than other women. They were usually concerned about issues involving their husband, partner or children (McKinlay and others, 1987b).

The authors also revealed that women who had less than a high school education and who were widowed, separated or divorced had a rate of depression approaching 23 percent, more than twice the rate of depression in all other categories (McKinlay and others, 1987). This finding underscores two important issues. First, women need strong relationships in their lives. Women who are widowed, separated or divorced may be lacking that relationship, as are women like Rebecca who are struggling in a difficult marriage. Education is also an important factor in women's well-being. Women with less than a high school education are most likely to suffer from the effects of poverty and job discrimination. The low rate of depression among women who had never been married has been consistently reported in literature on depression in women (so much for the old-maid myth).

In summary, there are multiple biological, psychological and sociological changes that affect women during the menopausal years. Much evidence suggests that effects of the psychological and sociological changes at midlife are in fact stronger than the biological changes alone that are associated with menopause. That still leaves us with menopausal women suffering from a depression rate of between 5 and 10 percent. We need to concern ourselves with the complicated assessment and treatment issues.

✦ TREATMENT FOR DEPRESSION

The most important thing to remember about the treatment of depression is that there is a variety of effective treatments available to you. First, if you look at the tables on depression, and find that you are suffering from dysthymia or a major depressive episode, you should seek psychological treatment. There are many types of qualified mental health professionals. The most important issue is that the person be experienced in treating depressed women. Depression is usually depression, and responds to specific types of psychotherapy, as we will describe shortly. Many other women choose to go to their primary care clinicians, who may be a family practitioner, general internist, gynecologist, or nurse practitioner to be diagnosed. Any woman seeking medical advice regarding depression needs to be as explicit as possible. For example, if there is a family member who has been depressed, your primary care clinician should know about it. Also, if there are problems in your marriage or relationship, that is significant information, not a cause for shame. Alcohol consumption, prescription and over-the-counter medications that you might be taking also need to be discussed.

Many drugs are commonly associated with depressive symptoms. The most common culprits are alcohol, benzodiazepines like Valium and Xanax, drugs used to treat hypertension and oral contraceptives. So, if you take any of these medications and you are depressed, you should discuss the situation with your physician.

Some women become depressed after starting HRT. It is the progesterone, not estrogen, that is the problem. If you have had previous problems with depression in response to oral contraceptives, you should inform your physician when trying to make a decision about hormone replacement therapy. The hormones used in earlier forms of birth control pills were at significantly higher doses than those used today in hormone replacement therapy. In addition, our situation at menopause leaves us in a state of estrogen deficiency. In other words, before menopause we were adding hormones to hormones when using birth control pills. During menopause, we are lacking in estrogen, so the body's response is different. Nonetheless, a previous depressive episode in association with oral contraceptive use should be discussed with a physician in order to provide the best care.

At Women's Health Associates, we work as a team in order to provide a comprehensive assessment of a patient's problem. Many women can clearly identify their depression and can pinpoint a psychosocial factor that is responsible for the depression. It is always important to be as thorough in diagnosis as possible. We have found, from time to time, that a woman who presents with depression actually has hypothyroidism (an underactive thyroid gland) or another medical problem. Similarly, some women go to their physicians for problems such as chronic back pain or headaches, and turn out to have depression associated with marital or other family or relationship problems. The overlap and interaction between medical and psychological problems is complicated. Research indicates that somewhere between 30 to 50 percent of depressions are misdiagnosed (Goldberg, 1988). At the same time, as we have reviewed, sometimes depression may be a part of a medical condition. We find that we present the biopsychosocial model to a woman and she can understand that there are numerous approaches to her depression, just as their are numerous factors causing the depression.

DEPRESSION VERSUS EXHAUSTION?

Many of our patients are working outside of the home, as well as bearing the largest share of the burden of household duties and remaining responsibilities for teens or adult children. It is for these women that we evaluate the difference between exhaustion and clinical depression. A recent national panel on sleep disorder reiterated that most Americans require seven to eight hours of sleep per night. However, most Americans do not get this much sleep. We have found that for many of our patients, giving up sleep is one of their first strategies for coping with an inordinately stressful and busy schedule. We have our patients fill out diaries tracking the amount of sleep they get, the intake of caffeine and sugar, and the amount of individual exercise. Here is Rebecca's schedule, before her divorce.

6:00 a.m.	Wake up, shower and get dressed
6:45 a.m.	Tidy up the house

7:15 a.m.	See that daughter is awake
7:30 a.m.	Prepare breakfast for family
8:00 a.m.	Phone call to mother
8:30 to 5:00 p.m.	Work
5:30 to 6:00 p.m.	Pick up daughter from sports, pick up groceries, return home
6:00 to 6:30 p.m.	Make dinner
6:30 to 6:45 p.m.	Eat dinner
6:45 to 7:30 p.m.	Clean up dishes, kitchen
7:30 to 8:30 p.m.	Call family members, regarding mother
8:30 to 9:30 p.m.	Tidy up the house
9:30 to 10:00 p.m.	Try to talk to daughter
10:00 to 10:05 p.m.	Talk to husband when he comes home
10:30 to 11:00 p.m.	Exhausted, both physically and mentally, attempt to read or engage in some form of personal relaxation
11:00 p.m.	Go to bed

If this hectic schedule looks familiar to you, you may be living the *Second Shift*, a term created by author Arlie Hochschild (Hochschild, 1989) for women who are employed and work one shift at work and another at home. We are never surprised that a woman with such a schedule might consume large amounts of caffeine and sugar to keep going during the day, or consume alcohol or be tempted by Valium or other drugs to relax at night. You might try filling out a daily diary to see how your own schedule measures up. Given these stresses, food and alcohol are two substances that women often use to help them get by.

THE DIETING DEPRESSION

With so many women dieting, the associated depression is understandable. It is clear that women's reactions to dieting are significant and may include irritability, anxiety and depression (Stunkard and Rush, 1974). Since women have been socialized from an early age to see food as nurturing and as something for which we are responsible, food has a primary role in women's lives. In addition, many women we see who are under severe stress use food, particularly simple sugars and carbohydrates, to feel better quickly. Indeed, the ingestion of sugar and carbohydrates can lead to a dramatic increase in blood sugar, which can make a woman feel much better. This is only temporary, because just as the blood sugar rises quickly, it drops quickly, precipitating symptoms of shakiness, fatigue, hunger and creating a vicious cycle. In this situation, dieting can be associated with feelings of deprivation and loss, which can in turn lead to sadness and chronic irritability. Chronic dieters are hyper-responsive to anxiety and other emotions (Polivy and Herman, 1985). Although a full-blown clinical depression, or major depressive episode, is not a typical response to dieting, such feelings of chronic sadness and irritability are quite common in women who are dieting. In this situation, we often find it helpful to adjust a woman's nutritional regimen by working with a nutritionist to move away from dieting as a lifestyle. We emphasize the positive role of exercise and a low-fat, not necessarily low-calorie diet.

ALCOHOL AND DEPRESSION

Many women turn to alcohol to reduce stress. In our practice, we've seen many women who use alcohol to treat their own sleep disturbances—one of the classic signs of anxiety or depression. This provides only short-term relief. In small amounts, alcohol does work as a sedative, but over time, consistent and heavy use can cause or worsen sleep problems. Alcohol and depression in women need to be evaluated. Dr. Barbara McCrady, Professor of Psychology and Clinical Director of the Center of Alcohol Studies at Rutgers University, suggests that 25 percent of alcoholic women have suffered from depression. A woman who abuses alcohol may find her depressive moods are worsened by the guilt and shame she feels about drinking (Tamerin and others, 1976). Dr. McCrady adds that after a month period of abstinence, if a woman is still depressed, or if it is clear that depression preceded alcohol abuse, then the depression should be treated (McCrady, 1988).

We work with women who have numerous responsibilities and stressors to try to help identify a part of their day during which they can reserve quality time for themselves. Even a half hour of quiet isolation, reading a book or taking a walk with a friend, can make all the difference. It is clear that women continue to provide the bulk of household work, as well as family obligations. This is true for most societies, despite the fact that women have continued to enter and stay in the workforce in record numbers.

✦ PSYCHOTHERAPY

Whether a woman is experiencing an adjustment problem, dysthymia or a major depression, as we discussed earlier, the most important thing to remember is that psychotherapy can usually provide effective and rapid treatment.

Psychotherapy is a structured process that is aimed at alleviating psychological pain. Most psychotherapy involves individual weekly sessions that are approximately forty-five to fifty minutes long. Psychotherapy is extremely effective in treating depression and is usually covered to some extent by health insurance.

There are many ways to find a good psychotherapist: The first step is to collect some names of qualified mental health professionals. A psychotherapist who specializes in treating depression is preferable. You will be surprised how many people have had contact with mental health professionals. Friends and relatives and members of the clergy can often give you referrals and may even be able to share with you a personal experience of psychotherapy. Usually, psychotherapists do not see *best* friends or close relatives of their present patients, but in that case, your friend's psychotherapist can recommend someone else.

Your family physician or health care provider may be another good resource and usually is familiar with qualified mental health professionals in your area. Remember to be clear if you ask them for a referral, and specify that you are interested in "psychotherapy." Some physicians hear a request for relief as a request for medication. Medication may not be necessary, and in fact could be counterproductive for some.

After getting names of good psychotherapists, you should make sure that person is a licensed health care professional. This is important in providing you with well-trained professionals, but also is often used by insurance companies in deciding whether your psychotherapy will be reimbursed. In addition, each state has a Board of Health that licenses health care providers, including psychiatrists, psychologists, social workers and psychiatric nurses. If there have been documented ethical complaints about a provider, the Board of Health often has that information. There is a pamphlet available, "Choosing a Psychotherapist," from the American Psychological Association, listed in the resource section of our book.

If you are seeking psychotherapy and you are a member of a minority group, it is often helpful to find a therapist from a similar background. Many women prefer to see a female psychotherapist. If that is not possible, however, it is often possible that a sensitive therapist of any background or gender can be helpful. Some of the best therapists we know take an approach that they will learn about the cultural differences from their patients, while being able to provide their own knowledge about treatment of depression.

Once you have found a psychotherapist, the next step is the initial consultation. During the first consultation it is very common to spend most of the time talking about symptoms and life issues. These life issues may involve your partner, parents and children, as well as recent life experiences. You should try to reveal any history of sexual abuse, physical abuse or neglect, and alcohol and drug abuse so that your therapist can be helpful to you. It is essential to discuss any suicidal thoughts or feelings that you may be having. Toward the end of the session, it is quite appropriate for you to ask the psychotherapist what they think will be helpful to you. If you are not comfortable with either the psychotherapist or the treatment plan, there is no reason to schedule a second session without at least getting a consultation from another psychotherapist. It is very common in psychotherapy for people to schedule first appointments, but to later decide that they would work better with another mental health professional. You should not feel nervous about changing if you find another psychotherapist with whom you feel more comfortable.

You will probably be apprehensive about your first consultation and that is okay. Once, years ago, Dr. Landau had an office in a building that housed several other psychotherapists as well. She was scheduled to see a new client. At the appointed hour, she went out to the waiting room and said, "Ms. Joanne Jones?" A woman in the waiting area answered, and Dr. Landau then introduced herself. The interview proceeded, but after several minutes, the woman's story did not sound like the one Dr. Landau remembered from their earlier phone conversation: Ever the astute clinician, Dr. Landau interrupted, "Excuse me, are you Joanne Jones?"

The anxious client responded, "No, but I'm so nervous I would have said 'yes' to anything!"

After showing her upstairs to another psychologist's office, Dr. Landau went back out into the waiting room—then fifteen minutes late—to find a mildly irritated but equally anxious Joanne Jones!

Whatever form of health insurance you may have, it usually includes some psychotherapy as part of the benefit package. We hope that ample mental health services with freedom of choice will be provided in any new health care reforms and that all Americans will have health insurance. If you have no health insurance, psychotherapy can be expensive, with hourly fees anywhere from $50 to over $100 per session. However, everyone can go to a local community mental health center. You may not be seen weekly on a long-term basis, but crisis intervention is usually available. In addition, there are agencies funded by religious groups and by the United Way, like Family Service Agencies, that also provide counseling and psychotherapy at an affordable cost. If you are not familiar with your local community mental health center, you can also contact the local branch of your National Association for Mental Health.

The types of psychotherapy that are most effective for depression have several factors in common. They focus on providing a depressed woman with alternatives to her feelings of hopelessness. In addition, most of these programs involve an active psychotherapist and are quite structured. Some psychotherapists tend to listen and reflect back to the client as the major treatment technique. This technique alone is not usually helpful when dealing with depression. After one or two sessions of gathering information, you should expect the psychotherapist to be interactive and focus on change. One of the best guides to one form of psychotherapy is Dr. David Burns' *Feeling Good, The New Mood Therapy*. This book, described in resources, details cognitive behavior therapy, which focuses on specific short-term goals and negative-thinking patterns that can both lead to depression and keep a woman depressed (Burns, 1980).

Other forms of individual psychotherapy that have proven to be effective with depressed woman are interpersonal psychotherapy, behavior therapy and feminist psychotherapy. If you want more detail about these forms of psychotherapy, the American Psychological Association publishes *Women and Depression: Risk Factors and Treatment Issues*. This book, edited by a group of eminent women psychologists, is the most up to date review of treatments for depression as they apply to women (McGrath and others, 1990).

If your problem is primarily marital (and most women know when this is the case), then you can consider marital therapy. An unhappy marriage can certainly either precipitate or worsen a depression. As women, we all too often accept most of the responsibility for a problematic relationship. By participating in long-term individual psychotherapy without addressing the problems of the marriage, it is clear that a woman will suffer unnecessarily. At times, women are so depressed and unable to function, that they are not able to address the marital problems right away. In that case, a course of individual psychotherapy, followed by marital psychotherapy, may well be beneficial.

✦ ANTIDEPRESSANT MEDICATION

Antidepressant medication can often be used to treat depression. Medication is best used in combination with psychotherapy. This has been supported by the work of many researchers. You are most likely to respond well to a medication when you have the symptoms of a major depression that we outlined earlier—if your depression is severe, if you have a family history of depression, or if you have responded well to medication in the past (Burns, 1980).

It is important not to see treatment for depression as either/or. Some people are unable to engage in psychotherapy without some medication to treat the biological symptoms such as sleep disturbance or weight loss. Many psychotherapists will see a woman individually for eight weeks before recommending medication. If you see a psychiatrist, she or he can prescribe antidepressant medication. Otherwise, your psychotherapist often works with a consulting psychiatrist. In some situations, your primary care physician may be comfortable prescribing an antidepressant medication. In both cases, it is important for your physician to remain in contact with your psychotherapist to provide the best coordinated health care.

There are dozens of different medications for depression. The first generation of antidepressants was the group of tricyclic antidepressants, so named because of their chemical structure. They had the advantage of being able to treat depression effectively and they are not expensive. The best way to take a tricyclic medication is to start with a small dose and work up to a larger dose as necessary. Many women report that they have taken tricyclics such as amitriptyline (Elavil) in the past, but that they had no positive response. In that case it is helpful for you to remember the highest dosage ever taken and the duration it was taken, because many women have been prescribed an inadequate amount for an inadequate time.

The medication receiving the most recent attention is fluoxetine, or Prozac. In a matter of two years, Prozac went from being newly introduced to the market to being the most frequently prescribed antidepressant medication in the country. One of the reasons that Prozac is so popular is that it is quite effective. In addition, it does not have some of the common side effects of the tricyclic antidepressants, including dry mouth, constipation, bladder problems and dizziness. In some cases, women feel agitated on Prozac. Prozac does occasionally have a side effect of making a person feel somewhat anxious or "hyper." Some of our patients who have had a negative reaction to Prozac describe feeling as if they have been consuming too much caffeine. If this feeling does not disappear over a matter of days, it should be discussed with your physician. Prozac has been seen as a wonder drug that not only treats women for depression but also helps them lose weight. An informal poll of the health providers at Women's Health Associates revealed that no one knew a woman who had actually lost weight on Prozac. On the other hand, none of the women treated with Prozac had gained weight, a common reaction to the tricyclic antidepressants!

There are many other types of antidepressant medications. One of the most important things to remember is that with modern medicine, if you are suffering from a severe depression, the combination of psychotherapy and medication can be extremely effective. It is important not to quit if either one or both of these attempts should fail the first time. You must not give up hope. With the wide range of psychotherapies and psychotherapists available, you should be able to get relief from depression. Other long-term problems may well take longer to change, but you can get relatively quick relief from your serious symptoms of depression within a matter of ten to twelve weeks.

✦ WHAT NOT TO DO WHEN YOU ARE DEPRESSED

The tragedy is that many women do nothing when they are suffering from depression. Most psychological problems are treated by primary care physicians, not mental health professionals, if they are treated at all. We as women are often more comfortable getting help for others than for ourselves. Reaching out for support from other women and from a mental health professional are the most effective steps you can take.

Just as there are social factors that might cause depression, so can social factors alleviate depression. One of the most important things to fight, especially at the beginning of the depressive episode, is a tendency toward isolation. If you feel depressed, *do not remain isolated and brood.* Depression can make you feel so bad that you don't feel you are even worthy of other people's time. Do not cut yourself off from friends and family. Doing so will not help you "sort things out," it will make you feel worse. Many women are particularly reticent about revealing their problems, because the problem often involves their husbands. They worry about betrayal, or their husbands have told them explicitly not to confide in anyone. This is not acceptable. You can find a trustworthy friend, family member, member of the clergy or doctor who may be helpful. Also, these resources can recommend a psychotherapist, if you decide to see one. On the other hand, if you can get over your initial lethargy and tendency toward being alone, talking with a close friend can be one of the most important outlets for depression. A study by Drs. Brown and Harris in Great Britain found that the presence of a close and confiding intimate person in a woman's life could protect her from depression when she would otherwise be likely to succumb (Brown and others, 1986).

Do not self-medicate with alcohol and other drugs. As we discussed before, many women try to treat themselves for fatigue by using large quantities of sugar and caffeine during the day. At night they may relax with a glass or two of wine, or perhaps a prescribed tranquilizer. These are dangerous habits and once started are very difficult to terminate. The studies on alcohol we discuss further in Chapter Eight reveal that even two drinks of alcohol per day can lead to medical problems in women (Tuyns and Pequinot, 1984). Alcohol may relax you and help you sleep—at first. However, after four hours or so, you will awaken because alcohol causes a sleep disturbance. Alcohol worsens depression, and you will be gaining another problem.

Xanax, a benzodiazepine, was first introduced as a wonder drug, able to treat both anxiety and depression. Over the long run, it has proven to be addictive. We have seen many women suffer tremendously from Xanax withdrawal. Valium, Librium and Ativan are also tranquilizers that should be used cautiously to treat anxiety, not depression.

An intriguing review article by Susan Nolen-Hoeksema of Stanford University helps us understand the isolation of depression when she links social and psychological factors. She suggests that when women begin to feel depressed, we turn inward, and by taking responsibility for relationships, often blame ourselves. Men, on the other hand, may tend to turn outward more, that is become involved with sports and other hobbies and distract themselves. Thus, they may have better ways of coping with depression than do women (Nolen-Hoeksema, 1987). Our work suggests that the female tendency toward analyzing relationships, combined with little power to create change in those relationships, can lead to feelings of helplessness and depression. These two separate styles of possible coping mechanisms for depression put women and men at cross purposes and relationship stress can follow.

Susan Nolen-Hoeksema's work suggests that men, who distract themselves by exercising or playing sports, may have a good idea here (Nolen-Hoeksema, 1987). *Do not remain sedentary if you are depressed.* Of course, if your sleep pattern has been disruptive, it is hard to maintain even your normal activities, and indeed this is one of the signs of depression. Some studies on running found that the release of endorphins was helpful in coping with depression. However, to the extent that you can control your behavior, the possibility of increased activity can be extremely successful. If you are like some of us and have never managed to experience this "runner's high," don't worry, try something else like walking, a dance class, basketball, or rollerblading. We discuss exercise in our chapter on health promotion, Chapter Ten.

We will leave you with one thought about treatment for depression—if you are feeling depressed, get some help and fight against the tendency to remain alone! Don't become one of all too many women who fail to receive help even though it is there.

✦ COMMUNICATION WITH YOUR HEALTH PROFESSIONAL

It is important to be as detailed as possible in talking with your physician. Your symptoms of depression may be elicited by your health professional. It is important to be as direct as possible about other issues. Some of the issues patients often have difficulty talking about include: sexual abuse, eating disorders, early childhood neglect and abuse, drug or alcohol abuse, sexual problems in a relationship, homosexuality and domestic violence. This information can provoke shame, and many people are reluctant to disclose it. The physician or other health care professional who is trying to assess your situation and make appropriate recommendations needs to know any permanent history.

You are most likely to get the best treatment if you are direct and open with your physician or health care provider. However, physicians are human, often make mistakes and may not be as sensitive as we would like them to be. For example, suppose you have been waiting for your physician for over a half hour. He or she comes into the examining room and in a hurried fashion, apologizes, and looks preoccupied. You try to bring up your issue of depression but you feel "brushed off" or minimized. It is important for you to be as direct as possible and to state, "I'm concerned that I've been depressed." Sometimes physicians in their attempt to be supportive, minimize problems. If this is the case, it is important to state again, ". . . but I know I'm having a problem here, and I think I could use a referral to a psychotherapist."

If after one or two attempts you feel that you are not being heard, you have several choices. First, you can try to make an appointment for another day, assuming that your physician may have had a couple of unusually busy days. Or, you could try to talk to your physician on the phone. If these approaches do not work, you could consider changing physicians. Some physicians are only comfortable in the biological sphere and are less comfortable in the psychosocial sphere. In that case, you might want to continue to work with your provider, but use other resources for obtaining psychological care.

✦ COMMUNICATION WITH YOUR FAMILY

We define family as people who are committed to one another, who love one another and who may or may not live together. A depressed member of a family can have a powerful negative effect on the family system. At the same time, an unresponsive family can increase a person's feeling of isolation, worthlessness, hopelessness and ultimately increase depression. One of the tragedies of depression is that a person feels completely isolated and this can become a self-fulfilling problem. This isolation leads to brooding, the brooding leads to further isolation, family members often become alienated from one another and the situation deteriorates. When we see a depressed person, we often have her family member join us for at least one visit. This helps us assess the situation and often helps to attempt to make changes in the family patterns.

Some of the simple strategies we use involve creating a situation where each member of the family can try to state clearly how they feel in the other's presence. In many marriages, or relationships of a long duration, the partners have stopped listening to one another or stopped talking. One of the most important and basic parts of communication is that of empathy, that is, not just stating you are sorry, but trying to actually understand how the other person feels, "putting yourself in their shoes." We recommend that a person try to respond with their feelings and not with judgments. Similarly, we encourage direct rather than indirect statements.

Using strategies based on the work of Deborah Tannen and others, we find that it is important for one spouse to be able to tell the other *exactly* what she needs. For example, many women want to have that empathic connection just to be heard and for their husband to understand them, rather than a quick solution. Many men, on the other hand, who are used to "report talk" as opposed to "rapport talk," try to solve the problem, by giving their wife a suggestion rather than an empathic connection (Tannen, 1990).

It is important to remember the children in a family suffering from depression. If a woman is feeling sad and hopeless, and continues to have the major amount of responsibility for her family—her work and the welfare of her children, as well as the care of the house—it is clear that something has to give. Children, even teenagers (especially teenagers!), are often particularly sensitive to the moods of their mother and will pick up feelings of depression. Similarly, marital problems, that are often associated with depression, will affect children very directly. If you are concerned about your children, it is important to mention your worries to your psychotherapist or health care provider in order to discuss the situation more fully.

Lesbian women have a specific set of needs with respect to depression. One of the most important problems for lesbian women is that of social isolation. When heterosexual women have problems, they may have an extended network to rely on, but some lesbian women who are closeted have fewer connections with which to explore their relationship issues. It is also clear that lesbians suffer from discrimination and prejudice. These additional factors can undoubtedly lead to increased stress. One of the few studies of lesbians, the National Lesbian Health Care Survey, found that half of the women seeking therapy saw depression as their major problem (National Institute of Mental Health, 1987). Just as with heterosexual women, involvement in a positive relationship with a partner has been related to low levels of depression in lesbian women. Similarly, the loss of a relationship is a risk factor for depression. This could be especially true for lesbians who may not be able to grieve openly and who have less social support. Communication problems are not absent from the lesbian community and in situations where the depressed person feels criticized by her partner, the patterns of isolation and hopelessness can be similarly devastating.

It is also important to explain depression to members of your family and close friends, and to remember that family members may have misinformation about depression as well. They might give you well-intentioned, but ineffective advice like "just pull yourself together and cope." Just pulling yourself together, still burdened with the same sociological, relationship and biological stressors, will only intensify your depression and make coping impossible. Communication, then, can be the first step toward obtaining support and breaking the cycle of depression.

✦ COMMUNICATING WITH FRIENDS

Studies of marriage reveal a paradox. In many marriages, a husband will be asked who his best friend is, only to reply that it is his wife. His wife, when asked the same question, will come back with the name of a woman friend. This is a generalization, but it is true for many women. In times of stress, they need to turn to someone who can share their feelings, who can help them solve problems and to whom they can feel connected. Unfortunately, in some marriages, the husband is not able, or willing, to participate in an intimate relationship to the same extent as his wife. Thus, women often turn to other women for emotional support. In other situations, a woman feels very well connected with her husband, but is in need of additional support also. It is this feeling of connectedness, as well as reciprocal problem solving, that can be a lifeline for many women. Many other mental health professionals have found that just helping a depressed woman reach out and develop new friendships is a powerful tool. Not only does it allow feelings of social support, but a woman may gain independence from her family and begin to feel more competent and effective outside of the home. In addition, she may get another perspective from someone who sees things in a slightly different fashion. Finally, this feeling of connectedness has the added benefit of increased social activity, as usually the women will begin to do things together—from walking to going to concerts, dropping by just to say hello and so on. Generations of women at home have found this connection through the coffee-klatsch of the 1950s, to the support groups or "networking" of the 1990s.

For many women suffering from poverty and discrimination, it is their connection with friends, usually other women and family members, that has gotten them through difficult times. Many single mothers develop cooperative relationships with other mothers in order to help provide emotionally for their children and for themselves. Women working outside of the home often find that if they have just one female colleague in their department or office, they can accomplish a lot of problem solving and benefit from mutual moral support. On numerous occasions, one of our colleagues has come into the conference room and closed the door quietly only to throw up her hands and say, "You won't believe what just happened!" This sharing of problems is not "male bashing," but a more general sharing of feelings and the difficulties in any particular job situation. This is particularly important in male-dominated settings, like medicine or architecture, or in settings where there are many women, such as libraries or schools that are populated by women but usually controlled by men.

We know that sharing your feelings of depression can often be difficult. Similarly, the process of psychotherapy is frightening to some. But if you break the cycle of secrecy and isolation, you can connect with friends and family or a psychotherapist, and you can recover from depression.

Psychotherapy can be difficult, but it can also change your life.

Rebecca's psychotherapy continued for several years. After some individual work, we referred her to a women's group and she came to see us less often. We have watched as she no longer defines herself as a failure and has grown more assertive, self-confident and comfortable with many newly discovered aspects of her personality. Just recently, during an individual session, she shared her feelings about her mother's recent death. Rebecca had cleaned out the family home, sorting through furniture, clothing and boxes. During this session, Rebecca brought out two photographs of her mother that she had found while cleaning. One was of her mother stepping out of a car on her wedding day. In this image, her mother appeared elegant, surrounded by onlookers, as she approached the church where the ceremony would take place. On her face, though, was an expression of profound sadness and fear. "But look at this," Rebecca added, and handed us the second picture.

The second photograph was of her mother during her high school years, participating in the long-jump during a track meet. Rebecca handled this snapshot very carefully, as if she were holding on to something precious. Even in the slightly faded black-and-white image, her mother's strong arms and legs, stretching out as she soared, offered the viewer a clear picture of her energetic joy. Rebecca, now at the age of fifty-five, is reclaiming her mother's spirit.

RESOURCES

In addition to communicating with your health care professional, family and friends about depression, there are numerous pamphlets available from a variety of mental health associations. For example, "Choosing a Therapist Who Is Right for You" is available from the American Psychological Association. The APA also publishes an excellent short book, *Women and Depression: Risk Factors and Treatment Issues*. The National Institute of Mental Health publishes a pamphlet on depression as does the National Association for Mental Health.

Reading many of these brochures can help you understand in greater depth both the nature of your depression and the resources available to you.

BOOKS

When Feeling Bad Is Good by Ellen McGrath, Ph.D. (New York: Henry Holt & Company, 1992). Dr. McGrath's *When Feeling Bad Is Good* is a great contribution to the field of self-help for depression. She is one of the psychologists who edited the American Psychological Association's Task Force on Depression. Her book is thorough and inclusive and deals with many women's issues directly.

Harriet Lerner's *The Dance of Anger, The Dance of Intimacy* and *The Dance of Deception* are transforming books. Many psychoanalytic, or psychodynamic, theorists believe that depression is anger turned inward. Although that is a somewhat simplistic assessment, it is clear that for women in particular, expressing feelings of anger directly is often not possible. Thus, sometimes we can become overwhelmed with feelings of hopelessness and inability to be effective. At other times we might be indirect in our anger. Dr. Lerner's books not only analyze these patterns but provide hopeful strategies for changing these behaviors.

ASSOCIATIONS

American Psychological Association
750 1st Street, NE
Washington, DC 20002-4242
(202) 336-5500

The APA publishes a short book, Women and Depression: Risk Factors and Treatment Issues, *which is available through their order department, as is a listing of their other publications, including pamphlets, books and journals. They also publish a pamphlet "Choosing a Psychotherapist." For referrals to psychologists, call your state psychological association.*

American Association for Marital and Family Therapists (AAMFT)
1100 17th St., NW, 10th Floor
Washington, DC 20036
(800) 374-2638

The AAMFT can provide you with a list of certified marital or family therapists in your area.

FEDERAL GOVERNMENT

National Institute of Mental Health
5600 Fishers Lane
Rockville, MD 20857
(301) 443-4513

NIMH publishes a number of free brochures on various mental health issues, including many on depression, in English and Spanish, as well as a listing of available books and pamphlets. They sponsor The Depression Awareness, Recognition, and Treatment (D/ART) Program, educating physicians and the public about depressive illness through educational materials and community outreach.

National Mental Health Association
Information Center
1021 Prince St.
Alexandria, VA 22314-2971
(703) 684-7722 or (800) 969-6642

Association with national affiliates that give information, referrals, and support concerning mental health issues. They have more than forty educational publications and a newsletter.

CHAPTER EIGHT

The Realities of Stress

LET'S FACE IT: YOU DON'T HAVE TO BE MENOPAUSAL TO KNOW STRESS. Much of the fuss about the stress during menopausal years has been exaggerated. Our approach is different. We know that there are some major transitions that occur during the menopausal years. But these transitions and changes are not crises. Moreover, solutions to stress can be quite pleasurable. For many women, midlife can be a time of self-discovery and fulfillment, a time to enjoy our past successes, make new plans and take more time for relaxing activities. In this chapter we will explore first the realities of the unique stresses today of menopausal women. We will outline the important connections between health and stress. By understanding the relationship between your health and personal stress, you will be better able to *enjoy* the middle years.

Each woman has a unique life plan. Some of us may be grandmothers at menopause, others may still have children in grammar school. Some of us will be advanced in a career, others may just be starting to work outside the home. Still others may continue or resume their education. If we are not what American society has dictated as the norm—that is, white, married women and mothers—we may meet with additional pressures from society. Some of us are women of color.

Some of us are lesbian women. Some of us are single parents or widows. All of us face adjustments and changes in midlife and can face stress. But none of this suggests that the transition of menopause has to be a crisis.

Our work with menopausal women has taught us about the positive force that women can mobilize at midlife. Stress can be an opportunity for change and growth. By the time we reach the menopausal years, our experiences, such as intimate relationships, childbirth, childrearing, work issues, as well as sexual harassment and discrimination (just to name a few), have given us the coping skills to tackle almost any challenge. Many women are unaware of the depth of their strengths and abilities. For these women, the menopausal years can serve to activate their true powers.

The next time you are feeling stressed, you might remember the experience of Lorraine Lengkeek and how she rose to the occasion. Lorraine was hiking with her husband down a trail in Glacier National Park, singing "How Great Thou Art," when her husband was attacked by a grizzly bear. Lorraine, a woman in her fifties, might well have felt stressed at this point; but Lorraine, a new menopausal heroine, fought off the bear by whacking it on the nose with her binoculars and then used her bra as a tourniquet to stop her husband's bleeding! We found this example in one of the Timex magazine advertisements, most of which we don't like because they involve stories of people being stuck on carnival rides and being inverted for a half hour at a time. But this one strikes us as a great example of a woman rising to deal with true adversity.

For most of us though, the psychological issues of midlife are certainly less dramatic than Lorraine's. Robin's story is more typical. Robin was a fifty-six-year-old woman who originally came to see us for her high blood pressure. She worked in her husband's construction business. With the declining economy of the late 1980s, she and her husband, James, were forced to sell the business. She went to work in another office but James could not find work. On January 1, 1990, when the governor of Rhode Island closed all the state savings and loans and froze all the accounts, Robin and James were left without access to their life savings. Her daughter divorced her husband and moved back home with two small children. James, still out of work, started to build a small addition to the house for the extra family but suffered a heart attack. Robin was left as the sole breadwinner of her family and spent her time worrying about finances, James, his health, her daughter, her grandchildren and the unfinished addition. We'll tell you more about Robin later.

Robin's situation of economic hardship and family worries is just one of the many possible problems of the menopausal years. The fact is that there is no one predictable pattern for women in the menopausal years. We have learned this by listening to the many different experiences of our patients. There is one thing we can expect during the menopausal years and that is change! Depending on your life plan, during this decade you may well: change jobs; see your children get married; become a grandparent; tend to the needs of elderly relatives; get a promotion. By understanding that these changes are part of the natural life process, you can use your internal and external resources to help you cope.

One study of midlife issues found that women's lives are more affected by the original choices they made with respect to their families. Women who had children when they were younger experienced a lessening of family burdens and some shifts in their outlook at midlife. On the other hand, if women had delayed childbearing, they might be grappling with some of the issues of childrearing and family concerns in their early and middle forties and might be dealing with their children's adolescence in their fifties. So these days the nest is not necessarily empty at menopause.

Many of our patients, heterosexual and lesbian, have no children and are in long-term relationships, growing old together as equal partners in life. "Reproductive versus nonreproductive life" has no meaning for them. More important dichotomies for most menopausal women include underpaid versus fairly paid, powerless versus powerful, employed versus unemployed or in a happy relationship versus in an abusive relationship.

Even the term "midlife crisis" has always been a controversial term, based more on theory rather than reality. Another problematic issue is the definition of midlife. While one writer, Elliot Jaques, suggested that age thirty-five is the beginning of the midlife crisis, others have written about people in their forties and early fifties (Jaques, 1965). Another way to look at midlife is not to use age as a marker, but rather a shift in outlook. This shift is moving away from viewing life as infinite to a focus on the time we have left.

For women, with an average life span being approximately eighty-two years, a chronological midpoint would be approximately in the early forties. If many women begin to struggle with midlife issues in their forties, by age fifty they have already made adjustments in their lives! Lynn, one of our patients, told us that at age fifty-three, "The forties were a hassle for me. My two children were coming and going, my husband was bored at work and I wanted time for *me*—to be myself, to get back to work. Now that I'm in my fifties, things have settled down. The kids moved away, my husband decided to work less and is volunteering at a vocational school and I'm teaching part-time. *Much* better!" A recent study of menopausal women reveals that women in their fifties feel better than they did in their forties. The women experienced a decrease in dependence and self-criticism, while simultaneously experiencing an increase in their self-confidence and ability to make decisions (Helson and Wink, 1992). So by the time of menopause, many women have experienced positive rather than negative changes.

❧ SYMPTOMS AS STRESSES

There are numerous biological changes that are common during midlife. The biological changes at midlife can trigger psychological issues. We have detailed the real changes that are a result of hormone changes during menopause. As we have discussed earlier, many of the biological changes are actually associated with aging and have little to do with estrogen deficiency and menopause. For example, over time our eyesight changes so that most of us need reading glasses by the time we are in our forties. Similarly, our hair begins to turn gray and we begin to develop wrinkles. All of this is true for men also. For some midlife women, the aging process is unacceptable.

Erik Erikson described the primary conflict around the biological issues as generativity versus self-absorption. Generativity is the process of transmitting values to the next generation. Erikson did not limit this to parenting or grandparenting exclusively, but included the activities of teaching and contributing to the younger generation through mentoring or other work. Erikson believed that at midlife we can lapse into self-absorption if this task of generativity is not mastered (Erikson, 1970). Preoccupation with too much attention to personal needs and possible changes in physical health can lead to brooding and turning inward. Then the biological changes can precipitate sadness and fear. On the other hand, if a midlife woman or man shifts toward generativity, an increased sense of command and contribution to society will follow. We have found that the more committed a woman is to her life, whether it's career, relationship or a political issue, the less she worries about the aging process.

Women's ability to focus on others allows us to have deeper, more intimate relationships and may lead us to be more naturally inclined toward generativity. The connectedness with family members allows our transitions at midlife to be more positive. These close relationships can serve as a counterpoint to the self-absorption that can take place at midlife. After all, the moments of closeness and intimacy, whether they come from parents, children, friends or lovers, are some of life's most meaningful. By the time we reach our menopausal years, we have become experts in relationships, and we can continue to benefit from them. Many modern psychologists place this ability to connect to others at the core of our development as women.

Self-absorption, on the other hand, begins when we try to fight the aging process. Jung noted that paying more attention to the inner world is a natural tendency during midlife. By this he meant the world of ideas and feelings, not the external physical and individual changes. Of course, a preoccupation with physical appearance is a natural tendency for women due to the intense media attention and socialization toward youthful sexuality. Although we completely understand when our patients come to us wanting a referral for cosmetic surgery, we have our doubts. Some magazine articles recommend that cosmetic eye surgery needs to begin in the early thirties. We have also seen young women who have had breast implants more than once by the time they are twenty. These women, at menopause, may be on their second, if not third generation of cosmetic surgery. All of us know the struggles we have with appearance, and few women are exempt from this worry. We also know that experimenting with appearance and makeup can be a creative activity for many women or an experience of "female bonding." Cosmetic surgery is quite different because it usually involves general anesthesia, with all of the risks of a major surgery, for the sake of delayed wrinkles. It seems that women are being exploited to see cosmetic surgery as a vehicle to permanent youthfulness.

The onset of symptoms of medical problems can also lead to anxiety. Here again, we have found that flexibility can be a woman's greatest coping strategy.

Samantha, one of our forty-five-year-old patients, had been diagnosed with multiple sclerosis ten years earlier. When the disease worsened, she did not panic. A single parent, she had raised her son alone despite tremendous financial turmoil and little support from the boy's father. Carl, her son, was off to college when Samantha was faced with her plans for her future. She quietly sold her home that had beautiful curving—but challenging—Victorian staircases. Even though she loved the aesthetics of her house, Samantha bought a new house with two apartments, had the first floor rebuilt to accommodate any possible change in her motor skills and used the second floor as an income property. She refers proudly to her recent project as, "my retirement plan." Samantha's flexibility and ability to face what her future may bring is just one dramatic example of the strengths of midlife women.

Her ability to think about retirement in the face of severe illness reflected the coping skills she had developed all those years as a single parent. Certainly, Samantha faced a potential midlife crisis, but she is using her problem-solving skills and her psychological resources to face each new challenge.

Certainly coping with multiple sclerosis is a particularly difficult situation. The more common biological stressors of midlife tend to be minor, yet troubling nonetheless. These may include changes in vision, early osteoarthritis, higher blood pressure, decreased caloric needs and reduced stamina. Most women adjust to these changes well. It is important to realize that social pressures that fight against graceful aging only add stress to the menopausal woman's life. We hope that as women continue to gain positions of power in the media, in government and in health care, that the social pressures will change. There are also a number of other social and sociological issues that can create stress during this developmental phase.

Some of the symptoms of menopause, usually hot flashes, can provide additional stress to a woman who is just barely able to manage the multiple roles she must juggle. Gloria came to see us because her twenty-three-year-old son was still demanding money from his parents and was unable to make a career choice. At the same time, her elderly mother needed to enter a nursing home, and Gloria was having difficulty arranging for the appropriate level of care. When she began to have unpredictable night sweats, she couldn't sleep and she felt completely "burnt out." Gloria had always been the family's "helper," but she began to suffer from role overload, as a wife, a parent and a daughter with tremendous demands. She found the hot flashes associated with menopause to be a terrible burden. Through our team approach, we helped her find appropriate resources for her mother and short term psychotherapy in order to help her set more limits with her son. She also decided to take a short term course of hormonal replacement therapy to manage her hot flashes.

HEADACHES

By far, the most common stress-related problem we see is the headache. In fact, Gloria originally came to us because of her headaches. Headaches are a problem for many menopausal women. Although the hormonal changes may be a factor for some women, stress also plays a role. Headaches are common in men, too. There are several categories of headaches. *Tension* headaches are the most common type of headache and are a result of the contraction of neck, scalp and facial muscles. Most people describe the pain as feeling like pressure is being applied to their head or sometimes their neck. These headaches also tend to coincide with periods of stress. If tension headaches become routine, they can then become *chronic*. These muscle-contraction headaches can also be caused by depression, anxiety, or other emotional factors.

A full 60 to 75 percent of people suffering from headaches are women (Andrasik and Kabela, 1988). Women suffer more often from *migraine* headaches than do men. A *classic migraine* headache is preceded by an "aura," or a warning that may be in the form of flashing lights or a temporary loss of vision which occurs between ten and thirty minutes before the headache begins. A *common migraine,* named so because it is much more common than classic migraines, is not preceded by an aura. The migraine process is not completely understood. It is believed that people who get migraine headaches have blood vessels that overreact or overdilate to certain triggers. These triggers can include stress as well as eating certain foods like chocolate, or the additive monosodium glutamate (MSG). It is the dilation that causes the throbbing pain of migraines. During the headache, many women will try to find a quiet, dark place to sleep. Both light and loud noise typically worsen the pain and sleeping seems to help. For some women, nausea and vomiting may also accompany the headache.

Gloria suffered from common migraine headaches. Some migraines reoccur around the time of menstrual periods and increase in frequency around the menopausal period. But the precise relationship between hormones and migraines is unclear. In some situations, the hormone progesterone can cause headaches. So, if your headaches began after you started a course of HRT, you should discuss them with your physician.

Migraine headaches may tend to occur in the pre- or perimenopausal periods rather than the postmenopausal period. Women who are between the ages of thirty and forty-nine and from lower-income households are at the highest risk for experiencing migraine headaches. The stress factor plays an important role once again.

Gloria got some relief of her migraine headaches by taking a medication that counteracts the vasodilation that occurs during the painful stage of the headache. These medications, the most common of which is ergotamine, should be taken during the early stages of a migraine headache. Ergotamine will not be effective if the migraine has been in progress for some time and it is contraindicated in certain medical conditions. For women who are troubled by severe and frequent migraines, preventive medications can be used, including propranolol and other Beta-blockers, medications that are also used to treat high blood pressure. One study at a headache clinic found that the most useful combination treatment for migraine headaches was propranolol and biofeedback (Margolis and Moses, 1992).

An international symposium of the World Health Organization and the World Psychiatric Association found that many people who had headaches also experienced a depression at the same time. It is not clear whether the depression caused the headache or whether the headache caused the depression, but it is clear that severe headaches tend to be associated with depression. Tricyclic antidepressant medication can be useful for some people with frequent headaches. Psychological consultation could be helpful to women either in sorting out the depression or in developing pain management strategies.

The treatment of tension or muscle-contraction headaches includes muscle relaxation, and many of the stress management procedures we outline in a bit. Nonsteroidal anti-inflammatory drugs (NSAIDs) like ibuprofen can be effective also. If you suffer from chronic headaches, try to become involved in a comprehensive program that will evaluate medical, nutritional and psychological factors. Be sure to avoid addictive painkillers like codeine and Percodan. They may work in the short run, but over time you will have a second problem—that of prescription drug abuse. A study of substance abusers found that almost 90 percent of them experience some type of headache. Of these substance abusers, women who had migraine headaches tended to develop their headaches first and then begin to crave pain medication. Others, who experienced tension headaches, tended to develop these headaches after using substances. Thus it is possible that substance abuse may cause tension headaches and that some of these headaches are caused by hangovers or withdrawal from prescription drugs (Andrasik and Kabela, 1988; El-Mallakh and Rif, 1987).

✦ Social Issues

The Juggling Act

Most menopausal women juggle work, family, friendship and leisure roles. At menopause, many women reevaluate the importance of these roles in their lives. Women who have functioned within a specific role for many years may decide to make changes at midlife. Juggling the different tasks within one job or role can be difficult enough and this is called "intra-role conflict." Not all changes within jobs lead to intrarole conflict, though. Some of the most pleasurable jobs allow different types of work. This protects an individual from boredom and allows for flexibility, creativity and a variety of interests. For example, Gail was a university professor who came to see us complaining of "post-tenure letdown." A quiet and diligent scholar, she had worked productively for over fifteen years, publishing a great deal of research. She had finally been promoted to full professor and had received tenure at a major university. She was now finding it difficult to concentrate and was beginning to question the validity of her previous choices that centered on research rather than on teaching. Fortunately her job was quite flexible and she was able to shift gears and devote more attention to her graduate students and undergraduates. By working with graduate students to develop their own research strategies, she became a major mentor and role model. This made her feel that she was making a contribution, within her larger career choice, but in a slightly different way.

A more common role conflict involves "inter-role conflict," that is when tensions occur between our *different* functions. Many women are so emotionally debilitated by family problems that it interferes with their work functioning. In other situations, the demands of a high-stress job leave a woman emotionally depleted and fatigued at the end of a long work day. This is particularly true for women who have careers that require tremendous amounts of responsibility without much financial reward. They are filling the "pink-collar" positions that make up the majority of the female workforce in this country. The women who hold these positions find their situation difficult to change and have an increased risk of heart disease that we discuss in Chapter Five, "Maintaining Our Health."

The plight of these stressed "pink-collar" workers is illustrated by one of our local manufacturers. This manufacturer had a large number of employees on strike, picketing daily outside the factory. Those with the signs, catchy phrases and bullhorns were not the female "pink collars" fed up with unfair treatment, but the male forklift workers who were determined to receive higher wages and an expanded benefits package. The others who deserved a pay increase and expanded benefits package remained inside the building, overworked, typing, answering the phone, correcting their boss's letters, making coffee, often doing their boss's personal chores and sundry other related tasks. These secretaries were being paid significantly less than the forklift workers. When a local resident near the factory was questioned as to why he thought the forklift workers, often with less education, were paid so much more, he responded, "They make the money for the company. Every time they lift a box to ship to a customer the company is making money." The company makes a lot of money from the secretary who processed the order, fixed the Xerox machine and produced the annual report.

The truth of the matter is that secretaries often have the very same financial responsibilities as forklift operators. Many of them are single, divorced or have husbands who are out of work, and most are struggling to make ends meet. The heavy workload these women handle on the job, combined with their barely livable salaries and numerous family responsibilities, leave them exhausted and stressed.

The multiple stresses experienced by clerical workers became clear to us recently when we met Claudette. Claudette was a fifty-five-year-old postmenopausal woman who came to us in a panic. She was referred by the Employee Assistance Program at a medical-secretarial agency, where she worked as a transcriptionist. The local business had recently merged with a larger company, and Claudette's job now required her to produce a certain number of typed lines per day. She had always been an extremely accurate typist, but was a bit slower than her colleagues. She made up for this shortcoming by helping others proofread and by working longer hours from time to time. Her new boss found this unacceptable and was quite critical of Claudette. Claudette was usually an accepting and cheerful woman who was a devout Roman Catholic; she was suffering from moderate hot flashes at night but had coped well, until recently when she felt increasingly anxious. When we first met her, her thinking was hard to follow and she was extremely tense and worried. Her blood pressure, usually a bit low, was now high, 140/102.

As a team we saw Claudette and learned the following: Claudette had untreated hyperthyroidism, which significantly increased her feelings of anxiety. In addition, she was separated from her husband, Louis, who had been laid off as a laborer in a warehouse, because of back problems. She had finally left him after thirty-three years because she "just couldn't take it anymore." They had experienced marital problems for many years, after they lost a three-year-old daughter to leukemia. Both she and her husband had been devastated by this tragedy, but Louis, always a quiet man, withdrew further and refused to get help. When she went to a pastoral counselor, Claudette became increasingly aware of her own neglected needs. This counseling relationship had restored her faith. Years earlier, when she went to her parish priest for help, he had only instructed her to pray and she became disillusioned. Over time, Louis began to drink too much, and became increasingly critical and possessive of Claudette. He questioned her every move and tried to prevent her from talking with her friends on the phone—her lifeline to support. She did not believe in divorce and she was terrified for both of them, because if she lost her job, neither of them would have health insurance.

Claudette's three children were struggling with their own families, and her youngest daughter had recently been traumatized when her husband beat her. The crisis at work had just "put [Claudette] over the edge." We helped Claudette take a short leave of absence, treated her thyroid condition, and saw her for a few sessions of psychotherapy. Claudette surprised us at how quickly she developed a more assertive manner. When we told her that we were so pleased with her quick change, Claudette reminded us that change often comes after extensive deliberation. "Getting something more for myself has been on my mind for years. You're just helping me act on these hopes. About five years ago, I realized that I don't have to be this way. I don't have to be the one to always take the overcooked part of the meat!" We met with her husband, and Claudette negotiated the conditions under which she would return home. He would have to agree to joint counseling, and she could use the telephone without his criticism. We referred Claudette and Louis to a family service agency.

We also referred Claudette's daughter to a domestic violence hotline. It would be easy to see Claudette's daughter as an unusual story, but unfortunately it is not. Many women have been battered, with an estimated 16 percent of women experiencing violence at home (Foley and Nechas, 1993). Most communities now have women's shelters and domestic-violence hotlines, so no longer do women need to suffer alone.

We also helped Claudette negotiate with her new boss, but the efforts were unsuccessful. She ultimately managed to find another job in a smaller company, where she could work at her own pace. Claudette's case is just one from our busy practice, and we know many other women who are trying to deal with inflexible jobs, problematic marriages and needy families.

The Support Gap and the Sandwich

Women are the emotional glue for most families. We serve as the support and confidantes for our friends and family members alike. Unfortunately, in some male-female relationships, this is a one-sided interaction, with women providing most of the emotional support but receiving much less. Women in relationships with men and sometimes even in relationships with other women, often suffer from a support gap, that is, they provide more support than they receive. Although many women feel connected to the men in their lives because the men confide in them, all too often there is little reciprocity. We have seen many women who go home after a long day's work to inquire about their husband's day, when the same question is never asked of them. The research on social support suggests that social support can be a major buffer to stress and can protect women from such stressful psychological conditions as depression (Brown and others, 1986). The cornerstone of social support is mutuality and expressiveness, where both partners have a meaningful relationship and commitment to one another. This is unfortunately not true for some women in their relationships with men. But, things are looking up as many men and women begin to change.

The issue of social support is also important for lesbian women. We have found that many lesbian women have strong social support networks within their relationships and within the lesbian community. However, being in a minority, they suffer additional social pressures, as well as discrimination and harassment. Women who have not "come out" often live in a certain amount of fear because of the possibility of exposure and resulting discrimination, and even losing their jobs.

The support gap often strikes women more intensely at the time of menopause, culminating in the problems of the "sandwich generation." Often, menopausal women have children who still need encouragement and support, and most women are happy to provide that support (especially if the child is now living outside the home). At the same time, women may be struggling to take care of elderly parents and in-laws. A woman in such a situation becomes "sandwiched" between the needs of the parents and children.

Gina, a recent patient of ours, is typical of the sandwich generation. Gina is a fifty-five-year-old courageous postmenopausal woman who was trying to keep her ninety-year-old mother out of a nursing home. Gina and Richard are a hardworking couple who are devoted to one another. Gina showed us many of her creative solutions to caring for her mother, who was suffering from Alzheimer's disease. She did orientation exercises with her mother, created skirts with rubber linings out of concern for her mother's incontinence, and coordinated a tremendous amount of social support for her mother. Gina was having additional difficulty comforting her newly divorced daughter, who was trying to support two children on a salary from Burger King. Like all too many women, her daughter was only receiving sporadic child-support payments of $50 a week. Gina was so sandwiched between the needs of her mother and her daughter that the main purpose of one of her office visits was to help gain access to social services from the Visiting Nurses Association for her mother and a community mental health center for her daughter.

Our staff meetings are full of descriptions of women, like Gina, who struggle to take care of their families and friends. Before the national family-leave policy, many women were forced to take time off from work to help find nursing homes for their parents or to take care of family members themselves. Although most women want to be helpful to their family, their goals are often unsupported by employment policies and by other family members. We know many women, forced to take time off from work, who find themselves punished. When they return, their responsibilities are often downgraded. Fortunately, the new federal legislation is beginning to change this situation, but many women are still perceived as not "committed to their careers" if they care for their families. Women provide the vast majority of care for the elderly. It is quite common for one sibling in a family, usually a daughter, to take on a larger proportion of the care for elderly parents, while others do very little.

THE POSITIVE SIDE OF JUGGLING

The work-home conflict, then, is a real one for many menopausal women. We should remember though, that we can all enjoy having multiple roles. Although a tremendous amount of attention has been given to the stress of work for women, there are many positive qualities of work. The majority of studies of women find that women enjoy work and enjoy the flexibility, autonomy and the independence that it offers them (Barnett and others, 1987).

Similarly, most women enjoy their children. Adjustment to midlife and the issue of adult children is often quite variable. Women have different feelings about their grown children based on many factors—how they feel as mothers, the nature of their relationships with their adult children and finally, the way the children leave home. Indeed, women have mixed feelings about the "empty nest." For many women, their children have filled the intimacy gap in their marriages. Other women raise their children alone. Still others have a solid relationship with their spouse or partner, but also have been very child-centered. The close connection with young children is emotionally exhausting but also intense and loving. Sue Miller, in her insightful novel, *For Love*, describes the change for one woman, a single mother watching her son become a man:

"What she'd felt in recent years, though, particularly since Ryan had gone off to college, was how absolute the ending to that mother-child romance was. It astonished her, given how central it had been in her life, given how much of her emotion had been taken up by Ryan—by love for him and anger at him and sadness with him and pride in him—how suddenly gone he was. All of that world was. She'd had a sense, the last few times he'd been home for a stretch, that there was some new relationship unfolding, something that, with luck, might look finally like a friendship. But mostly what she felt was the absence in herself of the old mothering emotions. Not that she loved him less. Not that at all. But that the kind of love was different. Less consuming . . . She was, on the whole, glad for this" (Miller, 1993, p. 80).

As we have discussed in the previous chapter, this does not mean that women become clinically depressed when their children leave home. Just that life changes. Some children leave home to go to college at age eighteen and then work for a few years and either establish a career track or return to graduate school. The entire family may see this as a positive change and an accomplishment. On the other hand, children who are not college-bound must struggle with the issues of careers at an early age and their separation may be less predictable. Sometimes they can find secure and well-paid jobs, but sometimes they can't. Given the recent crises in economics in America, it can be difficult for these children to find work and the stress on the entire family multiplies; and it is often the mother who bears the major responsibility for supporting the family through these changes.

In fact, the returns to the nest or "boomerangers" account for some eleven million young men and women in their twenties who try to leave home and then decide to come back. Although 34 percent of them are students, others are single people with full- or part-time jobs or are unemployed. One of the issues here is delayed marriage. The median age of marriage is at present twenty-six years for men and twenty-four years for women, a full four years later than the same statistics of the 1960s (Quinn, 1993). So, actually, many menopausal women are still helping their boomerang children.

✦ CRISES OF MIDLIFE

DEATH OF A SPOUSE

Conflicts at work and home can usually be managed. Most women overcome their anxieties about midlife and enjoy aging. The normal psychology and stresses of midlife are usually a series of small changes and most women do not find them to be particularly traumatic. Yet, there are some crises at midlife that can be traumatic and difficult. One such crisis is the death of a spouse or partner. Since women tend to marry older men, widowhood is something that many women begin to confront during the menopausal years. For women who become widowed, they often lose instrumental support, that is help with their pragmatic details of life, as well as emotional support. For many women, they also lose the social structure of couples that have held their social life together. The phases of grief and loss include numbness, yearning, protest, despair and recovery (Kübler-Ross, 1982). Although all women do not experience the stages in that order, they do tend to be common in the grieving process. Pathological grief that does not resolve after a couple of years can often turn into a midlife depression, and depression can be successfully treated with the proper combination of assessment and psychotherapy. We describe this in detail in Chapter Seven.

Gladys, the women you met in our first chapter, lost her husband to a heart attack three years after we first met. Even though Gladys had a good job and a supportive extended family, she went through a difficult time, financially and psychologically. About eighteen months after her husband died, she told us, "I guess I know I can get by now, but it's still hard, every single day."

There are now numerous support groups for widows that we have detailed in our section on resources. The social support provided by other women can help in coping with the feelings of loss and detachment. Support groups can be very beneficial in providing practical issues also. Women tend to share resources and problem-solving strategies and can be very creative in their work together.

Lesbian women who lose their partners often find that society at large does not allow them to experience the same grieving process. This was dramatic in a case where one woman who was suffering from a serious stroke was not allowed access to her lover when her family discovered their relationship. It took a protracted legal battle for these women to be able to live out the rest of their days together. Disruption of this grieving process can also make the loss more difficult for women recovering from the death of their partner. Most recently, some religious institutions have reached out to gay people to allow these rituals and social transitions to be truly inclusive.

Most menopausal women, however, do not experience widowhood but begin to worry about the health problems of their husband. The thought of widowhood becomes a reality for the first time. This was true in the case of Robin who needed to nurse her husband after his heart attack and had to confront her fears of possible loss.

DIVORCE/MARITAL ALIENATION

A more common problem during midlife is marital alienation and divorce. Longitudinal studies of marriages find that the highest peak time for divorce is seven years into a marriage. This usually occurs in the thirties, since most Americans still marry in their mid-twenties. There is, however, a second peak time for divorce, and that is around midlife. While good marriages tend to get better over time, problematic marriages often cannot tolerate the stresses associated with developmental life changes. One study of divorce found that the most frequent reason for divorce during midlife is extramarital affairs, either long-term or more recent in nature. Seventy-five percent of the people in the same study reported long-term difficulties but waited for either the children to leave or for other social changes to occur before the divorce took place (Kaslow, 1981).

A less dramatic but more common change is marital alienation. This alienation may involve a woman whose identity has been centered on raising the children, and who may not have received enough credit for it, from her husband or from the larger society. The lack of validation, combined with the loss of emotional connection to children, may make the adjustment to the menopausal transition more difficult. This situation can lead to sadness about the "empty nest" unless the couple make some adjustments.

Another similar pattern involves the changing needs of the midlife husband. Having accomplished his career goals, he may look to his wife for more shared leisure time. The wife may be freed from the burden of the children (sometimes), and want to go off to college, or open a business, or continue her career path. If a couple cannot negotiate these different expectations, marital stress can be debilitating. As people grow and face the changes of midlife, there are often changes in the original marital contract. The most common change is that when the couple married, the woman agreed to stay home and take care of the children. As the children grew older, however, the woman wanted more contact outside the home and had career goals. Often these changes necessitate changes in the marital contract—who does the housework, who does the grocery shopping and so on. Couples who are flexible take a logical approach to this and problem-solve together. Gina and Richard have used this problem-solving approach to their family life over the years.

Other couples, who have never been able to negotiate problems, find such changes too difficult and the marriage deteriorates. This is extremely problematic since so many people reevaluate their lives at midlife, and this naturally leads to changes in the marital contract. Too many of our midlife depressed women have husbands who are extremely rigid and unyielding, resistant to such changes. In other couples, the partners drift apart quietly and without conflict, each of them aware of their alienation, but not knowing what to do about it. Sophia and Preston, a midlife couple, are trapped in a rigid marriage in Whitney Otto's book *How to Make an American Quilt*. Sophia can't seem to escape from her inflexibility with her family and turns to other women, quietly:

> "Sophia wants to tell Preston that she loves him, wants to be less rule-bound with her children, but instead she spends one night a week piecing together bits of fabric with a group of women. As if she could piece together all the things she feels inside, stitch them together and make everything seem whole and right" (Otto, 1991, p. 76).

FINANCIAL DIFFICULTIES

Financial difficulties have become an increasingly prevalent problem in American society. This has been true for single women, single mothers and for the legions of women who have jobs where they are subject to sexual discrimination and harassment. Many of the women who are "pink-collar" workers are married to men who are "blue-collar" workers. We have found that many women in this situation have come to us, experiencing extreme stress related to their husband's work problems or unemployment.

Many of their husbands have been let go from their jobs unexpectedly. This can be particularly difficult for a single-career family where the men are employed and the women work at home. Gina's husband, Richard, has been a foreman in a rug-weaving plant for twenty-five years, and was looking forward to five more years before his retirement. Richard and Gina both believed that the company would take care of them, as it had their parents before them, but it was sold to a larger company and moved to Georgia. Richard and Gina could not leave their multiple responsibilities, and they were left without his full retirement pay. We find that many men and women like Gina and Richard face a new world of mergers and escalating health care costs. Many of the men are unemployed with few new job skills and with tremendous burdens for the financial security of their family.

Unemployment has a negative effect not only on the man who may be the single wage earner, but on the family as well. In many families, women are willing to go back to work and do so. This often has a beneficial effect on the family system. The husband feels relieved and both partners feel that they can share in the responsibilities for family finances. Yet in others, it is difficult for the man to accept his wife's work. Some men see this as a threat to their masculinity, or they begrudgingly *allow* their wives to "work outside the home," but do nothing to participate in the maintenance of family responsibilities, such as household chores, shopping and so on. Claudette's husband, Louis, became more controlling and jealous with her after he lost his job. Open communication and the ability to problem-solve play the key factors here in helping families contend with the changes of financial and employment difficulties.

Retirement and unemployment are not just men's issues. Married women, as well as single women, need the money they earn. Since many women have taken time off from work over the years because of their families, they have less Social Security and less income to save for retirement. According to *The Women's Encyclopedia of Health and Emotional Healing,* the average age that an American woman is widowed is fifty-six but does not become eligible for Social Security's widow's benefits until age sixty (Foley and Nechas, 1993). Even though many of us are intimidated by financial planning, the time to plan for retirement is now.

HISTORY OF PREVIOUS TRAUMA

As we spent more time with Claudette, she revealed to us something she had never told anyone in all of her fifty-five years—that she was sexually molested by a neighbor when she was eleven. This trauma had affected almost every aspect of her life, from her sexuality to her raising her children to dealing with authority. New research has found histories of sexual and physical trauma in women who come for treatment of substance abuse, chronic pain, sexual problems and a number of psychological disorders. Since most women never get psychotherapy and since these experiences are associated with guilt and shame, many women cannot reveal their pain at all, or wait until their middle years to do so. This may be especially true for women in their forties or fifties today with early experiences of abuse, when they had essentially no formal resources for help during childhood.

Judith Lewis Herman, a psychiatrist at Harvard Medical School, has written an eloquent, moving and informative book, *Trauma and Recovery*. It was our patient Claudette who first brought in Dr. Herman's book. This was a welcomed reference, since we were already familiar with Dr. Herman's work in the area of sexual abuse (Herman, 1992). Bringing us the book also made it easier for Claudette to tell us about her own story.

✦ STRESS MANAGEMENT

Any of you who have read women's magazines or health magazines in the past ten years can now be called stress experts. Stress management ranks up there with topics like "ten new luscious chocolate desserts" and "trim five inches from your thighs" as popular cover stories. The double bind created by placing these two stories on the same magazine cover is bound to increase stress in all of us, but that is another story (see our discussion of weight problems). Articles about women who have totally managed their stress down to the smallest detail have become burdensome in themselves. Even Candice Bergen in a televised interview in 1991 revealed that she had felt better immediately once she had stopped reading articles about how well Jane Pauley manages her life!

The first step in coping with stress is to identify it. We help our patients by providing them with assessments, using several questionnaires and strategies. These self-analysis tools provide new knowledge, and as you know by now, one of our strongest beliefs is that knowledge is power. So many women come to us with vague feelings of uneasiness or physical complaints. They know something is wrong, but they don't know what. One of our first steps in working together is to find out what specific stresses affect them. One helpful exercise is the pie chart. First, a woman lists the ways she may spend her time—work, spending time with family members, household chores, friends, leisure activities, self-improvement. The next step is to create a pie chart with sections devoted to how much time is spent per week on each activity. After that, the woman rank orders these behaviors as to their importance in her life. A second pie chart represents the way she would like to spend her time based on her values.

You might try this exercise yourself after referring to Molly's pie chart in Table 8-1. Molly was a forty-eight-year-old woman who was beginning to have hot flashes and entered psychotherapy because she felt "spacey and disconnected." Molly indeed was entering the menopausal phase but was not interested in hormone replacement therapy at the time. After she was evaluated medically, she began to see one of our psychologists. We found that although Molly was the mother of four teenage children, she also worked twenty hours a week. In addition, her husband, who was a highly paid, alcoholic executive, firmly believed that work was fine as long as "Molly did what she was supposed to do first." When we looked at Molly's pie chart we found that she was spending long hours outside her paid job, tidying up the house, preparing dinner, and waiting for her husband to come home. He often was late, without calling to let her know when he would be home.

Molly found that a full 75 percent of her time was devoted to working, taking care of the house, doing chores, preparing meals and waiting for her husband. Only 25 percent of her time remained for her other roles as colleague, friend, family member and person interested in maintaining her health. By actually looking at how she now spent her time, Molly realized the discrepancies between it and what she really wanted to do. Her priorities were to pull away from the lives of her children and husband. Her children had moved on to late adolescence and were beginning college. Her husband, despite her numerous attempts to involve him in therapy, continued to live an isolated and alcoholic existence. These discrepancies helped Molly examine the choices she needed to make to enter the next phase of her life.

It was a long process for Molly to come to the shocking realization that she had spent so much of her time on other people's needs without receiving much in return. Not that she didn't value taking care of her husband and children, but the extent to which she neglected her own needs had never been so apparent. She had been suffering from dysthymia, a chronic type of depression, for many years but merely added that to the list of negative feelings about herself, rather than being able to take charge of her life and make some significant changes. However, with continued psychotherapy, she was able to join an Al-Anon group, spend more time with her women friends and examine her dependence—financial and emotional—on her husband.

TABLE 8-1
MOLLY'S PIE CHARTS

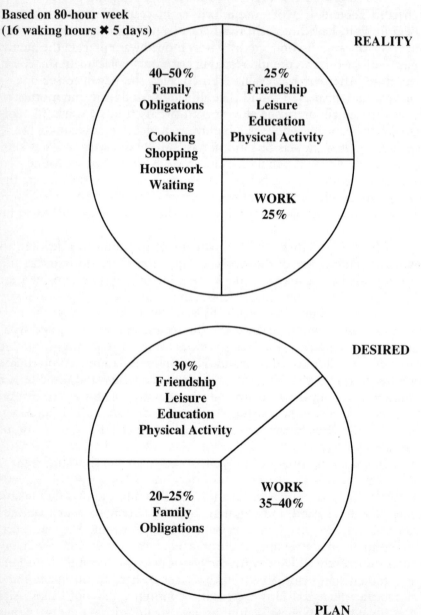

Based on 80-hour week
(16 waking hours ✖ 5 days)

REALITY

40–50%
Family
Obligations

Cooking
Shopping
Housework
Waiting

25%
Friendship
Leisure
Education
Physical Activity

WORK
25%

DESIRED

30%
Friendship
Leisure
Education
Physical Activity

20–25%
Family
Obligations

WORK
35–40%

PLAN
• **Cut back on family chores**
• **Take classes in order to**
expand job possibilities

✦ THE MIND/BODY CONNECTION

We see stress management as an integral part of our practice. This is because we do not engage in the typical mind verses body dichotomy, but see the mind/body connection every day in our practice. It is now very clear that stress can affect health negatively. This is not just some fuzzy philosophical belief but a growing area of medical science. People who have been widowed or suffered the death of their partner have a higher likelihood of dying during the six months after that loss. Six months after a divorce or marital separation is a time of more frequent visits to physicians and to emergency rooms. The link between the mind and the body may well be our immune system that controls the body and protects us against the possibility of infection or viruses. The relatively new field of psychoneuroimmunology (longest word in the book) has lead to medical breakthroughs in understanding this connection. In *Healing and the Mind,* Bill Moyers interviews numerous researchers who have shown the connection between stress and the immune system, where increased stress can interfere with the immune system's ability to work (Moyers, 1993). Similarly, decreasing stress can improve health. There are numerous stress management strategies. Here are but a few:

Deep muscle relaxation involves at least two components. First, it involves taking slow, deep breaths in order to control the rhythm of your breathing. You will be surprised at how relaxing it can be to take a few minutes for yourself and just think "Breathe in—pause—breathe out." You then consecutively and systematically tense and relax the various muscle groups throughout your body. Meditation often leads to relaxation. Meditation is a sense of complete concentration. It usually involves deep relaxation first and then includes trying to close your eyes and focus completely on a single word that you repeat over and over.

We are fond of using imagery as a technique. It, too, involves deep breathing exercises but adds a visual image that you can conjure up by concentrating. This is essentially a form of creative memory. You try to remember a time when you experienced either complete relaxation or joy. By conjuring up the physical details of that memory and even perhaps the smells and feelings that go along with it, you can create a state of intense relaxation.

Biofeedback is a way of measuring relaxation. The biofeedback machine involves measuring your heart, blood pressure and skin response. Bill Moyers describes his experience of being hooked up to a biofeedback machine. In working with Doctor Karen Olness, professor of pediatrics at Case Western Reserve University, she asks him to recite the Gettysburg address and when he stumbles after several sentences, he sees the line measuring his heart rate bouncing. She then asks him to imagine a comfortable scene and he does so: "I close my eyes again, in my mind I am standing on a peak near the Western slope of the Rockies. I have been to this spot only once a dozen years ago but the experience is as immediate and exhilarating in my mind's eye as it was that day when my friend and I paused to catch our breath and found ourselves silently, slowly, turning in a circle, complete circle—black elk's great hoop—and seeing as far as one could see nothing but sky and clouds and mountains, a 360-degree prospect as pure as Eden, as peaceful as a baby's breath . . . I look, the little white line moves serenely across the screen like a sailboat on the waveless horizon" (Moyers, 1993, p. 173). The biofeedback machine then was able to let him know how he had reached a state of relaxation. Now, few of us have such a rich and evocative way to recall experiences, but relaxation techniques like biofeedback can be helpful to everyone.

Any number of these techniques can improve your ability to cope with stress and you need to find the one that works best for you. Many women prefer the less structured and more interpersonal approach available in psychotherapy. Psychotherapy can often provide tremendous relief from stress and is discussed in great detail in our chapter on depression. Short term psychotherapy can help a woman identify her stressors and take a direct and problem-solving approach. Many women accomplish this in ten sessions or less.

In addition to the specific techniques of coping, there are many *attitudes* and psychological attributes that we need to add to our lifestyle to cope with stress. We have suggested several possible books and tapes in our resource section. Here are some of the attitudes and techniques then that we use with women in our practice. A few of them are very common; others are contrary to what you might expect.

ATTITUDE

Stress management should not be stressful. Review what you have learned about yourself in the pie chart or in discussions with a friend or psychotherapist and make some small adjustments first. In fact, an overly detailed and *heroic* approach to stress is counterproductive. Flexibility is the key. When we try to do too much of the "right thing," whether it is lowering cholesterol or reducing stress, we can become too rigid, preoccupied and more stressed.

Although stress can be difficult during menopause, women who directly confront their particular stresses feel more in control and more powerful. An attitude of taking control and making small changes can be most beneficial. You can be creative and imaginative in changing your life. The last thing we want to do is to increase your stress with our stress management advice. So think about our suggestions, but use them in combination with your own good common sense.

FLEXIBILITY

Our belief in flexibility dictates that we need to avoid an "either/or" approach. This "either/or" thinking is associated with stress in a number of ways. One of the most common areas is women and their weight. Judith Rodin, a psychologist and president of the University of Pennsylvania, has described women's weight issues as a "chronic stressor" in women's lives (Rodin and others, 1985, p. 267). Our preoccupation with what we eat, our weight, and how we look, can lead to a vicious cycle of dieting and bingeing or alternating between dieting and thinking of normal eating as "breaking a diet." Thus, many of us are either "on a diet" or "off a diet." It is this type of either/or thinking that is sure to destroy any hope for normal eating behavior.

An inflexible either/or approach can make your life worse! This is related to the superwoman role. Let's face it, most of us are not superwoman. There are many successful women who are hard driving, organized and who pay great attention to detail. This drive is related to the Type A personality that we discussed in the healthy hearts chapter. But other times this behavior is a woman's best attempt at coping with the many different jobs in her life. It is not helpful for us to tell you to stop if this lifestyle is working for you. On the other hand, many women who are superorganized suffer from being perfectionists and too self-critical. Their either/or system leads them to feel that they are either on top of things or failing.

DECREASING PERFECTIONISM

Many of us suffer from perfectionism. This can be a particular challenge to menopausal women. How can we manage our household responsibilities, deal with elderly family members, work and relate to our own friends and family? There is no way we can all be perfect at all these roles. There is no reason we have to have a perfectly clean house or apartment. Nor can we be perfectly available to our children and friends, particularly if needs are competing. One of the ways to correct this thinking is to ask ourselves, "What is the worst thing that could happen if I don't do this perfectly?" By applying this test, very few tasks will be as important as we think. The worst thing that can happen if we don't have a clean house is that there will be some extra dust. The worst thing that can happen if we don't complete a report in a day is that it will be a day late.

It is more difficult to change our thinking about relationships. Being perfectionistic about our relationships can be extremely damaging. Among other things, we do not have total control over our relationships. As women we somehow take the rap for the behavior of our grown children, as if we had total control of their environment as they were growing up. Children in their late teens and twenties are now individuals who have their own behaviors and these behaviors lead to many consequences, most of which we cannot control. When we combine our perfectionism with our feeling of total responsibility for the family's welfare we can easily become overwhelmed. We must divest ourselves of it.

We mentioned Gloria, earlier, who felt sandwiched between her son and her mother. Gloria is an example of a woman who was preoccupied with her grown children's lives. We understand her worries because that's what good mothers are supposed to do, of course! And it's hard to turn off these concerns when a child reaches some arbitrary age. But Gloria was still worrying about her thirty-year-old daughter, who was overweight and not married. After discussing the family situation with her, it became clear that her daughter Janet was probably the happiest of the three siblings. She had a well-paid, highly innovative job that allowed her to travel. She had many friends and was quite active in community theater. Yet, Gloria was struggling with the belief that not only should all her children be married, but that she had the responsibility for making this happen.

We need to work together as women to get rid of our perfectionism and need to be superwomen. These are difficult times and most women are just trying to get by. Let's move beyond "having it all." Nobody "has it all." The myriad of articles in magazines that promise the ability to have a high-paying job with an easy family life and few stresses promise more than society has been able to deliver. The implication here is that if we don't have it all, it may be our fault. Susan Faludi in her groundbreaking book *Backlash* has documented that for many of us liberation has not arrived and yet is being blamed for a tremendous amount of social ills (Faludi, 1991). This focus on women who "have it all" only fosters competition among women. We need to stop competing with one another and continue to cooperatively solve problems.

SENSE OF HUMOR

Numerous writers from Norman Cousins to Joan Borysenko (as well as Joan Rivers) have suggested that laughter is often our best medicine. Laughter reduces stress both psychologically and physiologically. There is probably nothing better in alleviating stress than a good dose of laughter. It can help us cope from everyday life to serious illness. In *On Women Turning Fifty,* Cathleen Rountree talks with Ruth Zaporah, a teacher and dancer. Zaporah has had previous struggles with migraine headaches, depression and divorce. Here's what she says about her fifties: "In my fifties I feel ripely quiet. Life seems much simpler: I am more appreciative. More of life seems funny to me, humorous and light. I consistently have a good time. It hasn't always been like that" (Rountree, 1993, p. 59).

So, why not rent the videotape or read the screenplay of Jane Wagner and Lily Tomlin's *The Search for Intelligent Life in the Universe?* Or, watch "The Mary Tyler Moore Show." Or, if you're a more scholarly type, read one of Shakespeare's comedies. Or, go see a performance artist, like Julie Goell in *Women in a Suitcase.* Read social and political essays, like Barbara Ehrenreich's hilarious *The Worst Years of Our Lives.* We hope you're beginning to add to the list.

One night, after giving a seminar on menopause, the three of us were completely exhausted, having gone through a long day of numerous family, teaching, and clinical responsibilities. At the end of the session, just when all of the women from the audience had left, one of us literally collapsed to the floor in order to demonstrate her fatigue, sending the other two into peals of laughter. This released all of our stress from the evening and prompted us to spend another half hour together talking, laughing and sharing the day's news.

WORK CAN BE FUN

Enjoy work. Here is a surprise. Most of what we read about women's work stress suggests that work is an "add on" that women do only after meeting all other family responsibilities. All too often that is the case. Work is also usually described as something that is inherently stressful and inherently in conflict with our roles as mothers. Yet sociologists Roselyn C. Barnett and Grace Baruch describe how multiple roles can actually be helpful to women. This supposedly negative role of women as workers is in contrast to the real data. Being a paid employee is associated with positive mental health and general health benefits for women (Barnett and others, 1987).

Women who are employed usually enjoy the challenges of their careers. All too often, women have more control over their work life than they do over their home life. Although we love our families, it is very common for women to comment that going to work is a vacation compared to family responsibilities! Remember Robin, the woman whose husband lost the construction business? Over time, she obtained a bookkeeping job in a small firm. She came to love the new work and social contacts she made and as she grew more independent, helped her family deal with their financial crises. She and her family are still struggling financially, but psychologically, they are coping well.

EDUCATION

Many women do not choose to work outside the home after their children are grown. They continue their involvement in educational activities and social-service or volunteer organizations and are happy doing so. Others feel a sense of malaise or emptiness during the menopausal period. For many women, the menopausal years are a time for a renewed interest in education. After Gloria began to give up her worries about her children, she looked to do more with her spare time. After so many years out of paid employment, however, Gloria felt particularly inferior compared to other women in the adult education programs she would attend. She finally found a book club that was small and included many women whom she knew. After several months, she gained self-confidence and re-enrolled in an undergraduate program in liberal arts. Many universities now have special programs for women who are returning to school, like Brown University's Resumed Undergraduate Education program. Education of any type can be helpful to many women at menopause and provides roles and benefits similar to those of paid employment.

EXPAND YOUR LEISURE AND CREATIVE ACTIVITIES

Reading alone can be a pleasant distraction from the stresses of everyday life. We've mentioned many books already. Many of our patients have also enjoyed Amy Tan's *The Kitchen God's Wife,* classics like *Tar Baby* or anything written by Toni Morrison, mysteries by Sue Grafton and Amanda Cross and nonfiction, like Gloria Steinem's *Revolution from Within.* Joining a book club is also a way to combine meeting new people with expanding your reading list.

Music is one of life's most powerful stress relievers. Writing this book has, of course, been stressful at times. We discovered a new coffee house where the sound of jazz fills the room. Often we meet there to discuss the book, and at other times one of us may go there alone and jot down some notes while sipping coffee and listening to Ella Fitzgerald. You might prefer classical, folk or rock. Whatever you do, if you find that the music has the calm and relaxing, or passionate and exciting feeling that we can all identify with, then you are not stressed at that time.

Writing can be a soothing and creative pastime. It can be yours alone or you might want to share it. Keep a journal, write down a story, even a play or a poem. Don't worry about whether it's "good" or not; it's yours.

Other creative arts can serve as a relief and an alternative force to stress. Explore painting, sketching, sculpture; put some rhinestones on an old T-shirt! One of our patients discovered pottery at menopause. She described the incredible relaxing quality of the hum of the potter's wheel and the feel of the clay.

We discuss physical activity in our chapter on healthy aging, and remember that any physical activity is beneficial and can be pleasurable. The artist Coeleen Kiebert started bodysurfing in her fifties (Rountree, 1993). You do not need to bodysurf or even jog three miles, you can walk. None of these activities work of course, unless you give yourself the time. Enjoying leisure activities, on a regular basis, can be as effective at managing stress as a formal program.

THE IMPORTANCE OF RELIGIOUS BELIEFS AND COMMITMENT

Many women in midlife are searching for depth and meaning, as well as for intimacy. Many reevaluate the role of formal religion at midlife. This seems to come with wisdom and with the inevitable confrontation with the reality of the limits of human life. Some spiritual life helps us with the confrontation with death and suffering that we experience more as we get older. With the generation of our parents now dying or near the end of the natural life span, we are now becoming the senior and responsible generation.

Herbert Benson, after writing *The Relaxation Response,* published *Beyond the Relaxation Response,* because the previous book neglected the issue of commitment. Stress management can be very effective, but most people at midlife also benefit from a deeply felt set of values and beliefs. These commitments can be formal religion, a sense of spirituality, a devotion to a humanitarian cause or to the larger community. Many women return to their religious traditions or find new types of commitments when confronted by illness and mortality. Gloria became more active in her synagogue, especially the Social Action Committee. As she worked, she began to feel her considerable energies in a new, deeper way. She also enjoyed the time spent with other clergy and lay members of the synagogue.

Healing and the Mind pays a great deal of attention to eastern religions only, but the fact is that prayer and meditation are major components of most religions. From the prayers of Christianity and Judaism to those of Islam, Buddhism and other eastern religions, contemplation and peaceful meditation are seen as important (Moyers, 1993). Having or developing an awareness of a larger reality is one way of understanding that the individual life has meaning and significance beyond the actual years of active living. Such a sense of meaning and/or the spiritual dimension of life is valuable and helpful for many people.

Much of the writing about midlife has a religious and existential focus. Erik Erikson, for example, wrote that healthy children will not fear life if their elders have enough integrity not to fear death (Erikson, 1950). The poet Audre Lorde fought a fourteen-year struggle with cancer and died while we were writing this book. Throughout her ordeal, Audre Lorde continued to write poetry. She described herself as "a Black, Lesbian, Feminist, Warrior Poet, fighting the good fight in spite of all" (Morgan, 1993, p. 58).

KNOWING WHEN TO GET ADDITIONAL HELP

Despite all of our efforts, stress can become too much. Although most of us suffer from a certain amount of normal stress, at some point stress can become severe. Many women experience severe physical tension. Quite a few women come to see us, suffering from tension headaches, gastrointestinal problems and backaches. Many medical conditions like asthma, headaches and irritable bowel syndrome are exacerbated by stress. Since part of our evaluation has always been to combine the medical with the psychological, here are some of the symptoms that may suggest your stress level is too high.

AVOID SELF-MEDICATION

In addition to prescription medication, sometimes women turn to alcohol to relieve headaches, stress, or anxiety. This is particularly problematic for women, who experience the adverse affects of alcohol more readily than men. Women have higher blood alcohol levels than men after drinking the same amount of alcohol even when weight differences are considered (Jones and Jones, 1976). Partially as a consequence of this, women develop such alcohol-related diseases as liver disease and hypertension earlier than men (Tuyns and Pequinot, 1984). Most women find it shocking to discover that as little as two alcoholic drinks per day can be dangerous. The real danger in using alcohol for stress is that it works, at least in the short run. It is, after all, a depressant, not unlike Valium. The use of alcohol to reduce stress or to get to sleep is risky not only because of the biological consequences, but also because of psychological dependence. Many women start drinking at particularly stressful times, for example during a divorce. The pattern of drinking continues well after the stressful period has passed. We often ask our patients if they use alcohol to alleviate stress. If they do, this is a real warning of a possible problem, and we suggest other stress-management strategies.

✦ UNPRODUCTIVE WORRYING

Stress also affects the cognitive realm—the way we think. We have discussed some of the thinking problems above, such as the either/or problem or the problem of perfectionism. Psychologist Albert Ellis suggests that it is not the events that happen to us that cause stress, but our *thinking* about the event. Albert Ellis calls this the ABC model, where A is an activating event, B is our thinking about the event and C are the feelings and behaviors that result (Ellis and Harper, 1975). We see many women who are suffering from their thoughts about an event. For example, a secretary in one of the hospitals was severely chastised by one of her bosses on a regular basis. Lucy was in the category of pink-collar worker who was at greater risk of cardiovascular disease because her job required lots of responsibility but gave her little power. She came to us with severe feelings of worthlessness and stress. She felt anxiety before going to work and was finding herself drinking two daily gin and tonics to unwind after work. When we talked to her at length, we found that her intervening thinking, the B of the ABC model, was that surely if she were a better secretary, her boss would not reprimand her (see Figure 8-1). Surely if she were more organized this wouldn't happen. Lucy began to learn that when she talked more and more about her boss's behavior, the behavior had less to do with her than it did with her boss. We helped her change her thinking pattern to, "I've done a decent job, this is an unacceptable reprimand." Over time, Lucy began to talk to other people and understand the unrealistic demands of her job. She was transferred to another department with a more collaborative management, continues to work effectively, and no longer needs alcohol to relax after work.

Many women with cognitive stress become burdened with preoccupation that can become obsessive and brooding. This occurs when

FIGURE 8-1

LUCY'S FAULTY THINKING

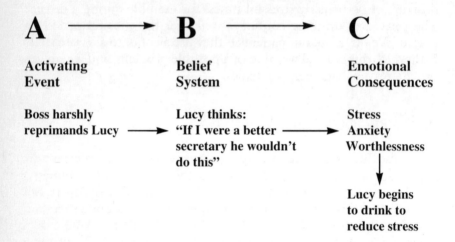

A ──────▶ B ──────▶ C

Activating Event	Belief System	Emotional Consequences
Boss harshly reprimands Lucy ──▶	Lucy thinks: "If I were a better ──▶ secretary he wouldn't do this"	Stress Anxiety Worthlessness

Lucy begins to drink to reduce stress

CORRECTION TO FAULTY THINKING

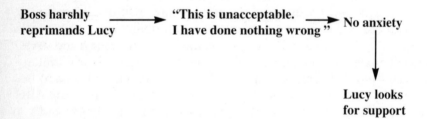

Boss harshly reprimands Lucy ──────▶ "This is unacceptable. I have done nothing wrong" ──────▶ No anxiety

Lucy looks for support

you continue to think about a problem over and over without making any headway. For some women with these cognitive problems, their mind is actually too active and too busy for them to relax enough to engage in muscle-relaxation procedures. They find it difficult to concentrate on the tapes. In this situation, there are other possibilities. Alternative activities like exercise, music or dance can engage the mind and distract a woman from her worries.

Closely related to unproductive worrying is one of the most common psychological problems for women, *anxiety*. Anxiety can take many forms, from panic attacks, agoraphobia, to free-floating anxiety. Many menopausal women have a feeling of foreboding or dis-ease just before a hot flash. When we explain to our patients that this brief experience is a natural precursor to a flash, they feel a sense of relief. Other women have a panicky feeling, which, combined with the heart palpitations, seems a bit like a panic attack. If you are having these symptoms at times other than a flash, then you may be suffering from some type of anxiety disorder. Treatments for anxiety, like those for depression, have made great advances recently, and help is available.

There are many avenues for help. Stress-management programs are available in many facilities. Your employer may have an employee assistance program (EAP). These programs are confidential, and usually provide general stress-management programs on an individual or group basis. They are not seen as "psychological malfunctioning" and most enlightened employers now see that stress management can only improve an employee's work rather than detract from it. Health maintenance organizations (HMOs) often have stress-management programs as well. Many social service agencies and community centers offer programs for managing stress also. These usually are not expensive and reduce visits to the doctors by providing alternative forms for reducing stress and anxiety.

If you find that you are suffering from some of the symptoms of anxiety and depression that we outline, then it is helpful to get in touch with a mental health professional. We detail this process in the chapter on depression. Almost every form of health insurance provides some mental health coverage. Whether you have a depression, an anxiety problem, or feel a general sense of stress, you may well benefit from meeting with the mental health professional. Many times you will feel relief after only a few sessions.

✦ COMMUNICATION

GET HELP AT HOME, AS WELL

Many menopausal women are working too hard at home. The 1980 census found that the average number of hours that a man contributed to household chores and child-care in a given week was eight. Women working full-time also worked another twenty hours at home. Arlie Hochschild details this situation in her moving book *The Second Shift* (Hochschild, 1989). The facts are that most working women work a full shift at work and another shift at home. Menopausal women are no exception. Although the caretaking demands for young children usually do not exist, the household duties remain. Some women have less energy at menopause and others are justifiably fed up!

A first strategy in obtaining help around the house is to renegotiate the household duties with your partner. Many women find this difficult to do for several reasons. First, many of us have been brought up to believe that the house is our territory. Hochschild describes one couple, both of whom were professional, where the woman did the inside chores while the man did the outside chores. The couple distorted the division of responsibilities as an equal split, even though the indoor chores involved vacuuming, cleaning, washing the dishes, cleaning the bathrooms and food preparation. Her husband's chores, on the other hand, involved mowing the lawn, doing the laundry and taking out the trash (Hochschild, 1989). Not quite a fifty-fifty split. Many women are afraid to address this issue with their husband for fear of causing conflict. Some of them have tried to discuss these issues in the past with little success. Many of them have difficulty confronting the fact that their husband is quite unwilling to be cooperative.

We have seen many women, however, who learn to negotiate more forcefully at midlife. Conflict need not be frightening, particularly if there are no children in the home. In addition, many women are able to give up the notion that conflict is bad, especially when it can lead to a more equitable division of labor and a more comfortable partnership. Many women regain some power in the marriage at midlife primarily because they have stopped being afraid of conflict. If such accommodations are not made, many women have been extremely creative in getting help in other ways. For example, some families form meal cooperatives, when one family, instead of making one meal, will make four and share with other families. Then on other nights of the week, the same family has no cooking to do. Other women learn to share cleaning and organizational resources as well.

Finally, it is important to remember that there are *many avenues for help*. For a number of reasons, many women do not go to stress-management or psychotherapy programs. We wish this were not true because so many women could benefit from these programs. Often women turn to their families and friends for support and this, too, is beneficial.

It is also important to keep all of this stress business in perspective. At the end of his midlife crisis article, Eliot Jaques reminds us of the gains of midlife: "The gain is in the deepening of awareness, understanding, and self-realization. Genuine values can be cultivated—of wisdom, fortitude and courage, deeper capacity for love and affection and human insight and hopefulness and enjoyment" (Jaques, 1965, p. 513). Remember his words. So, the next time you're feeling stressed, also remember Lorraine fighting off that bear, and Samantha taking charge of her MS. Remember Gladys who managed to go on, despite the loss of her husband, and Robin who took charge of her family. And Gina and Richard, working together through unemployment and family illness. And remember Audre Lorde, looking death right in the eye and still rejoicing in each day. These women are in all of us.

RESOURCES

In addition to the books we mentioned so far, here are some excellent resources on stress.

BOOKS

Joan Borysenko's *Minding the Body, Mending the Mind* (New York: Bantam, 1988) is a book based on the psychologist's work at the Deaconess Hospital.

Mind/Body Medicine (Yonkers, NY: Consumer Reports Book, 1993) is edited by Daniel Goleman, Ph.D., a psychologist who is an editor of *Psychology Today,* and Joel Gurin, the science editor of *Consumer Reports.* This is a well-written and extremely informative book, with contributions from many of the leading authorities in health care.

Mastering Stress: A Lifestyle Approach, by David H. Barlow, Ph.D., and Ronald M. Rapee, Ph.D., is a manual on stress reduction, available from the Learn Education Center of Dallas, Texas. This a clear and concise book, written by two leading experts in the area of stress and anxiety.

Trusting Ourselves: The Complete Guide to Emotional Well-Being for Women (New York: Atlantic Monthly Press, 1991) is written by Karen Johnson, M.D., former women's health editor of *Medical Self-Care.* This book addresses the issues of stress, anxiety depression and relaxation, and is accessible and informative.

Beyond the Relaxation Response was published in 1984 (New York: New York Times Book Company). Written by Dr. Herbert Benson and William Proctor, it emphasizes the importance of personal commitment to the basic issue of attaining relaxation.

Women's Encyclopedia of Health and Emotional Healing (Emmaus, Pennsylvania: Rodale Press, 1993) is edited by Denise Foley, Eileen Nechas and the editors of *Prevention* magazine. Hundreds of women who are health care professionals and other experts collaborated to produce this book that covers everything from anger to wrinkles.

AUDIOTAPES

There are many commercially produced tapes on stress management available. You need to find the one that is most effective with your individual needs. Jon Kabat-Zinn, Ph.D., has led meditation groups at Massachusetts Medical Center's Stress Reduction Clinic. His tapes can be ordered from P.O. Box 547, Lexington, MA 02173.

VIDEOTAPES

Bill Moyers's series on PBS, *Healing and the Mind,* is available on videocassette.

PAMPHLETS

The National Institute of Mental Health publishes a booklet titled "Plain Talk About Handling Stress." It is available by writing to Information Resources Branch, Room 15C-05, Office of Scientific Information NIMH-5600 Fishers Lane, Rockville, MD 20857.

CHAPTER NINE

Hysterectomy

YOU MIGHT BE WONDERING WHY WE HAVE INCLUDED A CHAPTER ON hysterectomy. After all, this is a book on the natural process of menopause, not on women's surgery. Our reason is inescapable: by the age of sixty, one-third of American women will have had hysterectomies (Carlson, Nichols and Schiff, 1993, p. 856). Some studies even suggest that the lifetime rate is as high as 58 percent. The ovaries are often routinely removed at the time of hysterectomy in premenopausal women, which causes menopause and its associated symptoms to occur earlier than they would naturally. Hysterectomy is the second most common operation performed on women, the first being a Caesarean section (Carlson and others, 1993, p. 856). Given these statistics, we hope that you can see how important it is to become well informed on the conditions which may lead to a recommendation for hysterectomy and to understand fully what the procedure involves.

Hysterectomy is major surgery. It involves general anesthesia, an incision, and the surgical removal of the uterus and cervix. It is often combined with an oophorectomy, which involves the removal of the ovaries. Abdominal hysterectomy usually requires four to five days of inpatient hospitalization, followed by months of recovery. Vaginal hysterectomy often results in a one- or two-day hospital stay. This major surgery has associated biological, psychological and sexual changes. A decision of this magnitude should be made conservatively and with great attention to your own personal medical symptoms.

A recent major review in the prestigious *New England Journal of Medicine* documented that a tremendous number of physicians are unsure about appropriate indications for hysterectomy. Drs. Carlson, Schiff and Nichols of Massachusetts General Hospital conclude that there are difficulties in diagnosis of the conditions that lead to hysterectomy, as well as a lack of information on the probable outcomes. They add that more attention should be given to alternative treatments. Finally, they conclude that women's preferences are not always taken into account. You need to know all you can before choosing a hysterectomy because this is an area where medical practice is rapidly changing (Carlson and others, 1993, pp. 856–860).

There is tremendous variation in rates of hysterectomy within our country. Women in the South have more hysterectomies than women in the North. One study revealed that in Maine, 70 percent of women in one city had hysterectomies whereas another city had a figure of 20 percent! In addition, African-American women have hysterectomies more often than white women. Hysterectomy is so common among African-American women in the South that it has been referred to as "a Mississippi appendectomy" (Morgan, 1982). Although African-American women tend to have fibroids more often than white women, hysterectomy may not be the most appropriate treatment for fibroids that are not life-threatening. These economic, regional, and racial differences need to be researched further. It is also clear that physicians' and patients' individual beliefs about hysterectomy must be factors. All the more reason for you to be an educated consumer when it comes to gynecological problems.

In the state of Florida, the average cost of a hysterectomy is over $10,000 (Health Survey, 1993). In other parts of the country, the cost is considerably less. Given the fact that so many hysterectomies are unnecessary, the cost to health insurance carriers, and ultimately to all of us, is enormous. With hospital costs of over five billion dollars on a yearly basis, it is financially wise to reevaluate hysterectomy as a routine surgical procedure.

Your individual health insurance plan plays a large role in how you are treated and advised. Research has shown that women whose insurance companies reimburse on a fee-for-service basis, have hysterectomies more often than women who are in health-maintenance organizations. Among the Western countries, the United States has the highest rate of hysterectomy, with Norway, Sweden and the United Kingdom having the lowest rates. Interestingly, those European countries also have national health insurance that monitors rates of hysterectomies as well as appropriate indications before the surgery can be performed. Unfortunately, there is no evidence that women in the United States have any improved health benefits from the high rate of hysterectomy. So the decision to have a hysterectomy and oophorectomy should be individually based on a woman's medical history, as well as her concerns.

We have provided Table 9-1 to help you understand the vocabulary that your doctor may use. Physicians use the term "total hysterectomy" to mean the removal of the uterus and cervix. If the hysterectomy is not total, it is called "subtotal" or "supercervical" and in that situation the uterus is removed and the cervix remains. The removal of the ovaries is called an oophorectomy. The removal of both the ovaries and the fallopian tubes is called a bilateral salpingo oophorectomy. Table 9-1 can clarify for you which organs have been left in and which organs come out in these various operations.

In our practice we have noticed a disturbing fact. Many women who have had a hysterectomy and/or an oophorectomy, do not know which type of surgery they have had. They may have heard the term

Table 9-1

Medical Term	Uterus	Cervix	Fallopian Tubes	Ovaries
Subtotal, partial or supracervical hysterectomy	OUT	IN	IN	IN
Total hysterectomy	OUT	OUT	IN	IN
Oophorectomy	IN	IN	OUT	OUT
Total hysterectomy & bilateral salpingo oophorectomy	OUT	OUT	OUT	OUT

"total hysterectomy" and falsely believed that their ovaries have been removed as well. It is critically important for you to know whether the cervix or ovaries have been left intact. As you know from Chapter One, your ovaries produce not only the female hormones estrogen and progesterone, but also the male hormone testosterone, as well as other hormones. Unlike the gradual changes that are experienced during a natural menopause, oophorectomy leads to the abrupt cessation of hormone production. Women who have had this operation experience a sudden and dramatic drop in their hormones, which can cause hot flashes. The beneficial effects of the hormone estrogen in preventing osteoporosis and cardiovascular disease are therefore lost with surgical menopause, sometimes for no good reason. Then the question of whether or not to take hormone replacement therapy becomes crucial.

You may be surprised to discover that there are relatively few medical conditions for which elective hysterectomy is the only, or even the best option. There is no disagreement that hysterectomy is indicated in the following circumstances: invasive cervical or endometrial cancers, massive hemorrhage, uterine rupture, or severe uncontrollable infection (Cutler and Garcia, 1992). These clear indications for hysterectomy are listed in Table 9-2. Many of these cases are medical emergencies and will be done quickly, as well they should be.

Elective hysterectomy, which is surgery that is planned and not an emergency, may be offered for a variety of conditions. Other conditions for which hysterectomies have traditionally been performed are: fibroids, abnormal bleeding, endometriosis, chronic pelvic pain, en-

---

Table 9–2

INDICATIONS FOR HYSTERECTOMY

- Invasive cervical or endometrial cancer

- Massive hemorrhage

- Uterine rupture

- Severe uncontrollable infection

dometrial hyperplasia and genital prolapse. These indications are listed in Table 9-3 along with their alternative treatments. In each of these situations you need to discuss with your physician whether an alternative treatment is available. If it is available, you should consider it before deciding on a hysterectomy.

Of the hysterectomies performed in this country, 30 percent are for leiomyomas or fibroids. Fibroids are benign, not cancerous, overgrowth of smooth muscle tissue. Fibroids grow out of the wall of the uterus and can be as large as a football. There is a very small chance (less than 1 percent) of fibroids progressing to a type of cancer called leiomyosarcoma (Leibsohn and others, 1990). Some women may have multiple smaller fibroids in the uterine wall. Many women—in fact 30 percent of all women over forty years old—have fibroids, but have never experienced any symptoms. A smaller number of women will have symptoms such as bleeding, pelvic or back pain and later be told that they have fibroids. In most cases fibroids shrink at the time of menopause, because of the decreasing estrogen levels.

Not all bleeding is caused by fibroids alone. Other causes of bleeding include polyps, endometriosis, endometrial or cervical cancer and finally "dysfunctional uterine bleeding." We have always been troubled by this latter term because it seems like another harsh medical term that stigmatizes women's problems. Other similar terms include "incompetent cervix," "ovarian failure," and one of our own personal favorites "elderly first-time mothers" coined for pregnant women over the age of thirty-five. Dysfunctional uterine bleeding refers to excessive bleeding (either increased quantity, frequency or both) not related to fibroids, polyps, endometriosis, cancer, pregnancy, etc. This bleeding is presumed to be related to hormonal changes or imbalance and is actually more likely to occur in the perimenopausal period. Although it is often a reflection of changing menstrual cycles, it can also indicate something more serious like endometrial cancer. Therefore, abnormal bleeding needs to be fully evaluated by your doctor.

Another cause of hysterectomy (20 percent of all cases) is endometriosis. Symptoms of endometriosis (notably pelvic pain) are caused by the migration of tissue that normally lines the uterus to other organs in the pelvis. Although the number of hysterectomies for endometriosis is increasing, there are many new alternative treatments that are showing promise. Another bit of good news is that endometriosis is usually cured by menopause.

Genital prolapse (or pelvic relaxation), which is sagging of the rectum, urethra, or uterus through a weakened pelvic floor, is the reason given for about 15 percent of all hysterectomies. The two remaining reasons given for hysterectomy are chronic pelvic pain and endometrial hyperplasia. Chronic pelvic pain is one of the more complicated issues, and the underlying cause needs to be fully explored before hysterectomy should be recommended. Endometrial hyperplasia is the accumulation of the lining of the uterus, often related to a relative excess of estrogen. Although this condition accounts for almost 6 percent of hysterectomies, hysterectomy is not necessary in most of these cases (Carlson and others, 1993, p. 856).

Most women are unaware of the alternatives to hysterectomy. Medical technology has provided us with tremendous advances in the treatment of endometriosis and fibroids, conditions that have previously made up 50 percent of indications for the operation. If a hysterectomy is recommended to you, it is critically important that you get a second opinion. We will discuss this further in the communications section. Taking into consideration the inconsistent and often high rates of hysterectomy, it seems unlikely that women are participating enough in the informed consent process. Informed consent is an analysis with your physicians of the alternatives to hysterectomy, as well as the benefits and the risks involved. This should not be just signing a paper, but a lengthy discussion that allows you to see what your choices are and to talk over your concerns.

In addition to medical reasons, many experts believe that there are sexual and psychological reasons to avoid a hysterectomy if it is not truly necessary (Cutler, 1990). The wholesale removal of the uterus, as well as the resulting changes in the ligaments and the nerves in the area, can lead to changes in the sexual experience. The more we learn about sexual functioning, we know that the uterus, cervix and ovaries may be important sexual as well as reproductive organs. At one time, women were told what kind of orgasm to have, primarily by the orthodox psychoanalysts. The best orgasm, we were told, was the "mature vaginal" orgasm, in contrast to the "immature clitoral" orgasm. Now we know that women have a wide variety of sexual experiences (Masters and others, 1970). Linda Ellerbee once said that, "The best time to laugh is anytime you can" (ABC News, 1993). The same can be said for having any kind of orgasm. Many women experience some feeling of uterine contractions during orgasm and have had some cervical stimulation during intercourse. Thus, the removal of the uterus may have specific sexual implications.

Psychologically, hysterectomy is a major surgical procedure and can be very disruptive to a woman's life, involving several months of recovery. The literature on the association between hysterectomy and depression is complicated, as we will discuss. Although hysterectomy and oophorectomy do not necessarily cause depression in most women, they are major surgeries, with all that is involved. For some women, the loss of their reproductive organs may have a symbolic as well as a biological significance. In some cultures "no periods" implies "not feminine." One of our favorite gynecologists has even seen some patients whose husbands left them after a hysterectomy. Rather than experiencing a natural and gradual menopause, a woman literally wakes up to find that she can no longer choose to bear children. Overall, then, we do not view the reproductive organs as "not necessary anyway" as many of our menopausal patients have been told as a justification for a hysterectomy and oophorectomy.

Oophorectomy to Prevent Ovarian Cancer

Prevention of cancer is one of the common reasons for recommending oophorectomy. This may be an alternative for women who have strong family histories of ovarian cancer and who have completed their families. Doctors Winifred Cutler and Celso-Ramón García report that the recommendation of routinely removing the ovaries in the average woman was based on a false statistic that was reported in a medical journal. This statistic suggested that there would be a 5 percent chance that an ovary would become cancerous over a woman's lifetime. When Doctors Cutler and García checked this fact, they found that the true rate was only one-tenth this amount. Thus, they have suggested that routine removal of ovaries in the average woman was unfounded (Cutler and García, 1992, p. 216).

Many women continue to be fearful of ovarian cancer specifically because it often lacks symptoms. Elizabeth, one of our patients, was told that the removal of her ovaries would alleviate her fear. Since she had no family history of ovarian cancer, the oophorectomy was being suggested to her for primarily psychological reasons. This suggestion was made without any psychological evaluation. The recommendation failed to consider the psychological impact of oophorectomy itself, and the fact that Elizabeth might certainly have gone on to worry about other forms of cancer, such as breast or colon cancer. These cancers are actually more common, but no reasonable person would suggest removing these organs ahead of time. In fact, removal of the ovaries does not absolutely guarantee the prevention of ovarian cancer if any bit of tissue remains.

One scenario for removing a woman's ovaries, or performing oophorectomy, occurs when the woman is having a hysterectomy for another reason. She then may decide or be advised that she may as well take out her ovaries to "prevent ovarian cancer." Women who are perimenopausal are sometimes told that "they don't need the organs anymore anyway." For women in general, a large number of healthy ovaries will be removed in order to prevent one case of ovarian cancer. Granted, ovarian cancer, a silent killer, is a truly terrifying fear. By now we all know the case of Gilda Radner, whose story exemplifies a woman's worst nightmare; a fear that a recurrent abdominal symptom, however vague, could actually be invasive cancer. But, the chances for the average woman who has no symptoms getting ovarian cancer are very small.

For women who do have strong family histories of ovarian cancer—that is, two first-degree relatives (mother, sisters) who have suffered from the disease—the situation is different. They face a more complicated decision involving whether or not to have the hysterectomy and oophorectomy to avoid cancer but risk the complications of the surgery. These women with strong family histories of ovarian cancer, who may have a risk of ovarian cancer up to 50 percent, are in a different situation than the thousands of American women who may undergo unnecessary oophorectomies.

What about women over the age of forty-five? There is some disagreement within the field about this. Drs. Cutler and García conclude that "the ovaries should not be removed unless they are diseased" (Cutler and García, 1992, p. 207). Doctors Carlson, Nichols and Schiff write that conserving the ovaries is "recommended for women under the age of forty-five and oophorectomy is recommended for women over the age of fifty. For women forty-five to fifty years of age, the decision should be individualized with consideration given to the patient's menopausal status, the risk of ovarian cancer and the ability to take estrogen replacement therapy" (Carlson and others, 1993, p. 859). So, the choice of surgically removing your ovaries depends on your age group and your individual medical situation, and should be discussed with your doctor.

✦ ALTERNATIVES TO HYSTERECTOMY

There is now a wide variety of alternative treatments for conditions that once led to hysterectomy. These treatments are summarized in Table 9-3. Fibroids, a common reason for hysterectomy, can sometimes be removed surgically without removing the entire uterus. This procedure is called myomectomy. It is technically more difficult, however, and has a higher risk for recurrence of fibroids. For these reasons, few people would consider this operation postmenopausally. If fibroids are big enough to obstruct bowel or urinary functioning, cause pain or persistent bleeding with anemia, and have not responded to other medical treatments, hysterectomy may well be the best alternative.

While a large percentage of white and African-American women approaching menopause may have fibroids, most have no symptoms. Since fibroids are stimulated by the hormone estrogen, they may subs-

---

Table 9–3

COMMON CONDITIONS ASSOCIATED WITH HYSTERECTOMY AND ALTERNATIVE TREATMENTS

Condition	Treatment
Fibroids (uterine leiomyomas)	Monitor During Menopausal Period Myomectomy
Dysfunctional Uterine Bleeding	Hormonal Treatment Endometrial Ablation
Endometrial Hyperplasia	Dilation and Curettage (D&C) Progestin Therapy and Monitoring
Endometriosis	Hormone Suppression Using Danazol
Genital Prolapse	Pessary, Topical Estrogen and Exercises
Chronic Pelvic Pain	Comprehensive Evaluation and Treatment, Including Psychological Nonsteroidal Anti-inflammatory Drugs

tantially decrease in size as estrogen declines during your natural menopause. So, one course of action, if your fibroids are not too troubling, is to monitor them over the perimenopausal period and to see if the situation improves. In addition, there are several drugs that can shrink fibroid tumors, a class of agents called gonadotropin-releasing hormone (GnRH) agonists. These drugs are known to decrease the size of fibroids, but in most cases they will grow back after the treatment is discontinued. In addition, there are side effects, including hot flashes and bone loss. However, the medication may be helpful in the short-term until the onset of menopause, or in cases to reduce the fibroids enough to enable a vaginal hysterectomy (Adamson, 1992). This medical treatment could avoid an unnecessary hysterectomy. However, this drug is very expensive—$375 per shot (monthly) and some insurance plans do not cover it.

A fibroid can be located by using a pelvic ultrasound or sonogram and it can be monitored to see how the treatment is proceeding. Gynecologists frequently express the size of a fibroid in terms of pregnancy, for example, ten weeks (odd but true). Laser surgery for fibroids causes less bleeding than traditional myomectomy and uses a device called a hysterascope, which allows the surgeon to look into the uterus itself. However, this procedure is indicated primarily for smaller fibroids, and only ones protruding substantially into the uterine cavity.

The first step in evaluating abnormal uterine bleeding is an endometrial biopsy. This involves taking a piece of the lining of the uterus. It is performed in a doctor's office and causes some minimal discomfort and bleeding. If an endometrial biopsy is normal, many women may choose to monitor the situation with the support of their primary professional. Some bleeding may be controlled by repeated short courses of progesterone treatment. A new technique has been developed that is called endometrial ablation, which shows increasing promise for perimenopausal women. This procedure uses either a high-frequency electrical current or a laser to destroy the endometrium or the lining of the uterus. To date, endometrial ablation is effective in its ability to stop unnecessary bleeding and preserve the uterus. There is limited experience with women in the perimenopausal years, but some studies suggest that this procedure can be used prior to taking HRT. Both myomectomies and endometrial ablation are new and very specialized techniques. So, you need to find surgeons who have performed many of these procedures. These gynecologic surgeons are often affiliated with medical schools.

Endometriosis is another condition that often improves at the time of menopause. This occurs because the monthly cycles of the building up of the endometrial lining begin to diminish and ultimately stop. So endometriosis may improve through your menopausal years. Endometrial ablation can also be used for endometriosis. In addition, medical alternatives include taking the medications Danazol or Lupron.

Genital prolapse occurs when the muscles of the pelvic floor are so weakened that they sag. Many women describe this as a feeling of heaviness or "drooping." This can occur in women who have had multiple pregnancies. One way to prevent prolapse is by taking care of ourselves during pregnancy and childbirth.

But for some of us, by now "the horse is out of the barn," since our childbearing years are long gone. So what can be done if there are symptoms of prolapse? First, it is never too late to try the Kegel's exercises. The Kegel's exercises we outlined in Chapter Three are a key part of maintaining our pelvic muscles. These are often used in combination with a vaginal pessary—a device that holds the uterus in place. Susanne Morgan in her book *Coping with a Hysterectomy,* also suggests certain yoga positions, or kneeling on the floor with your chest down to relieve discomfort (Morgan, 1982). Finally, there are surgical alternatives to hysterectomy. Gynecological surgeons can perform a suspension operation to lift and reattach the uterus.

Chronic pelvic pain is one of the most troubling reasons for hysterectomy. Chronic pelvic pain is defined as pain that has lasted at least six months. Chronic pelvic pain may have any number of gynecological causes or may be related to other medical problems, like irritable bowel syndrome or inflammatory bowel disease. Psychological factors may also play a role. One study found that almost 40 percent of women with chronic pelvic pain had experienced physical trauma as children (Rector, 1990, p. 117). Unless a precise cause for the pain has been found, such as an unusually large fibroid, it seems quite risky to have a hysterectomy. Chronic pelvic pain, like any aspect of sexuality, may involve more than the genital organs, including past history, attitudes and overall physical health. Unfortunately many women who have pelvic pain before hysterectomy, have pelvic pain after hysterectomy. One study found that 22 percent had persistent pelvic pain even after the surgery. Another found that a high percentage of women with pelvic pain had histories of sexual and/or physical abuse (Caldirola, 1983; Herman, 1986). It is tragic to think that these women may not have been evaluated thoroughly before experiencing a possibly unnecessary and ineffective operation for their presenting problem.

Chronic pelvic pain is sometimes linked to depression and depression has, in turn, been linked to hysterectomy. A study by the McKinlay group found that normal menopause is not associated with depression, but that hysterectomy is. This study found that 18 percent of women who had experienced hysterectomies were depressed. Since the McKinlays were able to follow these women before and after their hysterectomies, they were also able to pinpoint an additional concern. Many of the woman were depressed *prior* to their hysterectomies (McKinlay and others, 1987). Women who were depressed might have experienced more pains and gynecological problems. These chronic symptoms might have led them to visit numerous doctors, ultimately leading to the chain of events resulting in hysterectomy. The problem here is, of course, that the depression may be worsened by hysterectomy and oophorectomy. So it looks, once again, like depressed women may be especially prone to unnecessary medical procedures, including hysterectomies.

Given the fact that chronic pelvic pain and depression may ultimately lead to unnecessary hysterectomy, it is important that women be evaluated comprehensively. So, if your physician recommends a psychiatric evaluation as one part of a comprehensive evaluation for chronic pelvic pain, you should not be offended. Try to be open to it as part of a thorough assessment, because if there is a psychological component to chronic pelvic pain, it should be treated. If it is not treated, hysterectomy could make the problem worse. So, it is important to try to be open to psychological treatments as well as medical treatments. This is not to say that you should accept *only* a psychological evaluation for chronic pelvic pain. Too many women have experienced the "There, there dear, it's all in your head" approach and know that it is demeaning and often a manifestation of a physician's frustration.

◆ ALTERNATIVES TO OOPHORECTOMY TO PREVENT OVARIAN CANCER

This is an area in which more work is needed. Early detection of ovarian cancer is crucial. Some gynecologists now recommend a combination of ultrasound and a blood test called CA125 in order to monitor the possibility of ovarian cancer in high-risk patients. However, this technology is just developing. CA125 was actually developed in order to monitor the *progress* of treatment for ovarian cancer after it has been diagnosed, not to predict the development of it. An additional problem with this blood test is that it has a high degree of false positives, meaning that in many women, the blood level is elevated, even though there is no cancer present. Thus, sometimes the use of this blood test can increase fear in women unnecessarily and may even lead to unnecessary oophorectomy. We hope there will soon be further development in the technology to detect ovarian cancer early.

Overall though, many hysterectomies and oophorectomies are being performed for unclear reasons. We know, too, that there are alternative treatments for many of the conditions that once automatically led to hysterectomy. Many of you may feel that "just taking it all out," especially during the menopausal years is a good idea. We believe that you need to be aware of the advances in medical treatment and that you should consider alternatives. Using this new information, you will be better able to make your decision.

✦ COMMUNICATION

Hysterectomies are sometimes necessary. Alicia's story points out the importance of doctor-patient communication, even when there is agreement that a woman needs a hysterectomy.

Alicia, our fifty-one-year-old patient, first came to see us six months after her hysterectomy. Her story reveals the importance of communication, not only between doctor and patient, but between a woman and her family. Alicia was "fed-up," to put it in her own words, with her gynecologist and his office. For fifteen years she had gone to see him, but been mildly irritated when he was more apt to talk about books, or recent vacation plans, than to concentrate on Alicia's concerns about her health. She knew that her doctor was trying to build rapport, but he was not meeting her needs, since she wanted to ask more detailed questions about a variety of gynecological concerns. She became somewhat resentful when she reached the menopausal years and began to have questions about her hot flashes and, as time passed, irregular bleeding.

Alicia had been married to Brian, her college sweetheart, for thirty years and was content. Together they had raised three children. However, she did express concern about their communication. She was a bit frustrated by always being the one to initiate conversations about feelings. He used "report talk," whereas Alicia needed "rapport talk." Alicia did mention that if she and Brian were to enter a discussion about politics, he would suddenly spend up to an hour exhausting them both while expounding on his distrust and disgust of the system. When it came to concerns about her health care, the only response Alicia could get from Brian centered around whether or not the local democratic representative in their district could be beaten.

When Alicia was about fifty she began to have irregular and heavy bleeding. She thought about reporting it to her doctor, but waited a few months because she thought it was just her menopause. When she finally did go to her doctor, he did a pelvic exam and then recommended that she have an endometrial biopsy. Alicia had no idea what an endometrial biopsy was. When she asked him if anything was seriously wrong he answered, "Don't worry about anything. In ninety-nine percent of these cases nothing is wrong." When she then asked about what an endometrial biopsy was, or what he was looking for, he told her again not to worry and left the office. Alicia then questioned the nurse in the office, hoping to get a little more information as she had in earlier years. This day, however, the nurse was too busy to answer her questions. As Alicia left the office, she looked back at the nurse and receptionist with a feeling of sadness and frustration.

Alicia came home in need of reassurance and comfort that Brian was unable to give. When Alicia told Brian of the endometrial biopsy, he replied by saying, "Don't get yourself worked up over nothing."

"But this is serious," she asserted.

"It'll be fine," Brian responded, feeling that he had adequately addressed his wife's fears. He was not aware, as many spouses are not, that his wife wanted to talk about this situation in some depth. Brian felt that if he did not have hard information about this medical condition, he could not talk to her about it. He was unfortunately not aware that just the process of sharing her fears would have made Alicia feel better.

Because she could not find comfort in Brian, Alicia chose to turn to a neighborhood friend whom she saw occasionally for coffee, or for dinner when their husbands were out of town. She felt supported as she shared her fears while her friend listened. She then turned to her daughter, Norma, but having been the mother for so many years, her long-distance phone call across country to her eldest daughter turned into a counseling session for Norma's failing marriage. But at least the conversation with Norma took Alicia's mind off the possibility of that dreaded word, cancer, for a moment. But on the whole, Alicia found little comfort from her friends and family, and spent a great deal of the following week anxious about what tomorrow would bring.

Because Alicia's doctor was off on the day that she was scheduled for her endometrial biopsy, one of his partners performed it. Alicia was on the examining table, nervous, waiting in her hospital johnny when the surgeon came in. This was their entire conversation: He walked in saying, "Endometrial biopsy. Please scoot down into the stirrups. Just relax. Okay. Bye."

At this point, Alicia felt a combination of such rage and fear that she was literally speechless. As much as she had had concerns about her regular physician, he did, at least, treat her as a person and tried his best to communicate. This person had literally spoken fewer than a dozen words to her in their entire encounter for a procedure that hurt a bit and could have meant a serious life-threatening condition.

Alicia's rage spilled over when the worst of her fears were validated and her gynecologist told her that the results of her pathology test indicated invasive uterine cancer, but that they should be able to "take care of it with a hysterectomy." She finally asserted herself and insisted that the gynecologist sit with her and Brian and spend some time going over her questions and concerns. Alicia was quick to point out that she felt that having Brian along during those consultations made the doctor more apt to take her requests seriously. When at home, Alicia addressed her fears and panic with Brian. When Brian started sounding "just like my doctor," Alicia told him that she needed his help and understanding now more than ever, and that he must give it his best shot. As the days passed, Brian learned to listen a bit more and tried his best to share feelings.

When the surgery was over, her gynecologist commented that he was "almost 99 percent certain" that he had gotten it all. Not realizing his earlier similar remark, suggesting that he was 99 percent certain that she did not have cancer. This response had a strong negative effect on Alicia. "What if he didn't get it all?" she thought. "Did he say that to everybody? What if I am in the one percent?" But her doctor was gone long before she could articulate any of these fears.

Alicia's recovery was long and tedious. It gave her enough time, however, to think about the fact that she wanted a new doctor. Having seen the movie *Network* when she first came to us she said, "I'm mad as hell and I'm not going to take it anymore!" By the time Alicia came to us, she and Brian had found a few more things to talk about. Because Alicia and Brian had always had an affectionate and sexual life together, they found ways to stay in touch while Alicia was recovering. Often that would mean sitting close together on the back porch and reading, while Brian gave his wife a shoulder massage. She was happy also that Norma came to visit from San Francisco, partly to get away from her marriage, and both Brian and Norma took care of the household chores and made sure that Alicia received a good amount of rest.

As part of Alicia's recovery, she was given a course of radiation therapy, and Brian was actively involved, helping her understand and deal with her concerns every step of the way. Because Alicia had been fifty-one, she accepted the recommendation that her ovaries also be removed. She was started on estrogen replacement therapy soon after the operation. Alicia chose the patch and has adjusted well to the therapy.

Now it is five years later and Alicia and Brian talk of all that had happened to her. They often speak of the hysterectomy and how it had saved Alicia's life. Brian, having witnessed an event that could have taken his wife away from him, grew to listen and appreciate the time that they had together even more. He completely understood Alicia's need to find a different doctor, listened and offered his opinion as she began to learn more about prevention and maintenance of her health.

Alicia learned to be more assertive in her health care. When she comes to Women's Health Associates, she often has a list of concerns written on a pad that she checks off one by one as they have been answered. She credits her hysterectomy with saving her life, and her previous gynecologist's attitude to making her the "demanding patient" she has become.

Alicia's case points out the different dynamics in doctor-patient relationships. Alicia's first gynecologist undoubtedly meant well in his rapport-building chats, but what this particular patient wanted was a slightly more detailed discussion of medical care. The second surgeon's attitude toward Alicia during the endometrial biopsy, however, left us speechless, as it did her. There is no justification for not discussing a procedure, no matter how hurried a physician might be. Even given these problems, Alicia had no doubt that her hysterectomy had been the right course of action.

It is a little more complicated when hysterectomy is an option, but not absolutely necessary. You can look at the list of medical reasons to consider hysterectomy and the alternative treatments on Table 9-3. This is just a beginning list and undoubtedly as treatments develop, you will be able to add to it. You can also investigate alternative treatments by contacting a women's health practice or a major university-affiliated hospital that deals in women's surgery.

After reviewing this chapter, if you do not find that you have enough information, you might seek additional resources to answer your specific questions. There are several excellent books addressing hysterectomy. *Hysterectomy, Before and After* was written by Dr. Winifred Cutler, a reproductive biologist who has written extensively on menopause and hysterectomy. She has been involved in independent research and is a faculty member of a medical school. Dr. Cutler's writing style on hysterectomy is both detailed and clear. The book will inform you as to every aspect of the changes that you will experience. Another book that focuses on alternatives to hysterectomy is *You Don't Need a Hysterectomy* by Ivan K. Strausz, M.D. (Reading, MA:

Addison-Wesley, 1993). *Ourselves Growing Older,* published by the Boston Women's Health Collective, is one of their most recent books to help educate women to be good health consumers. It summarizes much of the medical treatment but focuses more on alternatives to hysterectomy.

With these resources and others, you will get a wide range of information that can help you make an informed decision. After you have looked at the alternative treatments, if you are still considering a hysterectomy, you should get an independent second opinion. Your second opinion can come from another gynecologist who is certified by the American Board of Obstetrics and Gynecology. Another possibility is an internist, certified by the American Board of Internal Medicine. Many internists, especially those specializing in endocrinology, can suggest nonsurgical approaches to your problem. Most insurance companies now require this precaution, and this is good because women do not want to offend their doctors. This fear of giving offense is one of our worst enemies when it comes to getting good medical care. Alicia might well have been able to work things out with her first gynecologist if she had been able to talk about her concerns with him. Wanting a second opinion is a perfectly acceptable course of action and you should get another point of view before deciding upon hysterectomy. This means that you should not ask your doctor for the name of a close colleague. You might ask friends, or contact your local university hospital, in order to get a true independent second opinion.

Here is the problem in seeking a medical opinion, or any opinion regarding health care. If you go to a psychologist, she or he will probably recommend psychological treatment. As one of our colleagues put it, "If you go to Midas, you get a muffler." If you go to a surgeon, she or he may well recommend surgical treatment. For that reason, it might be best to talk to a primary care doctor or a gynecologist who does not perform hysterectomies, a general internist or family practitioner. By talking to one of these doctors about your condition, whether it is endometriosis, pelvic pain, or fibroids, you may get a true second point of view. A medical approach may be entirely different from a surgical approach. It is worth taking this additional time to think through your individual situation before making an important decision like this.

After obtaining a second opinion, and/or returning to your first physician, you might want to take a family member or friend with you. You need to know what specific condition you have, and can review alternatives to hysterectomy by asking what will happen if you do not have a hysterectomy. As we have discussed in earlier chapters, making serious decisions about your health care can increase your anxiety. Also, your anxiety can interfere with your ability to process information. That is what friends and family are for, to help you in this situation. Even though Brian was not a big talker, his mere presence signified to Alicia's doctor that this was an important situation. Also, Brian's support gave Alicia more confidence and a feeling that she was cared for. In addition, since hysterectomy requires an extensive recovery period, it is important for your family and friends to be informed so that they can be prepared to be supportive.

Talk to women who have had a hysterectomy. With the numbers we have discussed, it shouldn't be hard to find one. You will find a range of opinions about the procedure. Take Connie, for example, who after two years of completely unpredictable vaginal bleeding, was determined to have a hysterectomy. A busy, fifty-year-old educational administrator, Connie was fed up with the drug therapy and several dilation and curettage procedures that she had had in the last two years. When her gynecologist suggested that she should have a hysterectomy, she leapt at the chance and checked herself into a hospital three days before Christmas.

Unfortunately, the hospital was somewhat understaffed during the holidays, especially with respect to nurses. Connie was in a fair amount of pain after the operation, and found it difficult to get her nurses' attention during those moments when she needed assistance the most. Her friend Margaret, who was a particularly resourceful teacher on school break, moved into the adjacent bed in this two-bed room, put on a nightgown and pretended to be a patient so that she could take care of Connie twenty-four hours a day. Although Connie's nurses were aware that Margaret was only there to support her friend, they welcomed the intrusion. In addition to nursing Connie, Margaret brought in several magazines and favorite books, and when her friend was not resting, she would try to help her pass the time with inspiring stories and articles. Connie continued to improve and was able to leave the hospital several days after Christmas. She has had an excellent recovery and complains only of a little bit of weight gain. She is particularly grateful to Margaret for her supportive care.

This story points out the need for support from family and friends. Of course, it is not necessary to go to such lengths as Margaret did, but certainly your family and friends can pool together to support, encourage and listen to you during such an important time.

In addition, many hospitals have prehysterectomy groups that provide support and information that can help you make a decision.

✦ IF YOU DECIDE TO HAVE A HYSTERECTOMY

Our emphasis in this chapter has been prevention because of our strong feelings about the number of unnecessary hysterectomies. Nonetheless, we are aware that many times hysterectomy, even an elective hysterectomy, is indicated. Either medical treatments have failed, or you and your doctor have discussed it and opted for hysterectomy, knowing all the alternatives as well as the risks and benefits. Still, it's a good idea to prepare yourself for any surgery by understanding what will happen.

If you decide to have a hysterectomy, find a surgeon who is extremely experienced. You have the right to know how many procedures the surgeon has done. You have the right to know what hospital he or she uses, and you have the right to know what to expect. As a patient, remember that informed consent does not mean signing a piece of paper the day before surgery, as is usual procedure. It means having a full understanding of what the surgery involves and what the possible outcomes can be. Some hysterectomies are performed vaginally, but the majority are performed abdominally. In abdominal hysterectomy, the uterus is removed through an incision in the abdomen. In vaginal hysterectomy, an incision is made through the vagina and around the cervix. Although vaginal hysterectomy has a higher rate of infection, abdominal hysterectomy leaves an external scar. The type of surgery frequently is related to the reason for the hysterectomy. Some women choose to donate blood before their surgery. Both operations are major surgery, usually requiring general anesthesia and an inpatient hospitalization of one to two days for vaginal hysterectomy and four to five days for abdominal hysterectomy. Other forms of anesthesia, spinal or epidural can also be used.

You should know how much the hysterectomy will cost. In these days of cost containment, it is likely that your hysterectomy will need to be pre-authorized by any health plan. Nonetheless, even given this, there are often additional costs to a hospitalization that you should know about. This will help you do the appropriate financial planning.

The immediate surgical recovery period also means abstaining from sexual intercourse. You should not feel pressured to resume sexual activity until you feel comfortable. Preparation for surgery should involve your partner, so that there is an understanding of the sense of the delicate nature of hysterectomy. If a couple communicates well and shows consideration, then they are more likely to show a good adjustment after the operation. It is most important here that women not resume sexual activity until they feel comfortable and until their partner fully understands their physical and psychological needs related to the hysterectomy.

DEPRESSION AFTER HYSTERECTOMY

Although depression can occur in some women after a hysterectomy, you do not need to see it as inevitable. As we mentioned, the McKinlays found that many of the women who were depressed after a hysterectomy also had oophorectomies and may have been depressed before. Dr. Carlson and her colleague found no association in general between hysterectomy and depression.

There are several issues for you to consider. First, if you have an oophorectomy as well as a hysterectomy, your estrogen level will plummet. Thus, you will not experience a slow reduction as we have described in natural menopause; you will go cold turkey! So, the issue of hormone replacement therapy is quite different. So if you opt against hormone replacement therapy after an oophorectomy, you should try to use some of the alternative treatments for hot flashes in order to minimize your discomfort.

You will be less likely to become depressed if you plan your surgery carefully, provide yourself with ample social support, and allow yourself to explore any psychological issues that may arise.

✦ COMMUNICATING WITH YOUR FAMILY

It is important for your family to know that abdominal hysterectomy is a major operation. In addition to the recovery period, one study found that it took women a full thirteen months, on the average, to feel that they had gotten back to normal. This was in contrast to other operations, including gallbladder or appendectomy, where it only took 4.2 months, on average, to recover. The support of your family and friends is crucial in such a long recovery period.

We have found that many families have difficulty in reacting to the disability (even if temporary) of the mother, and even when the children are long since out of the house and grown with their own children. Sometimes denial sets in. The best way to cope with Mom's problem is to pretend that it doesn't exist. This might work well for everyone but Mom. Everyone goes back to business as usual, and unfortunately that often means that Mom is back to work at home entirely too soon. Don't do it! Household chores are often more strenuous than jobs outside the home. Everyone can learn to pitch in, and you need to take it slow after major surgery. Ask your family to treat you as you have treated them when they have been sick. Take it slow, and over time you will know how much you are capable of doing. It will not take thirteen months to make it back to your daily routine— most women can do so after two to three months, but your body will let you know when you've done too much. Talking to one of the nurses can be informative and supportive. This can be extremely helpful when you are planning your recovery period. Each woman is different, but you may begin to know what to expect in terms of when you would be able to get back to your daily routine, how you will feel and so on.

Again, it is a good idea to talk to a woman who has had a hysterectomy. You may be reluctant to do so. You may feel that you probably will not need it or that hysterectomy is a private matter. Nonetheless, talking with other women about a problem has a long history of serving women well. You will be relieved to know that your lack of sexual interest may be short-term, or that another woman has benefited from hormone replacement therapy. The reactions of other women's family members may be similar to yours. Women who have recovered from the hysterectomy often feel better by being able to share their knowledge with other women.

Try to become physically active as soon as you can after the procedure. This does not mean jumping on the StairMaster the day after surgery! By beginning to walk around your room as soon as you can, you will have a smoother recovery. Walking not only begins to help you regain use of your muscles, but will also help your gastrointestinal tract get moving, which can be a problem sometimes after surgery. As you feel better and can get more exercise on a daily basis, you will find that your mood will improve as well. This activity will also help you to firm muscles, and it can help in dealing with the mood changes that you may experience as a result of the operation.

If you have had an oophorectomy and you are perimenopausal, you need to consider the issue of hormone replacement therapy. You will probably have hot flashes, since they are reported by up to 70 percent of women after a hysterectomy. If, on the other hand, you are already postmenopausal and hot-flash free, you will not redevelop hot flashes because the reduction of hormones has already occurred. This is because the hot flashes associated with oophorectomy are triggered by the sudden reduction in estrogen from high premenopausal levels to low levels. The most important thing is to take care of yourself. This is major surgery, and you will recover. It will take time, and support will help. In the words of Alicia, "After all I've been through, I'm going to enjoy this recovery now."

✦ RESOURCES

"Come on up, I'll be your lifeline." This refrain from a poignant Holly Near song summarizes our feeling about social support for women who have had hysterectomies. We have identified other resources as well. You and your family, your relationship with your physician, and books can all help you not only decide whether to have a hysterectomy, but can help you plan ahead and minimize any disruption that the surgery might cause.

Through the hospital's social service or nursing department, you can often get in touch with a woman who has had a hysterectomy and is willing to volunteer her time to talk with you. Many communities have cancer support groups for women who have had breast or ovarian cancer. In some communities, specific hysterectomy support groups are also offered. Kara told us this story:

> The hysterectomy support group is small. Six women are sitting around a table drinking coffee and tea. Joanne, the social worker who leads the group, has sensitively put away the childbirth education materials used by another group that utilizes the same conference room. She usually begins the group with an open-ended question of how things have been going. This group has been together and meeting for six months. Two of the members have only been out of the hospital for several weeks. Two others have been out for several months and the "grandmothers" have been involved with numerous hysterectomy support groups over the years, having had their hysterectomies five years ago.

Kara is a forty-five-year-old African-American woman who had a hysterectomy because of recurrent fibroids that did not respond to medical treatment. Her surgery consisted of the removal of her uterus and her ovaries. The fibroids had been a problem all of her life, even preventing a normal pregnancy. Fortunately, she and her husband were able to adopt a healthy baby girl and Ruth was now a fun-loving ten-year-old who liked to rollerblade and play computer games.

Kara and her husband Roy have been having a difficult time more recently. Kara is having a slow recovery from her hysterectomy three months ago. She hasn't been able to pay as much attention to Ruth or Roy as she had in the past. She seems distracted and tired all of the time. As a self-employed business woman, she had lost a significant amount of money by taking two months off after the operation. Now that she was back to work, she felt a bit better but still hadn't regained her old passion for the "big sell." Roy, an insurance agent, always tried to be supportive of his wife, but he was having difficulty understanding her adjustment.

Sally, one of the older women in the group, asked her, "I'm wondering if this is raising old feelings of sadness for you?" Kara's eyes began to fill with tears. She hadn't realized that in addition to the normal adjustment after hysterectomy, she would be reliving some of her feelings of sadness over the infertility issue of earlier years. To be sure, she was a devoted and involved mother, and Ruthy was the center of her existence. Still, the hospital held for her many sad associations of feelings of loss, of anxiety and of tremendous disappointment.

The other women in the group were very protective of Kara. It was as if all their maternal feelings erupted at once and came to her aid. This feeling of connectedness and recognition that other women knew what she was going through helped Kara to sort out her feelings with the group over time. Some of the other members, those who had had children and those who hadn't, were able to share with her their feelings about the childbearing part of their life being over, and somewhat suddenly also.

One night the unthinkable happened. Some of the husbands of women in the group became interested enough to form a "men's group." These men decided to share their feeling of anxiety and concern for their wives when they did not know what to do. Many of these men had not been in a group with other men discussing anything related to their family since their childbirth education classes, which may have been anywhere from ten to twenty years ago, and some of them had never been in a group before. At the end of one of these evenings, the two groups and the couples were able to share their variety of experiences. It was somehow consoling to Roy to hear Jeff, the husband of another woman in the group, say that after a year his wife was back to her old self.

Kara's situation makes the point that although women don't tend to get depressed after a hysterectomy in general, the experience can bring out previous psychological issues. Undoubtedly, a woman having a hysterectomy at age forty-five is in a completely different category than a woman at the age of twenty-eight or thirty-eight. By forty-five she has either had her children or probably resolved the issue of childbearing in her life. But sometimes previous experiences with sexuality, infertility or hospitals themselves can lead to an awakening of old psychological pain. In such a case, the value of meeting with other women to discuss the situation is enormous. At other times, talking with an individual volunteer might also be helpful. If the pain becomes severe or if a symptom such as anxiety or depression occurs, then you can also discuss the situation with a mental health professional. But talking with other women is often the first step.

We have found that normal menopause also evokes these psychological issues in some women. This is especially true when there are unresolved issues concerning motherhood, abortion or infertility. Once again, sharing your concerns with a friend, participating in a support group or seeing a psychologist or other mental health professional will help.

CHAPTER TEN

Promoting a Healthy Lifestyle

PLEASE DON'T WORRY, THIS IS NOT A CHAPTER WHERE WE WILL INSIST that you eat huge quantities of oat bran and fish oil, work out with weights five times a week, jog three or four miles a day and abstain from all alcohol and sugar. Although, if you can do those things, by all means, carry on. However, most of our lives are full of responsibilities, time restrictions and old habits that make such a regimented diet and exercise program impractical. As you read on, keep in mind that our intention is not to burden you with unrealistic suggestions, but to give you a set of principles and ideas that, combined with your own good judgment, you can use to develop a plan that works for you.

Midlife is an ideal time for us to refocus on our health. Freed from some of the burdens of family responsibilities, we can now spend some of our time on planning for the future. We don't want to merely focus on longevity or the length of our life, but to improve the quality of our lives as well. None of us would look forward to living into her eighties if it means being severely crippled by osteoporosis or serious cardiovascular problems. Fortunately, with a careful assessment, and by setting some priorities, each of us can devise a plan that will improve and promote health throughout the next phase of our lives.

Prevention of illness is one of the most overlooked areas of medicine and all of health care. Unfortunately, only 1 to 3 percent of the American health care expenditures goes for preventive services. Given the clear link between such issues as smoking, substance abuse and lack of exercise to so many health problems, this small percentage reflects a problem in the priorities of the American health care system. By developing a good health-maintenance plan, you can do a lot to help prevent the development of serious illness. It's time to focus on healthy living.

There are six components of the Women's Health Promotion Plan. They are: routine health *Screening*, increased *Exercise*, *Relaxation*, *Eliminating* or reducing problematic behaviors, proper *Nutrition* and *Expanding* your social support system. We used the acronym SERENE, so that you can remember these five areas. We settled on "serene" for a very specific reason. One of the most important elements to a lifestyle focusing on health promotion is to remember to enjoy and accept life. As you will see, we believe that you should take control of your own health, especially in the area of promotion. But most importantly, we should all try to experience our middle years to the fullest, and take time to relax and enjoy our lives.

Before attending to any one of these six components, we need to look at some principles of change. You will have the best opportunity to change your life if you use these principles as a foundation. They are based on many years of psychological research investigating behavioral and cognitive factors in how people change. Each of these principles is well documented as having a positive effect on health promotion.

PRINCIPLE #1
Develop a realistic, specific and positive plan. At first, you might want to target only one or two behavior changes, like reducing the fat in your diet, for example. These targeted behaviors should have realistic goals. If, for example, you have always been overweight, do not try to lose forty pounds in two months. A realistic weight goal is especially important to women given our American socialization and emphasis on being too thin. In the areas of smoking cessation and alcohol treatment, most people feel that abstinence is the appropriate goal.

PRINCIPLE #2
Take small steps. Your changes can be small, but steady. You are not going to go from a diet of daily croissants to one of celery sticks. But, if you plan carefully and steadily, you will be able to make changes over the long run. Exercise plans, for example, have been found to fail

more often when they are overly heroic and intense. You need to walk before you can run, and so on.

PRINCIPLE #3

Think positive. This is not just some "don't worry, be happy" or Pollyanna approach, but once again is based on ample psychological research. We do not believe, though, that people who think certain ways or have certain personality styles are responsible for developing cancer. There is no evidence that this is true and this incorrect interpretation of the mind-body connection literature has been hurtful to many people with cancer. As we have discussed before, by trying to lower our stress levels, and maintaining an attitude of positive coping, we can improve our health. It is clear that as we age, we will encounter some health problems. With any luck, these health problems will be minor. But when coping with these problems, whether they are elevated blood pressure or increased stress, seeing them as a challenge and something that we can control is important. Stress is often a result of a lack of control in your life. By creating your own health-promotion plan with a positive attitude, you will be able to maintain control and feel better.

PRINCIPLE #4

Your commitment to change is key. After reviewing this chapter, you might choose only one or two categories to begin your health promotion plan. But make a firm commitment to do so. Many people find that, for example, choosing a quit date when they want to stop smoking is helpful if they do it long in advance and have a well-thought-out plan. This is also why so many smoking cessation programs are overwhelmed by new recruits shortly after the New Year. There is nothing wrong with New Year's resolutions, we just hope that you will be able to stick to them. By committing yourself to one or two areas for change, you are more likely to succeed.

PRINCIPLE #5

Restructure your environment to help you change. You can do this through small but steady changes. If you have targeted alcohol or smoking as your problem, you can limit your exposure by avoiding bars, restaurants and friends who continue to abuse those substances. If you are trying to cut back on fat, don't go to that Dunkin Donuts where you have always eaten a double-chocolate donut and assume that you will just buy coffee. In the area of exercise, find an exercise that is comfortable and easily available. By making these environmental changes, you can help yourself follow through with your health-promotion plan.

PRINCIPLE #6

Provide yourself with ample reinforcement. Most of these behaviors have provided you with good feelings over the years. Food may have provided you with comfort, nicotine may have helped you feel more energetic, alcohol may have reduced anxiety. We understand this and know that this is why it is so difficult to give up so many of these behaviors. So, you need to fight fire with fire by developing a system of rewards. Try to structure the rewards frequently. For example, many women will buy themselves a new wardrobe once they have lost twenty or thirty pounds. But it is a long time between cutting down on some of those favorite foods and any significant weight change. A better strategy might be to buy yourself a new mystery novel on a weekly basis, or to go to a self-help group for support on a daily basis. So you can get rewards from yourself and from others.

PRINCIPLE #7

Try to avoid all-or-nothing thinking and other unhelpful cognitive styles. All-or-nothing thinking is perhaps the most destructive when it comes to changing difficult behaviors. Most of us know full well how it feels to have been successfully dieting for several days or weeks, or even months, only to experience a loss of control with resulting feelings of disappointment. Many women feel that they are either "on a diet" or "off a diet." It's important to rethink these changes as part of a new lifestyle. You are likely to slip up now and then. But by seeing the slipups as one bit of behavior and your next meal, or the next hour without cigarettes as one bit of behavior, you are less likely to be overwhelmed by your feelings and to go into an actual relapse. This is where the Alcoholics Anonymous motto of "One Day at a Time" got started and can be helpful to you when trying to conquer these difficult changes.

PRINCIPLE #8

Try to find a doctor who will help you in your efforts by focusing on prevention and support. Many doctors are less attentive to these issues than they should be. This is a result of a lack of training, as well as their need to attend to people who are suffering from acute illness. But with some care, you can find a doctor who will support your efforts. Many doctors at HMOs are more involved in preventive medicine. Yet you also need someone who can help you feel good and reinforce the changes that need to be made. Your doctor can assist by helping you access self-help groups and university-affiliated behavioral medicine programs for your specific problem, and by just plain praising you when you have lost five pounds or abstained from alcohol or not smoked a cigarette for a month. Remember the other members of your health care team, including nurses, exercise physiologists, nutritionists and health psychologists, or other mental health professionals who can help you in this area.

James O. Prochaska, a clinical psychologist at the University of Rhode Island and his colleagues Drs. Carlo DiClemente and John Norcross have addressed the issue of relapse in their comprehensive analysis of how people change (Prochaska and others, 1992). Their stages of change model helps us to understand how to change some problematic behaviors like smoking and substance abuse. These researchers have studied thousands of people who are trying to change their problematic behaviors. They emphasize that people don't just change, but rather go through a set of predictable stages. The stages of change are: precontemplation, contemplation, preparation, action, maintenance and termination. Precontemplation is the stage where a person does not intend to change a behavior during the next six months. At this stage, many people do not have the problematic behavior identified as an issue. A women enters the contemplation stage when she has identified the problem and has begun to think about changing. Preparation involves planning to take action in the near future, like the next month, and may involve making some small changes already. The action stage is the time when a woman begins to change her problematic behavior. Maintenance involves maintaining the changed behavior. Most people feel that a behavior change should be maintained for six months before termination from a treatment program should be considered.

A major point of the stages of change model is that relapse is quite common. We do not emphasize this because we want to discourage you, but so you can understand that relapse is understandable. Most people, who relapse after trying to change their behavior, go back to an earlier stage of the model, but they don't go back to the precontemplation stage. In the area of smoking cessation, for example, people may make on the average between three or four attempts to change before attaining long-term maintenance. If you relapse, all that means is that you need to go over your plan and modify it. Try to identify what went wrong and plan your next attempt by addressing the problem. For example, you might find that you were able to maintain an exercise program during the summer, but as winter came, your exercise decreased. Your next exercise plan could include moving permanently to California or Florida, but that is probably not practical. So, you have to work harder on identifying an indoor exercise strategy that is affordable and comfortable for you.

By understanding the stages of change, you are more likely to find the appropriate treatment plan for you. For example, if you do not believe that you are drinking too much and your partner feels that you are, then an assessment of your drinking behavior by your primary care provider or a qualified substance abuse counselor may be helpful. If you identify where you are in the stages of change, you will be able to find the best target behaviors for you to change and to develop an appropriate treatment plan. You might be better off choosing a plan for which you are already prepared rather than a change about which you are ambivalent. For example, many people who are going from the contemplation to preparation stage go through a list of pros and cons. If, at the present time, your pros and cons are evenly balanced, then beginning a program based on behavior change may not be successful. This model shows great promise in helping us understand how people change.

Our work with Teresa exemplifies the attitudes of many midlife women when it comes to exercise and health promotion. Teresa has been our patient for many years. A sociologist, she appears on our public television and radio stations often as a consultant on sociological issues, especially the American family. At the age of fifty-one, Teresa feels that she has reached her prime. Teresa is witty, vivacious, committed to a number of feminist activities, and is particularly gifted at creating "sound bites" that are so valued by television.

Teresa grew up in a traditional Mexican/American family in Southern California. As one of three children, she was always very close to her siblings and her parents and committed to a family life. She came to the East coast after meeting her husband, Don, at UCLA. She moved to this area when Don was offered a professorship at a university. Teresa and Don have two children, Mark and Paula. As a young wife and mother, she opted to concentrate her energies on her family and home, taking graduate-level courses throughout their elementary school years and always maintaining that she would return to school full-time one day when her children were older. She was devoted to them, and she and her husband spent many hours following their sports, debates and other school activities.

When Mark and Paula reached high school, Teresa wanted to pursue her earlier interests. She kept that promise to herself and went back to school at the age of thirty-eight to obtain a doctorate in sociology.

She enjoyed graduate school, made many new friends, and finished her doctorate in four years. She states that she is fortunate to have a husband who has always been supportive of her aspirations, and admiring of her strong commitment to herself, her career and her family. Now, after almost ten years of publishing, she is in a tenured position at a local college. This tenure gives her the freedom to explore other professional activities like providing public information, a task that she always enjoyed tremendously. She is often called upon when some new study is released to explain the practical implications for American families.

Each time we meet with Teresa we are amazed at how well organized she is, planning her career and family-time down to the smallest detail. Although she credits this as the secret to her success, she recognizes that she has a tendency to be a little rigid. We discovered that Teresa has also been rigid in her diet. For the past twenty years, and perhaps most of her adult life, she has counted calories (Note: Technically a calorie is a unit of energy. What most of us refer to as a calorie is actually 1000 kilocalories, or a Calorie. Now that you know this bit of nutritional trivia, we will go back to using the word that you know best, calorie) and been careful to keep track of her daily intake of food. Teresa is a tall, large-boned woman. She comes to us normally for routine screening and health maintenance, rarely having any major medical complaints. But this past year was different for Teresa; she found that her normal dieting pattern was no longer working. For example, in the past, if she knew that she and her husband were going out to dinner on a Saturday night, she would be very careful to eat less during the week before and after. So, if she had gained a pound over the weekend, she could take it off within another week or so. This plan suddenly came to a screeching halt over the past year, and she gained five pounds. For a woman who was concerned about her weight and interested in her appearance because of her media exposure, this was a crushing blow.

When Teresa expressed her frustrations to us, we explained that over time the body's metabolism changes. The bad news is that not only does our metabolism slow down, and therefore we need fewer calories to maintain a certain weight, but in addition, if we do not exercise, our body weight will consist of a higher percentage of fat and a lower percentage of muscle, regardless of how muscular we may have been before. Teresa, never at a loss for words exclaimed, "Oh, wouldn't you just know it—all those cheesecakes I left by the side of the road and I'm still in trouble! Celery sticks and diet root beer for the rest of my life I suppose!"

We reassured Teresa that we were not going to suggest some rigid diet, where all she could have were vegetable sticks for snacks and a powdered shake in place of her morning muffin. We emphasized that although her diet was important, the role of exercise or physical activity could be a major player in her battle against the weight gain and in maintaining a good fat/muscle ratio. We recommended that Teresa work with an exercise physiologist to come up with an exercise program that would be suitable for her lifestyle. At first, she was extremely reluctant. She had never had the time for exercise and had functioned quite well with her previous plan. She was not particularly interested in becoming a "jock" at this point in her life. We reassured her that she need not resemble a woman in the "Just Do It!" sneaker commercial to reap the benefits of increased physical activity. After several conversations, she relented and met with an exercise physiologist and nutritionist; it was during that time that we discovered how Teresa's adolescence played a large part in her fear of exercise.

We also found out that Teresa's nutritional plan was quite sound. Fortunately, she had avoided the trap of so many women of alternating fasting with binging, or in depriving herself of calcium. She drank very little alcohol, consuming one to two glasses of wine on a weekly basis, if she and her husband went out to dinner. Although Teresa's calcium intake was more than the average American woman, she was still only consuming about 800 mg a day, and so we suggested that she use a calcium supplement. She decided to purchase large quantities of calcium carbonate–based antacids and would keep them in her purse so she could "pop one or two a day from time to time." We found that her diet was also high in fruits and vegetables, had an adequate amount of protein, and was overall a low-fat diet. Not that she didn't enjoy eating out and straying occasionally, but this was her general nutritional plan. Teresa, who likes to verbally spar with us, pointed out that she had an advantage growing up in California, where she developed an early appreciation of fruits and vegetables rather than the late conversions of so many people recently.

During those sessions, when we examined her attitude toward exercise, it became clear that she was similar to so many other women in the menopausal age group that we had known in our practice, having gone to junior and senior high school in the mid- to late fifties, when there was virtually no emphasis on women's health education in the schools. We laughed as Teresa shared with us her stories of the familiar dreaded gymsuit, a "tasteful" navy blue with capped sleeves and a built in belt that all the girls loathed. Besides feeling a bit silly in the exercise uniform, Teresa was never particularly coordinated and did her best just to get through the physical education class without too much embarrassment. She focused her skills and energies instead on academic events and the school chorus. Of course this was well before Title IX, the section of the Education Amendments of 1972 that outlawed sexual discrimination, so no attention was played to women's sports at all, and this was fine with Teresa. She preferred cheering in the stands and wearing her high school boyfriend's letter sweater on Fridays.

Further evaluation revealed that Teresa had also experienced what, for her, was a traumatic event in her early years. When Teresa was in the seventh grade, she and her family lived in a rural area where there were very few teachers. Therefore, her school system had hired two part-time physical education teachers from a local university. These were, unfortunately, attractive and flirtatious young men in their early twenties who had little or no experience teaching, but were physical education majors. The girls in the class, of course, developed mad crushes on these two young men. They were in a bind, wanting to do well in sports, but were afraid of looking silly during class. Teresa's fear and lack of coordination came out in an acrobatics class when she was awkwardly attempting a cartwheel which resulted in an embarrassing fall on the mat and a rip in the fashionable gymsuit. Although the teacher did, at first, rush to her side to make sure that she was not hurt, his response was to tease her, and even referred to the traumatic episode quite a few times throughout the semester. Teresa, of course, was mortified. She still could feel a slight twinge of embarrassment when she recounted the episode so many years later. She remembers her feelings more than the details of the event. She has wondered, over the years, whether the young men were engaged in good-natured teasing, or whether there was an element of prejudice involved, since she was one of the few Chicanas in a class dominated by Anglo girls. But overall, she still remembers her humiliation and this has carried over to her feelings about organized exercise.

Teresa had developed her tendency at that early age to compartmentalize things—to separate them into categories in order to cope. She quickly categorized physical education as a time where she could be humiliated and embarrassed. Physical education, as we have discussed in Chapter Four, "went off the list" for Teresa and many other women, never to return. Activity and physical education had a similar role in her life during college, where she was allowed to choose from several courses and thus chose shuffleboard, badminton and bowling. She preferred the games as they were less intimidating, shared activities that were already the source of humor among the other young women.

It took several sessions for Teresa to expand her view of physical education to include activities such as walking and swimming, as well as noncompetitive sports that she could share with other friends and her husband. After a careful analysis of her lifestyle, two things became clear. One was that now that she and her husband had more shared time, they were open to a joint activity. Don was a similarly intellectual and nonathletic man who maintained his health by walking to and from the university. He too knew he needed more physical activity, and over time, he and Teresa began to play tennis together on a weekly basis. One or two hours of tennis once a week is not enough to maintain bone mass or cardiovascular fitness, so we encouraged Teresa to find additional activities which she could add to her routine.

It was in fact a disagreement between Teresa and Don that finally helped her find her own exercise routine. Teresa was open to tennis as it would mean shared time with her husband, and now that Mark and Paula needed her less, she could relax and enjoy these activities. But, just as her career was taking off, Don insisted on getting a dog. Teresa knew this could mean trouble and her response was somewhat predictable: Although she had no interest in a dog, after a few months of heated debates on the issue, she realized that it was extremely important to her husband.

After extensive negotiations, Teresa agreed that she would try to be kind to the dog, but that she would not take major responsibility for feeding or other maintenance chores. Little did she know how attached she would become to the dog over time! Ultimately, Teresa's attachment to the new addition, a friendly copper-and-white Spaniel named Quayle, led her to begin walking their new pet. She not only walked Quayle, but she began to walk her a mile a day, twice a day, and was able to see the results of this added exercise within a few months. It is gratifying to us to see Teresa walking on a local bike-path trail, wearing her bulky parka and ski cap, with her dog in the midst of the harsh New England winters. Teresa found at this late date that walking was something that she could do not only to "help the damn dog," but to maintain her weight and her health as well.

After six months, not only was Teresa walking, but she was actually intermittently jogging a bit. After six months she came into see us once and exclaimed, "Not only am I developing muscles, but I think I may have felt one or two endorphins!"

✦ SCREENING

Although Teresa was a sedentary woman and needed to work on that area of her health, she represents the new breed of American women interested in health as she reaches her middle years. She knows it is very important to monitor health during the menopausal years in order to be screened for certain diseases and to maintain our present level of functioning. If you look at Table 10-1, you will find the screening plan that we recommend for the midlife woman.

One of the most critical screening procedures for women is the mammogram. There is some controversy, but the American Cancer Society recommends that women aged forty-five to fifty have mammograms every other year and that women after the age of fifty have annual mammograms (American Cancer Society, 1988). Unfortunately, despite these recommendations, it is clear that mammograms are underutilized. Only 25 percent of women above the age of fifty report having *ever had* a mammogram (Jacobs Institute, 1992). The rates of mammography in African-American and Hispanic women are even lower. In a recent review by the National Cancer Institute, less than 50 percent of white women had more than one mammogram (National Cancer Institute, 1990).

These low rates of screening reflect several problems. One study of women's decisions about mammograms suggested that women who had a positive orientation about mammograms and their value in health care were more likely to use mammography as part of their routine health screening (Rakowski and others, 1992). In the National Cancer Institute study, women who had not had a mammogram listed "not having thought about it" as their most common reason followed by "doctor never recommended it." This is a tragedy.

Some women falsely believe that having a mammogram will actually cause cancer and are afraid of mammograms. Although some women find them unpleasant, they are certainly not painful, especially when you go to a radiological facility that specializes in women. Some of these facilities offer reading materials and herbal tea while you wait for the results and the technicians are particularly sensitive to women.

The same NCI report found that women report that only 52 to 80 percent of them have had a breast exam by a health care provider in the last year (National Cancer Institute, 1990). We held a panel discussion recently of women medical students and physicians in training and they all commented that they had never been taught to examine the breast. As one recent editorial in the *Annals of Internal Medicine* put it: "Almost every internist, regardless of subspeciality, makes sure the patients blood pressure is taken routinely" with a resultant reduction in cardiovascular disease and death. "We can make similar strides in breast-cancer deaths if only we remember the breast is close to the heart" (Fletcher, 1992).

Table 10–1

HEALTH SCREENING FOR WOMEN AGES 45–55

	Appropriate Office Visit	Lab Test	Other
Yearly	Breast exam	Stool for testing	Mammogram
	Pelvic exam	Occult blood (ages > 50)	(ages 50–55 only)
	Pap test		
	Blood pressure		
	Dental prophylaxis		
Every other year			Mammogram
			(ages 45–50—only with no family
			history of breast cancer)
Every 5 years	Full physical exam	Serum cholesterol	
		Glucose	
Every 5–10 years	Screening for vision/		
	Glaucoma		

Other areas of prevention should be part of regular health screening. You should have your blood pressure checked as part of your annual physical. Control of blood pressure is one of the major goals in preventing heart attacks and other cardiovascular problems. Your doctor will also order routine blood tests and screening for blood in the stool, a way to detect colorectal cancer. We also need to pay attention to regular dental and periodontal care. This involves checkups to see that your gums are not receding over time. Your dentist or periodontist may recommend X rays periodically.

Most of these screening procedures will be scheduled in your doctor's office, but it is possible that this will not happen. Offices are usually happy to remind you of your screening procedures, but, you may miss your physical or have to cancel an appointment. You can take charge of your own health by writing everything down on your calendar at the office or at home.

Self-awareness is useful in many areas, including early detection of possible malignancies. Remember to follow the American Cancer Society's acronym of CAUTION: The American Cancer Society's early warning sign of cancer.

C. *Change in bowel habits*
A. *A sore that does not heal*
U. *Unusual bleeding or discharge*
T. *Thickening or lump in the breast or elsewhere*
I. *Indigestion or difficulty in swallowing*
O. *Obvious change in a wart or mole*
N. *Nagging cough or hoarseness*

Any of the CAUTION acronym changes mean that you should contact your primary care physician right away to investigate them further. Self-awareness and monitoring really pays off. One of our patients, Elizabeth, saw a public service announcement about skin cancer. She then found a tiny malignancy—a melanoma on her leg—and proceeded to have it removed. That was five years ago. Elizabeth is doing fine and uses a #30 skin block, or wears long sleeves and a hat when she goes out into the sun.

✦ PHYSICAL ACTIVITY AND EXERCISE

Teresa is like so many of us: she's struggled with her weight for years mainly by restricting her food intake. Exercise was just never part of her life. Teresa is not alone. Only 22 percent of Americans engage in thirty or more minutes of light to moderate physical activity five or more times per week. And as we get older, we tend to exercise even less. We've been told to "take it easy" so often that many people falsely believe that we require less exercise as we age. The truth is just the opposite: most of us exercise less than we should. Physical activity is associated with increased life expectancy. It can also help prevent and manage some diseases, promote cardiovascular fitness, maintain muscle mass and strength, help control body weight and improve feelings of competence and reduce stress. A very impressive list of benefits! Overall, physical activity and exercise cannot only lengthen our lives, but can enhance the quality of life at every stage.

You might remember, from our chapter on healthy bones, that physical activity is any movement that uses energy. Exercise, on the other hand, is leisure-time physical activity that is structured and designed to improve physical fitness. Remember that even if you are not interested in exercise, that a physically active lifestyle can pay off. Figure 10-1 depicts the benefits of physical activity and exercise.

Regular physical activity can improve many aspects of our health. However, any physical activity is useful in maintaining a level of fitness

FIGURE 10-1

GENERAL BENEFITS OF PHYSICAL ACTIVITY/EXERCISE

Habitual Physical Activity/Exercise

⟶ **Physical/Physiological Benefits**

⟶ **Health Benefits**
   Health Maintenance
   Disease Prevention

⟶ **Daily Living Benefits**

⟶ **Emotional Benefits**

 IMPROVED
QUALITY
OF LIFE

and can even improve our health to some extent. At any rate, a physically active lifestyle is associated with reduced morbidity and mortality. Dr. Steven Blair's research has followed more than ten thousand men and three thousand women over an eight-year period. The results were clear. People who had the lowest levels of physical fitness were more likely to die than those in the moderate or high-fitness categories. Small steps can be life-saving (Blair and others, 1989).

Women in the menopausal years have specific concerns. Table 10-2 is the exercise program for general fitness. You can use this as a basic plan. The specific plans for healthy hearts and healthy bones are included in chapters Four and Five. Many women in their fifties, sixties and seventies complete marathons and triathlons and compete in master's level competitions in swimming, tennis and other sports. Compared to sedentary people, these women almost always have a lower percentage of body fat, more energy, stronger muscles and less fatigue from normal daily activities.

One of the best examples of the value of consistent exercise is Tina Turner, who at the age of fifty-three is still a major force in rock and roll and is literally kicking up her heels. Despite her history of a hard life and a physically abusive marriage with Ike Turner, she is now thriving. When asked, Turner denies having any plastic surgery. She responds to the question with, "Look, this is me . . . I've been singing and dancing and that's exercise—thirty-five years, it's got to do something. I have muscle from control" (Orth, 1993).

Now we know that you are probably thinking, "Yeah, right. I'm really going to become a master swimmer or dancer like Tina Turner at this age." It is true that few of us will become master athletes or rock and roll stars. But, we can make some significant changes. First, you can work on increasing your daily physical activity. Here are the basics:

- Walk, don't drive, whenever you can.
- Use your lunch hour to walk.
- Take the stairs instead of the elevator.
- Don't stack things up at the foot of the stairs—take steps, don't "save steps."
- Take walking tours of cities where you live or travel.
- If you go to a shopping mall, don't waste time and emotional energy circling the parking lot for the ideal space. Use the physical energy and walk those extra yards.
- Consider walking when you visit a friend instead of, or in addition to, eating.
- Remember some of your high school dates? You didn't just go

Table 10–2

FIT PROGRAM FOR
GENERAL HEALTH
PHYSICAL ACTIVITY/EXERCISE PLANS

Purpose:	General health benefits
	Energy expenditure
	Enjoyment, feeling better
Frequency:	Start: 2–3 times per week
	Goal: 5 times per week
Intensity:	Light to Moderate
	(60% Max HR +)
Time:	Start: 10–20 minutes per session
	Goal: 30–60 minutes per session
Types:	Any physical activity
	Any recreational activity
	Walking, brisk walking, gardening

out to dinner or the movies or theater, you bowled, or went miniature-golfing. Try them again.

So physical activity can be part of your routine, and you will find that this change in your lifestyle can pay off. A second change is to do a *thorough* search for an enjoyable exercise. If this has been one of your areas for commitment, make a real attempt to find one that is fun for you and easily available. Many of us still have haunting memories of those navy blue gymsuits. In these days of the mirrored health clubs, we can be equally put off by overly thin young women in Spandex. But let's face it: most of us are not exercising now as a way to meet lovers. So we should try to attend to the exercise facilities and not be distracted by some of the other interpersonal games that are going on. The most important elements of success are to get comfortable and to get started! Be creative. You don't need to go to an aerobics class or jog, you can: go mall-walking, tap dance, swim, cross-country ski, the list is endless. Even a little change can help. Some studies find that the people who benefit the most from increased physical activity were those who went from being completely sedentary to being somewhat active. You do not need to be Jane Fonda or a marathon runner. Even Jane Fonda has reduced her number of workouts from five hours a day to a mere four hours per week (Boston Globe, 1993). Being a slightly more active you is a good start, and in many cases can have significant health benefits.

If you do begin an exercise plan, you need to consider your goals. Look at Table 10-3 for a reference. If you want some small benefit from increased activity, just get moving (walk, even garden) on a daily or at least every-other-day basis for thirty to sixty minutes. You can also take children to the park, play with them, push them on the swings. Do some errands by walking rather than driving, or use Don's example and get a dog that needs walking. Figure 10-2 illustrates a typical session. Remember, start slowly!

✦ RELAXATION

By now you are probably beginning to feel some stress. You may feel like we are pressuring you with all of these principles, and that you will not be able to change. You may even be discouraged. Let's take a break. Take heart, you are in control. You will be able to choose what and how much you want to change, and develop a reasonable plan. We are just covering all the bases. But, since you may be feeling a little stressed and burdened with information, now is a good time to remind you of the importance of relaxation.

The need for relaxation is universal. You don't need to be unusually stressed to have the need to relax. For most women in their midlife years, daily life alone has enough hassles to merit relaxation. We have discussed stress-management procedures in our chapter on stress, but we'll take the time to remind you again of our need for routine relaxation.

You need to find at least fifteen to thirty minutes a day where you can incorporate relaxation techniques into your life. It should be part of your daily routine. Many women incorporate relaxation into their lunch breaks. It doesn't matter when, as long as you use a consistent technique that you believe you will be able to stick to. Here are some key elements: Find a comfortable position and make sure that the temperature is suitable. Eliminate other possible distractions and responsi-

Table 10–3

DEVELOPING YOUR
PHYSICAL ACTIVITY/EXERCISE PLAN

Identify Your Reason to Exercise

•Optimal cardiovascular fitness and health benefits?
•Energy expenditure for weight control?
•Minimum activity for health benefits?
•Enjoyment, feeling better?
•Prevention of osteoporosis?

Considerations for a Physical Activity/Exercise Plan

•Frequency
•Intensity
•Time
•Type

Getting Ready—Check with Physician

•Obtain information about community programs and facilities; select location
•Get proper clothing (shoes, comfortable clothing)
•Identify convenient days and times
•Make arrangements with friend(s) if desired
•Determine a consistent time and days
•Set a starting date—mark it on calendar

Implement Plan

Use Friends and Family for Supports

bilities before you begin. Breathe slowly and deeply. Close your eyes for a few minutes. Be consistent; it may take time to remember how to relax! In *Mind-Body Medicine,* Dr. Herbert Benson, the developer of the Relaxation Response, points out that it is the end point of feeling

FIGURE 10-2

TYPICAL COMBINATION "EXERCISE" SESSION—FOR THE WOMAN WHO WANTS IT ALL
(60 min)

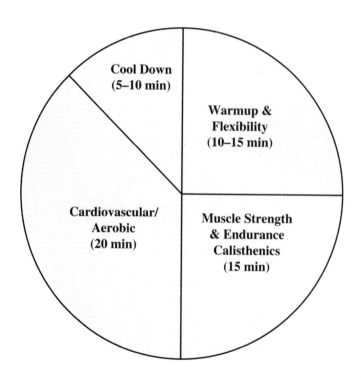

DEVELOPING A PLAN WITH VARIETY

Weekly Schedule for General Exercise & Fitness

- Two days per week — Exercise session
- Two days per week — Physical activity (walking, jogging)
- One day per week — Special activity based on personal interests
(swimming, golf, etc.)

relaxed and calm that is the goal (Benson, 1993). How we get there can differ and you should explore the possibilities from transcendental meditation to Zen, to progressive relaxation, prayer or imagery in order to attain that state.

By incorporating relaxation into your daily life, you will be better able to face some of the tasks of career and family life. You will also be better at maintaining an exercise or behavior change program. Dance, listen to music, meditate, enjoy sex, read a good book, or even a bad book. Do something that takes you away from the daily struggles that life can bring. We all tend to get so preoccupied with the tasks of the day, that we forget this important part of our health. Just remember that relaxation is as important as any other part of the health-management plan and it needs to have high priority in structuring your life and incorporating it into a daily routine.

✦ ELIMINATING OR REDUCING PROBLEMATIC BEHAVIORS

Smoking, substance abuse and binge-eating are the three problematic behaviors which have particular implications for women. All three of these behaviors are difficult to change because they involve properties of addiction. All three can feel good because they provide relaxation or distraction from stress quickly. But, in the long-term, these quick fixes from problematic behaviors have negative health consequences. Women often begin these behaviors for specific psychological reasons, such as reducing anxiety or fighting off depression. Over time, the behaviors become reinforcing in themselves. We know full well how difficult it is to change any of these behaviors, but the health benefits and psychological benefits are so strong that we hope you will try.

SMOKING

Teresa was fortunate in that she had not developed the habit of smoking, and therefore, did not have to worry about smoking cessation. She describes a humorous episode from her first year of college that illustrates the power of reinforcement and punishment. It was quite common at her college for the women in her dormitory to relax after dinner with a cigarette, over coffee. Teresa, like many women in their first year of college, longed to be included and to be sophisticated. In addition, smoking was becoming associated with the pleasure of good conversation, and an excellent cup of coffee. Teresa began to see smoking as part of the sophisticated style and so one night after dinner, she joined the other young women by lighting up. However, just as she did so, someone called her to the phone. She exited the dining hall, holding her cigarette and opening the heavy fire door. While doing so, she managed to smash one of her fingers on the other hand at the same time. ("Let's face it," she said. "Coordination is not one of my strong suits!") This led to an emergency visit to the infirmary, where a physician actually had to drill a small hole in her fingernail to release the pressure from the blood that was rushing to her finger. Teresa, knowing the principles of behavior modification, laughed as she shared this story with us saying, "Talk about major punishment. I never lit up again."

But for many women, smoking continues to be a major health hazard. Although the overall prevalence of smoking has declined in the United States since 1965, 26 percent of all Americans continue to smoke. It is predicted that by the mid 1990s, there will be as many women as men smoking (Burmen and Gritz, 1990).

The hazards of smoking are numerous and frightening. It is lung cancer, not breast cancer, that is the major cause of death by cancer among women. Smoking also increases your risk of cardiovascular disease (the major cause of death in women over the age of forty), oral cancers, and other related lung cancers (American Cancer Society, 1988). If you combined deaths due to alcohol, AIDS, fire, suicide, homicide, automobile accidents, as well as cocaine and heroin, you would still not reach the number of deaths that are attributable to cigarette smoking. That figure is now one in seven (Warner, 1991). Smoking also increases the aging process and brings on an earlier menopause. Women who smoke reach menopause, on the average, one to two years earlier than women who have never smoked. Smoking is also associated with an increased risk for osteoporosis. Finally there is good evidence that smoking causes wrinkles.

Since women's risk of heart disease increases after menopause, the interaction between smoking and cardiovascular reactivity to stress is important. The connections here are unclear for menopausal women, but it is quite possible that smoking increases reactivity to stress (Dembroski and others, 1985).

Second-hand smoke is an additional health problem. By smoking, you are exposing the people who live with you to an elevated risk of lung cancer (Brownson and others, 1992). Second-hand smoke has been identified as a major public health problem. Restaurants and corporations are making every effort to limit smoking as much as possible.

We know that for those of you who do smoke, you are well aware of the hazards and health problems related to smoking. Some of you have been smoking for years and are heavy smokers. Smoking is an extremely difficult behavior to change. Women continue to smoke for a variety of reasons, including nicotine addiction, weight control, psychological dependence, positive associations with smoking, as well as using smoking as a coping mechanism (Rigotti, 1992). So we understand the many reasons for your smoking. We just want you to consider quitting.

One of the primary concerns for women is that they are afraid they will gain weight if they stop smoking. We have listened to women worry about this many times, and there is good reason. Many women actually endorse smoking as a weight-loss strategy (Klesges and Klesges, 1988). Weight gain is, indeed, a legitimate concern since there is evidence that smokers who quit gain an average of five pounds (Rigotti, 1992). One of the Surgeon General's reports found that 75 percent of people who quit smoking did, indeed, gain weight (U.S. Surgeon General, 1990). The reasons for this are not completely clear, but may involve a reduced metabolic rate after withdrawal from nicotine, as well as eating more sweets during withdrawal.

The fear of weight gain is intense for many women. But you have to remember that there are things you can do within a smoking-cessation program to address this issue. Probably the most beneficial strategy would be to incorporate exercise into your smoking-cessation program. Exercise can use more calories and provide you with another stress-reducing mechanism. This is significant, since women also use smoking to cope with stress, and therefore may show more stress if they withdraw. Women who experience time pressure, whether they are working at home or outside of the home, are most likely to be smokers (Chesney, 1991). A final problem is that women have difficulty giving up smoking because they feel less confident that they will succeed.

It is clear then that women who smoke have special needs. We know that nicotine is one of the most difficult drugs to conquer. But we also know that many women manage to successfully quit smoking. Remember that there are many people who quit smoking on their own. We read less about these women because most researchers deal with people who come to formal smoking programs for guidance, and these people are usually those who have had more difficulty. So there are many success stories.

Dr. David Abrams and his associates have also conceptualized smoking as part of the way people try to cope with stress (Abrams and others, 1987). If you are one of the women who is concerned about her weight, as well as stress management, then you should know that there are many advances in smoking programs that can be helpful to you. Remember that you are not alone, and that many women need several attempts before they can finally quit smoking. Behavioral programs that combine stress management and weight-control procedures are offered at many university-affiliated hospitals. These programs are usually run by health psychologists and help you construct a careful analysis of the circumstances under which you smoke, the reasons for smoking and any past attempts at ending smoking that have not worked. The needs of women smokers are now finally being addressed in these assessments. By participating in such a program, you will be able to find other coping mechanisms for dealing with stress and weight control. If you have had problems with depression, smoking cessation may be extremely difficult for you. Some women who smoke and have a history of depression may experience symptoms of depression when they quit. This is all the more reason to be involved in a comprehensive smoking-cessation program.

One component of a smoking-cessation program that many women find helpful is nicotine replacement. This is especially helpful for women who are heavy smokers and who have smoked for many years. Many midlife women are in this category. The two methods of nicotine replacement are nicotine gum and the transdermal nicotine patch. It is best, however, to combine the gum or the patch with a multifaceted behavioral program as we have described. Your primary care physician can help you with the use of nicotine gum or the nicotine patch. It is important to set a quit date and to then be sure you have stopped smoking before adding nicotine to your system. The advantage of the gum is that it is a habit that can replace lighting up during the situations when you have smoked before. The patch, on the other hand, is applied on a daily basis and provides continuous absorption to keep the blood level of nicotine at a consistent level.

Over time, you do want to withdraw from nicotine as well, and therefore you can use the patch or the gum to gradually withdraw from nicotine, after you have broken the habit of smoking itself. You can try to structure your environment to avoid cigarettes by avoiding places where other people smoke, by informing your friends of your quit date, and by developing alternative behaviors, whether it is the gum, sipping herbal tea, or leaving situations with which you have associated smoking in the past.

If your first attempt to quit smoking is not a complete success, remember that you are not alone. Many women and men who try to stop smoking need several attempts to finally quit. If you go back to the stages of change model, you will see that this is part of the relapse that is quite possible during the change of any addictive behavior. This does not mean that you are lazy, stupid or have poor willpower, many of the unhelpful labels that we apply to ourselves when trying to change an addictive behavior. It means that you are making an extremely important but difficult change in order to improve your health and the health of those around you.

ALCOHOL

Eileen has been our patient for three years. When she first came to us, she did not perceive her drinking patterns as a problem. She and her husband would have a drink when they came home from work and one with dinner. It was only occasionally, on special holidays or weekends, that she might have an additional glass of wine, but never more than four on any particular evening.

When we discussed her family history, Eileen readily acknowledged that her father had had a problem with alcohol. She described him as a "functional alcoholic who went to work every day and rarely became truly drunk until his later years." It was in these later years that alcohol became more of a problem. Eileen's mother, who she describes as "a woman whose home could pass the old-fashioned white-glove test," drank much less and managed to keep the home together, despite her husband's frequent drunken episodes.

Eileen is now fifty, has two children ages nineteen and seventeen and is happily married to Roger, her second husband, who is an accountant. She is a buyer for a chain of women's clothing stores and describes herself as fairly stressed by the pressures at work and at home. She and Roger very much enjoy their evening drink together and see it as a time to relax and discuss the events of the day. Eileen is in very good health, although she acknowledges that she could certainly exercise more and be more careful in her diet. She comes to our Women's Health Associates for her yearly exam and a discussion regarding mammography for women fifty years old. Eileen has learned that she needs an annual mammogram now that she is fifty years old, but she is surprised when we discuss alcohol with her.

Eileen is fairly typical of American women, many of whom drink one to two alcoholic beverages a day. What Eileen did not know before she came to our practice was that for women drinking in this range, there are some well-established health risks. First, let's start with the basics. A drink is a drink is a drink. That is, one drink is equivalent to five ounces of wine, twelve ounces of beer, or a cocktail mixed with a shot or one and a half ounces of hard liquor. Many people assume that wine and beer, because of their lower alcohol content are less of a problem than hard liquor, but the lower alcohol content is usually offset by drinking a larger quantity. Any drink that is concocted with more than the standard quantity of alcohol is obviously comparable to more than one alcoholic beverage.

Eileen could not understand how drinking one or two drinks an evening could possibly be dangerous, particularly when she had seen her father drink for years in the range of six to ten cocktails an evening. This exemplifies one of the many inequities between the genders. While men can consume up to four drinks a day without experiencing long-term health consequences, women run the risk of experiencing the complications of alcohol by drinking over one and a half to two drinks a day. We now know that women absorb alcohol to a greater extent than men and have higher blood levels of alcohol even when differences in body weight are considered. So for any equivalent amount of alcohol consumed, a woman is going to experience the immediate effects to a much greater extent than a man. This becomes particularly important when considering the immediate consequences of driving while intoxicated.

The differences in the immediate effects carry over to differences in long-term effects. Women develop health complications of alcohol use after drinking for a much shorter time and at a much lower level than men. This is true for liver disease, ulcer disease, gastrointestinal bleeding and the neurologic effects of alcohol. Women who drink more than the equivalent of one and half to two drinks a day, increase their risk of developing alcohol liver damage after ten years. Eileen found this a shocking statistic, especially since Roger had been told by his physician to drink two drinks a day to elevate his HDL, the good part of his cholesterol. This is another area where the advice given to men may have one risk-benefit analysis, whereas the risks and benefits for women are quite different. Though it is true that alcohol has been shown to have some beneficial effect on cholesterol, the amount of alcohol that is recommended to achieve this benefit may put women at risk for a number of other complications. In the larger picture, the risk-benefit analysis of drinking for women makes it unwise to recommend this approach.

There are also a number of complications of alcohol use which are specifically problematic for women. Even at what some women see as low levels of alcohol consumption, women may increase their risk of developing breast cancer. This was demonstrated in several studies where women who drank in the range of even one drink per day were shown to increase their risk of breast cancer, up to one and a half times the rate of nondrinkers or moderate drinkers. For women who may already have an increased risk of breast cancer because of a family history, this is particularly important. The increased risk of breast cancer from hormone replacement is approximately equivalent to that which is conferred by drinking four or more drinks per week. Somehow, the information about estrogen and breast cancer has received much more attention than the information about alcohol and its link to breast cancer.

Osteoporosis is another condition related to alcohol consumption. Alcohol abuse increases the chance that a woman will develop osteoporosis as well as hip fractures in her lifetime. Coupled with cigarette smoking, these are two very preventable risk factors for osteoporosis. We may not be able to change our family history, but we certainly can try to change the behaviors which put us at an increased risk for this debilitating disease.

There are also a number of gynecologic problems associated with alcohol consumption. Many of these may have particular importance at the time of menopause. For example, irregular or heavy menstrual bleeding has been associated with heavy drinking. Many perimenopausal women have these symptoms anyway and it is likely that alcohol could worsen them. Although the obstetrical complications of alcohol are unlikely to be your primary concern during the perimenopausal period, they are well documented also.

Eileen was concerned about the health risks of drinking at her current level, but was reluctant to agree to give up her nightly two drinks. She saw these drinks as her reward at the end of what were often very hectic and stressful days. We discussed with her at some length the dangers of using alcohol as a relaxant medication. The dependence on alcohol for relaxation was already beginning to disrupt Eileen's sleep, but she did not understand this until we explained it to her. She would indeed feel relaxed right before going to bed, after drinking with Roger, but she was beginning to wake up in the middle of the night and did not understand that this could be a result of the alcohol. When alcohol enters the bloodstream, it does cause relaxation. However, approximately four hours later, when the alcohol level goes down, one becomes dehydrated and is often awakened.

In addition, Eileen was already at significant high risk of developing true alcohol dependence because of her father's history of alcoholism. Alcoholism is an inheritable disease, and it is particularly true that women who have alcoholic fathers are very much at risk of developing alcoholism. Women who use alcohol to improve their daily functioning seem to be at more of a risk of developing problems. Women who use alcohol to relax, to get to sleep, or to be more sociable have been shown to have higher rates of alcoholism than women who do not use alcohol in these ways. Although Eileen was controlling her alcohol consumption at that point in time, she did run significant risk of having future problems. It was also striking that she was so reluctant to consider giving up her nightly drinks. This reaction in and of itself indicated a potential dependence on alcohol that was more significant than she had ever realized. When we last talked with Eileen, she had reached the planning stage of her behavior change and was going to an Alcoholics Anonymous meeting with Roger. They were both considering abstaining from alcohol, and Eileen wanted to learn more about the impact of her father on her own drinking and family life.

In addition to family history and the use of alcohol as a medication, there are other factors which put women at an increased risk for developing alcoholism. Women who are married to or living with an alcoholic are at increased risk of developing problems with alcohol. Although there is some conflicting evidence, lesbian women may be at a higher risk of developing alcoholism than are heterosexual women. Some have suggested that this is a result of the discrimination and social stress of being in a minority group. There is considerable concern that the rates of alcoholism among African-American and Hispanic women are increasing in the United States, and the tragic high rate of alcohol abuse among Native Americans is well documented. There is, in general, a higher rate of alcoholism among people from Eileen's Irish background, as well as French and German backgrounds.

For any particular woman, it is important to make a very detailed assessment of these risk factors. Although drinking may not be a significant problem now, it may become one in the future. There have been a number of questionnaires which have been developed to assess whether a woman has a problem with alcohol. Most of these questionnaires rely on information pertaining to problems with relationships that have developed, rather than the health problems that tend to occur late in the course of alcoholism. One questionnaire, which many physicians find useful, is called the CAGE Questionnaire and consists of four questions (Ewing, 1984). The questions are:

1. Have you ever tried to *Cut down* on your drinking?

2. Have you ever been *Annoyed by* criticism about your drinking?

3. Have you ever felt *Guilty* about your drinking?

4. Have you ever had an *Eye-opener* or an early-morning drink to treat a hangover?

Any positive response to these questions requires careful consideration of your drinking patterns. If you previously cut down on your alcohol consumption because of pregnancy, this may or may not represent a cause for concern. On the other hand, if you have tried to cut down on your alcohol consumption because you perceive that it was causing some problems in your life, this may be more significant. If you have two or more positive responses to these questions, you may have a problem with drinking, and you should consider getting an evaluation from a substance-abuse counselor or a mental health professional specializing in substance abuse.

If you suspect you have a problem with alcohol, or others are concerned about your drinking, it is important that you seek help. Although not all physicians are equipped to treat alcohol-related problems, they should be aware of resources within your community. There are a number of different types of treatment for alcohol abuse, including the self-help groups which rely on group process. The most familiar of the self-help groups is Alcoholics Anonymous, and it has been extremely helpful for many people dealing with alcohol problems. There are literally hundreds of meetings in any geographic area every week. There are meetings for women only, meetings which provide child-care, meetings for lesbians, and nonsmoking meetings, to name a few. Studies have shown that women do respond better to self-help programs and to all female groups (Jarvis, 1992). There is also a specific self-help group for women only called Women for Sobriety, which may meet in your area as well.

Many women also choose to see an alcohol counselor alone, in addition to self-help groups. The counselor can help to establish a treatment plan and monitor and support you through the recovery process. Alcohol counselors usually work closely with self-help groups and other resources in the community.

For some women, it is important that they be out of their usual situation in order to gain the most from treatment. Inpatient or residential treatment programs have been designed specifically for this purpose. Most of these programs involve hospitalization that is devoted to therapy and education about alcohol and its effects. Families and significant others are usually encouraged to participate in the program because long-term recovery depends not only on the individual with a drinking problem but also on their family and friends. Most residential programs also arrange for continued treatment after discharge in an outpatient setting.

Relapse may occur, of course, but treatment for alcoholism can be remarkably successful, and most people can look forward to happier and healthier lives in recovery.

SUBSTANCE ABUSE

Just as women are not immune to alcoholism neither are they immune to problems with other drugs which have the potential to be addictive. While only 5 percent of all women compared to 8 percent of all men reported using illegal drugs according to one survey, it is true that women abuse prescription drugs at a higher rate than men (National Institute on Drug Abuse, 1990). It is estimated that nearly half of women alcoholics are also dependent on other drugs, most commonly, sleeping pills or tranquilizers used for anxiety.

Not surprisingly, the factors which put women at risk for drug abuse include a family history of drug abuse, early age of onset of alcohol or other drug use, having a significant other who abuses drugs, and having been prescribed a mood-altering drug. We certainly can't do anything about our family history nor can we do anything about the age at which we might have begun drinking or using other drugs, but we do have some control over our significant others and our use of prescription drugs. Certainly no one begins taking a medication with the intention of becoming addicted to it. However, the path to addiction can be very insidious. There are extremely few women who do not have a complaint which could warrant the use of an addictive medication. Anxiety, insomnia, weight problems and chronic pain are all conditions that could be treated with medications which have addictive potential. Everyone is now aware of the dangers of Valium, which was prescribed too often to women with anxiety and stress. Only after a number of years of experience with the drug did it become clear that it was highly addictive for those who took it on a long-term basis.

Amphetamines were also used extensively in the past to treat weight problems, and many women became hooked on these uppers which gave them seemingly boundless energy and birdlike appetites. Narcotic pain medications used over the long-term can be addictive as well. This is not to say that pain medicine should be avoided altogether, but rather that any pain which has a potential to be chronic, such as long-standing lower-back pain or osteoarthritis, should be treated with medications that are nonaddictive, when possible. Although most health care providers are now aware of the addictive potential of many drugs, it is important that you question your physician and/or pharmacist when you are prescribed a new medication. If you do discover that there is the potential for addiction, you may ask for an alternative treatment, or reassurance that your treatment will be short-term and will not pose any long-term problems.

If you are worried that you may have developed an addiction to a particular medication, or to a nonprescription drug, it is absolutely important that you share this concern with your clinician. As in the case of alcoholism, physicians and other health care professionals may or may not be knowledgeable enough to establish a treatment plan with you, but they should be able to refer you to the appropriate resources. In the case of some drugs, it is important that the dose be gradually tapered rather than abruptly stopped in order to avoid symptoms of drug withdrawal. This can usually be done with the advice of your physician, counselor or in an inpatient setting designed for drug detoxification. The principles of drug treatment are similar to those of alcohol treatment and include self-help programs, including Narcotics Anonymous, drug counselors for outpatient treatment and residential programs for inpatient treatment. There is help available if you need it and want it. Remember the stages of change presented earlier in this chapter. The key is to move from precontemplation to action. Relapses may occur but should not be seen as signs of failure or reasons to lose hope.

✦ OVEREATING AND WEIGHT-LOSS PROGRAMS

American society, in general, and the medical profession, in particular, have been especially critical of overweight women. In fact, we find that most women are uncomfortable with their bodies. Most of us believe that we are too heavy or too thin, too flat-chested, or too full-figured. The pages of most women's magazines are filled with photographs of models who resemble boys or waifs, a completely unrealistic "look" for the majority of women. We only know a few women who have somehow escaped from the anxiety about body image.

Overweight people are one of the few remaining categories where prejudice is socially acceptable. You need only to look at any television program to see that overweight women and men take the brunt of numerous jokes. Midlife women, already subjected to discrimination, can be especially targeted for hurtful remarks when they are over-weight. We are reminded of a visiting dignitary who came to one of our graduate programs in the early seventies and informed us that the women's movement would never take off because "after forty, women's hips spread." We knew even back then that this made no sense, particularly coming from a man who, although quite accomplished in his career, was not exactly Robert Redford.

Being overweight also continues to be seen as a character flaw, rather than a problem. This prejudice continues, even after progress has been made in other addictive behaviors, like alcohol abuse. This bias goes on despite the fact that it is clear that genetics play an important role in the determination of body weight and shape. In addition, little thought is sometimes given to the fact that treatment for obesity has usually not been very successful and has involved high rates of relapse. Treatment for overweight women is now somewhat controversial. Several psychologists who pioneered research on the efficacy of weight-loss treatments are now recommending caution in dieting. Drs. Susan and Orville Wooley believe that obesity alone should not be targeted for change. They recommend changes in eating behaviors like lowering cholesterol as a target behavior, rather than weight loss per se (Wooley and Wooley, 1979).

There are many hazards to being significantly overweight, as we have discussed in earlier chapters. Being moderately or severely overweight is associated with hazardous hypertension, cardiovascular disease, gallbladder disease, diabetes, musculoskeletal problems and certain types of cancer. These associations have not been found for slightly overweight people. So in many cases, weight loss is a good idea. However, overweight women have special concerns, including the hazards of weight cycling, or what is known as "yo-yo dieting" (Ernsberger and Nelson, 1988). By the time they reach midlife, many women have gained and lost weight a number of times, and these failures themselves have certain psychological hazards (Wadden and others, 1988). Many of these women, rather than understanding that being overweight is a complex and difficult set of behaviors to change, believe that *they* are failures and have resulting feelings of sadness and discouragement.

Nonetheless, many midlife women continue to try to lose weight. Others are trying to avoid the weight gain that is often associated with menopause. We believe that the first step should be to use the stages of change model that we have discussed. If there are other parts of our health-promotion plan where you have already begun to take action, it might make sense to follow through with those first. It doesn't make sense to tackle the weight problem again if you are not convinced and committed at this time.

What if you reach the preparation stage and you are only mildly overweight? You may be interested in losing weight primarily because of concerns about your appearance; then, you might consider an exercise program. One of our patients, Jeanette, is a fifty-four-year-old women who had a long history of being overweight and made multiple attempts to diet. She had previously lost between five and ten pounds, only to regain them over the last five years. She was frustrated because, as she got older, she noted it was even more difficult to lose weight than before. Jeanette decided that rather than change her diet, she would make a concerted and consistent effort to increase her physical activity level. Specifically, she had read that if she walked three miles a day, four or five times a week, she could lose ten pounds in a year. When we saw Jeanette for the first time she had been on her exercise program for less than a month. However, now a year has passed and Jeanette has indeed lost nine pounds without making any changes in her eating behavior. Jeanette has had great difficulty in sticking to her exercise plan but has managed to do so. She now wants to continue to exercise to maintain her weight loss.

Dr. Kelly Brownell of Yale University recommends that the key to successful treatment is a careful assessment in matching the patient to the treatment plan (Brownell and Wadden, 1991). The best place to have your weight-loss plan assessed is a comprehensive program, usually in departments of behavioral medicine in university-affiliated hospitals. These programs ensure that you will be able to be evaluated comprehensively, where the biological, psychological and social issues can all be considered in your treatment. Dr. Matthew Clark and associates at Brown University Medical School completed a review of all the literature on treatment of obesity and suggest that the following factors should be considered: First, it is important to have a psychological assessment. Two of the most important psychological issues are binge eating and a history of physical and sexual abuse. Some women who struggle with their weight are binge eaters and may require treatment for depression, not just another diet. Binge eating involves eating large quantities of food at a sitting and feeling out of control. This is now seen as a separate type of eating disorder that requires specific treatment. Some studies have found that up to 30 percent of women in weight-control programs have true eating disorders or another psychological problem (Clark and others, 1993). In addition, some women use food to treat their depressions. They may have had depressive episodes in response to dieting in the past. Finally, many women who have histories of sexual abuse, substance-abuse problems or anxiety, also need comprehensive psychological care. Additional parts of an evaluation should include a physical examination, laboratory tests and a nutritional and exercise assessment. Such an assessment will help you identify what your target behaviors are in order to provide an effective treatment program.

Components of a weight-reduction program usually involve behavior therapy, nutritional counseling and an increased exercise and physical activity program. Some recommend the use of a very low-calorie diet for people who have a lot of weight to lose. It should be noted that these programs need to be combined with a comprehensive treatment approach to maximize the possibility of long-term maintenance. Most experts, at this time, do not recommend surgery for obesity. The use of medications depends on the extent of weight loss necessary and should be carefully monitored. You should be especially wary of medications that can be addictive and affect the central nervous system.

Suppose you live in an area without a comprehensive weight-loss program? Remember, let the buyer beware, and use your own good common sense. Few weight-reduction programs have been evaluated scientifically and many of them spend a fortune on advertising, often using celebrities. Yet, do you really want to go on a liquid protein diet, and follow in the footsteps of Oprah Winfrey and proudly show off weight loss in a pair of tight black jeans, only to gain it all back in a few months time? Every weight expert we know shuddered and was concerned for Oprah when she announced her supposedly permanent new shape. You should be especially cautious about crash diets and programs that ask for a lot of money at the beginning of the plan. Some of these programs will give you a rationale that large amounts of money are needed "up front," in order to prevent you from dropping out easily. Although there is some truth to that, many programs for losing weight are quite similar and large amounts of money do not guarantee a good program. You want a program to focus on gradual nutritional planning, behavior modification and increased physical activity and exercise.

Consumer Reports analyzed the responses of 95,000 of their readers in order to evaluate commercial diet programs. Their results were sobering: Most of the people regained their lost weight within a year (Losing Weight, 1993). Among the top diet programs, there were no differences in helping people lose weight or keep it off. Members of Weight Watchers, however, reported the greatest level of satisfaction with the program. Although only 6 percent of the readers had been to hospital-based weight-reduction programs, these programs did as well as the others and received fewer complaints than other programs.

There were two particularly interesting results of this study. First, more than 25 percent of the people did not even meet the criteria for being overweight. More evidence that many of us are dieting unnecessarily. In addition, another 25 percent of the group did maintain weight loss, but the study could not determine what led to these successes.

In our experience, there are two key elements to keeping weight off. The first is as you know by now, a physically active lifestyle. The second is to identify and act on your need for social support, one of our favorite topics, which is more complicated when it comes to losing weight and maintaining weight loss. Although having a weight-loss or maintenance partner is usually helpful, a woman needs to decide if she prefers what Drs. Brownell and Rodin call a solo or a social plan (Brownell and Rodin, 1990). They found that some individuals do better with a buddy, whereas others preferred to lose weight alone. So look for support if you need it.

If, after an assessment, you are still unsure about the pros and cons of losing weight and are still in the contemplation stage, and if you have made multiple attempts to lose weight by dieting, you might consider an exercise/physical activity program. Some women break out of the diet habit by beginning a low-fat, rather than a low-calorie diet. The fact is that there are no easy answers to losing weight. One of the problems in losing weight is that the goal cannot be abstinence, as it can be in smoking cessation or substance-abuse programs. We cannot eliminate food from our environment. Thus, the exposure to temptation is frequent. In addition, gaining some weight as we age is to be expected. Thus, we should try to break out of the "you can never be too thin" mentality.

What if you are only ten pounds overweight and your physician is pushing you to lose weight? We have had many women come to us with this concern recently. Many of them have no other health-risk factors and are in good shape, but just tend to be heavier, as do many members of their family. Given the fact that we now know there is some genetic basis to being overweight and the fact that treatment for obesity is usually not successful for long-term maintenance, it seems that these women are being unfairly pressured. As much as we hope that you will be able to lose weight if you decide to do so, the fact is that this is still an area with a lot of relapse. Finally, some of the most recent research suggests that gaining a little weight as we get older may have protective health benefits like fewer hot flashes (Erlik and others, 1982). So this may be an opportunity for you to be assertive with your physician by suggesting that you do not feel this is a problem that you want to work on at this time and stressing your reasons for your beliefs.

Unfortunately, some health care providers are not as sensitive in this area as they could be. They may be unaware of the number of times you have tried to lose weight and your feelings about it. Your feelings are an important part of your health. It is appropriate and even necessary for you to share any feelings you may have with regard to your weight and past attempts at dieting. Remember that a healthy lifestyle overall is more important than the numbers on the scale.

✦ NUTRITION

As we have discussed in the previous section about overeating, all too many menopausal women have been prisoners of the calorie count for decades. By the time we reach midlife, many women have been dieting for a full thirty years. Most menopausal women are therefore experts in calories and calorie counting. This preoccupation tends to be destructive rather than beneficial. So we are not going to deal with calories. A better approach is to look at the components of nutrition that are necessary for good health during the menopausal years and to target problem areas. The components of good nutrition for midlife women are: a balanced diet, adequate calcium, lower fat consumption, avoidance of alcohol and caffeine and simple sugar, and adequate water intake.

Remember the four basic food groups that we learned in elementary school? Well you can forget them now, because the U.S. Department of Agriculture has launched a new food guide referred to as the new food pyramid. The pyramid (Figure 10-3) emphasizes for us, once again, that Americans have been eating too much meat. The foundation of our diet should be in the complex carbohydrates—the bread, rice, cereal and pasta group. Complex carbohydrates should compose from 55 to 60 percent of our diet. The next level of our diet should be composed of three to five daily servings of vegetables and two to four servings of fruit. We should be eating less of the proteins such as meat, poultry, fish and beans. Finally, we should eat very few fats, oils and sweets.

When the food pyramid was first released, Teresa laughed and mentioned that if she ate all of the servings of those foods, even as they were described, she would end up "looking like a pyramid." She has described her own dietary needs as "the shrinking pyramid." But the pyramid is a definite improvement over the old four food groups in that it emphasizes an increased intake of fiber and carbohydrates as an important component.

The American Dietetic Association has also suggested that within

Figure 10–3

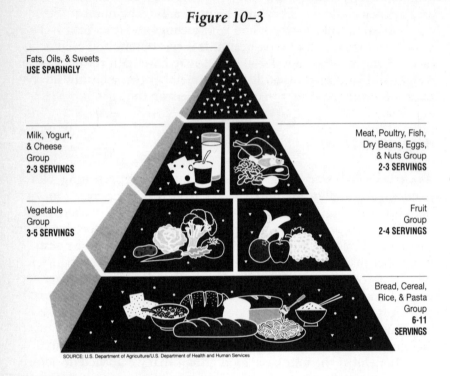

Fats, Oils, & Sweets
USE SPARINGLY

Milk, Yogurt,
& Cheese
Group
2-3 SERVINGS

Meat, Poultry, Fish,
Dry Beans, Eggs,
& Nuts Group
2-3 SERVINGS

Vegetable
Group
3-5 SERVINGS

Fruit
Group
2-4 SERVINGS

Bread, Cereal,
Rice, & Pasta
Group
**6-11
SERVINGS**

SOURCE: U.S. Department of Agriculture/U.S. Department of Health and Human Services

each of these groups, there are also variations in the amount of fats. Many sauces and additives contain lots of fat, and we should focus on keeping fat and cholesterol low, limiting excessive sodium and simple sugar and eating a broad variety of fruits and vegetables (1992a).

THE FAT QUESTION

Reducing fat is one of the most important changes for general health benefits and specifically for cardiovascular health. Two of the most important changes that we can make are to reduce the amount of red meat and to avoid high-fat dairy products. Many women have given up red meat entirely, but we must also be careful of high-fat dairy foods. In some gourmet ice cream, for example, 50 percent of the total calories is from fat, whereas in low-fat frozen yogurts only 6 percent of the calories comes from fat. So yes, you might want to give up chocolate-chip cookie dough ice cream and replace it with low-fat chocolate yogurt.

It is important to be careful about hidden fats. Fast-food and prepared foods are often extremely high in their fat and salt content. We should be eating no more than 30 percent of fat in our diet, and many nutritionists suggest that this figure should be closer to 25 percent for better health promotion. You can actually calculate the percentage of your calories that are fat, relatively easily. One gram of fat has nine calories. Most prepared foods now include a nutritional analysis that will list this figure. For example, one serving of a flavored cracker may have 50 calories. If the cracker serving has 2 grams of fat, then 2 (grams) × 9 (calories per gram of fat) = 18, or 18 of those 50 calories consists of fat. This is 36 percent of the total serving. This is actually a high figure for a cracker, especially when you compare it to a saltine, which has zero grams of fat. It is important then to read the label and not just assume that crackers, as a general rule, are all low-fat.

Another approach is to add up your grams of fat for the day. A 1,500 daily calorie diet could have about 40 grams of fat per day if you are aiming for the 25-percent figure. These quick calculations can help you make significant and consistent changes in your nutritional planning.

Beware of food labeling. The Food and Drug Administration has been mandated to develop a system of food labeling. This legislation is aimed at promoting consistency in labeling. In addition, the FDA will be cracking down on the terms that are vastly overused like "low-fat," and "light." They are in the process of providing definitions so that a company cannot slap a new label on an old product. We have all also seen the labeling that suggests that one serving of a coffee cake will have only 100 calories, only to find that that particular serving may be one-twentieth of a small cake (a tiny bite!). Another example is that a "light" hot dog may have a full two-thirds of its calories derived from fat. That may be "light" compared to other hot dogs that have 95 percent fat, but remember that we are aiming for less than 30 percent of our total daily calories to be derived from fat. You can accomplish a lot just by selecting low-fat foods. For example, one ounce of potato chips can have 10 grams (25 percent of your daily "fat allowance") of fat (Friedman, 1993, p. 1). Low-fat and no-fat muffins can replace the greasy ones. Frozen pizzas can vary from 5 grams of fat per slice (tofu or vegetarian), to about 13 to 14 grams (extra cheese or many "deluxe" toppings) (Friedman, 1993, p. 3). You can substitute a cup of unbuttered popcorn and eliminate fat.

The question of omega-3 fatty acid that is found in fish oils received attention when it was found that heart disease is quite rare among the Greenland Eskimos. Several studies suggested that these omega-3 fatty acids reduce the level of triglycerides which contribute to heart disease. In addition, there is some evidence that they reduce the tendency to form blood clots as well. Yet, most nutritionists agree that fish oil supplements are not necessary, but that eating fish two or three times a week is a good idea. This is true because fish is a good source of protein and also a natural source of the omega-3 fatty acids.

Adequate Calcium

Don't forget your calcium. As a result of inadequate calcium intake in youth and young adulthood, most of us reach the menopausal years with a low peak bone mass. In addition, as we age, our ability to absorb calcium decreases, especially at the time of menopause. This is particularly true for women after the age of fifty, but begins during the menopausal years. Remember, the calcium needs for perimenopausal women are somewhere about 1,200 mg per day. For the postmenopausal women, the suggestion is 1,500 mg per day.

One of the problems here is that women have long avoided dairy products because of a concern about gaining weight. As we discussed in our chapter on healthy bones, we can get enough calcium by replacing milk with skim milk, ice cream with low-fat yogurt, by eating a calcium-rich diet and by taking calcium supplements. Other vitamins and minerals can also be taken in a one-a-day supplement. This may be necessary because in our quest to cut calories, many women do not eat enough fruits and vegetables which greatly limits intake of vitamins and minerals (Winick, 1992).

The Iron Question

Sometimes women who are chronically dieting have an inadequate vitamin and mineral intake, especially iron. For perimenopausal women who are still menstruating, the recommended daily allowance of iron is 18 mg per day. Unfortunately, this would require an average caloric intake of 3,000 calories a day of a mixed, well-balanced diet! Obviously, this caloric requirement would lead to obesity over time, given the average activity level of most American women.

Until recently, it was believed that women who are premenopausal should be taking iron supplements. However, recent studies suggested that high iron stores have been associated with increased risk of heart attacks. Women's low stores of iron might protect us from heart disease before menopause. For that reason, women who have lower than the recommended intake of iron, but are not having any symptoms, may not benefit from iron supplements. This is clearly an area to watch for future developments.

H_2O

One of the healthiest choices that we can all make is to drink more water. Water makes up about 60 percent of our body and is needed for our body to function properly. The rule is that we should be drinking about four eight-ounce cups of water for every 1,000 calories we consume. For most women, that would be between six to eight glasses of water per day. This is particularly important because we tend to get dehydrated as we get older. Adequate intake of water can improve our skin, and can also keep us from overeating. Yet most of us have difficulty drinking this much water. Here are a few suggestions to make it easier: First, try replacing some of your caffeinated beverages with ice water. Because some of our tap water may contain contaminates, or may just "taste funny," using bottled water can help us feel more like drinking the water we need. It is as easy to order ice water when you are out to eat at a restaurant as it is to order a soda, and it is almost always free! Second, think about adding a water cooler to the office coffee room. We did this in both of our offices and it has had great results. You might also try drinking small amounts of water at a time. A three-and-a-half-ounce paper cup, for example, does not seem as overwhelming as an eight- or ten-ounce glass. Finally, you can follow the model of the character Susan Silverman in the Robert Parker novels about Spencer. Susan is prone to sipping warm water, perhaps with a bit of lemon or honey, while she is having those long intimate conversations with Spencer. You will be surprised how easy a habit that is to develop (the water, not the relationship with Spencer), especially during the winter.

CUT DOWN ON CAFFEINE AND ALCOHOL

With any luck, while you are drinking more water, you will be drinking less caffeine. Caffeine should really be limited to a maximum of two to three cups per day. Too much caffeine can inhibit the absorption of certain foods and can make us anxious and edgy. One study found that even people who drank between two and three cups of coffee per day experienced some symptoms of withdrawal when the caffeine was taken away. The symptoms included moderate to severe headaches, feeling depressed and feeling fatigued. This does not mean that caffeine should be avoided at all costs, but that we should be careful. In addition, the use of caffeine should be evaluated if you have a problem like headaches, anxiety or depression. It is often present in pain relievers and some other medications. Many over-the-counter weight-loss drugs are composed of high amounts of caffeine. Not only is caffeine a stimulant, it is also a diuretic. Therefore, all the good you do by drinking water can be undone if you match it with an amount of caffeine that depletes your system of water. Many women use both coffee and caffeinated diet sodas to get going during the day. Although we can certainly understand the need for coffee first thing in the morning, perhaps after one or two cups, you can stop. Diet sodas have recently become available in decaffeinated varieties so you can enjoy the taste without the caffeine or calories.

Alcohol abuse is associated with undernutrition. This is true because alcohol consumption affects the stomach, small intestine, pancreas, as well as the liver. It can also cause diarrhea which can result in the loss of nutrients. In addition to these problems, many women who drink too much are not eating a balanced diet. So we need to look at alcohol consumption when we are evaluating our overall nutritional status.

If you make up a new nutritional plan, try to remember our general rules. Try to make moderate rather than severe changes. You are unlikely to go from a diet that is composed of too much fat and simple sugar to an intense low-fat high-fiber diet. But, if you move toward lower-fat and higher-carbohydrate foods, you are more likely to succeed. You may make different choices over a given week. If you know that you are going to a party and it is likely that you will eat a favorite problematic food, it is okay to eat some as long as you try to balance out your diet at another time during the week. You can try to balance your diet over the course of any given week. You don't have to give up favorite problematic foods forever. If you limit your portions and only eat high-fat foods or sweets now and then, you can still continue to maintain a balanced diet.

✦ EXPANDING YOUR SOCIAL NETWORK

Social support is one of the most clearly beneficial factors in all health research. Expanding a social network can take many other forms. Many women have a strong network within their nuclear or extended family. Others have long-term friendships. Social support has been positively associated with everything from maintaining exercise programs to coping with chronic illness. In almost every area that we have described so far, you can find a social support system, whether it is working with a friend who has a similar problem, or participating in a formal self-help group. In the United States more than fifteen million people attend about 500,000 different self-help groups each week. In California alone, 4,600 self-help groups are listed (de Turenne, 1993). Most local newspapers devote a page to self-help groups on a daily or weekly basis. Self-help groups are now part of our culture and also part of a long tradition. We have, therefore, included self-help groups related to health promotion at the end of this chapter. We will discuss more general self-help groups and social-support groups in the next chapter. It is clear that despite the diversity of social networks, these links have been a particularly powerful source of strength for women.

Another way to expand our social network is by giving something back to the larger community. Erik Erikson suggests that the task of midlife is to struggle with the issues of self-absorption as opposed to generativity. Self-absorption can develop out of isolation. Without meaningful relationships, we can begin to turn inward and brood about the narcissistic losses of middle age. The growth-promoting aspect of generativity is the sharing with a younger generation the knowledge that comes with age. In this way, a woman in midlife can connect with others. Many women do so, through their paid employment, volunteer work, mentoring or grandparenting. So much for Helene Deutsch's nonsense that we have ended our service to the species. A study of menopausal women validated the importance of generativity, finding that when women had a commitment, whether it was paid employment or not, they reported fewer menopausal symptoms.

Hortence Powdermaker was an anthropologist who wrote about the importance of connection. In her description of life as an anthropologist, she too described her fear about doing field work in the Pacific. Her feelings of panic finally dissipated when she began to talk with one of the islanders. Her words can help all of us: "I was no longer alone. I had friends and went to bed and fell asleep almost immediately. No more thoughts of madness or leaving entered my mind. Several years later, I learned that a definition of panic is a state of unrelatedness" (Conway, 1992, p. 247). By remaining connected to others and expanding our social support, health promotion can become a new lifestyle.

You have now read about six components of the Women's Health Promotion Plan. But if your New Year's resolution was to attempt all six at once, it would be difficult to follow through. If, on the other hand, you use your own good common sense and identify one or two of these components with your primary care clinician, you are more likely to succeed. Please don't view us as the health police patrol, whose purpose is to remove all happiness and pleasure from your life. Use stress management, relaxation and pleasurable activities as the foundation. We don't want you to view the menopausal years as restriction and suffering, but we do want you to incorporate some of these changes into your lifestyle.

Keep in mind that no matter what changes or lifestyle we adopt, it is most important to enjoy life. Dr. Teresa Bernardez, a psychiatrist, gave a fascinating lecture to the Menninger's Institute on "Women and Self-Esteem" in 1989. She points out that we have enough struggles in midlife, and that to completely restrict our food intake and to make food a constant preoccupation is a tremendous loss for many women. She describes coming to the United States from her native Argentina in the 1950s and expecting to see a lot of free, comfortable, Katharine Hepburn-like women in comfortable slacks. In contrast, she found women whom she described as trapped in girdles, with hair that was controlled by lacquered layers of hair spray and a life of constant preoccupation with eating and not eating. Dr. Bernardez reminds all of us that food is extremely enjoyable for women, and that we can combine some good health habits with periodic relaxation and enjoyment (Bernardez, 1990).

RESOURCES

GENERAL RESOURCES

Melpomene
Melpomene Institute
1010 University Ave.
St. Paul, MN 55104
(612) 642-1951

Journal on women's health research; 3 journals a year with a membership to the Institute for $32. It includes profiles of older women, information on health, research and aging.

Prevention
Box 181
Emmaus, PA 18099-0181

A monthly magazine for $19.97 a year. Easy reading on nutrition, exercise, health-screening and maintenance.

Radiance Magazine
PO Box 31703
Oakland, CA 94604
(415) 482-0680

A quarterly magazine for large women, giving resources and information on health, including older women's health, fashion, politics, entertainment. $15 a year.

University of California at Berkeley Wellness Letter
PO Box 420148
Palm Coast, FL 32142
(904) 445-6414

Newsletter on nutrition, fitness, stress management and health. Somewhat technical and very informative. 12 issues for $24 a year.

HEALTH-SCREENING

Dial-a-Hearing Screening Test
(800) 222-EARS

This number, open Monday to Friday 9–6, EST, will connect you to an operator who will give you a local number to call. This number is a recorded hearing test consisting of 8 tones, with instructions. Operators also provide referrals.

EXERCISE

Living with Exercise, by Steven N. Blair. Dr. Blair is a major researcher in the area of physical fitness at the Institute for Aerobics Research in Dallas, Texas. Dr. Blair writes, "You don't have to be an Olympic champion to receive health benefits from physical fitness." His book is extremely valuable because of its approach. He emphasizes physical activities that are moderate, stressing that you do not need to begin to train for the Olympics, even though you have been a couch potato for most of your life. He takes a behavioral approach, helping you outline the rewards of exercise while eliminating the barriers. Finally, he focuses on increasing your physical activity as part of your daily life-style.

The American Volkksport is an association committed to promoting health and fitness through noncompetitive, safe sporting activities. They publish the *American Wanderer,* a bimonthly newspaper for $12 a year, with news on their groups and events. They can also send you a list of local walking clubs. An individual yearly membership is $20.

Rockport's Complete Book of Fitness Walking by Dr. James M. Rippe and Ann Ward, Ph.D. (New York: Prentice Hall Press, 1989).

Prevention Walking Club
Rodale Press
Box 6099
Emmaus, PA 18099
(800) 441-7761

A $9.97 membership includes a quarterly newsletter and annual magazine, both about various aspects of walking.

RELAXATION

There are many books dealing with the issue of relaxation. Some of the better ones include:

Beyond the Relaxation Response by Herbert Benson with William Proctor (New York: New York Times Book Company, 1984).

Mind/Body Medicine is an edited book, published by *Consumer Reports.* Some of the leading experts on psychoneuroimmunolgy present their views on how stress affects our health

Healthy Pleasures by Robert Ornstein and David Sobel presents a comfortable nonthreatening approach to lifestyle change. The upbeat tone helps us avoid the feelings at being trapped by the "health police" (Reading, MA: Addison-Wesley Publishing Co., Inc., 1989).

ELIMINATING OR REDUCING PROBLEMATIC BEHAVIORS—OVEREATING

Dr. Kelly Brownell and Dr. Judith Rodin have participated in research on obesity for many years. Two of the books that we have found helpful are: *The LEARN Program for Weight Control* by Dr. Brownell and *The Weight Maintenance Survival Guide* by Drs. Brownell and Rodin. The value of these books is that they are based on behavioral research and take a safe and gradual approach to weight loss. In addition, they are extremely sensitive to women's issues and to the concerns about weight-cycling that can also be hazardous.

ALCOHOL ABUSE

Alcoholics Anonymous or AA, the grandparent of self-help groups, is usually listed in the front of the telephone book and often on the pages of local newspapers. If, however, you cannot find a group in your area, you can check with the General Service Office at P.O. Box 459, Grand Central Station, New York, NY 10016—(212)-686-1100. Some women find AA to be too male-dominated and are more comfortable in groups where there are more women. This varies on a group by group basis.

Another group that works with women alone is called Women For Sobriety, P.O. Box 618, Quaker Town Pennsylvania, 18951—(800) 333-1606.

SMOKING

The American Lung Association provides pamphlets about quitting smoking. Your local affiliate can also send you a list of smoke-free restaurants in your area.

NUTRITION

Jane Brody is one of the best health writers around. Her articles in the *New York Times* are always balanced and practical. One of her books that is extremely helpful is called *Jane Brody's Nutrition Book* (New York: Bantam Books, 1987).

For women interested in vegetarianism, an interesting magazine is *Vegetarian Times,* published in Mount Morris, Illinois. This old guard vegetarian monthly magazine includes health topics, humane issues, vegetarian product information and recipes, but also covers educational articles promoting healthy lifestyles.

Fast Vegetarian Feasts, by Martha Rose Shulman (New York: Dial Press, 1982). This book proves that vegetarian cooking can be quick. It also includes menus.

Moosewood Cookbook, this meatless cookbook is one of the oldest and most popular, and has been recently revised to reflect the lower calorie approach. Written by Mollie Katzen (The Ten Speed Press, Berkeley California, 1993).

Tufts University Diet and Nutrition Letter
203 Harrison Ave.
Boston, MA 02111
(800) 274-7581

Newsletter that reviews studies, and gives the latest information on nutrition and health in a rather off-the-cuff, skeptical style. $20 a year for 12 issues.

← *CHAPTER ELEVEN*

Resources

So there it is. Now you know almost everything we know about menopause. You know that menopause does not need to be a time of multiple symptoms and deteriorating health. Menopause is not necessarily a time of significant losses. Menopause does not need to be a time when we retreat from society and withdraw into invisibility. Menopause is a time of new freedom from concerns about birth control, freedom from fulfilling but often draining family responsibilities, freedom to have more power to choose everything from our friends to our health care providers, and freedom to explore new ways of living.

Menopause is not merely a hormonal event, nor is it a negative event. Women need to be viewed as whole people, affected by our biology, yes, but by psychology, sociology and the political environment as well. As health care professionals we do see some women who are suffering from troubling symptoms at menopause. We know from our work with patients and our review of the research that problems associated with menopause can be treated effectively, and therefore that menopause is not a particularly troubling time for most women.

This chapter will help you get the most out of your own resources.

When it comes to coping with issues around menopause and dealing with other problems, women have long turned to one another for strength and guidance. We can turn inward to trust our own feelings, and we can turn outward to other women and resources that can be extremely beneficial. Intuitively you will know how to approach certain problems. If you trust your feelings, you will know what your needs are, and your emotional response to many suggestions or ideas about solutions can tell you a lot. This chapter will provide you with resources, but remember that you are your own best health expert.

Two of the most important resources in dealing with the menopausal years are maintenance of good health and focusing on relationships. By maintaining good health, we can promote a lifestyle that prevents as much disease as possible. Focusing on health, rather than illness, also helps us keep an optimistic and coping attitude, instead of focusing on the next phase of life as a series of losses and symptoms. By using the preventive strategies we detailed in the previous chapter, we can continue to lead, not only long, but active and healthy lives. Part of that lifestyle involves developing a women's health team, which we will describe shortly. By maximizing our choices and obtaining as much information as possible, women can work with a primary care provider to develop a healthy lifestyle and flourish during the menopausal years.

Whatever problems we face in life, our relationships and social connections can help us. In every area of women's health from depression to maintenance of exercise routines to dealing with the issue of hormone replacement therapy, women have received support from their relationships with others. These relationships can consist of our family, our friends, our health care providers and self-help groups. If you combine the information that you have taken away from this book, with an assertive attitude toward your own health care and an openness to relationships that can provide you with a feeling of support, you will be well able to cope with whatever life brings. These principles can continue to guide you long after you finish reading this book.

◆ CREATING YOUR OWN WOMEN'S HEALTH TEAM

One of the most significant, positive changes you can make is to take charge of your own health care. You can do this by creating your own women's health team, maintaining a healthy attitude, becoming an educated health consumer and accessing resources.

As we write this book, the health care system in the United States is under intense scrutiny and in the midst of revolutionary change. This change is necessary because of the escalating health care costs that threaten our economic livelihood. We know all too many women who have been shut out of good health care because they lack health insurance. This may be due to poverty, unemployment, inadequate health benefits or the results of a divorce. We should all recognize the impact of the "feminization of poverty"—that is, the fact that most of the people on welfare in the United States are women and their children, and older women as well. As women entering the menopausal years, we must remember that we are the largest segment of the American population and that as we age, we must continue to develop political power so that no woman or man is shut out of the health care system.

We hope that any changes in the health care system will support an effort to emphasize the role of primary care providers. Primary care professionals are the key to women's health during the menopausal years. A primary care provider can help us process the explosion of new information and access appropriate resources when necessary. By creating a partnership in which a woman makes her own health care decision with her primary care provider, health care costs can be maintained, with the best possible health resulting.

Given the changes in the health care system, there is tremendous uncertainty about what types of health insurance will be available, and what will be included in health care coverage. Nonetheless, whether your health insurance is provided on a fee-for-service basis, or in a health-maintenance organization, or in a primary care clinic, you can use certain principles to guide you.

The first principle is to develop a good relationship or partnership with your health care professional. This significant relationship must be based on mutual respect and the ability to talk over the rapidly developing information regarding choices and health care for women in today's changing world. All too often, we have heard our patients say, "I can't really talk with my doctor, but I don't want to hurt his or her feelings" or "My doctor really doesn't have the time to talk to me much." Although we understand the stresses in being a doctor, we know that it is not a woman's job to take care of her doctor, or to worry about taking up too much time. We see many confident and successful women who may be assertive in their everyday lives, but who are still anxious when they need a few moments time from their physicians. It is imperative that we stop feeling like we are "wasting the doctor's time" or that "the doctor has more important things to do than listen to me complain." Spending productive time with our doctor is a meaningful activity, since communication is the key to understanding and the road to prevention and healing. You need to be able to feel free to share your feelings with your physician and to feel comfortable asking questions. Your doctor does not need to be your best friend, but there should be a minimal amount of tension and an attitude of mutual respect, and the ability to share feelings as well as information.

Remember to focus on your own communication skills. The more prepared you are for the office visit, the more you will get out of it. This means first thinking through what your goals are. If there is information that you want to explore during an office visit, you can state that as soon as possible. If, on the other hand, you have several symptoms or problems that are of concern, try to emphasize the ones that are most bothersome or cause you the most anxiety. You might want to review some of the interactions we describe in other chapters of this book to help you along.

Your primary care professional should coordinate your health care. This means providing referrals to appropriate subspecialties and helping you understand their role in your health care. Too many of our patients who have had extensive medical evaluations for infertility, cancer or cardiac problems have stated that the most troubling part of these experiences was dealing with the health care system in general. Trying to coordinate these various specialists is a difficult proposition and your primary care provider should be able to do it for you.

It is important that your health care focus on health, not on illness alone. You probably knew this by now, since in every chapter we have emphasized the issue of prevention. The lifestyle changes that we have outlined are sometimes difficult. But, once they have been established as part of your daily routine, they can make all the difference in your menopausal years. We know that we can reduce the risk of heart disease in women if we begin early. We know that exercise and the appropriate calcium intake, as well as hormone replacement therapy, can reduce the risk of osteoporosis. We know that exercising and eliminating substance abuse can make us all feel better. This emphasis on a healthy lifestyle should be one of your health care provider's values as well.

Do not hesitate to involve a health psychologist or mental health professional. Women tend to use the mental health care system more than men. This is not evidence of some growing mental illness in women, but is a strength. We can conclude from these numbers that most women know when they need help, and we should all trust our instincts and access the mental health system when necessary. Counseling or psychotherapy can make all the difference when coping with stress, family problems or depression. Still, national estimates are that only 8 percent of people with psychological problems receive the appropriate care. Your primary care provider should have a positive attitude toward psychological care as well. Usually, he or she can help you find a competent psychotherapist when necessary. If not, you can refer to our chapter on depression for other ways to access the system of psychological care.

You should be able to have some choice in selecting your primary care provider. This includes choosing a female clinician. Medicine has long been dominated by male physicians. For too many years, women did not have access to female psychologists or physicians. Fortunately, the situation changed rapidly in the last twenty years, with 30 percent of the graduates of medical schools and more than half of the graduate schools of doctoral programs in psychology being female. But female gender alone does not guarantee either an attitude of mutual respect or necessarily an expertise or interest in women's health. This was summed up to us once when one of our patients who was thinking of going to a female gynecologist was told by a close friend, "If you are the type of woman who wants a woman doctor, that woman doctor is not the right one for you!" Complicated, but we knew what she meant.

A significant part of the women's health approach involves a woman's family. Whether your family includes a spouse, partner, children, or a close friend, these people are important resources, not a burden to your health care. Your family should feel comfortable, accompanying you to appointments and even meeting with the doctor when you are either feeling anxious or perhaps facing a major crisis. Most primary care providers are eager to include your family, so you should not hesitate to do so.

✦ THE ROLE OF MENOPAUSE CLINICS

Menopause clinics are springing up everywhere, and we are somewhat concerned about this popular trend. If a menopause clinic involves the comprehensive and interdisciplinary approach we have described, with attention to doctor-patient communication, then it is likely to be an excellent facility for you. However, some menopause clinics focus exclusively on the issue of hormone replacement therapy, and may even involve unnecessary testing (for example, bone densitometry for every woman). Other such clinics are primarily screening centers, but do not offer continuing primary care for women. Your best bet for finding comprehensive care, is to look for a women's health associates practice, using the same principles that we have described above. In addition, the North American Menopause Society (NAMS) can provide you with a resources list for your area. These resources provide the type of professional services available from NAMS members. NAMS is composed of professionals from many disciplines and has national as well as regional meetings to disseminate new treatments and advances in research.

Whether you choose a menopause clinic or a women's health practice, a primary care provider or an individual in an HMO, you should consider scheduling a first meeting essentially as a consultation. This may not always be feasible, depending on your health insurance plan or financial situation. If you can, use that meeting to get a feeling for your comfort level with the provider and to share expectations of what the relationship will be. Ultimately, you are the best judge of your relationship with your primary care provider. If, after two visits you are uncomfortable, be sure to seek out another health care provider or facility.

Be sure to avail yourself of the resources in your community. Although many of the resources such as health education and behavioral medicine programs may be out there, you may not know about them if you do not seek them out.

Above all, do not let yourself become invisible. Most health care providers respect their patients and know that good communication with an actively involved patient may require extra time, but ultimately is worthwhile. If you are treated without respect, you should work with a patient advocate if you are in an HMO or clinic, or find another primary care doctor if your insurance is fee for service. In most cases you will be able to work things out by taking an informed and assertive approach to your own health care. If all else fails, you may need to risk being labeled cranky, or even a "bitch," when your health is at stake. As U.S. Supreme Court Justice Ruth Ginsburg has been quoted, "Better bitch than mouse" (Rosen, 1993).

❖ BECOMING AN EDUCATED CONSUMER

Every Thursday morning on the morning news programs and radio shows, we learn the results of the most recent medical breakthroughs, possible cures and hazards. Often, a doctor of one sort or another is brought on the program for approximately three to four minutes to explain an article published in a medical journal. At times, this overload of information can become unbelievably confusing—do this, don't do that, take this, stay away from that. A prime example was described by

Dr. James Muller, a cardiologist at Harvard Medical School. He was listening to a talk show in which a caller drew a conclusion from two separate studies that had been reported. One study had suggested that heart attacks tended to occur in the morning, another that eating grapes could reduce the risk of heart attacks. Conclusion? "The best way to stay healthy was to stay in bed, eating grapes, until noon" (Rosenthal, 1993). Although such a lifestyle has a certain appeal, this example illustrates how we can make false conclusions when we receive just a little information!

But how can we make sense of these new articles, facts and findings? The best advice is "Do not panic!" over tomorrow's miracle cure or killer. It is rare that the results of one study alone are enough to necessitate a major change in your lifestyle. It is also true that sometimes the media picks up studies that are more sensational than they are reputable. However, if you begin to hear the same results over and over again, then it is time to take notice. Talk all of this new information over with your clinician. In addition, there are several good health magazines that can help you process the information. We list some of them in the back of this chapter, but one of the best is *Prevention*. It tends to review current and reputable articles, rather than the most sensational ones.

We appreciate and respect your interest in understanding the literature. We know that the traditional medical establishment has not paid enough attention to women's health until recently, and so women have needed to be active consumers of information. We do *not* think that you should take a passive view, but should remember to try not to be frightened based on one study. There are several questions you can ask when trying to understand the results of medical literature. One issue involved in understanding the study includes methodology, or how the study was conducted. You need to know if the study is a new study, or has it been done before with other people? The most notorious examples here were many of the cardiovascular studies that were done only on men, ignoring the issue of women's health. Another example is the exaggeration of a study that commented on women's declining fertility in their thirties. The original overly dramatized study was actually based on a small group of French women whose chief complaint was the couple's infertility—hardly a group from which to generalize to the larger American society.

Remember also that association does not mean causation. If we see that, for example, baldness is *associated* with heart disease, that does not mean that baldness causes heart disease in general. Nor does it mean that if someone you know is bald, he will suffer a heart attack.

It may be, for example, some underlying factor that affects most bald men that may also be associated with heart disease. There are a few factors that we know are directly causal. (One thing we do know for sure, however, is that smoking causes lung cancer, the cancer most likely to kill women. So we will take this opportunity to ask you again to quit smoking if you are a smoker.) But in general, Dr. Muller rightly cautions us that we shouldn't "live off tidbits of epidemiological data." Epidemiological studies merely point in certain directions. It takes much more careful study to understand how and why certain medical problems occur.

Risk factors can help us make general decisions, but do not completely protect us from illness, nor do they always apply to any individual woman. For example, let's say that your risk of getting bitten by a mosquito was .0001. If a new study came out and found that women who wore perfume increased their risk tenfold, this could be met with quite a bit of excitement. But that still only increases the risk of that individual to .001, that is, only one out of a thousand women would still be bitten by the mosquito. So, in this situation, the numbers can tell you a lot. Scientists, like other people, have points of view, and so they can use numbers in many ways. You can use your own common sense to help you decide how much or how little the risk factors or numbers involved in a study apply to you.

Note who paid for the study. The publicized study linking baldness to heart attacks was funded by the UpJohn Corporation, which wanted to prove that it was the baldness and not minoxidil, the drug produced by UpJohn to treat baldness, that was associated with heart attacks. More importantly, studies that have been funded by pharmaceutical companies that produce hormone replacement drugs, or institutes which rely on these companies for a large proportion of their income, should also be viewed accordingly.

Remember again to think over your concerns and bring them up with your primary care provider. Some women prefer not to follow the psychological and medical literature and prefer to let their primary care provider let them know appropriate new information. But most of our patients are avid consumers of health news. Most physicians and psychologists enjoy talking over these findings with their patients and are usually prepared to do so.

✦ ACCESSING RESOURCES

There are a number of general resources for the menopausal woman. These resources have been included at the end of this chapter.

There are two resources that we find are vastly underutilizied. Both of them are good examples of taxpayers' dollars at work, something we do not hear much about these days. Both of them are practically free, and readily available. First, on the local level, ask your librarian. Some of you may remember how exciting it was to walk into a library when you were ten or eleven years old and suddenly realized the amount of information that could be found there. If you were very lucky, you met a friendly, rather than intimidating librarian, who could show you available resources and answer your questions. Guess what? She (or he) is still around! You just need to find the library where she works. This is, after all, what reference librarians do best. For you, it costs nothing. It is easy, and there is usually a public library nearby.

On the federal level, one of our exciting discoveries was the Bureau of Public Documents (U.S. Government Printing Office, Superintendent of Documents, Mail Stop: SSOP, Washington, D.C. 20402-9328). You can obtain a monthly list of documents that are published. They are quite wide ranging and informative, from growing lima beans to an excellent review of the hormone replacement therapy literature. So you can keep up with what the government is publishing on a regular basis and order these documents for a minimal cost.

✦ RESOURCES

We have selected several resources for you in a number of categories. This list is not meant to be exhaustive, but rather is included to give you an idea of some of the best resources available.

BOOKS

The Columbia University 40+ Guide to Good Health (Fairfield, OH: Consumer Reports Books, 1993). This book is published by the Columbia University School of Public Health faculty. It debunks many of the myths of aging and provides coping strategies, biological and psychological problems.

ASSOCIATIONS

AARP—American Association of Retired People
601 E St., NW
Washington DC 20049
(202) 434-2277

We know that you are probably not retired yet, but the AARP works to enhance the quality of life for older people through education and policy change and has more than 33 million members over 50. One program within the Association is the Women's Initiative, which focuses specifically on older women's issues. Members receive a bimonthly magazine, Modern Maturity, *and a newspaper with information about the AARP's activities and achievements,* The AARP Bulletin, *eleven times a year. Other free publications are available on a variety of topics, including exercise, diet, older women's health concerns, mental health, and the health needs of various ethnic groups.*

American Board of Medical Specialties
1007 Church Street, Suite 404
Evanston, IL 60201-5913
1-800-776-CERT—certification line
(708) 491-9091—number for the Board

Call or write to find out if a doctor is board-certified. The board also offers a pamphlet, "Which Medical Specialist for You?," describing medical specialties, for $1.50.

American Board of Obstetrics and Gynecology
4225 Roosevelt Way NE, Suite 305
Seattle, WA 98105
(206) 547-4884

This is a certifying board: call or write to find out if a gynecologist is certified.

American Cancer Society
1599 Clifton Rd., NE
Atlanta, GA 30329
(800) ACS-2345—This number connects you to your state office.

Check your white pages for the nearest local office.
The ACS provides information, guidance, support groups, and referrals to other community resources. They can send you free pamphlets and factsheets on mammograms, breast self-exams, Pap smears, reproductive cancer, and general cancer information.

American College of Obstetricians and Gynecologists (ACOG)
409 12th St, SW
Washington, DC 20024
(202) 638-5577

The ACOG can give you a listing of board-certified physicians in your area. They also offer a number of free patient-education pamphlets on menopause and related issues, osteoporosis, hysterectomy, and fitness and exercise.

American Dental Association
211 E. Chicago Ave.
Chicago, IL 60611
(312) 440-2500

The ADA can give you a listing of dentists in your area. They also publish free pamphlets on dentures, diet and dental health, and dental tips for older adults.

American Dietetic Association
216 W Jackson Blvd, Suite 800
Chicago, IL 60606

This association and its newsletter are geared toward dieticians, but brochures on dietetics and nutrition are also available for consumers.

Gray Panthers
1424 16th St, NW, Suite 602
Washington DC 20036
(202) 347-6471

A coalition of activists that promotes the concerns of older people. The group has a newsletter and other publications on a variety of issues.

Health/PAC (Policy Advisory Center)
853 Broadway, Suite 1607
NY, NY 10003
(212) 614-1660

The Center is a nonprofit advocate for progressive health policy. They publish a quarterly journal on health care policy, HealthPAC Bulletin, *for $35 a year, $22.50 for people with low income. The group also sponsors seminars on health care and policy.*

National Senior Citizens' Law Center
1815 H Street, NW, Suite 700
Washington, DC 20006
(202) 887-5280

This is a legal-service support center which advocates for low-income older clients and offers referrals.

North American Menopause Society
University Hospitals of Cleveland
2074 Abington Rd.
Cleveland, OH 44106
(216) 844-3334

The NAMS has publications on menopause, a listing of literature about menopause, and lists of menopause clinics across the country.

Older Women's League (OWL)
666 11th St, NW, Suite 700
Washington, DC 20001
(202) 783-6686

OWL lobbies for the needs of older women. They have a referral resource file for support groups, and will answer your letters and questions. They sponsor the Campaign for Women's Health, which lobbies and publishes the newsletter "Women's Health," and also put out a bimonthly newspaper, The Owl Observer. *They are in the process of publishing a brochure on menopause.*

Women's Action Alliance
370 Lexington Ave, Suite 603
NY, NY 10017
(212) 532-8330

A nonprofit group working for positive change and self-determination for girls and women. Women's health is one of their focuses but nothing on menopause has been published. The Alliance has a publication catalog.

FEDERAL GOVERNMENT

National Cancer Institute
9000 Rockville Pike
Building 31, Room 10A24
Bethesda, MD 20892
(800) 4-CANCER—number answered regionally

The NCI has a listing of free publications which you can order, in English or Spanish, on smoking, nutrition, breast cancer, cancer tests for those over 65, and mammograms. It also sponsors the Cancer Information Service: free cancer information and support from trained counselors, referrals to physicians, quit smoking counseling, and resources for medical care and counseling.

The Cancer Information Service
Office of Cancer Communications
333 Cedar Street, LEPH 139
PO Box 3333
New Haven, CT 06510

National Heart, Lung, and Blood Institute
9000 Rockville Pike
Building 31, Room 4A-21
Bethesda, MD 20892
(301) 951-3260

The institute publishes a directory of resources for relevant health concerns, including somewhat technical-free pamphlets and factsheets on healthy eating, weight loss and exercise.

National Institute on Aging
Information Center
PO Box 8057
Gaithersburg, MD 20898-8057
(800) 222-2225

The institute publishes a very complete resource directory for Women's Health and Aging, the pamphlet "The Menopause Time of Life," and a series of factsheets or Age Pages on menopause and other aspects of aging, exercise, and nutrition. They also sponsor workshops on menopause.

INFORMATION CENTERS/CLEARINGHOUSES

Boston Women's Health Book Collective
240A M Street
Davis Square
Somerville, MA 02114
(617) 625-0271

A medical consumer organization that publishes books and brochures on women's health issues. They have available a listing of their publications and services and literature packets on a variety of women's health topics, including HRT and menopause.

Center for Medical Consumers
237 Thompson St
NY, NY 10012
(212) 674-7105

The center has a library and a monthly newsletter, "Health Facts," which includes information for menopausal women. A pamphlet on the benefits and risks of mammography screening, "Mammography Screening: A Decision-Making Guide," is available for $5.

Consumer Information Center
PO Box 100
Pueblo, CO 81002
(719) 948-3334

They have a listing of publications, the Consumer Information Catalog of government publications, covering a lot of topics, including health, aging, exercise, and nutrition.

National Council on Patient Information and Education
666 11th St, NW #810
Washington, DC 20001

The council publishes "Medicines: What Every Woman Should Know," a pamphlet on proper use and behavior related to medicines.

National Institute on Drug Abuse
Prepares the brochure "Elder-Ed: Using Your Medicines Wisely." To receive it, write to:

Government Printing Office
710 N Capitol St, NW
Washington, DC 20402
(Stock No 00017002400969—$4.75)

National Self-Help Clearinghouse
25 W 43rd St, Room 620
NY, NY 10036
(212) 642-2944

The clearinghouse is a databank and "switchboard" for information and referrals to self-help groups. It publishes manuals, training materials and group-starting materials, as well as a quarterly newsletter, "Self-Help Reporter," for $10.

National Women's Health Network
1325 G Street, NW, Lower Level
Washington, DC 20077-2052
(202) 293-6045

A member-based educational organization and clearinghouse for information on women's health. They have a database of current resources, 56 literature packets available for $8 each on women's health issues, a free directory of publications, pamphlets, and factsheets available, and can provide referrals. A $25 membership includes the "National Women's Health Report," a bimonthly newsletter. They also publish "The Network News," a newsletter on women's health and resources.

National Women's Health Resource Center
2440 M St, NW, Suite 325
Washington, DC 20037
(202) 293-6045

An information clearinghouse on women's health, focusing on public education, clinical services, and research. The Center publishes a newsletter, "National Women's Health Report." They publish a brochure on HRT and sponsor conferences and seminars on menopause.

Santa Fe Health Education Project
PO Box 577
Santa Fe, NM 87502
(505) 982-3236 or 982-9520

They publish a newsletter, "Healthletters," with bilingual health information for women. "Menopause—a Self-Care Manual" is also available for $3.85.

Vintage 45 Press
PO Box 266
Orinda, CA 94563-0266

Publishes a Selected Booklist catalog, with books on all aspects of being an older woman, including one on menopause.

Self-Help Groups

Red Hot Mamas
Connecticut Center for Menopause Management
Ridgefield, CT
(203) 431-3902

The Red Hot Mamas was founded by Karen Giblin. They offer support groups in Connecticut and can help women establish new chapters.

Supportive Older Women's Network (SOWN)
2805 N 47th Street
Philadelphia, PA 19131
(215) 477-6000

Helps women over 60 with aging-related concerns through support groups, consultation, and outreach programs. The Network also puts out a newsletter, "The Sounding Board," and publishes guidelines for developing a group.

Pharmaceutical Company Publications

US Pharmacopeial Convention, Inc.
Drug Information Division
12601 Twinbrook Parkway
Rockville, MD 20852

Publishes the USP Catalog of patient education materials, such as "About Your Medicines," a book on common prescription drugs, patient education leaflets, and computer products.

Bristol-Myers Squibb
PO Box 907
Spring House, PA 19477-9945
(800) 937-4025

Offers a free newsletter on aging, menopause and HRT, "Transitions," put out by company that makes ESTRACE, a brand of estradiol.

Newsletters

Consumer Reports Health Letter
Consumer Union of US, Inc.
101 Truman Avenue
Yonkers, NY 10703-1057

Information on prevention, risks, treatment of various health issues with a focus on keeping the consumer informed.

Johns Hopkins Medical Letter: Health After 50
PO Box 420176
Palm Coast, FL 32142

12 issues of medical information on women's health and older people's medical concerns for $24.

Network
National Gray Panther Newsletter
3635 Chestnut St.
Philadelphia, PA 19104

Bimonthly newsletter on aging, health care, political action, and local chapter activities.

MAGAZINES/PERIODICALS

Lear's
PO Box 420353
Palm Coast, FL 32142-9648

Monthly magazine geared toward older women with articles on entertainment, health, fashion, politics, money. $18 a year.

Hippocrates
301 Howard Street, Suite 1800
San Francisco, CA 94105

Monthly magazine of health information.

Menopause Management
9 Mt. Pleasant Turnpike
Denville, NJ 07834
(201) 361-1280

Magazine endorsed by the North American Menopause Society with articles on all aspects of menopause: symptoms, prevention, treatment, lifestyle. Primarily oriented to health care professionals. Published bimonthly for $25 a year.

Midlife Wellness Center for Climacteric Studies
University of Florida
901 NW 8th Ave, Suite B1
Gainesville, FL 32601

Quarterly journal on menopause and aging for health professionals and the general public.

CHAPTER TWELVE

Moving On

As you know by now, we see the menopausal years as exciting and full of a new sense of freedom. Yet, the negative views of the menopausal years persist in medical literature, in the popular media and within all of us. There is, of course, a long history of bashing the menopausal woman, and older women. But the combination of the negative attitude with medicalization of women's lives has a particularly destructive effect. This combination can be traced back many centuries. Our job, as women today, is to fight it every step of the way, in every form we see it.

In 1816, French physician C.P.L. de Gardanne described a syndrome called "De la ménépausie ou de l'age critique des femmes" (Gardanne, 1821). Over one hundred pages of the manuscript is dedicated to a myriad of illnesses that may accompany menopause, including hemorrhoids, rebellion and severe mental illness. If we were to read *La Ménépausie* today, and take it to heart, we would conclude that menopause was merely a batch of horrifying symptoms that would make us deteriorate over time, filling the remainder portion of our lives with misery.

Our experience has provided us with a much more optimistic outlook. We know that women are strong, and that they have most likely survived many life crises by the time they reach menopause. But if you are still a nonbeliever, consider the following women. Many of these women's stories have been collected and edited in an excellent book by Jill Ker Conway, the first woman president of Smith College and a professor at the Massachusetts Institute of Technology. In *Written by Herself,* we can learn about the stories of women of all ages (Conway, 1992).

• Marian Anderson, who died while we were working on this book, was the first black person to sing at the Metropolitan Opera Company on January 7, 1955. She describes her anxiety and excitement over this accomplishment.

> ". . . Mother arrived, and she threw her arms around me and whispered in my ear, 'We thank the Lord.' Her only words before the performance had been, 'Mother is praying for you,' and after it she just stood there, and though she is not outwardly demonstrative, I could see that there was a light around her face. She did not know much about opera, but she knew the significance of what was going on that night and she was profoundly moved by it. If she had said more she would have said, 'My cup runneth over' " (Anderson, 1992, p. 97).

Marian Anderson was fifty-three on that exciting night.

• Ruth Bader Ginsburg was one of ten women in her law school class of five hundred from the late 1950s. She was elected to the law reviews of both Harvard and Columbia University. Proposed by one of her Harvard Law School professors as a potential clerk to Justice Felix Frankfurter, the justice told Professor Albert Sacks that "while the candidate was impressive, he was not ready to hire a woman" (Lewis, 1993). Ruth Bader Ginsburg became the first tenured female law professor at Columbia. Judge Ginsburg credits her mother as "the bravest and strongest person I have known, who was taken from me much too soon. I pray that I may be all that she would have been, had she lived in an age when women could inspire and achieve, and daughters are cherished as much as sons. I look forward to working to the best of my ability for the advancement of the law in the service of society" (Lewis, 1993). You know where Ruth Bader Ginsburg, now in her sixties, is today.

• Cecilia Payne Gaposchkin became the professor and chairman of the Department of Anthropology at Harvard University at the age of fifty-six. She had a loving family life, and had worked at Harvard for many decades. Perhaps some of her energy was fueled by the discrimination she faced. Despite the fact that she was an accomplished woman who had received her Ph.D. from Radcliffe in 1925 and had written extensively, her salary from the Harvard Observatory had to be paid directly from her mentor, Harlow Cheply. For twenty years she was not paid a fair salary and her courses were not even listed in the catalogue. Cecilia, too, has words of wisdom, "On the material side, being a woman has been a great disadvantage. It is a tale of low salary, lack of status, and slow advancement . . . it is a case of survival, not of the fittest, but of the most doggedly persistent. I was not consciously aiming at the point I finally reached. I simply went on plotting, rewarded by the beauty of the scenery, toward an unexpected goal. . . . Your reward will be the widening of the horizon as you climb. And if you achieve that reward, you will ask no other" (Gaposchkin, 1992, p. 282).

• Vida Dutton Scudder challenged the conventions of society when she opposed Wellesley College's accepting money from the Rockefeller family because she felt it was tainted, and when she addressed workers who were on strike in Lawrence, Massachusetts. All this occurred in 1912, when Scudder was fifty-one years old (Scudder, 1992, p. 333).

• In July 1966, Nien Cheng survived the loss of her husband and the prejudices of Chinese society. Nien Cheng saw her house ransacked and lived more than six years in solitary confinement because she refused to confess that she was an enemy of the state. She was fifty-one when she was arrested. Her imprisonment was followed by the tragic discovery of the death of her daughter. Nien Cheng pursued the mysterious details of her daughter's death for over a decade, until she discovered that her daughter had been murdered. She, like the mothers of the Plaza de Mayo in Argentina, would not let the matter drop. She came to the United States and wrote the book *Life and Death in Shanghai,* as a testament to her daughter. She writes, "I live a full and busy life. Only sometimes I feel a haunting sadness. At dusk, when the day is fading away and the level of my physical energy is at a low ebb, I may find myself depressed and nostalgic. But the next morning I invariably wake up with a renewed optimism to welcome the day as another opportunity given me by God for enlightenment and experience. . . . I feel a compulsion to speak out and let those who have the good fortune to live in freedom know what my life was like during those dark days in Maoist China" (Cheng, 1988, p. 538).

• The photographer and writer Margaret Bourke-White was in her late forties when she was an official army and air force photographer during World War II, and much of her work was published by *Life* magazine. She was at the peak of her career when she reached her mid-fifties, and even when she was diagnosed with Parkinson's disease, fought against it by using photographs of people during rehabilitation to encourage others. Bourke-White chose never to marry and wrote this, "Mine is a life into which marriage doesn't fit very well. If I had children, I would have chartered a widely different life, drawn creative inspiration from them and shaped my work to them. Perhaps I would have worked on children's books rather than going to wars. It must be a fascinating thing to watch a growing child absorb his expanding world. One life is not better than the other, it is just a different life. . . . There is a richness in a life where you stand on your own feet, although it imposes a certain creed. There must be no demands, others have the right to be as free as you are. You must be able to take disappointments gallantly. You set your own ground rules, and if you follow them, there are great rewards" (Bourke-White, 1992, p. 453).

• Frances Sherwood is a fifty-three-year-old woman who is a professor, and mother of three grown children. She wrote a brilliant novel based on the life of eighteenth-century feminist Mary Wollstonecraft. The novel was rejected by four agents. Frances Sherwood then sent her manuscript directly to a publisher and her novel was published in 1993. The title of her novel? *Vindication* (Olshan, 1993).

• Maya Angelou was named one of the one hundred most influential American women in 1983 when she was fifty-five. Author of *I Know Why the Caged Bird Sings,* this gifted poet and writer was asked to create a poem especially for the inauguration of President Clinton when she was sixty-five years old.

We read frequently that women used to die in their forties and fifties, and that perhaps we were never meant to live another forty years without estrogen. But these statistics have an artificially low average age of death because they include many women who died during childbirth. Although our life spans are increasing, there have always been thriving older women around, if only we would pay attention to them, and heed their words. Like Ellen Glasgow: "Yes, I have had my life, I have known ecstasy, I have known anguish, I have loved, and I have been loved. With one I loved, I have watched the light breaking over the Alps. If I pass through, 'the dark night of the soul,' I have had a far off glimpse of the illumination beyond. For an infinitesimal point of time, or eternity, I have caught a gleam, or imagined I caught a gleam, of the mystic vision. It was enough, and now it is over. Not for everything that the world could give me would I consent to live over my life unchanged, or to bring back unchanged my youth" (Glasgow, 1992, p. 400).

Did these women have hot flashes? Probably. Did some of them have headaches or other difficulties? Maybe. Did they survive and flourish? Most definitely, and we are the better for it. Knowing now what we know about menopause, perhaps it is time to treat our symptoms seriously when we should, and then to move ahead with the strength that women share.

APPENDIX A
MISCELLANEOUS PROBLEMS
AND SYMPTOMS

In this appendix we have included a variety of symptoms and problems that have been reported by our menopausal patients and in the medical literature. If a symptom has not been covered in a previous chapter, you will be able to find a description of it here. We have titled this appendix "Miscellaneous Problems and Symptoms" because these are less frequently reported. However, we know that any symptom that is *yours* is extremely important. "Miscellaneous" certainly does not imply minor. Some of the symptoms listed below may be your only, or most troubling, symptom of menopause.

There is a danger, however, in listing every problem that has ever been reported by menopausal women. Many women do not have regular health care prior to menopause. We go to the obstetrician when we are pregnant, we may go to a gynecologist for routine pelvic exams and Pap smears, but often we do not obtain ongoing health care. It is often during the menopausal years that some women will visit a physician regularly for the first time in their lives. This is good for any individual woman's health, but it leads to certain problems in research and misrepresenting the "typical menopausal woman." There have been too few studies of the menopausal women who choose not to visit physicians, so it is difficult to obtain the "normal picture." One study of Swedish women found that a full 35 percent of menopausal women did not experience any changes other than cessation of the menstrual cycle. The remaining 65 percent reported changes in weight gain and redistribution of body fat, some changes in skin or hair and stiffness of the joints. But, the vast majority of these women did not see that these symptoms had any negative effect on their life (Collins, 1992).

We should not generalize to all women from the small groups of women who begin to visit doctors at the time of menopause, or from other women who may be visiting doctors very frequently.

There are some difficulties with the symptoms mentioned in this chapter as well. Because of the lack of research on women's health issues, we do not know which problems are common to all women, which are a function of aging, and which are associated specifically with menopause. This appendix will try to sort through these factors. Still, there has been so little research on women, that we will not be able to give you all the answers at this point in time.

What we can give you is an assurance that any discomfort from these miscellaneous symptoms can, for the most part, be treated effectively. Part of our major motivation for writing this book was our emotional reaction to other books about menopause that literally listed dozens of problems potentially associated with menopause, without listing their relative frequency. Many of the problems that were listed were equally common to aging men, but were presented as menopausal problems. We ask one favor of you. *Do not* read this appendix and believe that you *will necessarily* experience any or all of these problems and symptoms. Be reassured that it is extremely unlikely that you would experience more than one or two of them, and even if you do, most women have found that these problems are not severe and can be managed quite well. Rather, use this appendix as a reference point for miscellaneous symptoms that you did not find in other chapters.

A good reference is the *Johns Hopkins Medical Handbook: One Hundred Major Medical Disorders* of people over the age of fifty. This is a detailed and accessible book that is an excellent reference. It provides discussions of the major problems of midlife people and also provides an additional section on resources for treatment.

✦ BACK PAIN

Fifty to eighty percent of Americans complain of back pain at some time. Back pain actually represents a large category of problems. We found that for most women chronic back pain can occur at any time. Low back pain can also be aggravated by osteoarthritis or rheumatoid arthritis. It is important to read the chapter on osteoporosis to understand the necessity for trying to maintain our bone mass as much as possible. Chronic back pain can be improved by weight loss, as well as by exercise.

Acute back pain, which may be mild or severe, is usually the result of an injury, an accident or a ruptured disc. It is important to consult your physician as soon as possible when experiencing acute back pain. The most likely treatment for acute back pain is actual bed rest for several days. We don't know many women who follow these instructions, given their multiple roles and the demands of daily household responsibilities; however, it is extremely important to treat acute back pain with care. Heat treatments are often recommended. We find that many people misunderstand the use of heat treatments. Do not use heat for more than fifteen minutes at a time. Alternate heat treatment with rest in order to benefit from it.

Exercise can prevent chronic back pain. By exercising, we strengthen our back and abdominal muscles. It is also important to maintain good posture and to be cautious in lifting heavy objects. Bending the knees instead of the back and holding an object close to the body is the most important precaution to take. We find that many women, believing that they are immune from heart disease, will shovel snow on a regular basis. They do this to prevent their husbands from experiencing a sudden heart attack. But shoveling snow is one of the most dangerous exercises with respect to back pain. If it is not possible to get help in shoveling snow, it is important for women to use as much caution as men in approaching the task, to use good posture and to do small amounts of lifting at any one time.

✦ BREAST CHANGES

Our breasts are composed of glandular tissue and fat. Glandular tissue reacts to the presence or absence of hormones. This is one of the reasons that hormone replacement therapy is not indicated for women who have breast cancer. Estrogen can stimulate the growth of cancer in these glands.

Just as our breasts can become swollen and retain water prior to our menstrual period, hormones can affect the breasts at menopause as well. After the production of estrogen slows, the glandular tissue in the breasts shrinks. At the same time there are ligaments, Cooper's ligaments, that continue to support the breast tissue. Over time, they lose some of their elasticity and begin to lengthen, thus our breasts tend to become somewhat smaller and sag. Although estrogen replacement therapy may reverse this situation somewhat, this cosmetic concern should not be a major factor in making the decision whether or not to begin hormone replacement therapy.

✦ CHEST PAIN

See Chapter Five, on healthy hearts.

✦ CHOLESTEROL

Cholesterol is one of the fats found in all of the body's cells. Elevated cholesterol is associated with the development of atherosclerosis. Since an elevated cholesterol is associated with a higher risk of cardiovascular disease, it is important to maintain a low-fat diet and to exercise. We discuss the cardiovascular risks in Chapter Five, our chapter on healthy hearts, and the importance of diet and exercise more in our chapter on prevention, Chapter Ten.

✦ FATIGUE

Fatigue is one of the most common complaints of not only menopausal women but of all women. Fatigue can be the result of any number of conditions, including depression and stress. It is clear that women who suffer from hot flashes may have their sleep disturbed and that insomnia leads to fatigue. A woman who had been functioning quite well may now need more sleep or feel overwhelmed at times during the day. Thus, the treatment of hot flashes may effectively treat the insomnia and the resulting fatigue. Menopause can be a time of increased vulnerability. Women who are entering the perimenopausal period seem to develop and report more symptoms than women either before menopause or after menopause. For some women, fatigue is just the natural response to unrealistic responsibilities in and out of the home, combined with emotional burdens.

✦ FOOT PROBLEMS

There are some changes in the structure of our feet that are associated with aging, unrelated to menopause. The skin becomes more easily dehydrated and less elastic over time. Our feet become more susceptible to infections from bacteria or fungus. At the same time, the soles and heels of our feet lose some of their padding fat and calluses can develop on these weight-bearing points. These changes can actually lead to change in shoe size. This should not be a cause for concern. Walking, foot massage and a consultation with a podiatrist might be helpful.

A persistent complaint of having cold feet may be due to poor circulation. This may be a result of artherosclerosis or also could be a sign of diabetes. Any consistent complaints of feelings of coldness or numbness of the extremities should be a cause for concern.

✦ HAIR CHANGES

Most of the changes in our hair over time are due to the natural aging process. After approximately age forty, our hair tends to become dryer and often begins to turn gray. There is a tremendous amount of variability in this process. We all know people who begin to turn gray in their twenties, and others who have only a few gray hairs into their sixties. But eventually we all become gray, men and women alike. Poor nutrition can lead to brittle hair, and this is a separate problem not associated with aging. Sometimes thyroid conditions can affect hair and cause noticeable changes. The concerns with hair changes are primarily cosmetic and we are concerned that some of our patients worry excessively about these changes. They are not indicating any medical problem.

Hirsutism is the growth of excessive dark hair. As the female hormone estrogen decreases, the relative amount of testosterone, the male hormone, increases. Some hair is responsive to hormonal changes and will therefore become excessive and thicker. Our patients complain when they develop excessive hair on their faces. This can usually be managed though, with hair removal or bleaching techniques, and tends not to be a major problem for most women. Hirsutism is also sometimes associated with obesity. The interaction between obesity and the related hormonal changes in menopause can worsen this situation.

✦ HEADACHES

Headaches are one of the most common problems of Americans. There are several categories of headaches, including migraines and tension. In addition, substance abuse can be a factor here, as a possible cause or when a woman may turn to pain killers for relief. Headaches are described in greater detail in Chapter Eight, our chapter on stress.

✦ INSOMNIA

Insomnia is one of life's most frustrating problems. All of us have trouble falling asleep from time to time, and as we age our sleep becomes more disrupted. One study by the National Institute of Health found that more than half of the people over the age of sixty-five experienced some sleep disturbance (Foley and Nechas, 1993). We find that many menopausal women who complain of insomnia are having problems with night sweats. A night sweat is a hot flash that occurs at night and often awakens a woman. In a study of normal menopause, the McKinlay group found that women who experienced hot flashes were twice as likely to report insomnia as women who did not. This can be an extremely disruptive experience and some women have tremendous difficulty getting back to sleep. Estrogen replacement therapy is an effective treatment for hot flashes and will reduce night sweats and the resulting insomnia. Vitamin E and other treatments have not been thoroughly evaluated, but can provide some relief for many women. Wearing cotton bedclothes can also help.

However, since some insomnia and sleep disruption are also associated with the aging process, it is important to take other precautions as well. There are several behavioral techniques we can use. First, get up at the same time every day regardless of what time you went to sleep. Try not to go to bed unless you are sleepy. Exercise regularly and avoid caffeine within six hours of bedtime. Try an hour of relaxation before getting into bed. Use your bed only for sleeping—not for reading or doing paperwork. You want to develop a strong association between the bed and sleeping. The only exception to the rule is sex.

The elimination of naps is needed in order to reestablish a consistent sleep cycle. It is extremely important to avoid using alcohol or sleeping medications to treat this problem. Although both may seem to work, they are associated with significant problems if used consistently. Most physicians will not prescribe sleep preparations for more than several nights and of course it is extremely important never to mix a sleeping pill with alcohol.

✦ JOINT PAIN

Joint pain is often caused by an inflammation of the joints called arthritis. There are two major types of arthritis, rheumatoid and osteoarthritis. Arthritis can occur in any joint but is commonly found in the hips, feet, spine and knees. Many women also complain of arthritis in their finger joints. *Osteoarthritis* is associated with the aging process and is common to most people over the age of sixty. In a normal joint, the ends of bones are covered by cartilage, a rubbery, protective coating. This cartilage cushions the area between the bones. The bones are held together by ligaments and tendons. Over time, the joint tissue breaks down, the cartilage can soften and become frayed and loses its elasticity. In some cases, sections of the cartilage actually wear away. This leads the unprotected bones to rub together with any movement and cause pain. When the cartilage deteriorates, a joint may change its shape, with the bone ends thickening. These changes cause pain.

There is no evidence that osteoarthritis is associated with menopause. It is associated with the aging process in that it is rarely reported by people under the age of forty unless the joints have had overuse or injuries. There is also some evidence that people who are overweight are more likely to have arthritis because of the extra pressure on the knees and the hips—the weight-bearing joints. When osteoarthritis is diagnosed in these joints, weight loss is often recommended to reduce the wear and tear on the joints and the resulting pain.

Rheumatoid arthritis is a different problem. It is a systemic disease and affects the entire body. Although rheumatoid arthritis tends to affect women more than men and begins in the forties and fifties, it is not specifically associated with menopause either. Rather than being caused by a breakdown of cartilage, in rheumatoid arthritis the lining or membrane between the joints becomes inflamed and the joints can appear to be swollen. Rheumatoid arthritis often causes redness and warmth whereas osteoarthritis does not cause redness. Osteoarthritis is usually limited to specific joints whereas rheumatoid arthritis affects many joints. Rheumatoid arthritis causes a more general feeling of sickness and fatigue. Your doctor can make the distinction between rheumatoid and osteoarthritis by testing your sedimentation rate, using a simple blood test. In addition, the morning pain associated with osteoarthritis tends not to last more than thirty minutes, whereas with rheumatoid arthritis it lasts much longer. Osteoarthritis is less common in the wrist, elbow, shoulder and ankle joints. The pain associated with osteoarthritis gets better with time and hand functioning is maintained. In rheumatoid arthritis there is a loss of grip strength. Osteoarthritis can also be confirmed by X-ray findings that show bone and cartilage overgrowth and narrowing of joint spaces.

Treatment of arthritis begins with the appropriate diagnosis. It is important to seek treatment because arthritis can be one of the most chronic and crippling diseases. Arthritis responds to several forms of treatment. Both types of arthritis respond to the nonsteroidal, anti-inflammatory drugs which are known by the acronym NSAID. Ibuprofen is the most common of the NSAIDs, but your doctor can help you choose one of the others as well. One of the problems with the NSAIDs is that they have many side effects that affect the gastrointestinal system. These include mild stomach pain, as well as nausea and vomiting. The chronic use of the NSAIDs can sometimes lead to ulcers. It is important to take them with a full meal and to drink plenty of liquids.

Aspirin is actually the oldest and most common NSAID. Like other NSAIDs it can cause gastrointestinal side effects which may be partially avoided with the buffered form. One problem with aspirin, however, is that the dose required is somewhere between 3 and 6 grams or nine to eighteen pills per day. Many women who may be dieting or concerned about their weight, do not have the regular eating habits necessary to appropriately take this much aspirin. For many women, it is difficult to take medications more than three times a day, so that taking pills every four hours is unthinkable.

Although there is no treatment that can prevent or reverse osteoarthritis at this time, it is important that we try to keep up with our daily activities.

Exercise can be alternated with rest in order to maintain our level of functioning. Swimming is a particularly good exercise for women with arthritis, since it takes all of the weight off the joints and allows movement and muscle development with less pain.

✦ MEMORY LOSS

Some perimenopausal women complain of problems with memory loss. However, so do many mid-life men! The ability to memorize and process new information can decline with age in both men and women. This should not be accepted as a normal part of aging, since memory loss can be a symptom of depression, stress, substance abuse, vitamin deficiency or a side effect of medication. Additionally, the sleep disruption associated with hot flashes and night sweats can also negatively affect one's ability to concentrate, and hence remember.

As research on menopause and aging progresses, we are beginning to learn more. Some researchers believe that estrogen can enhance cognitive functioning in postmenopausal women, but overall, the results of studies have been variable. Some authors have gone so far as to suggest that post-menopause HRT will decrease the likelihood of developing dementia or Alzheimer's Disease, but to date, there is no definitive answer.

✦ MOOD CHANGES

Many women experience mood changes around the time of menopause. The perimenopausal period is often associated with feelings of emotional instability. Others believe that the hormonal factors themselves may lead to some emotional malaise, but this has not yet been documented. Some women feel irritable or describe themselves as nervous, as we have discussed in Chapter Seven, "Myths of Depression." Most of these changes are mild, time-linked, and do not affect women at menopause any more often than women at other ages. However, if changes in your mood are disruptive and long lasting, it is time to consult a mental health professional. Our chapter on depression discusses this in great detail.

✦ SKIN CHANGES

Some women complain of itchy or uncomfortable feelings of dry skin. This can be combated by using milder soaps and moisturizers. One of the most important changes we can make during the menopausal years is to drink large quantities of water.

There are also age-related changes in pigmentation such as liver spots and "ruby spots." These are groups of dilated capillaries that can appear on the face, neck, arms and legs. Environmental conditions can also lead to dry skin. The most obvious culprit here is sun, and if by now you haven't restricted your exposure to the sun, menopause is a good time to do so. Using a sunscreen and avoiding direct exposure to the sun by wearing protective clothing and sunglasses is wise. Even when swimming, it is important to use sunscreen.

With skin cancers accounting for more than half of the malignancies in the United States each year, it is important to learn to examine ourselves for moles that are asymmetrical, with irregular borders, with a color that is not uniform and with a diameter that is larger than the size of a pencil eraser. Any change in a wart or mole represents an early warning sign of skin cancer—the O in the American Cancer Society's CAUTION.

The American Cancer Society's early warning signs of cancer:

C. *Change in bowel habits.*
A. *A sore that does not heal.*
U. *Unusual bleeding or discharge.*
T. *Thickening or lump in the breast or elsewhere*
I. *Indigestion or difficulty in swallowing.*
O. *Obvious changes in a wart or mole.*
N. *Nagging cough or hoarseness.*

Some women describe a feeling of pins and needles or a sense of tingling. A small number of menopausal women report experiencing that insects are crawling on their skin. This is called formication. One study found that 20 percent of women experienced formication around the time of their last period, but only 10 percent of them described the problem over time. Like many menopausal symptoms, the cause is unknown, but thankfully it tends to be a short-lived problem.

✦ PALPITATIONS

See the chapter on healthy hearts, Chapter Five.

✦ VISION CHANGES

Most of us will eventually need to use reading glasses, but menopause cannot be blamed for this. Men and women alike have changes in their vision, beginning approximately at age forty. This is because, as we age, the lens of our eye begins to lose some of its elasticity. We find it increasingly difficult to focus on objects that are near. This gradual farsightedness is known as presbyopia, the visual change associated with aging.

Although corrective reading glasses can be purchased over the counter at almost any pharmacy, it is important to begin to check in regularly with an ophthalmologist. An ophthalmologist can begin to screen for other eye problems associated with aging such as glaucoma and cataracts. In addition, the farsightedness does change over time and prescription lenses will need to be adjusted accordingly.

Some of us will experience a disruption in our vision. Behind the lens of our eye is a large compartment filled with a clear fluid called the *vitreous humor*. When tiny bits of material drift in this clear fluid, we may see spots or strings dropping down into our field of vision. These are called "floaters." These are usually harmless but should be discussed with an ophthalmologist. If you experience any sudden change in vision (including an increase in floaters) you should seek medical attention immediately.

✦ WEIGHT LOSS

If you have experienced a sudden or significant weight loss, and you have not been dieting or exercising more, then it is important to consult with a physician as this can be a symptom of a serious problem. Thyroid disease and diabetes can also cause unexpected weight loss.

✦ WEIGHT GAIN

At midlife our metabolism slows down, making it more likely for us to gain weight if we continue to eat as we have previously. Obesity can contribute to the development of diabetes, heart disease, high blood pressure and joint pain. However, many women diet unnecessarily because of unrealistic standards. Weight gain at midlife is expected and natural. If you are concerned about this, you are more likely to successfully maintain your weight with increased exercise than by rigid dieting. We discuss the possibilities of healthy eating behaviors and exercise in our chapter on prevention.

Gaining weight, of course, can lead to a thickening around our abdomens. It is important to note that abdominal and pelvic disorders (including ovarian cancer) sometimes manifest themselves by the sudden distention of the abdomen. If you have not been gaining weight because of lack of exercise or overeating, a sudden bloated feeling or change in your abdomen should prompt you to schedule a visit with your physician for a complete evaluation including a pelvic exam.

There are some reports of weight gain with hormone replacement therapy and this is a great concern to menopausal women. This may be caused by fluid retention and is believed to be associated with the hormone progesterone rather than estrogen. Some researchers have also suggested that hormones can also make a person hungrier and can lead to overeating if control is not maintained. Weight gain is discussed thoroughly in Chapter Five, "Healthy Hearts" and Chapter Ten, "Promoting a Healthy Lifestyle."

APPENDIX B
"TOWN MEETING" QUESTIONS

As we met with women in our "menopause town meetings," we began to compile the most common questions. Here they are, along with the corresponding page numbers.

❦ TOWN MEETING: WOMEN'S HEALTH QUESTIONS

HORMONE REPLACEMENT THERAPY

Do I have to take progesterone with estrogen?   pp. 149, 160–161

Doesn't estrogen cause breast cancer?   pp. 149–153

Can I stop taking estrogen suddenly if I don't like it?   p. 144

What is the advantage of the estrogen patch?   pp. 140–141

Will estrogen prevent me from getting heart disease?   pp. 118–119, 128, 146

Will estrogen make me look younger?   p. 147

If I take HRT, do I have to have my periods back?   pp. 155–156

Can I take HRT before my periods end if I'm having hot flashes?   p. 143

I've heard you should start taking HRT right at menopause to prevent osteoporosis. When is it too late to start?   pp. 103–104, 146

Can I take HRT if I have fibroids?   p. 154

Should I have my estrogen level checked?   pp. 48–49, 138

My doctor says my FSH is high—what does that mean?   p. 138

SEX

Will sex change at menopause?   pp. 29, 31–33, 61–65, 69–72

I'm having problems with vaginal dryness, but I don't want to take estrogen.
   What can I do?   pp. 77, 161–162, 166

I've just begun to have a little urinary incontinence. Will that continue?
   pp. 72–73

What are Kegel's exercises?   pp. 75–76

I've lost interest in sex. Is that part of menopause?   pp. 79, 83, 176–177

How will I know when I don't need to use contraceptives anymore?
   pp. 77–78

SYMPTOMS

I'm only forty-six and I'm having hot flashes. But my periods are coming
   more frequently, not less. I thought hot flashes came at menopause?
   pp. 24, 27, 42–49

Can vitamin E stop hot flashes?   pp. 53–54

What can I do about headaches?   pp. 226–229, 333

I've been feeling really irritable lately. Is that normal?   p. 336

My skin feels weird. What could it be?   pp. 147, 336–337

Will I get facial hair at menopause? Will estrogen prevent this?   p. 333

Why am I forgetting things like phone numbers and lists?   p. 336

GENERAL HEALTH

Usually I can crash off a few pounds in a week or two. Now that I'm fifty, I
   can't seem to do it. Why is this true?   pp. 117, 265–266, 338

I've heard that one or two drinks can help me prevent heart disease and help
   me relax. Is this true?   pp. 98, 127, 282–287

Do I need to eat a low-fat diet if I'm in good health?   pp. 124–127, 294–296

How much exercise do I really need?   pp. 56, 100–102, 123–125, 225, 271–276

I've been reading a lot about heart disease. What can I do to prevent it?   pp. 121–127, 278–298

I've tried to stop smoking three times. I feel like giving up. Any ideas?   pp. 121–122, 263–264, 278–282

If I swim three times a week, will that prevent osteoporosis?   pp. 100–102

If I take HRT, do I need to worry about osteoporosis?   pp. 95–104

Does everyone get osteoporosis?   pp. 88–90, 91–93, 98, 107

How much calcium should I be consuming?   pp. 95–97

Should I be taking vitamin D in addition to calcium?   pp. 96–98

I don't like dairy products. How else can I take in enough calcium?   pp. 96–97

I went to a menopause clinic and they said I need to have the density of my bones measured. I'm in good health. Do I really need this?   pp. 93–94

Should I have my cholesterol checked?   pp. 115–116, 124–126, 270

Psychological Issues

Will I get depressed at menopause?   pp. 29–31, 168–170, 258

Don't most women have midlife crises?   pp. 201–203, 212–216

How can I handle family stress? I thought it would be over by now.   pp. 184–185, 208–212, 231–233

Will estrogen help me if I'm depressed?   pp. 171, 178–179

What can I do about anxiety?   pp. 219–226, 230–231

I need some psychological help, but I don't have insurance coverage for it. What can I do?   pp. 188–189, 199, 232–233

What's all this I read about Prozac? Is it a wonder drug? Is it addictive?   pp. 189–191

If I had PMS, should I expect the same at menopause?   pp. 30, 178

I have a lot of "down" days—is that depression or normal mood swings?   pp. 173–179

Hysterectomy

What is the difference between a hysterectomy and having my ovaries removed?   pp. 235–238

I had a hysterectomy five years ago. How will that affect my menopause?   pp. 140, 158, 247–250

My doctor is suggesting that I have a hysterectomy because of my fibroids. I'm forty-three. Are there other treatments available?   pp. 239–241, 242–244

I'm almost fifty and I am having a hysterectomy. Should I have my ovaries removed too?   pp. 242, 250–252

My doctor says I should have a hysterectomy because of my pelvic pain. I want to get a second opinion, but I don't want to hurt his feelings.   pp. 16–17, 240–241, 245–246, 251–252

If I have had a hysterectomy, how will I know I'm going through menopause?   pp. 27–28, 45, 140, 143–145

Health-Care and Doctor-Patient Communication

My doctor doesn't seem to listen to me. What can I do?   pp. 15–18, 36–38, 106, 111–112, 193–194, 307–309

I'm fifteen pounds overweight, and my doctor keeps telling me to lose weight. I've tried every diet there is. What should I say?   pp. 292–293

My doctor says I need to do "weight-bearing exercise." Isn't all exercise weight-bearing?   pp. 100, 102

I'm worried about heart disease, but my doctor thinks I'm silly to worry.   pp. 111–112, 129–130

I can't understand my doctor's answers to my questions. What should I do?   pp. 15–17, 37–38, 128–129, 193–194, 250, 307–309

General

Is there any way to predict when I will go through menopause?   pp. 24, 40, 142

Can a blood test predict when I'll go through menopause?   pp. 138, 142

When does menopause occur?   pp. 24–25, 27, 142

✦ REFERENCES

ABC News. (1993). *Prime Time Live,* 6. Transcript #304. New York.

Abrams, D.B., Monti, P., Pinto, R., and Elder, J. (1987). Psychological stress and coping in smokers who relapse or quit. *Health Psychology, 6,* 289–303.

Adamson, G.D. (1992). Treatment of uterine fibroids: Current findings with gonadotropin-releasing hormone agonists. *Am J Obstet Gynecol, 166,* 746–51.

Albrecht, B.H., Schiff, I., Tulchinsky, D., and Ryan, K.J. (1980). Objective evidence that placebo and oral medroxyprogesterone acetate therapy diminish menopausal vasomotor flushes. *Am. J. Obstet. Gynecol. 139:* 631–635.

American Cancer Society. (1988). Summary of current guidelines for the cancer related checkup: recommendations. New York: American Cancer Society.

American Heart Association. (1989). Women and heart disease. Summary of proceedings. Meeting, Washington, D.C.

American Psychiatric Association. (1987). *Diagnostic and Statistical Manual of Mental Disorders.* Third Revised ed., Washington, D.C.: The American Psychiatric Associations.

Anderson, M. (1992). My Lord, what a morning. In J.K. Conway (Ed.), *Written by Herself,* pp. 55–97. New York: Vintage Books, A Division of Random House.

Andrasik, F., and Kabela, E. (1988). Headaches. In E.A. Blechman and K.D. Brownell (Eds.), *Handbook of Behavioral Medicine for Women,* pp. 206–221. New York: Pergamon Press.

Aneshensel, C. (1986). Marital and employment role-strain, social support and depression among adult women. In S. Hobfoll (Ed.), *Stress, Social Support, and Women,* pp. 99–114. Washington, D.C.: Hemisphere.

Are You Eating Right? *Consumer Reports,* October 1992a, 647.

Associated Press. (1993, March). U.S. health study to involve 160,000 women at 16 centers. *New York Times,* p. A21.

Avis, N.E., and McKinlay, S.M. (1990). Health care utilization among mid-aged women. In M. Flint, F. Kronenberg, and W. Utian (Eds.) *Multidisciplinary perspectives on menopause,* pp. 228–256. New York: New York Academy of Sciences.

Bachmann, G.A. and Leiblum, S.R. (1991). Sexuality in sexagenarian women. *Maturitas, 13,* 43–50.

Barnett, R., Biener, L. and G. Baruch. (1987). *Gender and Stress.* New York: The Free Press.

Barrett-Connor, E. and Bush, T.L. (1991). Estrogen and coronary heart disease in women. *JAMA, 265,* 14: 1861.

Beckman, H.B. and Frankel, R.M. (1984). The effect of physician behavior on the collection of data. *Annals of Internal Medicine, 101,* 692–697.

Bell, S.E. (1990). The medicalization of menopause. In Formanek, R. (Ed.), *The Meaning of Menopause: Historical, Medical and Clinical Perspectives.* Hillsdale, N.J.: The Analytic Press.

Benson, H. (1993). The relaxation response. In D. Goleman and J. Gurin (Eds.), *Mind/Body Medicine: How to Use Your Mind for Better Health.* Yonkers: Consumers Union of United States, Inc.

Bergkvist, L. (1989). The risk of breast cancer after estrogen and estrogen-progestin replacement. *NEJM, 321,* 293–297.

Bernardez, T. (1990). Older women: Inventing our lives. In *Seventh Annual Women in Context Conference in Topeka, Kansas,* The Menninger Foundation.

Blair, S.N., Kohl, H.W., and Paffenbarger, D.G. (1989). Physical fitness and all-cause mortality: a prospective study of healthy men and women. *JAMA, 262,* 2395–2401.

Blumstein, P. and Schwartz, P. (1983). *American Couples.* New York: William Morrow and Company.

Boston Globe, Quote unquote, p. 30, January 4, 1993.

Bourke-White, M. (1992). Portrait of myself. In J.K. Conway (Ed.), *Written By Herself,* pp. 423–453. New York: Vintage Books, A Division of Random House.

Brown, G.W., Bifulco, A., Harris, T.O., and Bridge, L. (1986). Life stress, chronic subclinical symptoms and vulnerability to clinical depression. *The Journal of Affective Disorders, 11,* 1–19.

Brownell, K.D. and Rodin, J. (1990). *The Weight Maintenance Survival Guide.* Dallas: Brownell & Hager.

Brownell, K.D. and Wadden, T.A. (1991). The heterogeneity of obesity: fitting treatments to individuals. *Behavior Therapy, 22,* 153–177.

Brownson, R.C., Alavanja, M.C.R., Hock, E.T., and Loy, T.S. (1992). Passive smoking and lung cancer in nonsmoking women. *American Journal of Public Health, 82* (11), 1525–1530.

Budoff, P.W. (1983). *No More Hot Flashes: And Other Good News.* New York: Warner Books.

Bullock, J.L. (1975). Use of medroxyprogesterone acetate to prevent menopausal symptoms. *Obstetrics and Gynecology, 46* (2), 165–68.

Burmen, B. and Gritz, E. (1990). Women and smoking: Current trends. *Journal of Substance Abuse 3,* 221–238.

Burns, D.D. (1980). *Feeling Good: The New Mood Therapy.* New York: William Morrow & Company.

Bush, T.L. (1991). Epidemiology of cardiovascular disease in women. In G.P. Redmond (Ed.), *Lipids and Women's Health,* pp. 6–20. New York: Springer-Verlag.

Byyny, R. and Speroff, L. (1990). *A Clinical Guide for the Care of Older Women.* Baltimore: Williams & Wilkins.

Caldirola, D. (1983). Incest and pelvic pain. *Health and Social Work, 4,* 309.

Carlson, K.J., Nichols, D.H., and Schiff, I. (1993). Indications for hysterectomy. *New England Journal of Medicine,* 856–860.

Cheng, N. (1988). *Life and Death in Shanghai.* New York: Viking Penguin.

Chesney, M.A. (1991). Women, work-related stress and smoking. In M. Frankenhaeuser, U. Lundberg & M.A. Chesney (Eds.), *Women, Work and Health,* pp. 139–55. New York: Plenum Press.

Clark, M.M., Ruggiero, L., Pera, V., Goldstein, M.G., and Abrams, D.B. (1993). Assessment, classification, and treatment of obesity: a behavioral medicine perspective. In A. Stoudemire and B.S. Fogel (Eds.), *The Psychiatric Care of the Medical Patient,* New York: Oxford University Press.

Clayden, J.R., Bel, J.W. and Pollard. (1974). Menopausal flushing: Double blind trial of a non-hormonal medication. *British Medical Journal 1,* 409–412.

Collins, A. (1992). Emotional responses and symptomatic changes during transition to menopause. In K. Wijma and B. von Schoultz (Eds), *Advances in Psychosomatic Obstetrics and Gynecology.* Park Ridge, N.J.: Parthenon.

Conway, J.K. (Ed.) (1992). *Written By Herself.* New York: Vintage Books, A Division of Random House.

Cooper, Kenneth, H. (1989). *Preventing Osteoporosis.* New York: Bantam Books.

Cutler, W. and Garcia, C. (1992). *Menopause: A Guide for Women and the Men Who Love Them.* New York: W.W. Norton & Company.

Dembroski, T.M, MacDouguel, J.M., and Cardozo, S. (1985). Selective cardiovascular effects of stress and cigarette smoking in young females. *Health Psychology, 4,* 153–167.

de Turenne, Veronique. (1993, March 24). Support groups link people in similar situations. *Sarasota Herald-Tribune,* 1E, 4E.

Deutsch, H. (1945). *Psychology of women.* Vol. ii. New York: Grune & Stratton.

Deykin, E. (1966). The empty nest: Psychological aspects of conflict between depressed women and their grown children. *American Journal of Psychiatry,* 1422–1425.

Doress, P.B., Siegal, D.L., and The Midlife and Older Women Book Project. (1987). *Ourselves, Growing Older: Women, Aging with Knowledge and Power.* New York: Simon & Schuster/Touchstone Books.

Douglas, P., Clarkson, T.B., Flowers, N.C., and Hajjar, K.A. (1992). Exercise and atherosclerotic heart disease in women. *Medicine and Science in Sports and Exercise* 24 (6): S26.

Dukes, M.N.G. (Ed.) (1992). *Meyler's Side Effects of Drugs: An Encyclopedia of Adverse Reactions and Interactions.* Amsterdam: Elsevier.

Eaker, E.D. and Castelli, W.P. (1987). Coronary heart disease and its risk factors among women in the Framingham study. In E.D. Eaker, B. Packard, N.K. Wenger, T.B. Clarkson, and H.A. Tyroler (Eds.). *Coronary Heart Disease in Women: Proceedings of an N.I.H. Workshop,* pp.122–130. New York: Haymarket Doyma, Inc.

Ellis, A. and Harper, R.A. (1975). *A New Guide to Rational Living.* North Hollywood: Wilshire Book Company.

El-Mallakh, N. and Rif, S. (1987). Marijuana and migraine. *Headache,* 8, 442–444.

Erikson, E. (1950). *Childhood and Society.* New York: W.W. Norton.

Erikson, E. (1970). *Identity Through the Life Cycle.* 2nd ed. New York: W.W. Norton.

Erlik, Y., Meldrum, D.R., and Judd, H.L. (1982). Estrogen levels in postmenopausal women with hot flushes. *Obstetrics and Gynecology, 59:* 403.

Erlik, Y., Tatryn, I.V., Meldrum, D.R., Lomax, P., Bajorek, J.G., and Judd, H.L. (1981). Association of waking episodes with menopausal hot flushes. *JAMA, 245:* 1744.

Ernsberger, P. and Nelson, D.O. (1988). Refeeding hypertension and dietary obesity. *American Journal of Physiology, 254,* R47–55.

Ernster, V.L. (1988). Benefits and risks of menopausal estrogen and/or progestin use. *Preventative Medicine 17,* 301–323.

Ettinger, B., Genant, H.K., and Cann, C.E. (1987). Postmenopausal bone loss is prevented by treatment with low-dosage estrogen with calcium. *Annals of Int. Med., 106,* 40–45.

Ewing, J.A. (1984). Detecting alcoholism: The cage questionnaire. *JAMA, 252,* 1905–1907.

Faludi, S. (1991). *Backlash: The Undeclared War Against American Women.* New York: Crown.

Fleming, L.A. (1992). Osteoporosis: Clinical features, prevention and treatment. *J. Gen Int Med, 7,* 554–561.

Fletcher, S.W. (1992). The breast is close to the heart. *Annals of Internal Medicine, 117,* 969–971.

Foley, D. and Nechas, E. (Eds.) (1993). *Women's Encyclopedia of Health and Emotional Healing.* Emmaus, Pa.: Rodale Press.

Friedman, M. and Rosenman, R.H. (1974). *Type A Behavior and Your Heart.* New York: Knopf.

Friedman, R.M. (Ed.) Pizza: however you slice it. (1993, June). *University of California at Berkeley Wellness Letter,* 3.

Friedman, R.M. (Ed.) (1993, June). Fascinating facts. *University of California at Berkeley Wellness Letter,* 1.

Gaposchkin, C.P. (1992). An autobiography and other recollections. In J. K. Conway (Ed.), *Written By Herself,* pp. 248–282. New York: Vintage Books, A Division of Random House.

Gardanne, Ch.P.L de. (1821). *De la ménépausie ou de l'age critique des femmes.* Paris: Chez Mequignon, Marvis, Libraire.

Gershoff, S.N. (Ed.) (1992, July). How many calories? More than the label says. *Tufts University Diet & Nutrition Letter, 10* (7), 1–2.

Glasgow, E.A.G. (1992). The woman within. In J. K. Conway (Ed.), *Written By Herself,* pp.372–400. New York: Vintage Books, A Division of Random House.

Goldberg, R.J. (1988). Depression in primary care: DSM-III diagnoses and other depressive syndromes. *Clinical Reviews, 3,* 491–497.

Goleman, D. and Gurin, J. (1993). *Mind Body Medicine.* Yonkers: Consumers Union of United States, Inc.

Grady, D., Rubin, S., and Petitti, D. (1992). Hormone therapy to prevent disease and prolong life in postmenopausal women. *Annals of Internal Medicine, 117,* 1016–1037.

Greenwood, S. (1984). *Menopause Naturally: Preparing for the Second Half of Life.* Volcano, CA: Volcano Press.

Greer, G. (1970). *The Female Eunuch.*

Greer, G. (1992). *The Change: Women, Aging and the Menopause.* New York: Alfred A. Knopf.

Hallstrom, T. (1977). Sexuality in the climacteric. *Clinics in Obstetrics and Gynecology 4,* 227–239.

Harris, R.B., Laws, A., and Reddy, V. (1990). Are women using post-menopausal estrogen? A community survey. *American Journal of Public Health, 80* (1): 1266–1268.

Haynes, S.G., Feinleib, and Kannel, W.B. (1980). The relationship of psychosocial factors to coronary heart disease in the Framingham study. III. Eight-year incidence of coronary heart disease. *Am J Epidemiol, 111* (1): 37–58.

Health Survey. (1993, March 24). *Sarasota Herald Tribune,* 1.

Helson, R. and Wink, P. (1992). Personality change in women from the early 40s to the early 50s. *Psycholog-Aging, 7* (1): 46–55.

Henderson, I.C. and Wender, R.C. (1991). Breast cancer. *Am Cancer Soc Newsletter,* 2, 1.

Henrich, J.B. (1992). The postmenopausal estrogen/breast cancer controversy. *JAMA, 268* (14): 1900–1902.

Herman, J.L. (1986). Long-term effects of incestuous abuse in childhood. American Journal of Psychiatry, *143:* 1493.

Herman, J.L. (1992). *Trauma and Recovery.* Cambridge: Harvard University Press.

Hochschild, A. (1989). *The Second Shift: Working Parents and the Revolution at Home.* New York: Viking Penguin, Inc.

Hunter, M. (1990). Emotional well-being, sexual behaviour and hormone replacement therapy. *Maturitas, 12,* 299–314.

J.S. (1992). ERT: Helping Women Decide. *Journal Watch, 10* (5): 39–40.

Jacobs Institute of Women's Health. (1992). Mammography Attitudes and Usage. Washington, D.C.: Jacobs Institute of Women's Health.

Jaques, E. (1965). Death and the midlife crisis. *International Journal of Psychoanalysis, 46,* (4): 502–513.

Jarvis, J. (1992). Gender of problem drinkers points to different treatment needs. *Br. J. Addiction, 87,* 1249.

Jones, B.M. and Jones, M.K. (1976). Male and female intoxication levels for three alcohol doses or do women really get higher than men? *Alcohol Technical Reports, 5,* 11.

Jones, K.P., Ravnikar, V., and Schiff, I. (1985). A preliminary evaluation of the effect of lofexitine on vasomotor flushes in postmenopausal women. *Maturitas, 7,* 135–139.

Kaplan, A. G. (1986). The "self-in-relation": Implications for depression in women. *Psychotherapy: Theory, Research, and Practice, 23,* 235–242.

Kaslow, F.W. (1981). Divorce and Divorce Therapy. In A. Gurman and D. Kniskern (Eds.), *Handbook of Family Therapy.* New York: Brunner/Mazel.

Katz, L. (1992). Beyond the hot flash. *Seasons,* 4–7.

Kegel, A.M. (1951). Physiologic therapy for urinary stress incontinence. *Journal of Am. Medical Assoc., 146,* 915–917.

Keeping your weight steady found better than "yo-yo" dieting. (1993, January 17). *Providence Journal*.

Klesges, R.C. and Klesges, L.M. (1988). Cigarette smoking as a dieting strategy in a university population. *International Journal of Eating Disorders*, *7*, 413–419.

Kronenberg, F. (1990). Hot Flashes: Epidemiology and Physiology. In *Annals of New York Academy of Sciences* 56–86.

Kronenberg, F. (1993, May 21). Menopausal hot flashes. Paper presented at Menopause: The Background and Skills for Effective Therapy. Symposium of the North American Menopause Society.

Kübler-Ross, E. *Living with Death and Dying*. New York: Macmillan, 1982

LeGuin, U. (Summer 1976). The space crone. *The Co-Evolution Quarterly*.

Leibsohn, S., d'Ablaing, G., Mishell, D.R. and Schlaerth, J.B. (1990). Leiomyosarcoma in a series of hysterectomies performed for presumed uterine leiomyomas. *Am J Obstet Gynecol, 162*, 968–976.

Lewis, N.A. (1993, June 15). "Clinton Names Ruth Ginsburg, Advocate for Women, To Court." *New York Times*, A1, A23.

Lindsay, R. (1991). Estrogens, bone mass, and osteoporotic fracture. *Am. J. Medicine, 91*, 10S–12S.

Lipid Research Clinic Program. (1984). The lipid research clinics coronary primary prevention trial results. *JAMA, 251*, 351–364.

Lock, M. (1991). Contested meanings of the menopause. *The Lancet, 337*, 1270–1272.

Loo, C. (1988). Sociocultural barriers to the achievement of Asian American women. *Annual Meeting of the American Psychological Association*. Paper presented at the meeting of the American Psychological Association, Atlanta, GA.

Losing Weight: What Works. What doesn't. *Consumer Reports*, June 1993, 347–357.

Lutter, J. (1992). A question of age: similarities and differences of melpomene members across the lifespan. *Melpomene, 11* (1): 28–34.

Mahowald, M. (1992). Beyond Motherhood: Ethical Issues. In *3rd Annual Meeting of the North American Menopause Society* (p. 56). Cleveland, Ohio: Case Western Reserve University.

Manson, J., Stampfer, M., Colditz, G., Willett, W., Rosner, B., Speizer, F., and Hennekens, C. (1991). A prospective study of aspirin use and primary prevention of cardiovascular disease in women. *JAMA, 266* (4): 521–527.

Margolis, S., and Moses, H. (1992). Headaches. In *The Johns Hopkins Medical Handbook*, pp. 120–131. New York: Rebus, Inc.

Masters, W., and Johnson, V. (1970). *Human Sexual Inadequacy*. Boston: Little Brown & Co.

McCrady, B.S. (1988). Alcoholism. In E.A. Blechman and K.D. Brownell

(Eds.), *Handbook of Behavioral Medicine for Women*, pp. 356–368. New York: Pergamon.

McGill, H.C. (1989). Sex steroid hormone receptors in the cardiovascular system. *Postgrad Medicine*, 64–8.

McGrath, E., Keita, G.P., Strickland, B.R. and Russo, N.F. (1990). *Women and Depression*. Washington, D.C.: American Psychological Association.

McKinlay, J., McKinlay, S., & Brambilla, D. (1987). Health status and utilization behavior associated with menopause. *American Journal of Epidemiology, 125,* 110–121.

McKinlay, J., McKinlay, S., & Brambilla, D. (1987). The relative contributions of endocrine changes and social circumstances to depression in mid-aged women. *Journal of Health and Social Behavior, 28,* 345–363.

Miller, S. (1993). *For Love*. New York: HarperCollins.

Mills, P.K., Beeson, W.L., Phillips R.L., & Fraser, G.E. (1989). Prospective study of exogenous hormone use and breast cancer in seventh day adventists. *Cancer, 64,* 591–597.

Morgan R. (Ed.) (1993). Audre Lorde obituary. *Ms. 3* (5), 58.

Morgan, S. (1982). *Coping with a Hysterectomy*. New York: The Dial Press.

Moyers, B. (1993). *Healing and the Mind*. New York: Bantam Doubleday Dell.

Nabulsi, A.A., Folsom, A.R., White, A., & Patsch, W. (1993). Association of hormone replacement therapy with various cardiovascular risk factors in postmenopausal women. *The New England Journal of Medicine, 328,* 1069–75.

Nachtigall, L. & Heilman, J.R. (1991). *Estrogen: The Facts that Can Change Your Life*. New York: HarperCollins.

National Cancer Institute. (1990). The NCI breast cancer screening consortium screening mammography: A missed opportunity?: Results of the NCI Breast Cancer Screening Consortium and National Health Interview survey studies. *JAMA 264,* 54–58.

National Institute on Drug Abuse Sample Size and US Population Size Tables. (1990). National Household Survey on Drug Abuse: Population estimates, 17.

National Institute of Mental Health. (1987). National Lesbian Health Care Survey. Washington, D.C.: The U.S. Dept. of Health and Human Services, 1987.

National Osteoporosis Foundation. (1991). Boning up on osteoporosis: A guide to prevention and treatment. Washington, D.C.: National Osteoporosis Foundation.

Neaton, J.D., Lewis, H.K., Wentworth, D., & Borhani, N.O. (1984). Total and cardiovascular mortality in relation to cigarette smoking, serum cholesterol concentration, and diastolic blood pressure among black and white males followed up for five years. *Am Heart Journal, 108,* 759.

Nolen-Hoeksema, S. (1987). Sex differences in unipolar depression: Evidence and theory. *Psychological Bulletin, 101,* 259–282.

Olshan, J. (1993, June 28). Picks & Pans: Pages. *People,* p. 10.

Orlander, J., Jick, S., Dean, A., & Jick, H. (1992). Urinary tract infections and estrogen use in older women. *JAGS, 40* (8), 817–820.

Orlandi, M.A. (1987). Gender differences in smoking cessation. *Women's Health.*

Orth, M. (1993, May). The lady has legs. *Vanity Fair, 171.*

Otto, W. (1991). *How to Make an American Quilt.* New York: Ballantine Books.

Parke, E. (1991). A funny thing happened on my way to middle age. In D. Taylor and A.C. Sumrall (Eds.), *Women of the 14th Moon,* p. 7. Freedom: The Crossing Press.

Perspectives. (1993, July 12). *Newsweek.*

Petitti, D.B., Sydney, S., & Pearlman, J.A. (1988). Increased risk of cholecystectomy in users of supplemental estrogen. *Gastroenterology, 94,* 91–95.

Polivy, V. & Herman, C.P. (1985). Dieting and binging. *American Psychologist, 40,* 193–201.

Prochaska, J.P., Norcross, J.C. and DiClemente, C. (1992). In search of how people change: Applications to addictive behaviors. *American Psychologist, 47* (9), 1102–1114.

Quinn, J.B. (1993, April 5). What's for dinner, mom? *Newsweek,* p. 68.

Rakowski, W., Dube, C.E., Marcus, B.H., Prochaska, J.O. (1992). Assessing elements of women's decisions about mammography. *Health Psychology, 11,* 111–188.

Ravnikar, V.A. (1987). Compliance with hormonal therapy. *American Journal of Obstetrics and Gynecology, 156,* 1332–1334.

Ravnikar, V. (1990). Physiology and treatment of hot flushes. *Obstetrics & Gynecology, 75,* 3S–8S.

Rector, R.C. (Ed.) (1990). *Chronic Pelvic Pain Clinical OB:GYN.* Vol. 33. New York: Lippincott.

Rigotti, N. (1992). Smoking cessation strategies for women. Paper presented at *Harvard Medical School Continuing Education Course Primary Care of Women.* Boston, MA.

Rodin, J., Silberstein, L.R., & Striegel-Moore, R.H. (1985). Women and weight: A normative discontent. In T.B. Sonderegger (Ed.), *Nebraska Symposium on Motivation: Psychology and Gender, 32* (pp. 267–301). Lincoln: University of Nebraska Press, 1985.

Rosen, J. (1993, August 2). Book of Ruth. *The New Republic,* pp. 19–31.

Rosenthal, E. (1993, March 21). Conversations: James E. Muller. *New York Times.*

Rothert, M. (1991). Perspectives and issues in studying patients decision making. In M.L. Grady (Ed.), *Primary Care Research: Theory and*

Methods, (pp. 175–179). Rockville: Agency for Health Care Policy Research.

Rountree, C. (1993). *On Women Turning 50: Celebrating Mid Life Discoveries.* San Francisco: HarperSanFrancisco.

Russo, N.F. & Olmedo, E.L. (1983). Women's utilization of outpatient psychiatric services: Some emerging priorities for rehabilitation psychologists. *Rehabilitation Psychology, 28,* 141–155.

Sachs, J. (1991). *What Women Should Know About Menopause.* New York: Bantam Doubleday Dell Publishing Group, Inc.

Salonen, J.T., Nyyssonen, K., Korpela, H., Tuomilehto, J., Seppanen, R. & Salonen, R. (1992). High stored iron levels are associated with excess risk of myocardial infarction in eastern Finnish men. *Circulation, 86,* 803–811.

Schiff, I. and Walsh, B. (1989). Hot flashes. In C.B. Hammond, F. Haseltine, and I. Schiff (Eds.). *Menopause: Evaluation, Treatment and Health Concerns.* New York: Wiley, 1989

Schiff, I., Tulchinsky, D., Cramer, D., & Ryan, K. (1980). Oral medroxyprogesterone in the treatment of postmenopausal symptoms. *JAMA, 244,* 1443–1445.

Schmidt, P. & Rubinow, D. (1991). Menopause-related affective disorders: a justification for further study. *American Journal of Psychiatry, 148,* 844–852.

Scudder, V.D. (1992). Modeling my life. In J.K. Conway (Ed.), *Written by Herself,* pp. 333–371. New York: Vintage Books.

Sheehy, G. (1991). *The Silent Passage.* New York: Random House.

Sheehy, G. (1992, May 14). The silent passage: Menopause. *Vanity Fair,* p. 6.

Sherwin B. (Chair) (1993, September). Menopausal depression: Myth or realty? Symposium conducted at the Fourth Annual Meeting of the North American Menopause Society, San Diego.

Stampfer, M.J. (1991). Postmenopausal estrogen therapy and cardiovascular disease. *The New England Journal of Medicine, 325,* 756–62.

Stampfer, M.J., Graham, A.C., Willett, W.C., Rosner, B., Speizer, F.E., & Hennekens, C.H. (1987). Coronary heart disease risk factors in women: The Nurses' Health Study experience. In E.D. Eaker, B. Packard, B. Packard, N.K. Wenger, T.B. Clarkson, and H.A. Tyroler (Eds.), *Coronary Heart Disease in Women: Proceedings of an N.I.H. Workshop* (pp. 112–116). New York: Haymarket Doyma, Inc.

Stampfer, M.J., Hennekens, C.H., Manson, J.E., Colditz, G.A., Rosner, B., and Willett, W.C. (1993). Vitamin E. consumption and the risk of coronary disease in women. *The New England Journal of Medicine,* 1444–1449.

Stark, M. (November, 1992). Ask your doctor. *Boston Magazine, 84,* 11: 67–69.

Stunkard, A.J. and Rush, J. (1974). Dieting and depression reexamined: A critical review of untoward responses during weight reduction for obesity. *Annals of Internal Medicine, 81,* 526–533.

Sturdee, D.W., Wilson, K.A., Pipili, E., & Crocker, A.D. (1978). Physiological aspects of menopausal hot flush. *British Medical Journal, 2,* 79–80.

Swartzman, L., Edelberg, R., & Kemmann, E. (1990). Impact of stress on objectively recorded menopausal hot flushes and on flush report bias. *Health Psychology, 9,* 529–545.

Tamerin, J.S., Tolor, A., & Harrington, B. (1976). Sex differences in alcoholics: A comparison of male and female alcoholics and spouse perceptions. *American Journal of Drug and Alcohol Abuse, 3,* 457–472.

Tannen, D. (1990). *You Just Don't Understand.* New York: Ballantine Books.

Taylor, D. and Sumrall, A.C. (Eds.). (1991). *Women of the 14th Moon.* Freedom: The Crossing Press.

Todd, A.D. (1989). *Intimate Adversaries: Cultural Conflict Between Doctors and Women Patients.* Philadelphia: University of Pennsylvania Press.

Tuyns, A.J. & Pequinot, G. (1984). Greater risk of ascitic cirrhosis in females in relation to alcohol consumption. *International Journal of Epidemiology, 13,* 53.

United States Congress, Office of Technology Assessment. (1992). *The Menopause, Hormone Therapy, and Women's Health.* (OTA-BP-BA-88) Washington, D.C.: U.S. Government Printing Office.

United States Surgeon General. (1990). *The Health Consequences of Smoking Cessation.* U.S. Dept. of Health and Human Services: Public Health Service, Office on Smoking and Health.

U.S. Dept. of Health and Human Services. (1988). Indian Health Service: Chart Series Book. Washington, D.C.: The United States Government Printing Office.

Wadden, T.A., Stunkard, A.J., & Liebschutz. (1988). Three year follow-up of the treatment of obesity by very low calorie diet, behavior therapy and their combination. *Journal of Consulting and Clinical Psychology, 56,* 926–928.

Walling, M., Anderson, B., & Johnson, S. (1990). Hormonal replacement therapy for postmenopausal women: A review of sexual outcomes and related gynecologic effects. *Archives of Sexual Behavior, 19,* 135.

Warner, K.E. (1991). Health and economic implications of a tobacco free society. *Journal of the American Medical Association, 258* (15): 2080–2088.

Weissman, M.M. (1980). The treatment of depressed women: the efficacy of psychotherapy. In C.L. Heckerman (Ed.), *The Evolving Female: Women in a Psychosocial Context* (pp. 307–324). New York: Human Sciences Press.

Weissman, M.M. & Klerman, G. (1985). Sex differences and the epidemiology of depression. *Arch Gen Psychiatry, 34,* 98–111.

Wenger, N.K., Speroff, L., & Packard, B. (1993). Cardiovascular health and disease in women. *The New England Journal of Medicine, 329,* 247–256.

Wilson, R.A. (1966). *Feminine Forever.* New York: M. Evans.

Winick. (1992). Nutritional Needs of the Menopausal Woman. Paper Presented at the North American Menopause Association. Cleveland, Ohio.

Wolfe, L. (1992, October 12). New York Woman. *New York,* pp. 46–55.

Wooley, S.C. & Wooley, O.W. (1979). Obesity and Women: I. A Closer Look at the Facts. *Women's Studies International Quarterly, 2,* 69–79.

Ylikorkala, O., Kuusi, T., Tikkanen, M.J., and Vinikka, L. (1987). Desogestertrel- and levonorgestrel-containing oral contraceptives have different effects on urinary excretion of prostacyclin metabolites and serum high density lipoproteins. *J. Clin. Endocrinol. Metab., 65,* 1238–42.

Young, R.L., Kumar, N.S., & Goldzieher. (1990). Management of menopause when estrogen cannot be used. *Drugs, 40* (2), 220–230.

 *GLOSSARY*

amenorrhea: Absence of the menses.

androgen: A class of male hormones including testosterone.

anemia: A condition in which the blood is deficient of red cells, hemoglobin or total volume.

artery: A vessel through which the blood passes away from the heart to the various parts of the body.

atherosclerosis: A condition characterized by thickening and loss of elasticity of the arterial walls.

atrophy: A wasting away; a diminution in the size of a cell, tissue, organ, or part.

beta-blockers: A class of drugs used for a variety of conditions including cardiovascular health.

bilateral oophorectomy: Surgical removal of both ovaries.

biopsychosocial: Pertaining to the interactions between mind, body and society in the formation and continuation of the personality.

cardiovascular disease: Diseases pertaining to the heart and blood vessels.

cervix: The lower and narrow end of the uterus which protrudes into the vagina.

chemotherapy: The use of chemical agents in the treatment of a disease, usually cancer.

cholesterol: A pearly fatlike steroid substance which circulates within the bloodstream and is found in foods.

conjugated estrogen: A form of estrogen therapy commonly derived from the urine of pregnant mares.

depression, major: A psychiatric disorder that includes depressed mood or markedly diminished interest and three of the following symptoms: The symptoms have occurred for two weeks and are a change from usual functioning. They include: changes in weight or sleep and agitation or retardation, fatigue or loss of energy, feelings of worthlessness, inability to concentrate and recurrent thoughts of death or suicide.

diabetes (diabetes mellitus): A disease that occurs when insulin is absent or ineffective. Insulin is the hormone that processes sugar.

diuretic: Tending to increase the flow of urine.

dyspareunia: Difficult or painful coitus/intercourse in women.

dysthymic disorder: A chronic condition that includes symptoms of sadness or irritability and at least two of the following symptoms: changes in appetite, sleep, energy level or concentration and low self-esteem and feelings of hopelessness.

endometriosis: The migration of tissue that normally lines the uterus to other organs.

endometrium: The lining of the uterus.

epidemiology: A branch of medical science that deals with the incidence, distribution and control of a disease in a population.

epithelium, vaginal: The tissue lining of the vagina.

estrogen: A female sex hormone. It is responsible for the development of the female secondary sex characteristics.

extrusion: A form that is pushed or pressed out.

fallopian tube: The pair of tubes through which eggs are transported from the ovary to the uterus.

fibroids: Benign, not cancerous, overgrowth of smooth muscle tissue in the uterine wall.

follicle: The structure on the ovary surface that nurtures a ripening oocyte. At ovulation the follicle ruptures and the oocyte is released.

FSH: Follicle-stimulating hormone. This hormone is produced in the pituitary gland and stimulates estrogen production in the ovary. A high level of FSH is associated with low levels of estrogen.

hot flash: Subjective experience of intense warmth throughout the upper body.

hot flush: The objective change during a hot flash that produces visable redness of the upper chest, neck and face followed by perspiration.

HRT (Hormone Replacement Therapy): Usually including both estrogen and progesterone.

hypertension: An elevation of the blood pressure.

hypothalamus: The portion of the diencephalon (part of the brain) that regulates many vital functions.

hysterectomy: Surgical removal of the uterus.

incontinence: Inability to control urination.

invasive: Tending to invade healthy tissue.

lactose: A type of sugar present in milk.

LH: Luteinizing hormone produced by the pituitary gland to act on the ovaries.

menarche: The establishment or beginning of menstruation.

menopause: The cessation of menstruation.

oocyte: Immature eggs produced by the ovaries.

osteoarthritis: A chronic process that wears away the cartilage between the bones, leading to joint stiffness and pain.

osteoporosis: A condition of bone thinning that can lead to fractures.

ovaries: The female reproductive organs that produce eggs and the female sex hormones.

perimenopausal: The time around the menopause when menstrual cycles begin to be irregular.

postmenopausal: Occurring after the menopause.

progesterone: One of the principal female hormones. Progesterone causes the lining of the uterus to shed in the absence of a fertilized egg.

regimen: A strictly regulated scheme of diet, exercise, or medication designed to achieve certain ends.

sonogram: See ultrasound.

stress: The sum of the biological reactions to any adverse stimulus, physical, mental, or emotional, internal or external, that tends to disturb the organism's equilibrium.

symptom: The subjective experience of a disease

syndrome: A group of symptoms that produce a pattern typical of a particular disease.

thyroid: The endocrine gland lying at the base of the neck that produces thyroid hormone. Thyroid hormone regulates metabolism.

ultrasound: Diagnostic technique for the examination of internal body structures that involves an image created by ultrasonic or echo waves.

urethra: The canal that carries urine from the bladder to the exterior of the body.

urinary stress incontinence: Involuntary escape of urine due to strain on the orifice of the bladder, as in coughing or sneezing.

uterus *pl. uteri:* The hollow muscular female organ located in the pelvis where a fetus can grow.

vasoconstriction: Reversible narrowing of blood vessels which decreases the blood delivered to an area.

vasodilation: Reversable expansion of a vessel that increases blood flow; **re-**

flex vasodilation, vasodilation occurring as a reflex to a stimulus, or after an initial vasoconstrictive response.

vasodilator: A medication that widens blood vessels and increases blood flow.

vertebra *pl. vertebrae:* Any of the thirty-three bones of the spine, including the seven cervical, twelve thoracic, five lumbar, five sacral, and four coccygeal vertebrae.

❧ INDEX

Drs. Landau, Cyr and Moulton founded Women's Health
Associates, an interdisciplinary group practice affiliated with the
Division of General Internal Medicine, Rhode Island Hospital,
Brown University School of Medicine.

Correspondence can be directed to:

Division of General Internal Medicine
Rhode Island Hospital
593 Eddy Street
Providence, R.I. 02903
or telephone
(401) 273-2828 (Dr. Landau)
or
(401) 444–5344 (Drs. Cyr and Moulton)